P9-AFB-647

ALL GLORY TO ŚRĪ GURU AND GAURĀṄGA

ŚRĪMAD BHĀGAVATAM

of

KṚṢṆA-DVAIPĀYANA VYĀSA

यस्यात्मबुद्धिः कुणपे त्रिधातुके
स्वधीः कलत्रादिषु भौम इज्यधीः ।
यत्तीर्थबुद्धिः सलिले न कर्हिचिज्
जनेष्वभिज्ञेषु स एव गोखरः ॥१३॥

yasyātma-buddhiḥ kuṇape tri-dhātuke
sva-dhīḥ kalatrādiṣu bhauma ijya-dhīḥ
yat-tīrtha-buddhiḥ salile na karhicij
janeṣv abhijñeṣu sa eva go-kharaḥ

(p. 455)

BOOKS by
His Divine Grace
A. C. Bhaktivedanta Swami Prabhupāda

Bhagavad-gītā As It Is
Śrīmad-Bhāgavatam, cantos 1-10 (12 vols.)
Śrī Caitanya-caritāmṛta (17 vols.)
Teachings of Lord Caitanya
The Nectar of Devotion
The Nectar of Instruction
Śrī Īśopaniṣad
Easy Journey to Other Planets
Kṛṣṇa Consciousness: The Topmost Yoga System
Kṛṣṇa, The Supreme Personality of Godhead (3 vols.)
Perfect Questions, Perfect Answers
Teachings of Lord Kapila, the Son of Devahūti
Transcendental Teachings of Prahlāda Mahārāja
Dialectic Spiritualism—A Vedic View of Western Philosophy
Teachings of Queen Kuntī
Kṛṣṇa, the Reservoir of Pleasure
The Science of Self-Realization
The Path of Perfection
Search for Liberation
Life Comes from Life
The Perfection of Yoga
Beyond Birth and Death
On the Way to Kṛṣṇa
Geetār-gan (Bengali)
Vairāgya-vidyā (Bengali)
Buddhi-yoga (Bengali)
Bhakti-ratna-boli (Bengali)
Rāja-vidyā: The King of Knowledge
Elevation to Kṛṣṇa Consciousness
Kṛṣṇa Consciousness: The Matchless Gift
Back to Godhead magazine (founder)

A complete catalog is available upon request.

Bhaktivedanta Book Trust
Hare Krishna Land
Juhu, Bombay-400 049

Bhaktivedanta Book Trust
1A, Rainey Park
Calcutta-700 019

ŚRĪMAD BHĀGAVATAM

Tenth Canto
"The Summum Bonum"

(Part Four—Chapters 70–90)

With the Original Sanskrit Text, Its Roman Transliteration, Synonyms, Translation and Elaborate Purports

by disciples of

His Divine Grace
A.C. Bhaktivedanta Swami Prabhupāda
Founder-*Ācārya* of the International Society for Krishna Consciousness

THE BHAKTIVEDANTA BOOK TRUST
Los Angeles · London · Stockholm · Bombay · Sydney

Readers interested in the subject matter of this book
are invited by the International Society for Krishna Consciousness
to correspond with its Secretary at either of the following addresses:

International Society for Krishna Consciousness
Hare Krishna Land
Juhu, Bombay-400 049

Bhaktivedanta Book Trust
Hare Krishna Land
Juhu, Bombay-400 049

First Indian Printing 1992 / 2000 Copies
Second Indian Printing 1995 / 2000 Copies
Third Indian Printing 1997 / 2000 Copies
Fourth Indian Printing 1998 / 2000 Copies

© 1987 Bhaktivedanta Book Trust International
All Rights Reserved
Printed in India
at Rekha Printers Pvt. Ltd., New Delhi-110 020

Library of Congress Cataloging in Publication Data (Revised)

Śrīmad-Bhāgavatam.

In English and Sanskrit.
Translation of: Bhāgavatapurāṇa
10th canto, v.2-12th canto by disciples of His Divine Grace A. C. Bhaktivedanta Swami Prabhupāda.
Includes index.
Contents: 1st canto. Creation— 2nd canto. The cosmic manifestation— 3rd canto. The status quo (2 v)— 4th canto. The creation of the fourth order (2 v)— 5th canto. The creative impetus— 6th canto. Prescribed duties for mankind— 7th canto. The science of God— 8th canto. Withdrawal of the cosmic creations— 9th canto. Liberation— 10th canto. The summum bonum (4 v)— 11th canto. General history (2 v)— 12th canto. The age of deterioration.
1. Purāṇas. Bhāgavatapurāṇa—Criticism, interpretation, etc.
I. A. C. Bhaktivedanta Swami Prabhupāda, 1896-1977.
BL1140.4.B432E5 1987 294.5'925 87-25585
ISBN 0-89213-264-7 (v. 15)

The Bhaktivedanta Book Trust
Śrīmad-Bhāgavatam Translation and Editorial Board

Hridayānanda dāsa Goswami
Project Director, Translator, Commentator and Editor in Chief

Gopīparāṇadhana dāsa Adhikārī
Translator, Commentator and Sanskrit Editor

Draviḍa dāsa Brahmacārī
English Editor

Table of Contents

CHAPTER SEVENTY-ONE
The Lord Travels to Indraprastha

CHAPTER SEVENTY-TWO
The Slaying of the Demon Jarāsandha

CHAPTER SEVENTY-FOUR
The Deliverance of Śiśupāla at the Rājasūya Sacrifice

CHAPTER SEVENTY-FIVE
Duryodhana Humiliated

CHAPTER SEVENTY–SIX
The Battle Between Śālva and the Vṛṣṇis

CHAPTER SEVENTY–SEVEN
Lord Kṛṣṇa Slays the Demon Śālva

CHAPTER SEVENTY-EIGHT
The Killing of Dantavakra, Vidūratha and Romaharṣaṇa

CHAPTER SEVENTY-NINE
Lord Balarāma Goes on Pilgrimage

CHAPTER EIGHTY
The Brāhmaṇa Sudāmā Visits Lord Kṛṣṇa in Dvārakā

CHAPTER EIGHTY–ONE
The Lord Blesses Sudāmā Brāhmaṇa

CHAPTER EIGHTY-TWO
Kṛṣṇa and Balarāma Meet the Inhabitants of Vṛndāvana

CHAPTER EIGHTY-THREE
Draupadī Meets the Queens of Kṛṣṇa

CHAPTER EIGHTY-FOUR
The Sages' Teachings at Kurukṣetra

CHAPTER EIGHTY–FIVE
Lord Kṛṣṇa Instructs Vasudeva and Retrieves Devakī's Sons

CHAPTER EIGHTY-SIX
Arjuna Kidnaps Subhadrā, and Kṛṣṇa Blesses His Devotees

CHAPTER EIGHTY-SEVEN
The Prayers of the Personified Vedas

CHAPTER EIGHTY-EIGHT
Lord Śiva Saved from Vṛkāsura

CHAPTER EIGHTY-NINE
Kṛṣṇa and Arjuna Retrieve a Brāhmaṇa's Sons

CHAPTER NINETY

Summary of Lord Kṛṣṇa's Glories

Preface

nama oṁ viṣṇu-pādāya kṛṣṇa-preṣṭhāya bhū-tale
śrīmate bhaktivedānta-svāmin iti nāmine

I offer my most respectful obeisances at the lotus feet of His Divine Grace A. C. Bhaktivedanta Swami Prabhupāda, who is very dear to Lord Kṛṣṇa on this earth, having taken shelter at His lotus feet.

namas te sārasvate deve gaura-vāṇī-pracāriṇe
nirviśeṣa-śūnyavādi-pāścātya-deśa-tāriṇe

I offer my most respectful obeisances unto the lotus feet of His Divine Grace A. C. Bhaktivedanta Swami Prabhupāda, who is the disciple of Śrīla Bhaktisiddhānta Sarasvatī Ṭhākura and who is powerfully distributing the message of Caitanya Mahāprabhu and thus saving the fallen Western countries from impersonalism and voidism.

Śrīmad-Bhāgavatam, with authorized translation and elaborate purports in the English language, is the great work of His Divine Grace Oṁ Viṣṇupāda Paramahaṁsa Parivrājakācārya Aṣṭottara-śata Śrī Śrīmad A. C. Bhaktivedanta Swami Prabhupāda, our beloved spiritual master. Our present publication is a humble attempt by his servants to complete his most cherished work of *Śrīmad-Bhāgavatam*. Just as one may worship the holy Ganges River by offering Ganges water unto the Ganges, similarly, in our attempt to serve our spiritual master, we are offering to him that which he has given to us.

Śrīla Prabhupāda came to America in 1965, at a critical moment in the history of America and the world in general. The story of Śrīla Prabhupāda's arrival and his specific impact on world civilization, and especially Western civilization, has been brilliantly documented by Satsvarūpa dāsa Goswami. From Satsvarūpa Goswami's authorized biography of Śrīla Prabhupāda, called *Śrīla Prabhupāda-līlāmṛta*, the reader can fully understand Śrīla Prabhupāda's purpose, desire and mission in presenting *Śrīmad-Bhāgavatam*. Further, in Śrīla Prabhupāda's own preface to the *Bhāgavatam* (reprinted as the foreword in this volume), he clearly states that this transcendental literature will provoke a cultural revolution in the world, and that is now underway. I do not wish to be redundant by repeating what Śrīla Prabhupāda has so eloquently stated in his preface, or that which has been so abundantly documented by Satsvarūpa Goswami in his authorized biography.

It is necessary to mention, however, that *Śrīmad-Bhāgavatam* is a completely transcendental, liberated sound vibration coming from the spiritual world. And, being absolute, it is not different from the Absolute Truth Himself, Lord Śrī Kṛṣṇa. By understanding *Śrīmad-Bhāgavatam,* consisting of twelve cantos, the reader acquires perfect knowledge, by which he or she may live peacefully and progressively on the earth, attending to all material necessities and simultaneously achieving supreme spiritual liberation. As we have worked to prepare this and other volumes of *Śrīmad-Bhāgavatam,* our intention has always been to faithfully serve the lotus feet of our spiritual master, carefully trying to translate and comment exactly as he would have, thus preserving the unity and spiritual potency of this edition of *Śrīmad-Bhāgavatam.* In other words, by our strictly following the disciplic succession, called in Sanskrit *guru-paramparā,* this edition of the *Bhāgavatam* will continue to be throughout its volumes a liberated work, free from material contamination and capable of elevating the reader to the kingdom of God.

Our method has been to faithfully follow the commentaries of previous *ācāryas* and exercise a careful selectivity of material based on the example and mood of Śrīla Prabhupāda. One may write transcendental literature only by the mercy of the Supreme Personality of Godhead, Śrī Kṛṣṇa, and the authorized, liberated spiritual masters coming in disciplic succession. Thus we humbly fall at the lotus feet of the previous *ācāryas,* offering special gratitude to the great commentators on the *Bhāgavatam,* namely Śrīla Śrīdhara Svāmī, Śrīla Jīva Gosvāmī, Śrīla Viśvanātha Cakravartī Ṭhākura and Śrīla Bhaktisiddhānta Sarasvatī Gosvāmī, the spiritual master of Śrīla Prabhupāda. We also offer our obeisances at the lotus feet of Śrīla Vīrarāghavācārya, Śrīla Vijayadhvaja Ṭhākura and Śrīla Vaṁśīdhara Ṭhākura, whose commentaries have also helped in this work. Additionally, we offer our humble obeisances at the lotus feet of the great *ācārya* Śrīla Madhva, who has made innumerable learned comments on *Śrīmad-Bhāgavatam.* We further offer our humble obeisances at the lotus feet of the Supreme Personality of Godhead, Śrī Kṛṣṇa Caitanya Mahāprabhu, and to all of His eternally liberated followers, headed by Śrīla

Nityānanda Prabhu, Advaita Prabhu, Gadādhara Prabhu, Śrīvāsa Ṭhākura and the six Gosvāmīs, namely Śrīla Rūpa Gosvāmī, Śrīla Sanātana Gosvāmī, Śrīla Raghunātha dāsa Gosvāmī, Śrīla Raghunātha Bhaṭṭa Gosvāmī, Śrīla Jīva Gosvāmī and Śrīla Gopāla Bhaṭṭa Gosvāmī. Finally we offer our most respectful obeisances at the lotus feet of the Absolute Truth, Śrī Śrī Rādhā and Kṛṣṇa, and humbly beg for Their mercy so that this great work of *Śrīmad-Bhāgavatam* can be quickly finished. *Śrīmad-Bhāgavatam* is undoubtedly the most important book in the universe, and the sincere readers of *Śrīmad-Bhāgavatam* will undoubtedly achieve the highest perfection of life, Kṛṣṇa consciousness.

In conclusion, I again remind the reader that *Śrīmad-Bhāgavatam* is the great work of His Divine Grace A. C. Bhaktivedanta Swami Prabhupāda, and that the present volume is the humble attempt of his devoted servants.

Hare Kṛṣṇa

Hridayananda dāsa Goswami

Preface

Nityānanda Prabhu, Advaita Prabhu, Gadādhara Prabhu, Śrīvāsa Ṭhākura and the six Gosvāmīs, namely Śrīla Rūpa Gosvāmī, Śrīla Sanātana Gosvāmī, Śrīla Raghunātha dāsa Gosvāmī, Śrīla Raghunātha Bhaṭṭa Gosvāmī, Śrīla Jīva Gosvāmī and Śrīla Gopāla Bhaṭṭa Gosvāmī. Finally we offer our most respectful obeisances at the lotus feet of the Absolute Truth, Śrī Śrī Rādhā and Kṛṣṇa, and humbly beg for Their mercy so that this great work of Śrīmad-Bhāgavatam can be quickly finished. Śrīmad-Bhāgavatam is undoubtedly the most important book in the universe, and the sincere readers of Śrīmad-Bhāgavatam will undoubtedly achieve the highest perfection of life, Kṛṣṇa consciousness.

In conclusion, I again remind the reader that Śrīmad-Bhāgavatam is the great work of His Divine Grace A. C. Bhaktivedanta Swami Prabhupāda, and that the present volume is the humble attempt of his devoted servants.

Hare Kṛṣṇa

Hridayānanda dāsa Gosvāmī

Foreword

We must know the present need of human society. And what is that need? Human society is no longer bounded by geographical limits to particular countries or communities. Human society is broader than in the Middle Ages, and the world tendency is toward one state or one human society. The ideals of spiritual communism, according to *Śrīmad-Bhāgavatam*, are based more or less on the oneness of the entire human society, nay, of the entire energy of living beings. The need is felt by great thinkers to make this a successful ideology. *Śrīmad-Bhāgavatam* will fill this need in human society. It begins, therefore, with an aphorism of Vedānta philosophy, *janmādy asya yataḥ*, to establish the ideal of a common cause.

Human society, at the present moment, is not in the darkness of oblivion. It has made rapid progress in the fields of material comforts, education and economic development throughout the entire world. But there is a pinprick somewhere in the social body at large, and therefore there are large-scale quarrels, even over less important issues. There is need of a clue as to how humanity can become one in peace, friendship and prosperity with a common cause. *Śrīmad-Bhāgavatam* will fill this need, for it is a cultural presentation for the respiritualization of the entire human society.

Śrīmad-Bhāgavatam should be introduced also in the schools and colleges, for it is recommended by the great student-devotee Prahlāda Mahārāja in order to change the demoniac face of society:

kaumāra ācaret prājño
dharmān bhāgavatān iha
durlabhaṁ mānuṣaṁ janma
tad apy adhruvam artha-dam
(*Bhāg*. 7.6.1)

Disparity in human society is due to lack of principles in a godless civilization. There is God, or the Almighty One, from whom everything emanates, by whom everything is maintained and in whom everything is merged to rest. Material science has tried to find the ultimate source of creation very insufficiently, but it is a fact that there is one ultimate source of everything that be. This ultimate source is explained rationally and authoritatively in the beautiful *Bhāgavatam,* or *Śrīmad-Bhāgavatam.*

Śrīmad-Bhāgavatam is the transcendental science not only for knowing the ultimate source of everything but also for knowing our relation with Him and our duty toward perfection of the human society on the basis of this perfect knowledge. It is powerful reading matter in the Sanskrit language, and it is now rendered into English elaborately so that simply by a careful reading one will know God perfectly well, so much so that the reader will be sufficiently educated to defend himself from the onslaught of atheists. Over and above this, the reader will be able to convert others to accepting God as a concrete principle.

Śrīmad-Bhāgavatam begins with the definition of the ultimate source. It is a bona fide commentary on the *Vedānta-sūtra* by the same author, Śrīla Vyāsadeva, and gradually it develops into nine cantos up to the highest state of God realization. The only qualification one needs to study this great book of transcendental knowledge is to proceed step by step cautiously and not jump forward haphazardly, as with an ordinary book. It should be gone through chapter by chapter, one after another. The reading matter is so arranged with the original Sanskrit text, its roman transliteration, synonyms, translation and purports so that one is sure to become a God-realized soul at the end of finishing the first nine cantos.

The Tenth Canto is distinct from the first nine cantos because it deals directly with the transcendental activities of the Personality of Godhead, Śrī Kṛṣṇa. One will be unable to capture the effects of the Tenth Canto without going through the first nine cantos. The book is complete in twelve cantos, each independent, but it is good for all to read them in small installments one after another.

I must admit my frailties in presenting *Śrīmad-Bhāgavatam,* but still I am hopeful of its good reception by the thinkers and leaders of society on the strength of the following statement of *Śrīmad-Bhāgavatam* (1.5.11):

tad-vāg-visargo janatāgha-viplavo
yasmin prati-ślokam abaddhavaty api
nāmāny anantasya yaśo 'ṅkitāni yat
śṛṇvanti gāyanti gṛṇanti sādhavaḥ

"On the other hand, that literature which is full of descriptions of the transcendental glories of the name, fame, forms, pastimes, etc., of the unlimited Supreme Lord is a different creation, full of transcendental words directed toward bringing about a revolution in the impious lives of this world's misdirected civilization. Such transcendental literatures, even though imperfectly composed, are heard, sung and accepted by purified men who are thoroughly honest."

Oṁ tat sat

A. C. Bhaktivedanta Swami

His Divine Grace
A. C. Bhaktivedanta Swami Prabhupāda
Founder-Ācārya of the International Society for Krishna Consciousness

PLATE ONE: Bhīma and Jarāsandha swung their clubs at each other with such force that the weapons were crushed and broken as they struck their shoulders, hips and collarbones. (*p. 106*)

PLATE TWO: At the magnificent Rājasūya sacrifice performed by King Yudhiṣṭhira, Lord Kṛṣṇa received the honor of first worship. (*pp.158-9*)

PLATE THREE: Wicked Śiśupāla became infuriated by the honor shown to Lord Kṛṣṇa and began hurling insults at Him. At first the Lord said nothing, while several members of the assembly covered their ears and walked out and

the Pāṇḍavas took up their weapons and prepared to kill the offender. Checking His devotees, the Lord then sent forth His razor-sharp disc and beheaded the evil son of Damaghoṣa. (*p. 169*)

PLATE FOUR: After seating His friend Sudāmā on His consort's bed, the Lord offered him various tokens of respect and personally bathed his feet. (*p. 322*)

PLATE FIVE: When Kṛṣṇa and Sudāmā were *brahmacārī* students at the school of Sāndīpani Muni, they once got caught in a violent unseasonal storm while fetching firewood. (*pp. 331-3*)

PLATE SIX: The foremost of warriors, Lord Paraśurāma, slew all the kings in the world and created huge lakes from their blood at Samanta-pañcaka. (*p. 376*)

PLATE SEVEN: After fighting the Lord for twenty-seven days, Jāmbavān came to his senses and offered both the Syamantaka jewel and his daughter Jāmbavatī to Him as tokens of reverence. (*p. 418*)

PLATE EIGHT: When Lord Kṛṣṇa met the cowherd girls of Vṛndāvana at Kurukṣetra after a long separation, He instructed them in *jñāna-yoga* so that they could see Him everywhere. But the *gopīs,* who were completely immersed in pure love for Him, simply prayed, "Dear Lord, great *yogīs* and philosophers

meditate on Your lotus feet, which are the only shelter for those suffering in material existence. But even though we are only ordinary cowherd girls engaged in household affairs, we wish that those lotus feet may also be awakened within our hearts." (*p. 406*)

PLATE NINE: After killing the demon Bhauma, Lord Kṛṣṇa liberated 16,100 princesses from his prison and married them all. (*p. 439*)

PLATE TEN: When she saw her long-lost children, Devakī felt overwhelming maternal affection for them. (*p. 544*)

PLATE ELEVEN: In His magnificent city of Dvārakā, Lord Kṛṣṇa would enjoy with each of His 16,108 queens in her own palace. On the grounds of these palaces were clear ponds fragrant with the pollen of many lotuses, and the Lord would enter those ponds and enjoy sporting in the water with His wives. As

musicians, singers and poets glorified Him, the Lord would squirt water at His consorts, and they would squirt Him back, laughing all the while. In this way He enjoyed Himself like the king of elephants in the company of his bevy of she-elephants. *(pp. 802-6)*

PLATE TWELVE: Śrutadeva was so overjoyed to see Lord Kṛṣṇa and the sages accompanying him that he began to dance, waving his shawl. (*p. 576*)

Introduction

"This *Bhāgavata Purāṇa* is as brilliant as the sun, and it has arisen just after the departure of Lord Kṛṣṇa to His own abode, accompanied by religion, knowledge, etc. Persons who have lost their vision due to the dense darkness of ignorance in the age of Kali shall get light from this *Purāṇa*." (*Śrīmad-Bhāgavatam* 1.3.43)

The timeless wisdom of India is expressed in the *Vedas*, ancient Sanskrit texts that touch upon all fields of human knowledge. Originally preserved through oral tradition, the *Vedas* were first put into writing five thousand years ago by Śrīla Vyāsadeva, "the literary incarnation of God." After compiling the *Vedas*, Vyāsadeva set forth their essence in the aphorisms known as *Vedānta-sūtras*. *Śrīmad-Bhāgavatam* (*Bhāgavata Purāṇa*) is Vyāsadeva's commentary on his own *Vedānta-sūtras*. It was written in the maturity of his spiritual life under the direction of Nārada Muni, his spiritual master. Referred to as "the ripened fruit of the tree of Vedic literature," *Śrīmad-Bhāgavatam* is the most complete and authoritative exposition of Vedic knowledge.

After compiling the *Bhāgavatam*, Vyāsa imparted the synopsis of it to his son, the sage Śukadeva Gosvāmī. Śukadeva Gosvāmī subsequently recited the entire *Bhāgavatam* to Mahārāja Parīkṣit in an assembly of learned saints on the bank of the Ganges at Hastināpura (now Delhi). Mahārāja Parīkṣit was the emperor of the world and was a great *rājarṣi* (saintly king). Having received a warning that he would die within a week, he renounced his entire kingdom and retired to the bank of the Ganges to fast until death and receive spiritual enlightenment. The *Bhāgavatam* begins with Emperor Parīkṣit's sober inquiry to Śukadeva Gosvāmī: "You are the spiritual master of great saints and devotees. I am therefore begging you to show the way of perfection for all persons, and especially for one who is about to die. Please let me know what a man should hear, chant, remember and worship, and also what he should not do. Please explain all this to me."

Śukadeva Gosvāmī's answer to this question, and numerous other questions posed by Mahārāja Parīkṣit, concerning everything from the nature of the self to the origin of the universe, held the assembled sages in rapt attention continuously for the seven days leading up to the king's death. The sage Sūta Gosvāmī, who was present in that assembly when Śukadeva Gosvāmī first recited *Śrīmad-Bhāgavatam,* later repeated the *Bhāgavatam* before a gathering of sages in the forest of Naimiṣāraṇya. Those sages, concerned about the spiritual welfare of the people in general, had gathered to perform a long, continuous chain of sacrifices to counteract the degrading influence of the incipient age of Kali. In response to the sages' request that he speak the essence of Vedic wisdom, Sūta Gosvāmī repeated from memory the entire eighteen thousand verses of *Śrīmad-Bhāgavatam,* as spoken by Śukadeva Gosvāmī to Mahārāja Parīkṣit.

The reader of *Śrīmad-Bhāgavatam* hears Sūta Gosvāmī relate the questions of Mahārāja Parīkṣit and the answers of Śukadeva Gosvāmī. Also, Sūta Gosvāmī sometimes responds directly to questions put by Śaunaka Ṛṣi, the spokesman for the sages gathered at Naimiṣāraṇya. One therefore simultaneously hears two dialogues: one between Mahārāja Parīkṣit and Śukadeva Gosvāmī on the bank of the Ganges, and another between Sūta Gosvāmī and the sages at Naimiṣāraṇya forest, headed by Śaunaka Ṛṣi. Furthermore, while instructing King Parīkṣit, Śukadeva Gosvāmī often relates historical episodes and gives accounts of lengthy philosophical discussions between such great souls as Nārada Muni and Vasudeva. With this understanding of the history of the *Bhāgavatam,* the reader will easily be able to follow its intermingling of dialogues and events from various sources. Since philosophical wisdom, not chronological order, is most important in the text, one need only be attentive to the subject matter of *Śrīmad-Bhāgavatam* to fully appreciate its profound message.

The translators of this edition compare the *Bhāgavatam* to sugar candy—wherever you taste it, you will find it equally sweet and relishable. Therefore, to taste the sweetness of the *Bhāgavatam,* one may begin by reading any of its volumes. After such an introductory taste, however, the serious reader is best advised to go back to the First Canto and then proceed through the *Bhāgavatam,* canto after canto, in its natural order.

This edition of the *Bhāgavatam* is the first complete English translation of the important text with an elaborate commentary, and it is the first widely available to the English-speaking public. The first twelve volumes (Canto One through Part One of Canto Ten) are the product of the scholarly and devotional effort of His Divine Grace A. C. Bhaktivedanta

Swami Prabhupāda, the founder-*ācārya* of the International Society for Krishna Consciousness and the world's most distinguished teacher of Indian religious and philosophical thought.

Śrīla Prabhupāda began his *Śrīmad-Bhāgavatam* in mid-1962 in Vṛndavana, India, the land most sacred to Lord Kṛṣṇa. With no assistants and limited funds, but with an abundance of devotion and determination, he was able to publish the First Canto (then in three volumes) by early 1965. After coming to the United States later that year, Śrīla Prabhupāda continued his commentated translation of the *Bhāgavatam,* and over the next twelve years, while developing his growing Kṛṣṇa consciousness movement and traveling incessantly, he produced twenty-seven more volumes. These were all edited, illustrated, typeset, proofread and indexed by his disciples, members of the Bhaktivedanta Book Trust (BBT). Throughout all of these volumes (totaling twelve in the present edition), Śrīla Prabhupāda's pure devotion to Lord Kṛṣṇa, his consummate Sanskrit scholarship and his intimate familiarity with Vedic culture and thought, and with modern life, combine to reveal to the Western reader a magnificent exposition of this important classic.

After Śrīla Prabhupāda's departure from this world in 1977, his monumental work of translating and commenting on *Śrīmad-Bhāgavatam* was continued by his disciples, headed by Hridayānanda dāsa Goswami, Gopīparāṇadhana dāsa Adhikārī and Draviḍa dāsa Brahmacārī—all seasoned BBT workers. Relying on the same Sanskrit editions of *Śrīmad-Bhāgavatam* that Śrīla Prabhupāda had used, Hridayānanda dāsa Goswami and Gopīparāṇadhana dāsa translated the Sanskrit text and added commentary. Then they turned over the manuscript to Draviḍa dāsa for final editing and production. In this way the concluding six volumes were published.

Readers will find this work of value for many reasons. For those interested in the classical roots of Indian civilization, it serves as a vast detailed reservoir of information on virtually every one of its aspects. For students of comparative philosophy and religion, the *Bhāgavatam* offers a penetrating view into the meaning of India's profound spiritual heritage. To sociologists and anthropologists, the *Bhāgavatam* reveals the practical workings of a peaceful, prosperous and scientifically organized Vedic culture, whose institutions were integrated on the basis of a highly developed spiritual world view. Students of literature will discover the *Bhāgavatam* to be a masterpiece of majestic poetry. For students of psychology, the text provides important perspectives on the nature of consciousness, human behavior and the philosophical study of identity. Finally, to those seeking spiritual insight, the *Bhāgavatam* offers simple and practical guidance for attainment of the highest self-knowledge and realization of the Absolute Truth. The entire eighteen-volume text, presented by the Bhaktivedanta Book Trust, promises to occupy a significant place in the intellectual, cultural and spiritual life of modern man for a long time to come.

—The Publishers

CHAPTER SEVENTY

Lord Kṛṣṇa's Daily Activities

This chapter describes Lord Śrī Kṛṣṇa's daily activities and two proposals placed before Him—one by a messenger from Dvārakā and another by the sage Nārada.

In the early hours of the morning, Lord Kṛṣṇa would rise from bed and bathe Himself in clear water. After executing the dawn rituals and other religious duties, He would offer oblations into the sacred fire, chant the Gāyatrī *mantra,* worship and pay tribute to the demigods, sages and forefathers, and offer respects to learned *brāhmaṇas*. Then He would touch auspicious substances, decorate Himself with celestial ornaments and gratify His subjects by giving them whatever they desired.

The Lord's chariot driver, Dāruka, would bring His chariot, and the Lord would mount it and drive to the royal assembly hall. When He would take His seat in the assembly, surrounded by the Yādavas, He would appear like the moon surrounded by the circle of stars called *nakṣatras*. Bards would recite His praises to the accompaniment of drums, cymbals, *vīṇās* and other instruments.

On one occasion, the doorkeepers escorted a messenger into the assembly hall. The messenger offered prostrated obeisances to the Lord and then, standing with joined palms, addressed Him: "O Lord, Jarāsandha has captured twenty thousand kings and is holding them prisoner. Please do something, for these kings are all Your surrendered devotees."

Just at that moment Nārada Muni appeared. Lord Śrī Kṛṣṇa and all the members of the assembly stood up and offered obeisances to Nārada by bowing their heads. The sage accepted a seat, and then Lord Kṛṣṇa gently questioned him: "Since you travel all over the universe, please inform Us what the Pāṇḍava brothers are planning to do." Nārada then praised the Supreme Lord and replied, "King Yudhiṣṭhira desires to perform the Rājasūya sacrifice. For this he requests Your sanction and presence. Many demigods and illustrious kings will come just to see You."

Understanding that the Yādavas wanted Him to defeat Jarāsandha, Lord Kṛṣṇa asked His wise minister Uddhava to determine which of the two matters at hand—the defeat of Jarāsandha or the Rājasūya sacrifice—should be attended to first.

TEXT 1

श्रीशुक उवाच
अथोषस्युपवृत्तायां कुक्कुटान् कूजतोऽशपन् ।
गृहीतकण्ठ्यः पतिभिर्माधव्यो विरहातुराः ॥१॥

śrī-śuka uvāca
athoṣasy upavṛttāyāṁ
kukkuṭān kūjato 'śapan
gṛhīta-kaṇṭhyaḥ patibhir
mādhavyo virahāturāḥ

śrī-śukaḥ uvāca—Śukadeva Gosvāmī said; *atha*—then; *uṣasi*—the dawn; *upavṛttāyām*—as it was approaching; *kukkuṭān*—the roosters; *kūjataḥ*—who were crowing; *aśapan*—cursed; *gṛhīta*—being held; *kaṇṭhyaḥ*—whose necks; *patibhiḥ*—by their husbands (Lord Kṛṣṇa in His multiple manifestations); *mādhavyaḥ*—the wives of Lord Kṛṣṇa; *viraha*—over separation; *āturāḥ*—agitated.

TRANSLATION

Śukadeva Gosvāmī said: As dawn approached, the wives of Lord Mādhava, each embraced around the neck by her husband, cursed the crowing roosters. The ladies were disturbed that now they would be separated from Him.

PURPORT

This description of Lord Kṛṣṇa's daily activities starts with the crowing of the rooster. Lord Kṛṣṇa's wives knew that the Lord would dutifully get up and perform His prescribed morning rituals, and thus they were agitated at their coming separation from Him and cursed the roosters.

TEXT 2

वयांस्यरोरुवन् कृष्णं बोधयन्तीव वन्दिनः ।
गायत्स्वलिष्वनिद्राणि मन्दारवनवायुभिः ॥२॥

vayāṁsy aroruvan kṛṣṇaṁ
bodhayantīva vandinaḥ
gāyatsv aliṣv anidrāṇi
mandāra-vana-vāyubhiḥ

vayāṁsi—birds; *aroruvan*—sounded loudly; *kṛṣṇam*—Lord Kṛṣṇa; *bodhayanti*—waking; *iva*—as if; *vandinaḥ*—bards; *gāyatsu*—as they sang; *aliṣu*—bees; *anidrāṇi*—aroused from sleep; *mandāra*—of *pārijāta* trees; *vana*—from the garden; *vāyubhiḥ*—by the breeze.

TRANSLATION

The bees' buzzing, caused by the fragrant breeze from the *parijāta* garden, roused the birds from sleep. And when the birds began to sing loudly, they woke Lord Kṛṣṇa like court poets reciting His glories.

TEXT 3

मुहूर्तं तं तु वैदर्भी नामृष्यदतिशोभनम् ।
परिरम्भणविश्लेषात्प्रियबाह्वन्तरं गता ॥३॥

muhūrtaṁ taṁ tu vaidarbhī
nāmṛṣyad ati-śobhanam
parirambhaṇa-viśleṣāt
priya-bāhv-antaraṁ gatā

muhūrtam—time of the day; *tam*—that; *tu*—but; *vaidarbhī*—Queen Rukmiṇī; *na amṛṣyat*—did not like; *ati*—very; *śobhanam*—auspicious; *parirambhaṇa*—of His embrace; *viśleṣāt*—because of the loss; *priya*—of her beloved; *bāhu*—the arms; *antaram*—between; *gatā*—situated.

TRANSLATION

Lying in her beloved's arms, Queen Vaidarbhī did not like this most auspicious hour, for it meant she would lose His embrace.

PURPORT

Śrīla Śrīdhara Svāmī explains that the reaction of Queen Vaidarbhī, Rukmiṇī-devī, shows the attitude of all the queens.

TEXTS 4–5

ब्राह्मे मुहूर्त उत्थाय वार्युपस्पृश्य माधवः ।
दध्यौ प्रसन्नकरण आत्मानं तमसः परम् ॥४॥
एकं स्वयंज्योतिरनन्यमव्ययं
स्वसंस्थया नित्यनिरस्तकल्मषम् ।
ब्रह्माख्यमस्योद्भवनाशहेतुभिः
स्वशक्तिभिर्लक्षितभावनिर्वृतिम् ॥५॥

brāhme muhūrta utthāya
vāry upaspṛśya mādhavaḥ
dadhyau prasanna-karaṇa
ātmānaṁ tamasaḥ param

ekaṁ svayaṁ-jyotir ananyam avyayaṁ
sva-saṁsthayā nitya-nirasta-kalmaṣam
brahmākhyam asyodbhava-nāśa-hetubhiḥ
sva-śaktibhir lakṣita-bhāva-nirvṛtim

brāhme muhūrte—during the most suitable period of the day for spiritual activity, before sunrise; *utthāya*—rising; *vāri*—water; *upaspṛśya*—touching; *mādhavaḥ*—Lord Kṛṣṇa; *dadhyau*—meditated; *prasanna*—clear; *karaṇaḥ*—His mind; *ātmānam*—upon Himself; *tamasaḥ*—ignorance; *param*—beyond; *ekam*—exclusive; *svayam-jyotiḥ*—self-luminous; *ananyam*—without another; *avyayam*—infallible; *sva-saṁsthayā*—by His own nature; *nitya*—perpetually; *nirasta*—dispelling; *kalmaṣam*—contamination; *brahma-ākhyam*—known as Brahman, the Absolute

Truth; *asya*—of this (universe); *udbhava*—of creation; *nāśa*—and destruction; *hetubhiḥ*—by the causes; *sva*—His own; *śaktibhiḥ*—energies; *lakṣita*—manifest; *bhāva*—existence; *nirvṛtim*—joy.

TRANSLATION

Lord Mādhava would rise during the *brāhma-muhūrta* period and touch water. With a clear mind He would then meditate upon Himself, the single, self-luminous, unequaled and infallible Supreme Truth, known as Brahman, who by His very nature ever dispels all contamination, and who through His personal energies, which cause the creation and destruction of this universe, manifests His own pure and blissful existence.

PURPORT

Viśvanātha Cakravartī Ṭhākura points out that the word *bhāva* in this verse indicates the created beings. Thus the compound word *lakṣita-bhāva-nirvṛtim* means that Lord Kṛṣṇa gives pleasure to the created beings through His various energies. Of course, the soul is never created, but our material, conditioned existence is created by the interaction of the Lord's energies.

One who is favored by the Lord's internal potency can understand the nature of the Absolute Truth; this understanding is called Kṛṣṇa consciousness. In *Bhagavad-gītā* Lord Kṛṣṇa explains that His energies are divided into inferior and superior, or material and spiritual, potencies. The *Brahma-saṁhitā* further explains that the material potency acts like a shadow, following the movements of the spiritual reality, which is the Lord Himself and His spiritual potency. When one is favored by Lord Kṛṣṇa, He reveals Himself to the surrendered soul, and thus the same creation that formerly covered the soul becomes an impetus for spiritual enlightenment.

TEXT 6

अथाप्लुतोऽम्भस्यमले यथाविधि
क्रियाकलापं परिधाय वाससी ।
चकार सन्ध्योपगमादि सत्तमो
हुतानलो ब्रह्म जजाप वाग्यतः ॥६॥

athāpluto 'mbhasy amale yathā-vidhi
kriyā-kalāpaṁ paridhāya vāsasī
cakāra sandhyopagamādi sattamo
hutānalo brahma jajāpa vāg-yataḥ

atha—then; *āplutaḥ*—having bathed; *ambhasi*—in water; *amale*—pure; *yathā-vidhi*—according to Vedic rules; *kriyā*—of rituals; *kalāpam*—the entire sequence; *paridhāya*—after dressing; *vāsasī*—in lower and upper garments; *cakāra*—He executed; *sandhyā-upagama*—worship at dawn; *ādi*—and so on; *sat-tamaḥ*—the most saintly of personalities; *huta*—having offered oblations; *analaḥ*—to the sacred fire; *brahma*—the *mantra* of the *Vedas* (namely Gāyatrī); *jajāpa*—He chanted quietly; *vāk*—speech; *yataḥ*—controlling.

TRANSLATION

That most saintly of personalities would then bathe in sanctified water, dress Himself in lower and upper garments and perform the entire sequence of prescribed rituals, beginning with worship at dawn. After offering oblations into the sacred fire, Lord Kṛṣṇa would silently chant the Gāyatrī *mantra*.

PURPORT

Śrīdhara Svāmī points out that since Lord Kṛṣṇa was in the disciplic succession from Kaṇva Muni, He offered oblations to the fire before sunrise. Then He chanted the Gāyatrī *mantra*.

TEXTS 7–9

उपस्थायार्कमुद्यन्तं तर्पयित्वात्मनः कलाः ।
देवानृषीन् पितॄन् वृद्धान् विप्रानभ्यर्च्य चात्मवान् ॥७॥
धेनूनां रुक्मशृंगीनां साध्वीनां मौक्तिकस्रजाम् ।
पयस्विनीनां गृष्टीनां सवत्सानां सुवाससाम् ॥८॥
ददौ रूप्यखुराग्राणां क्षौमाजिनतिलैः सह ।
अलंकृतेभ्यो विप्रेभ्यो बद्वं बद्वं दिने दिने ॥९॥

upasthāyārkam udyantaṁ
tarpayitvātmanaḥ kalāḥ
devān ṛṣīn pitṝn vṛddhān
viprān abhyarcya cātmavān

dhenūnāṁ rukma-śṛṅgīnāṁ
sādhvīnāṁ mauktika-srajām
payasvinīnāṁ gṛṣṭīnāṁ
sa-vatsānāṁ su-vāsasām

dadau rūpya-khurāgrāṇāṁ
kṣaumājina-tilaiḥ saha
alaṅkṛtebhyo viprebhyo
badvaṁ badvaṁ dine dine

upasthāya—worshiping; *arkam*—the sun; *udyantam*—rising; *tarpayitvā*—propitiating; *ātmanaḥ*—His own; *kalāḥ*—expansions; *devān*—the demigods; *ṛṣīn*—sages; *pitṝn*—and forefathers; *vṛddhān*—His elders; *viprān*—and *brāhmaṇas; abhyarcya*—worshiping; *ca*—and; *ātma-vān*—self-possessed; *dhenūnām*—of cows; *rukma*—(covered with) gold; *śṛṅgīnām*—whose horns; *sādhvīnām*—good-natured; *mauktika*—of pearls; *srajām*—with necklaces; *payasvinīnām*—giving milk; *gṛṣṭīnām*—having given birth only once; *sa-vatsānām*—together with their calves; *su-vāsasām*—nicely dressed; *dadau*—He gave; *rūpya*—(covered with) silver; *khura*—of their hooves; *agrāṇām*—the fronts; *kṣauma*—linen; *ajina*—deerskins; *tilaiḥ*—and sesame seeds; *saha*—together with; *alaṅkṛtebhyaḥ*—who were given ornaments; *viprebhyaḥ*—to learned *brāhmaṇas; badvam badvam*—(one hundred and seven) groups of 13,084 (thus totaling 1,400,000); *dine-dine*—each day.

TRANSLATION

Each day the Lord worshiped the rising sun and propitiated the demigods, sages and forefathers, who are all His expansions. The self-possessed Lord would then carefully worship His elders and the *brāhmaṇas*. To those well-attired *brāhmaṇas* He would offer herds of tame and peaceful cows with gold-plated horns and pearl necklaces. These cows were also dressed in fine cloth, and the

fronts of their hooves were plated with silver. Providers of abundant milk, they had each given birth only once and were accompanied by their calves. Daily the Lord gave many groups of 13,084 cows to the learned *brāhmaṇas,* together with linen, deerskins and sesame seeds.

PURPORT

Śrīdhara Svāmī quotes several Vedic scriptures to show that in the context of Vedic ritual, a *badva* here refers to 13,084 cows. The words *badvaṁ badvaṁ dine dine* indicate that Lord Kṛṣṇa would give the learned *brāhmaṇas* many such groups of cows on a daily basis. Śrīdhara Svāmī further gives evidence that the usual practice for great saintly kings in previous ages was to give 107 such *badva,* or groups of 13,084 cows. Thus the total number of cows given in this sacrifice, known as Mañcāra, is 14 lakhs, or 1,400,000.

The words *alaṅkṛtebhyo viprebhyaḥ* indicate that in Lord Kṛṣṇa's kingdom the *brāhmaṇas* were given nice clothes and ornaments and were thus well attired.

In *Kṛṣṇa, the Supreme Personality of Godhead,* Śrīla Prabhupāda writes with striking and profound insight on these pastimes of Lord Kṛṣṇa. The reader is strongly urged to study this book, which contains an invaluable wealth of information and commentary on the pastimes described in the Tenth Canto of *Śrīmad-Bhāgavatam.* Our humble attempt here can never equal the consummate purity and skill of our great master. Still, as a service offered at his lotus feet, we are simply presenting the original Sanskrit text of the Tenth Canto, word-for-word meanings, a clear translation and essential commentary, for the most part based on the statements of the great spiritual masters in our line.

TEXT 10

गोविप्रदेवतावृद्धगुरून् भूतानि सर्वशः ।
नमस्कृत्यात्मसम्भूतीर्मंगलानि समस्पृशत् ॥१०॥

go-vipra-devatā-vṛddha-
gurūn bhūtāni sarvaśaḥ

namaskṛtyātma-sambhūtīr
maṅgalāni samaspṛśat

go—to the cows; *vipra*—*brāhmaṇas; devatā*—demigods; *vṛddha*—elders; *gurūn*—and spiritual masters; *bhūtāni*—to living beings; *sarvaśaḥ*—all; *namaskṛtya*—offering obeisances; *ātma*—to His own; *sambhūtīḥ*—expanded manifestations; *maṅgalāni*—auspicious things (such as a brown cow); *samaspṛśat*—He touched.

TRANSLATION

Lord Kṛṣṇa would offer obeisances to the cows, *brāhmaṇas* and demigods, His elders and spiritual masters, and all living beings—all of whom are expansions of His supreme personality. Then He would touch auspicious things.

TEXT 11

आत्मानं भूषयामास नरलोकविभूषणम् ।
वासोभिर्भूषणैः स्वीयैर्दिव्यस्रगनुलेपनैः ॥११॥

ātmānaṁ bhūṣayām āsa
nara-loka-vibhūṣaṇam
vāsobhir bhūṣaṇaiḥ svīyair
divya-srag-anulepanaiḥ

ātmānam—Himself; *bhūṣayām āsa*—He decorated; *nara-loka*—of human society; *vibhūṣaṇam*—the very ornament; *vāsobhiḥ*—with clothes; *bhūṣaṇaiḥ*—and jewelry; *svīyaiḥ*—belonging to Himself; *divya*—divine; *srak*—with flower garlands; *anulepanaiḥ*—and ointments.

TRANSLATION

He would decorate His body, the very ornament of human society, with His own special clothes and jewelry and with divine flower garlands and ointments.

PURPORT

Śrīdhara Svāmī points out that the Lord's "own garments and ornaments" include the Lord's well-known yellow garments, the Kaustubha gem and so on.

TEXT 12

अवेक्ष्याज्यं तथादर्शं गोवृषद्विजदेवताः ।
कामांश्च सर्ववर्णानां पौरान्तःपुरचारिणाम् ।
प्रदाप्य प्रकृतीः कामैः प्रतोष्य प्रत्यनन्दत ॥१२॥

avekṣyājyaṁ tathādarśam
go-vṛṣa-dvija-devatāḥ
kāmāṁś ca sarva-varṇānāṁ
paurāntaḥ-pura-cāriṇām
pradāpya prakṛtīḥ kāmaiḥ
pratoṣya pratyanandata

avekṣya—looking; *ājyam*—at purified butter; *tathā*—and also; *ādarśam*—at a mirror; *go*—cows; *vṛṣa*—bulls; *dvija*—*brāhmaṇas; devatāḥ*—and demigods; *kāmān*—desired objects; *ca*—and; *sarva*—all; *varṇānām*—to the members of the social classes; *paura*—in the city; *antaḥ-pura*—and in the palace; *cāriṇām*—living; *pradāpya*—arranging to give; *prakṛtīḥ*—His ministers; *kāmaiḥ*—with fulfillment of their desires; *pratoṣya*—fully satisfying; *pratyanandata*—He greeted them.

TRANSLATION

He would then look at ghee, a mirror, the cows and bulls, the *brāhmaṇas* and the demigods and see to it that the members of all the social classes living in the palace and throughout the city were satisfied with gifts. After this He would greet His ministers, gratifying them by fulfilling all their desires.

TEXT 13

संविभज्याग्रतो विप्रान् स्रक्ताम्बूलानुलेपनैः ।
सुहृदः प्रकृतीर्दारानुपायुंक्त ततः स्वयम् ॥१३॥

saṁvibhajyāgrato viprān
srak-tāmbūlānulepanaiḥ
suhṛdaḥ prakṛtīr dārān
upāyuṅkta tataḥ svayam

saṁvibhajya—distributing; *agrataḥ*—first; *viprān*—to the *brāhmaṇas*; *srak*—garlands; *tāmbūla*—betel nut; *anulepanaiḥ*—and sandalwood paste; *suhṛdaḥ*—to His friends; *prakṛtīḥ*—to His ministers; *dārān*—to His wives; *upāyuṅkta*—He partook; *tataḥ*—then; *svayam*—Himself.

TRANSLATION

After first distributing flower garlands, *pān* and sandalwood paste to the *brāhmaṇas*, He would give these gifts to His friends, ministers and wives, and finally He would partake of them Himself.

TEXT 14

तावत्सूत उपानीय स्यन्दनं परमाद्भुतम् ।
सुग्रीवाद्यैर्हयैर्युक्तं प्रणम्यावस्थितोऽग्रतः ॥१४॥

tāvat sūta upānīya
syandanaṁ paramādbhutam
sugrīvādyair hayair yuktaṁ
praṇamyāvasthito 'grataḥ

tāvat—by then; *sūtaḥ*—His chariot driver; *upānīya*—having brought; *syandanam*—His chariot; *parama*—supremely; *adbhutam*—wonderful; *sugrīva-ādyaiḥ*—named Sugrīva and so on; *hayaiḥ*—with His horses; *yuktam*—yoked; *praṇamya*—bowing down; *avasthitaḥ*—standing; *agrataḥ*—before Him.

TRANSLATION

By then the Lord's driver would have brought His supremely wonderful chariot, yoked with Sugrīva and His other horses. His charioteer would bow down to the Lord and then stand before Him.

TEXT 15

गृहीत्वा पाणिना पाणी सारथेस्तमथारुहत् ।
सात्यक्युद्धवसंयुक्तः पूर्वाद्रिमिव भास्करः ॥१५॥

gṛhītvā pāṇinā pāṇī
sārathes tam athāruhat
sātyaky-uddhava-saṁyuktaḥ
pūrvādrim iva bhāskaraḥ

gṛhītvā—taking; *pāṇinā*—with His hand; *pāṇī*—the hands; *sāratheḥ*—of His chariot driver; *tam*—it; *atha*—then; *āruhat*—He mounted; *sātyaki-uddhava*—by Sātyaki and Uddhava; *saṁyuktaḥ*—joined; *pūrva*—of the east; *adrim*—the mountain; *iva*—as if; *bhāskaraḥ*—the sun.

TRANSLATION

Holding on to His charioteer's hands, Lord Kṛṣṇa would mount the chariot, together with Sātyaki and Uddhava, just like the sun rising over the easternmost mountain.

PURPORT

The *ācāryas* point out that the Lord's chariot driver would stand with joined palms and that the Lord, holding on to his joined hands with His right hand, would mount the chariot.

TEXT 16

ईक्षितोऽन्तःपुरस्त्रीणां सव्रीडप्रेमवीक्षितैः ।
कृच्छ्राद्विसृष्टो निरगाज्जातहासो हरन्मनः ॥१६॥

īkṣito 'ntaḥ-pura-strīṇāṁ
sa-vrīḍa-prema-vīkṣitaiḥ
kṛcchrād visṛṣṭo niragāj
jāta-hāso haran manaḥ

īkṣitaḥ—looked upon; *antaḥ-pura*—of the palace; *strīṇām*—of the women; *sa-vrīḍa*—shy; *prema*—and loving; *vīkṣitaiḥ*—by glances; *kṛcchrāt*—with difficulty; *visṛṣṭaḥ*—getting free; *niragāt*—He went out; *jāta*—appeared; *hāsaḥ*—a smile; *haran*—removing; *manaḥ*—their minds.

TRANSLATION

The palace women would look upon Lord Kṛṣṇa with shy, loving glances, and thus He would get free from them only with difficulty. He would then set off, His smiling face captivating their minds.

PURPORT

Śrīla Viśvanātha Cakravartī describes this scene as follows: "The shy, loving glances of the palace women, hinting at their agitation, implied, 'How can we tolerate this torment of being separated from You?' The idea here is that because the Lord was captured by their affection, He smiled, indicating 'My dear restless ladies, you are so overwhelmed by this little bit of separation. I am coming back later today to enjoy with you.' And then, with His smile captivating their minds, He got away only with difficulty, freeing Himself from the bondage of their loving glances."

TEXT 17

सुधर्माख्यां सभां सर्वैर्वृष्णिभिः परिवारितः ।
प्राविशद्यन्निविष्टानां न सन्त्यंग षड्रूर्मयः ॥१७॥

sudharmākhyāṁ sabhāṁ sarvair
vṛṣṇibhiḥ parivāritaḥ
prāviśad yan-niviṣṭānāṁ
na santy aṅga ṣaḍ ūrmayaḥ

sudharmā-ākhyām—known as Sudharmā; *sabhām*—the royal assembly hall; *sarvaiḥ*—by all; *vṛṣṇibhiḥ*—the Vṛṣṇis; *parivāritaḥ*—attended; *prāviśat*—He entered; *yat*—which; *niviṣṭānām*—for those who have entered; *na santi*—do not occur; *aṅga*—my dear King (Parīkṣit); *ṣaṭ*—the six; *ūrmayaḥ*—waves.

TRANSLATION

The Lord, attended by all the Vṛṣṇis, would enter the Sudharmā assembly hall, which protects those who enter it from the six waves of material life, dear King.

PURPORT

Śrīla Prabhupāda writes, "It may be remembered that the Sudharmā assembly house was taken away from the heavenly planet and was reestablished in the city of Dvārakā. The specific significance of the assembly house was that anyone who entered it would be free from the six kinds of material pangs, namely hunger, thirst, lamentation, illusion, old age and death. These are the whips of material existence, and as long as one remained in that assembly house of Sudharmā, he would not be affected by these six material whips."

In this regard, Śrīdhara Svāmī and Viśvanātha Cakravartī explain that when Lord Kṛṣṇa would exit separately from each of His many palaces, each individual form would be visible to the persons present on those particular palace grounds and to the neighboring residents, but not to others. Then, at the gateway path of the Sudharmā assembly hall, all the forms of the Lord would merge into a single form, and thus He would enter the hall.

TEXT 18

तत्रोपविष्टः परमासने विभुर्
बभौ स्वभासा ककुभोऽवभासयन् ।
वृतो नृसिंहैर्यदुभिर्यदूत्तमो
यथोडुराजो दिवि तारकागणैः ॥१८॥

tatropaviṣṭaḥ paramāsane vibhur
babhau sva-bhāsā kakubho 'vabhāsayan
vṛto nṛ-siṁhair yadubhir yadūttamo
yathoḍu-rājo divi tārakā-gaṇaiḥ

tatra—there; *upaviṣṭaḥ*—seated; *parama-āsane*—on His exalted throne; *vibhuḥ*—the almighty Supreme Lord; *babhau*—shone; *sva*—with His own; *bhāsā*—effulgence; *kakubhaḥ*—all the quarters of the sky;

avabhāsayan—making glow; *vṛtaḥ*—surrounded; *nṛ*—among men; *simhaiḥ*—by lions; *yadubhiḥ*—by the Yadus; *yadu-uttamaḥ*—the most excellent of the Yadus; *yathā*—like; *uḍu-rājaḥ*—the moon; *divi*—in the sky; *tārakā-gaṇaiḥ*—(surrounded) by the stars.

TRANSLATION

As the almighty Supreme Lord would seat Himself upon His exalted throne there in the assembly hall, He shone with His unique effulgence, illuminating all the quarters of space. Surrounded by the Yadus, lions among men, that best of the Yadus appeared like the moon amidst many stars.

TEXT 19

तत्रोपमन्त्रिणो राजन्नानाहास्यरसैर्विभुम् ।
उपतस्थुर्नटाचार्या नर्तक्यस्ताण्डवैः पृथक् ॥१९॥

tatropamantriṇo rājan
nānā-hāsya-rasair vibhum
upatasthur naṭācāryā
nartakyas tāṇḍavaiḥ pṛthak

tatra—there; *upamantriṇaḥ*—the jesters; *rājan*—O King; *nānā*—with various; *hāsya*—joking; *rasaiḥ*—moods; *vibhum*—the Supreme Lord; *upatasthuḥ*—they served; *naṭa-ācāryāḥ*—expert entertainers; *nartakyaḥ*—female dancers; *tāṇḍavaiḥ*—with energetic dances; *pṛthak*—separately.

TRANSLATION

And there, O King, jesters would entertain the Lord by displaying various comic moods, expert entertainers would perform for Him, and female dancers would dance energetically.

PURPORT

Śrīla Viśvanātha Cakravartī points out that the word *naṭācāryāḥ* refers, among other things, to expert magicians. All of these different entertainers, one after the other, would perform for the Lord in the assembly of great kings.

TEXT 20

मृदंगवीणामुरजवेणुतालदरस्वनैः ।
ननृतुर्जगुस्तुष्टुवुश्च सूतमागधवन्दिनः ॥२०॥

mṛdaṅga-vīṇā-muraja-
veṇu-tāla-dara-svanaiḥ
nanṛtur jagus tuṣṭuvuś ca
sūta-māgadha-vandinaḥ

mṛdaṅga—of *mṛdaṅga* drums; *vīṇā*—*vīṇās; muraja*—and of *murajas,* another kind of drum; *veṇu*—of flutes; *tāla*—cymbals; *dara*—and conchshells; *svanaiḥ*—with the sounds; *nanṛtuḥ*—they danced; *jaguḥ*—sang; *tuṣṭuvuḥ*—offered praise; *ca*—and; *sūta*—bards; *māgadha*—reciters of history; *vandinaḥ*—and panegyrists.

TRANSLATION

These performers would dance and sing to the sounds of *mṛdaṅgas, vīṇās, murajas,* flutes, cymbals and conchshells, while professional poets, chroniclers and panegyrists would recite the Lord's glories.

TEXT 21

तत्राहुर्ब्राह्मणाः केचिदासीना ब्रह्मवादिनः ।
पूर्वेषां पुण्ययशसां राज्ञां चाकथयन् कथाः ॥२१॥

tatrāhur brāhmaṇāḥ kecid
āsīnā brahma-vādinaḥ
pūrveṣāṁ puṇya-yaśasāṁ
rājñāṁ cākathayan kathāḥ

tatra—there; *āhuḥ*—spoke; *brāhmaṇāḥ*—*brāhmaṇas; kecit*—some; *āsīnāḥ*—seated; *brahma*—in the *Vedas; vādinaḥ*—fluent; *pūrveṣām*—of those of the past; *puṇya*—pious; *yaśasām*—whose fame; *rājñām*—of kings; *ca*—and; *ākathayan*—they recounted; *kathāḥ*—stories.

TRANSLATION

Some *brāhmaṇas* sitting in that assembly hall would fluently chant Vedic *mantras*, while others recounted stories of past kings of pious renown.

TEXT 22

तत्रैकः पुरुषो राजन्नागतोऽपूर्वदर्शनः ।
विज्ञापितो भगवते प्रतीहारैः प्रवेशितः ॥२२॥

tatraikaḥ puruṣo rājann
āgato 'pūrva-darśanaḥ
vijñāpito bhagavate
pratīhāraiḥ praveśitaḥ

tatra—there; *ekaḥ*—one; *puruṣaḥ*—person; *rājan*—O King (Parīkṣit); *āgataḥ*—did come; *apūrva*—never before; *darśanaḥ*—whose appearance; *vijñāpitaḥ*—announced; *bhagavate*—to the Supreme Lord; *pratīhāraiḥ*—by the doorkeepers; *praveśitaḥ*—made to enter.

TRANSLATION

Once a certain person arrived in the assembly, O King, who had never been seen there before. The doorkeepers announced him to the Lord and then escorted him inside.

TEXT 23

स नमस्कृत्य कृष्णाय परेशाय कृताञ्जलिः ।
राज्ञामावेदयद्दुःखं जरासन्धनिरोधजम् ॥२३॥

sa namaskṛtya kṛṣṇāya
pareśāya kṛtāñjaliḥ
rājñām āvedayad duḥkhaṁ
jarāsandha-nirodha-jam

saḥ—he; *namaskṛtya*—after bowing down; *kṛṣṇāya*—to Lord Kṛṣṇa; *para-īśāya*—the Supreme Personality of Godhead; *kṛta-añjaliḥ*—with joined palms; *rājñām*—of the kings; *āvedayat*—he submitted; *duḥkham*—the suffering; *jarāsandha*—by Jarāsandha; *nirodha-jam*—due to imprisonment.

TRANSLATION

That person bowed down to Kṛṣṇa, the Supreme Personality of Godhead, and with joined palms he described to the Lord how a number of kings were suffering because Jarāsandha had imprisoned them.

TEXT 24

ये च दिग्विजये तस्य सन्नतिं न ययुर्नृपाः ।
प्रसह्य रुद्धास्तेनासन्नयुते द्वे गिरिव्रजे ॥२४॥

ye ca dig-vijaye tasya
sannatiṁ na yayur nṛpāḥ
prasahya ruddhās tenāsann
ayute dve girivraje

ye—those who; *ca*—and; *dik-vijaye*—during the conquest of all directions; *tasya*—by him (Jarāsandha); *sannatim*—complete subservience; *na yayuḥ*—did not accept; *nṛpāḥ*—kings; *prasahya*—by force; *ruddhāḥ*—made captive; *tena*—by him; *āsan*—they were; *ayute*—ten thousands; *dve*—two; *giri-vraje*—in the fortress known as Girivraja.

TRANSLATION

Twenty thousand kings who had refused to submit absolutely to Jarāsandha during his world conquest had been forcibly imprisoned by him in the fortress named Girivraja.

PURPORT

Śrīla Viśvanātha Cakravartī points out that these kings refused the payment of tribute and other forms of submission to Jarāsandha. Also, there is a well-known account in the *Mahābhārata* and other literatures that Jarāsandha desired to worship Mahā-bhairava by offering him the lives of one hundred thousand kings in sacrifice.

TEXT 25

राजान ऊचुः
कृष्ण कृष्णाप्रमेयात्मन् प्रपन्नभयभञ्जन ।
वयं त्वां शरणं यामो भवभीताः पृथग्धियः ॥२५॥

rājāna ūcuḥ
kṛṣṇa kṛṣṇāprameyātman
prapanna-bhaya-bhañjana
vayaṁ tvāṁ śaraṇaṁ yāmo
bhava-bhītāḥ pṛthag-dhiyaḥ

rājānaḥ—the kings; *ūcuḥ*—said; *kṛṣṇa kṛṣṇa*—O Kṛṣṇa, Kṛṣṇa; *aprameya-ātman*—O immeasurable Soul; *prapanna*—of those who are surrendered; *bhaya*—the fear; *bhañjana*—O You who destroy; *vayam*—we; *tvām*—to You; *śaraṇam*—for shelter; *yāmaḥ*—have come; *bhava*—of material existence; *bhītāḥ*—afraid; *pṛthak*—separate; *dhiyaḥ*—whose mentality.

TRANSLATION

The kings said [as related through their messenger]: O Kṛṣṇa, Kṛṣṇa, O immeasurable Soul, destroyer of fear for those surrendered to You! Despite our separatist attitude, we have come to You for shelter out of fear of material existence.

PURPORT

Śrīdhara Svāmī explains that the kings present their entreaty in this and the following five verses. In this verse they take shelter of the Lord, in the next three verses they describe their fear, and in the last two verses they make their prayerful request.

TEXT 26

लोको विकर्मनिरतः कुशले प्रमत्तः
कर्मण्ययं त्वदुदिते भवदर्चने स्वे ।

यस्तावदस्य बलवानिह जीविताशां
सद्यश्छिनत्त्यनिमिषाय नमोऽस्तु तस्मै ॥२६॥

loko vikarma-nirataḥ kuśale pramattaḥ
karmaṇy ayaṁ tvad-udite bhavad-arcane sve
yas tāvad asya balavān iha jīvitāśāṁ
sadyaś chinatty animiṣāya namo 'stu tasmai

lokaḥ—the whole world; *vikarma*—to sinful activities; *nirataḥ*—always attached; *kuśale*—which are for their benefit; *pramattaḥ*—bewildered; *karmaṇi*—about duties; *ayam*—this (world); *tvat*—by You; *udite*—spoken; *bhavat*—of You; *arcane*—the worship; *sve*—their own (beneficial engagement); *yaḥ*—who; *tāvat*—inasmuch; *asya*—of this (world); *bala-vān*—powerful; *iha*—in this life; *jīvita*—for longevity; *āśām*—hope; *sadyaḥ*—suddenly; *chinatti*—cuts off; *animiṣāya*—to "unblinking" time; *namaḥ*—obeisances; *astu*—may there be; *tasmai*—to Him.

TRANSLATION

People in this world are always engaged in sinful activities and are thus bewildered about their real duty, which is to worship You according to Your commandments. This activity would truly bring them good fortune. Let us offer our obeisances unto the all-powerful Lord, who appears as time and suddenly cuts down one's stubborn hope for a long life in this world.

PURPORT

Lord Kṛṣṇa states in the *Bhagavad-gītā* (9.27),

yat karoṣi yad aśnāsi
yaj juhoṣi dadāsi yat
yat tapasyasi kaunteya
tat kuruṣva mad-arpaṇam

"Whatever you do, whatever you eat, whatever you offer or give away, and whatever austerities you perform—do that, O son of Kuntī, as an offering to Me."

This is the Supreme Lord's commandment, but people in general are bewildered and neglect this auspicious activity, preferring instead to perform sinful activities that lead them to terrible suffering. The Kṛṣṇa consciousness movement is working to enlighten the world about this most essential activity of loving service to the Lord.

TEXT 27

लोके भवान् जगदिनः कलयावतीर्णः
सद्रक्षणाय खलनिग्रहणाय चान्यः ।
कश्चित्त्वदीयमतियाति निदेशमीश
किं वा जनः स्वकृतमृच्छति तन्न विद्मः ॥२७॥

loke bhavāñ jagad-inaḥ kalayāvatīrṇaḥ
sad-rakṣaṇāya khala-nigrahaṇāya cānyaḥ
kaścit tvadīyam atiyāti nideśam īśa
kiṁ vā janaḥ sva-kṛtam ṛcchati tan na vidmaḥ

loke—into this world; *bhavān*—You; *jagat*—of the universe; *inaḥ*—the predominator; *kalayā*—with Your expansion Baladeva, or with Your time potency; *avatīrṇaḥ*—having descended; *sat*—the saintly; *rakṣaṇāya*—to protect; *khala*—the wicked; *nigrahaṇāya*—to subdue; *ca*—and; *anyaḥ*—other; *kaścit*—someone; *tvadīyam*—Your; *atiyāti*—transgresses; *nideśam*—the law; *īśa*—O Lord; *kim vā*—or else; *janaḥ*—a person; *sva*—by himself; *kṛtam*—created; *ṛcchati*—obtains; *tat*—that; *na vidmaḥ*—we do not understand.

TRANSLATION

You are the predominating Lord of the universe and have descended into this world with Your personal power to protect the saintly and suppress the wicked. We cannot understand, O Lord, how anyone can transgress Your law and still continue to enjoy the fruits of his work.

PURPORT

Śrīdhara Svāmī explains that the kings were bewildered by the suffering that had come upon them. They state here that since the Lord has descended to this world to protect the pious and punish the wicked, how is it that Jarāsandha, who brazenly transgressed the order of the Lord, continued to perform his wicked activities, whereas the kings were put into a miserable condition? Viśvanātha Cakravartī Ṭhākura similarly states that the kings could not understand how Jarāsandha, who harassed the saintly devotees and nourished the envious, could continue to prosper, whereas the kings were being tormented by the wicked Jarāsandha. Similarly Śrīla Prabhupāda quotes the kings as follows in *Kṛṣṇa, the Supreme Personality of Godhead:* "My dear Lord, You are the proprietor of all the worlds, and You have incarnated Yourself along with Your plenary expansion Lord Balarāma. It is said that Your appearance in this incarnation is for the purpose of protecting the faithful and destroying the miscreants. Under the circumstances, how is it possible that miscreants like Jarāsandha can put us into such deplorable conditions of life against Your authority? We are puzzled at the situation and cannot understand how it is possible. It may be that Jarāsandha has been deputed to give us such trouble because of our past misdeeds, but we have heard from revealed scriptures that anyone who surrenders unto Your lotus feet immediately becomes immune to the reactions of sinful life. . . . [We] therefore . . . wholeheartedly offer ourselves unto Your shelter, and we hope that Your Lordship will now give us full protection."

TEXT 28

स्वप्नायितं नृपसुखं परतन्त्रमीश
शश्वद्भयेन मृतकेन धुरं वहामः ।
हित्वा तदात्मनि सुखं त्वदनीहलभ्यं
क्लिश्यामहेऽतिकृपणास्तव माययेह ॥२८॥

svapnāyitaṁ nṛpa-sukhaṁ para-tantram īśa
śaśvad-bhayena mṛtakena dhuraṁ vahāmaḥ
hitvā tad ātmani sukhaṁ tvad-anīha-labhyaṁ
kliśyāmahe 'ti-kṛpaṇās tava māyayeha

svapnāyitam—like a dream; *nṛpa*—of kings; *sukham*—the happiness; *para-tantram*—conditional; *īśa*—O Lord; *śaśvat*—perpetually; *bhayena*—

full of fear; *mṛtakena*—with this corpse; *dhuram*—burden; *vahāmaḥ*—we carry; *hitvā*—rejecting; *tat*—that; *ātmani*—within the self; *sukham*—happiness; *tvat*—done for You; *anīha*—by selfless works; *labhyam*—to be obtained; *kliśyāmahe*—we suffer; *ati*—extremely; *kṛpaṇāḥ*—wretched; *tava*—Your; *māyayā*—with the illusory energy; *iha*—in this world.

TRANSLATION

O Lord, with this corpselike body, always full of fear, we bear the burden of the relative happiness of kings, which is just like a dream. Thus we have rejected the real happiness of the soul, which comes by rendering selfless service to You. Being so very wretched, we simply suffer in this life under the spell of Your illusory energy.

PURPORT

After expressing their doubts in the previous verse, the kings herein admit that actually they are suffering because of their own foolishness, having given up the eternal happiness of the soul in exchange for the temporary, conditional happiness of a so-called kingly position. Most people make a similar mistake, desiring wealth, power, prestige, aristocratic family and so on, in exchange for their own soul. The kings admit that they have fallen under the spell of the Lord's illusory energy and have mistaken the tremendous anxiety of political leadership for happiness.

TEXT 29

तन्नो भवान् प्रणतशोकहराङ्घ्रियुग्मो
बद्धान् वियुङ्क्ष्व मगधाह्वयकर्मपाशात् ।
यो भूभुजोऽयुतमतंगजवीर्यमेको
बिभ्रद् रुरोध भवने मृगराडिवावीः ॥२९॥

tan no bhavān praṇata-śoka-haraṅghri-yugmo
baddhān viyuṅkṣva magadhāhvaya-karma-pāśāt
yo bhū-bhujo 'yuta-mataṅgaja-vīryam eko
bibhrad rurodha bhavane mṛga-rāḍ ivāvīḥ

tat—therefore; *naḥ*—us; *bhavān*—Your good self; *praṇata*—of those who have surrendered; *śoka*—the sorrow; *hara*—which remove; *aṅghri*—of feet; *yugmaḥ*—whose pair; *baddhān*—bound; *viyuṅkṣva*—please release; *magadha-āhvaya*—going by the name Magadha (Jarāsandha); *karma*—of fruitive work; *pāśāt*—from the fetters; *yaḥ*—who; *bhū-bhujaḥ*—kings; *ayuta*—ten thousand; *matam*—maddened; *gaja*—of elephants; *vīryam*—the prowess; *ekaḥ*—alone; *bibhrat*—wielding; *rurodha*—imprisoned; *bhavane*—in His residence; *mṛga-rāṭ*—the lion, king of the animals; *iva*—just as; *aviḥ*—sheep.

TRANSLATION

Therefore, since Your feet relieve the sorrow of those who surrender to them, please release us prisoners from the shackles of *karma*, manifest as the King of Magadha. Wielding alone the prowess of ten thousand maddened elephants, he has locked us up in his house just as a lion captures sheep.

PURPORT

The kings here pray for the Lord to release them from the bondage of *karma* created by the Lord's material potency. The kings make it clear that Jarāsandha is so powerful that there is no hope for them to escape by their own power.

TEXT 30

यो वै त्वया द्विनवकृत्व उदात्तचक्र
भग्नो मृधे खलु भवन्तमनन्तवीर्यम् ।
जित्वा नृलोकनिरतं सकृदूढदर्पो
युष्मत्प्रजा रुजति नोऽजित तद्विधेहि ॥३०॥

yo vai tvayā dvi-nava-kṛtva udātta-cakra
bhagno mṛdhe khalu bhavantam ananta-vīryam
jitvā nṛ-loka-niratam sakṛd ūḍha-darpo
yuṣmat-prajā rujati no 'jita tad vidhehi

yaḥ—who; *vai*—indeed; *tvayā*—by You; *dvi*—twice; *nava*—nine; *kṛtvaḥ*—times; *udātta*—upraised; *cakra*—O You whose disc weapon;

bhagnaḥ—crushed; *mṛdhe*—in battle; *khalu*—surely; *bhavantam*—You; *ananta*—unlimited; *vīryam*—whose power; *jitvā*—defeating; *nṛ-loka*—in human affairs; *niratam*—absorbed; *sakṛt*—only once; *ūḍha*—inflated; *darpaḥ*—whose pride; *yuṣmat*—Your; *prajāḥ*—subjects; *rujati*—torments; *naḥ*—us; *ajita*—O unconquerable one; *tat*—that; *vidhehi*—please rectify.

TRANSLATION

O wielder of the disc! Your strength is unlimited, and thus seventeen times You crushed Jarāsandha in battle. But then, absorbed in human affairs, You allowed him to defeat You once. Now he is so filled with pride that he dares to torment us, Your subjects. O unconquerable one, please rectify this situation.

PURPORT

The word *nṛ-loka-niratam* indicates that the Lord was absorbed in playing within the world of human beings. Thus, while acting like a human king He allowed Jarāsandha to be victorious in a single battle after the Lord had crushed him seventeen times. The kings here imply that Jarāsandha is especially harassing them because they are souls surrendered to Lord Kṛṣṇa. Therefore they beg the Lord, "O You who hold the *cakra* weapon high, please make the proper arrangement."

Śrīla Prabhupāda expresses the kings' feelings as follows: "My dear Lord, You have already fought with Jarāsandha eighteen times consecutively, out of which You have defeated him seventeen times by surpassing his extraordinary powerful position. But in Your eighteenth fight You exhibited Your human behavior, and thus it appeared that You were defeated. My dear Lord, we know very well that Jarāsandha cannot defeat You at any time, because Your power, strength, resources and authority are all unlimited. No one can equal You or surpass You. The appearance of defeat by Jarāsandha in the eighteenth engagement is nothing but an exhibition of human behavior. Unfortunately, foolish Jarāsandha could not understand Your tricks, and he has since then become puffed up over his material power and prestige. Specifically, he has arrested us and imprisoned us, knowing fully that as Your devotees, we are subordinate to Your sovereignty."

TEXT 31

दूत उवाच
इति मागधसंरुद्धा भवद्दर्शनकाङ्‌क्षिणः ।
प्रपन्नाः पादमूलं ते दीनानां शं विधीयताम् ॥३१॥

dūta uvāca
iti māgadha-saṁruddhā
bhavad-darśana-kāṅkṣiṇaḥ
prapannāḥ pāda-mūlaṁ te
dīnānāṁ śaṁ vidhīyatām

dūtaḥ uvāca—the messenger said; *iti*—thus; *māgadha*—by Jarāsandha; *saṁruddhāḥ*—imprisoned; *bhavat*—of You; *darśana*—for the sight; *kāṅkṣiṇaḥ*—anxiously awaiting; *prapannāḥ*—surrendered; *pāda*—of the feet; *mūlam*—to the base; *te*—Your; *dīnānām*—to the pitiable; *śam*—benefit; *vidhīyatām*—please bestow.

TRANSLATION

The messenger continued: This is the message of the kings imprisoned by Jarāsandha, who all hanker for Your audience, having surrendered to Your feet. Please bestow good fortune on these poor souls.

TEXT 32

श्रीशुक उवाच
राजदूते ब्रुवत्येवं देवर्षिः परमद्युतिः ।
बिभ्रत्पिंगजटाभारं प्रादुरासीद्यथा रविः ॥३२॥

śrī-śuka uvāca
rāja-dūte bruvaty evaṁ
devarṣiḥ parama-dyutiḥ
bibhrat piṅga-jaṭā-bhāraṁ
prādurāsīd yathā raviḥ

śrī-śukaḥ uvāca—Śukadeva Gosvāmī said; *rāja*—of the kings; *dūte*—the messenger; *bruvati*—having spoken; *evam*—in this manner; *deva*—of the demigods; *ṛṣiḥ*—the sage (Nārada Muni); *parama*—supreme;

dyutiḥ—whose effulgence; *bibhrat*—wearing; *piṅga*—yellowish; *jaṭā*—of matted locks; *bhāram*—a mass; *prādurāsīt*—appeared; *yathā*—like; *raviḥ*—the sun.

TRANSLATION

Śukadeva Gosvāmī said: When the kings' messenger had thus spoken, the sage of the demigods, Nārada, suddenly appeared. Bearing a mass of golden matted locks on his head, the supremely effulgent sage entered like the brilliant sun.

TEXT 33

तं दृष्ट्वा भगवान् कृष्णः सर्वलोकेश्वरेश्वरः ।
ववन्द उत्थितः शीर्ष्णा ससभ्यः सानुगो मुदा ॥३३॥

taṁ dṛṣṭvā bhagavān kṛṣṇaḥ
sarva-lokeśvareśvaraḥ
vavanda utthitaḥ śīrṣṇā
sa-sabhyaḥ sānugo mudā

tam—him; *dṛṣṭvā*—seeing; *bhagavān*—the Supreme Lord; *kṛṣṇaḥ*—Kṛṣṇa; *sarva*—of all; *loka*—worlds; *īśvara*—of the controllers; *īśvaraḥ*—the supreme controller; *vavanda*—offered His respects; *utthitaḥ*—standing up; *śīrṣṇā*—with His head; *sa*—along with; *sabhyaḥ*—the members of the assembly; *sa*—along with; *anugaḥ*—His followers; *mudā*—joyfully.

TRANSLATION

Lord Kṛṣṇa is the worshipable master of even planetary rulers like Lord Brahmā and Lord Śiva, yet as soon as He saw that Nārada Muni had arrived, He joyfully stood up along with His ministers and secretaries to receive the great sage and offer His respectful obeisances by bowing His head.

PURPORT

This translation is based on Śrīla Prabhupāda's *Kṛṣṇa, the Supreme Personality of Godhead.* The word *mudā* indicates that Lord Kṛṣṇa was delighted to see that Nārada had arrived.

TEXT 34

सभाजयित्वा विधिवत्कृतासनपरिग्रहम् ।
बभाषे सुनृतैर्वाक्यैः श्रद्धया तर्पयन्मुनिम् ॥३४॥

sabhājayitvā vidhi-vat
kṛtāsana-parigraham
babhāṣe sunṛtair vākyaiḥ
śraddhayā tarpayan munim

sabhājayitvā—worshiping; *vidhi-vat*—according to scriptural injunctions; *kṛta*—to him (Nārada) who had done; *āsana*—of a seat; *parigraham*—acceptance; *babhāṣe*—He (Lord Kṛṣṇa) spoke; *su-nṛtaiḥ*—truthful and pleasing; *vākyaiḥ*—with words; *śraddhayā*—with reverence; *tarpayan*—gratifying; *munim*—the sage.

TRANSLATION

After Nārada had accepted the seat offered to him, Lord Kṛṣṇa honored the sage according to scriptural injunctions and, gratifying him with His reverence, spoke the following truthful and pleasing words.

TEXT 35

अपि स्विदद्य लोकानां त्रयाणामकुतोभयम् ।
ननु भूयान् भगवतो लोकान् पर्यटतो गुणः ॥३५॥

api svid adya lokānāṁ
trayāṇām akuto-bhayam
nanu bhūyān bhagavato
lokān paryaṭato guṇaḥ

api svit—certainly; *adya*—today; *lokānām*—of the worlds; *trayāṇām*—three; *akutaḥ-bhayam*—complete freedom from fear; *nanu*—indeed; *bhūyān*—great; *bhagavataḥ*—of the powerful personality; *lokān*—throughout all the planetary systems; *paryaṭataḥ*—who travels; *guṇaḥ*—the quality.

TRANSLATION

[Lord Kṛṣṇa said:] It is certain that today the three worlds have attained freedom from all fear, for that is the influence of such a great personality as you, who travel at will throughout all the worlds.

TEXT 36

न हि तेऽविदितं किञ्चिल्लोकेष्वीश्वरकर्तृषु ।
अथ पृच्छामहे युष्मान् पाण्डवानां चिकीर्षितम् ॥३६॥

na hi te 'viditaṁ kiñcil
lokeṣv īśvara-kartṛṣu
atha pṛcchāmahe yuṣmān
pāṇḍavānāṁ cikīrṣitam

na—not; *hi*—indeed; *te*—to you; *aviditam*—unknown; *kiñcit*—anything; *lokeṣu*—within the worlds; *īśvara*—the Supreme Lord; *kartṛṣu*—whose maker; *atha*—thus; *pṛcchāmahe*—let Us inquire; *yuṣmān*—from you; *pāṇḍavānām*—of the sons of Pāṇḍu; *cikīrṣitam*—about the intentions.

TRANSLATION

There is nothing unknown to you within God's creation. Therefore please tell Us what the Pāṇḍavas intend to do.

TEXT 37

श्रीनारद उवाच
दृष्टा मया ते बहुशो दुरत्यया
माया विभो विश्वसृजश्च मायिनः ।
भूतेषु भूमंश्चरतः स्वशक्तिभिर्
वह्नेरिव च्छन्नरुचो न मेऽद्भुतम् ॥३७॥

śrī-nārada uvāca
dṛṣṭā mayā te bahuśo duratyayā
māyā vibho viśva-sṛjaś ca māyinaḥ
bhūteṣu bhūmaṁś carataḥ sva-śaktibhir
vahner iva cchanna-ruco na me 'dbhutam

śrī-nāradaḥ uvāca—Śrī Nārada said; *dṛṣṭā*—seen; *mayā*—by me; *te*—Your; *bahuśaḥ*—many times; *duratyayā*—insurmountable; *māyā*—power of illusion; *vibho*—O almighty one; *viśva*—of the universe; *sṛjaḥ*—of the creator (Lord Brahmā); *ca*—and; *māyinaḥ*—of the bewilderer (You); *bhūteṣu*—among the created beings; *bhūman*—O all-encompassing one; *carataḥ*—(of You) who move; *sva*—Your own; *śaktibhiḥ*—by energies; *vahneḥ*—of fire; *iva*—as; *channa*—covered; *rucaḥ*—whose light; *na*—not; *me*—for me; *adbhutam*—amazing.

TRANSLATION

Śrī Nārada said: I have seen many times the insurmountable power of Your Māyā, O almighty one, by which You bewilder even the creator of the universe, Brahmā. O all-encompassing Lord, it does not surprise me that You disguise Yourself by Your own energies while moving among the created beings, as a fire covers its own light with smoke.

PURPORT

When Lord Kṛṣṇa questioned Nārada Muni about the intentions of the Pāṇḍavas, the sage replied that the Lord is Himself all-powerful and all-knowing, even to the extent that He can bewilder the creator of the universe, Brahmā. Nārada understood that Lord Kṛṣṇa desired to kill Jarāsandha and was thus beginning to arrange for this pastime by inquiring from Nārada about the Pāṇḍavas' intentions. Understanding the Lord's own intention, Nārada was not astonished when Lord Kṛṣṇa humbly requested information from him.

TEXT 38

तवेहितं कोऽर्हति साधु वेदितुं
स्वमाययेदं सृजतो नियच्छतः ।

यद्विद्यमानात्मतयावभासते
तस्मै नमस्ते स्वविलक्षणात्मने ॥३८॥

tavehitaṁ ko 'rhati sādhu vedituṁ
sva-māyayedaṁ sṛjato niyacchataḥ
yad vidyamānātmatayāvabhāsate
tasmai namas te sva-vilakṣaṇātmane

tava—Your; *īhitam*—purpose; *kaḥ*—who; *arhati*—is able; *sādhu*—properly; *veditum*—to understand; *sva*—by Your own; *māyayā*—material energy; *idam*—this (universe); *sṛjataḥ*—who creates; *niyacchataḥ*—and withdraws; *yat*—which; *vidyamāna*—to exist; *ātmatayā*—by relation to You, the Supersoul; *avabhāsate*—appears; *tasmai*—to Him; *namaḥ*—obeisances; *te*—to You; *sva*—by Your own nature; *vilakṣaṇa-ātmane*—inconceivable.

TRANSLATION

Who can properly understand Your purpose? With Your material energy You expand and also withdraw this creation, which thus appears to have substantial existence. Obeisances to You, whose transcendental position is inconceivable.

PURPORT

Śrīla Prabhupāda explains Nārada's realization as follows: "My dear Lord, by Your inconceivable potencies You create this cosmic manifestation, maintain it and again dissolve it. It is by dint of Your inconceivable potency only that this material world, although a shadow representation of the spiritual world, appears to be factual. No one can understand what You plan to do in the future. Your transcendental position is always inconceivable to everyone. As far as I am concerned, I can simply offer my respectful obeisances unto You again and again."

The word *sva-vilakṣaṇātmane* also indicates that Lord Kṛṣṇa has His own unique nature and characteristics. No one is equal to God or greater than God.

TEXT 39

जीवस्य यः संसरतो विमोक्षणं
न जानतोऽनर्थवहाच्छरीरतः ।
लीलावतारैः स्वयशः प्रदीपकं
प्राज्वालयत्त्वा तमहं प्रपद्ये ॥३९॥

jīvasya yaḥ saṁsarato vimokṣaṇaṁ
na jānato 'nartha-vahāc charīrataḥ
līlāvatāraiḥ sva-yaśaḥ pradīpakaṁ
prājvālayat tvā tam ahaṁ prapadye

jīvasya—for the conditioned living being; *yaḥ*—He (the Supreme Lord) who; *saṁsarataḥ*—(the conditioned soul) caught in the cycle of birth and death; *vimokṣaṇam*—liberation; *na jānataḥ*—not knowing; *anartha*—unwanted things; *vahāt*—which brings; *śarīrataḥ*—from the material body; *līlā*—for pastimes; *avatāraiḥ*—by His appearances in this world; *sva*—His own; *yaśaḥ*—fame; *pradīpakam*—the torch; *prājvālayat*—made to blaze; *tvā*—You; *tam*—that Lord; *aham*—I; *prapadye*—approach for shelter.

TRANSLATION

The living being caught in the cycle of birth and death does not know how he can be delivered from the material body, which brings him so much trouble. But You, the Supreme Lord, descend to this world in various personal forms, and by performing Your pastimes You illumine the soul's path with the blazing torch of Your fame. Therefore I surrender unto You.

PURPORT

Śrīla Prabhupāda writes, "[Nārada said,] In the bodily concept of knowledge, everyone is driven by material desires, and thus everyone develops new material bodies one after another in the cycle of birth and death. Being absorbed in such a concept of existence, one does not know how to get out of the encagement of the material body. Out of Your causeless mercy, my Lord, You descend to exhibit Your different transcendental pastimes, which are illuminating and full of glory. Therefore I have no alternative but to offer my respectful obeisances unto You. My dear Lord, You are the Supreme, Parabrahman, and Your pastimes as an ordinary human are another tactical resource, exactly like a play on the stage, in which an actor plays parts different from his own identity."

TEXT 40

अथाप्याश्रावये ब्रह्म नरलोकविडम्बनम् ।
राज्ञः पैतृष्वस्रेयस्य भक्तस्य च चिकीर्षितम् ॥४०॥

athāpy āśrāvaye brahma
nara-loka-viḍambanam
rājñaḥ paitṛ-ṣvasreyasya
bhaktasya ca cikīrṣitam

atha api—nonetheless; *āśrāvaye*—I shall tell; *brahma*—O Supreme Truth; *nara-loka*—of human society; *viḍambanam*—(to You) who imitate; *rājñaḥ*—of the King (Yudhiṣṭhira); *paitṛ*—of Your father; *svasreyasya*—of the sister's son; *bhaktasya*—Your devotee; *ca*—and; *cikīrṣitam*—the intentions.

TRANSLATION

Nonetheless, O Supreme Truth playing the part of a human being, I shall tell You what Your devotee Yudhiṣṭhira Mahārāja, the son of Your father's sister, intends to do.

TEXT 41

यक्ष्यति त्वां मखेन्द्रेण राजसूयेन पाण्डवः ।
पारमेष्ठ्यकामो नृपतिस्तद् भवाननुमोदताम् ॥४१॥

yakṣyati tvāṁ makhendreṇa
rājasūyena pāṇḍavaḥ
pārameṣṭhya-kāmo nṛpatis
tad bhavān anumodatām

yakṣyati—he will perform sacrifice; *tvām*—unto You; *makha*—of fire sacrifices; *indreṇa*—with the greatest; *rājasūyena*—known as Rājasūya; *pāṇḍavaḥ*—the son of Pāṇḍu; *pārameṣṭhya*—uncontested dominion; *kāmaḥ*—desiring; *nṛ-patiḥ*—the King; *tat*—that; *bhavān*—You; *anumodatām*—please sanction.

TRANSLATION

Desiring unrivaled sovereignty, King Yudhiṣṭhira intends to worship You with the greatest fire sacrifice, the Rājasūya. Please bless his endeavor.

PURPORT

King Yudhiṣṭhira is described here as *pārameṣṭhya-kāma,* or "desiring *pārameṣṭhya.*" The word *pārameṣṭhya* means "unrivaled supremacy" and also indicates "the Supreme Personality of Godhead, who stands at the very height of all existence." Therefore, Śrīla Prabhupāda translates Nārada's message as follows: "You have inquired about Your cousins the Pāṇḍavas in the role of their well-wisher, and therefore I shall let You know about their intentions. Now please hear me. First of all, may I inform You that King Yudhiṣṭhira has all material opulences that are possible to achieve in the highest planetary system, Brahmaloka. He has no material opulence for which to aspire, and yet he wants to perform the Rājasūya sacrifice only to get Your association and to please You. . . . He wants to worship You in order to achieve Your causeless mercy, and I beg to request You to fulfill his desires."

Since the word *pārameṣṭhya* may also indicate the position of Lord Brahmā, the term *pārameṣṭhya-kāma* is taken here by Śrīla Prabhupāda to indicate not only that King Yudhiṣṭhira desired Lord Kṛṣṇa's association and mercy but also that King Yudhiṣṭhira himself possessed *pārameṣṭhya,* all the opulences of Lord Brahmā.

TEXT 42

तस्मिन् देव क्रतुवरे भवन्तं वै सुरादयः ।
दिदृक्षवः समेष्यन्ति राजानश्च यशस्विनः ॥४२॥

tasmin deva kratu-vare
bhavantaṁ vai surādayaḥ
didṛkṣavaḥ sameṣyanti
rājānaś ca yaśasvinaḥ

tasmin—in that; *deva*—O Lord; *kratu*—of sacrifices; *vare*—best; *bhavantam*—You; *vai*—indeed; *sura*—demigods; *ādayaḥ*—and other exalted personalities; *didṛkṣavaḥ*—eager to see; *sameṣyanti*—will all come; *rājānaḥ*—kings; *ca*—also; *yaśasvinaḥ*—glorious.

TRANSLATION

O Lord, exalted demigods and glorious kings, eager to see You, will all come to that best of sacrifices.

PURPORT

The *ācāryas* explain that Nārada here means to say that since all the great personalities will come especially to see Lord Kṛṣṇa, He should also come to that sacrifice.

TEXT 43

श्रवणात्कीर्तनाद्ध्यानात्पूयन्तेऽन्तेवसायिनः ।
तव ब्रह्ममयस्येश किमुतेक्षाभिमर्शिनः ॥४३॥

śravaṇāt kīrtanād dhyānāt
pūyante 'nte-vasāyinaḥ
tava brahma-mayasyeśa
kim utekṣābhimarśinaḥ

śravaṇāt—from hearing; *kīrtanāt*—chanting; *dhyānāt*—and meditating; *pūyante*—become purified; *ante-vasāyinaḥ*—outcastes; *tava*—about You; *brahma-mayasya*—the full manifestation of the Absolute Truth; *īśa*—O Lord; *kim uta*—what then to speak of; *īkṣā*—those who see; *abhimarśinaḥ*—and touch.

TRANSLATION

O Lord, even outcastes are purified by hearing and chanting Your glories and meditating upon You, the Absolute Truth. What then to speak of those who see and touch You?

PURPORT

Śrīla Śrīdhara Svāmī interprets the word *brahma-mayasya* to mean *brahma-ghana-mūrteḥ,* "of the concentrated form of the Absolute Truth."

TEXT 44

यस्यामलं दिवि यशः प्रथितं रसायां
भूमौ च ते भुवनमंगल दिग्वितानम् ।
मन्दाकिनीति दिवि भोगवतीति चाधो
गंगेति चेह चरणाम्बु पुनाति विश्वम् ॥४४॥

yasyāmalaṁ divi yaśaḥ prathitaṁ rasāyāṁ
bhūmau ca te bhuvana-maṅgala dig-vitānam
mandākinīti divi bhogavatīti cādho
gaṅgeti ceha caraṇāmbu punāti viśvam

yasya—whose; *amalam*—spotless; *divi*—in heaven; *yaśaḥ*—fame; *prathitam*—disseminated; *rasāyām*—in the subterranean region; *bhūmau*—on the earth; *ca*—and; *te*—Your; *bhuvana*—for all the worlds; *maṅgala*—O creator of good fortune; *dik*—in or of the universal directions; *vitānam*—the expansion, or decorative canopy; *mandākinī iti*—called Mandākinī; *divi*—in heaven; *bhogavatī iti*—called Bhogavatī; *ca*—and; *adhaḥ*—below; *gaṅgā iti*—called Gaṅgā; *ca*—and; *iha*—here, on the earth; *caraṇa*—from Your feet; *ambu*—the water; *punāti*—purifies; *viśvam*—the whole universe.

TRANSLATION

My dear Lord, You are the symbol of everything auspicious. Your transcendental name and fame is spread like a canopy all over the universe, including the higher, middle and lower planetary systems. The transcendental water that washes Your lotus

feet is known in the higher planetary systems as the Mandākinī River, in the lower planetary systems as the Bhogavatī and in this earthly planetary system as the Ganges. This sacred, transcendental water flows throughout the entire universe, purifying wherever it goes.

PURPORT

This translation is based on Śrīla Prabhupāda's *Kṛṣṇa*. Śrīdhara Svāmī mentions that the word *dig-vitānam* indicates that Lord Kṛṣṇa's transcendental glories spread throughout the universe like a cooling canopy over the universal directions. In other words, the whole world can find shelter under the cooling shade of the Lord's lotus feet. Thus the Lord is *bhuvana-maṅgala*, the symbol of everything auspicious for this world.

TEXT 45

श्रीशुक उवाच
तत्र तेष्वात्मपक्षेष्वगृणत्सु विजिगीषया ।
वाचः पेशैः स्मयन् भृत्यमुद्धवं प्राह केशवः ॥४५॥

śrī-śuka uvāca
tatra teṣv ātma-pakṣeṣv a-
gṛṇatsu vijigīṣayā
vācaḥ peśaiḥ smayan bhṛtyam
uddhavaṁ prāha keśavaḥ

śrī-śukaḥ uvāca—Śukadeva Gosvāmī said; *tatra*—there; *teṣu*—they (the Yādavas); *ātma*—His own; *pakṣeṣu*—supporters; *agṛṇatsu*—not agreeing; *vijigīṣayā*—because of their desire to conquer (Jarāsandha); *vācaḥ*—of speech; *peśaiḥ*—with charming usage; *smayan*—smiling; *bhṛtyam*—to His servant; *uddhavam*—Śrī Uddhava; *prāha*—spoke; *keśavaḥ*—Lord Kṛṣṇa.

TRANSLATION

Śukadeva Gosvāmī said: When His supporters, the Yādavas, objected to this proposal out of eagerness to defeat Jarāsandha, Lord Keśava turned to His servant Uddhava and, smiling, addressed him with fine words.

PURPORT

Śrīla Prabhupāda explains, "Just before the great sage Nārada arrived in the Sudharmā assembly house of Dvārakā, Lord Kṛṣṇa and His ministers and secretaries had been considering how to attack the kingdom of Jarāsandha. Because they were seriously considering this subject, Nārada's proposal that Lord Kṛṣṇa go to Hastināpura for Mahārāja Yudhiṣṭhira's great Rājasūya sacrifice did not much appeal to them. Lord Kṛṣṇa could understand the intentions of His associates because He is the ruler of even Lord Brahmā. Therefore, in order to pacify them, He smilingly [spoke] to Uddhava."

Śrīla Viśvanātha Cakravartī points out that the Lord smiled because He was about to demonstrate Uddhava's brilliant ability to give counsel in difficult situations.

TEXT 46

श्रीभगवानुवाच
त्वं हि नः परमं चक्षुः सुहृन्मन्त्रार्थतत्त्ववित् ।
अथात्र ब्रूह्यनुष्ठेयं श्रद्दध्मः करवाम तत् ॥४६॥

śrī-bhagavān uvāca
tvaṁ hi naḥ paramaṁ cakṣuḥ
suhṛn mantrārtha-tattva-vit
athātra brūhy anuṣṭheyaṁ
śraddadhmaḥ karavāma tat

śrī-bhagavān uvāca—the Personality of Godhead said; *tvam*—you; *hi*—indeed; *naḥ*—Our; *paramam*—supreme; *cakṣuḥ*—eye; *suhṛt*—well-wishing friend; *mantra*—of counsel; *artha*—the value; *tattva-vit*—who knows perfectly; *atha*—thus; *atra*—in this regard; *brūhi*—please say; *anuṣṭheyam*—what is to be done; *śraddadhmaḥ*—We have trust; *karavāma*—We will carry out; *tat*—that.

TRANSLATION

The Personality of Godhead said: You are indeed Our best eye and closest friend, for you know perfectly the relative value of various kinds of counsel. Therefore please tell Us what should be done in this situation. We trust your judgment and shall do as you say.

TEXT 47

इत्युपामन्त्रितो भर्त्रा सर्वज्ञेनापि मुग्धवत् ।
निदेशं शिरसाधाय उद्धवः प्रत्यभाषत ॥४७॥

ity upāmantrito bhartrā
sarva-jñenāpi mugdha-vat
nideśaṁ śirasādhāya
uddhavaḥ pratyabhāṣata

iti—thus; *upāmantritaḥ*—requested; *bhartrā*—by his master; *sarva-jñena*—all-knowing; *api*—even though; *mugdha*—perplexed; *vat*—as if; *nideśam*—the order; *śirasā*—on his head; *ādhāya*—taking; *uddhavaḥ*—Uddhava; *pratyabhāṣata*—replied.

TRANSLATION

[Śukadeva Gosvāmī continued:] Thus requested by his master, who, though omniscient, acted as if perplexed, Uddhava took this order upon his head and replied as follows.

Thus end the purports of the humble servants of His Divine Grace A. C. Bhaktivedanta Swami Prabhupāda to the Tenth Canto, Seventieth Chapter, of the Śrīmad-Bhāgavatam, *entitled "Lord Kṛṣṇa's Daily Activities."*

CHAPTER SEVENTY-ONE

The Lord Travels to Indraprastha

This chapter relates how Lord Kṛṣṇa followed Uddhava's advice and went to Indraprastha, where the Pāṇḍavas celebrated His arrival with great festivity.

Wise Uddhava, knowing Lord Kṛṣṇa's inner desire, advised the Lord as follows: "By conquering all directions and then performing the Rājasūya sacrifice, King Yudhiṣṭhira will fulfill all his purposes—defeating Jarāsandha, protecting those who have taken shelter of You, and executing the Rājasūya-yajña. Thus the Yādavas' powerful enemy will be destroyed and the imprisoned kings freed, and both deeds will glorify You.

"King Jarāsandha can be killed only by Bhīma, and since Jarāsandha is very devoted to the *brāhmaṇas,* Bhīma should disguise himself as a *brāhmaṇa,* go to Jarāsandha and beg a fight from him. Then, in Your presence, Bhīma will defeat the demon."

Nārada Muni, the Yādava elders and Lord Kṛṣṇa all praised Uddhava's plan, and Lord Kṛṣṇa proceeded to mount His chariot and head for Indraprastha, followed by His devoted queens. Soon Lord Kṛṣṇa arrived in that city. Hearing of the Lord's arrival, King Yudhiṣṭhira immediately came out of the city to greet Him. Yudhiṣṭhira repeatedly embraced Lord Kṛṣṇa, losing external consciousness in his ecstasy. Then Bhīmasena, Arjuna, Nakula, Sahadeva and others each embraced or bowed down to Him, as was appropriate.

After Lord Kṛṣṇa had properly greeted everyone, He entered the city as a fanfare of many musical instruments played and reverential hymns were chanted. The women of the city scattered flowers down from the rooftops, remarking on the extreme good fortune of the Lord's queens.

Śrī Kṛṣṇa entered the royal palace and offered respects to Queen Kuntīdevī, who embraced her nephew, and Draupadī and Subhadrā offered obeisances to the Lord. Kuntīdevī then requested Draupadī to worship Lord Kṛṣṇa's wives.

The Supreme Personality of Godhead, Śrī Kṛṣṇa, gratified King Yudhiṣṭhira by remaining there for some months. During this stay He enjoyed strolling here and there. He would drive on chariots with Arjuna, followed by many warriors and soldiers.

TEXT 1

श्रीशुक उवाच
इत्युदीरितमाकर्ण्य देवर्षेरुद्धवोऽब्रवीत् ।
सभ्यानां मतमाज्ञाय कृष्णस्य च महामतिः ॥१॥

śrī-śuka uvāca
ity udīritam ākarṇya
devarṣer uddhavo 'bravīt
sabhyānāṁ matam ājñāya
kṛṣṇasya ca mahā-matiḥ

śrī-śukaḥ uvāca—Śukadeva Gosvāmī said; *iti*—thus; *udīritam*—that which was stated; *ākarṇya*—hearing; *deva-ṛṣeḥ*—by Nārada. the sage of the demigods; *uddhavaḥ*—Uddhava; *abravīt*—spoke; *sabhyānām*—of the members of the royal assembly; *matam*—the opinion; *ājñāya*—understanding; *kṛṣṇasya*—of Lord Kṛṣṇa; *ca*—and; *mahā-matiḥ*—great-minded.

TRANSLATION

Śukadeva Gosvāmī said: Having thus heard the statements of Devarṣi Nārada, and understanding the opinions of both the assembly and Lord Kṛṣṇa, the great-minded Uddhava began to speak.

TEXT 2

श्रीउद्धव उवाच
यदुक्तमृषिना देव साचिव्यं यक्ष्यतस्त्वया ।
कार्यं पैतृष्वस्रेयस्य रक्षा च शरणैषिणाम् ॥२॥

śrī-uddhava uvāca
yad uktam ṛṣinā deva
sācivyaṁ yakṣyatas tvayā

kāryaṁ paitṛ-ṣvasreyasya
rakṣā ca śaraṇaiṣiṇām

śrī-uddhavaḥ uvāca—Śrī Uddhava said; *yat*—what; *uktam*—was stated; *ṛṣinā*—by the sage (Nārada); *deva*—O Lord; *sācivyam*—assistance; *yakṣyataḥ*—to him who intends to perform sacrifice (Yudhiṣṭhira); *tvayā*—by You; *kāryam*—should be rendered; *paitṛ-ṣvasreyasya*—to Your father's sister's son; *rakṣā*—protection; *ca*—also; *śaraṇa*—shelter; *eṣiṇām*—for those who desire.

TRANSLATION

Śrī Uddhava said: O Lord, as the sage advised, You should help Your cousin fulfill his plan for performing the Rājasūya sacrifice, and You should also protect the kings who are begging for Your shelter.

PURPORT

Devarṣi Nārada wanted Lord Kṛṣṇa to go to Indraprastha and help His cousin Yudhiṣṭhira perform the Rājasūya sacrifice. At the same time, the members of the royal assembly strongly desired that He defeat Jarāsandha and rescue the kings he was holding prisoner. The great-minded Uddhava could understand that Lord Kṛṣṇa desired to do both things, and thus he intelligently advised how both these purposes could be simultaneously accomplished.

TEXT 3

यष्टव्यं राजसूयेन दिक्चक्रजयिना विभो ।
अतो जरासुतजय उभयार्थो मतो मम ॥३॥

yaṣṭavyaṁ rājasūyena
dik-cakra-jayinā vibho
ato jarā-suta-jaya
ubhayārtho mato mama

yaṣṭavyam—sacrifice should be performed; *rājasūyena*—with the Rājasūya ritual; *dik*—of directions; *cakra*—the complete circle; *jayinā*—by one who has conquered; *vibho*—O almighty one; *ataḥ*—therefore;

jarā-suta—of the son of Jarā; *jayaḥ*—the conquest; *ubhaya*—both; *arthaḥ*—having the purposes; *mataḥ*—opinion; *mama*—my.

TRANSLATION

Only one who has conquered all opponents in every direction can perform the Rājasūya sacrifice, O almighty one. Thus, in my opinion, conquering Jarāsandha will serve both purposes.

PURPORT

Śrī Uddhava here explains that only one who has conquered all directions is entitled to perform the Rājasūya sacrifice. Therefore Lord Kṛṣṇa should immediately accept the invitation to participate in the sacrifice, but then He should arrange to kill Jarāsandha as a necessary prerequisite. In this way the kings' request for protection would be fulfilled automatically. If the Lord would thus adhere to a single policy—namely, seeing that the Rājasūya sacrifice was performed properly—all purposes would be fulfilled.

According to Śrīla Rūpa Gosvāmī in his *Bhakti-rasāmṛta-sindhu,* one of Lord Kṛṣṇa's qualities is *catura,* "clever," which means that He can perform various types of work at the same time. Thus the Lord could certainly have solved the dilemma of how to simultaneously satisfy King Yudhiṣṭhira's desire to perform the Rājasūya sacrifice and the imprisoned kings' desire for freedom. But Kṛṣṇa wanted to give His dear devotee Uddhava the credit for the solution, and thus He pretended to be perplexed.

TEXT 4

अस्माकं च महानर्थो ह्येतेनैव भविष्यति ।
यशश्च तव गोविन्द राज्ञो बद्धान् विमुञ्चतः ॥४॥

asmākaṁ ca mahān artho
hy etenaiva bhaviṣyati
yaśaś ca tava govinda
rājño baddhān vimuñcataḥ

asmākam—for us; *ca*—and; *mahān*—great; *arthaḥ*—a gain; *hi*—indeed; *etena*—by this; *eva*—even; *bhaviṣyati*—there will be; *yaśaḥ*—

glory; *ca*—and; *tava*—for You; *govinda*—O Govinda; *rājñaḥ*—the kings; *baddhān*—imprisoned; *vimuñcataḥ*—who will release.

TRANSLATION

By this decision there will be great gain for us, and You will save the kings. Thus, Govinda, You will be glorified.

TEXT 5

स वै दुर्विषहो राजा नागायुतसमो बले ।
बलिनामपि चान्येषां भीमं समबलं विना ॥५॥

sa vai durviṣaho rājā
nāgāyuta-samo bale
balinām api cānyeṣāṁ
bhīmaṁ sama-balaṁ vinā

saḥ—he, Jarāsandha; *vai*—indeed; *durviṣahaḥ*—invincible; *rājā*—king; *nāga*—elephants; *ayuta*—to ten thousand; *samaḥ*—equal; *bale*—in strength; *balinām*—among powerful men; *api*—indeed; *ca*—and; *anyeṣām*—others; *bhīmam*—Bhīma; *sama-balam*—equal in strength; *vinā*—except for.

TRANSLATION

The invincible King Jarāsandha is as strong as ten thousand elephants. Indeed, other powerful warriors cannot defeat him. Only Bhīma is equal to him in strength.

PURPORT

Śrīdhara Svāmī explains that the Yādavas were extremely eager to kill Jarāsandha, and thus to caution them Śrī Uddhava spoke this verse. Jarāsandha's death could come only at the hand of Bhīma. Śrīla Viśvanātha Cakravartī adds that Uddhava had previously deduced this from the *Jyotī-rāga* and other astrological scriptures he had learned from his teacher Bṛhaspati.

TEXT 6

द्वैरथे स तु जेतव्यो मा शताक्षौहिणीयुतः ।
ब्राह्मण्योऽभ्यर्थितो विप्रैर्न प्रत्याख्याति कर्हिचित् ॥६॥

dvai-rathe sa tu jetavyo
mā śatākṣauhiṇī-yutaḥ
brāhmaṇyo 'bhyarthito viprair
na pratyākhyāti karhicit

dvai-rathe—in combat involving only two chariots; *saḥ*—he; *tu*—but; *jetavyaḥ*—is to be defeated; *mā*—not; *śata*—by one hundred; *akṣauhiṇī*—military divisions; *yutaḥ*—joined; *brāhmaṇyaḥ*—devoted to brahminical culture; *abhyarthitaḥ*—entreated; *vipraiḥ*—by *brāhmaṇas; na pratyākhyāti*—does not refuse; *karhicit*—ever.

TRANSLATION

He will be defeated in a match of single chariots, not when he is with his hundred military divisions. Now, Jarāsandha is so devoted to brahminical culture that he never refuses requests from *brāhmaṇas*.

PURPORT

It might be argued that since only Bhīma could equal Jarāsandha in personal strength, Jarāsandha would be more powerful when supported by his huge army. Therefore, Uddhava here recommends single combat. But how could Jarāsandha be persuaded to give up the support of his powerful army? Here Uddhava gives the clue: Jarāsandha will never refuse a request from *brāhmaṇas,* since he is devoted to brahminical culture.

TEXT 7

ब्रह्मवेषधरो गत्वा तं भिक्षेत वृकोदरः ।
हनिष्यति न सन्देहो द्वैरथे तव सन्निधौ ॥७॥

brahma-veṣa-dharo gatvā
taṁ bhikṣeta vṛkodaraḥ
haniṣyati na sandeho
dvai-rathe tava sannidhau

brahma—of a *brāhmaṇa; veṣa*—the dress; *dharaḥ*—wearing; *gatvā*—going; *tam*—to him, Jarāsandha; *bhikṣeta*—should beg; *vṛka-udaraḥ*—Bhīma; *haniṣyati*—he will kill him; *na*—no; *sandehaḥ*—doubt; *dvai-rathe*—in one-on-one chariot combat; *tava*—Your; *sannidhau*—in the presence.

TRANSLATION

Bhīma should go to him disguised as a *brāhmaṇa* and beg charity. Thus he will obtain single combat with Jarāsandha, and in Your presence Bhīma will no doubt kill him.

PURPORT

The idea is that Bhīma should beg as charity a one-to-one fight with Jarāsandha.

TEXT 8

निमित्तं परमीशस्य विश्वसर्गनिरोधयोः ।
हिरण्यगर्भः शर्वश्च कालस्यारूपिणस्तव ॥८॥

nimittaṁ param īśasya
viśva-sarga-nirodhayoḥ
hiraṇyagarbhaḥ śarvaś ca
kālasyārūpiṇas tava

nimittam—the instrument; *param*—merely; *īśasya*—of the Supreme Lord; *viśva*—of the universe; *sarga*—in the creation; *nirodhayoḥ*—and the annihilation; *hiraṇyagarbhaḥ*—Lord Brahmā; *śarvaḥ*—Lord Śiva; *ca*—and; *kālasya*—of time; *arūpiṇaḥ*—formless; *tava*—Your.

TRANSLATION

Even Lord Brahmā and Lord Śiva act only as Your instruments in cosmic creation and annihilation, which are ultimately done by You, the Supreme Lord, in Your invisible aspect of time.

PURPORT

Uddhava here explains that in fact Lord Kṛṣṇa Himself will cause the death of Jarāsandha, and Bhīma will merely be the instrument. The Supreme Lord, through His invisible potency of time, creates and annihilates the entire cosmic situation, whereas great demigods such as Lord Brahmā and Lord Śiva are merely the instruments of the Lord's will. Therefore Bhīma will have no difficulty acting as the Lord's instrument to kill the powerful Jarāsandha. In this way, by the Lord's arrangement, His devotee Bhīma will be glorified.

TEXT 9

गायन्ति ते विशदकर्म गृहेषु देव्यो
राज्ञां स्वशत्रुवधमात्मविमोक्षणं च ।
गोप्यश्च कुञ्जरपतेर्जनकात्मजायाः
पित्रोश्च लब्धशरणा मुनयो वयं च ॥९॥

gāyanti te viśada-karma gṛheṣu devyo
rājñāṁ sva-śatru-vadham ātma-vimokṣaṇaṁ ca
gopyaś ca kuñjara-pater janakātmajāyāḥ
pitroś ca labdha-śaraṇā munayo vayaṁ ca

gāyanti—they sing; *te*—Your; *viśada*—spotless; *karma*—deeds; *gṛheṣu*—in their homes; *devyaḥ*—the godly wives; *rājñām*—of the kings; *sva*—of their; *śatru*—enemy; *vadham*—the killing; *ātma*—of themselves; *vimokṣaṇam*—the deliverance; *ca*—and; *gopyaḥ*—the cowherd girls of Vraja; *ca*—and; *kuñjara*—of the elephants; *pateḥ*—of the lord; *janaka*—of King Janaka; *ātma-jāyāḥ*—of the daughter (Sītādevī, the wife of Lord Rāmacandra); *pitroḥ*—of Your parents; *ca*—and; *labdha*—who have attained; *śaraṇāḥ*—shelter; *munayaḥ*—sages; *vayam*—we; *ca*—also.

TRANSLATION

In their homes, the godly wives of the imprisoned kings sing of Your noble deeds—about how You will kill their husbands' enemy and deliver them. The *gopīs* also sing Your glories—how You killed the enemy of the elephant king, Gajendra; the enemy of Sītā, daughter of Janaka; and the enemies of Your own parents as well. So also do the sages who have obtained Your shelter glorify You, as do we ourselves.

PURPORT

Great sages and devotees had informed the grief-stricken wives of the imprisoned kings that Lord Kṛṣṇa would arrange for the killing of Jarāsandha and would thus save them from their crisis. These godly women would thus sing the glories of the Lord at home, and when their children would cry for their fathers, their mothers would tell them, "Child, do not cry. Śrī Kṛṣṇa will save your father." In fact, the Lord has saved many devotees in the past, as described here.

TEXT 10

जरासन्धवधः कृष्ण भूर्यर्थायोपकल्पते ।
प्रायः पाकविपाकेन तव चाभिमतः क्रतुः ॥१०॥

jarāsandha-vadhaḥ kṛṣṇa
bhūry-arthāyopakalpate
prāyaḥ pāka-vipākena
tava cābhimataḥ kratuḥ

jarāsandha-vadhaḥ—the killing of Jarāsandha; *kṛṣṇa*—O Kṛṣṇa; *bhūri*—immense; *arthāya*—value; *upakalpate*—will produce; *prāyaḥ*—certainly; *pāka*—of accumulated *karma; vipākena*—as the reaction; *tava*—by You; *ca*—and; *abhimataḥ*—favored; *kratuḥ*—the sacrifice.

TRANSLATION

O Kṛṣṇa, the killing of Jarāsandha, which is certainly a reaction of his past sins, will bring immense benefit. Indeed, it will make possible the sacrificial ceremony You desire.

PURPORT

Śrīdhara Svāmī explains that the word *bhūry-artha,* "immense benefit," signifies that with the death of Jarāsandha it will become easy to kill the demon Śiśupāla and to realize other objectives. The great commentator Śrīdhara Svāmī further explains that the term *pāka* indicates that the kings will be saved as a result of their piety, and that the term *vipākena* indicates that Jarāsandha will die as a result of his wickedness. In either case, the plan Uddhava has proposed is most favorable for the execution of the great Rājasūya sacrifice, desired by both the Lord and His pure devotees the Pāṇḍavas, headed by King Yudhiṣṭhira.

TEXT 11

श्रीशुक उवाच

इत्युद्धववचो राजन् सर्वतोभद्रमच्युतम् ।
देवर्षिर्यदुवृद्धाश्च कृष्णश्च प्रत्यपूजयन् ॥११॥

śrī-śuka uvāca
ity uddhava-vaco rājan
sarvato-bhadram acyutam
devarṣir yadu-vṛddhāś ca
kṛṣṇaś ca pratyapūjayan

śrī-śukaḥ uvāca—Śukadeva Gosvāmī said; *iti*—thus stated; *uddhava-vacaḥ*—the words of Uddhava; *rājan*—O King (Parīkṣit); *sarvataḥ*—in all ways; *bhadram*—auspicious; *acyutam*—infallible; *deva-ṛṣiḥ*—the sage of the demigods, Nārada; *yadu-vṛddhāḥ*—the Yadu elders; *ca*—and; *kṛṣṇaḥ*—Lord Kṛṣṇa; *ca*—and also; *pratyapūjayan*—praised it in response.

TRANSLATION

Śukadeva Gosvāmī said: O King, Devarṣi Nārada, the Yadu elders and Lord Kṛṣṇa all welcomed Uddhava's proposal, which was entirely auspicious and infallible.

PURPORT

Śrīla Śrīdhara Svāmī explains that the term *acyutam* indicates that Uddhava's proposal was "fortified by logical reasoning." Furthermore,

Śukadeva Gosvāmī specifically indicates by the term *yadu-vṛddhāḥ* that it was the senior members, not the junior ones, who welcomed the proposal. Young princes such as Aniruddha did not like Uddhava's proposal, since they were eager to fight Jarāsandha's army immediately.

TEXT 12

अथादिशत्प्रयाणाय भगवान् देवकीसुतः ।
भृत्यान् दारुकजैत्रादीननुज्ञाप्य गुरून् विभुः ॥१२॥

athādiśat prayāṇāya
bhagavān devakī-sutaḥ
bhṛtyān dāruka-jaitrādīn
anujñāpya gurūn vibhuḥ

atha—then; *ādiśat*—ordered; *prayāṇāya*—in preparation for leaving; *bhagavān*—the Supreme Lord; *devakī-sutaḥ*—the son of Devakī; *bhṛtyān*—His servants; *dāruka-jaitra-ādīn*—headed by Dāruka and Jaitra; *anujñāpya*—taking permission; *gurūn*—from His superiors; *vibhuḥ*—the almighty one.

TRANSLATION

The almighty Personality of Godhead, the son of Devakī, begged His superiors for permission to leave. Then He ordered His servants, headed by Dāruka and Jaitra, to prepare for departure.

PURPORT

The superiors mentioned here are personalities such as Vasudeva, Lord Kṛṣṇa's father.

TEXT 13

निर्गमय्यावरोधान् स्वान्ससुतान् सपरिच्छदान् ।
संकर्षणमनुज्ञाप्य यदुराजं च शत्रुहन् ।
सूतोपनीतं स्वरथमारुहद् गरुडध्वजम् ॥१३॥

nirgamayyāvarodhān svān
sa-sutān sa-paricchadān
saṅkarṣaṇam anujñāpya
yadu-rājaṁ ca śatru-han
sūtopanītaṁ sva-ratham
āruhad garuḍa-dhvajam

nirgamayya—making go; *avarodhān*—wives; *svān*—His; *sa*—with; *sutān*—their sons; *sa*—with; *paricchadān*—their baggage; *saṅkarṣaṇam*—Lord Balarāma; *anujñāpya*—taking leave of; *yadu-rājam*—the King of the Yadus (Ugrasena); *ca*—and; *śatru-han*—O killer of enemies (Parīkṣit); *sūta*—by His driver; *upanītam*—brought; *sva*—His; *ratham*—chariot; *āruhat*—He mounted; *garuḍa*—of Garuḍa; *dhvajam*—whose flag.

TRANSLATION

O slayer of enemies, after He had arranged for the departure of His wives, children and baggage and taken leave of Lord Saṅkarṣaṇa and King Ugrasena, Lord Kṛṣṇa mounted His chariot, which had been brought by His driver. It flew a flag marked with the emblem of Garuḍa.

PURPORT

Having accepted Uddhava's proposal, Lord Kṛṣṇa first proceeded with His wives, family and entourage to the royal city of Indraprastha, the capital of the Pāṇḍavas. The rest of this chapter describes Lord Kṛṣṇa's journey to that city and how He was received there by His loving devotees. In Indraprastha Lord Kṛṣṇa explained to the Pāṇḍavas His plan to first kill Jarāsandha and then perform the Rājasūya sacrifice, and with their full agreement He proceeded, with Bhīmasena, to settle accounts with the wicked king.

Viśvanātha Cakravartī Ṭhākura explains that Lord Kṛṣṇa's wives had also been invited to the Rājasūya sacrifice and were eager to go. The description of the colorful royal procession begins with the following verse.

TEXT 14

ततो रथद्विपभटसादिनायकैः
करालया परिवृत आत्मसेनया ।
मृदंगभेर्यानकशंखगोमुखैः
प्रघोषघोषितककुभो निरक्रमत् ॥१४॥

tato ratha-dvipa-bhaṭa-sādi-nāyakaiḥ
karālayā parivṛta ātma-senayā
mṛdaṅga-bhery-ānaka-śaṅkha-gomukhaiḥ
praghoṣa-ghoṣita-kakubho nirakramat

tataḥ—then; *ratha*—of His chariots; *dvipa*—elephants; *bhaṭa*—infantry; *sādi*—and cavalry; *nāyakaiḥ*—with leaders; *karālayā*—fearsome; *parivṛtaḥ*—surrounded; *ātma*—personal; *senayā*—by His army; *mṛdaṅga*—by *mṛdaṅga* drums; *bherī*—*bherī* horns; *ānaka*—kettledrums; *śaṅkha*—conchshells; *go-mukhaiḥ*—and *gomukha* horns; *praghoṣa*—by the resounding; *ghoṣita*—filled with vibrations; *kakubhaḥ*—all directions; *nirakramat*—He went out.

TRANSLATION

As the vibrations resounding from *mṛdaṅgas, bherīs,* kettledrums, conchshells and *gomukhas* filled the sky in all directions, Lord Kṛṣṇa set out on His journey. He was accompanied by the chief officers of His corps of chariots, elephants, infantry and cavalry and surrounded on all sides by His fierce personal guard.

TEXT 15

नृवाजिकाञ्चनशिबिकाभिरच्युतं
सहात्मजाः पतिमनु सुव्रता ययुः ।
वराम्बराभरणविलेपनस्रजः
सुसंवृता नृभिरसिचर्मपाणिभिः ॥१५॥

nṛ-vāji-kāñcana-śibikābhir acyutaṁ
sahātmajāḥ patim anu su-vratā yayuḥ
varāmbarābharaṇa-vilepana-srajaḥ
su-saṁvṛtā nṛbhir asi-carma-pāṇibhiḥ

nṛ—human; *vāji*—with powerful carriers; *kāñcana*—golden; *śibikābhiḥ*—with palanquins; *acyutam*—Lord Kṛṣṇa; *saha-ātmajāḥ*—along with their children; *patim*—their husband; *anu*—following; *su-vratāḥ*—His faithful wives; *yayuḥ*—went; *vara*—fine; *ambara*—whose clothes; *ābharaṇa*—ornaments; *vilepana*—fragrant oils and ointments; *srajaḥ*—and garlands; *su*—well; *saṁvṛtāḥ*—encompassed; *nṛbhiḥ*—by soldiers; *asi*—swords; *carma*—and shields; *pāṇibhiḥ*—in whose hands.

TRANSLATION

Lord Acyuta's faithful wives, along with their children, followed the Lord on golden palanquins carried by powerful men. The queens were adorned with fine clothing, ornaments, fragrant oils and flower garlands, and they were surrounded on all sides by soldiers carrying swords and shields in their hands.

PURPORT

According to Śrīdhara Svāmī, the word *vāji* indicates that some of Lord Kṛṣṇa's queens were transported by horse-drawn conveyances.

TEXT 16

नरोष्ट्रगोमहिषखराश्वतर्यनः-
करेणुभिः परिजनवारयोषितः ।
स्वलंकृताः कटकुटिकम्बलाम्बराद्य्-
उपस्करा ययुरधियुज्य सर्वतः ॥१६॥

naroṣṭra-go-mahiṣa-kharāśvatary-anaḥ-
kareṇubhiḥ parijana-vāra-yoṣitaḥ
sv-alaṅkṛtāḥ kaṭa-kuṭi-kambalāmbarādy-
upaskarā yayur adhiyujya sarvataḥ

nara—by human carriers; *uṣṭra*—camels; *go*—bulls; *mahiṣa*—buffalo; *khara*—donkeys; *aśvatarī*—mules; *anaḥ*—bullock carts; *kareṇubhiḥ*—and female elephants; *parijana*—of the household; *vāra*—and of public use; *yoṣitaḥ*—the women; *su-alaṅkṛtāḥ*—well decorated; *kaṭa*—made of grass; *kuṭi*—huts; *kambala*—blankets; *ambara*—clothing; *ādi*—and so on; *upaskarāḥ*—whose paraphernalia; *yayuḥ*—they went; *adhiyujya*—having loaded; *sarvataḥ*—on all sides.

TRANSLATION

On all sides proceeded finely adorned women—attendants of the royal household, as well as courtesans. They rode on palanquins and camels, bulls and buffalo, donkeys, mules, bullock carts and elephants. Their conveyances were fully loaded with grass tents, blankets, clothes and other items for the trip.

PURPORT

Śrīla Viśvanātha Cakravartī explains that the household attendants mentioned here included washerwomen and other helpers.

TEXT 17

बलं बृहद्ध्वजपटछत्रचामरैर्
वरायुधाभरणकिरीटवर्मभिः ।
दिवांशुभिस्तुमुलरवं बभौ रवेर्
यथार्णवः क्षुभिततिमिंगिलोर्मिभिः ॥१७॥

balaṁ bṛhad-dhvaja-paṭa-chatra-cāmarair
varāyudhābharaṇa-kirīṭa-varmabhiḥ
divāṁśubhis tumula-ravaṁ babhau raver
yathārṇavaḥ kṣubhita-timiṅgilormibhiḥ

balam—the army; *bṛhat*—huge; *dhvaja*—with flagpoles; *paṭa*—banners; *chatra*—umbrellas; *cāmaraiḥ*—and yak-tail fans; *vara*—excellent; *āyudha*—with weapons; *ābharaṇa*—jewelry; *kirīṭa*—helmets; *varmabhiḥ*—and armor; *divā*—during the day; *aṁśubhiḥ*—by the rays;

tumula—tumultuous; *ravam*—whose sound; *babhau*—shone brilliantly; *raveḥ*—of the sun; *yathā*—like; *arṇavaḥ*—an ocean; *kṣubhita*—agitated; *timiṅgila*—whose *timiṅgila* fish; *ūrmibhiḥ*—and waves.

TRANSLATION

The Lord's army boasted royal umbrellas, *cāmara* fans and huge flagpoles with waving banners. During the day the sun's rays reflected brightly from the soldiers' fine weapons, jewelry, helmets and armor. Thus Lord Kṛṣṇa's army, noisy with shouts and clatter, appeared like an ocean stirring with agitated waves and *timiṅgila* fish.

TEXT 18

अथो मुनिर्यदुपतिना सभाजितः
प्रणम्य तं हृदि विदधद्विहायसा ।
निशम्य तद्व्यवसितमाहृतार्हणो
मुकुन्दसन्दरशननिर्वृतेन्द्रियः ॥१८॥

atho munir yadu-patinā sabhājitaḥ
praṇamya taṁ hṛdi vidadhad vihāyasā
niśamya tad-vyavasitam āhṛtārhaṇo
mukunda-sandaraśana-nirvṛtendriyaḥ

atha u—and then; *muniḥ*—the sage (Nārada); *yadu-patinā*—by Kṛṣṇa, the Lord of the Yadus; *sabhājitaḥ*—honored; *praṇamya*—bowing down; *tam*—to Him; *hṛdi*—in his heart; *vidadhat*—placing Him; *vihāyasā*—through the sky; *niśamya*—having heard; *tat*—His; *vyavasitam*—affirmed intention; *āhṛta*—having accepted; *arhaṇaḥ*—worship; *mukunda*—of Lord Kṛṣṇa; *sandaraśana*—by the meeting; *nirvṛta*—peaceful; *indriyaḥ*—whose senses.

TRANSLATION

Honored by Śrī Kṛṣṇa, the chief of the Yadus, Nārada Muni bowed down to the Lord. All of Nārada's senses were satisfied by his meeting with Lord Kṛṣṇa. Thus, having heard the decision of

the Lord and having been worshiped by Him, Nārada placed Him firmly within his heart and departed through the sky.

TEXT 19

राजदूतमुवाचेदं भगवान् प्रीणयन् गिरा ।
मा भैष्ट दूत भद्रं वो घातयिष्यामि मागधम् ॥१९॥

rāja-dūtam uvācedaṁ
bhagavān prīṇayan girā
mā bhaiṣṭa dūta bhadraṁ vo
ghātayiṣyāmi māgadham

rāja—of the kings; *dūtam*—to the messenger; *uvāca*—He said; *idam*—this; *bhagavān*—the Supreme Lord; *prīṇayan*—pleasing him; *girā*—with His words; *mā bhaiṣṭa*—do not fear; *dūta*—O messenger; *bhadram*—may there be all good; *vaḥ*—for you; *ghātayiṣyāmi*—I shall arrange for the killing; *māgadham*—of the King of Magadha (Jarāsandha).

TRANSLATION

With pleasing words the Lord addressed the messenger sent by the kings: "My dear messenger, I wish all good fortune to you. I shall arrange for the killing of King Māgadha. Do not fear."

PURPORT

The statement *mā bhaiṣṭa*, "do not fear," is in the plural, being intended for both the messenger and the kings. Similarly, the expression *bhadraṁ vaḥ*, "blessings unto you," is also in the plural, expressing a similar intent.

TEXT 20

इत्युक्तः प्रस्थितो दूतो यथावदवदन्नृपान् ।
तेऽपि सन्दर्शनं शौरेः प्रत्यैक्षन् यन्मुमुक्षवः ॥२०॥

ity uktaḥ prasthito dūto
yathā-vad avadan nṛpān
te 'pi sandarśanaṁ śaureḥ
pratyaikṣan yan mumukṣavaḥ

iti—thus; *uktaḥ*—addressed; *prasthitaḥ*—departed; *dūtaḥ*—the messenger; *yathā-vat*—accurately; *avadat*—he told; *nṛpān*—the kings; *te*—they; *api*—and; *sandarśanam*—the audience; *śaureḥ*—of Lord Kṛṣṇa; *pratyaikṣan*—awaited; *yat*—because; *mumukṣavaḥ*—being eager for liberation.

TRANSLATION

Thus addressed, the messenger departed and accurately relayed the Lord's message to the kings. Eager for freedom, they then waited expectantly for their meeting with Lord Kṛṣṇa.

PURPORT

The great Vaiṣṇava scholar Śrīla Jīva Gosvāmī comments here that by force of circumstances the kings began focusing their attention on Lord Kṛṣṇa alone.

TEXT 21

आनर्तसौवीरमरूंस्तीर्त्वा विनशनं हरिः ।
गिरीन्नदीरतीयाय पुरग्रामव्रजाकरान् ॥२१॥

ānarta-sauvīra-marūṁs
tīrtvā vinaśanaṁ hariḥ
girīn nadīr atīyāya
pura-grāma-vrajākarān

ānarta-sauvīra-marūn—Ānarta (the province of Dvārakā), Sauvīra (eastern Gujarat) and the desert (of Rajasthan); *tīrtvā*—crossing through; *vinaśanam*—Vinaśana, the district of Kurukṣetra; *hariḥ*—Lord Kṛṣṇa; *girīn*—hills; *nadīḥ*—and rivers; *atīyāya*—passing; *pura*—cities; *grāma*—villages; *vraja*—cow pastures; *ākarān*—and quarries.

TRANSLATION

As He traveled through the provinces of Ānarta, Sauvīra, Marudeśa and Vinaśana, Lord Hari crossed rivers and passed mountains, cities, villages, cow pastures and quarries.

TEXT 22

ततो दृषद्वतीं तीर्त्वा मुकुन्दोऽथ सरस्वतीम् ।
पञ्चालानथ मत्स्यांश्च शक्रप्रस्थमथागमत् ॥२२॥

tato dṛṣadvatīṁ tīrtvā
mukundo 'tha sarasvatīm
pañcālān atha matsyāṁś ca
śakra-prastham athāgamat

tataḥ—then; *dṛṣadvatīm*—the river Dṛṣadvati; *tīrtvā*—crossing; *mukundaḥ*—Lord Kṛṣṇa; *atha*—then; *sarasvatīm*—the river Sarasvatī; *pañcālān*—the Pañcāla province; *atha*—then; *matsyān*—the Matsya province; *ca*—also; *śakra-prastham*—to Indraprastha; *atha*—and; *āgamat*—He came.

TRANSLATION

After crossing the rivers Dṛṣadvatī and Sarasvatī, He passed through Pañcāla and Matsya and finally came to Indraprastha.

TEXT 23

तमुपागतमाकर्ण्य प्रीतो दुर्दर्शनं नृणाम् ।
अजातशत्रुर्निरगात्सोपध्यायः सुहृद्वृतः ॥२३॥

tam upāgatam ākarṇya
prīto durdarśanaṁ nṛṇām
ajāta-śatrur niragāt
sopadhyāyaḥ suhṛd-vṛtaḥ

tam—Him; *upāgatam*—arrived; *ākarṇya*—hearing; *prītaḥ*—pleased; *durdarśanam*—rarely seen; *nṛṇām*—by humans; *ajāta-śatruḥ*—King Yudhiṣṭhira, whose enemy was never born; *niragāt*—came out; *sa*—with; *upadhyāyaḥ*—his priests; *suhṛt*—by relatives; *vṛtaḥ*—surrounded.

TRANSLATION

King Yudhiṣṭhira was delighted to hear that the Lord, whom human beings rarely see, had now arrived. Accompanied by his priests and dear associates, the King came out to meet Lord Kṛṣṇa.

TEXT 24

गीतवादित्रघोषेण ब्रह्मघोषेण भूयसा ।
अभ्ययात्स हृषीकेशं प्राणाः प्राणमिवादृतः ॥२४॥

gīta-vāditra-ghoṣeṇa
brahma-ghoṣeṇa bhūyasā
abhyayāt sa hṛṣīkeśaṁ
prāṇāḥ prāṇam ivādṛtaḥ

gīta—of song; *vāditra*—and instrumental music; *ghoṣeṇa*—with the sound; *brahma*—of the *Vedas;* *ghoṣeṇa*—with the sound; *bhūyasā*—abundant; *abhyayāt*—went forth; *saḥ*—he; *hṛṣīkeśam*—to Lord Kṛṣṇa; *prāṇāḥ*—the senses; *prāṇam*—consciousness, or the air of life; *iva*—as; *ādṛtaḥ*—reverential.

TRANSLATION

As songs and musical instruments resounded along with the loud vibration of Vedic hymns, the King went forth with great reverence to meet Lord Hṛṣīkeśa, just as the senses go forth to meet the consciousness of life.

PURPORT

Lord Kṛṣṇa is here described as Hṛṣīkeśa, the Lord of the senses, and King Yudhiṣṭhira's rushing to the Lord is compared to the senses eagerly joining the consciousness of life. Without consciousness, the senses are useless; indeed, the senses function through consciousness. Similarly, when the individual souls are bereft of Kṛṣṇa consciousness, love of God, they enter into a useless and illusory struggle called material existence. Pure devotees like King Yudhiṣṭhira are never bereft of the Lord's association, for they keep Him always within their heart, and yet they feel special ecstasy when they see the Lord after long separation, as described here.

TEXT 25

दृष्ट्वा विक्लिन्नहृदयः कृष्णं स्नेहेन पाण्डवः ।
चिराद्दृष्टं प्रियतमं सस्वजेऽथ पुनः पुनः ॥२५॥

dṛṣṭvā viklinna-hṛdayaḥ
kṛṣṇaṁ snehena pāṇḍavaḥ
cirād dṛṣṭaṁ priyatamaṁ
sasvaje 'tha punaḥ punaḥ

dṛṣṭvā—seeing; *viklinna*—melted; *hṛdayaḥ*—his heart; *kṛṣṇam*—Lord Kṛṣṇa; *snehena*—with affection; *pāṇḍavaḥ*—the son of Pāṇḍu; *cirāt*—after a long time; *dṛṣṭam*—seen; *priya-tamam*—his dearmost friend; *sasvaje*—he embraced Him; *atha*—thereupon; *punaḥ punaḥ*—again and again.

TRANSLATION

The heart of King Yudhiṣṭhira melted with affection when he saw his dearmost friend, Lord Kṛṣṇa, after such a long separation, and he embraced the Lord again and again.

TEXT 26

दोर्भ्यां परिष्वज्य रमामलालयं
मुकुन्दगात्रं नृपतिर्हताशुभः ।
लेभे परां निर्वृतिमश्रुलोचनो
हृष्यत्तनुर्विस्मृतलोकविभ्रमः ॥२६॥

dorbhyāṁ pariṣvajya ramāmalālayaṁ
mukunda-gātraṁ nṛ-patir hatāśubhaḥ
lebhe parāṁ nirvṛtim aśru-locano
hṛṣyat-tanur vismṛta-loka-vibhramaḥ

dorbhyām—with his arms; *pariṣvajya*—embracing; *ramā*—of the goddess of fortune; *amala*—faultless; *alayam*—the abode; *mukunda*—of Lord Kṛṣṇa; *gātram*—the body; *nṛ-patiḥ*—the king; *hata*—destroyed; *aśubhaḥ*—all of whose bad fortune; *lebhe*—achieved; *parām*—the highest; *nirvṛtim*—joy; *aśru*—tears; *locanaḥ*—in whose eyes; *hṛṣyat*—exhilarated; *tanuḥ*—whose body; *vismṛta*—forgetting; *loka*—of the mundane realm; *vibhramaḥ*—the illusory affairs.

TRANSLATION

The eternal form of Lord Kṛṣṇa is the everlasting residence of the goddess of fortune. As soon as King Yudhiṣṭhira embraced Him, the King became free of all the contamination of material existence. He immediately felt transcendental bliss and merged in an ocean of happiness. There were tears in his eyes, and his body shook due to ecstasy. He completely forgot that he was living in this material world.

PURPORT

The above translation is taken from Śrīla Prabhupāda's *Kṛṣṇa*.

TEXT 27

तं मातुलेयं परिरभ्य निर्वृतो
भीमः स्मयन् प्रेमजलाकुलेन्द्रियः ।
यमौ किरीटी च सुहृत्तमं मुदा
प्रवृद्धबाष्पाः परिरेभिरेऽच्युतम् ॥२७॥

taṁ mātuleyaṁ parirabhya nirvṛto
bhīmaḥ smayan prema-jalākulendriyaḥ
yamau kirīṭī ca suhṛttamaṁ mudā
pravṛddha-bāṣpāḥ parirebhire 'cyutam

tam—Him; *mātuleyam*—his mother's brother's son; *parirabhya*—embracing; *nirvṛtaḥ*—filled with joy; *bhīmaḥ*—Bhīmasena; *smayan*—laughing; *prema*—due to love; *jala*—with the water (tears); *ākula*—filled; *indriyaḥ*—whose eyes; *yamau*—the twins (Nakula and Sahadeva); *kirīṭī*—Arjuna; *ca*—and; *suhṛt-tamam*—their dearmost friend; *mudā*—with pleasure; *pravṛddha*—profuse; *bāṣpāḥ*—whose tears; *parirebhire*—they embraced; *acyutam*—the infallible Lord.

TRANSLATION

Then Bhīma, his eyes brimming with tears, laughed with joy as he embraced his maternal cousin, Kṛṣṇa. Arjuna and the twins—Nakula and Sahadeva—also joyfully embraced their dearmost friend, the infallible Lord, and they cried profusely.

TEXT 28

अर्जुनेन परिष्वक्तो यमाभ्यामभिवादितः ।
ब्राह्मणेभ्यो नमस्कृत्य वृद्धेभ्यश्च यथार्हतः ।
मानिनो मानयामास कुरुसृञ्जयकैकयान् ॥२८॥

arjunena pariṣvakto
yamābhyām abhivāditaḥ
brāhmaṇebhyo namaskṛtya
vṛddhebhyaś ca yathārhataḥ
mānino mānayām āsa
kuru-sṛñjaya-kaikayān

arjunena—by Arjuna; *pariṣvaktaḥ*—embraced; *yamābhyām*—by the twins; *abhivāditaḥ*—offered obeisances; *brāhmaṇebhyaḥ*—to the *brāhmaṇas; namaskṛtya*—bowing down; *vṛddhebhyaḥ*—to the elders; *ca*—and; *yathā-arhataḥ*—according to etiquette; *māninaḥ*—the honorable ones; *mānayām āsa*—He honored; *kuru-sṛñjaya-kaikayān*—the Kurus, Sṛñjayas and Kaikayas.

TRANSLATION

After Arjuna had embraced Him once more and Nakula and Sahadeva had offered Him their obeisances, Lord Kṛṣṇa bowed

down to the *brāhmaṇas* and elders present, thus properly honoring the respectable members of the Kuru, Sṛñjaya and Kaikaya clans.

PURPORT

Śrīla Śrīdhara Svāmī mentions that since Arjuna was considered Lord Kṛṣṇa's social equal, when Arjuna tried to bow down to Him, Lord Kṛṣṇa held Arjuna by his arms so that he could only embrace Him. The twins, however, being junior cousins, bowed down and grasped Lord Kṛṣṇa's feet.

TEXT 29

सूतमागधगन्धर्वा वन्दिनश्चोपमन्त्रिण: ।
मृदंगशंखपटहवीणापणवगोमुखै: ।
ब्राह्मणाश्चारविन्दाक्षं तुष्टुवुर्ननृतुर्जगु: ॥२९॥

sūta-māgadha-gandharvā
vandinaś copamantriṇaḥ
mṛdaṅga-śaṅkha-paṭaha-
vīṇā-paṇava-gomukhaiḥ
brāhmaṇāś cāravindākṣaṁ
tuṣṭuvur nanṛtur jaguḥ

sūta—bards; *māgadha*—chroniclers; *gandharvāḥ*—demigods known for their singing; *vandinaḥ*—eulogists; *ca*—and; *upamantriṇaḥ*—jesters; *mṛdaṅga*—with *mṛdaṅga* drums; *śaṅkha*—conchshells; *paṭaha*—kettledrums; *vīṇā*—*vīṇās; paṇava*—a smaller drum; *gomukhaiḥ*—and *gomukha* horns; *brāhmaṇāḥ*—*brāhmaṇas; ca*—as well; *aravinda-akṣam*—the lotus-eyed Lord; *tuṣṭuvuḥ*—glorified with hymns; *nanṛtuḥ*—danced; *jaguḥ*—sang.

TRANSLATION

Sūtas, Māgadhas, Gandharvas, Vandīs, jesters and *brāhmaṇas* all glorified the lotus-eyed Lord—some reciting prayers, some dancing and singing—as *mṛdaṅgas*, conchshells, kettledrums, *vīṇās, paṇavas* and *gomukhas* resounded.

TEXT 30

एवं सुहृद्भिः पर्यस्तः पुण्यश्लोकशिखामणिः ।
संस्तूयमानो भगवान् विवेशालंकृतं पुरम् ॥३०॥

evaṁ suhṛdbhiḥ paryastaḥ
puṇya-śloka-śikhāmaṇiḥ
saṁstūyamāno bhagavān
viveśālaṅkṛtaṁ puram

evam—thus; *su-hṛdbhiḥ*—by His well-wishing relatives; *paryastaḥ*—surrounded; *puṇya-śloka*—of persons of pious renown; *śikhā-maṇiḥ*—the crest jewel; *saṁstūyamānaḥ*—being glorified; *bhagavān*—the Supreme Lord; *viveśa*—entered; *alaṅkṛtam*—decorated; *puram*—the city.

TRANSLATION

Thus surrounded by His well-wishing relatives and praised on all sides, Lord Kṛṣṇa, the crest jewel of the justly renowned, entered the decorated city.

PURPORT

Śrīla Prabhupāda writes, "While Lord Kṛṣṇa was entering the city, all the people were talking among themselves about the glories of the Lord, praising His transcendental name, quality, form, etc."

TEXTS 31–32

संसिक्तवर्त्म करिणां मदगन्धतोयैश्
चित्रध्वजैः कनकतोरणपूर्णकुम्भैः ।
मृष्टात्मभिर्नवदुकूलविभूषणस्रग्-
गन्धैर्नृभिर्युवतिभिश्च विराजमानम् ॥३१॥
उद्दीप्तदीपबलिभिः प्रतिसद्म जाल-
निर्यातधूपरुचिरं विलसत्पताकम् ।
मूर्धन्यहेमकलशै रजतोरुशृंगैर्
जुष्टं ददर्श भवनैः कुरुराजधाम ॥३२॥

saṁsikta-vartma kariṇāṁ mada-gandha-toyaiś
citra-dhvajaiḥ kanaka-toraṇa-pūrṇa-kumbhaiḥ
mṛṣṭātmabhir nava-dukūla-vibhūṣaṇa-srag-
gandhair nṛbhir yuvatibhiś ca virājamānam

uddīpta-dīpa-balibhiḥ prati-sadma jāla-
niryāta-dhūpa-ruciraṁ vilasat-patākam
mūrdhanya-hema-kalaśai rajatoru-śṛṅgair
juṣṭaṁ dadarśa bhavanaiḥ kuru-rāja-dhāma

saṁsikta—sprinkled with water; *vartma*—whose roads; *kariṇām*—of elephants; *mada*—of the liquid exuding from their foreheads; *gandha*—fragrant; *toyaiḥ*—with the water; *citra*—colorful; *dhvajaiḥ*—with flags; *kanaka*—golden; *toraṇa*—with gateways; *pūrṇa-kumbhaiḥ*—and full waterpots; *mṛṣṭa*—decorated; *ātmabhiḥ*—whose bodies; *nava*—new; *dukūla*—with fine garments; *vibhūṣaṇa*—ornaments; *srak*—flower garlands; *gandhaiḥ*—and aromatic sandalwood paste; *nṛbhiḥ*—with men; *yuvatibhiḥ*—with young women; *ca*—also; *virājamānam*—resplendent; *uddīpta*—lit; *dīpa*—with lamps; *balibhiḥ*—and offerings of tribute; *prati*—each; *sadma*—home; *jāla*—from the holes of latticed windows; *niryāta*—drifting; *dhūpa*—with incense smoke; *ruciram*—attractive; *vilasat*—waving; *patākam*—with banners; *mūrdhanya*—on the roofs; *hema*—gold; *kalaśaiḥ*—with domes; *rajata*—of silver; *uru*—large; *śṛṅgaiḥ*—with platforms; *juṣṭam*—adorned; *dadarśa*—He saw; *bhavanaiḥ*—with homes; *kuru-rāja*—of the King of the Kurus; *dhāma*—the domain.

TRANSLATION

The roads of Indraprastha were sprinkled with water perfumed by the liquid from elephants' foreheads, and colorful flags, golden gateways and full waterpots enhanced the city's splendor. Men and young girls were beautifully arrayed in fine, new garments, adorned with flower garlands and ornaments, and anointed with aromatic sandalwood paste. Every home displayed glowing lamps and respectful offerings, and from the holes of the latticed windows drifted incense, further beautifying the city. Banners waved, and the roofs were decorated with golden domes on broad silver bases. Thus Lord Kṛṣṇa saw the royal city of the King of the Kurus.

PURPORT

Śrīla Prabhupāda adds in this connection: "Lord Kṛṣṇa thus entered the city of the Pāṇḍavas, enjoyed the beautiful atmosphere and slowly proceeded ahead."

TEXT 33

प्राप्तं निशम्य नरलोचनपानपात्रम्
औत्सुक्यविश्लथितकेशदुकूलबन्धाः ।
सद्यो विसृज्य गृहकर्म पतींश्च तल्पे
द्रष्टुं ययुर्युवतयः स्म नरेन्द्रमार्गे ॥३३॥

prāptaṁ niśamya nara-locana-pāna-pātram
autsukya-viślathita-keśa-dukūla-bandhāḥ
sadyo visṛjya gṛha-karma patīṁś ca talpe
draṣṭuṁ yayur yuvatayaḥ sma narendra-mārge

prāptam—arrived; *niśamya*—hearing; *nara*—of men; *locana*—of the eyes; *pāna*—of drinking; *pātram*—the object, or reservoir; *autsukya*—out of their eagerness; *viślathita*—loosened; *keśa*—their hair; *dukūla*—of their dresses; *bandhāḥ*—and the knots; *sadyaḥ*—immediately; *visṛjya*—abandoning; *gṛha*—of the household; *karma*—their work; *patīn*—their husbands; *ca*—and; *talpe*—in bed; *draṣṭum*—to see; *yayuḥ*—went; *yuvatayaḥ*—the young girls; *sma*—indeed; *nara-indra*—of the king; *mārge*—onto the road.

TRANSLATION

When the young women of the city heard that Lord Kṛṣṇa, the reservoir of pleasure for human eyes, had arrived, they hurriedly went onto the royal road to see Him. They abandoned their household duties and even left their husbands in bed, and in their eagerness the knots of their hair and garments came loose.

TEXT 34

तस्मिन् सुसंकुल इभाश्वरथद्विपद्भिः
कृष्णं सभार्यमुपलभ्य गृहाधिरूढाः ।

नार्यो विकीर्य कुसुमैर्मनसोपगुह्य
सुस्वागतं विदधुरुत्स्मयवीक्षितेन ॥३४॥

tasmin su-saṅkula ibhāśva-ratha-dvipadbhiḥ
kṛṣṇaṁ sa-bhāryam upalabhya gṛhādhirūḍhāḥ
nāryo vikīrya kusumair manasopaguhya
su-svāgataṁ vidadhur utsmaya-vīkṣitena

tasmin—on that (road); *su*—very; *saṅkule*—crowded; *ibha*—with elephants; *aśva*—horses; *ratha*—chariots; *dvi-padbhiḥ*—and foot soldiers; *kṛṣṇam*—Lord Kṛṣṇa; *sa-bhāryam*—with His wives; *upalabhya*—catching sight of; *gṛha*—of the homes; *adhirūḍhāḥ*—having climbed to the tops; *nāryaḥ*—the women; *vikīrya*—scattering; *kusumaiḥ*—flowers; *manasā*—in their minds; *upaguhya*—embracing Him; *su-svāgatam*—heartfelt welcome; *vidadhuḥ*—they gave Him; *utsmaya*—broadly smiling; *vīkṣitena*—with their glances.

TRANSLATION

The royal road being quite crowded with elephants, horses, chariots and foot soldiers, the women climbed to the top of their houses, where they caught sight of Lord Kṛṣṇa and His queens. The city ladies scattered flowers upon the Lord, embraced Him in their minds and expressed their heartfelt welcome with broadly smiling glances.

PURPORT

Śrīla Śrīdhara Svāmī comments that the ladies communicated through their affectionate glances, their eager inquiries as to the comfort of Lord Kṛṣṇa's trip, and so on. In other words, in their ecstasy they intensely desired to serve the Lord.

TEXT 35

ऊचुः स्त्रियः पथि निरीक्ष्य मुकुन्दपत्नीस्
तारा यथोडुपसहाः किमकार्यमूभिः ।

यच्चक्षुषां पुरुषमौलिरुदारहास-
लीलावलोककलयोत्सवमातनोति ॥३५॥

ūcuḥ striyaḥ pathi nirīkṣya mukunda-patnīs
tārā yathoḍupa-sahāḥ kim akāry amūbhiḥ
yac cakṣuṣāṁ puruṣa-maulir udāra-hāsa-
līlāvaloka-kalayotsavam ātanoti

ūcuḥ—said; *striyaḥ*—the women; *pathi*—upon the road; *nirīkṣya*—seeing; *mukunda*—of Lord Kṛṣṇa; *patnīḥ*—the wives; *tārāḥ*—stars; *yathā*—like; *uḍu-pa*—the moon; *sahāḥ*—accompanying; *kim*—what; *akāri*—was done; *amūbhiḥ*—by them; *yat*—since; *cakṣuṣām*—for their eyes; *puruṣa*—of men; *mauliḥ*—the diadem; *udāra*—wide; *hāsa*—with smiles; *līlā*—playful; *avaloka*—of His glances; *kalayā*—with a small portion; *utsavam*—a festival; *ātanoti*—He bestows.

TRANSLATION

Observing Lord Mukunda's wives passing on the road like stars accompanying the moon, the women exclaimed, "What have these ladies done so that the best of men bestows upon their eyes the joy of His generous smiles and playful sidelong glances?"

TEXT 36

तत्र तत्रोपसंगम्य पौरा मंगलपाणयः ।
चक्रुः सपर्यां कृष्णाय श्रेणीमुख्या हतैनसः ॥३६॥

tatra tatropasaṅgamya
paurā maṅgala-pāṇayaḥ
cakruḥ saparyāṁ kṛṣṇāya
śreṇī-mukhyā hatainasaḥ

tatra tatra—in various places; *upasaṅgamya*—approaching; *paurāḥ*—citizens of the city; *maṅgala*—auspicious offerings; *pāṇayaḥ*—in their hands; *cakruḥ*—performed; *saparyām*—worship; *kṛṣṇāya*—for Lord

Kṛṣṇa; *śreṇī*—of occupational guilds; *mukhyāḥ*—the leaders; *hata*—eradicated; *enasaḥ*—whose sins.

TRANSLATION

In various places citizens of the city came forward holding auspicious offerings for Lord Kṛṣṇa, and sinless leaders of occupational guilds came forward to worship the Lord.

PURPORT

Śrīla Prabhupāda writes, "While Lord Kṛṣṇa was thus passing on the road, at intervals some of the opulent citizens, who were all rich, respectable and freed from sinful activities, presented auspicious articles to the Lord, just to offer Him a reception to the city. Thus they worshiped Him as humble servitors."

TEXT 37

अन्तःपुरजनैः प्रीत्या मुकुन्दः फुल्ललोचनैः ।
ससम्भ्रमैरभ्युपेतः प्राविशद् राजमन्दिरम् ॥३७॥

antaḥ-pura-janaiḥ prītyā
mukundaḥ phulla-locanaiḥ
sa-sambhramair abhyupetaḥ
prāviśad rāja-mandiram

antaḥ-pura—of the imperial precinct; *janaiḥ*—by the people; *prītyā*—lovingly; *mukundaḥ*—Lord Kṛṣṇa; *phulla*—blossoming; *locanaiḥ*—whose eyes; *sa-sambhramaiḥ*—in a flurry; *abhyupetaḥ*—approached with greetings; *prāviśat*—He entered; *rāja*—royal; *mandiram*—the palace.

TRANSLATION

With wide-open eyes, the members of the royal household came forward in a flurry to lovingly greet Lord Mukunda, and thus the Lord entered the royal palace.

TEXT 38

पृथा विलोक्य भ्रात्रेयं कृष्णं त्रिभुवनेश्वरम् ।
प्रीतात्मोत्थाय पर्यंकात्ससनुषा परिषस्वजे ॥३८॥

pṛthā vilokya bhrātreyaṁ
kṛṣṇaṁ tri-bhuvaneśvaram
prītātmotthāya paryaṅkāt
sa-snuṣā pariṣasvaje

pṛthā—Queen Kuntī; *vilokya*—seeing; *bhrātreyam*—her brother's son; *kṛṣṇam*—Lord Kṛṣṇa; *tri-bhuvana*—of the three worlds; *īśvaram*—the master; *prīta*—full of love; *ātmā*—whose heart; *utthāya*—rising; *paryaṅkāt*—from her couch; *sa-snuṣā*—together with her daughter-in-law (Draupadī); *pariṣasvaje*—embraced.

TRANSLATION

When Queen Pṛthā saw her nephew Kṛṣṇa, the master of the three worlds, her heart became filled with love. Rising from her couch with her daughter-in-law, she embraced the Lord.

PURPORT

Queen Kuntī's daughter-in-law is the famous Draupadī.

TEXT 39

गोविन्दं गृहमानीय देवदेवेशमादृतः ।
पूजायां नाविदत्कृत्यं प्रमोदोपहतो नृपः ॥३९॥

govindaṁ gṛham ānīya
deva-deveśam ādṛtaḥ
pūjāyāṁ nāvidat kṛtyaṁ
pramodopahato nṛpaḥ

govindam—Lord Kṛṣṇa; *gṛham*—to His quarters; *ānīya*—bringing; *deva*—of all gods; *deva-īśam*—the Supreme God and controller; *ādṛtaḥ*—

reverential; *pūjāyām*—in the ritual worship; *na avidat*—did not know; *kṛtyam*—the details of performance; *pramoda*—by his great joy; *upahataḥ*—overwhelmed; *nṛpaḥ*—the King.

TRANSLATION

King Yudhiṣṭhira respectfully brought Lord Govinda, the Supreme God of gods, to his personal quarters. The King was so overcome with joy that he could not remember all the rituals of worship.

PURPORT

Śrīla Prabhupāda writes, "As he brought Kṛṣṇa within the palace, King Yudhiṣṭhira became so confused in his jubilation that he practically forgot what he was to do at that time in order to receive Kṛṣṇa and worship Him properly."

TEXT 40

पितृष्वसुर्गुरुस्त्रीणां कृष्णश्चक्रेऽभिवादनम् ।
स्वयं च कृष्णया राजन् भगिन्या चाभिवन्दितः ॥४०॥

pitṛ-ṣvasur guru-strīṇāṁ
kṛṣṇaś cakre 'bhivādanam
svayaṁ ca kṛṣṇayā rājan
bhaginyā cābhivanditaḥ

pitṛ—His father's; *svasuḥ*—of the sister (Kuntī); *guru*—of His elders; *strīṇām*—and of the wives; *kṛṣṇaḥ*—Lord Kṛṣṇa; *cakre*—performed; *abhivādanam*—offering of obeisances; *svayam*—Himself; *ca*—and; *kṛṣṇayā*—by Kṛṣṇā (Draupadī); *rājan*—O King (Parīkṣit); *bhaginyā*—by His sister (Subhadrā); *ca*—also; *abhivanditaḥ*—bowed down to.

TRANSLATION

Lord Kṛṣṇa bowed down to His aunt and the wives of His elders, O King, and then Draupadī and the Lord's sister bowed down to Him.

PURPORT

Śrīla Prabhupāda writes, "Lord Kṛṣṇa delightfully offered His respectful obeisances to Kuntī and other elderly ladies of the palace. His younger sister, Subhadrā, was also standing there with Draupadī, and both offered their respectful obeisances unto the lotus feet of the Lord."

TEXTS 41–42

श्वश्र्वा सञ्चोदिता कृष्णा कृष्णपत्नीश्च सर्वशः ।
आनर्च रुक्मिणीं सत्यां भद्रां जाम्बवतीं तथा ॥४१॥
कालिन्दीं मित्रविन्दां च शैब्यां नाग्नजितीं सतीम् ।
अन्याश्चाभ्यागता यास्तु वासःस्रङ्मण्डनादिभिः ॥४२॥

śvaśrvā sañcoditā kṛṣṇā
kṛṣṇa-patnīś ca sarvaśaḥ
ānarca rukmiṇīṁ satyāṁ
bhadrāṁ jāmbavatīṁ tathā

kālindīṁ mitravindāṁ ca
śaibyāṁ nāgnajitīṁ satīm
anyāś cābhyāgatā yās tu
vāsaḥ-sraṅ-maṇḍanādibhiḥ

śvaśrvā—by her mother-in-law (Kuntī); *sañcoditā*—encouraged; *kṛṣṇā*—Draupadī; *kṛṣṇa-patnīḥ*—Kṛṣṇa's wives; *ca*—and; *sarvaśaḥ*—all of them; *ānarca*—she worshiped; *rukmiṇīm*—Rukmiṇī; *satyām*—Satyabhāmā; *bhadrām jāmbavatīm*—Bhadrā and Jāmbavatī; *tathā*—also; *kālindīm mitravindām ca*—Kālindī and Mitravindā; *śaibyām*—the descendant of King Śibi; *nāgnajitīm*—Nāgnajitī; *satīm*—chaste; *anyāḥ*—others; *ca*—as well; *abhyāgatāḥ*—those who had come there; *yāḥ*—who; *tu*—and; *vāsaḥ*—with clothing; *srak*—flower garlands; *maṇḍana*—jewelry; *ādibhiḥ*—and so on.

TRANSLATION

Encouraged by her mother-in-law, Draupadī worshiped all of Lord Kṛṣṇa's wives, including Rukmiṇī; Satyabhāmā; Bhadrā;

Jāmbavatī; Kālindī; Mitravindā, the descendant of Śibi; the chaste Nāgnajitī; and the other queens of the Lord who were present. Draupadī honored them all with such gifts as clothing, flower garlands and jewelry.

TEXT 43

सुखं निवासयामास धर्मराजो जनार्दनम् ।
ससैन्यं सानुगामत्यं सभार्यं च नवं नवम् ॥४३॥

sukhaṁ nivāsayām āsa
dharma-rājo janārdanam
sa-sainyaṁ sānugāmatyaṁ
sa-bhāryaṁ ca navaṁ navam

sukham—comfortably; *nivāsayām āsa*—accommodated; *dharma-rājaḥ*—the king of religiosity, Yudhiṣṭhira; *janārdanam*—Lord Kṛṣṇa; *sa-sainyam*—with His army; *sa-anuga*—with His servants; *amatyam*—and ministers; *sa-bhāryam*—with His wives; *ca*—and; *navam navam*—newer and newer.

TRANSLATION

King Yudhiṣṭhira arranged for Kṛṣṇa's rest and saw to it that all who came along with Him—namely His queens, soldiers, ministers and secretaries—were comfortably situated. He arranged that they would experience a new feature of reception every day while staying as guests of the Pāṇḍavas.

PURPORT

This translation is taken from Śrīla Prabhupāda's *Kṛṣṇa.*

TEXTS 44–45

तर्पयित्वा खाण्डवेन वह्निं फाल्गुनसंयुतः ।
मोचयित्वा मयं येन राज्ञे दिव्या सभा कृता ॥४४॥

उवास कतिचिन्मासान् राज्ञः प्रियचिकीर्षया ।
विहरन् रथमारुह्य फाल्गुनेन भटैर्वृतः ॥४५॥

tarpayitvā khāṇḍavena
vahniṁ phālguna-saṁyutaḥ
mocayitvā mayaṁ yena
rājñe divyā sabhā kṛtā

uvāsa katicin māsān
rājñaḥ priya-cikīrṣayā
viharan ratham āruhya
phālgunena bhaṭair vṛtaḥ

tarpayitvā—satisfying; *khāṇḍavena*—with the Khāṇḍava forest; *vahnim*—the fire-god; *phālguna*—by Arjuna; *saṁyutaḥ*—accompanied; *mocayitvā*—saving; *mayam*—the demon Maya; *yena*—by whom; *rājñe*—for the King (Yudhiṣṭhira); *divyā*—celestial; *sabhā*—assembly hall; *kṛtā*—made; *uvāsa*—He resided; *katicit*—several; *māsān*—months; *rājñaḥ*—to the King; *priya*—pleasure; *cikīrṣayā*—with a desire to give; *viharan*—sporting; *ratham*—His chariot; *āruhya*—riding; *phālgunena*—with Arjuna; *bhaṭaiḥ*—by guards; *vṛtaḥ*—surrounded.

TRANSLATION

Desiring to please King Yudhiṣṭhira, the Lord resided at Indraprastha for several months. During His stay, He and Arjuna satisfied the fire-god by offering him the Khāṇḍava forest, and they saved Maya Dānava, who then built King Yudhiṣṭhira a celestial assembly hall. The Lord also took the opportunity to go riding in His chariot in the company of Arjuna, surrounded by a retinue of soldiers.

PURPORT

Śrīla Prabhupāda writes in *Kṛṣṇa*, "It was during this time that Lord Śrī Kṛṣṇa, with the help of Arjuna, for the satisfaction of the fire-god, Agni, allowed Agni to devour the Khāṇḍava forest. During the forest fire, Kṛṣṇa saved the demon Mayāsura, who was hiding in the forest. Upon being saved, Mayāsura felt obliged to the Pāṇḍavas and Lord Kṛṣṇa, and he constructed a wonderful assembly house within the city of Hastināpura. In this way, Lord Kṛṣṇa, in order to please King Yudhiṣṭhira, remained in the city of Hastināpura for several months. During His stay, He enjoyed strolling here and there. He used to drive on chariots along with Arjuna, and many warriors and soldiers used to follow them."

Thus end the purports of the humble servants of His Divine Grace A. C. Bhaktivedanta Swami Prabhupāda to the Tenth Canto, Seventy-first Chapter, of the Śrīmad-Bhāgavatam, *entitled "The Lord Travels to Indraprastha."*

CHAPTER SEVENTY-TWO

The Slaying of the Demon Jarāsandha

This chapter describes how Lord Kṛṣṇa heard King Yudhiṣṭhira's request and then arranged for Bhīmasena to defeat Jarāsandha.

One day King Yudhiṣṭhira addressed Lord Kṛṣṇa as He sat in the royal assembly: "My Lord, I wish to perform the Rājasūya sacrifice. In this sacrifice people uninterested in Your devotional service will be able to see firsthand the superiority of Your devotees and the inferiority of nondevotees. They will also be able to see Your lotus feet."

Lord Kṛṣṇa extolled Yudhiṣṭhira's proposition: "Your scheme is so excellent that it will spread your fame throughout the universe. Indeed, all living beings should desire that this sacrifice be performed. To make this sacrifice possible, however, you must first defeat all the kings of the earth and collect all the necessary paraphernalia."

Satisfied with Lord Kṛṣṇa's words, King Yudhiṣṭhira sent his brothers to conquer the various directions. After they had conquered—or won the fealty of—the kings in their assigned directions, they brought back abundant wealth to Yudhiṣṭhira. They informed him, however, that Jarāsandha could not be defeated. As King Yudhiṣṭhira pondered how he could subdue Jarāsandha, Śrī Kṛṣṇa revealed to him the means for doing so, following the previous advice of Uddhava.

Bhīma, Arjuna and Śrī Kṛṣṇa then disguised themselves as *brāhmaṇas* and went to the palace of Jarāsandha, who was very devoted to the brahminical class. They introduced themselves as *brāhmaṇas* to King Jarāsandha, flattering him by praising his reputation for hospitality, and requested him to grant their desire. Seeing the marks of bowstrings on their limbs, Jarāsandha concluded that they were warriors and not *brāhmaṇas*, but still, even though fearful, he promised to fulfill whatever desire they might have. At that point Lord Kṛṣṇa discarded His disguise and asked Jarāsandha to fight Him in one-to-one combat. But Jarāsandha refused, claiming that Kṛṣṇa was a coward because He had once fled the battlefield. Jarāsandha also declined to fight Arjuna on the plea that he was inferior in age and size. But Bhīma he considered a worthy opponent.

Thus Jarāsandha handed Bhīma a club and took up another himself, and they all went outside the city to begin the fight.

After the fight had gone on for some time, it became clear that the two opponents were too equally matched for either to gain victory. Lord Kṛṣṇa then split a small tree branch in half, thus showing Bhīma how to kill Jarāsandha. Bhīma threw Jarāsandha to the ground, stepped on one of his legs, seized the other with his arms and proceeded to tear him apart from his genitals to his head.

Seeing Jarāsandha dead, his relatives and subjects cried out in lamentation. Lord Kṛṣṇa then appointed Jarāsandha's son ruler of Magadha and released the kings Jarāsandha had imprisoned.

TEXTS 1–2

श्रीशुक उवाच
एकदा तु सभामध्य आस्थितो मुनिभिर्वृतः ।
ब्राह्मणैः क्षत्रियैर्वैश्यैर्भ्रातृभिश्च युधिष्ठिरः ॥१॥
आचार्यैः कुलवृद्धैश्च ज्ञातिसम्बन्धिबान्धवैः ।
शृण्वतामेव चैतेषामाभाष्येदमुवाच ह ॥२॥

śrī-śuka uvāca
ekadā tu sabhā-madhya
āsthito munibhir vṛtaḥ
brāhmaṇaiḥ kṣatriyair vaiśyair
bhrātṛbhiś ca yudhiṣṭhiraḥ

ācāryaiḥ kula-vṛddhaiś ca
jñāti-sambandhi-bāndhavaiḥ
śṛṇvatām eva caiteṣām
ābhāṣyedam uvāca ha

śrī-śukaḥ uvāca—Śukadeva Gosvāmī said; *ekadā*—once; *tu*—and; *sabhā*—of the royal assembly; *madhye*—in the midst; *āsthitaḥ*—seated; *munibhiḥ*—by sages; *vṛtaḥ*—surrounded; *brāhmaṇaiḥ kṣatriyaiḥ vaiśyaiḥ*—by *brāhmaṇas, kṣatriyas* and *vaiśyas; bhrātṛbhiḥ*—by his brothers; *ca*—and; *yudhiṣṭhiraḥ*—King Yudhiṣṭhira; *ācāryaiḥ*—by his spiritual masters; *kula*—of the family; *vṛddhaiḥ*—by the elders; *ca*—also; *jñāti*—by blood relatives; *sambandhi*—in-laws; *bāndhavaiḥ*—and friends; *śṛṇvatām*—

as they listened; *eva*—indeed; *ca*—and; *eteṣām*—all of them; *ābhāṣya*—addressing (Lord Kṛṣṇa); *idam*—this; *uvāca ha*—he said.

TRANSLATION

Śukadeva Gosvāmī said: One day, as King Yudhiṣṭhira sat in the royal assembly surrounded by eminent sages, *brāhmaṇas, kṣatriyas* and *vaiśyas,* and also by his brothers, spiritual masters, family elders, blood relations, in-laws and friends, he addressed Lord Kṛṣṇa as everyone listened.

TEXT 3

श्रीयुधिष्ठिर उवाच
क्रतुराजेन गोविन्द राजसूयेन पावनीः ।
यक्ष्ये विभूतीर्भवतस्तत्सम्पादय नः प्रभो ॥३॥

śrī-yudhiṣṭhira uvāca
kratu-rājena govinda
rājasūyena pāvanīḥ
yakṣye vibhūtīr bhavatas
tat sampādaya naḥ prabho

śrī-yudhiṣṭhiraḥ uvāca—Śrī Yudhiṣṭhira said; *kratu*—of major fire sacrifices; *rājena*—with the king; *govinda*—O Kṛṣṇa; *rājasūyena*—named Rājasūya; *pāvanīḥ*—purifying; *yakṣye*—I wish to worship; *vibhūtīḥ*—the opulent expansions; *bhavataḥ*—of Yourself; *tat*—that; *sampādaya*—please allow to happen; *naḥ*—for us; *prabho*—O master.

TRANSLATION

Śrī Yudhiṣṭhira said: O Govinda, I desire to worship Your auspicious, opulent expansions by the Rājasūya sacrifice, the king of Vedic ceremonies. Please make our endeavor a success, my Lord.

PURPORT

Śrīla Śrīdhara Svāmī states that the word *vibhūtīḥ* refers to Lord Kṛṣṇa's expansions (*aṁśān*), and Śrīla Viśvanātha Cakravartī Ṭhākura further explains that here the word *vibhūtīḥ* refers to Lord Kṛṣṇa's opulent expansions within this world, such as the demigods and other empowered beings. Thus Śrīla Prabhupāda treats this verse as follows in *Kṛṣṇa, the Supreme Personality of Godhead:* "My dear Lord Kṛṣṇa, the sacrifice known as the Rājasūya *yajña* is to be performed by the emperor, and it is considered to be the king of all sacrifices. By performing this sacrifice, I wish to satisfy all the demigods, who are Your empowered representatives within this material world, and I wish that You will kindly help me in this great adventure so that it may be successfully executed. As far as the Pāṇḍavas are concerned, we have nothing to ask from the demigods. We are personally satisfied by being Your devotees. As you say in the *Bhagavad-gītā,* 'Persons who are bewildered by material desires worship the demigods,' but our purpose is different. I want to perform this Rājasūya sacrifice and invite the demigods to show them that they have no power independent of You. They are all Your servants, and You are the Supreme Personality of Godhead. Foolish persons with a poor fund of knowledge consider Your Lordship an ordinary human being. Sometimes they try to find fault in You, and sometimes they defame You. Therefore I wish to perform the Rājasūya *yajña.* I wish to invite all the demigods, beginning from Lord Brahmā, Lord Śiva and other exalted chiefs of the heavenly planets, and in that great assembly of the demigods from all parts of the universe, I want to substantiate that You are the Supreme Personality of Godhead and that everyone is Your servant."

TEXT 4

त्वत्पादुके अविरतं परि ये चरन्ति
ध्यायन्त्यभद्रनशने शुचयो गृणन्ति ।
विन्दन्ति ते कमलनाभ भवापवर्गम्
आशासते यदि त आशिष ईश नान्ये ॥४॥

tvat-pāduke aviratam pari ye caranti
dhyāyanty abhadra-naśane śucayo gṛṇanti
vindanti te kamala-nābha bhavāpavargam
āśāsate yadi ta āśiṣa īśa nānye

tvat—Your; *pāduke*—slippers; *aviratam*—constantly; *pari*—fully; *ye*—who; *caranti*—serve; *dhyāyanti*—meditate upon; *abhadra*—of inauspicious things; *naśane*—which (cause) the destruction; *śucayaḥ*—purified; *gṛṇanti*—and describe in their words; *vindanti*—obtain; *te*—they; *kamala*—(like a) lotus; *nābha*—O You whose navel; *bhava*—of material life; *apavargam*—the cessation; *āśāsate*—harbor desires; *yadi*—if; *te*—they; *āśiṣaḥ*—(attain) the desired objects; *īśa*—O Lord; *na*—not; *anye*—other persons.

TRANSLATION

Purified persons who constantly serve, meditate upon and glorify Your shoes, which destroy everything inauspicious, are sure to obtain freedom from material existence, O lotus-naveled one. Even if they desire something in this world, they obtain it, whereas others—those who do not take shelter of You—are never satisfied, O Lord.

PURPORT

Śrīla Prabhupāda writes in this connection that liberated, Kṛṣṇa conscious persons "do not even desire to become freed from this material existence or to enjoy material opulences; their desires are fulfilled by Kṛṣṇa conscious activities. As far as we [King Yudhiṣṭhira] are concerned, we are fully surrendered unto Your lotus feet, and by Your grace we are so fortunate to see You personally. Therefore, naturally we have no desire for material opulences. The verdict of the Vedic wisdom is that You are the Supreme Personality of Godhead. I want to establish this fact, and I also want to show the world the difference between accepting You as the Supreme Personality of Godhead and accepting You as an ordinary powerful historical person. I wish to show the world that one can attain the highest perfection of life simply by taking shelter at Your lotus feet, exactly as one can satisfy the branches, twigs, leaves and flowers of an entire tree simply by watering the root. Thus, if one takes to Kṛṣṇa consciousness, his life becomes fulfilled both materially and spiritually."

Śrīla Viśvanātha Cakravartī similarly explains King Yudhiṣṭhira's statement: "We feel no great urgency to perform the Rājasūya sacrifice, nor do we have any personal interest, since we are already seeing Your lotus feet and by Your boundless mercy have been taken into Your personal association. But in this world there are some whose hearts are contaminated and who thus think You are not the Supreme Personality of Godhead but an ordinary man. Or else they find fault with You and even criticize You. This is an arrow piercing our hearts.

"Therefore, to extract this arrow from our heart, we must call to this place—on the pretext of the Rājasūya—Brahmā, Rudra and other wise *brahmacārīs* and demigods who reside in each of the fourteen planetary systems. When such an exalted congregation has assembled, it will be incumbent upon them to first arrange for the *agra-pūjā,* or the first worship for the most worthy person present. And when they are directly shown that You, Lord Kṛṣṇa, are the Supreme Personality of Godhead, the arrow piercing our heart will be removed."

TEXT 5

तद्देवदेव भवतश्चरणारविन्द-
सेवानुभावमिह पश्यतु लोक एषः ।
ये त्वां भजन्ति न भजन्त्युत वोभयेषां
निष्ठां प्रदर्शय विभो कुरुसृञ्जयानाम् ॥५॥

tad deva-deva bhavataś caraṇāravinda-
sevānubhāvam iha paśyatu loka eṣaḥ
ye tvāṁ bhajanti na bhajanty uta vobhayeṣāṁ
niṣṭhāṁ pradarśaya vibho kuru-sṛñjayānām

tat—therefore; *deva-deva*—O Lord of lords; *bhavataḥ*—Your; *caraṇa-aravinda*—to the lotus feet; *sevā*—of service; *anubhāvam*—the power; *iha*—in this world; *paśyatu*—may they see; *lokaḥ*—the populace; *eṣaḥ*—this; *ye*—who; *tvām*—You; *bhajanti*—worship; *na bhajanti*—do not worship; *uta vā*—or else; *ubhayeṣām*—of both; *niṣṭhām*—the status; *pradarśaya*—please show; *vibho*—O all-powerful one; *kuru-sṛñjayānām*—of the Kurus and Sṛñjayas.

TRANSLATION

Therefore, O Lord of lords, let the people of this world see the power of devotional service rendered to Your lotus feet. Please show them, O almighty one, the position of those Kurus and Sṛñjayas who worship You, and the position of those who do not.

PURPORT

Here we clearly see the heart of a preacher. The great devotee Yudhiṣṭhira Mahārāja implores Lord Kṛṣṇa to demonstrate plainly the result of worshiping Him and the result of not worshiping Him. If the people of the world could understand this, they could begin to recognize that Kṛṣṇa is the Supreme Personality of Godhead and that everyone's ultimate self-interest lies in surrendering to Him. As confirmed by great authorities, Yudhiṣṭhira Mahārāja is a pure devotee of the Lord, and thus his actual motivation in discharging his duties as a king was to establish the supremacy of Lord Kṛṣṇa as the Supreme Personality of Godhead. This is the real purport of the activities of the Pāṇḍavas, which are described in both the *Śrīmad-Bhāgavatam* and the *Mahābhārata.*

TEXT 6

न ब्रह्मणः स्वपरभेदमतिस्तव स्यात्
सर्वात्मनः समदृशः स्वसुखानुभूतेः ।
संसेवतां सुरतरोरिव ते प्रसादः
सेवानुरूपमुदयो न विपर्ययोऽत्र ॥६॥

na brahmaṇaḥ sva-para-bheda-matis tava syāt
sarvātmanaḥ sama-dṛśaḥ sva-sukhānubhūteḥ
saṁsevatāṁ sura-taror iva te prasādaḥ
sevānurūpam udayo na viparyayo 'tra

na—not; *brahmaṇaḥ*—of the Absolute Truth; *sva*—of own; *para*—and other's; *bheda*—differential; *matiḥ*—mentality; *tava*—of You; *syāt*—there can be; *sarva*—of all beings; *ātmanaḥ*—of the Soul; *sama*—equal; *dṛśaḥ*—whose vision; *sva*—within Himself; *sukha*—of happiness; *anubhūteḥ*—whose experience; *saṁsevatām*—for those who properly worship; *sura-taroḥ*—of the heavenly desire tree; *iva*—as if; *te*—Your; *prasādaḥ*—grace; *sevā*—with the service; *anurūpam*—in accordance; *udayaḥ*—desirable results; *na*—not; *viparyayaḥ*—contradiction; *atra*—in this.

TRANSLATION

Within Your mind there can be no such differentiation as "This one is mine, and that is another's," because You are the Supreme Absolute Truth, the Soul of all beings, always equipoised and enjoying transcendental happiness within Yourself. Just like the heavenly desire tree, You bless all who properly worship You, granting their desired fruits in proportion to the service they render You. There is nothing wrong in this.

PURPORT

Śrīla Śrīdhara Svāmī explains that a desire tree has no material attachments or partiality but simply bestows its fruits upon those who deserve them, and not upon others. Jīva Gosvāmī Prabhupāda adds that a desire tree does not think, "This person is fit to worship me, but that other person is not." Rather, a desire tree is satisfied with all who properly serve it. And the Lord acts in the same way, as explained here by King Yudhiṣṭhira.

Śrīla Viśvanātha Cakravartī adds that no one should accuse Lord Kṛṣṇa of being envious of one person and showing favoritism toward another. Since the Lord is *sva-sukhānubhūti,* experiencing His own happiness within Himself, He has nothing to gain or lose in relation to conditioned souls. Rather, He reciprocates according to how they approach Him. Śrīla Prabhupāda very nicely sums up this point as follows in his rendering of King Yudhiṣṭhira's statement: "If one takes to Kṛṣṇa consciousness, his life becomes fulfilled both materially and spiritually. This does not mean that You are partial to the Kṛṣṇa conscious person and indifferent to the non-Kṛṣṇa conscious person. You are equal to everyone; that is Your declaration. You cannot be partial to one and not interested in others, because You are sitting in everyone's heart as the Supersoul and giving everyone the respective results of his fruitive activities. You give every living entity the chance to enjoy this material world as he desires. As the Supersoul, You are sitting in the body along with the living entity, giving him the results of his own actions as well as opportunities to turn toward Your devotional service by developing Kṛṣṇa consciousness. You openly declare that one should surrender unto You, giving up all other engagements, and that You will take charge of him, giving him relief from the reactions of all sins. You are like the desire tree in the heavenly planets, which awards benediction according to one's desires. Everyone is free to achieve the highest perfection, but if one does not so desire, then Your awarding of lesser benedictions is not due to partiality."

TEXT 7

श्रीभगवानुवाच
सम्यग् व्यवसितं राजन् भवता शत्रुकर्शन ।
कल्याणी येन ते कीर्तिर्लोकाननुभविष्यति ॥७॥

śrī-bhagavān uvāca
samyag vyavasitaṁ rājan
bhavatā śatru-karśana
kalyāṇī yena te kīrtir
lokān anubhaviṣyati

śrī-bhagavān uvāca—the Supreme Lord said; *samyak*—perfectly; *vyavasitam*—determined; *rājan*—O King; *bhavatā*—by you; *śatru*—of enemies; *karśana*—O tormentor; *kalyāṇī*—auspicious; *yena*—by which; *te*—your; *kīrtiḥ*—fame; *lokān*—all the worlds; *anubhaviṣyati*—it will see.

TRANSLATION

The Supreme Personality of Godhead said: Your decision is perfect, O King, and thus your noble fame will spread to all the worlds, O tormentor of your enemies.

PURPORT

Lord Kṛṣṇa here concurs with King Yudhiṣṭhira's decision that the Rājasūya sacrifice should be performed. The Lord further agrees that there is nothing unfair in the fact that one result is achieved by those who worship Him, and another by those who do not. The great *Bhāgavatam* commentators point out that by addressing King Yudhiṣṭhira as *śatru-karśana*, "tormentor of enemies," Lord Kṛṣṇa is imparting to him the potency to conquer all the enemy kings. Thus Kṛṣṇa predicted that King Yudhiṣṭhira's noble fame would spread to all the worlds, and in fact it has.

TEXT 8

ऋषीणां पितृदेवानां सुहृदामपि नः प्रभो ।
सर्वेषामपि भूतानामीप्सितः क्रतुराडयम् ॥८॥

ṛṣīṇāṁ pitṛ-devānāṁ
suhṛdām api naḥ prabho
sarveṣām api bhūtānām
īpsitaḥ kratu-rāḍ ayam

ṛṣīṇām—for the sages; *pitṛ*—departed forefathers; *devānām*—and demigods; *suhṛdām*—for the friends; *api*—also; *naḥ*—our; *prabho*—O master; *sarveṣām*—for all; *api*—as well; *bhūtānām*—living beings; *īpsitaḥ*—desirable; *kratu*—of major Vedic sacrifices; *rāṭ*—king; *ayam*—this.

TRANSLATION

Indeed, My lord, for the great sages, the forefathers and the demigods, for Our well-wishing friends and, indeed, for all living beings, the performance of this king of Vedic sacrifices is desirable.

TEXT 9

विजित्य नृपतीन् सर्वान् कृत्वा च जगतीं वशे ।
सम्भृत्य सर्वसम्भारानाहरस्व महाक्रतुम् ॥९॥

vijitya nṛpatīn sarvān
kṛtvā ca jagatīṁ vaśe
sambhṛtya sarva-sambhārān
āharasva mahā-kratum

vijitya—conquering; *nṛ-patīn*—the kings; *sarvān*—all; *kṛtvā*—making; *ca*—and; *jagatīm*—the earth; *vaśe*—under your control; *sambhṛtya*—collecting; *sarva*—all; *sambhārān*—the paraphernalia; *āharasva*—execute; *mahā*—great; *kratum*—the sacrifice.

TRANSLATION

First conquer all kings, bring the earth under your control and collect all the required paraphernalia; then execute this great sacrifice.

TEXT 10

एते ते भ्रातरो राजल्ँ लोकपालांशसम्भवाः ।
जितोऽस्म्यात्मवता तेऽहं दुर्जयो योऽकृतात्मभिः ॥१०॥

ete te bhrātaro rājal̐
loka-pālāṁśa-sambhavāḥ
jito 'smy ātmavatā te 'haṁ
durjayo yo 'kṛtātmabhiḥ

ete—these; *te*—your; *bhrātaraḥ*—brothers; *rājan*—O King; *loka*—of the planets; *pāla*—from the ruling demigods; *aṁśa*—as partial expansions; *sambhavāḥ*—born; *jitaḥ*—conquered; *asmi*—am; *ātma-vatā*—self-controlled; *te*—by you; *aham*—I; *durjayaḥ*—unconquerable; *yaḥ*—who; *akṛta-ātmabhiḥ*—by those who have not conquered their senses.

TRANSLATION

These brothers of yours, O King, have taken birth as partial expansions of the demigods ruling various planets. And you are so self-controlled that you have conquered even Me, who am unconquerable for those who cannot control their senses.

PURPORT

Śrīla Prabhupāda writes in *Kṛṣṇa,* "It is said that Bhīma was born of the demigod Vāyu and that Arjuna was born of the demigod Indra, whereas King Yudhiṣṭhira himself was born of the demigod Yamarāja." Śrīla Prabhupāda goes on to state, "Lord Kṛṣṇa told King Yudhiṣṭhira that He becomes conquered by the love of one who has conquered his senses. One who has not conquered his senses cannot conquer the Supreme Personality of Godhead. This is the secret of devotional service.

To conquer the senses means to engage them constantly in the service of the Lord. The specific qualification of all the Pāṇḍava brothers was that they always engaged their senses in the service of the Lord. One who thus engages his senses becomes purified, and with purified senses one can actually render service to the Lord. The Lord can thus be conquered by the devotee through loving transcendental service."

TEXT 11

न कश्चिन्मत्परं लोके तेजसा यशसा श्रिया ।
विभूतिभिर्वाभिभवेद्देवोऽपि किमु पार्थिवः ॥११॥

na kaścin mat-paraṁ loke
tejasā yaśasā śriyā
vibhūtibhir vābhibhaved
devo 'pi kim u pārthivaḥ

na—not; *kaścit*—any person; *mat*—to Me; *param*—one who is dedicated; *loke*—in this world; *tejasā*—by his strength; *yaśasā*—fame; *śriyā*—beauty; *vibhūtibhiḥ*—opulences; *vā*—or; *abhibhavet*—can overcome; *devaḥ*—a demigod; *api*—even; *kim u*—what to speak of; *pārthivaḥ*—a ruler of the earth.

TRANSLATION

No one in this world, even a demigod—what to speak of an earthly king—can defeat My devotee with his strength, beauty, fame or riches.

PURPORT

Here Lord Kṛṣṇa assures King Yudhiṣṭhira that he will have no problem conquering the worldly kings, since the King is a pure devotee and the Lord's pure devotees can never be conquered, even by the demigods, what to speak of earthly kings. Although materialists are proud of their power, fame, beauty and opulence, they can never surpass the pure devotees of the Lord in any of these categories.

TEXT 12

श्रीशुक उवाच
निशम्य भगवद्गीतं प्रीत: फुल्लमुखाम्बुज: ।
भ्रातॄन् दिग्विजयेऽयुंक्त विष्णुतेजोपबृंहितान् ॥१२॥

śrī-śuka uvāca
niśamya bhagavad-gītaṁ
prītaḥ phulla-mukhāmbujaḥ
bhrātṝn dig-vijaye 'yuṅkta
viṣṇu-tejopabṛṁhitān

śrī-śukaḥ uvāca—Śrī Śuka said; *niśamya*—hearing; *bhagavat*—of the Supreme Lord; *gītam*—the song; *prītaḥ*—pleased; *phulla*—blossoming; *mukha*—his face; *ambujaḥ*—lotuslike; *bhrātṝn*—his brothers; *dik*—of all the directions; *vijaye*—in the conquest; *ayuṅkta*—engaged; *viṣṇu*—of Lord Viṣṇu; *tejaḥ*—with the potency; *upabṛṁhitān*—fortified.

TRANSLATION

Śukadeva Gosvāmī said: Upon hearing these words sung by the Supreme Lord, King Yudhiṣṭhira became joyful, and his face blossomed like a lotus. Thus he sent forth his brothers, who were empowered with Lord Viṣṇu's potency, to conquer all directions.

TEXT 13

सहदेवं दक्षिणस्यामादिशत्सह सृञ्जयै: ।
दिशि प्रतीच्यां नकुलमुदीच्यां सव्यसाचिनम् ।
प्राच्यां वृकोदरं मत्स्यै: केकयै: सह मद्रकै: ॥१३॥

sahadevaṁ dakṣiṇasyām
ādiśat saha sṛñjayaiḥ
diśi pratīcyāṁ nakulam
udīcyāṁ savyasācinam
prācyāṁ vṛkodaraṁ matsyaiḥ
kekayaiḥ saha madrakaiḥ

sahadevam—Sahadeva; *dakṣiṇasyām*—to the south; *ādiśat*—he ordered; *saha*—with; *sṛñjayaiḥ*—the warriors of the Sṛñjaya clan; *diśi*—to the direction; *pratīcyām*—western; *nakulam*—Nakula; *udīcyām*—to the north; *savyasācinam*—Arjuna; *prācyām*—to the east; *vṛkodaram*—Bhīma; *matsyaiḥ*—the Matsyas; *kekayaiḥ*—the Kekayas; *saha*—together with; *madrakaiḥ*—and the Madrakas.

TRANSLATION

He sent Sahadeva to the south with the Sṛñjayas, Nakula to the west with the Matsyas, Arjuna to the north with the Kekayas, and Bhīma to the east with the Madrakas.

TEXT 14

ते विजित्य नृपान् वीरा आजह्रुर्दिग्भ्य ओजसा ।
अजातशत्रवे भूरि द्रविणं नृप यक्ष्यते ॥१४॥

te vijitya nṛpān vīrā
ājahrur digbhya ojasā
ajāta-śatrave bhūri
draviṇaṁ nṛpa yakṣyate

te—they; *vijitya*—defeating; *nṛpān*—kings; *vīrāḥ*—the heroes; *ājahruḥ*—brought; *digbhyaḥ*—from the different directions; *ojasā*—by their personal strength; *ajāta-śatrave*—to Yudhiṣṭhira Mahārāja, whose enemy was never born; *bhūri*—abundant; *draviṇam*—wealth; *nṛpa*—O King (Parīkṣit); *yakṣyate*—who was intending to perform sacrifice.

TRANSLATION

After defeating many kings with their prowess, these heroic brothers brought back abundant wealth for Yudhiṣṭhira Mahārāja, who was intent on performing the sacrifice, O King.

PURPORT

Śrīla Prabhupāda writes, "It may be noted that by dispatching his younger brothers to conquer in different directions, King Yudhiṣṭhira did not actually intend that they declare war with the kings. Actually, the brothers started for different directions to inform the respective kings about King Yudhiṣṭhira's intention to perform the Rājasūya sacrifice. The kings were thus informed that they were required to pay taxes for the execution of the sacrifice. This payment of taxes to Emperor Yudhiṣṭhira meant that the king accepted his subjugation before him. In case of a king's refusal to act accordingly, there was certainly a fight. Thus by their influence and strength, the brothers conquered all the kings in different directions, and they were able to bring in sufficient taxes and presentations. These were brought before King Yudhiṣṭhira by his brothers."

TEXT 15

श्रुत्वाजितं जरासन्धं नृपतेर्ध्यायतो हरिः ।
आहोपायं तमेवाद्य उद्धवो यमुवाच ह ॥१५॥

śrutvājitaṁ jarāsandhaṁ
nṛpater dhyāyato hariḥ
āhopāyaṁ tam evādya
uddhavo yam uvāca ha

śrutvā—hearing; *ajitam*—unconquered; *jarāsandham*—Jarāsandha; *nṛpateḥ*—the King; *dhyāyataḥ*—as he pondered; *hariḥ*—Lord Kṛṣṇa; *āha*—told; *upāyam*—the means; *tam*—to him; *eva*—indeed; *ādyaḥ*—the original person; *uddhavaḥ*—Uddhava; *yam*—which; *uvāca ha*—had spoken.

TRANSLATION

When King Yudhiṣṭhira heard that Jarāsandha remained undefeated, he set to pondering, and then the primeval Lord, Hari, told him the means Uddhava had described for defeating Jarāsandha.

TEXT 16

भीमसेनोऽर्जुनः कृष्णो ब्रह्मलिंगधरास्त्रयः ।
जग्मुर्गिरिव्रजं तात बृहद्रथसुतो यतः ॥१६॥

bhīmaseno 'rjunaḥ kṛṣṇo
brahma-liṅga-dharās trayaḥ
jagmur girivrajaṁ tāta
bṛhadratha-suto yataḥ

bhīmasenaḥ arjunaḥ kṛṣṇaḥ—Bhīmasena, Arjuna and Kṛṣṇa; *brahma*—of *brāhmaṇas; liṅga*—the guises; *dharāḥ*—wearing; *trayaḥ*—the three; *jagmuḥ*—went; *girivrajam*—to the fortress city Girivraja; *tāta*—my dear (Parīkṣit); *bṛhadratha-sutaḥ*—the son of Bṛhadratha (Jarāsandha); *yataḥ*—where.

TRANSLATION

Thus Bhīmasena, Arjuna and Kṛṣṇa disguised themselves as *brāhmaṇas* and went to Girivraja, my dear King, where the son of Bṛhadratha was to be found.

TEXT 17

ते गत्वातिथ्यवेलायां गृहेषु गृहमेधिनम् ।
ब्रह्मण्यं समयाचेरन् राजन्या ब्रह्मलिंगिनः ॥१७॥

te gatvātithya-velāyāṁ
gṛheṣu gṛha-medhinam
brahmaṇyaṁ samayāceran
rājanyā brahma-liṅginaḥ

te—they; *gatvā*—going; *ātithya*—for receiving uninvited guests; *velāyām*—at the appointed hour; *gṛheṣu*—in his residence; *gṛha-medhinam*—from the religious householder; *brahmaṇyam*—respectful to *brāhmaṇas; samayāceran*—begged; *rājanyāḥ*—the kings; *brahma-liṅginaḥ*—appearing with the signs of *brāhmaṇas.*

TRANSLATION

Disguised as *brāhmaṇas,* the royal warriors approached Jarāsandha at home during the appointed hour for receiving guests. They submitted their entreaty to that dutiful householder, who was especially respectful to the brahminical class.

PURPORT

Śrīla Prabhupāda writes, "King Jarāsandha was a very dutiful householder, and he had great respect for the *brāhmaṇas*. He was a great fighter, a *kṣatriya* king, but he was never neglectful of the Vedic injunctions. According to Vedic injunctions, the *brāhmaṇas* are considered to be the spiritual masters of all other castes. Lord Kṛṣṇa, Arjuna and Bhīmasena were actually *kṣatriyas*, but they dressed themselves as *brāhmaṇas*, and at the time when King Jarāsandha was to give charity to the *brāhmaṇas* and receive them as guests, they approached him."

TEXT 18

राजन् विद्ध्यतिथीन् प्राप्तानर्थिनो दूरमागतान् ।
तन्नः प्रयच्छ भद्रं ते यद्वयं कामयामहे ॥१८॥

rājan viddhy atithīn prāptān
arthino dūram āgatān
tan naḥ prayaccha bhadraṁ te
yad vayaṁ kāmayāmahe

rājan—O King; *viddhi*—please know; *atithīn*—guests; *prāptān*—arrived; *arthinaḥ*—desirous of gain; *dūram*—from far away; *āgatān*—come; *tat*—that; *naḥ*—to us; *prayaccha*—please grant; *bhadram*—all good; *te*—unto you; *yat*—whatever; *vayam*—we; *kāmayāmahe*—are desiring.

TRANSLATION

[Kṛṣṇa, Arjuna and Bhīma said:] O King, know us to be needy guests who have come to you from afar. We wish all good unto you. Please grant us whatever we desire.

TEXT 19

किं दुर्मर्षं तितिक्षूणां किमकार्यमसाधुभिः ।
किं न देयं वदान्यानां कः परः समदर्शिनाम् ॥१९॥

kiṁ durmarṣaṁ titikṣūṇāṁ
kim akāryam asādhubhiḥ
kiṁ na deyaṁ vadānyānāṁ
kaḥ paraḥ sama-darśinām

kim—what; *durmarṣam*—intolerable; *titikṣūṇām*—for the patient; *kim*—what; *akāryam*—impossible to do; *asādhubhiḥ*—for the impious; *kim*—what; *na deyam*—impossible to give away; *vadānyānām*—for the generous; *kaḥ*—who; *paraḥ*—separate; *sama*—equal; *darśinām*—for those whose vision.

TRANSLATION

What can the tolerant not bear? What will the wicked not do? What will the generous not give in charity? And who will those of equal vision see as an outsider?

PURPORT

In the previous verse, Lord Kṛṣṇa and the two Pāṇḍava brothers, Bhīma and Arjuna, requested Jarāsandha to grant them whatever they asked of him. Here they explain why there is no need for them to specify their desire.

The *ācāryas* comment on this verse as follows: Jarāsandha might be thinking, "What if you request my son, from whom separation would be intolerable?"

To this possible objection Kṛṣṇa and the Pāṇḍavas reply, "For a tolerant person, nothing is intolerable."

Similarly, Jarāsandha could object, "What if you ask me to give my body or my precious jewels and other ornaments, which are meant to be given to my sons, not to ordinary beggars?"

To this they reply, "For the generous, what is not to be donated in charity?" In other words, everything is to be given.

Jarāsandha might also object that he could be giving charity to his enemies. To this his guests counter with the statement *kaḥ paraḥ sama-darśinām:* "For those with equal vision, who is a stranger?"

Thus Śrī Kṛṣṇa and the Pāṇḍavas encouraged Jarāsandha to simply agree to grant their request without further discussion.

TEXT 20

योऽनित्येन शरीरेण सतां गेयं यशो ध्रुवम् ।
नाचिनोति स्वयं कल्पः स वाच्यः शोच्य एव सः ॥२०॥

yo 'nityena śarīreṇa
satāṁ geyaṁ yaśo dhruvam
nācinoti svayaṁ kalpaḥ
sa vācyaḥ śocya eva saḥ

yaḥ—who; *anityena*—temporary; *śarīreṇa*—with the material body; *satām*—by saints; *geyam*—to be glorified; *yaśaḥ*—fame; *dhruvam*—permanent; *na ācinoti*—does not acquire; *svayam*—himself; *kalpaḥ*—capable; *saḥ*—he; *vācyaḥ*—contemptible; *śocyaḥ*—pitiable; *eva*—indeed; *saḥ*—he.

TRANSLATION

He indeed is to be censured and pitied who, though able to do so, fails to achieve with his temporary body the lasting fame glorified by great saints.

TEXT 21

हरिश्चन्द्रो रन्तिदेव उञ्छवृत्तिः शिबिर्बलिः ।
व्याधः कपोतो बहवो ह्यध्रुवेण ध्रुवं गताः ॥२१॥

hariścandro rantideva
uñchavṛttiḥ śibir baliḥ
vyādhaḥ kapoto bahavo
hy adhruveṇa dhruvaṁ gatāḥ

hariścandraḥ rantidevaḥ—Hariścandra and Rantideva; *uñcha-vṛttiḥ*—Mudgala, who lived by gathering grains left behind in the fields after the harvest; *śibiḥ baliḥ*—Śibi and Bali; *vyādhaḥ*—the hunter; *kapotaḥ*—the pigeon; *bahavaḥ*—many; *hi*—indeed; *adhruveṇa*—by the temporary; *dhruvam*—to the permanent; *gatāḥ*—went.

TRANSLATION

Hariścandra, Rantideva, Uñchavṛtti Mudgala, Śibi, Bali, the legendary hunter and pigeon, and many others have attained the permanent by means of the impermanent.

PURPORT

Here Lord Kṛṣṇa and the two Pāṇḍavas are pointing out to Jarāsandha that one can use the temporary material body to achieve a permanent situation in life. Because Jarāsandha was a materialist, they appealed to his natural interest in the heavenly planets, where life lasts so long that it appears permanent to people on earth.

Śrīla Śrīdhara Svāmī briefly summarizes the history of the personalities mentioned in this verse: "To pay off his debts to Viśvāmitra, Hariścandra sold everything he had, including his wife and children. Yet even after attaining the status of a *caṇḍāla,* he did not become discouraged; thus he went to heaven, together with all the inhabitants of Ayodhyā. Rantideva, after going without even water for forty-eight days, somehow obtained some food and water, but then some beggars came and he gave it all away to them. In this way he attained Brahmaloka. Mudgala followed the practice of gathering grains left behind in the fields after the harvest. Yet still he was hospitable toward uninvited guests, even after his family had been suffering in poverty for six months. Thus he also went to Brahmaloka.

"To protect a pigeon who had taken shelter of him, King Śibi gave his own flesh to a hawk and attained heaven. Bali Mahārāja gave all his property to Lord Hari when the Lord disguised Himself as a dwarf *brāhmaṇa* (Vāmanadeva), and so Bali gained the Lord's personal association. The pigeon and his mate gave their own flesh to a hunter as a show of hospitality, and thus they were taken to heaven in a celestial airplane. When the hunter understood their situation in the mode of goodness, he also became renounced, and thus he gave up hunting and went off to perform severe austerities. Because he was freed of all sins, after his body burned to death in a forest fire he was elevated to heaven. Thus many personalities have attained enduring life on higher planets by means of the temporary material body."

TEXT 22

श्रीशुक उवाच
स्वरैराकृतिभिस्तांस्तु प्रकोष्ठैर्ज्याहतैरपि ।
राजन्यबन्धून् विज्ञाय दृष्टपूर्वानचिन्तयत् ॥२२॥

śrī-śuka uvāca
svarair ākṛtibhis tāṁs tu
prakoṣṭhair jyā-hatair api
rājanya-bandhūn vijñāya
dṛṣṭa-pūrvān acintayat

śrī-śukaḥ uvāca—Śukadeva Gosvāmī said; *svaraiḥ*—by their voices; *ākṛtibhiḥ*—their bodily statures; *tān*—them; *tu*—however; *prakoṣṭhaiḥ*—by (seeing) their forearms; *jyā*—by bowstrings; *hataiḥ*—imprinted; *api*—even; *rājanya*—of royalty; *bandhūn*—as family members; *vijñāya*—recognizing; *dṛṣṭa*—seen; *pūrvān*—previously; *acintayat*—he considered.

TRANSLATION

Śukadeva Gosvāmī said: From the sound of their voices, their physical stature and the marks of bowstrings on their forearms, Jarāsandha could tell that his guests were of the royal order. He began to think he had seen them somewhere before.

PURPORT

The *ācāryas* point out that Jarāsandha had seen Lord Kṛṣṇa, Bhīmasena and Arjuna at Draupadī's *svayaṁ-vara* ceremony. Since they had come begging in the guise of *brāhmaṇas*, Jarāsandha thought they must be low-class *kṣatriyas*, as indicated here by the word *rājanya-bandhūn*.

TEXT 23

राजन्यबन्धवो ह्येते ब्रह्मलिंगानि बिभ्रति ।
ददानि भिक्षितं तेभ्य आत्मानमपि दुस्त्यजम् ॥२३॥

rājanya-bandhavo hy ete
brahma-liṅgāni bibhrati
dadāni bhikṣitaṁ tebhya
ātmānam api dustyajam

rājanya-bandhavaḥ—relatives of *kṣatriyas; hi*—indeed; *ete*—these; *brahma*—of *brāhmaṇas; liṅgāni*—the signs; *bibhrati*—they are wearing; *dadāni*—I should give; *bhikṣitam*—what is begged; *tebhyaḥ*—to them; *ātmānam*—my own body; *api*—even; *dustyajam*—impossible to give up.

TRANSLATION

[Jarāsandha thought:] These are surely members of the royal order dressed as *brāhmaṇas,* but still I must grant their request for charity, even if they beg me for my own body.

PURPORT

Here Jarāsandha reveals his strong commitment to charity, especially when begged by *brāhmaṇas.*

TEXT 24–25

बलेर्नु श्रूयते कीर्तिर्वितता दिक्ष्वकल्मषा ।
ऐश्वर्याद् भ्रंशितस्यापि विप्रव्याजेन विष्णुना ॥२४॥
श्रियं जिहीर्षतेन्द्रस्य विष्णवे द्विजरूपिणे ।
जानन्नपि महीं प्रादाद्वार्यमाणोऽपि दैत्यराट् ॥२५॥

baler nu śrūyate kīrtir
vitatā dikṣv akalmaṣā
aiśvaryād bhraṁśitasyāpi
vipra-vyājena viṣṇunā

śriyaṁ jihīrṣatendrasya
viṣṇave dvija-rūpiṇe
jānann api mahīṁ prādād
vāryamāṇo 'pi daitya-rāṭ

baleḥ—of Bali; *nu*—is it not so; *śrūyate*—are heard; *kīrtiḥ*—the glories; *vitatā*—widespread; *dikṣu*—in all directions; *akalmaṣā*—spotless; *aiśvaryāt*—from his powerful position; *bhraṁśitasya*—who was made to fall; *api*—even though; *vipra*—of a *brāhmaṇa; vyājena*—in the guise; *viṣṇunā*—by Lord Viṣṇu; *śriyam*—the opulence; *jihīrṣatā*—who wanted to take away; *indrasya*—of Indra; *viṣṇave*—to Viṣṇu; *dvija-rūpiṇe*—appearing as a *brāhmaṇa; jānan*—aware; *api*—although; *mahīm*—the whole earth; *prādāt*—he gave; *vāryamāṇaḥ*—being forbidden; *api*—even; *daitya*—of the demons; *rāṭ*—the king.

TRANSLATION

Indeed, the spotless glories of Bali Mahārāja are heard throughout the world. Lord Viṣṇu, wishing to recover Indra's opulence from Bali, appeared before him in the guise of a *brāhmaṇa* and made him fall from his powerful position. Though aware of the ruse and forbidden by his *guru*, Bali, king of the demons, still gave Viṣṇu the whole earth in charity.

TEXT 26

जीवता ब्राह्मणार्थाय को न्वर्थः क्षत्रबन्धुना ।
देहेन पतमानेन नेहता विपुलं यशः ॥२६॥

jīvatā brāhmaṇārthāya
ko nv arthaḥ kṣatra-bandhunā
dehena patamānena
nehatā vipulaṁ yaśaḥ

jīvatā—who is alive; *brāhmaṇa-arthāya*—for the benefit of *brāhmaṇas; kaḥ*—what; *nu*—at all; *arthaḥ*—use; *kṣatra-bandhunā*—with a fallen *kṣatriya; dehena*—by his body; *patamānena*—about to fall; *na īhatā*—who is not endeavoring; *vipulam*—for extensive; *yaśaḥ*—glory.

TRANSLATION

What is the use of an unqualified *kṣatriya* who goes on living but fails to gain everlasting glory by working with his perishable body for the benefit of *brāhmaṇas*?

TEXT 27

इत्युदारमतिः प्राह कृष्णार्जुनवृकोदरान् ।
हे विप्रा व्रियतां कामो ददाम्यात्मशिरोऽपि वः ॥२७॥

ity udāra-matiḥ prāha
kṛṣṇārjuna-vṛkodarān
he viprā vriyatāṁ kāmo
dadāmy ātma-śiro 'pi vaḥ

iti—thus; *udāra*—generous; *matiḥ*—whose mentality; *prāha*—said; *kṛṣṇa-arjuna-vṛkodarān*—to Kṛṣṇa, Arjuna and Bhīma; *he viprāḥ*—O learned *brāhmaṇas; vriyatām*—let it be chosen; *kāmaḥ*—what you desire; *dadāmi*—I will give; *ātma*—my own; *śiraḥ*—head; *api*—even; *vaḥ*—to you.

TRANSLATION

[Śukadeva Gosvāmī continued:] Thus making up his mind, the generous Jarāsandha addressed Kṛṣṇa, Arjuna and Bhīma: "O learned *brāhmaṇas*, choose whatever you wish. I will give it to you, even if it is my own head."

TEXT 28

श्रीभगवानुवाच
युद्धं नो देहि राजेन्द्र द्वन्द्वशो यदि मन्यसे ।
युद्धार्थिनो वयं प्राप्ता राजन्या नान्यकाङ्क्षिणः ॥२८॥

śrī-bhagavān uvāca
yuddhaṁ no dehi rājendra
dvandvaśo yadi manyase
yuddhārthino vayaṁ prāptā
rājanyā nānya-kāṅkṣiṇaḥ

śrī-bhagavān uvāca—the Supreme Lord (Kṛṣṇa) said; *yuddham*—battle; *naḥ*—to us; *dehi*—please give; *rāja-indra*—O exalted King; *dvandvaśaḥ*—as a one-on-one duel; *yadi*—if; *manyase*—you think it proper; *yuddha*—for a fight; *arthinaḥ*—desirous; *vayam*—we; *prāptāḥ*—have come here; *rājanyāḥ*—members of the royal order; *na*—not; *anya*—anything else; *kāṅkṣiṇaḥ*—wanting.

TRANSLATION

The Supreme Lord said: O exalted King, give us battle in the form of a duel, if you think it fitting. We are princes and have come to beg a fight. We have no other request to make of you.

TEXT 29

असौ वृकोदरः पार्थस्तस्य भ्रातार्जुनो ह्ययम् ।
अनयोर्मातुलेयं मां कृष्णं जानीहि ते रिपुम् ॥२९॥

asau vṛkodaraḥ pārthas
tasya bhrātārjuno hy ayam
anayor mātuleyaṁ māṁ
kṛṣṇaṁ jānīhi te ripum

asau—that one; *vṛkodaraḥ*—Bhīma; *pārthaḥ*—the son of Pṛthā; *tasya*—his; *bhrātā*—brother; *arjunaḥ*—Arjuna; *hi*—indeed; *ayam*—this other; *anayoḥ*—of the two of them; *mātuleyam*—the maternal cousin; *mām*—Me; *kṛṣṇam*—Kṛṣṇa; *jānīhi*—please know; *te*—your; *ripum*—enemy.

TRANSLATION

Over there is Bhīma, son of Pṛthā, and this is his brother Arjuna. Know Me to be their maternal cousin, Kṛṣṇa, your enemy.

TEXT 30

एवमावेदितो राजा जहासोच्चैः स्म मागधः ।
आह चामर्षितो मन्दा युद्धं तर्हि ददामि वः ॥३०॥

evam āvedito rājā
jahāsoccaiḥ sma māgadhaḥ

āha cāmarṣito mandā
yuddhaṁ tarhi dadāmi vaḥ

evam—thus; *āveditaḥ*—invited; *rājā*—the King; *jahāsa*—laughed; *uccaiḥ*—out loud; *sma*—indeed; *māgadhaḥ*—Jarāsandha; *āha*—he said; *ca*—and; *amarṣitaḥ*—intolerant; *mandāḥ*—O fools; *yuddham*—battle; *tarhi*—then; *dadāmi*—I will give; *vaḥ*—to you.

TRANSLATION

[Śukadeva Gosvāmī continued:] Thus challenged, Magadharāja laughed out loud and contemptuously said, "All right, you fools, I'll give you a fight!

PURPORT

Śrīla Viśvanātha Cakravartī comments that Jarāsandha felt inner satisfaction because he thought that his enemies had been humiliated by having to dress like *brāhmaṇas* to approach him. Thus the *ācārya* understands Jarāsandha's mind as follows: "O weak ones, forget the botheration of fighting. Why not just accept my head? By dressing yourselves as *brāhmaṇas* begging charity, you have made your heroism set like the sun, but if somehow you have not lost your courage, I will give you battle."

The *ācārya* finally points out that the goddess of learning intends the phrase *amarṣito mandāḥ* to read *amarṣito 'mandāḥ*. In other words, Lord Kṛṣṇa and the Pāṇḍavas are *amandāḥ*, "never foolish." And that is why they chose the best tactic for doing away once and for all with the cruel Jarāsandha.

TEXT 31

न त्वया भीरुणा योत्स्ये युधि विक्लवतेजसा ।
मथुरां स्वपुरीं त्यक्त्वा समुद्रं शरणं गतः ॥३१॥

na tvayā bhīruṇā yotsye
yudhi viklava-tejasā
mathurāṁ sva-purīṁ tyaktvā
samudraṁ śaraṇaṁ gataḥ

na—not; *tvayā*—with You; *bhīruṇā*—cowardly; *yotsye*—I will fight; *yudhi*—in battle; *viklava*—impaired; *tejasā*—whose strength; *mathurām*—Mathurā; *sva*—Your own; *purīm*—city; *tyaktvā*—leaving; *samudram*—to the ocean; *śaraṇam*—for shelter; *gataḥ*—gone.

TRANSLATION

"But I will not fight with You, Kṛṣṇa, for You are a coward. Your strength abandoned You in the midst of battle, and You fled Your own capital of Mathurā to take shelter in the sea.

TEXT 32

अयं तु वयसातुल्यो नातिसत्त्वो न मे समः ।
अर्जुनो न भवेद्योद्धा भीमस्तुल्यबलो मम ॥३२॥

ayaṁ tu vayasātulyo
nāti-sattvo na me samaḥ
arjuno na bhaved yoddhā
bhīmas tulya-balo mama

ayam—this; *tu*—on the other hand; *vayasā*—in age; *atulyaḥ*—unequal; *na*—not; *ati*—much; *sattvaḥ*—having strength; *na*—not; *me*—to me; *samaḥ*—evenly matched; *arjunaḥ*—Arjuna; *na bhavet*—should not be; *yoddhā*—the contender; *bhīmaḥ*—Bhīma; *tulya*—equal; *balaḥ*—in strength; *mama*—with me.

TRANSLATION

"As for this one, Arjuna, he is not as old as I, nor is he very strong. Since he is no match for me, he should not be the contender. Bhīma, however, is as strong as I am."

TEXT 33

इत्युक्त्वा भीमसेनाय प्रादाय महतीं गदाम् ।
द्वितीयां स्वयमादाय निर्जगाम पुराद् बहिः ॥३३॥

ity uktvā bhīmasenāya
prādāya mahatīṁ gadām
dvitīyāṁ svayam ādāya
nirjagāma purād bahiḥ

iti—thus; *uktvā*—saying; *bhīmasenāya*—to Bhīmasena; *prādāya*—giving; *mahatīm*—a large; *gadām*—club; *dvitīyām*—another; *svayam*—himself; *ādāya*—taking; *nirjagāma*—he went out; *purāt*—from the city; *bahiḥ*—to the outside.

TRANSLATION

Having said this, Jarāsandha offered Bhīmasena a huge club, took up another himself and went outside the city.

TEXT 34

ततः समेखले वीरौ संयुक्तावितरेतरम् ।
जघ्नतुर्वज्रकल्पाभ्यां गदाभ्यां रणदुर्मदौ ॥३४॥

tataḥ samekhale vīrau
saṁyuktāv itaretaram
jaghnatur vajra-kalpābhyāṁ
gadābhyāṁ raṇa-durmadau

tataḥ—then; *samekhale*—on the level fighting grounds; *vīrau*—the two heroes; *saṁyuktau*—engaged; *itara-itaram*—each other; *jaghnatuḥ*—struck; *vajra-kalpābhyām*—like lightning bolts; *gadābhyām*—with their clubs; *raṇa*—by the fight; *durmadau*—driven to a mad fury.

TRANSLATION

The two heroes thus began battling each other on the level fighting grounds outside the city. Maddened with the fury of combat, they struck each other with their lightning-bolt-like clubs.

TEXT 35

मण्डलानि विचित्राणि सव्यं दक्षिणमेव च ।
चरतोः शुशुभे युद्धं नटयोरिव रंगिणोः ॥३५॥

maṇḍalāni vicitrāṇi
savyaṁ dakṣiṇam eva ca
caratoḥ śuśubhe yuddhaṁ
naṭayor iva raṅgiṇoḥ

maṇḍalāni—arcs; *vicitrāṇi*—skillful; *savyam*—to the left; *dakṣiṇam*—to the right; *eva ca*—also; *caratoḥ*—of them who were moving; *śuśubhe*—appeared splendid; *yuddham*—the fight; *naṭayoḥ*—of actors; *iva*—like; *raṅgiṇoḥ*—on a stage.

TRANSLATION

As they skillfully circled left and right, like actors dancing on a stage, the fight presented a magnificent spectacle.

PURPORT

Jarāsandha and Bhīma here demonstrate their expertise in the use of clubs. Thus it can be understood that both fighters were fearless and steady even in the rage of battle.

TEXT 36

ततश्चटचटाशब्दो वज्रनिष्पेषसन्निभः ।
गदयोः क्षिप्तयो राजन् दन्तयोरिव दन्तिनोः ॥३६॥

tataś caṭa-caṭā-śabdo
vajra-niṣpeṣa-sannibhaḥ
gadayoḥ kṣiptayo rājan
dantayor iva dantinoḥ

tataḥ—then; *caṭa-caṭā-śabdaḥ*—the clattering sound; *vajra*—of lightning; *niṣpeṣa*—the crash; *sannibhaḥ*—resembling; *gadayoḥ*—of their clubs; *kṣiptayoḥ*—being swung; *rājan*—O King (Parīkṣit); *dantayoḥ*—of the tusks; *iva*—as if; *dantinoḥ*—of elephants.

TRANSLATION

When Jarāsandha's and Bhīmasena's clubs loudly collided, O King, the sound was like the impact of the big tusks of two fighting elephants, or the crash of a thunderbolt in a flashing electrical storm.

PURPORT

This translation is based on Śrīla Prabhupāda's *Kṛṣṇa.*

TEXT 37

ते वै गदे भुजजवेन निपात्यमाने
अन्योन्यतोऽंसकटिपादकरोरुजत्रुम् ।
चूर्णीबभूवतुरुपेत्य यथार्कशाखे
संयुध्यतोर्द्विरदयोरिव दीप्तमन्व्योः ॥३७॥

te vai gade bhuja-javena nipātyamāne
anyonyato 'ṁsa-kaṭi-pāda-karoru-jatrum
cūrṇī-babhūvatur upetya yathārka-śākhe
saṁyudhyator dviradayor iva dīpta-manvyoḥ

te—they; *vai*—indeed; *gade*—the two clubs; *bhuja*—of their arms; *javena*—by the rapid force; *nipātyamāne*—being powerfully swung; *anyonyataḥ*—against one another; *aṁsa*—their shoulders; *kaṭi*—hips; *pāda*—feet; *kara*—hands; *ūru*—thighs; *jatrum*—and collarbones; *cūrṇī*—crushed; *babhūvatuḥ*—became; *upetya*—contacting; *yathā*—as; *arka-śākhe*—two branches of *arka* trees; *saṁyudhyatoḥ*—fighting vigorously; *dviradayoḥ*—of a pair of elephants; *iva*—as; *dīpta*—inflamed; *manvyoḥ*—whose anger.

TRANSLATION

They swung their clubs at each other with such speed and force that as the clubs struck their shoulders, hips, feet, hands, thighs

and collarbones, the weapons were crushed and broken like branches of *arka* trees with which two enraged elephants furiously attack each other.

TEXT 38

इत्थं तयोः प्रहतयोर्गदयोर्नृवीरौ
क्रुद्धौ स्वमुष्टिभिरयःस्परशैरपिष्टाम् ।
शब्दस्तयोः प्रहरतोरिभयोरिवासीन्
निर्घातवज्रपरुषस्तलताडनोत्थः ॥३८॥

itthaṁ tayoḥ prahatayor gadayor nṛ-vīrau
kruddhau sva-muṣṭibhir ayaḥ-sparaśair apiṣṭām
śabdas tayoḥ praharator ibhayor ivāsīn
nirghāta-vajra-paruṣas tala-tāḍanotthaḥ

ittham—in this manner; *tayoḥ*—their; *prahatayoḥ*—being ruined; *gadayoḥ*—the clubs; *nṛ*—among human beings; *vīrau*—the two great heroes; *kruddhau*—angry; *sva*—their own; *muṣṭibhiḥ*—with the fists; *ayaḥ*—like iron; *sparaśaiḥ*—whose touch; *apiṣṭām*—they battered; *śabdaḥ*—the sound; *tayoḥ*—of them; *praharatoḥ*—striking; *ibhayoḥ*—of two elephants; *iva*—as; *āsit*—became; *nirghāta*—crashing; *vajra*—like thunder; *paruṣaḥ*—harsh; *tala*—of their palms; *tāḍana*—by the hitting; *utthaḥ*—raised.

TRANSLATION

Their clubs thus ruined, those great heroes among men angrily pummeled each other with their iron-hard fists. As they slapped each other, the sound resembled the crash of elephants colliding or harsh thunderclaps.

TEXT 39

तयोरेवं प्रहरतोः समशिक्षाबलौजसोः ।
निर्विशेषमभूद्युद्धमक्षीणजवयोर्नृप ॥३९॥

tayor evaṁ praharatoḥ
sama-śikṣā-balaujasoḥ
nirviśeṣam abhūd yuddham
akṣīṇa-javayor nṛpa

tayoḥ—of the two; *evam*—thus; *praharatoḥ*—striking; *sama*—equal; *śikṣā*—whose training; *bala*—strength; *ojasoḥ*—and stamina; *nirviśeṣam*—indecisive; *abhūt*—was; *yuddham*—the fight; *akṣīṇa*—undiminished; *javayoḥ*—whose exertion; *nṛpa*—O King.

TRANSLATION

As they thus fought, this contest between opponents of equal training, strength and stamina reached no conclusion. And so they kept on fighting, O King, without any letup.

PURPORT

Some *ācāryas* include the following two verses in the text of this chapter, and Śrīla Prabhupāda has also translated them in *Kṛṣṇa:*

evaṁ tayor mahā-rāja
yudhyatoḥ sapta-viṁśatiḥ
dināni niragaṁs tatra
suhṛd-van niśi tiṣṭhatoḥ

ekadā mātuleyaṁ vai
prāha rājan vṛkodaraḥ
na śakto 'haṁ jarāsandhaṁ
nirjetuṁ yudhi mādhava

"Thus, O King, they continued to fight for twenty-seven days. At the end of each day's fighting, both lived at night as friends in Jarāsandha's palace. Then on the twenty-eighth day, O King, Vṛkodara [Bhīma] told his maternal cousin, 'Mādhava, I cannot defeat Jarāsandha in battle.'"

TEXT 40

शत्रोर्जन्ममृती विद्वाञ्जीवितं च जराकृतम् ।
पार्थमाप्याययन् स्वेन तेजसाचिन्तयद्धरिः ॥४०॥

śatror janma-mṛtī vidvāñ
jīvitaṁ ca jarā-kṛtam
pārtham āpyāyayan svena
tejasācintayad dhariḥ

śatroḥ—of the enemy; *janma*—the birth; *mṛtī*—and death; *vidvān*—knowing; *jīvitam*—the bringing to life; *ca*—and; *jarā*—by the demoness Jarā; *kṛtam*—done; *pārtham*—Bhīma, the son of Pṛthā; *āpyāyayan*—empowering; *svena*—with His own; *tejasā*—potency; *acintayat*—thought; *hariḥ*—Lord Kṛṣṇa.

TRANSLATION

Lord Kṛṣṇa knew the secret of His enemy Jarāsandha's birth and death, and also how he had been given life by the demoness Jarā. Considering all this, Lord Kṛṣṇa imparted His special power to Bhīma.

PURPORT

Śrīla Prabhupāda writes that Lord Kṛṣṇa "knew the mystery of the birth of Jarāsandha. Jarāsandha was born in two different parts from two different mothers. When his father saw that the baby was useless, he threw the two parts in the forest, where they were later found by a black-hearted witch named Jarā. She managed to join the two parts of the baby from top to bottom. Knowing this, Lord Kṛṣṇa therefore also knew how to kill him."

TEXT 41

सञ्चिन्त्यारिवधोपायं भीमस्यामोघदर्शनः ।
दर्शयामास विटपं पाटयन्निव संज्ञया ॥४१॥

sañcintyāri-vadhopāyaṁ
bhīmasyāmogha-darśanaḥ
darśayām āsa viṭapaṁ
pāṭayann iva saṁjñayā

sañcintya—having thought; *ari*—their enemy; *vadha*—for killing; *upāyam*—about the means; *bhīmasya*—to Bhīma; *amogha-darśanaḥ*—

the Supreme Lord, whose vision is infallible; *darśayām āsa*—showed; *viṭapam*—a tree branch; *pāṭayan*—tearing apart; *iva*—as if; *saṁjñayā*—as a sign.

TRANSLATION

Having determined how to kill the enemy, that Lord of infallible vision made a sign to Bhīma by tearing in half a small branch of a tree.

TEXT 42

तद्विज्ञाय महासत्त्वो भीमः प्रहरतां वरः ।
गृहीत्वा पादयोः शत्रुं पातयामास भूतले ॥४२॥

tad vijñāya mahā-sattvo
bhīmaḥ praharatāṁ varaḥ
gṛhītvā pādayoḥ śatruṁ
pātayām āsa bhū-tale

tat—that; *vijñāya*—understanding; *mahā*—great; *sattvaḥ*—whose strength; *bhīmaḥ*—Bhīma; *praharatām*—of fighters; *varaḥ*—the best; *gṛhītvā*—seizing; *pādayoḥ*—by the feet; *śatrum*—his enemy; *pātayām āsa*—he made him fall; *bhū-tale*—to the ground.

TRANSLATION

Understanding this sign, mighty Bhīma, the best of fighters, seized his opponent by the feet and threw him to the ground.

TEXT 43

एकं पादं पदाक्रम्य दोर्भ्यामन्यं प्रगृह्य सः ।
गुदतः पाटयामास शाखामिव महागजः ॥४३॥

ekaṁ pādaṁ padākramya
dorbhyām anyaṁ pragṛhya saḥ
gudataḥ pāṭayām āsa
śākhām iva mahā-gajaḥ

ekam—one; *pādam*—leg; *padā*—with his foot; *ākramya*—standing on top of; *dorbhyām*—with his two hands; *anyam*—the other; *pragṛhya*—taking hold of; *saḥ*—he; *gudataḥ*—beginning from the anus; *pāṭayām āsa*—tore him asunder; *śākhām*—a tree branch; *iva*—as; *mahā*—great; *gajaḥ*—an elephant.

TRANSLATION

Bhīma pressed down on one leg with his foot while grabbing Jarāsandha's other leg in his hands, and just as a great elephant might break the branch of a tree, Bhīma tore Jarāsandha apart from the anus upward.

TEXT 44

एकपादोरुवृषणकटिपृष्ठस्तनांसके ।
एकबाह्वक्षिभ्रूकर्णे शकले ददृशुः प्रजाः ॥४४॥

eka-pādoru-vṛṣaṇa-
kaṭi-pṛṣṭha-stanāṁsake
eka-bāhv-akṣi-bhrū-karṇe
śakale dadṛśuḥ prajāḥ

eka—with one; *pāda*—leg; *ūru*—thigh; *vṛṣaṇa*—testicle; *kaṭi*—hip; *pṛṣṭha*—side of the back; *stana*—chest; *aṁsake*—and shoulder; *eka*—with one; *bāhu*—arm; *akṣi*—eye; *bhrū*—eyebrow; *karṇe*—and ear; *śakale*—two pieces; *dadṛśuḥ*—saw; *prajāḥ*—the citizens.

TRANSLATION

The King's subjects then saw him lying in two separate pieces, each with a single leg, thigh, testicle, hip, shoulder, arm, eye, eyebrow and ear, and with half a back and chest.

TEXT 45

हाहाकारो महानासीन्निहते मगधेश्वरे ।
पूजयामासतुर्भीमं परिरभ्य जयाच्युतौ ॥४५॥

hāhā-kāro mahān āsīn
nihate magadheśvare
pūjayām āsatur bhīmaṁ
parirabhya jayācyutau

hāhā-kāraḥ—a cry of lamentation; *mahān*—great; *āsīt*—arose; *nihate*—having been killed; *magadha-īśvare*—the lord of the Magadha province; *pūjayām āsatuḥ*—the two of them honored; *bhīmam*—Bhīma; *parirabhya*—embracing; *jaya*—Arjuna; *acyutau*—and Kṛṣṇa.

TRANSLATION

With the death of the lord of Magadha, a great cry of lamentation arose, while Arjuna and Kṛṣṇa congratulated Bhīma by embracing him.

TEXT 46

सहदेवं तत्तनयं भगवान् भूतभावनः ।
अभ्यषिञ्चदमेयात्मा मगधानां पतिं प्रभुः ।
मोचयामास राजन्यान् संरुद्धा मागधेन ये ॥४६॥

sahadevaṁ tat-tanayaṁ
bhagavān bhūta-bhāvanaḥ
abhyaṣiñcad ameyātmā
magadhānāṁ patiṁ prabhuḥ
mocayām āsa rājanyān
saṁruddhā māgadhena ye

sahadevam—named Sahadeva; *tat*—his (Jarāsandha's); *tanayam*—son; *bhagavān*—the Personality of Godhead; *bhūta*—of all living beings; *bhāvanaḥ*—the sustainer; *abhyaṣiñcat*—coronated; *ameya-ātmā*—the immeasurable one; *magadhānām*—of the Magadhas; *patim*—as the master; *prabhuḥ*—the Lord; *mocayām āsa*—He released; *rājanyān*—the kings; *saṁruddhāḥ*—imprisoned; *māgadhena*—by Jarāsandha; *ye*—who.

TRANSLATION

The immeasurable Supreme Personality of Godhead, the sustainer and benefactor of all living beings, coronated Jarāsandha's son, Sahadeva, as the new ruler of the Magadhas. The Lord then freed all the kings Jarāsandha had imprisoned.

PURPORT

Śrīla Prabhupāda writes, "Although Jarāsandha was killed, neither Kṛṣṇa nor the two Pāṇḍava brothers made a claim to the throne. Their purpose in killing Jarāsandha was to stop him from creating a disturbance against the proper discharge of world peace. A demon always creates disturbances, whereas a demigod always tries to keep peace in the world. The mission of Lord Kṛṣṇa is to give protection to the righteous persons and to kill the demons who disturb a peaceful situation. Therefore Lord Kṛṣṇa immediately called for the son of Jarāsandha, whose name was Sahadeva, and with due ritualistic ceremonies He asked him to occupy the seat of his father and reign over the kingdom peacefully. Lord Kṛṣṇa is the master of the whole cosmic creation, and He wants everyone to live peacefully and execute Kṛṣṇa consciousness. After installing Sahadeva on the throne, He released all the kings and princes who had been imprisoned unnecessarily by Jarāsandha."

Thus end the purports of the humble servants of His Divine Grace A. C. Bhaktivedanta Swami Prabhupāda to the Tenth Canto, Seventy-second Chapter, of the Śrīmad-Bhāgavatam, *entitled "The Slaying of the Demon Jarāsandha."*

CHAPTER SEVENTY–THREE

Lord Kṛṣṇa Blesses the Liberated Kings

This chapter relates how Lord Śrī Kṛṣṇa, after freeing the kings imprisoned by Jarāsandha, mercifully gave them His audience and bestowed royal gifts upon them.

When Lord Kṛṣṇa freed the 20,800 kings Jarāsandha had imprisoned, they immediately fell to the ground to pay Him obeisances. Then they stood with joined palms and began to pray to Him. Seeing their imprisonment as an act of mercy by the Lord to smash their false pride, the kings prayed only to be granted whatever would facilitate their perpetual remembrance of His lotus feet.

The Lord assured the kings that their prayer would be fulfilled. He instructed them, "Worship Me by performing Vedic sacrifices, and protect your subjects in accordance with the principles of religion. Fixing your minds on Me, beget progeny, and remain always equipoised in happiness and distress. Thus at the end of your lives you will surely attain Me."

Lord Kṛṣṇa then saw to it that the kings were properly bathed and dressed, and He had Sahadeva offer them flower garlands, sandalwood pulp, fine clothing and other things suitable for kings. After having them adorned with jewels and golden ornaments, He seated them on chariots and sent them off to their respective kingdoms. In accordance with the orders the Lord had given them, they began to carry out their various duties once again.

Lord Kṛṣṇa, Bhīma and Arjuna then departed for Indraprastha, where they met with King Yudhiṣṭhira and related to him everything that had happened.

TEXTS 1–6

श्रीशुक उवाच

अयुते द्वे शतान्यष्टौ निरुद्धा युधि निर्जिताः ।
ते निर्गता गिरिद्रोण्यां मलिना मलवाससः ॥१॥

क्षुत्क्षामाः शुष्कवदनाः संरोधपरिकर्शिताः ।
ददृशुस्ते घनश्यामं पीतकौशेयवाससम् ॥२॥
श्रीवत्सांकं चतुर्बाहुं पद्मगर्भारुणेक्षणम् ।
चारुप्रसन्नवदनं स्फुरन्मकरकुण्डलम् ॥३॥
पद्महस्तं गदाशंखरथांगैरुपलक्षितम् ।
किरीटहारकटककटिसूत्रांगदाञ्चितम् ॥४॥
भ्राजद्वरमणिग्रीवं निवीतं वनमालया ।
पिबन्त इव चक्षुर्भ्यां लिहन्त इव जिह्वया ॥५॥
जिघ्रन्त इव नासाभ्यां रम्भन्त इव बाहुभिः ।
प्रणेमुर्हतपाप्मानो मूर्धभिः पादयोर्हरेः ॥६॥

śrī-śuka uvāca
ayute dve śatāny aṣṭau
niruddhā yudhi nirjitāḥ
te nirgatā giridroṇyāṁ
malinā mala-vāsasaḥ

kṣut-kṣāmāḥ śuṣka-vadanāḥ
saṁrodha-parikarśitāḥ
dadṛśus te ghana-śyāmaṁ
pīta-kauśeya-vāsasam

śrīvatsāṅkaṁ catur-bāhuṁ
padma-garbhāruṇekṣaṇam
cāru-prasanna-vadanaṁ
sphuran-makara-kuṇḍalam

padma-hastaṁ gadā-śaṅkha-
rathāṅgair upalakṣitam
kirīṭa-hāra-kaṭaka-
kaṭi-sūtrāṅgadāñcitam

bhrājad-vara-maṇi-grīvaṁ
nivītaṁ vana-mālayā

pibanta iva cakṣurbhyāṁ
lihanta iva jihvayā

jighranta iva nāsābhyāṁ
rambhanta iva bāhubhiḥ
praṇemur hata-pāpmāno
mūrdhabhiḥ pādayor hareḥ

śrī-śukaḥ uvāca—Śukadeva Gosvāmī said; *ayute*—ten thousands; *dve*—two; *śatāni*—hundreds; *aṣṭau*—eight; *niruddhāḥ*—imprisoned; *yudhi*—in battle; *nirjitāḥ*—defeated; *te*—they; *nirgatāḥ*—coming out; *giridroṇyām*—in the fortress of Giridroṇī, Jarāsandha's capital; *malināḥ*—dirty; *mala*—dirty; *vāsasaḥ*—whose clothes; *kṣut*—by hunger; *kṣāmāḥ*—emaciated; *śuṣka*—dried up; *vadanāḥ*—faces; *saṁrodha*—by their bondage; *parikarśitāḥ*—greatly weakened; *dadṛśuḥ*—saw; *te*—they; *ghana*—like a cloud; *śyāmam*—dark blue; *pīta*—yellow; *kauśeya*—of silk; *vāsasam*—whose clothing; *śrīvatsa*—by the distinctive sign known as Śrīvatsa; *aṅkam*—marked; *catuḥ*—four; *bāhum*—having arms; *padma*—of a lotus; *garbha*—like the whorl; *aruṇa*—pink; *īkṣaṇam*—eyes; *cāru*—charming; *prasanna*—and pleasant; *vadanam*—face; *sphurat*—gleaming; *makara*—shaped like sea monsters; *kuṇḍalam*—with earrings; *padma*—a lotus; *hastam*—in His hand; *gadā*—by His club; *śaṅkha*—conchshell; *ratha-aṅgaiḥ*—and disc weapon; *upalakṣitam*—identified; *kirīṭa*—with a helmet; *hāra*—jeweled necklace; *kaṭaka*—gold bracelets; *kaṭi-sūtra*—belt; *aṅgada*—and armlets; *añcitam*—decorated; *bhrājat*—brilliant; *vara*—excellent; *maṇi*—a jewel (the Kaustubha); *grīvam*—on His neck; *nivītam*—hanging (from His neck); *vana*—of forest flowers; *mālayā*—with a garland; *pibantaḥ*—drinking; *iva*—as if; *cakṣurbhyām*—with their eyes; *lihantaḥ*—licking; *iva*—as if; *jihvayā*—with their tongues; *jighrantaḥ*—smelling; *iva*—as if; *nāsābhyām*—with their nostrils; *rambhantaḥ*—embracing; *iva*—as if; *bāhubhiḥ*—with their arms; *praṇemuḥ*—they bowed down; *hata*—destroyed; *pāpmānaḥ*—whose sins; *mūrdhabhiḥ*—with their heads; *pādayoḥ*—at the feet; *hareḥ*—of Lord Kṛṣṇa.

TRANSLATION

Śukadeva Gosvāmī said: Jarāsandha had defeated 20,800 kings in combat and thrown them into prison. As these kings emerged from the Giridroṇī fortress, they appeared dirty and shabbily

dressed. They were emaciated by hunger, their faces were dried up, and they were greatly weakened by their long imprisonment.

The kings then beheld the Lord before them. His complexion was dark blue like the color of a cloud, and He wore a yellow silk garment. He was distinguished by the Śrīvatsa mark on His chest, His four mighty arms, the pinkish hue of His eyes, which resembled the whorl of a lotus, His lovely, cheerful face, His gleaming *makara* earrings and the lotus, club, conchshell and disc in His hands. A helmet, a jeweled necklace, a golden belt, and golden bracelets and armlets decorated His form, and on His neck He wore both the brilliant, precious Kaustubha gem and a garland of forest flowers. The kings seemed to drink His beauty with their eyes, lick Him with their tongues, relish His fragrance with their nostrils and embrace Him with their arms. Their past sins now eradicated, the kings all bowed down to Lord Hari, placing their heads at His feet.

TEXT 7

कृष्णसन्दर्शनाह्लादध्वस्तसंरोधनक्लमाः ।
प्रशशंसुर्हृषीकेशं गीर्भिः प्राञ्जलयो नृपाः ॥७॥

kṛṣṇa-sandarśanāhlāda-
dhvasta-saṁrodhana-klamāḥ
praśaśaṁsur hṛṣīkeśaṁ
gīrbhiḥ prāñjalayo nṛpāḥ

kṛṣṇa-sandarśana—of seeing Lord Kṛṣṇa; *āhlāda*—by the ecstasy; *dhvasta*—eradicated; *saṁrodhana*—of imprisonment; *klamāḥ*—whose weariness; *praśaśaṁsuḥ*—they praised; *hṛṣīkā-īśam*—the supreme master of the senses; *gīrbhiḥ*—with their words; *prāñjalayaḥ*—with joined palms; *nṛpāḥ*—the kings.

TRANSLATION

The ecstasy of beholding Lord Kṛṣṇa having dispelled the weariness of their imprisonment, the kings stood with joined palms and offered words of praise to that supreme master of the senses.

TEXT 8

राजान ऊचुः
नमस्ते देवदेवेश प्रपन्नार्तिहराव्यय ।
प्रपन्नान् पाहि नः कृष्ण निर्विण्णान् घोरसंसृतेः ॥८॥

rājāna ūcuḥ
namas te deva-deveśa
prapannārti-harāvyaya
prapannān pāhi naḥ kṛṣṇa
nirviṇṇān ghora-saṁsṛteḥ

rājānaḥ ūcuḥ—the kings said; *namaḥ*—obeisances; *te*—to You; *deva*—of the demigods; *deva*—of the lords; *īśa*—O Supreme Lord; *prapanna*—of those who are surrendered; *ārti*—of the distress; *hara*—O remover; *avyaya*—O inexhaustible one; *prapannān*—surrendered; *pāhi*—please save; *naḥ*—us; *kṛṣṇa*—O Kṛṣṇa; *nirviṇṇān*—despondent; *ghora*—terrible; *saṁsṛteḥ*—from material existence.

TRANSLATION

The kings said: Obeisances to You, O Lord of the ruling demigods, O destroyer of Your surrendered devotees' distress. Since we have surrendered to You, O inexhaustible Kṛṣṇa, please save us from this terrible material life, which has made us so despondent.

TEXT 9

नैनं नाथानुसूयामो मागधं मधुसूदन ।
अनुग्रहो यद् भवतो राज्ञां राज्यच्युतिर्विभो ॥९॥

nainaṁ nāthānusūyāmo
māgadhaṁ madhusūdana
anugraho yad bhavato
rājñāṁ rājya-cyutir vibho

na—not; *enam*—with this; *nātha*—O master; *anusūyāmaḥ*—do we find fault; *māgadham*—the King of Magadha; *madhusūdana*—O Kṛṣṇa;

anugrahaḥ—mercy; *yat*—since; *bhavataḥ*—Your; *rājñām*—of kings; *rājya*—from their dominion; *cyutiḥ*—the falling; *vibho*—O almighty one.

TRANSLATION

O master, Madhusūdana, we do not blame this King of Magadha, since it is actually by Your mercy that kings fall from their royal position, O almighty Lord.

PURPORT

It is significant that upon seeing Lord Kṛṣṇa and thus becoming purified of their sins, the kings did not feel any mundane hatred or bitterness toward Jarāsandha, who had imprisoned them. Simply by seeing Lord Kṛṣṇa, the kings came to the position of Kṛṣṇa consciousness and spoke these verses, which show deep spiritual wisdom.

TEXT 10

राज्यैश्वर्यमदोन्नद्धो न श्रेयो विन्दते नृपः ।
त्वन्मायामोहितोऽनित्या मन्यते सम्पदोऽचलाः ॥१०॥

rājyaiśvarya-madonnaddho
na śreyo vindate nṛpaḥ
tvan-māyā-mohito 'nityā
manyate sampado 'calāḥ

rājya—with sovereignty; *aiśvarya*—and opulence; *mada*—by the intoxication; *unnaddhaḥ*—becoming unrestrained; *na*—does not; *śreyaḥ*—real benefit; *vindate*—obtain; *nṛpaḥ*—a king; *tvat*—Your; *māyā*—by the potency of illusion; *mohitaḥ*—deluded; *anityāḥ*—temporary; *manyate*—he thinks; *sampadaḥ*—assets; *acalāḥ*—permanent.

TRANSLATION

Infatuated with his opulence and ruling power, a king loses all self-restraint and cannot obtain his true welfare. Thus bewildered by Your illusory energy, he imagines his temporary assets to be permanent.

PURPORT

The word *unnaddha* indicates that one who is intoxicated by false pride goes beyond the boundaries of proper behavior. Human life is meant to be governed by *dharma*, spiritual principles for gradual advancement to the perfection of Kṛṣṇa consciousness. Blinded by wealth and power, however, a foolish person does not hesitate to act whimsically, against the laws of nature and God. Unfortunately, this is now the situation in the prosperous Western countries.

TEXT 11

मृगतृष्णां यथा बाला मन्यन्त उदकाशयम् ।
एवं वैकारिकीं मायामयुक्ता वस्तु चक्षते ॥११॥

mṛga-tṛṣṇāṁ yathā bālā
manyanta udakāśayam
evaṁ vaikārikīṁ māyām
ayuktā vastu cakṣate

mṛga-tṛṣṇām—a mirage; *yathā*—as; *bālāḥ*—men of childish intelligence; *manyante*—consider; *udaka*—of water; *āśayam*—a reservoir; *evam*—in the same way; *vaikārikīm*—subject to transformations; *māyām*—the material illusion; *ayuktāḥ*—those who lack discrimination; *vastu*—substance; *cakṣate*—see as.

TRANSLATION

Just as men of childish intelligence consider a mirage in the desert to be a pond of water, so those who are irrational look upon the illusory transformations of Māyā as substantial.

TEXTS 12–13

वयं पुरा श्रीमदनष्टदृष्टयो
जिगीषयास्या इतरेतरस्पृधः ।
घ्नन्तः प्रजाः स्वा अतिनिर्घृणाः प्रभो
मृत्युं पुरस्त्वाविगणय्य दुर्मदाः ॥१२॥

त एव कृष्णाद्य गभीररंहसा
दुरन्तवीर्येण विचालिताः श्रियः ।
कालेन तन्वा भवतोऽनुकम्पया
विनष्टदर्पाश्चरणौ स्मराम ते ॥१३॥

vayaṁ purā śrī-mada-naṣṭa-dṛṣṭayo
jigīṣayāsyā itaretara-spṛdhaḥ
ghnantaḥ prajāḥ svā ati-nirghṛṇāḥ prabho
mṛtyuṁ puras tvāvigaṇayya durmadāḥ

ta eva kṛṣṇādya gabhīra-raṁhasā
duranta-vīryeṇa vicālitāḥ śriyaḥ
kālena tanvā bhavato 'nukampayā
vinaṣṭa-darpāś caraṇau smarāma te

vayam—we; *purā*—previously; *śrī*—of opulence; *mada*—by the intoxication; *naṣṭa*—lost; *dṛṣṭayaḥ*—whose sight; *jigīṣayā*—with the desire of conquering; *asyāḥ*—this (earth); *itara-itara*—with one another; *spṛdhaḥ*—quarreling; *ghnantaḥ*—attacking; *prajāḥ*—citizens; *svāḥ*—our own; *ati*—extremely; *nirghṛṇāḥ*—cruel; *prabho*—O Lord; *mṛtyum*—death; *puraḥ*—in front; *tvā*—You; *avigaṇayya*—disregarding; *durmadāḥ*—arrogant; *te*—they (ourselves); *eva*—indeed; *kṛṣṇa*—O Kṛṣṇa; *adya*—now; *gabhīra*—mysterious; *raṁhasā*—whose movement; *duranta*—irresistible; *vīryeṇa*—whose power; *vicālitāḥ*—forced to depart; *śriyaḥ*—from our opulence; *kālena*—by time; *tanvā*—Your personal form; *bhavataḥ*—Your; *anukampayā*—by the mercy; *vinaṣṭa*—destroyed; *darpāḥ*—whose pride; *caraṇau*—the two feet; *smarāma*—may we remember; *te*—Your.

TRANSLATION

Previously, blinded by the intoxication of riches, we wanted to conquer this earth, and thus we fought one another to achieve victory, mercilessly harassing our own subjects. We arrogantly disregarded You, O Lord, who stood before us as death. But now, O Kṛṣṇa, that powerful form of Yours called time, moving mysteriously and irresistibly, has deprived us of our opulences. Now that You have mercifully destroyed our pride, we beg simply to remember Your lotus feet.

TEXT 14

अथो न राज्यं मृगतृष्णिरूपितं
देहेन शश्वत्पतता रुजां भुवा ।
उपासितव्यं स्पृहयामहे विभो
क्रियाफलं प्रेत्य च कर्णरोचनम् ॥१४॥

atho na rājyaṁ mṛga-tṛṣṇi-rūpitaṁ
dehena śaśvat patatā rujāṁ bhuvā
upāsitavyaṁ spṛhayāmahe vibho
kriyā-phalaṁ pretya ca karṇa-rocanam

atha u—henceforward; *na*—not; *rājyam*—kingdom; *mṛga-tṛṣṇi*—like a mirage; *rūpitam*—which appears; *dehena*—by the material body; *śaśvat*—perpetually; *patatā*—subject to demise; *rujām*—of diseases; *bhuvā*—the birthplace; *upāsitavyam*—to be served; *spṛhayāmahe*—do we hanker for; *vibho*—O almighty Lord; *kriyā*—of pious work; *phalam*—the fruit; *pretya*—having passed to the next life; *ca*—and; *karṇa*—for the ears; *rocanam*—enticement.

TRANSLATION

Never again will we hanker for a miragelike kingdom—a kingdom that must be slavishly served by this mortal body, which is simply a source of disease and suffering and which is declining at every moment. Nor, O almighty Lord, will we hanker to enjoy the heavenly fruits of pious work in the next life, since the promise of such rewards is simply an empty enticement for the ears.

PURPORT

One must work very hard to maintain a kingdom or political sovereignty. And yet the body, which works so hard to maintain one's political power, is itself doomed. At every moment the mortal body moves toward death, and all along the way the body is subject to many painful diseases. The whole affair of mundane power is thus a waste of time for the pure soul, who needs to revive his dormant Kṛṣṇa consciousness.

The Vedic scriptures and other religious scriptures contain many promises of prosperity and heavenly enjoyment in the next life for one who acts piously in this life. Such promises are pleasing to the ears, but they are nothing more than that. Material enjoyment, whether in heaven or in hell, is a type of illusion for the pure soul. By the personal association of Lord Kṛṣṇa, the fortunate kings have now realized the higher spiritual reality beyond the phantasmagoria of the material creation.

TEXT 15

तं नः समादिशोपायं येन ते चरणाब्जयोः ।
स्मृतिर्यथा न विरमेदपि संसरतामिह ॥१५॥

taṁ naḥ samādiśopāyaṁ
yena te caraṇābjayoḥ
smṛtir yathā na viramed
api saṁsaratām iha

tam—that; *naḥ*—to us; *samādiśa*—please instruct; *upāyam*—the means; *yena*—by which; *te*—Your; *caraṇa*—of the feet; *abjayoḥ*—lotuslike; *smṛtiḥ*—remembrance; *yathā*—as; *na viramet*—may not cease; *api*—even; *saṁsaratām*—for those traveling through the cycle of birth and death; *iha*—in this world.

TRANSLATION

Please tell us how we may constantly remember Your lotus feet, though we continue in the cycle of birth and death in this world.

PURPORT

One can constantly remember the Lord only by His mercy. Such remembrance is the easy method to obtain supreme liberation, as explained in *Bhagavad-gītā* (8.14):

ananya-cetāḥ satataṁ
yo māṁ smarati nityaśaḥ
tasyāhaṁ sulabhaḥ pārtha
nitya-yuktasya yoginaḥ

"For one who always remembers Me without deviation, I am easy to obtain, O son of Pṛthā, because of his constant engagement in devotional service."

The words *api saṁsaratām iha* indicate that the kings were approaching Lord Kṛṣṇa not merely for liberation but rather for the boon of always being able to remember His lotus feet. Such constant remembrance is a symptom of love, and love of Godhead is the actual goal of life.

TEXT 16

कृष्णाय वासुदेवाय हरये परमात्मने ।
प्रणतक्लेशनाशाय गोविन्दाय नमो नमः ॥१६॥

kṛṣṇāya vāsudevāya
haraye paramātmane
praṇata-kleśa-nāśāya
govindāya namo namaḥ

kṛṣṇāya—to Kṛṣṇa; *vāsudevāya*—the son of Vasudeva; *haraye*—the Supreme Lord, Hari; *parama-ātmane*—the Supersoul; *praṇata*—of those who have surrendered; *kleśa*—of the distress; *nāśāya*—to the destroyer; *govindāya*—to Govinda; *namaḥ namaḥ*—repeated obeisances.

TRANSLATION

Again and again we offer our obeisances unto Lord Kṛṣṇa, Hari, the son of Vasudeva. That Supreme Soul, Govinda, vanquishes the suffering of all who surrender to Him.

TEXT 17

श्रीशुक उवाच
संस्तूयमानो भगवान् राजभिर्मुक्तबन्धनैः ।
तानाह करुणस्तात शरण्यः श्लक्ष्णया गिरा ॥१७॥

śrī-śuka uvāca
saṁstūyamāno bhagavān
rājabhir mukta-bandhanaiḥ

tān āha karuṇas tāta
śaraṇyaḥ ślakṣṇayā girā

śrī-śukaḥ uvāca—Śukadeva Gosvāmī said; *saṁstūyamānaḥ*—being nicely praised; *bhagavān*—the Supreme Lord; *rājabhiḥ*—by the kings; *mukta*—freed; *bandhanaiḥ*—from their bondage; *tān*—to them; *āha*—He spoke; *karuṇaḥ*—merciful; *tāta*—my dear (King Parīkṣit); *śaraṇyaḥ*—the giver of shelter; *ślakṣṇayā*—with gentle; *girā*—words.

TRANSLATION

Śukadeva Gosvāmī said: Thus the kings, now freed from bondage, glorified the Supreme Lord. Then, my dear Parīkṣit, that merciful bestower of shelter spoke to them in a gentle voice.

TEXT 18

श्रीभगवानुवाच
अद्य प्रभृति वो भूपा मय्यात्मन्यखिलेश्वरे ।
सुदृढा जायते भक्तिर्बाढमाशंसितं तथा ॥१८॥

śrī-bhagavān uvāca
adya prabhṛti vo bhūpā
mayy ātmany akhileśvare
su-dṛḍhā jāyate bhaktir
bāḍham āśaṁsitaṁ tathā

śrī-bhagavān uvāca—the Supreme Lord said; *adya prabhṛti*—beginning from now; *vaḥ*—your; *bhū-pāḥ*—O kings; *mayi*—for Me; *ātmani*—the Self; *akhila*—of all; *īśvare*—the controller; *su*—very; *dṛḍhā*—firm; *jāyate*—will arise; *bhaktiḥ*—devotion; *bāḍham*—assuredly; *āśaṁsitam*—what is desired; *tathā*—so.

TRANSLATION

The Supreme Personality of Godhead said: From now on, my dear kings, you will have firm devotion to Me, the Supreme Self and the Lord of all that be. I assure you this will come to pass, just as you desire.

TEXT 19

दिष्टया व्यवसितं भूपा भवन्त ऋतभाषिणः ।
श्रीयैश्वर्यमदोन्नाहं पश्य उन्मादकं नृणाम् ॥१९॥

diṣṭyā vyavasitaṁ bhūpā
bhavanta ṛta-bhāṣiṇaḥ
śrīy-aiśvarya-madonnāhaṁ
paśya unmādakaṁ nṛṇām

diṣṭyā—fortunate; *vyavasitam*—your resolve; *bhūpāḥ*—O kings; *bhavantaḥ*—you; *ṛta*—truthfully; *bhāṣiṇaḥ*—speaking; *śrī*—of opulence; *aiśvarya*—and power; *mada*—due to the intoxication; *unnāham*—lack of restraint; *paśye*—I see; *unmādakam*—maddening; *nṛṇām*—for human beings.

TRANSLATION

Fortunately you have come to the proper conclusion, my dear kings, and what you have spoken is true. I can see that human beings' lack of self-restraint, which arises from their intoxication with opulence and power, simply leads to madness.

TEXT 20

हैहयो नहुषो वेणो रावणो नरकोऽपरे ।
श्रीमदाद् भ्रंशिताः स्थानाद्देवदैत्यनरेश्वराः ॥२०॥

haihayo nahuṣo veṇo
rāvaṇo narako 'pare
śrī-madād bhraṁśitāḥ sthānād
deva-daitya-nareśvarāḥ

haihayaḥ nahuṣaḥ veṇaḥ—Haihaya (Kārtavīrya), Nahuṣa and Veṇa; *rāvaṇaḥ narakaḥ*—Rāvaṇa and Naraka; *apare*—others also; *śrī*—due to opulence; *madāt*—because of their intoxication; *bhraṁśitāḥ*—made to fall; *sthānāt*—from their positions; *deva*—of demigods; *daitya*—demons; *nara*—and men; *īśvarāḥ*—rulers.

TRANSLATION

Haihaya, Nahuṣa, Veṇa, Rāvaṇa, Naraka and many other rulers of demigods, men and demons fell from their elevated positions because of infatuation with material opulence.

PURPORT

As described by Śrīdhara Svāmī, because Haihaya stole the desire cow of Lord Paraśurāma's father, Jamadagni, Paraśurāma killed him and his impudent sons. Nahuṣa became puffed up when he temporarily assumed the post of Indra. When out of pride Nahuṣa ordered some *brāhmaṇas* to carry him in a palanquin to an illicit meeting with Lord Indra's chaste wife, Śacī, the *brāhmaṇas* made him fall down from his position and become an old man. King Veṇa was similarly mad, and when he insulted the *brāhmaṇas* they killed him by loud incantations of the syllable *hum*. Rāvaṇa was a famous ruler of the Rākṣasas, but out of lust he kidnapped mother Sītā, and thus her husband, Lord Rāmacandra, killed him. Naraka was a ruler of the Daityas who dared to steal mother Aditi's earrings, and for his offense he was also killed. Thus throughout history powerful leaders have fallen from their positions because they became intoxicated with their so-called opulence.

TEXT 21

भवन्त एतद्विज्ञाय देहाद्युत्पाद्यमन्तवत् ।
मां यजन्तोऽध्वरैर्युक्ताः प्रजा धर्मेण रक्ष्यथ ॥२१॥

bhavanta etad vijñāya
dehādy utpādyam anta-vat
māṁ yajanto 'dhvarair yuktāḥ
prajā dharmeṇa rakṣyatha

bhavantaḥ—you; *etat*—this; *vijñāya*—understanding; *deha-ādi*—the material body and so forth; *utpādyam*—subject to birth; *anta-vat*—having an end; *mām*—Me; *yajantaḥ*—worshiping; *adhvaraiḥ*—with Vedic sacrifices; *yuktāḥ*—having clear intelligence; *prajāḥ*—your citizens; *dharmeṇa*—according to religious principles; *rakṣyatha*—you should protect.

TRANSLATION

Understanding that this material body and everything connected with it have a beginning and an end, worship Me by Vedic sacrifices, and with clear intelligence protect your subjects in accordance with the principles of religion.

TEXT 22

सन्तन्वन्तः प्रजातन्तून् सुखं दुःखं भवाभवौ ।
प्राप्तं प्राप्तं च सेवन्तो मच्चित्ता विचरिष्यथ ॥२२॥

santanvantaḥ prajā-tantūn
sukhaṁ duḥkhaṁ bhavābhavau
prāptaṁ prāptaṁ ca sevanto
mac-cittā vicariṣyatha

santanvantaḥ—generating; *prajā*—of progeny; *tantūn*—lines; *sukham*—happiness; *duḥkham*—distress; *bhava*—birth; *abhavau*—and death; *prāptam prāptam*—as they are encountered; *ca*—and; *sevantaḥ*—accepting; *mat-cittāḥ*—with minds fixed on Me; *vicariṣyatha*—you should go about.

TRANSLATION

As you live your lives, begetting generations of progeny and encountering happiness and distress, birth and death, always keep your minds fixed on Me.

TEXT 23

उदासीनाश्च देहादावात्मारामा धृतव्रताः ।
मय्यावेश्य मनः सम्यङ् मामन्ते ब्रह्म यास्यथ ॥२३॥

udāsīnāś ca dehādāv
ātmārāmā dhṛta-vratāḥ
mayy āveśya manaḥ samyaṅ
mām ante brahma yāsyatha

udāsīnāḥ—indifferent; *ca*—and; *deha-ādau*—to the body and so on; *ātma-ārāmāḥ*—self-satisfied; *dhṛta*—holding firmly; *vratāḥ*—to your vows; *mayi*—upon Me; *āveśya*—concentrating; *manaḥ*—the mind; *samyak*—completely; *mām*—to Me; *ante*—in the end; *brahma*—the Absolute Truth; *yāsyatha*—you will go.

TRANSLATION

Be detached from the body and everything connected to it. Remaining self-satisfied, steadfastly keep your vows while concentrating your minds fully on Me. In this way you will ultimately attain Me, the Supreme Absolute Truth.

TEXT 24

श्रीशुक उवाच
इत्यादिश्य नृपान् कृष्णो भगवान् भुवनेश्वरः ।
तेषां न्ययुंक्त पुरुषान् स्त्रियो मज्जनकर्मणि ॥२४॥

śrī-śuka uvāca
ity ādiśya nṛpān kṛṣṇo
bhagavān bhuvaneśvaraḥ
teṣāṁ nyayuṅkta puruṣān
striyo majjana-karmaṇi

śrī-śukaḥ uvāca—Śukadeva Gosvāmī said; *iti*—thus; *ādiśya*—ordering; *nṛpān*—the kings; *kṛṣṇaḥ*—Kṛṣṇa; *bhagavān*—the Supreme Lord; *bhuvana*—of all the worlds; *īśvaraḥ*—the master; *teṣām*—of them; *nyayuṅkta*—engaged; *puruṣān*—menservants; *striyaḥ*—and women; *majjana*—of cleansing; *karmaṇi*—in the work.

TRANSLATION

Śukadeva Gosvāmī said: Having thus instructed the kings, Lord Kṛṣṇa, the supreme master of all the worlds, engaged male and female servants in bathing and grooming them.

TEXT 25

सपर्यां कारयामास सहदेवेन भारत ।
नरदेवोचितैर्वस्त्रैर्भूषणैः स्रग्विलेपनैः ॥२५॥

saparyāṁ kārayām āsa
sahadevena bhārata
naradevocitair vastrair
bhūṣaṇaiḥ srag-vilepanaiḥ

saparyām—service; *kārayām āsa*—He had done; *sahadevena*—by Sahadeva, the son of Jarāsandha; *bhārata*—O descendant of Bharata; *nara-deva*—kings; *ucitaiḥ*—befitting; *vastraiḥ*—with clothing; *bhūṣaṇaiḥ*—ornaments; *srak*—flower garlands; *vilepanaiḥ*—and sandalwood paste.

TRANSLATION

O descendant of Bharata, the Lord then had King Sahadeva honor them with offerings of clothing, jewelry, garlands and sandalwood paste, all suitable for royalty.

TEXT 26

भोजयित्वा वरान्नेन सुस्नातान् समलंकृतान् ।
भोगैश्च विविधैर्युक्तांस्ताम्बूलाद्यैर्नृपोचितैः ॥२६॥

bhojayitvā varānnena
su-snātān samalaṅkṛtān
bhogaiś ca vividhair yuktāṁs
tāmbūlādyair nṛpocitaiḥ

bhojayitvā—feeding; *vara*—excellent; *annena*—with food; *su*—properly; *snātān*—bathed; *samalaṅkṛtān*—well decorated; *bhogaiḥ*—with objects of enjoyment; *ca*—and; *vividhaiḥ*—various; *yuktān*—bestowed; *tāmbūla*—betel nut; *ādyaiḥ*—and so on; *nṛpa*—kings; *ucitaiḥ*—befitting.

TRANSLATION

After they had been properly bathed and adorned, Lord Kṛṣṇa saw to it that they dined on excellent food. He also presented them with various items befitting the pleasure of kings, such as betel nut.

TEXT 27

ते पूजिता मुकुन्देन राजानो मृष्टकुण्डलाः ।
विरेजुर्मोचिताः क्लेशात्प्रावृडन्ते यथा ग्रहाः ॥२७॥

te pūjitā mukundena
rājāno mṛṣṭa-kuṇḍalāḥ
virejur mocitāḥ kleśāt
prāvṛḍ-ante yathā grahāḥ

te—they; *pūjitāḥ*—honored; *mukundena*—by Lord Kṛṣṇa; *rājānaḥ*—the kings; *mṛṣṭa*—gleaming; *kuṇḍalāḥ*—whose earrings; *virejuḥ*—appeared splendid; *mocitāḥ*—released; *kleśāt*—from their distress; *prāvṛṭ*—of the rainy season; *ante*—at the end; *yathā*—as; *grahāḥ*—the planets (such as the moon).

TRANSLATION

Honored by Lord Mukunda and freed from tribulation, the kings shone splendidly, their earrings gleaming, just as the moon and other celestial bodies shine brilliantly in the sky at the end of the rainy season.

TEXT 28

रथान् सदश्वानारोप्य मणिकाञ्चनभूषितान् ।
प्रीणय्य सुनृतैर्वाक्यैः स्वदेशान् प्रत्ययापयत् ॥२८॥

rathān sad-aśvān āropya
maṇi-kāñcana-bhūṣitān
prīṇayya sunṛtair vākyaiḥ
sva-deśān pratyayāpayat

rathān—chariots; *sat*—fine; *aśvān*—with horses; *āropya*—having them mount; *maṇi*—with jewels; *kāñcana*—and gold; *bhūṣitān*—decorated; *prīṇayya*—gratifying; *sunṛtaiḥ*—with pleasant; *vākyaiḥ*—words; *sva*—to their own; *deśān*—kingdoms; *pratyayāpayat*—He sent off.

TRANSLATION

Then the Lord arranged for the kings to be seated on chariots drawn by fine horses and adorned with jewels and gold, and pleasing them with gracious words, He sent them off to their own kingdoms.

TEXT 29

त एवं मोचिताः कृच्छ्रात्कृष्णेन सुमहात्मना ।
ययुस्तमेव ध्यायन्तः कृतानि च जगत्पतेः ॥२९॥

ta evaṁ mocitāḥ kṛcchrāt
kṛṣṇena su-mahātmanā
yayus tam eva dhyāyantaḥ
kṛtāni ca jagat-pateḥ

te—they; *evam*—thus; *mocitāḥ*—freed; *kṛcchrāt*—from difficulty; *kṛṣṇena*—by Kṛṣṇa; *su-mahā-ātmanā*—the greatest of personalities; *yayuḥ*—they went; *tam*—on Him; *eva*—alone; *dhyāyantaḥ*—meditating; *kṛtāni*—the deeds; *ca*—and; *jagat-pateḥ*—of the Lord of the universe.

TRANSLATION

Thus liberated from all difficulty by Kṛṣṇa, the greatest of personalities, the kings departed, and as they went they thought only of Him, the Lord of the universe, and of His wonderful deeds.

TEXT 30

जगदुः प्रकृतिभ्यस्ते महापुरुषचेष्टितम् ।
यथान्वशासद् भगवांस्तथा चक्रुरतन्द्रिताः ॥३०॥

jagaduḥ prakṛtibhyas te
mahā-puruṣa-ceṣṭitam
yathānvaśāsad bhagavāṁs
tathā cakrur atandritāḥ

jagaduḥ—told; *prakṛtibhyaḥ*—to their ministers and other associates; *te*—they (the kings); *mahā-puruṣa*—of the Supreme Person; *ceṣṭitam*—the activities; *yathā*—as; *anvaśāsat*—He instructed; *bhagavān*—the Lord; *tathā*—so; *cakruḥ*—they did; *atandritāḥ*—without becoming lax.

TRANSLATION

The kings told their ministers and other associates what the Personality of Godhead had done, and then they diligently carried out the orders He had imparted to them.

TEXT 31

जरासन्धं घातयित्वा भीमसेनेन केशवः ।
पार्थाभ्यां संयुतः प्रायात्सहदेवेन पूजितः ॥३१॥

jarāsandhaṁ ghātayitvā
bhīmasenena keśavaḥ
pārthābhyāṁ saṁyutaḥ prāyāt
sahadevena pūjitaḥ

jarāsandham—Jarāsandha; *ghātayitvā*—having had killed; *bhīmasenena*—by Bhīmasena; *keśavaḥ*—Lord Kṛṣṇa; *pārthābhyām*—by the two sons of Pṛthā (Bhīma and Arjuna); *saṁyutaḥ*—accompanied; *prāyāt*—He departed; *sahadevena*—by Sahadeva; *pūjitaḥ*—worshiped.

TRANSLATION

Having arranged for Bhīmasena to kill Jarāsandha, Lord Keśava accepted worship from King Sahadeva and then departed with the two sons of Pṛthā.

TEXT 32

गत्वा ते खाण्डवप्रस्थं शंखान् दध्मुर्जितारयः ।
हर्षयन्तः स्वसुहृदो दुर्हृदां चासुखावहाः ॥३२॥

gatvā te khāṇḍava-prasthaṁ
śaṅkhān dadhmur jitārayaḥ
harṣayantaḥ sva-suhṛdo
durhṛdāṁ cāsukhāvahāḥ

gatvā—arriving; *te*—they; *khāṇḍava-prastham*—at Indraprastha; *śaṅkhān*—their conchshells; *dadhmuḥ*—blew; *jita*—having defeated; *arayaḥ*—their enemy; *harṣayantaḥ*—delighting; *sva*—their; *suhṛdaḥ*—well-wishers; *durhṛdām*—to their enemies; *ca*—and; *asukha*—displeasure; *āvahāḥ*—bringing.

TRANSLATION

When they arrived at Indraprastha, the victorious heroes blew their conchshells, bringing joy to their well-wishing friends and sorrow to their enemies.

TEXT 33

तच्छ्रुत्वा प्रीतमनस इन्द्रप्रस्थनिवासिनः ।
मेनिरे मागधं शान्तं राजा चाप्तमनोरथः ॥३३॥

tac chrutvā prīta-manasa
indraprastha-nivāsinaḥ
menire māgadhaṁ śāntaṁ
rājā cāpta-manorathaḥ

tat—that; *śrutvā*—hearing; *prīta*—pleased; *manasaḥ*—in their hearts; *indraprastha-nivāsinaḥ*—the residents of Indraprastha; *menire*—understood; *māgadham*—Jarāsandha; *śāntam*—put to rest; *rājā*—the King (Yudhiṣṭhira); *ca*—and; *āpta*—achieved; *manaḥ-rathaḥ*—whose desires.

TRANSLATION

The residents of Indraprastha were very pleased to hear that sound, for they understood that now the King of Magadha had been put to rest. King Yudhiṣṭhira felt that his desires were now fulfilled.

TEXT 34

अभिवन्द्याथ राजानं भीमार्जुनजनार्दनाः ।
सर्वमाश्रावयां चक्रुरात्मना यदनुष्ठितम् ॥३४॥

abhivandyātha rājānaṁ
bhīmārjuna-janārdanāḥ
sarvam āśrāvayāṁ cakrur
ātmanā yad anuṣṭhitam

abhivandya—offering their respects; *atha*—then; *rājānam*—the King; *bhīma-arjuna-janārdanāḥ*—Bhīma, Arjuna and Kṛṣṇa; *sarvam*—everything; *āśrāvayām cakruḥ*—they told; *ātmanā*—by themselves; *yat*—what; *anuṣṭhitam*—executed.

TRANSLATION

Bhīma, Arjuna and Janārdana offered their respects to the King and informed him fully about what they had done.

TEXT 35

निशम्य धर्मराजस्तत्केशवेनानुकम्पितम् ।
आनन्दाश्रुकलां मुञ्चन् प्रेम्णा नोवाच किञ्चन ॥३५॥

niśamya dharma-rājas tat
keśavenānukampitam
ānandāśru-kalāṁ muñcan
premṇā novāca kiñcana

niśamya—hearing; *dharma-rājaḥ*—the king of religion, Yudhiṣṭhira; *tat*—that; *keśavena*—by Lord Kṛṣṇa; *anukampitam*—the mercy;

ānanda—of ecstasy; *aśru-kalām*—tears; *muñcan*—shedding; *premṇā*—out of love; *na uvāca*—he did not say; *kiñcana*—anything.

TRANSLATION

Upon hearing their account of the great favor Lord Keśava had mercifully shown him, King Dharmarāja shed tears of ecstasy. He felt such love that he could not say anything.

Thus end the purports of the humble servants of His Divine Grace A. C. Bhaktivedanta Swami Prabhupāda to the Tenth Canto, Seventy-third Chapter, of the Śrīmad-Bhāgavatam, *entitled "Lord Kṛṣṇa Blesses the Liberated Kings."*

CHAPTER SEVENTY-FOUR

The Deliverance of Śiśupāla at the Rājasūya Sacrifice

This chapter describes how Lord Kṛṣṇa received the honor of first worship during the Rājasūya sacrifice, and how He killed Śiśupāla.

After glorifying Lord Kṛṣṇa, King Yudhiṣṭhira selected qualified *brāhmaṇas* such as Bharadvāja, Gautama and Vasiṣṭha to serve as the priests of the Rājasūya sacrifice. Then many exalted guests of all the four social orders arrived to see the sacrificial performance.

As the sacrifice proceeded, the ritual of "first worship" had to be performed, and the members of the assembly were called upon to decide who would receive this honor. Sahadeva spoke up: "Śrī Kṛṣṇa, the Supreme Lord, is indeed the most exalted person, for He Himself comprises all the deities worshiped by Vedic sacrifice. In His role as the Supersoul in the heart, He arranges for everyone in the universe to engage in his particular kind of work, and by His mercy alone human beings can perform various kinds of pious activities and receive the resultant benefits. One who worships Him worships all living entities. Surely Lord Kṛṣṇa should be worshiped first."

Nearly everyone in the assembly agreed with Sahadeva's proposal and loudly congratulated him. Thus King Yudhiṣṭhira happily worshiped Lord Kṛṣṇa. After bathing His feet, the King took the wash water and sprinkled it on his head, and his wives, younger brothers, ministers and relatives also sprinkled that water on their heads. Then everyone shouted, "All victory, all victory!" and bowed down to Lord Kṛṣṇa as flowers rained down from above.

Śiśupāla, however, could not tolerate this worship and glorification of Śrī Kṛṣṇa. He stood up from his seat and harshly rebuked the wise elders for choosing Kṛṣṇa to be worshiped first. "After all," he said, "this Kṛṣṇa is outside the system of Vedic social and spiritual orders and the society of respectable families. He follows no principles of religion and has no good qualities."

Even as Śiśupāla continued to blaspheme Him in this way, Lord Kṛṣṇa remained silent. But many members of the assembly covered their ears and quickly left the hall, while the Pāṇḍava brothers raised their weapons and prepared to kill Śiśupāla. Lord Kṛṣṇa stopped them from attacking, however, and instead used His Sudarśana disc to decapitate the offender. At that moment an effulgent spark of light rose out of Śiśupāla's dead body and entered the transcendental body of Lord Kṛṣṇa. Having lived through three births as the enemy of the Lord, Śiśupāla now attained the liberation of *sāyujya,* merging into Him, by dint of his constant meditation on Him.

King Yudhiṣṭhira then distributed profuse gifts to the respected guests of the assembly and to the priests, and finally he executed the purificatory oblations known as the *prāyaścitta-homa,* which counteract errors made during the sacrifice. Yudhiṣṭhira's Rājasūya sacrifice having now been completed, Lord Kṛṣṇa took His leave from the King and set off for Dvārakā in the company of His wives and ministers.

Duryodhana could not bear to see this abundant manifestation of King Yudhiṣṭhira's prosperity, but apart from him, everyone happily praised the glories of the Rājasūya sacrifice and of the Lord of all sacrifices, Śrī Kṛṣṇa.

TEXT 1

श्रीशुक उवाच

एवं युधिष्ठिरो राजा जरासन्धवधं विभोः ।
कृष्णस्य चानुभावं तं श्रुत्वा प्रीतस्तमब्रवीत् ॥१॥

śrī-śuka uvāca
evaṁ yudhiṣṭhiro rājā
jarāsandha-vadhaṁ vibhoḥ
kṛṣṇasya cānubhāvaṁ tam
śrutvā prītas tam abravīt

śrī-śukaḥ uvāca—Śukadeva Gosvāmī said; *evam*—thus; *yudhiṣṭhiraḥ*—Yudhiṣṭhira; *rājā*—the King; *jarāsandha-vadham*—the killing of Jarāsandha; *vibhoḥ*—of the almighty; *kṛṣṇasya*—Lord Kṛṣṇa; *ca*—and; *anubhāvam*—the (display of) power; *tam*—that; *śrutvā*—hearing of; *prītaḥ*—pleased; *tam*—Him; *abravīt*—he addressed.

TRANSLATION

Śukadeva Gosvāmī said: Having thus heard of the killing of Jarāsandha, and also of almighty Kṛṣṇa's wonderful power, King Yudhiṣṭhira addressed the Lord as follows with great pleasure.

TEXT 2

श्रीयुधिष्ठिर उवाच
ये स्युस्त्रैलोक्यगुरवः सर्वे लोका महेश्वराः ।
वहन्ति दुर्लभं लब्ध्वा शिरसैवानुशासनम् ॥२॥

śrī-yudhiṣṭhira uvāca
ye syus trai-lokya-guravaḥ
sarve lokā maheśvarāḥ
vahanti durlabhaṁ labdhvā
śirasaivānuśāsanam

śrī-yudhiṣṭhiraḥ uvāca—Śrī Yudhiṣṭhira said; *ye*—who; *syuḥ*—there are; *trai-lokya*—of the three worlds; *guravaḥ*—spiritual masters; *sarve*—all; *lokāḥ*—(the inhabitants of) the planets; *mahā-īśvarāḥ*—and the great controlling demigods; *vahanti*—they carry; *durlabham*—rarely obtained; *labdhvā*—having obtained; *śirasā*—on their heads; *eva*—indeed; *anuśāsanam*—(Your) command.

TRANSLATION

Śrī Yudhiṣṭhira said: All the exalted spiritual masters of the three worlds, together with the inhabitants and rulers of the various planets, carry on their heads Your command, which is rarely obtained.

PURPORT

Śrīla Prabhupāda renders Mahārāja Yudhiṣṭhira's statement as follows: "My dear Kṛṣṇa, O eternal form of bliss and knowledge, all the exalted directors of the affairs of this material world, including Lord Brahmā, Lord Śiva and King Indra, are always anxious to receive and carry out orders from You, and whenever they are fortunate enough to receive such orders, they immediately take them and keep them in their hearts.'"

TEXT 3

स भवानरविन्दाक्षो दीनानामीशमानिनाम् ।
धत्तेऽनुशासनं भूमंस्तदत्यन्तविडम्बनम् ॥३॥

sa bhavān aravindākṣo
dīnānām īśa-māninām
dhatte 'nuśāsanaṁ bhūmaṁs
tad atyanta-viḍambanam

saḥ—He; *bhavān*—Yourself; *aravinda-akṣaḥ*—the lotus-eyed Lord; *dīnānām*—of those who are wretched; *īśa*—rulers; *māninām*—who presume themselves; *dhatte*—takes upon Himself; *anuśāsanam*—the order; *bhūman*—O all-pervading one; *tat*—that; *atyanta*—extreme; *viḍambanam*—pretense.

TRANSLATION

That You, the lotus-eyed Supreme Lord, accept the orders of wretched fools who presume themselves rulers is a great pretense on Your part, O all-pervading one.

PURPORT

Śrīla Prabhupāda writes, "[Yudhiṣṭhira said,] 'O Kṛṣṇa, You are unlimited, and although we sometimes think of ourselves as royal kings and rulers of the world and become puffed up over our paltry positions, we are very poor in heart. Actually, we are fit to be punished by You, but the wonder is that instead of punishing us, You so kindly and mercifully accept our orders and carry them out properly. Others are very surprised that Your Lordship can play the part of an ordinary human, but we can understand that You are performing these activities just like a dramatic artist.'"

TEXT 4

न ह्येकस्याद्वितीयस्य ब्रह्मणः परमात्मनः ।
कर्मभिर्वर्धते तेजो ह्रसते च यथा रवेः ॥४॥

na hy ekasyādvitīyasya
brahmaṇaḥ paramātmanaḥ
karmabhir vardhate tejo
hrasate ca yathā raveḥ

na—not; *hi*—indeed; *ekasya*—of the one; *advitīyasya*—without a second; *brahmaṇaḥ*—the Absolute Truth; *parama-ātmanaḥ*—the Supreme Soul; *karmabhiḥ*—by activities; *vardhate*—increases; *tejaḥ*—the power; *hrasate*—diminishes; *ca*—and; *yathā*—as; *raveḥ*—of the sun.

TRANSLATION

But of course the power of the Absolute Truth, the Supreme Soul, the primeval one without a second, is neither increased nor diminished by His activities, any more than the sun's power is by its movements.

PURPORT

Śrīla Prabhupāda writes in *Kṛṣṇa:* "[King Yudhiṣṭhira said,] 'Your real position is always exalted, exactly like that of the sun, which always remains at the same temperature, both during the time of its rising and the time of its setting. Although we feel the difference in temperature between the rising and the setting sun, the temperature of the sun never changes. You are always transcendentally equipoised, and thus You are neither pleased nor disturbed by any condition of material affairs. You are the Supreme Brahman, the Personality of Godhead, and for You there are no relativities.'"

Śrīla Śrīdhara Svāmī quotes a similar statement from the Vedic *mantras: na karmaṇā vardhate no kanīyān* (*Śatapatha Brāhmaṇa* 14.7.2.28, *Taittirīya Brāhmaṇa* 3.12.9.7 and *Bṛhad-āraṇyaka Upaniṣad* 4.4.23). "He is not increased by His activities, nor does He become lesser." As explained here by King Yudhiṣṭhira, the Lord is one without a second.

There is no other entity in His supreme category, and thus it is simply by His causeless mercy that He agrees to carry out the orders of His pure devotees, like Mahārāja Yudhiṣṭhira. There is certainly no loss of status for the Supreme Personality of Godhead when He thus extends His causeless mercy to His surrendered devotees.

TEXT 5

न वै तेऽजित भक्तानां ममाहमिति माधव ।
त्वं तवेति च नानाधीः पशूनामिव वैकृती ॥५॥

na vai te 'jita bhaktānāṁ
mamāham iti mādhava
tvaṁ taveti ca nānā-dhīḥ
paśūnām iva vaikṛtī

na—not; *vai*—indeed; *te*—Your; *ajita*—O unconquerable one; *bhaktānām*—of the devotees; *mama aham iti*—"mine" and "I"; *mādhava*—O Kṛṣṇa; *tvam tava iti*—"you" and "yours"; *ca*—and; *nānā*—of differences; *dhīḥ*—mentality; *paśūnām*—of animals; *iva*—as if; *vaikṛtī*—perverted.

TRANSLATION

O unconquerable Mādhava, even Your devotees make no distinctions of "I" and "mine," "you" and "yours," for this is the perverted mentality of animals.

PURPORT

An ordinary person thinks, "I am so attractive, intelligent and wealthy that people should simply serve me and do what I want. Why should I obey anyone else?" This proud, separatist mentality is also found in animals who battle one another for supremacy. Such a mentality is conspicuously absent in the mind of an advanced devotee, and it is certainly absent in the sublime, omniscient mind of the Supreme Personality of Godhead.

TEXT 6

श्रीशुक उवाच
इत्युक्त्वा यज्ञिये काले वव्रे युक्तान् स ऋत्विजः ।
कृष्णानुमोदितः पार्थो ब्राह्मणान् ब्रह्मवादिनः ॥६॥

śrī-śuka uvāca
ity uktvā yajñiye kāle
vavre yuktān sa ṛtvijaḥ
kṛṣṇānumoditaḥ pārtho
brāhmaṇān brahma-vādinaḥ

śrī-śukaḥ uvāca—Śukadeva Gosvāmī said; *iti*—thus; *uktvā*—speaking; *yajñiye*—appropriate for the sacrifice; *kāle*—at the time; *vavre*—chose; *yuktān*—suitable; *saḥ*—he; *ṛtvijaḥ*—sacrificial priests; *kṛṣṇa*—by Lord Kṛṣṇa; *anumoditaḥ*—sanctioned; *pārthaḥ*—the son of Pṛthā (Yudhiṣṭhira); *brāhmaṇān*—*brāhmaṇas; brahma*—of the *Vedas; vādinaḥ*—expert authorities.

TRANSLATION

Śukadeva Gosvāmī said: Having said this, King Yudhiṣṭhira waited until the proper time for the sacrifice was at hand. Then with Lord Kṛṣṇa's permission he selected suitable priests, all expert authorities on the *Vedas*, to execute the sacrifice.

PURPORT

The great *Bhāgavatam* commentator Śrīdhara Svāmī explains that the proper time for the sacrifice mentioned here was the spring.

TEXTS 7–9

द्वैपायनो भरद्वाजः सुमन्तुर्गोतमोऽसितः ।
वसिष्ठश्च्यवनः कण्वो मैत्रेयः कवषस्त्रितः ॥७॥
विश्वामित्रो वामदेवः सुमतिर्जैमनिः क्रतुः ।
पैलः पराशरो गर्गो वैशम्पायन एव च ॥८॥

अथर्वा कश्यपो धौम्यो रामो भार्गव आसुरिः ।
वीतिहोत्रो मधुच्छन्दा वीरसेनोऽकृतव्रणः ॥९॥

dvaipāyano bharadvājaḥ
sumantur gotamo 'sitaḥ
vasiṣṭhaś cyavanaḥ kaṇvo
maitreyaḥ kavaṣas tritaḥ

viśvāmitro vāmadevaḥ
sumatir jaiminiḥ kratuḥ
pailaḥ parāśaro gargo
vaiśampāyana eva ca

atharvā kaśyapo dhaumyo
rāmo bhārgava āsuriḥ
vītihotro madhucchandā
vīraseno 'kṛtavraṇaḥ

dvaipāyanaḥ bharadvājaḥ—Dvaipāyana (Vedavyāsa) and Bharadvāja; *sumantuḥ gotamaḥ asitaḥ*—Sumantu, Gotama and Asita; *vasiṣṭhaḥ cyavanaḥ kaṇvaḥ*—Vasiṣṭha, Cyavana and Kaṇva; *maitreyaḥ kavaṣaḥ tritaḥ*—Maitreya, Kavaṣa and Trita; *viśvāmitraḥ vāmadevaḥ*—Viśvāmitra and Vāmadeva; *sumatiḥ jaiminiḥ kratuḥ*—Sumati, Jaimini and Kratu; *pailaḥ parāśaraḥ gargaḥ*—Paila, Parāśara and Garga; *vaiśampāyanaḥ*—Vaiśampāyana; *eva ca*—also; *atharvā kaśyapaḥ dhaumyaḥ*—Atharvā, Kaśyapa and Dhaumya; *rāmaḥ bhārgavaḥ*—Pāraśurāma, the descendant of Bhṛgu; *āsuriḥ*—Āsuri; *vītihotraḥ madhucchandāḥ*—Vītihotra and Madhucchandā; *vīrasenaḥ akṛtavraṇaḥ*—Vīrasena and Akṛtavraṇa.

TRANSLATION

He selected Kṛṣṇa-dvaipāyana, Bharadvāja, Sumantu, Gotama and Asita, along with Vasiṣṭha, Cyavana, Kaṇva, Maitreya, Kavaṣa and Trita. He also selected Viśvāmitra, Vāmadeva, Sumati, Jaimini, Kratu, Paila and Parāśara, as well as Garga, Vaiśampāyana, Atharvā, Kaśyapa, Dhaumya, Rāma of the Bhārgavas, Āsuri, Vītihotra, Madhucchandā, Vīrasena and Akṛtavraṇa.

PURPORT

King Yudhiṣṭhira invited all these exalted *brāhmaṇas* to act in different capacities as priests, advisers and so on.

TEXTS 10–11

उपहूतास्तथा चान्ये द्रोणभीष्मकृपादयः ।
धृतराष्ट्रः सहसुतो विदुरश्च महामतिः ॥१०॥
ब्राह्मणाः क्षत्रिया वैश्याः शूद्रा यज्ञदिदृक्षवः ।
तत्रेयुः सर्वराजानो राज्ञां प्रकृतयो नृप ॥११॥

upahūtās tathā cānye
droṇa-bhīṣma-kṛpādayaḥ
dhṛtarāṣṭraḥ saha-suto
viduraś ca mahā-matiḥ

brāhmaṇāḥ kṣatriyā vaiśyāḥ
śūdrā yajña-didṛkṣavaḥ
tatreyuḥ sarva-rājāno
rājñāṁ prakṛtayo nṛpa

upahūtāḥ—invited; *tathā*—also; *ca*—and; *anye*—others; *droṇa-bhīṣma-kṛpa-ādayaḥ*—headed by Droṇa, Bhīṣma and Kṛpa; *dhṛtarāṣṭraḥ*—Dhṛtarāṣṭra; *saha-sutaḥ*—together with his sons; *viduraḥ*—Vidura; *ca*—and; *mahā-matiḥ*—greatly intelligent; *brāhmaṇāḥ kṣatriyāḥ vaiśyāḥ śūdrāḥ*—*brāhmaṇas, kṣatriyas, vaiśyas* and *śūdras; yajña*—the sacrifice; *didṛkṣavaḥ*—eager to see; *tatra*—there; *īyuḥ*—came; *sarva*—all; *rājānaḥ*—kings; *rājñām*—of the kings; *prakṛtayaḥ*—the entourages; *nṛpa*—O King.

TRANSLATION

O King, others who were invited included Droṇa, Bhīṣma, Kṛpa, Dhṛtarāṣṭra with his sons, the wise Vidura, and many other *brāhmaṇas, kṣatriyas, vaiśyas* and *śūdras,* all eager to witness the sacrifice. Indeed, all the kings came there with their entourages.

TEXT 12

ततस्ते देवयजनं ब्राह्मणाः स्वर्णलांगलैः ।
कृष्ट्वा तत्र यथाम्नायं दीक्षयां चक्रिरे नृपम् ॥१२॥

tatas te deva-yajanaṁ
brāhmaṇāḥ svarṇa-lāṅgalaiḥ
kṛṣṭvā tatra yathāmnāyaṁ
dīkṣayāṁ cakrire nṛpam

tataḥ—then; *te*—they; *deva-yajanam*—the place for worshiping the demigods; *brāhmaṇāḥ*—the *brāhmaṇas; svarṇa*—gold; *lāṅgalaiḥ*—with plows; *kṛṣṭvā*—furrowing; *tatra*—there; *yathā-āmnāyam*—according to the standard authorities; *dīkṣayām cakrire*—they initiated; *nṛpam*—the King.

TRANSLATION

The *brāhmaṇa* priests then plowed the sacrificial ground with golden plowshares and initiated King Yudhiṣṭhira for the sacrifice in accordance with the traditions set down by standard authorities.

TEXTS 13–15

हैमाः किलोपकरणा वरुणस्य यथा पुरा ।
इन्द्रादयो लोकपाला विरिञ्चिभवसंयुताः ॥१३॥
सगणाः सिद्धगन्धर्वा विद्याधरमहोरगाः ।
मुनयो यक्षरक्षांसि खगकिन्नरचारणाः ॥१४॥
राजानश्च समाहूता राजपत्न्यश्च सर्वशः ।
राजसूयं समीयुः स्म राज्ञः पाण्डुसुतस्य वै ।
मेनिरे कृष्णभक्तस्य सूपपन्नमविस्मिताः ॥१५॥

haimāḥ kilopakaraṇā
varuṇasya yathā purā
indrādayo loka-pālā
viriñci-bhava-saṁyutāḥ

sa-gaṇāḥ siddha-gandharvā
vidyādhara-mahoragāḥ
munayo yakṣa-rakṣāṁsi
khaga-kinnara-cāraṇāḥ

rājānaś ca samāhūtā
rāja-patnyaś ca sarvaśaḥ
rājasūyaṁ samīyuḥ sma
rājñaḥ pāṇḍu-sutasya vai
menire kṛṣṇa-bhaktasya
sūpapannam avismitāḥ

haimāḥ—fashioned out of gold; *kila*—indeed; *upakaraṇāḥ*—utensils; *varuṇasya*—of Varuṇa; *yathā*—as; *purā*—in the past; *indra-ādayaḥ*—headed by Lord Indra; *loka-pālāḥ*—the rulers of planets; *viriñci-bhava-saṁyutāḥ*—including Lord Brahmā and Lord Śiva; *sa-gaṇāḥ*—with their attendants; *siddha-gandharvāḥ*—the Siddhas and Gandharvas; *vidyā-dhara*—the Vidyādharas; *mahā-uragāḥ*—and great serpents; *munayaḥ*—the exalted sages; *yakṣa-rakṣāṁsi*—the Yakṣa and Rākṣasa demons; *khaga-kinnara-cāraṇāḥ*—the celestial birds, the Kinnaras and the Cāraṇas; *rājānaḥ*—kings; *ca*—and; *samāhūtāḥ*—invited; *rāja*—of the kings; *patnyaḥ*—the wives; *ca*—also; *sarvaśaḥ*—from everywhere; *rājasūyam*—to the Rājasūya sacrifice; *samīyuḥ sma*—they came; *rājñaḥ*—of the King; *pāṇḍu-sutasya*—the son of Pāṇḍu; *vai*—indeed; *menire*—they considered; *kṛṣṇa-bhaktasya*—for the devotee of Lord Kṛṣṇa; *su-upapannam*—quite appropriate; *avismitāḥ*—not surprised.

TRANSLATION

The utensils used in the sacrifice were made of gold, just as in the ancient Rājasūya performed by Lord Varuṇa. Indra, Brahmā, Śiva and many other planetary rulers; the Siddhas and Gandharvas with their entourage; the Vidyādharas; great serpents; sages; Yakṣas; Rākṣasas; celestial birds; Kinnaras; Cāraṇas; and earthly kings—all were invited, and indeed they all came from every direction to the Rājasūya sacrifice of King Yudhiṣṭhira, the son of Pāṇḍu. They were not in the least astonished to see the opulence of the sacrifice, since it was quite appropriate for a devotee of Lord Kṛṣṇa.

PURPORT

Mahārāja Yudhiṣṭhira was universally famous as a great devotee of Lord Kṛṣṇa, and thus nothing was impossible for him.

TEXT 16

अयाजयन्महाराजं याजका देववर्चसः ।
राजसूयेन विधिवत्प्रचेतसमिवामराः ॥१६॥

ayājayan mahā-rājaṁ
yājakā deva-varcasaḥ
rājasūyena vidhi-vat
pracetasam ivāmarāḥ

ayājayan—they performed the sacrifice; *mahā-rājam*—for the great King; *yājakāḥ*—the sacrificial priests; *deva*—of demigods; *varcasaḥ*—possessing the power; *rājasūyena*—the Rājasūya; *vidhi-vat*—according to the prescriptions of the *Vedas; pracetasam*—Varuṇa; *iva*—as; *amarāḥ*—the demigods.

TRANSLATION

The priests, as powerful as gods, performed the Rājasūya sacrifice for King Yudhiṣṭhira in accordance with the Vedic injunctions, just as the demigods had previously performed it for Varuṇa.

TEXT 17

सूत्येऽहन्यवनीपालो याजकान् सदसस्पतीन् ।
अपूजयन्महाभागान् यथावत्सुसमाहितः ॥१७॥

sūtye 'hany avanī-pālo
yājakān sadasas-patīn
apūjayan mahā-bhāgān
yathā-vat su-samāhitaḥ

sūtye—of extracting the *soma* juice; *ahani*—on the day; *avanī-pālaḥ*—the King; *yājakān*—the sacrificers; *sadasaḥ*—of the assembly; *patīn*—the leaders; *apūjayat*—worshiped; *mahā-bhāgān*—greatly exalted; *yathā-vat*—correctly; *su-samāhitaḥ*—with careful attention.

TRANSLATION

On the day of extracting the *soma* juice, King Yudhiṣṭhira properly and very attentively worshiped the priests and the most exalted personalities of the assembly.

PURPORT

Śrīla Prabhupāda writes in *Kṛṣṇa:* "According to the Vedic system, whenever there is an arrangement for sacrifice, the members participating in the sacrifice are offered the juice of the *soma* plant. The juice of the *soma* plant is a kind of life-giving beverage. On the day of extracting the *soma* juice, King Yudhiṣṭhira very respectfully received the special priest who had been engaged to detect any mistake in the formalities of sacrificial procedures. The idea is that the Vedic *mantras* must be enunciated perfectly and chanted with the proper accent; if the priests who are engaged in this business commit any mistake, the checker, or referee priest, immediately corrects the procedure, and thus the ritualistic performances are perfectly executed. Unless it is perfectly executed, a sacrifice cannot yield the desired result. In this age of Kali there is no such learned *brāhmaṇa* or priest available; therefore, all such sacrifices are forbidden. The only sacrifice recommended in the *śāstras* is the chanting of the Hare Kṛṣṇa *mantra*."

TEXT 18

सदस्याग्र्यार्हणार्हं वै विमृशन्तः सभासदः ।
नाध्यगच्छन्ननैकान्त्यात्सहदेवस्तदाब्रवीत् ॥१८॥

sadasyāgryārhaṇārhaṁ vai
vimṛśantaḥ sabhā-sadaḥ
nādhyagacchann anaikāntyāt
sahadevas tadābravīt

sadasya—of the members of the assembly; *agrya*—first; *arhaṇa*—worship; *arham*—him who deserves; *vai*—indeed; *vimṛśantaḥ*—pondering over; *sabhā*—in the assembly; *sadaḥ*—those seated; *na adhyagacchan*—they could not come to a conclusion; *anaika-antyāt*—because of the great number (of qualified candidates); *sahadevaḥ*—Sahadeva, the younger brother of Mahārāja Yudhiṣṭhira; *tadā*—then; *abravīt*—spoke.

TRANSLATION

The members of the assembly then pondered over who among them should be worshiped first, but since there were many personalities qualified for this honor, they were unable to decide. Finally Sahadeva spoke up.

PURPORT

Śrīla Prabhupāda writes, "Another important procedure is that the most exalted personality in the assembly of such a sacrificial ceremony is first offered worship.... This particular ceremony is called *agra-pūjā*. *Agra* means 'first,' and *pūjā* means 'worship.' This *agra-pūjā* is similar to the election of the president. In the sacrificial assembly, all the members were very exalted. Some proposed to elect one person as the perfect candidate for accepting *agra-pūjā*, and others proposed someone else."

As the great *ācārya* Jīva Gosvāmī points out, Text 15 of this chapter states that the members of the assembly were not astonished at the opulence of the sacrifice, since they knew that King Yudhiṣṭhira was a devotee of Lord Kṛṣṇa. Still, Text 18 now states that the assembly could not select the most deserving candidate for being worshiped first. This indicates that many of the *brāhmaṇas* present were not fully realized transcendentalists but rather conventional *brāhmaṇas* uncertain of the supreme conclusion of Vedic wisdom.

Similarly, Ācārya Viśvanātha comments that the undecided members of the assembly were the less intelligent ones, and not such exalted personalities as Brahmā, Śiva and Dvaipāyana Vyāsadeva, who thought, "Since today no one is asking our opinion, why should we say anything? Furthermore, here is Sahadeva, who is renowned for his sharp skill in analyzing all sorts of circumstances. He can help appoint the person who is to be worshiped first. Only if he somehow fails to speak or cannot understand the situation will we speak up, despite no one's having inquired from us." Having made up their minds in this way, the greatest personalities remained silent. This is how Viśvanātha Cakravartī advises us to understand what occurred in the assembly.

TEXT 19

अर्हति ह्यच्युतः श्रैष्ठ्यं भगवान् सात्वतां पतिः ।
एष वै देवताः सर्वा देशकालधनादयः ॥१९॥

arhati hy acyutaḥ śraiṣṭhyaṁ
bhagavān sātvatāṁ patiḥ
eṣa vai devatāḥ sarvā
deśa-kāla-dhanādayaḥ

arhati—deserves; *hi*—indeed; *acyutaḥ*—infallible Kṛṣṇa; *śraiṣṭhyam*—the supreme position; *bhagavān*—the Supreme Lord; *sātvatām*—of the Yādavas; *patiḥ*—the chief; *eṣaḥ*—He; *vai*—certainly; *devatāḥ*—demigods; *sarvāḥ*—all; *deśa*—the place (for the sacrifice); *kāla*—the time; *dhana*—the material paraphernalia; *ādayaḥ*—and so on.

TRANSLATION

[Sahadeva said:] Certainly it is Acyuta, the Supreme Personality of Godhead and chief of the Yādavas, who deserves the highest position. In truth, He Himself comprises all the demigods worshiped in sacrifice, along with such aspects of the worship as the sacred place, the time and the paraphernalia.

TEXTS 20–21

यदात्मकमिदं विश्वं क्रतवश्च यदात्मकाः ।
अग्निराहुतयो मन्त्रा सांख्यं योगश्च यत्परः ॥२०॥
एक एवाद्वितीयोऽसावैतदात्म्यमिदं जगत् ।
आत्मनात्माश्रयः सभ्याः सृजत्यवति हन्त्यजः ॥२१॥

yad-ātmakam idaṁ viśvaṁ
kratavaś ca yad-ātmakāḥ

agnir āhutayo mantrā
sāṅkhyaṁ yogaś ca yat-paraḥ

eka evādvitīyo 'sāv
aitad-ātmyam idaṁ jagat
ātmanātmāśrayaḥ sabhyāḥ
sṛjaty avati hanty ajaḥ

yat-ātmakam—founded upon whom; *idam*—this; *viśvam*—universe; *kratavaḥ*—great sacrificial performances; *ca*—and; *yat-ātmakāḥ*—founded upon whom; *agniḥ*—the sacred fire; *āhutayaḥ*—the oblations; *mantrāḥ*—the incantations; *sāṅkhyam*—the doctrine of philosophic investigation; *yogaḥ*—the art of meditation; *ca*—and; *yat*—at whom; *paraḥ*—aimed; *ekaḥ*—one; *eva*—alone; *advitīyaḥ*—without a second; *asau*—He; *aitat-ātmyam*—founded upon Him; *idam*—this; *jagat*—universe; *ātmanā*—through Himself (i.e., His energies); *ātma*—Himself alone; *āśrayaḥ*—having as His shelter; *sabhyāḥ*—O members of the assembly; *sṛjati*—He creates; *avati*—maintains; *hanti*—and destroys; *ajaḥ*—the unborn.

TRANSLATION

This entire universe is founded upon Him, as are the great sacrificial performances, with their sacred fires, oblations and *mantras*. *Sāṅkhya* and *yoga* both aim toward Him, the one without a second. O assembly members, that unborn Lord, relying solely on Himself, creates, maintains and destroys this cosmos by His personal energies, and thus the existence of this universe depends on Him alone.

TEXT 22

विविधानीह कर्माणि जनयन् यदवेक्षया ।
ईहते यदयं सर्वः श्रेयो धर्मादिलक्षणम् ॥२२॥

vividhānīha karmāṇi
janayan yad-avekṣayā
īhate yad ayaṁ sarvaḥ
śreyo dharmādi-lakṣaṇam

vividhāni—various; *iha*—in this world; *karmāṇi*—material activities; *janayan*—generating; *yat*—by whose; *avekṣayā*—grace; *īhate*—endeavors; *yat*—inasmuch; *ayam*—this world; *sarvaḥ*—entire; *śreyaḥ*—for the ideals; *dharma-ādi*—religiosity and so on; *lakṣaṇam*—characterized as.

TRANSLATION

He creates the many activities of this world, and thus by His grace the whole world endeavors for the ideals of religiosity, economic development, sense gratification and liberation.

TEXT 23

तस्मात्कृष्णाय महते दीयतां परमार्हणम् ।
एवं चेत्सर्वभूतानामात्मनश्चार्हणं भवेत् ॥२३॥

tasmāt kṛṣṇāya mahate
dīyatāṁ paramārhaṇam
evaṁ cet sarva-bhūtānām
ātmanaś cārhaṇaṁ bhavet

tasmāt—therefore; *kṛṣṇāya*—to Lord Kṛṣṇa; *mahate*—the Supreme; *dīyatām*—should be given; *parama*—the greatest; *arhaṇam*—honor; *evam*—in this manner; *cet*—if; *sarva*—of all; *bhūtānām*—living beings; *ātmanaḥ*—of oneself; *ca*—and; *arhaṇam*—honoring; *bhavet*—will be.

TRANSLATION

Therefore we should give the highest honor to Kṛṣṇa, the Supreme Lord. If we do so, we will be honoring all living beings and also our own selves.

TEXT 24

सर्वभूतात्मभूताय कृष्णायानन्यदर्शिने ।
देयं शान्ताय पूर्णाय दत्तस्यानन्त्यमिच्छता ॥२४॥

sarva-bhūtātma-bhūtāya
kṛṣṇāyānanya-darśine
deyaṁ śāntāya pūrṇāya
dattasyānantyam icchatā

sarva—of all; *bhūta*—beings; *ātma*—the Soul; *bhūtāya*—who comprises; *kṛṣṇāya*—to Lord Kṛṣṇa; *ananya*—never as separate; *darśine*—who sees; *deyam*—(honor) should be given; *śāntāya*—to the peaceful; *pūrṇāya*—perfectly complete; *dattasya*—of what is given; *ānantyam*—unlimited increase; *icchatā*—by him who desires.

TRANSLATION

Anyone who wishes the honor he gives to be reciprocated infinitely should honor Kṛṣṇa, the perfectly peaceful and perfectly complete Soul of all beings, the Supreme Lord, who views nothing as separate from Himself.

PURPORT

Śrīla Prabhupāda writes as follows: "[Sahadeva said:] 'Ladies and gentlemen, it is superfluous to speak about Kṛṣṇa, because every one of you exalted personalities knows the Supreme Brahman, Lord Kṛṣṇa, for whom there are no material differences between body and soul, between energy and the energetic, or between one part of the body and another. Since everyone is part and parcel of Kṛṣṇa, there is no qualitative difference between Kṛṣṇa and all living entities. Everything is an emanation of Kṛṣṇa's energies, the material and spiritual energies. Kṛṣṇa's energies are like the heat and light of the fire; there is no difference between the quality of heat and light and the fire itself. . . . He should therefore be offered the first worship of this great sacrifice, and no one should disagree. . . . Kṛṣṇa is present as the Supersoul in every living being, and if we can satisfy Him, then automatically every living being becomes satisfied.'"

TEXT 25

इत्युक्त्वा सहदेवोऽभूत्तूष्णीं कृष्णानुभाववित् ।
तच्छ्रुत्वा तुष्टुवुः सर्वे साधु साध्विति सत्तमाः ॥२५॥

ity uktvā sahadevo 'bhūt
tūṣṇīṁ kṛṣṇānubhāva-vit
tac chrutvā tuṣṭuvuḥ sarve
sādhu sādhv iti sattamāḥ

iti—thus; *uktvā*—speaking; *sahadevaḥ*—Sahadeva; *abhūt*—became; *tūṣṇīm*—silent; *kṛṣṇa*—of Lord Kṛṣṇa; *anubhāva*—the influence; *vit*—who knew well; *tat*—this; *śrutvā*—hearing; *tuṣṭuvuḥ*—praised; *sarve*—all; *sādhu sādhu iti*—"excellent, excellent!"; *sat*—of saintly persons; *tamāḥ*—the best.

TRANSLATION

[Śukadeva Gosvāmī continued:] Having said this, Sahadeva, who understood Lord Kṛṣṇa's powers, fell silent. And having heard his words, all the saintly persons present congratulated him, exclaiming "Excellent! Excellent!"

TEXT 26

श्रुत्वा द्विजेरितं राजा ज्ञात्वा हार्दं सभासदाम् ।
समर्हयद्धृषीकेशं प्रीतः प्रणयविह्वलः ॥२६॥

śrutvā dvijeritaṁ rājā
jñātvā hārdaṁ sabhā-sadām
samarhayad dhṛṣīkeśaṁ
prītaḥ praṇaya-vihvalaḥ

śrutvā—hearing; *dvija*—by the *brāhmaṇas; īritam*—what was pronounced; *rājā*—the King, Yudhiṣṭhira; *jñātvā*—understanding; *hārdam*—the inner thoughts; *sabhā-sadām*—of the members of the assembly; *samarhayat*—fully worshiped; *hṛṣīkeśam*—Lord Kṛṣṇa; *prītaḥ*—pleased; *praṇaya*—by love; *vihvalaḥ*—overwhelmed.

TRANSLATION

The King was delighted to hear this pronouncement of the *brāhmaṇas*, from which he understood the mood of the entire

assembly. Overwhelmed with love, he fully worshiped Lord Kṛṣṇa, the master of the senses.

TEXTS 27–28

तत्पादाववनिज्यापः शिरसा लोकपावनीः ।
सभार्यः सानुजामात्यः सकुटुम्बो वहन्मुदा ॥२७॥
वासोभिः पीतकौषेयैर्भूषणैश्च महाधनैः ।
अर्हयित्वाश्रुपूर्णाक्षो नाशकत्समवेक्षितुम् ॥२८॥

tat-pādāv avanijyāpaḥ
śirasā loka-pāvanīḥ
sa-bhāryaḥ sānujāmātyaḥ
sa-kuṭumbo vahan mudā

vāsobhiḥ pīta-kauṣeyair
bhūṣaṇaiś ca mahā-dhanaiḥ
arhayitvāśru-pūrṇākṣo
nāśakat samavekṣitum

tat—His; *pādau*—feet; *avanijya*—washing; *āpaḥ*—the water; *śirasā*—on his head; *loka*—the world; *pāvanīḥ*—which purifies; *sa*—with; *bhāryaḥ*—his wife; *sa*—with; *anuja*—his brothers; *amātyaḥ*—and his ministers; *sa*—with; *kuṭumbaḥ*—his family; *vahan*—carrying; *mudā*—with pleasure; *vāsobhiḥ*—with garments; *pīta*—yellow; *kauṣeyaiḥ*—silk; *bhūṣaṇaiḥ*—with jewelry; *ca*—and; *mahā-dhanaiḥ*—precious; *arhayitvā*—honoring; *aśru*—with tears; *pūrṇa*—filled; *akṣaḥ*—whose eyes; *na aśakat*—he was unable; *samavekṣitum*—to look upon Him directly.

TRANSLATION

After bathing Lord Kṛṣṇa's feet, Mahārāja Yudhiṣṭhira joyfully sprinkled the water upon his own head, and then upon the heads of his wife, brothers, other family members and ministers. That water purifies the whole world. As he honored the Lord with presentations of yellow silken garments and precious jeweled ornaments, the King's tear-filled eyes prevented him from looking directly at the Lord.

TEXT 29

इत्थं सभाजितं वीक्ष्य सर्वे प्राञ्जलयो जनाः ।
नमो जयेति नेमुस्तं निपेतुः पुष्पवृष्टयः ॥२९॥

itthaṁ sabhājitaṁ vīkṣya
sarve prāñjalayo janāḥ
namo jayeti nemus taṁ
nipetuḥ puṣpa-vṛṣṭayaḥ

ittham—in this manner; *sabhājitam*—honored; *vīkṣya*—seeing; *sarve*—all; *prāñjalayaḥ*—with palms joined in supplication; *janāḥ*—the people; *namaḥ*—"obeisances to You"; *jaya*—"all victory to You"; *iti*—so saying; *nemuḥ*—they bowed down; *tam*—to Him; *nipetuḥ*—fell; *puṣpa*—of flowers; *vṛṣṭayaḥ*—showers.

TRANSLATION

When they saw Lord Kṛṣṇa thus honored, nearly all who were present joined their palms reverentially, exclaiming "Obeisances to You! All victory to You!" and then bowed down to Him. Flowers rained down from above.

TEXT 30

इत्थं निशम्य दमघोषसुतः स्वपीठाद्
उत्थाय कृष्णगुणवर्णनजातमन्युः ।
उत्क्षिप्य बाहुमिदमाह सदस्यमर्षी
संश्रावयन् भगवते परुषाण्यभीतः ॥३०॥

itthaṁ niśamya damaghoṣa-sutaḥ sva-pīṭhād
utthāya kṛṣṇa-guṇa-varṇana-jāta-manyuḥ
utkṣipya bāhum idam āha sadasy amarṣī
saṁśrāvayan bhagavate paruṣāṇy abhītaḥ

ittham—thus; *niśamya*—hearing; *damaghoṣa-sutaḥ*—the son of Damaghoṣa (Śiśupāla); *sva*—his; *pīṭhāt*—from the seat; *utthāya*—rising;

kṛṣṇa-guṇa—of the great qualities of Lord Kṛṣṇa; *varṇana*—by the descriptions; *jāta*—aroused; *manyuḥ*—whose anger; *utkṣipya*—waving; *bāhum*—his arms; *idam*—this; *āha*—he said; *sadasi*—in the midst of the assembly; *amarṣī*—intolerant; *saṁśrāvayan*—addressing; *bhagavate*—at the Supreme Lord; *paruṣāṇi*—harsh words; *abhītaḥ*—having no fear.

TRANSLATION

The intolerant son of Damaghoṣa became infuriated upon hearing the glorification of Lord Kṛṣṇa's transcendental qualities. He stood up from his seat and, angrily waving his arms, fearlessly spoke to the entire assembly the following harsh words against the Supreme Lord.

PURPORT

Śrīla Prabhupāda writes, "In that meeting, King Śiśupāla was also present. He was an avowed enemy of Kṛṣṇa for many reasons, especially because of Kṛṣṇa's having stolen Rukmiṇī from the marriage ceremony; therefore, he could not tolerate such honor to Kṛṣṇa and glorification of His qualities. Instead of being happy to hear the glories of the Lord, he became very angry."

Śrīla Viśvanātha Cakravartī mentions that the reason Śiśupāla did not object when Sahadeva proposed Kṛṣṇa for the *agra-pūjā* is that Śiśupāla wanted to ruin King Yudhiṣṭhira's sacrifice. If Śiśupāla had argued earlier against Lord Kṛṣṇa's receiving the first worship and another person had been selected, the sacrifice would have then proceeded normally. Therefore Śiśupāla allowed Kṛṣṇa to be selected, waited until the worship was over, and then spoke up, hoping in this way to demonstrate that the sacrifice was now spoiled. Thus he would ruin the endeavor of Mahārāja Yudhiṣṭhira. In this regard the *ācārya* quotes the following *smṛti* reference: *apūjyā yatra pūjyante pūjyānāṁ ca vyatikramaḥ.* "In the place where those who are not to be worshiped are worshiped, there is offense to those who are actually worshipable." There is also the following statement: *pratibadhnāti hi śreyaḥ pūjyāpūjya-vyatikramaḥ.* "Improperly understanding who is to be worshiped and who is not to be worshiped will impede one's progress in life."

TEXT 31

ईशो दुरत्ययः काल इति सत्यवती श्रुतिः ।
वृद्धानामपि यद् बुद्धिर्बालवाक्यैर्विभिद्यते ॥३१॥

īśo duratyayaḥ kāla
iti satyavatī śrutiḥ
vṛddhānām api yad buddhir
bāla-vākyair vibhidyate

īśaḥ—the supreme controller; *duratyayaḥ*—unavoidable; *kālaḥ*—time; *iti*—thus; *satya-vatī*—truthful; *śrutiḥ*—the revealed statement of the *Vedas; vṛddhānām*—of elder authorities; *api*—even; *yat*—since; *buddhiḥ*—the intelligence; *bāla*—of a boy; *vākyaiḥ*—by the words; *vibhidyate*—is diverted.

TRANSLATION

[Śiśupāla said:] The statement of the *Vedas* that time is the unavoidable controller of all has indeed been proven true, since the intelligence of wise elders has now become diverted by the words of a mere boy.

TEXT 32

यूयं पात्रविदां श्रेष्ठा मा मन्ध्वं बालभाषितम् ।
सदसस्पतयः सर्वे कृष्णो यत्सम्मतोऽर्हणे ॥३२॥

yūyaṁ pātra-vidāṁ śreṣṭhā
mā mandhvaṁ bāla-bhāṣitam
sadasas-patayaḥ sarve
kṛṣṇo yat sammato 'rhaṇe

yūyam—all of you; *pātra*—of worthy candidates; *vidām*—of knowers; *śreṣṭhāḥ*—the best; *mā mandhvam*—please do not heed; *bāla*—of a boy; *bhāṣitam*—the statements; *sadasaḥ-patayaḥ*—O leaders of the assembly; *sarve*—all; *kṛṣṇaḥ*—Kṛṣṇa; *yat*—the fact that; *sammataḥ*—chosen; *arhaṇe*—for being honored.

TRANSLATION

O leaders of the assembly, you know best who is a fit candidate for being honored. Therefore you should not heed the words of a child when he claims that Kṛṣṇa deserves to be worshiped.

TEXTS 33–34

तपोविद्याव्रतधरान् ज्ञानविध्वस्तकल्मषान् ।
परमर्षीन् ब्रह्मनिष्ठाल्ँ लोकपालैश्च पूजितान् ॥३३॥
सदस्पतीनतिक्रम्य गोपालः कुलपांसनः ।
यथा काकः पुरोडाशं सपर्यां कथमर्हति ॥३४॥

tapo-vidyā-vrata-dharān
jñāna-vidhvasta-kalmaṣān
paramarṣīn brahma-niṣṭhāl̐
loka-pālaiś ca pūjitān

sadas-patīn atikramya
gopālaḥ kula-pāṁsanaḥ
yathā kākaḥ puroḍāśaṁ
saparyāṁ katham arhati

tapaḥ—austerity; *vidyā*—Vedic knowledge; *vrata*—severe vows; *dharān*—who maintain; *jñāna*—by spiritual understanding; *vidhvasta*—eradicated; *kalmaṣān*—whose impurities; *parama*—topmost; *ṛṣīn*—sages; *brahma*—to the Absolute Truth; *niṣṭhān*—dedicated; *loka-pālaiḥ*—by the rulers of the planetary systems; *ca*—and; *pūjitān*—worshiped; *sadaḥ-patīn*—leaders of the assembly; *atikramya*—passing over; *gopālaḥ*—a cowherd; *kula*—of His family; *pāṁsanaḥ*—the disgrace; *yathā*—as; *kākaḥ*—a crow; *puroḍāśam*—the sacred rice cake (offered to the demigods); *saparyām*—worship; *katham*—how; *arhati*—deserves.

TRANSLATION

How can you pass over the most exalted members of this assembly—topmost sages dedicated to the Absolute Truth, endowed with powers of austerity, divine insight and strict adherence to

severe vows, sanctified by knowledge and worshiped even by the rulers of the universe? How does this cowherd boy, the disgrace of His family, deserve your worship, any more than a crow deserves to eat the sacred *puroḍāśa* rice cake?

PURPORT

The great commentator Śrīdhara Svāmī has analyzed Śiśupāla's words as follows. The term *go-pāla* means not only "cowherd" but also "protector of the *Vedas* and the earth." Similarly, *kula-pāṁsana* has a double meaning. Śiśupāla intended it to mean "the disgrace of His family," which is its meaning when divided as above. But the word may also be analyzed as *ku-lapām aṁsana,* giving a totally different meaning. *Kulapām* indicates those who prattle with crooked words contrary to the *Vedas,* and *aṁsana,* derived from the verb *aṁsayati,* means "destroyer." In other words, he was praising Lord Kṛṣṇa as "He who vanquishes all misguided and frivolous speculations about the nature of truth." Similarly, although Śiśupāla wanted to compare Lord Kṛṣṇa to a crow with the words *yathā kākaḥ,* these words may also be divided *yathā a-kākaḥ.* In that case, according to Śrīla Śrīdhara Svāmī, the word *kāka* is a combination of *ka* and *āka,* which indicate material happiness and misery. Thus Lord Kṛṣṇa is *akāka* in the sense that He is beyond all material misery and happiness, being on the pure, transcendental platform. Finally, Śiśupāla was right in saying the Lord Kṛṣṇa does not deserve merely the *puroḍāśa* rice cake, offered to the lesser demigods as a substitute for the heavenly beverage *soma.* In fact, Lord Kṛṣṇa deserves to receive everything that we possess, since He is the ultimate proprietor of everything, including ourselves. Thus we should give Lord Kṛṣṇa our life and soul, not merely a ritualistic offering of rice cakes.

TEXT 35

वर्णाश्रमकुलापेतः सर्वधर्मबहिष्कृतः ।
स्वैरवर्ती गुणैर्हीनः सपर्यां कथमर्हति ॥३५॥

varṇāśrama-kulāpetaḥ
sarva-dharma-bahiṣ-kṛtaḥ
svaira-vartī guṇair hīnaḥ
saparyāṁ katham arhati

varṇa—of the principles of the four occupational orders of society; *āśrama*—of the four spiritual orders; *kula*—and of proper family upbringing; *apetaḥ*—devoid; *sarva*—from all; *dharma*—codes of religious duty; *bahiḥ-kṛtaḥ*—excluded; *svaira*—independently; *vartī*—behaving; *guṇaiḥ*—qualities; *hīnaḥ*—lacking; *saparyām*—worship; *katham*—how; *arhati*—deserves.

TRANSLATION

How does one who follows no principles of the social and spiritual orders or of family ethics, who has been excluded from all religious duties, who behaves whimsically, and who has no good qualities—how does such a person deserve to be worshiped?

PURPORT

Śrīla Prabhupāda comments, "Actually, Kṛṣṇa does not belong to any caste, nor does He have to perform any occupational duty. It is stated in the *Vedas* that the Supreme Lord has nothing to do as His prescribed duty. Whatever has to be done on His behalf is executed by His different energies. . . . Śiśupāla indirectly praised Kṛṣṇa by saying that He is not within the jurisdiction of Vedic injunction. This is true because He is the Supreme Personality of Godhead. That He has no qualities means that Kṛṣṇa has no material qualities, and because He is the Supreme Personality of Godhead, He acts independently, not caring for conventions or social or religious principles."

TEXT 36

ययातिनैषां हि कुलं शप्तं सद्‌भिर्बहिष्कृतम् ।
वृथापानरतं शश्वत्सपर्यां कथमर्हति ॥३६॥

yayātinaiṣāṁ hi kulaṁ
śaptaṁ sadbhir bahiṣ-kṛtam
vṛthā-pāna-rataṁ śaśvat
saparyāṁ katham arhati

yayātinā—by Yayāti; *eṣām*—their; *hi*—indeed; *kulam*—dynasty; *śaptam*—was cursed; *sadbhiḥ*—by well-behaved persons; *bahiḥ-kṛtam*—

ostracized; *vṛthā*—wantonly; *pāna*—to drinking; *ratam*—addicted; *śaśvat*—always; *saparyām*—worship; *katham*—how; *arhati*—does He deserve.

TRANSLATION

Yayāti cursed the dynasty of these Yādavas, and ever since then they have been ostracized by honest men and addicted to liquor. How, then, does Kṛṣṇa deserve to be worshiped?

PURPORT

Śrīla Viśvanātha Cakravartī gives the inner meaning of the words of Śiśupāla to show how he continued unintentionally glorifying Lord Kṛṣṇa and His Yadu dynasty: "Even though the Yadus were cursed by Yayāti, they have been relieved [*bahiṣ-kṛtam*] of this curse by great saints, and consequently they have been raised to a position of royal sovereignty by such persons as Kārtavīrya. Thus they have become absorbed in *pāna*, protecting the earth. Considering all this, how does Kṛṣṇa, the chief of the Yadus, deserve useless [*vṛthā*] worship? Rather, He deserves opulent worship."

TEXT 37

ब्रह्मर्षिसेवितान् देशान् हित्वैतेऽब्रह्मवर्चसम् ।
समुद्रं दुर्गमाश्रित्य बाधन्ते दस्यवः प्रजाः ॥३७॥

brahmarṣi-sevitān deśān
hitvaite 'brahma-varcasam
samudraṁ durgam āśritya
bādhante dasyavaḥ prajāḥ

brahma-ṛṣi—by great *brāhmaṇa* sages; *sevitān*—graced; *deśān*—lands (like Mathurā); *hitvā*—abandoning; *ete*—these (Yādavas); *abrahma-varcasam*—where brahminical principles are not observed; *samudram*—the ocean; *durgam*—a fortress; *āśritya*—taking shelter of; *bādhante*—they cause trouble; *dasyavaḥ*—thieves; *prajāḥ*—to their subjects.

TRANSLATION

These Yādavas have abandoned the holy lands inhabited by saintly sages and have instead taken shelter of a fortress in the sea, a place where no brahminical principles are observed. There, just like thieves, they harass their subjects.

PURPORT

The words *brahmarṣi-sevitān deśān* ("holy lands inhabited by saintly sages") allude to the district of Mathurā. Śrīla Prabhupāda writes, "Śiśupāla went crazy because of Kṛṣṇa's being elected the supreme, first-worshiped person in that meeting, and he spoke so irresponsibly that it appeared that he had lost all his good fortune."

TEXT 38

एवमादीन्यभद्राणि बभाषे नष्टमंगलः ।
नोवाच किञ्चिद् भगवान् यथा सिंहः शिवारुतम् ॥३८॥

evam-ādīny abhadrāṇi
babhāṣe naṣṭa-maṅgalaḥ
novāca kiñcid bhagavān
yathā siṁhaḥ śivā-rutam

evam—such; *ādīni*—and more; *abhadrāṇi*—harsh words; *babhāṣe*—he spoke; *naṣṭa*—ruined; *maṅgalaḥ*—whose good fortune; *na uvāca*—He did not say; *kiñcit*—anything; *bhagavān*—the Supreme Lord; *yathā*—just as; *siṁhaḥ*—a lion; *śivā*—of a jackal; *rutam*—the cry.

TRANSLATION

[Śukadeva Gosvāmī continued:] Bereft of all good fortune, Śiśupāla spoke these and other insults. But the Supreme Lord said nothing, just as a lion ignores a jackal's cry.

TEXT 39

भगवन्निन्दनं श्रुत्वा दुःसहं तत्सभासदः ।
कर्णौ पिधाय निर्जग्मुः शपन्तश्चेदिपं रुषा ॥३९॥

bhagavan-nindanaṁ śrutvā
duḥsahaṁ tat sabhā-sadaḥ
karṇau pidhāya nirjagmuḥ
śapantaś cedi-paṁ ruṣā

bhagavat—of the Supreme Lord; *nindanam*—criticism; *śrutvā*—hearing; *duḥsaham*—intolerable; *tat*—that; *sabhā-sadaḥ*—the members of the assembly; *karṇau*—their ears; *pidhāya*—covering; *nirjagmuḥ*—went away; *śapantaḥ*—cursing; *cedi-pam*—the King of Cedi (Śiśupāla); *ruṣā*—angrily.

TRANSLATION

Upon hearing such intolerable blasphemy of the Lord, several members of the assembly covered their ears and walked out, angrily cursing the King of Cedi.

TEXT 40

निन्दां भगवतः शृण्वंस्तत्परस्य जनस्य वा ।
ततो नापैति यः सोऽपि यात्यधः सुकृताच्च्युतः ॥४०॥

nindāṁ bhagavataḥ śṛṇvaṁs
tat-parasya janasya vā
tato nāpaiti yaḥ so 'pi
yāty adhaḥ sukṛtāc cyutaḥ

nindām—criticism; *bhagavataḥ*—of the Supreme Lord; *śṛṇvan*—hearing; *tat*—to Him; *parasya*—who is dedicated; *janasya*—of a person; *vā*—or; *tataḥ*—from that place; *na apaiti*—does not go away; *yaḥ*—who; *saḥ*—he; *api*—indeed; *yāti*—goes; *adhaḥ*—down; *su-kṛtāt*—from the good results of his pious works; *cyutaḥ*—fallen.

TRANSLATION

Anyone who fails to immediately leave the place where he hears criticism of the Supreme Lord or His faithful devotee will certainly fall down, bereft of his pious credit.

TEXT 41

ततः पाण्डुसुताः क्रुद्धा मत्स्यकैकयसृञ्जयाः ।
उदायुधाः समुत्तस्थुः शिशुपालजिघांसवः ॥४१॥

tataḥ pāṇḍu-sutāḥ kruddhā
matsya-kaikaya-sṛñjayāḥ
udāyudhāḥ samuttasthuḥ
śiśupāla-jighāṁsavaḥ

tataḥ—then; *pāṇḍu-sutāḥ*—the sons of Pāṇḍu; *kruddhāḥ*—angered; *matsya-kaikaya-sṛñjayāḥ*—the Matsyas, Kaikayas and Sṛñjayas; *ut-āyudhāḥ*—holding up their weapons; *samuttasthuḥ*—stood; *śiśupāla-jighāṁsavaḥ*—desiring to kill Śiśupāla.

TRANSLATION

Then the sons of Pāṇḍu became furious, and together with the warriors of the Matsya, Kaikaya and Sṛñjaya clans, they rose up from their seats with weapons poised, ready to kill Śiśupāla.

TEXT 42

ततश्चैद्यस्त्वसम्भ्रान्तो जगृहे खड्गचर्मणी ।
भर्त्सयन् कृष्णपक्षीयान् राज्ञः सदसि भारत ॥४२॥

tataś caidyas tv asambhrānto
jagṛhe khaḍga-carmaṇī
bhartsayan kṛṣṇa-pakṣīyān
rājñaḥ sadasi bhārata

tataḥ—then; *caidyaḥ*—Śiśupāla; *tu*—but; *asambhrāntaḥ*—unshaken; *jagṛhe*—took up; *khaḍga*—his sword; *carmaṇī*—and shield; *bhartsayan*—insulting; *kṛṣṇa*—of Kṛṣṇa; *pakṣīyān*—the proponents; *rājñaḥ*—the kings; *sadasi*—in the assembly; *bhārata*—O descendant of Bharata.

TRANSLATION

Undaunted, Śiśupāla then took up his sword and shield in the midst of all the assembled kings, O Bhārata, and hurled insults at those who sided with Lord Kṛṣṇa.

TEXT 43

तावदुत्थाय भगवान् स्वान्निवार्य स्वयं रुषा ।
शिरः क्षुरान्तचक्रेण जहार पततो रिपोः ॥४३॥

tāvad utthāya bhagavān
svān nivārya svayaṁ ruṣā
śiraḥ kṣurānta-cakreṇa
jahāra patato ripoḥ

tāvat—at that point; *utthāya*—rising; *bhagavān*—the Supreme Lord; *svān*—His own (devotees); *nivārya*—stopping; *svayam*—Himself; *ruṣā*—angrily; *śiraḥ*—the head; *kṣura*—sharp; *anta*—whose edge; *cakreṇa*—with His disc weapon; *jahāra*—severed; *patataḥ*—attacking; *ripoḥ*—of His enemy.

TRANSLATION

At that point the Supreme Lord stood up and checked His devotees. He then angrily sent forth His razor-sharp disc and severed the head of His enemy as he was attacking.

PURPORT

Śrīla Viśvanātha Cakravartī Ṭhākura explains the Lord's action as follows: If Lord Kṛṣṇa had done nothing, there probably would have been a savage fight on the sacrificial grounds, and thus the whole ceremony would have been drenched in blood, spoiling the sanctified atmosphere. Therefore, in order to protect the Rājasūya sacrifice of Kṛṣṇa's beloved devotee Yudhiṣṭhira, the Lord immediately severed Śiśupāla's head with His razor-sharp disc in such a way that not a drop of blood fell within the sacrificial grounds.

TEXT 44

शब्दः कोलाहलोऽथासीच्छिशुपाले हते महान् ।
तस्यानुयायिनो भूपा दुद्रुवुर्जीवितैषिणः ॥४४॥

śabdaḥ kolāhalo 'thāsīc
chiśupāle hate mahān
tasyānuyāyino bhūpā
dudruvur jīvitaiṣiṇaḥ

śabdaḥ—a sound; *kolāhalaḥ*—uproar; *atha*—thereupon; *āsīt*—there was; *śiśupāle*—Śiśupāla; *hate*—being killed; *mahān*—huge; *tasya*—his; *anuyāyinaḥ*—followers; *bhūpāḥ*—kings; *dudruvuḥ*—fled; *jīvita*—their lives; *eṣiṇaḥ*—hoping to save.

TRANSLATION

When Śiśupāla was thus killed, a great roar and howl went up from the crowd. Taking advantage of that disturbance, the few kings who were supporters of Śiśupāla quickly left the assembly out of fear for their lives.

PURPORT

The above translation is taken from Śrīla Prabhupāda's *Kṛṣṇa, the Supreme Personality of Godhead.*

TEXT 45

चैद्यदेहोत्थितं ज्योतिर्वासुदेवमुपाविशत् ।
पश्यतां सर्वभूतानामुल्केव भुवि खाच्च्युता ॥४५॥

caidya-dehotthitaṁ jyotir
vāsudevam upāviśat
paśyatāṁ sarva-bhūtānām
ulkeva bhuvi khāc cyutā

caidya—of Śiśupāla; *deha*—from the body; *utthitam*—risen; *jyotiḥ*—a light; *vāsudevam*—Lord Kṛṣṇa; *upāviśat*—entered; *paśyatām*—as they watched; *sarva*—all; *bhūtānām*—living beings; *ulkā*—a meteor; *iva*—as if; *bhuvi*—on the earth; *khāt*—from the sky; *cyutā*—fallen.

TRANSLATION

An effulgent light rose from Śiśupāla's body and, as everyone watched, entered Lord Kṛṣṇa just like a meteor falling from the sky to the earth.

PURPORT

In this connection, the *ācāryas* remind us that Śiśupāla is actually one of the Lord's eternal associates playing the part of a belligerent demon. Thus to most observers it appeared that Śiśupāla achieved the impersonal liberation of merging into Lord Kṛṣṇa's bodily effulgence. In fact, after being liberated from his mortal frame, Śiśupāla returned to the side of his master, the Supreme Lord of the spiritual world. The following verse further explains this.

TEXT 46

जन्मत्रयानुगुणितवैरसंरब्धया धिया ।
ध्यायंस्तन्मयतां यातो भावो हि भवकारणम् ॥४६॥

janma-trayānuguṇita-
vaira-saṁrabdhayā dhiyā
dhyāyaṁs tan-mayatāṁ yāto
bhāvo hi bhava-kāraṇam

janma—births; *traya*—three; *anuguṇita*—extending through; *vaira*—by enmity; *saṁrabdhayā*—obsessed; *dhiyā*—with a mentality; *dhyāyan*—meditating; *tat-mayatām*—oneness with Him; *yātaḥ*—attained; *bhāvaḥ*—one's attitude; *hi*—indeed; *bhava*—of rebirth; *kāraṇam*—the cause.

TRANSLATION

Obsessed with hatred of Lord Kṛṣṇa throughout three lifetimes, Śiśupāla attained the Lord's transcendental nature. Indeed, one's consciousness determines one's future birth.

PURPORT

Śiśupāla and his friend Dantavakra, who will be killed by Kṛṣṇa in Chapter Seventy-eight, were previously Jaya and Vijaya, two gatekeepers in Vaikuṇṭha. Because of an offense, the four Kumāras cursed them to take three births in the material world as demons. The first birth was as Hiraṇyākṣa and Hiraṇyakaśipu, the second as Rāvaṇa and Kumbhakarṇa, and the third as Śiśupāla and Dantavakra. In each birth they were completely absorbed in enmity toward the Lord and were slain by Him.

Śrīla Prabhupāda explains the position of Śiśupāla as follows: "Although Śiśupāla acted as the enemy of Kṛṣṇa, he was not for a single moment out of Kṛṣṇa consciousness. He was always absorbed in thought of Kṛṣṇa, and thus he got first the salvation of *sāyujya-mukti*, merging into the existence of the Supreme, and finally became reinstated in his original position of personal service. The *Bhagavad-gītā* corroborates the fact that one who is absorbed in the thought of the Supreme Lord at the time of death immediately enters the kingdom of God after quitting his material body."

The Third and Seventh cantos of the *Śrīmad-Bhāgavatam* elaborately describe the incident wherein the Lord's personal associates were cursed to come to the material world as His enemies. In this connection, Śrīla Viśvanātha Cakravartī quotes the following verse (*Bhāg.* 7.1.47):

vairānubandha-tīvreṇa
dhyānenācyuta-sātmatām
nītau punar hareḥ pārśvaṁ
jagmatur viṣṇu-pārṣadau

"These two associates of Lord Viṣṇu—Jaya and Vijaya—maintained a feeling of enmity for a very long time. Because of always thinking of Kṛṣṇa in this way, they regained the shelter of the Lord, having returned home, back to Godhead."

TEXT 47

ऋत्विग्भ्यः ससदस्येभ्यो दक्षिणां विपुलामदात् ।
सर्वान् सम्पूज्य विधिवच्चक्रेऽवभृथमेकराट् ॥४७॥

ṛtvigbhyaḥ sa-sadasyebhyo
dakṣiṇāṁ vipulām adāt
sarvān sampūjya vidhi-vac
cakre 'vabhṛtham eka-rāṭ

ṛtvigbhyaḥ—to the priests; *sa-sadasyebhyaḥ*—along with the members of the assembly; *dakṣiṇām*—gifts in gratitude; *vipulām*—abundant; *adāt*—he gave; *sarvān*—all of them; *sampūjya*—properly worshiping; *vidhi-vat*—according to scriptural injunctions; *cakre*—executed; *avabhṛtham*—the purificatory bathing of the sponsor of the sacrifice and the washing of the sacrificial utensils that mark the end of a major sacrifice; *eka-rāṭ*—the emperor, Yudhiṣṭhira.

TRANSLATION

Emperor Yudhiṣṭhira gave generous gifts to the sacrificial priests and the members of the assembly, properly honoring them all in the manner prescribed by the *Vedas*. He then took the *avabhṛtha* bath.

TEXT 48

साधयित्वा क्रतुः राज्ञः कृष्णो योगेश्वरेश्वरः ।
उवास कतिचिन्मासान् सुहृद्भिरभियाचितः ॥४८॥

sādhayitvā kratuḥ rājñaḥ
kṛṣṇo yogeśvareśvaraḥ
uvāsa katicin māsān
suhṛdbhir abhiyācitaḥ

sādhayitvā—accomplishing; *kratuḥ*—the *soma* sacrifice; *rājñaḥ*—of the King; *kṛṣṇaḥ*—Lord Kṛṣṇa; *yoga-īśvara*—of the masters of mystic power; *īśvaraḥ*—the supreme master; *uvāsa*—resided; *katicit*—some; *māsān*—months; *su-hṛdbhiḥ*—by His well-wishers; *abhiyācitaḥ*—begged.

TRANSLATION

Thus Śrī Kṛṣṇa, the Lord of all masters of mystic *yoga*, saw to the successful execution of this great sacrifice on behalf of King

Yudhiṣṭhira. Afterwards, the Lord stayed with His intimate friends for a few months at their earnest request.

PURPORT

Although Lord Kṛṣṇa is the master of all masters of *yoga*, such as Lord Śiva, still He was controlled by King Yudhiṣṭhira's pure love. Thus the Lord personally saw to the successful completion of the King's sacrificial performance. And after that He agreed to stay with His dear friends in Indraprastha for a few more months.

TEXT 49

ततोऽनुज्ञाप्य राजानमनिच्छन्तमपीश्वरः ।
ययौ सभार्यः सामात्यः स्वपुरं देवकीसुतः ॥४९॥

tato 'nujñāpya rājānam
anicchantam apīśvaraḥ
yayau sa-bhāryaḥ sāmātyaḥ
sva-puraṁ devakī-sutaḥ

tataḥ—then; *anujñāpya*—requesting leave; *rājānam*—of the King; *anicchantam*—who did not want it; *api*—although; *īśvaraḥ*—the Supreme Lord; *yayau*—went; *sa-bhāryaḥ*—with His wives; *sa-amātyaḥ*—and with His ministers; *sva*—to His own; *puram*—city; *devakī-sutaḥ*—the son of Devakī.

TRANSLATION

Then the Lord, the son of Devakī, took the reluctant permission of the King and returned to His capital with His wives and ministers.

TEXT 50

वर्णितं तदुपाख्यानं मया ते बहुविस्तरम् ।
वैकुण्ठवासिनोर्जन्म विप्रशापात्पुनः पुनः ॥५०॥

varṇitaṁ tad upākhyānaṁ
mayā te bahu-vistaram
vaikuṇṭha-vāsinor janma
vipra-śāpāt punaḥ punaḥ

varṇitam—related; *tat*—that; *upākhyānam*—account; *mayā*—by me; *te*—to you; *bahu*—much; *vistaram*—in detail; *vaikuṇṭha-vāsinoḥ*—of the two residents of the eternal kingdom of God (namely, the doorkeepers Jaya and Vijaya); *janma*—the material birth; *vipra*—of *brāhmaṇas* (the four Kumāras); *śāpāt*—due to the curse; *punaḥ punaḥ*—again and again.

TRANSLATION

I have already described to you in detail the history of the two residents of Vaikuṇṭha who had to undergo repeated births in the material world because of being cursed by *brāhmaṇas.*

TEXT 51

राजसूयावभृथ्येन स्नातो राजा युधिष्ठिरः ।
ब्रह्मक्षत्रसभामध्ये शुशुभे सुरराडिव ॥५१॥

rājasūyāvabhṛthyena
snāto rājā yudhiṣṭhiraḥ
brahma-kṣatra-sabhā-madhye
śuśubhe sura-rāḍ iva

rājasūya—of the Rājasūya sacrifice; *avabhṛthyena*—by the final, *avabhṛtya* ritual; *snātaḥ*—bathed; *rājā yudhiṣṭhiraḥ*—King Yudhiṣṭhira; *brahma-kṣatra*—of *brāhmaṇas* and *kṣatriyas; sabhā*—of the assembly; *madhye*—in the midst; *śuśubhe*—he appeared brilliant; *sura*—of the demigods; *rāṭ*—the King (Lord Indra); *iva*—like.

TRANSLATION

Purified in the final, *avabhṛthya* ritual, which marked the successful completion of the Rājasūya sacrifice, King Yudhiṣṭhira shone among the assembled *brāhmaṇas* and *kṣatriyas* like the King of the demigods himself.

TEXT 52

राज्ञा सभाजिताः सर्वे सुरमानवखेचराः ।
कृष्णं क्रतुं च शंसन्तः स्वधामानि ययुर्मुदा ॥५२॥

rājñā sabhājitāḥ sarve
sura-mānava-khecarāḥ
kṛṣṇaṁ kratuṁ ca śaṁsantaḥ
sva-dhāmāni yayur mudā

rājñā—by the King; *sabhājitāḥ*—honored; *sarve*—all; *sura*—the demigods; *mānava*—humans; *khe-carāḥ*—and travelers of the sky (minor demigods and demons); *kṛṣṇam*—Lord Kṛṣṇa; *kratum*—the sacrifice; *ca*—and; *śaṁsantaḥ*—praising; *sva*—to their own; *dhāmāni*—domains; *yayuḥ*—went; *mudā*—happily.

TRANSLATION

The demigods, humans and residents of intermediate heavens, all properly honored by the King, happily set off for their respective domains while singing the praises of Lord Kṛṣṇa and the great sacrifice.

PURPORT

According to Śrīdhara Svāmī, the term *khecarāḥ* here refers to the *pramathas,* mystic *yogīs* who accompany Lord Śiva.

TEXT 53

दुर्योधनमृते पापं कलिं कुरुकुलामयम् ।
यो न सेहे श्रियं स्फीतां दृष्ट्वा पाण्डुसुतस्य ताम् ॥५३॥

duryodhanam ṛte pāpaṁ
kaliṁ kuru-kulāmayam

yo na sehe śriyaṁ sphītāṁ
dṛṣṭvā pāṇḍu-sutasya tām

duryodhanam—Duryodhana; *ṛte*—except; *pāpam*—sinful; *kalim*—the empowered expansion of the age of Kali; *kuru-kula*—of the Kuru dynasty; *āmayam*—the disease; *yaḥ*—who; *na sehe*—could not tolerate; *śriyam*—the opulences; *sphītām*—flourishing; *dṛṣṭvā*—seeing; *pāṇḍu-sutasya*—of the son of Pāṇḍu; *tām*—that.

TRANSLATION

[All were satisfied] except sinful Duryodhana, the personification of the age of quarrel and the disease of the Kuru dynasty. He could not bear to see the flourishing opulence of the son of Pāṇḍu.

PURPORT

Śrīla Prabhupāda writes, "Duryodhana by nature was very envious because of his sinful life, and he appeared in the dynasty of the Kurus as a chronic disease personified in order to destroy the whole family." Śrīla Śrīdhara Svāmī mentions that Duryodhana hated pure religious principles.

TEXT 54

य इदं कीर्तयेद्विष्णोः कर्म चैद्यवधादिकम् ।
राजमोक्षं वितानं च सर्वपापैः प्रमुच्यते ॥५४॥

ya idaṁ kīrtayed viṣṇoḥ
karma caidya-vadhādikam
rāja-mokṣaṁ vitānaṁ ca
sarva-pāpaiḥ pramucyate

yaḥ—who; *idam*—these; *kīrtayet*—chants; *viṣṇoḥ*—of Lord Viṣṇu; *karma*—activities; *caidya-vadha*—the killing of Śiśupāla; *ādikam*—and so on; *rāja*—of the kings (who were imprisoned by Jarāsandha); *mokṣam*—the deliverance; *vitānam*—the sacrifice; *ca*—and; *sarva*—from all; *pāpaiḥ*—sinful reactions; *pramucyate*—he is freed.

TRANSLATION

One who recites these activities of Lord Viṣṇu, including the killing of Śiśupāla, the deliverance of the kings and the performance of the Rājasūya sacrifice, is freed from all sins.

Thus end the purports of the humble servants of His Divine Grace A. C. Bhaktivedanta Swami Prabhupāda to the Tenth Canto, Seventy-fourth Chapter, of the Śrīmad-Bhāgavatam, *entitled "The Deliverance of Śiśupāla at the Rājasūya Sacrifice."*

CHAPTER SEVENTY–FIVE

Duryodhana Humiliated

This chapter describes the glorious conclusion of the Rājasūya sacrifice, and how Prince Duryodhana was humiliated in King Yudhiṣṭhira's palace.

At the time of Mahārāja Yudhiṣṭhira's Rājasūya sacrifice, many of his relatives and well-wishers endeavored to please him by performing necessary services. When the sacrifice was complete, the King adorned the priests, the exalted members of the assembly and his own relatives with fragrant sandalwood paste, flower garlands and fine clothing. Then they all went to the banks of the Ganges to perform the ritual bathing that marks the end of the sponsor's period of initiation for the sacrifice. Before the final bathing, there was much sporting in the river among the male and female participants. Sprinkled with aromatic water and other liquids, Draupadī and the other ladies appeared most beautiful, their faces shining with bashful laughter.

After the priests had executed the final rituals, the King and his queen, Śrīmatī Draupadī, bathed in the Ganges. Then all those present who belonged to the orders of *varṇāśrama* bathed. Yudhiṣṭhira put on new clothes and worshiped the learned *brāhmaṇas,* his family, friends and well-wishers, each in the particular manner suitable for them, and offered them all various gifts. The guests then departed for their homes. But King Yudhiṣṭhira was so anxious about his imminent separation from those who were dear to him that he compelled several of his relatives and closest friends, including Lord Kṛṣṇa, to remain in Indraprastha a bit longer.

King Yudhiṣṭhira's royal palace had been constructed by Maya Dānava, who had endowed it with many wonderful features and opulences. King Duryodhana burned with envy when he saw these riches. One day, Yudhiṣṭhira was seated with Lord Kṛṣṇa in his royal assembly hall. Attended by his subordinates and family members, he was manifesting magnificence equal to that of Lord Indra. At that time Duryodhana entered the hall in a fitful mood. Bewildered by the mystic craft of Maya Dānava, Duryodhana mistook parts of the solid floor for water and thus lifted his garment, while in one place he fell into the water, mistaking it for the solid floor. When Bhīmasena, the ladies of the court and the royal princes present saw this, they began to laugh. Although Mahārāja Yudhiṣṭhira tried to stop them, Lord Kṛṣṇa encouraged their laughter. Thoroughly embarrassed, Duryodhana left the assembly hall in a fury and immediately departed for Hastināpura.

TEXTS 1–2

श्रीराजोवाच
अजातशत्रोस्तं दृष्ट्वा राजसूयमहोदयम् ।
सर्वे मुमुदिरे ब्रह्मन्नृदेवा ये समागताः ॥१॥
दुर्योधनं वर्जयित्वा राजानः सर्षयः सुराः ।
इति श्रुतं नो भगवंस्तत्र कारणमुच्यताम् ॥२॥

śrī-rājovāca
ajāta-śatros taṁ dṛṣṭvā
rājasūya-mahodayam
sarve mumudire brahman
nṛ-devā ye samāgatāḥ

duryodhanaṁ varjayitvā
rājānaḥ sarṣayaḥ surāḥ
iti śrutaṁ no bhagavaṁs
tatra kāraṇam ucyatām

śrī-rājā uvāca—the King (Parīkṣit) said; *ajāta-śatroḥ*—of Yudhiṣṭhira, whose enemy was never born; *tam*—that; *dṛṣṭvā*—seeing; *rājasūya*—of the Rājasūya sacrifice; *mahā*—great; *udayam*—the festiveness; *sarve*—all; *mumudire*—were delighted; *brahman*—O *brāhmaṇa* (Śukadeva); *nṛ-devāḥ*—the kings; *ye*—who; *samāgatāḥ*—assembled; *duryodhanam*—Duryodhana; *varjayitvā*—excepting; *rājānaḥ*—kings; *sa*—together with; *ṛṣayaḥ*—sages; *surāḥ*—and demigods; *iti*—thus; *śrutam*—heard; *naḥ*—by us; *bhagavan*—my lord; *tatra*—for that; *kāraṇam*—the reason; *ucyatām*—please speak.

TRANSLATION

Mahārāja Parīkṣit said: O *brāhmaṇa*, according to what I have heard from you, all the assembled kings, sages and demigods were

delighted to see the wonderful festivities of King Ajātaśatru's Rājasūya sacrifice, with the sole exception of Duryodhana. Please tell me why this was so, my lord.

TEXT 3

श्रीबादरायणिरुवाच
पितामहस्य ते यज्ञे राजसूये महात्मनः ।
बान्धवाः परिचर्यायां तस्यासन् प्रेमबन्धनाः ॥३॥

śrī-bādarāyaṇir uvāca
pitāmahasya te yajñe
rājasūye mahātmanaḥ
bāndhavāḥ paricaryāyāṁ
tasyāsan prema-bandhanāḥ

śrī-bādarāyaṇiḥ uvāca—Śrī Bādarāyaṇi (Śukadeva Gosvāmī) said; *pitāmahasya*—of the grandfather; *te*—your; *yajñe*—at the sacrifice; *rājasūye*—the Rājasūya; *mahā-ātmanaḥ*—of the great soul; *bāndhavāḥ*—family members; *paricaryāyām*—in humble service; *tasya*—for him; *āsan*—were situated; *prema*—by love; *bandhanāḥ*—who were bound.

TRANSLATION

Śrī Bādarāyaṇi said: At the Rājasūya sacrifice of your saintly grandfather, his family members, bound by their love for him, engaged themselves in humble services on his behalf.

PURPORT

King Yudhiṣṭhira did not force his relatives to accept different tasks at the sacrifice. Rather, out of their love for him they volunteered for such duties.

TEXTS 4–7

भीमो महानसाध्यक्षो धनाध्यक्षः सुयोधनः ।
सहदेवस्तु पूजायां नकुलो द्रव्यसाधने ॥४॥

गुरुशुश्रूषणे जिष्णुः कृष्णः पादावनेजने ।
परिवेषणे द्रुपदजा कर्णो दाने महामनाः ॥५॥
युयुधानो विकर्णश्च हार्दिक्यो विदुरादयः ।
बाह्लीकपुत्रा भूर्याद्या ये च सन्तर्दनादयः ॥६॥
निरूपिता महायज्ञे नानाकर्मसु ते तदा ।
प्रवर्तन्ते स्म राजेन्द्र राज्ञः प्रियचिकीर्षवः ॥७॥

bhīmo mahānasādhyakṣo
dhanādhyakṣaḥ suyodhanaḥ
sahadevas tu pūjāyāṁ
nakulo dravya-sādhane

guru-śuśrūṣaṇe jiṣṇuḥ
kṛṣṇaḥ pādāvanejane
pariveṣaṇe drupada-jā
karṇo dāne mahā-manāḥ

yuyudhāno vikarṇaś ca
hārdikyo vidurādayaḥ
bāhlīka-putrā bhūry-ādyā
ye ca santardanādayaḥ

nirūpitā mahā-yajñe
nānā-karmasu te tadā
pravartante sma rājendra
rājñaḥ priya-cikīrṣavaḥ

bhīmaḥ—Bhīma; *mahānasa*—of the kitchen; *adhyakṣaḥ*—the supervisor; *dhana*—of the treasury; *adhyakṣaḥ*—the supervisor; *suyodhanaḥ*—Suyodhana (Duryodhana); *sahadevaḥ*—Sahadeva; *tu*—and; *pūjāyām*—in worshiping (guests as they arrived); *nakulaḥ*—Nakula; *dravya*—needed items; *sādhane*—in procuring; *guru*—of respectable elders; *śuśrūṣaṇe*—in serving; *jiṣṇuḥ*—Arjuna; *kṛṣṇaḥ*—Kṛṣṇa; *pāda*—feet; *avanejane*—in washing; *pariveṣaṇe*—in distributing (food); *drupada-jā*—the daughter of Drupada (Draupadī); *karṇaḥ*—Karṇa; *dāne*—in giving gifts; *mahā-manāḥ*—magnanimous; *yuyudhānaḥ vikarṇaḥ ca*—Yuyudhāna and

Vikarṇa; *hārdikyaḥ vidura-ādayaḥ*—Hārdikya (Kṛtavarmā), Vidura and others; *bāhlīka-putrāḥ*—the sons of Bāhlīka-rāja; *bhūri-ādyāḥ*—headed by Bhūriśravā; *ye*—who; *ca*—and; *santardana-ādayaḥ*—Santardana and so on; *nirūpitāḥ*—engaged; *mahā*—vast; *yajñe*—at the sacrifice; *nānā*—various; *karmasu*—in duties; *te*—they; *tadā*—at that time; *pravartante sma*—carried on; *rāja-indra*—O best of kings (Parīkṣit); *rājñaḥ*—of the King (Yudhiṣṭhira); *priya*—gratification; *cikīrṣavaḥ*—wishing to do.

TRANSLATION

Bhīma supervised the kitchen, Duryodhana looked after the treasury, while Sahadeva respectfully greeted the arriving guests. Nakula procured needed items, Arjuna attended the respectable elders, and Kṛṣṇa washed everyone's feet, while Draupadī served food, and generous Karṇa gave out the gifts. Many others, such as Yuyudhāna; Vikarṇa; Hārdikya; Vidura; Bhūriśravā and other sons of Bāhlīka; and Santardana, similarly volunteered for various duties during the elaborate sacrifice. They did so because of their eagerness to please Mahārāja Yudhiṣṭhira, O best of kings.

TEXT 8

ऋत्विक्सदस्यबहुवित्सु सुहृत्तमेषु
स्विष्टेषु सूनृतसमर्हणदक्षिणाभिः ।
चैद्ये च सात्वतपतेश्चरणं प्रविष्टे
चक्रुस्ततस्त्ववभृथस्नपनं द्युनद्याम् ॥८॥

ṛtvik-sadasya-bahu-vitsu suhṛttameṣu
sv-iṣṭeṣu sūnṛta-samarhaṇa-dakṣiṇābhiḥ
caidye ca sātvata-pateś caraṇaṁ praviṣṭe
cakrus tatas tv avabhṛtha-snapanaṁ dyu-nadyām

ṛtvik—the priests; *sadasya*—the prominent members of the assembly who helped officiate in the sacrifice; *bahu-vitsu*—those who were greatly learned; *suhṛt-tameṣu*—and the best well-wishers; *su*—well; *iṣṭeṣu*—being honored; *sūnṛta*—with pleasing words; *samarhaṇa*—auspicious offerings; *dakṣiṇābhiḥ*—and gifts expressing gratitude; *caidye*—the King of Cedi (Śiśupāla); *ca*—and; *sātvata-pateḥ*—of the Lord of the Sātvatas

(Kṛṣṇa); *caraṇam*—the feet; *praviṣṭe*—having entered; *cakruḥ*—they executed; *tataḥ*—then; *tu*—and; *avabhṛtha-snapanam*—the *avabhṛtha* bath, which completed the sacrifice; *dyu*—of heaven; *nadyām*—in the river (the Yamunā).

TRANSLATION

After the priests, the prominent delegates, the greatly learned saints and the King's most intimate well-wishers had all been properly honored with pleasing words, auspicious offerings and various gifts as remuneration, and after the King of Cedi had entered the lotus feet of the Lord of the Sātvatas, the *avabhṛtha* bath was performed in the divine river Yamunā.

PURPORT

The gifts offered to the distinguished guests included valuable jewelry.

TEXT 9

मृदंगशंखपणवधुन्धुर्यानकगोमुखाः ।
वादित्राणि विचित्राणि नेदुरावभृथोत्सवे ॥९॥

mṛdaṅga-śaṅkha-paṇava-
dhundhury-ānaka-gomukhāḥ
vāditrāṇi vicitrāṇi
nedur āvabhṛthotsave

mṛdaṅga—*mṛdaṅga* drums; *śaṅkha*—conchshells; *paṇava*—smaller drums; *dhundhuri*—a kind of large military drum; *ānaka*—kettledrums; *go-mukhāḥ*—a wind instrument; *vāditrāṇi*—music; *vicitrāṇi*—variegated; *neduḥ*—sounded; *āvabhṛtha*—of the *avabhṛtha* bath; *utsave*—during the celebration.

TRANSLATION

During the *avabhṛtha* celebration, the music of many kinds of instruments resounded, including *mṛdaṅgas*, conchshells, *paṇavas*, *dhundhuris*, kettledrums and *gomukha* horns.

TEXT 10

नार्तक्यो ननृतुर्हृष्टा गायका यूथशो जगुः ।
वीणावेणुतलोन्नादस्तेषां स दिवमस्पृशत् ॥१०॥

nārtakyo nanṛtur hṛṣṭā
gāyakā yūthaśo jaguḥ
vīṇā-veṇu-talonnādas
teṣāṁ sa divam aspṛśat

nārtakyaḥ—female dancers; *nanṛtuḥ*—danced; *hṛṣṭāḥ*—joyful; *gāyakāḥ*—singers; *yūthaśaḥ*—in groups; *jaguḥ*—sang; *vīṇā*—of *vīṇas; veṇu*—flutes; *tala*—and hand cymbals; *unnādaḥ*—the loud sound; *teṣām*—their; *saḥ*—it; *divam*—the heavens; *aspṛśat*—touched.

TRANSLATION

Female dancers danced with great joy, and choruses sang, while the loud vibrations of *vīṇās*, flutes and hand cymbals reached all the way to the heavenly regions.

TEXT 11

चित्रध्वजपताकाग्रैरिभेन्द्रस्यन्दनार्वभिः ।
स्वलंकृतैर्भटैर्भूपा निर्ययू रुक्ममालिनः ॥११॥

citra-dhvaja-patākāgrair
ibhendra-syandanārvabhiḥ
sv-alaṅkṛtair bhaṭair bhūpā
niryayū rukma-mālinaḥ

citra—of various colors; *dhvaja*—with flags; *patāka*—and banners; *agraiḥ*—excellent; *ibha*—with elephants; *indra*—lordly; *syandana*—chariots; *arvabhiḥ*—and horses; *su-alaṅkṛtaiḥ*—well ornamented; *bhaṭaiḥ*—with foot soldiers; *bhū-pāḥ*—the kings; *niryayuḥ*—departed; *rukma*—gold; *mālinaḥ*—wearing necklaces.

TRANSLATION

All the kings, wearing gold necklaces, then set off for the Yamunā. They had flags and banners of various colors and were accompanied by infantrymen and well-adorned soldiers riding lordly elephants, chariots and horses.

TEXT 12

यदुसृञ्जयकाम्बोजकुरुकेकयकोशलाः ।
कम्पयन्तो भुवं सैन्यैर्यजमानपुरःसराः ॥१२॥

yadu-sṛñjaya-kāmboja-
kuru-kekaya-kośalāḥ
kampayanto bhuvaṁ sainyair
yajamāna-puraḥ-sarāḥ

yadu-sṛñjaya-kāmboja—the Yadus, Sṛñjayas and Kāmbojas; *kuru-kekaya-kośalāḥ*—the Kurus, Kekayas and Kośalas; *kampayantaḥ*—making tremble; *bhuvam*—the earth; *sainyaiḥ*—with their armies; *yajamāna*—the performer of the sacrifice (Mahārāja Yudhiṣṭhira); *puraḥ-sarāḥ*—placing in their front.

TRANSLATION

The massed armies of the Yadus, Sṛñjayas, Kāmbojas, Kurus, Kekayas and Kośalas made the earth tremble as they followed Yudhiṣṭhira Mahārāja, the performer of the sacrifice, in procession.

TEXT 13

सदस्यर्त्विग्द्विजश्रेष्ठा ब्रह्मघोषेण भूयसा ।
देवर्षिपितृगन्धर्वास्तुष्टुवुः पुष्पवर्षिणः ॥१३॥

sadasyartvig-dvija-śreṣṭhā
brahma-ghoṣeṇa bhūyasā
devarṣi-pitṛ-gandharvās
tuṣṭuvuḥ puṣpa-varṣiṇaḥ

sadasya—the officiating witnesses; *ṛtvik*—the priests; *dvija*—and *brāhmaṇas; śreṣṭhāḥ*—most excellent; *brahma*—of the *Vedas; ghoṣeṇa*—with sounding; *bhūyasā*—abundant; *deva*—the demigods; *ṛṣi*—divine sages; *pitṛ*—forefathers; *gandharvāḥ*—and singers of heaven; *tuṣṭuvuḥ*—recited praises; *puṣpa*—flowers; *varṣiṇaḥ*—raining down.

TRANSLATION

The assembly officials, the priests and other excellent *brāhmaṇas* resoundingly vibrated Vedic *mantras*, while the demigods, divine sages, Pitās and Gandharvas sang praises and rained down flowers.

TEXT 14

स्वलंकृता नरा नार्यो गन्धस्रग्भूषणाम्बरैः ।
विलिम्पन्त्योऽभिषिञ्चन्त्यो विजह्रुर्विविधै रसैः ॥१४॥

sv-alaṅkṛtā narā nāryo
gandha-srag-bhūṣaṇāmbaraiḥ
vilimpantyo 'bhiṣiñcantyo
vijahrur vividhai rasaiḥ

su-alaṅkṛtāḥ—well decorated; *narāḥ*—men; *nāryaḥ*—and women; *gandha*—with sandalwood paste; *srak*—flower garlands; *bhūṣaṇa*—jewelry; *ambaraiḥ*—and clothing; *vilimpantyaḥ*—smearing; *abhiṣiñcantyaḥ*—and sprinkling; *vijahruḥ*—they played; *vividhaiḥ*—various; *rasaiḥ*—with liquids.

TRANSLATION

Men and women, all adorned with sandalwood paste, flower garlands, jewelry and fine clothing, sported by smearing and sprinkling one another with various liquids.

TEXT 15

तैलगोरसगन्धोदहरिद्रासान्द्रकुंकुमैः ।
पुम्भिर्लिप्ताः प्रलिम्पन्त्यो विजह्रुर्वारयोषितः ॥१५॥

taila-gorasa-gandhoda-
haridrā-sāndra-kuṅkumaiḥ
pumbhir liptāḥ pralimpantyo
vijahrur vāra-yoṣitaḥ

taila—with vegetable oil; *go-rasa*—yogurt; *gandha-uda*—perfumed water; *haridrā*—turmeric; *sāndra*—plentiful; *kuṅkumaiḥ*—and with vermilion powder; *pumbhiḥ*—by the men; *liptāḥ*—smeared; *pralimpantyaḥ*—smearing them in turn; *vijahruḥ*—played; *vāra-yoṣitaḥ*—the courtesans.

TRANSLATION

The men smeared the courtesans with plentiful oil, yogurt, perfumed water, turmeric and *kuṅkuma* powder, and the courtesans playfully smeared the men with the same substances.

PURPORT

Śrīla Prabhupāda describes this scene as follows: "The men and women of Indraprastha, their bodies smeared with scents and floral oils, were nicely dressed in colorful garments and decorated with garlands, jewels and ornaments. They were all enjoying the ceremony, and they threw on each other liquid substances like water, oil, milk, butter and yogurt. Some even smeared these on each other's bodies. In this way, they were enjoying the occasion. The professional prostitutes were also engaged by jubilantly smearing these liquid substances on the bodies of the men, and the men reciprocated in the same way. All the liquid substances had been mixed with turmeric and saffron, and their color was a lustrous yellow."

TEXT 16

गुप्ता नृभिर्निरगमन्नुपलब्धुमेतद्
देव्यो यथा दिवि विमानवरैर्नृदेव्यो ।
ता मातुलेयसखिभिः परिषिच्यमानाः
सव्रीडहासविकसद्वदना विरेजुः ॥१६॥

guptā nṛbhir niragamann upalabdhum etad
devyo yathā divi vimāna-varair nṛ-devyo
tā mātuleya-sakhibhiḥ pariṣicyamānāḥ
sa-vrīḍa-hāsa-vikasad-vadanā virejuḥ

guptāḥ—guarded; *nṛbhiḥ*—by soldiers; *niragaman*—they went out; *upalabdhum*—to see first-hand; *etat*—this; *devyaḥ*—the wives of the demigods; *yathā*—as; *divi*—in the sky; *vimāna*—on their airplanes; *varaiḥ*—excellent; *nṛ-devyaḥ*—the queens (of King Yudhiṣṭhira); *tāḥ*—they; *mātuleya*—by their maternal cousins (Lord Kṛṣṇa and His brothers, such as Gada and Sāraṇa); *sakhibhiḥ*—and by their friends (such as Bhīma and Arjuna); *pariṣicyamānāḥ*—being sprinkled; *sa-vrīḍa*—shy; *hāsa*—with smiles; *vikasat*—blossoming; *vadanāḥ*—whose faces; *virejuḥ*—they appeared splendid.

TRANSLATION

Surrounded by guards, King Yudhiṣṭhira's queens came out on their chariots to see the fun, just as the demigods' wives appeared in the sky in celestial airplanes. As maternal cousins and intimate friends sprinkled the queens with liquids, the ladies' faces bloomed with shy smiles, enhancing the queens' splendid beauty.

PURPORT

The maternal cousins referred to here are Lord Kṛṣṇa and such brothers of His as Gada and Sāraṇa, and the friends mentioned are such persons as Bhīma and Arjuna.

TEXT 17

ता देवरानुत सखीन् सिषिचुर्दृतीभिः
क्लिन्नाम्बरा विवृतगात्रकुचोरुमध्याः ।
औत्सुक्यमुक्तकवराच्च्यवमानमाल्याः
क्षोभं दधुर्मलधियां रुचिरैर्विहारैः ॥१७॥

tā devarān uta sakhīn siṣicur dṛtībhiḥ
klinnāmbarā vivṛta-gātra-kucoru-madhyāḥ
autsukya-mukta-kavarāc cyavamāna-mālyāḥ
kṣobhaṁ dadhur mala-dhiyāṁ rucirair vihāraiḥ

tāḥ—they, the queens; *devarān*—their husband's brothers; *uta*—and also; *sakhīn*—their friends; *siṣicuḥ*—they squirted; *dṛtībhiḥ*—with syringes; *klinna*—drenched; *ambarāḥ*—whose dresses; *vivṛta*—visible; *gātra*—whose arms; *kuca*—breasts; *ūru*—thighs; *madhyāḥ*—and waists; *autsukya*—due to their excitement; *mukta*—loosened; *kavarāt*—from the braids of their hair; *cyavamāna*—slipping; *mālyāḥ*—whose small flower garlands; *kṣobham*—agitation; *dadhuḥ*—they created; *mala*—dirty; *dhiyām*—for those whose consciousness; *ruciraiḥ*—charming; *vihāraiḥ*—with their play.

TRANSLATION

As the queens squirted water from syringes at their brothers-in-law and other male companions, their own garments became drenched, revealing their arms, breasts, thighs and waists. In their excitement, the flowers fell from their loosened braids. By these charming pastimes they agitated those with contaminated consciousness.

PURPORT

Śrīla Prabhupāda writes, "Such behavior between pure males and females is enjoyable, but persons who are materially contaminated become lustful."

TEXT 18

स सम्राड् रथमारुढः सदश्वं रुक्ममालिनम् ।
व्यरोचत स्वपत्नीभिः क्रियाभिः क्रतुराडिव ॥१८॥

sa samrāḍ ratham āruḍhaḥ
sad-aśvaṁ rukma-mālinam
vyarocata sva-patnībhiḥ
kriyābhiḥ kratu-rāḍ iva

saḥ—he; *samrāṭ*—the emperor, Yudhiṣṭhira; *ratham*—his chariot; *āruḍhaḥ*—mounted; *sat*—excellent; *aśvam*—whose horses; *rukma*—golden; *mālinam*—with hangings; *vyarocata*—he shone forth; *sva-patnībhiḥ*—with his wives; *kriyābhiḥ*—with its rituals; *kratu*—of sacrifices; *rāṭ*—the king (Rājasūya); *iva*—as if.

TRANSLATION

The emperor, mounted upon his chariot drawn by excellent horses wearing golden collars, appeared splendid in the company of his wives, just like the brilliant Rājasūya sacrifice surrounded by its various rituals.

PURPORT

King Yudhiṣṭhira with his queens appeared like the personified Rājasūya sacrifice surrounded by its beautiful rituals.

TEXT 19

पत्नीसंयाजावभृथ्यैश्चरित्वा ते तमृत्विजः ।
आचान्तं स्नापयां चक्रुर्गंगायां सह कृष्णया ॥१९॥

patnī-saṁyājāvabhṛthyaiś
caritvā te tam ṛtvijaḥ
ācāntaṁ snāpayāṁ cakrur
gaṅgāyāṁ saha kṛṣṇayā

patnī-saṁyāja—the ritual performed by the sponsor of the sacrifice and his wife consisting of oblations to Soma, Tvaṣṭā, the wives of certain demigods, and Agni; *avabhṛthyaiḥ*—and the rituals which solemnize the completion of the sacrifice; *caritvā*—having executed; *te*—they; *tam*—him; *ṛtvijaḥ*—the priests; *ācāntam*—having sipped water for purification; *snāpayām cakruḥ*—they had him bathe; *gaṅgāyām*—in the Ganges; *saha*—along with; *kṛṣṇayā*—Draupadī.

TRANSLATION

The priests led the King through the execution of the final rituals of *patnī-saṁyāja* and *avabhṛthya*. Then they had him and

Queen Draupadī sip water for purification and bathe in the Ganges.

TEXT 20

देवदुन्दुभयो नेदुर्नरदुन्दुभिभिः समम् ।
मुमुचुः पुष्पवर्षाणि देवर्षिपितृमानवाः ॥२०॥

deva-dundubhayo nedur
nara-dundubhibhiḥ samam
mumucuḥ puṣpa-varṣāṇi
devarṣi-pitṛ-mānavāḥ

deva—of demigods; *dundubhayaḥ*—kettledrums; *neduḥ*—resounded; *nara*—of human beings; *dundubhibhiḥ*—kettledrums; *samam*—together with; *mumucuḥ*—released; *puṣpa*—of flowers; *varṣāṇi*—downpours; *deva*—demigods; *ṛṣi*—sages; *pitṛ*—forefathers; *mānavāḥ*—and humans.

TRANSLATION

The kettledrums of the gods resounded, along with those of human beings. Demigods, sages, forefathers and humans all poured down showers of flowers.

TEXT 21

सस्नुस्तत्र ततः सर्वे वर्णाश्रमयुता नराः ।
महापातक्यपि यतः सद्यो मुच्येत किल्बिषात् ॥२१॥

sasnus tatra tataḥ sarve
varṇāśrama-yutā narāḥ
mahā-pātaky api yataḥ
sadyo mucyeta kilbiṣāt

sasnuḥ—bathed; *tatra*—there; *tataḥ*—after this; *sarve*—all; *varṇa-āśrama*—the social system of sanctified occupational and spiritual orders; *yutāḥ*—who belonged to; *narāḥ*—humans; *mahā*—greatly;

pātakī—one who is sinful; *api*—even; *yataḥ*—by which; *sadyaḥ*—immediately; *mucyeta*—can be freed; *kilbiṣāt*—from contamination.

TRANSLATION

All the citizens belonging to the various orders of *varṇa* and *āśrama* then bathed in that place, where even the most grievous sinner can immediately be freed from all sinful reactions.

TEXT 22

अथ राजाहते क्षौमे परिधाय स्वलंकृतः ।
ऋत्विक्सदस्यविप्रादीनानर्चाभरणाम्बरैः ॥२२॥

atha rājāhate kṣaume
paridhāya sv-alaṅkṛtaḥ
ṛtvik-sadasya-viprādīn
ānarcābharaṇāmbaraiḥ

atha—next; *rājā*—the King; *ahate*—unused; *kṣaume*—a pair of silken garments; *paridhāya*—putting on; *su-alaṅkṛtaḥ*—nicely ornamented; *ṛtvik*—the priests; *sadasya*—the officiating members of the assembly; *vipra*—the *brāhmaṇas; ādīn*—and others; *ānarca*—he worshiped; *ābharaṇa*—with ornaments; *ambaraiḥ*—and clothing.

TRANSLATION

Next the King put on new silken garments and adorned himself with fine jewelry. He then honored the priests, assembly officials, learned *brāhmaṇas* and other guests by presenting them with ornaments and clothing.

PURPORT

Śrīla Prabhupāda writes, "The King not only dressed himself and decorated himself, but he also gave clothing and ornaments to all the priests and to the others who had participated in the *yajñas*. In this way he worshiped them all."

TEXT 23

बन्धून् ज्ञातीन्नृपान्मित्रसुहृदोऽन्यांश्च सर्वशः ।
अभीक्ष्णं पूजयामास नारायणपरो नृपः ॥२३॥

bandhūñ jñātīn nṛpān mitra-
suhṛdo 'nyāṁś ca sarvaśaḥ
abhīkṣṇaṁ pūjayām āsa
nārāyaṇa-paro nṛpaḥ

bandhūn—his more distant relatives; *jñātīn*—his immediate family members; *nṛpān*—the kings; *mitra*—his friends; *suhṛdaḥ*—and well-wishers; *anyān*—others; *ca*—also; *sarvaśaḥ*—in all sorts of ways; *abhīkṣṇam*—constantly; *pūjayām āsa*—worshiped; *nārāyaṇa-paraḥ*—devoted to Lord Nārāyaṇa; *nṛpaḥ*—the King.

TRANSLATION

In various ways King Yudhiṣṭhira, who had totally dedicated his life to Lord Nārāyaṇa, continuously honored his relatives, his immediate family, the other kings, his friends and well-wishers, and all others present as well.

TEXT 24

सर्वे जनाः सुररुचो मणिकुण्डलस्रग्-
उष्णीषकञ्चुकदुकूलमहार्घ्यहाराः ।
नार्यश्च कुण्डलयुगालकवृन्दजुष्ट-
वक्त्रश्रियः कनकमेखलया विरेजुः ॥२४॥

sarve janāḥ sura-ruco maṇi-kuṇḍala-srag-
uṣṇīṣa-kañcuka-dukūla-mahārghya-hārāḥ
nāryaś ca kuṇḍala-yugālaka-vṛnda-juṣṭa-
vaktra-śriyaḥ kanaka-mekhalayā virejuḥ

sarve—all; *janāḥ*—the men; *sura*—like the demigods; *rucaḥ*—whose effulgent complexions; *maṇi*—jeweled; *kuṇḍala*—with earrings; *srak*—

flower garlands; *uṣṇīṣa*—turbans; *kañcuka*—jackets; *dukūla*—silk garments; *mahā-arghya*—very precious; *hārāḥ*—and pearl necklaces; *nāryaḥ*—the women; *ca*—and; *kuṇḍala*—of earrings; *yuga*—with pairs; *alaka-vṛnda*—and locks of hair; *juṣṭa*—adorned; *vaktra*—of whose faces; *śriyaḥ*—the beauty; *kanaka*—gold; *mekhalayā*—with belts; *virejuḥ*—shone brilliantly.

TRANSLATION

All the men there shone like demigods. They were adorned with jeweled earrings, flower garlands, turbans, waistcoats, silk *dhotīs* and valuable pearl necklaces. The lovely faces of the women were beautified by their matched earrings and locks of hair, and they all wore golden belts.

TEXTS 25–26

अथर्त्विजो महाशीलाः सदस्या ब्रह्मवादिनः ।
ब्रह्मक्षत्रियविट्शूद्रा राजानो ये समागताः ॥२५॥
देवर्षिपितृभूतानि लोकपालाः सहानुगाः ।
पूजितास्तमनुज्ञाप्य स्वधामानि ययुर्नृप ॥२६॥

athartvijo mahā-śīlāḥ
sadasyā brahma-vādinaḥ
brahma-kṣatriya-viṭ-śūdrā
rājāno ye samāgatāḥ

devarṣi-pitṛ-bhūtāni
loka-pālāḥ sahānugāḥ
pūjitās tam anujñāpya
sva-dhāmāni yayur nṛpa

atha—then; *ṛtvijaḥ*—the priests; *mahā-śīlāḥ*—of exalted character; *sadasyāḥ*—the officials of the sacrifice; *brahma*—of the *Vedas; vādinaḥ*—expert authorities; *brahma*—the *brāhmaṇas; kṣatriya*—*kṣatriyas; viṭ*—*vaiśyas; śūdrāḥ*—and *śūdras; ājānaḥ*—the kings; *ye*—who; *samāgatāḥ*—had come; *deva*—the demigods; *ṛṣi*—sages; *pitṛ*—forefathers;

bhūtāni—and ghostly spirits; *loka*—of the planets; *pālāḥ*—the rulers; *saha*—with; *anugāḥ*—their followers; *pūjitāḥ*—worshiped; *tam*—from him; *anujñāpya*—taking permission; *sva*—their own; *dhāmāni*—to the abodes; *yayuḥ*—they went; *nṛpa*—O King (Parīkṣit).

TRANSLATION

Then the highly cultured priests, the great Vedic authorities who had served as sacrificial witnesses, the specially invited kings, the *brāhmaṇas, kṣatriyas, vaiśyas, śūdras,* demigods, sages, forefathers and mystic spirits, and the chief planetary rulers and their followers—all of them, having been worshiped by King Yudhiṣṭhira, took his permission and departed, O King, each for his own abode.

TEXT 27

हरिदासस्य राजर्षे राजसूयमहोदयम् ।
नैवातृप्यन् प्रशंसन्तः पिबन्मर्त्योऽमृतं यथा ॥२७॥

hari-dāsasya rājarṣe
rājasūya-mahodayam
naivātṛpyan praśaṁsantaḥ
piban martyo 'mṛtaṁ yathā

hari—of Lord Kṛṣṇa; *dāsasya*—of the servant; *rāja-ṛṣeḥ*—of the saintly King; *rājasūya*—of the Rājasūya sacrifice; *mahā-udayam*—the great celebration; *na*—not; *eva*—indeed; *atṛpyan*—they became satiated; *praśaṁsantaḥ*—glorifying; *piban*—drinking; *martyaḥ*—a mortal man; *amṛtam*—immortal nectar; *yathā*—as.

TRANSLATION

As they all glorified the wonderful Rājasūya-yajña performed by that great saintly King and servant of Lord Hari, they were not satiated, just as an ordinary man is never satiated when drinking nectar.

TEXT 28

ततो युधिष्ठिरो राजा सुहृत्सम्बन्धिबान्धवान् ।
प्रेम्णा निवारयामास कृष्णं च त्यागकातरः ॥२८॥

tato yudhiṣṭhiro rājā
suhṛt-sambandhi-bāndhavān
premṇā nivārayām āsa
kṛṣṇaṁ ca tyāga-kātaraḥ

tataḥ—then; *yudhiṣṭhiraḥ rājā*—King Yudhiṣṭhira; *suhṛt*—his friends; *sambandhi*—family members; *bāndhavān*—and relatives; *premṇā*—out of love; *nivārayām āsa*—stopped them; *kṛṣṇam*—Lord Kṛṣṇa; *ca*—and; *tyāga*—by separation; *kātaraḥ*—distressed.

TRANSLATION

At that time Rājā Yudhiṣṭhira stopped a number of his friends, immediate family members and other relatives from departing, among them Lord Kṛṣṇa. Out of love Yudhiṣṭhira could not let them go, for he felt the pain of imminent separation.

TEXT 29

भगवानपि तत्रांग न्यावात्सीत्तत्प्रियंकरः ।
प्रस्थाप्य यदुवीरांश्च साम्बादींश्च कुशस्थलीम् ॥२९॥

bhagavān api tatrāṅga
nyāvātsīt tat-priyaṁ-karaḥ
prasthāpya yadu-vīrāṁś ca
sāmbādīṁś ca kuśasthalīm

bhagavān—the Supreme Lord; *api*—and; *tatra*—there; *aṅga*—my dear (King Parīkṣit); *nyāvātsīt*—remained; *tat*—for his (Yudhiṣṭhira's); *priyam*—pleasure; *karaḥ*—acting; *prasthāpya*—sending; *yadu-vīrān*—the heroes of the Yadu dynasty; *ca*—and; *sāmba-ādīn*—headed by Sāmba; *ca*—and; *kuśasthalīm*—to Dvārakā.

TRANSLATION

My dear Parīkṣit, the Supreme Lord remained there for some time to please the King, after first sending Sāmba and the other Yadu heroes back to Dvārakā.

TEXT 30

इत्थं राजा धर्मसुतो मनोरथमहार्णवम् ।
सुदुस्तरं समुत्तीर्य कृष्णेनासीद् गतज्वरः ॥३०॥

itthaṁ rājā dharma-suto
manoratha-mahārṇavam
su-dustaraṁ samuttīrya
kṛṣṇenāsīd gata-jvaraḥ

ittham—in this manner; *rājā*—the King; *dharma*—of the lord of religion (Yamarāja); *sutaḥ*—the son; *manaḥ-ratha*—of his desires; *mahā*—huge; *arṇavam*—the ocean; *su*—very; *dustaram*—difficult to cross; *samuttīrya*—successfully crossing; *kṛṣṇena*—through the agency of Lord Kṛṣṇa; *āsīt*—he became; *gata-jvaraḥ*—freed of his feverish condition.

TRANSLATION

Thus King Yudhiṣṭhira, the son of Dharma, was at last relieved of his burning ambition, having by the grace of Lord Kṛṣṇa successfully crossed the vast and formidable ocean of his desires.

PURPORT

The previous chapters of *Śrīmad-Bhāgavatam* clearly explain that King Yudhiṣṭhira intensely desired to demonstrate to the world the supremacy of Kṛṣṇa, the Supreme Personality of Godhead, and the blessings received by those who surrender to Him. To do this, King Yudhiṣṭhira performed the Rājasūya sacrifice, a very difficult task.

Śrīla Prabhupāda writes in this connection: "In the material world, everyone has a particular type of desire to be fulfilled, but one is never able to fulfill his desires to his full satisfaction. But King Yudhiṣṭhira, because of his unflinching devotion to Kṛṣṇa, could fulfill all his desires successfully by the performance of the Rājasūya sacrifice. From the description of the Rājasūya *yajña,* it appears that such a function is a great ocean of opulent desires. It is not possible for an ordinary man to cross over such an ocean; nevertheless, by the grace of Lord Kṛṣṇa, King Yudhiṣṭhira was able to cross over it very easily, and thus he became freed from all anxieties."

TEXT 31

एकदान्तःपुरे तस्य वीक्ष्य दुर्योधनः श्रियम् ।
अतप्यद् राजसूयस्य महित्वं चाच्युतात्मनः ॥३१॥

ekadāntaḥ-pure tasya
vīkṣya duryodhanaḥ śriyam
atapyad rājasūyasya
mahitvaṁ cācyutātmanaḥ

ekadā—one day; *antaḥ-pure*—within the palace; *tasya*—his (Mahārāja Yudhiṣṭhira's); *vīkṣya*—observing; *duryodhanaḥ*—Duryodhana; *śriyam*—opulence; *atapyat*—he was pained; *rājasūyasya*—of the Rājasūya sacrifice; *mahitvam*—the greatness; *ca*—and; *acyuta-ātmanaḥ*—of him (King Yudhiṣṭhira) whose very soul was Lord Acyuta.

TRANSLATION

One day Duryodhana, while observing the riches of King Yudhiṣṭhira's palace, felt greatly disturbed by the magnificence of both the Rājasūya sacrifice and its performer, the King, whose life and soul was Lord Acyuta.

TEXT 32

यस्मिन्नरेन्द्रदितिजेन्द्रसुरेन्द्रलक्ष्मीर्
नाना विभान्ति किल विश्वसृजोपक्लृप्ताः ।
ताभिः पतीन् द्रुपदराजसुतोपतस्थे
यस्यां विषक्तहृदयः कुरुराडतप्यत् ॥३२॥

yasmiṁs narendra-ditijendra-surendra-lakṣmīr
nānā vibhānti kila viśva-sṛjopakḷptāḥ
tābhiḥ patīn drupada-rāja-sutopatasthe
yasyāṁ viṣakta-hṛdayaḥ kuru-rāḍ atapyat

yasmin—in which (palace); *nara-indra*—of the kings among men; *ditija-indra*—of the kings of the demons; *sura-indra*—and of the kings of the demigods; *lakṣmīḥ*—the opulences; *nānā*—variegated; *vibhānti*—were manifest; *kila*—indeed; *viśva-sṛjā*—by the cosmic manufacturer (Maya Dānava); *upakḷptāḥ*—provided; *tābhiḥ*—with them; *patīn*—her husbands, the Pāṇḍavas; *drupada-rāja*—of King Drupada; *sutā*—the daughter, Draupadī; *upatasthe*—served; *yasyām*—to whom; *viṣakta*—attached; *hṛdayaḥ*—whose heart; *kuru-rāṭ*—the Kuru prince, Duryodhana; *atapyat*—lamented.

TRANSLATION

In that palace all the collected opulences of the kings of men, demons and gods were brilliantly manifest, having been brought there by the cosmic inventor, Maya Dānava. With those riches Draupadī served her husbands, and Duryodhana, the prince of the Kurus, lamented because he was very much attracted to her.

TEXT 33

यस्मिन् तदा मधुपतेर्महिषीसहस्रं
श्रोणीभरेण शनकैः क्वणदङ्घ्रिशोभम् ।
मध्ये सुचारु कुचकुंकुमशोणहारं
श्रीमन्मुखं प्रचलकुण्डलकुन्तलाढ्यम् ॥३३॥

yasmin tadā madhu-pater mahiṣī-sahasraṁ
śroṇī-bhareṇa śanakaiḥ kvaṇad-aṅghri-śobham
madhye su-cāru kuca-kuṅkuma-śoṇa-hāraṁ
śrīman-mukhaṁ pracala-kuṇḍala-kuntalāḍhyam

yasmin—in which; *tadā*—at that time; *madhu*—of Mathurā; *pateḥ*—of the Lord; *mahiṣī*—the queens; *sahasram*—thousands; *śroṇī*—of their hips; *bhareṇa*—with the weight; *śanakaiḥ*—slowly; *kvaṇat*—tinkling; *aṅghri*—of whose feet; *śobham*—the charm; *madhye*—at the middle (the waist); *su-cāru*—very attractive; *kuca*—from their breasts; *kuṅkuma*—with the *kuṅkuma* powder; *śoṇa*—reddened; *hāram*—whose pearl necklaces; *śrī-mat*—beautiful; *mukham*—whose faces; *pracala*—moving; *kuṇḍala*—with earrings; *kuntala*—and locks of hair; *āḍhyam*—richly endowed.

TRANSLATION

Lord Madhupati's thousands of queens were also staying in the palace. Their feet moved slowly, weighed down by their hips, and the bells on their feet tinkled charmingly. Their waists were very slender, the *kuṅkuma* from their breasts reddened their pearl necklaces, and their swaying earrings and flowing locks of hair enhanced the exquisite beauty of their faces.

PURPORT

Śrila Prabhupāda writes, "After looking at such beauties in the palace of King Yudhiṣṭhira, Duryodhana became envious. He became especially envious and lustful upon seeing the beauty of Draupadī because he had cherished a special attraction for her from the very beginning of her marriage with the Pāṇḍavas. In the marriage selection assembly of Draupadī, Duryodhana had also been present, and with other princes he had been very much captivated by the beauty of Draupadi, but he had failed to achieve her."

TEXTS 34–35

सभायां मयक्लृप्तायां क्वापि धर्मसुतोऽधिराट् ।
वृतोऽनुगैर्बन्धुभिश्च कृष्णेनापि स्वचक्षुषा ॥३४॥
आसीनः काञ्चने साक्षादासने मघवानिव ।
पारमेष्ठ्यश्रिया जुष्टः स्तूयमानश्च वन्दिभिः ॥३५॥

sabhāyāṁ maya-kḷptāyām
kvāpi dharma-suto 'dhirāṭ
vṛto 'nugair bandhubhiś ca
kṛṣṇenāpi sva-cakṣuṣā

āsīnaḥ kāñcane sākṣād
āsane maghavān iva
pārameṣṭhya-śriyā juṣṭaḥ
stūyamānaś ca vandibhiḥ

sabhāyām—in the assembly hall; *maya*—by Maya Dānava; *kḷptāyām*—constructed; *kva api*—on one occasion; *dharma-sutaḥ*—the son of Yamarāja (Yudhiṣṭhira); *adhirāṭ*—the emperor; *vṛtaḥ*—accompanied; *anugaiḥ*—by his attendants; *bandhubhiḥ*—by his family members; *ca*—and; *kṛṣṇena*—by Lord Kṛṣṇa; *api*—also; *sva*—his own; *cakṣuṣā*—eye; *āsīnaḥ*—seated; *kāñcane*—made of gold; *sākṣāt*—in person; *āsane*—on a throne; *maghavān*—Lord Indra; *iva*—as if; *pārameṣṭhya*—of Brahmā, or of supreme rulership; *śriyā*—with the opulences; *juṣṭaḥ*—joined; *stūyamānaḥ*—being praised; *ca*—and; *vandibhiḥ*—by the court poets.

TRANSLATION

It so happened that Emperor Yudhiṣṭhira, the son of Dharma, was sitting just like Indra on a golden throne in the assembly hall built by Maya Dānava. Present with him were his attendants and family members, and also Lord Kṛṣṇa, his special eye. Displaying the opulences of Brahmā himself, King Yudhiṣṭhira was being praised by the court poets.

PURPORT

Śrīla Śrīdhara Svāmī explains that Lord Kṛṣṇa is described here as Yudhiṣṭhira's special eye since He advised the King on what was beneficial and what was not.

TEXT 36

तत्र दुर्योधनो मानी परीतो भ्रातृभिर्नृप ।
किरीटमाली न्यविशदसिहस्तः क्षिपन् रुषा ॥३६॥

tatra duryodhano mānī
parīto bhrātṛbhir nṛpa
kirīṭa-mālī nyaviśad
asi-hastaḥ kṣipan ruṣā

tatra—there; *duryodhanaḥ*—Duryodhana; *mānī*—proud; *parītaḥ*—surrounded; *bhrātṛbhiḥ*—by his brothers; *nṛpa*—O King; *kirīṭa*—wearing a crown; *mālī*—and a necklace; *nyaviśat*—entered; *asi*—a sword; *hastaḥ*—in his hand; *kṣipan*—insulting (the doorkeepers); *ruṣā*—angrily.

TRANSLATION

Proud Duryodhana, holding a sword in his hand and wearing a crown and necklace, angrily went into the palace in the company of his brothers, O King, insulting the doorkeepers as he entered.

PURPORT

Śrīla Prabhupāda writes that Duryodhana "was always in an envious and angry mood, and therefore, on a slight provocation, he spoke sharply with the doorkeepers and became angry."

TEXT 37

स्थलेऽभ्यगृह्णाद्वस्त्रान्तं जलं मत्वा स्थलेऽपतत् ।
जले च स्थलवद् भ्रान्त्या मयमायाविमोहितः ॥३७॥

sthale 'bhyagṛhṇād vastrāntaṁ
jalaṁ matvā sthale 'patat
jale ca sthala-vad bhrāntyā
maya-māyā-vimohitaḥ

sthale—on solid ground; *abhyagṛhṇāt*—he picked up; *vastra*—of his garment; *antam*—the end; *jalam*—water; *matvā*—thinking; *sthale*—and in another place; *apatat*—he fell; *jale*—into water; *ca*—and; *sthala*—solid ground; *vat*—as if; *bhrāntyā*—by the illusion; *maya*—of Maya Dānava; *māyā*—by the magic; *vimohitaḥ*—bewildered.

TRANSLATION

Bewildered by the illusions created through Maya Dānava's magic, Duryodhana mistook the solid floor for water and lifted the end of his garment. And elsewhere he fell into the water, mistaking it for the solid floor.

TEXT 38

जहास भीमस्तं दृष्ट्वा स्त्रियो नृपतयोऽपरे ।
निवार्यमाणा अप्यंग राज्ञा कृष्णानुमोदिताः ॥३८॥

jahāsa bhīmas taṁ dṛṣṭvā
striyo nṛpatayo 'pare
nivāryamāṇā apy aṅga
rājñā kṛṣṇānumoditāḥ

jahāsa—laughed; *bhīmaḥ*—Bhīma; *tam*—him; *dṛṣṭvā*—seeing; *striyaḥ*—the women; *nṛ-patayaḥ*—kings; *apare*—and others; *nivāryamāṇāḥ*—being checked; *api*—even though; *aṅga*—my dear (Parīkṣit); *rājñā*—by the King (Yudhiṣṭhira); *kṛṣṇa*—by Lord Kṛṣṇa; *anumoditāḥ*—approved.

TRANSLATION

My dear Parīkṣit, Bhīma laughed to see this, and so did the women, kings and others. King Yudhiṣṭhira tried to stop them, but Lord Kṛṣṇa showed His approval.

PURPORT

Śrīla Viśvanātha Cakravartī mentions that King Yudhiṣṭhira tried to check the laughter by glancing at the women and Bhīma. Lord Kṛṣṇa, however, gave approval with a gesture of His eyebrows. The Lord had come to the earth to remove the burden of wicked kings, and this incident was not unrelated to the Lord's purpose.

TEXT 39

स व्रीडितोऽवाग्वदनो रुषा ज्वलन्
निष्क्रम्य तूष्णीं प्रययौ गजाह्वयम् ।
हाहेति शब्दः सुमहानभूत्सताम्
अजातशत्रुर्विमना इवाभवत् ।
बभूव तूष्णीं भगवान् भुवो भरं
समुज्जिहीर्षुर्भ्रमति स्म यद्दृशा ॥३९॥

sa vrīḍito 'vāg-vadano ruṣā jvalan
niṣkramya tūṣṇīṁ prayayau gajāhvayam
hā-heti śabdaḥ su-mahān abhūt satām
ajāta-śatrur vimanā ivābhavat
babhūva tūṣṇīṁ bhagavān bhuvo bharaṁ
samujjihīrṣur bhramati sma yad-dṛśā

saḥ—he, Duryodhana; *vrīḍitaḥ*—embarrassed; *avāk*—held down; *vadanaḥ*—whose face; *ruṣā*—with anger; *jvalan*—burning; *niṣkramya*—exiting; *tūṣṇīm*—silently; *prayayau*—he went off; *gaja-āhvayam*—to Hastināpura; *hā-hā iti*—"alas, alas"; *śabdaḥ*—the sound; *su-mahān*—very great; *abhūt*—arose; *satām*—from the saintly persons; *ajāta-śatruḥ*—King Yudhiṣṭhira; *vimanāḥ*—depressed; *iva*—somewhat; *abhavat*—became; *babhūva*—was; *tūṣṇīm*—silent; *bhagavān*—the Supreme Lord; *bhuvaḥ*—of the earth; *bharam*—the burden; *samujjihīrṣuḥ*—wanting to remove; *bhramati sma*—(Duryodhana) became deluded; *yat*—whose; *dṛśā*—by the glance.

TRANSLATION

Humiliated and burning with anger, Duryodhana turned his face down, left without uttering a word and went back to Hastināpura. The saintly persons present loudly cried out, "Alas, alas!" and King Yudhiṣṭhira was somewhat saddened. But the Supreme Lord, whose mere glance had bewildered Duryodhana, remained silent, for His intention was to remove the burden of the earth.

PURPORT

Śrīla Prabhupāda writes, "When Duryodhana left in such an angry mood, everyone regretted the incident, and King Yudhiṣṭhira also became very sorry. But despite all occurrences, Kṛṣṇa was silent. He did not say anything against or in favor of the incident. It appeared that Duryodhana had been put into illusion by the supreme will of Lord Kṛṣṇa, and this was the beginning of the enmity between the two sects of the Kuru dynasty. This appeared to be a part of Kṛṣṇa's plan in His mission to decrease the burden of the world."

TEXT 40

एतत्तेऽभिहितं राजन् यत्पृष्टोऽहमिह त्वया ।
सुयोधनस्य दौरात्म्यं राजसूये महाक्रतौ ॥४०॥

etat te 'bhihitaṁ rājan
yat pṛṣṭo 'ham iha tvayā
suyodhanasya daurātmyaṁ
rājasūye mahā-kratau

etat—this; *te*—to you; *abhihitam*—spoken; *rājan*—O King; *yat*—what; *pṛṣṭaḥ*—asked; *aham*—I; *iha*—in this regard; *tvayā*—by you; *suyodhanasya*—of Suyodhana (Duryodhana); *daurātmyam*—the dissatisfaction; *rājasūye*—during the Rājasūya; *mahā-kratau*—the great sacrifice.

TRANSLATION

I have now replied to your question, O King, concerning why Duryodhana was dissatisfied on the occasion of the great Rājasūya sacrifice.

Thus end the purports of the humble servants of His Divine Grace A. C. Bhaktivedanta Swami Prabhupāda to the Tenth Canto, Seventy-fifth Chapter, of the Śrīmad-Bhāgavatam, *entitled "Duryodhana Humiliated."*

CHAPTER SEVENTY-SIX

The Battle Between Śālva and the Vṛṣṇis

This chapter relates how the demon Śālva acquired a huge and terrifying airship, how he used it to attack the Vṛṣṇis in Dvārakā, and how Lord Pradyumna was taken from the battlefield during the fighting that ensued.

Śālva was one of the kings who had been defeated at the time of Rukmiṇī-devī's marriage. Having vowed then that he would rid the earth of all the Yādavas, he began worshiping Lord Śiva each day by eating only a palmful of dust. After a year had passed, Śiva appeared before Śālva and asked him to choose a benediction. Śālva begged for a flying machine that could go anywhere and that would strike terror into the hearts of demigods, demons and humans alike. Lord Śiva granted this request and had Maya Dānava construct for Śālva a flying iron city named Saubha. Śālva took this vehicle to Dvārakā, where he and his huge army laid siege to the city. From his airplane Śālva bombarded Dvārakā with tree trunks, boulders and other missiles, and he produced a mighty whirlwind that obscured everything with dust.

When Pradyumna, Sātyaki and the other Yadu heroes saw the plight of Dvārakā and her residents, they went out to do battle with Śālva's forces. Pradyumna, the best of warriors, destroyed with His divine weapons all of Śālva's illusory magic, and He also bewildered Śālva himself. Thus Śālva's airplane began wandering aimlessly on the earth, in the sky and on the tops of mountains. But then a follower of Śālva's named Dyumān struck Pradyumna on the chest with his club, whereupon Pradyumna's chariot driver, thinking his master seriously injured, carried Him from the battlefield. But Pradyumna quickly regained consciousness and sharply criticized His driver for doing this.

TEXT 1

श्रीशुक उवाच
अथान्यदपि कृष्णस्य शृणु कर्माद्भुतं नृप ।
क्रीडानरशरीरस्य यथा सौभपतिर्हतः ॥१॥

śrī-śuka uvāca
athānyad api kṛṣṇasya
śṛṇu karmādbhutaṁ nṛpa
krīḍā-nara-śarīrasya
yathā saubha-patir hataḥ

śrī-śukaḥ uvāca—Śukadeva Gosvāmī said; *atha*—now; *anyat*—another; *api*—yet; *kṛṣṇasya*—of Lord Kṛṣṇa; *śṛṇu*—please hear; *karma*—deed; *adbhutam*—wonderful; *nṛpa*—O King; *krīḍā*—for playing; *nara*—humanlike; *śarīrasya*—whose body; *yathā*—how; *saubha-patiḥ*—the lord of Saubha (Śālva); *hataḥ*—killed.

TRANSLATION

Śukadeva Gosvāmī said: Now please hear, O King, another wondrous deed performed by Lord Kṛṣṇa, who appeared in His humanlike body to enjoy transcendental pastimes. Hear how He killed the master of Saubha.

TEXT 2

शिशुपालसखः शाल्वो रुक्मिण्युद्वाह आगतः ।
यदुभिर्निर्जितः संख्ये जरासन्धादयस्तथा ॥२॥

śiśupāla-sakhaḥ śālvo
rukmiṇy-udvāha āgataḥ
yadubhir nirjitaḥ saṅkhye
jarāsandhādayas tathā

śiśupāla-sakhaḥ—a friend of Śiśupāla's; *śālvaḥ*—named Śālva; *rukmiṇī-udvāhe*—to Rukmiṇī's wedding; *āgataḥ*—having come; *yadubhiḥ*—by the Yadus; *nirjitaḥ*—defeated; *saṅkhye*—in battle; *jarāsandha-ādayaḥ*—Jarāsandha and others; *tathā*—as well.

TRANSLATION

Śālva was a friend of Śiśupāla's. When he attended the wedding of Rukmiṇī, the Yadu warriors defeated him in battle, along with Jarāsandha and the other kings.

TEXT 3

शाल्वः प्रतिज्ञामकरोच्छृण्वतां सर्वभूभुजाम् ।
अयादवां क्ष्मां करिष्ये पौरुषं मम पश्यत ॥३॥

śālvaḥ pratijñām akaroc
chṛṇvatāṁ sarva-bhūbhujām
ayādavāṁ kṣmāṁ kariṣye
pauruṣaṁ mama paśyata

śālvaḥ—Śālva; *pratijñām*—a promise; *akarot*—made; *śṛṇvatām*—as they listened; *sarva*—all; *bhū-bhujām*—the kings; *ayādavām*—devoid of Yādavas; *kṣmām*—the earth; *kariṣye*—I will make; *pauruṣam*—prowess; *mama*—my; *paśyata*—just see.

TRANSLATION

Śālva swore in the presence of all the kings: "I will rid the earth of Yādavas. Just see my prowess!"

TEXT 4

इति मूढः प्रतिज्ञाय देवं पशुपतिं प्रभुम् ।
आराधयामास नृपः पांशुमुष्टिं सकृद् ग्रसन् ॥४॥

iti mūḍhaḥ pratijñāya
devaṁ paśu-patiṁ prabhum
ārādhayām āsa nṛpaḥ
pāṁśu-muṣṭiṁ sakṛd grasan

iti—with these words; *mūḍhaḥ*—the fool; *pratijñāya*—having vowed; *devam*—the lord; *paśu-patim*—Śiva, the protector of animallike men; *prabhum*—his master; *ārādhayām āsa*—worshiped; *nṛpaḥ*—the King; *pāṁśu*—of dust; *muṣṭim*—a handful; *sakṛt*—once (daily); *grasan*—eating.

TRANSLATION

Having thus made his vow, the foolish King proceeded to worship Lord Paśupati [Śiva] as his deity by eating a handful of dust each day, and nothing more.

TEXT 5

संवत्सरान्ते भगवानाशुतोष उमापतिः ।
वरेण च्छन्दयामास शाल्वं शरणमागतम् ॥५॥

saṁvatsarānte bhagavān
āśu-toṣa umā-patiḥ
vareṇa cchandayām āsa
śālvaṁ śaraṇam āgatam

saṁvatsara—of a year; *ante*—at the end; *bhagavān*—the great lord; *āśu-toṣaḥ*—he who is quickly pleased; *umā-patiḥ*—the master of Umā; *vareṇa*—with a benediction; *chandayām āsa*—had him choose; *śālvam*—Śālva; *śaraṇam*—for shelter; *āgatam*—approached.

TRANSLATION

The great Lord Umāpati is known as "he who is quickly pleased," yet only at the end of a year did he gratify Śālva, who had approached him for shelter, by offering him a choice of benedictions.

PURPORT

Śālva worshiped Lord Śiva, who is famous as Āśutoṣa, "one who is quickly satisfied." And yet Lord Śiva did not come to Śālva for an entire year because, being *bhagavān,* a great, all-knowing personality, he understood that any benediction given to Lord Kṛṣṇa's enemy would be fruitless. Still, as stated by the words *śaraṇam āgatam,* Śālva had come to Lord Śiva for shelter, and thus to maintain the standard principle that a worshiper receives a benediction, Lord Śiva offered one to Śālva.

TEXT 6

देवासुरमनुष्याणां गन्धर्वोरगरक्षसाम् ।
अभेद्यं कामगं वव्रे स यानं वृष्णिभीषणम् ॥६॥

devāsura-manuṣyāṇāṁ
gandharvoraga-rakṣasām
abhedyaṁ kāma-gaṁ vavre
sa yānaṁ vṛṣṇi-bhīṣaṇam

deva—by demigods; *asura*—demons; *manuṣyāṇām*—and humans; *gandharva*—by Gandharvas; *uraga*—celestial serpents; *rakṣasām*—and Rākṣasa spirits; *abhedyam*—indestructible; *kāma*—at will; *gam*—traveling; *vavre*—chose; *saḥ*—he; *yānam*—a vehicle; *vṛṣṇi*—for the Vṛṣṇis; *bhīṣaṇam*—terrifying.

TRANSLATION

Śālva chose a vehicle that could be destroyed by neither demigods, demons, humans, Gandharvas, Uragas nor Rākṣasas, that could travel anywhere he wished to go, and that would terrify the Vṛṣṇis.

TEXT 7

तथेति गिरिशादिष्टो मयः परपुरंजयः ।
पुरं निर्माय शाल्वाय प्रादात्सौभमयस्मयम् ॥७॥

tatheti giriśādiṣṭo
mayaḥ para-puraṁ-jayaḥ
puraṁ nirmāya śālvāya
prādāt saubham ayas-mayam

tathā—so be it; *iti*—having thus said; *giri-śa*—by Lord Śiva; *ādiṣṭaḥ*—ordered; *mayaḥ*—Maya Dānava; *para*—of the enemy; *puram*—the cities; *jayaḥ*—who conquers; *puram*—a city; *nirmāya*—constructing; *śālvāya*—to Śālva; *prādāt*—he gave; *saubham*—named Saubha; *ayaḥ*—of iron; *mayam*—made.

TRANSLATION

Lord Śiva said, "So be it." On his order, Maya Dānava, who conquers his enemies' cities, constructed a flying iron city named Saubha and presented it to Śālva.

TEXT 8

स लब्ध्वा कामगं यानं तमोधाम दुरासदम् ।
ययौ द्वारवतीं शाल्वो वैरं वृष्णिकृतं स्मरन् ॥८॥

sa labdhvā kāma-gaṁ yānaṁ
tamo-dhāma durāsadam
yayau dvāravatīṁ śālvo
vairaṁ vṛṣṇi-kṛtaṁ smaran

saḥ—he; *labdhvā*—obtaining; *kāma-gam*—moving at his will; *yānam*—the vehicle; *tamaḥ*—of darkness; *dhāma*—abode; *durāsadam*—unapproachable; *yayau*—went; *dvāravatīm*—to Dvārakā; *śālvaḥ*—Śālva; *vairam*—the enmity; *vṛṣṇi-kṛtam*—shown by the Vṛṣṇis; *smaran*—remembering.

TRANSLATION

This unassailable vehicle was filled with darkness and could go anywhere. Upon obtaining it, Śālva went to Dvārakā, remembering the Vṛṣṇis' enmity toward him.

TEXTS 9–11

निरुध्य सेनया शाल्वो महत्या भरतर्षभ ।
पुरीं बभञ्जोपवनानुद्यानानि च सर्वशः ॥९॥
सगोपुराणि द्वाराणि प्रासादाट्टालतोलिकाः ।
विहारान् स विमानाग्र्यान्निपेतुः शस्त्रवृष्टयः ॥१०॥
शिलाद्रुमाश्चाशनयः सर्पा आसारशर्कराः ।
प्रचण्डश्चक्रवातोऽभूद् रजसाच्छादिता दिशः ॥११॥

nirudhya senayā śālvo
mahatyā bharatarṣabha
purīṁ babhañjopavanān
udyānāni ca sarvaśaḥ

sa-gopurāṇi dvārāṇi
prāsādāṭṭāla-tolikāḥ
vihārān sa vimānāgryān
nipetuḥ śastra-vṛṣṭayaḥ

śilā-drumāś cāśanayaḥ
sarpā āsāra-śarkarāḥ
pracaṇḍaś cakravāto 'bhūd
rajasācchāditā diśaḥ

nirudhya—besieging; *senayā*—with an army; *śālvaḥ*—Śālva; *mahatyā*—large; *bharata-ṛsabha*—O best of the Bharatas; *purīm*—the city; *babhañja*—he broke up; *upavanān*—the parks; *udyanāni*—gardens; *ca*—and; *sarvaśaḥ*—all around; *sa-gopurāṇi*—with towers; *dvārāṇi*—and gateways; *prāsāda*—mansions; *aṭṭāla*—observatories; *tolikāḥ*—and surrounding walls; *vihārān*—recreational areas; *saḥ*—he, Śālva; *vimāna*—of airships; *agryāt*—from the best; *nipetuḥ*—there fell; *śastra*—of weapons; *vṛṣṭayaḥ*—torrents; *śilā*—stones; *drumāḥ*—and trees; *ca*—also; *aśanayaḥ*—thunderbolts; *sarpāḥ*—snakes; *āsāra-śarkarāḥ*—and hailstones; *pracaṇḍaḥ*—fierce; *cakravātaḥ*—a whirlwind; *abhūt*—arose; *rajasā*—with dust; *ācchāditāḥ*—covered; *diśaḥ*—all the directions.

TRANSLATION

Śālva besieged the city with a large army, O best of the Bharatas, decimating the outlying parks and gardens, the mansions along with their observatories, towering gateways and surrounding walls, and also the public recreational areas. From his excellent airship he threw down a torrent of weapons, including stones, tree trunks, thunderbolts, snakes and hailstones. A fierce whirlwind arose and blanketed all directions with dust.

TEXT 12

इत्यर्द्यमाना सौभेन कृष्णस्य नगरी भृशम् ।
नाभ्यपद्यत शं राजंस्त्रिपुरेण यथा मही ॥१२॥

ity ardyamānā saubhena
kṛṣṇasya nagarī bhṛśam
nābhyapadyata śaṁ rājaṁs
tri-pureṇa yathā mahī

iti—thus; *ardyamānā*—tormented; *saubhena*—by the airplane Saubha; *kṛṣṇasya*—of Lord Kṛṣṇa; *nagarī*—the city; *bhṛśam*—terribly; *na abhyapadyata*—could not have; *śam*—peace; *rājan*—O King; *tri-pureṇa*—by the three aerial cities of the demons; *yathā*—as; *mahī*—the earth.

TRANSLATION

Thus terribly tormented by the airship Saubha, Lord Kṛṣṇa's city had no peace, O King, just like the earth when it was attacked by the three aerial cities of the demons.

TEXT 13

प्रद्युम्नो भगवान् वीक्ष्य बाध्यमाना निजाः प्रजाः ।
मा भैष्टेत्यभ्यधाद्वीरो रथारूढो महायशाः ॥१३॥

pradyumno bhagavān vīkṣya
bādhyamānā nijāḥ prajāḥ
mā bhaiṣṭety abhyadhād vīro
rathārūḍho mahā-yaśāḥ

pradyumnaḥ—Pradyumna; *bhagavān*—the Lord; *vīkṣya*—seeing; *bādhyamānāḥ*—being harassed; *nijāḥ*—His own; *prajāḥ*—subjects; *mā bhaiṣṭa*—do not fear; *iti*—thus; *abhyadhāt*—addressed; *vīraḥ*—the great hero; *ratha*—on His chariot; *ārūḍhaḥ*—mounted; *mahā*—immense; *yaśāḥ*—whose glory.

TRANSLATION

Seeing His subjects so harassed, the glorious and heroic Lord Pradyumna told them, "Do not fear," and mounted His chariot.

TEXTS 14–15

सात्यकिश्चारुदेष्णश्च साम्बोऽक्रूरः सहानुजः ।
हार्दिक्यो भानुविन्दश्च गदश्च शुकसारणौ ॥१४॥
अपरे च महेष्वासा रथयूथपयूथपाः ।
निर्ययुर्दंशिता गुप्ता रथेभाश्वपदातिभिः ॥१५॥

sātyakiś cārudeṣṇaś ca
sāmbo 'krūraḥ sahānujaḥ
hārdikyo bhānuvindaś ca
gadaś ca śuka-sāraṇau

apare ca maheṣv-āsā
ratha-yūthapa-yūthapāḥ
niryayur daṁśitā guptā
rathebhāśva-padātibhiḥ

sātyakiḥ cārudeṣṇaḥ ca—Sātyaki and Cārudeṣṇa; *sāmbaḥ*—Sāmba; *akrūraḥ*—and Akrūra; *saha*—with; *anujaḥ*—younger brothers; *hārdikyaḥ*—Hārdikya; *bhānuvindaḥ*—Bhānuvinda; *ca*—and; *gadaḥ*—Gada; *ca*—and; *śuka-sāraṇau*—Śuka and Sāraṇa; *apare*—others; *ca*—also; *mahā*—eminent; *iṣv-āsāḥ*—archers; *ratha*—of chariot (warriors); *yūthapa*—of the leaders; *yūtha-pāḥ*—the leaders; *niryayuḥ*—they went out; *daṁśitāḥ*—wearing armor; *guptāḥ*—protected; *ratha*—by (soldiers on) chariots; *ibha*—elephants; *aśva*—and horses; *padātibhiḥ*—and by foot soldiers.

TRANSLATION

The chief commanders of the chariot warriors—Sātyaki, Cārudeṣṇa, Sāmba, Akrūra and his younger brothers, along with Hārdikya, Bhānuvinda, Gada, Śuka and Sāraṇa—went out of the city with many other eminent bowmen, all girded in armor and

protected by contingents of soldiers riding on chariots, elephants and horses, and also by companies of infantry.

TEXT 16

ततः प्रववृते युद्धं शाल्वानां यदुभिः सह ।
यथासुराणां विबुधैस्तुमुलं लोमहर्षणम् ॥१६॥

tataḥ pravavṛte yuddhaṁ
śālvānāṁ yadubhiḥ saha
yathāsurāṇāṁ vibudhais
tumulaṁ loma-harṣaṇam

tataḥ—then; *pravavṛte*—began; *yuddham*—a battle; *śālvānām*—of the followers of Śālva; *yadubhiḥ saha*—with the Yadus; *yathā*—just like; *asurāṇām*—of the demons; *vibudhaiḥ*—with the demigods; *tumulam*—tumultuous; *loma-harṣaṇam*—making bodily hair stand on end.

TRANSLATION

A tumultuous, hair-raising battle then commenced between Śālva's forces and the Yadus. It equaled the great battles between the demons and demigods.

TEXT 17

ताश्च सौभपतेर्माया दिव्यास्त्रै रुक्मिणीसुतः ।
क्षणेन नाशयामास नैशं तम इवोष्णगुः ॥१७॥

tāś ca saubha-pater māyā
divyāstrai rukmiṇī-sutaḥ
kṣaṇena nāśayām āsa
naiśaṁ tama ivoṣṇa-guḥ

tāḥ—those; *ca*—and; *saubha-pateḥ*—of the master of Saubha; *māyāḥ*—the magic illusions; *divya*—divine; *astraiḥ*—with weapons; *rukmiṇī-sutaḥ*—the son of Rukmiṇī (Pradyumna); *kṣaṇena*—in an instant; *nāśayām āsa*—destroyed; *naiśam*—of the night; *tamaḥ*—the darkness; *iva*—as; *uṣṇa*—warm; *guḥ*—whose rays (the sun).

TRANSLATION

With His divine weapons Pradyumna instantly destroyed all of Śālva's magic illusions, in the same way that the warm rays of the sun dissipate the darkness of night.

TEXTS 18–19

विव्याध पञ्चविंशत्या स्वर्णपुंखैरयोमुखैः ।
शाल्वस्य ध्वजिनीपालं शरैः सन्नतपर्वभिः ॥१८॥
शतेनाताडयच्छाल्वमेकैकेनास्य सैनिकान् ।
दशभिर्दशभिर्नेतॄन् वाहनानि त्रिभिस्त्रिभिः ॥१९॥

vivyādha pañca-viṁśatyā
svarṇa-puṅkhair ayo-mukhaiḥ
śālvasya dhvajinī-pālaṁ
śaraiḥ sannata-parvabhiḥ

śatenātāḍayac chālvam
ekaikenāsya sainikān
daśabhir daśabhir netṝn
vāhanāni tribhis tribhiḥ

vivyādha—He shot; *pañca*—five; *viṁśatyā*—plus twenty; *svarṇa*—gold; *puṅkhaiḥ*—whose shafts; *ayaḥ*—iron; *mukhaiḥ*—whose heads; *śālvasya*—of Śālva; *dhvajinī-pālam*—the commander-in-chief; *śaraiḥ*—with arrows; *sannata*—level; *parvabhiḥ*—whose joints; *śatena*—with one hundred; *atāḍayat*—He struck; *śālvam*—Śālva; *eka-ekena*—with one each; *asya*—his; *sainikān*—officers; *daśabhiḥ daśabhiḥ*—with ten each; *netṝn*—the chariot drivers; *vāhanāni*—the carriers; *tribhiḥ tribhiḥ*—with three each.

TRANSLATION

Lord Pradyumna's arrows all had gold shafts, iron heads and perfectly smooth joints. With twenty-five of them He struck down

Śālva's commander-in-chief [Dyumān], and with one hundred He struck Śālva himself. Then He pierced Śālva's officers with one arrow each, his chariot drivers with ten arrows each, and his horses and other carriers with three arrows each.

TEXT 20

तदद्भुतं महत्कर्म प्रद्युम्नस्य महात्मनः ।
दृष्ट्वा तं पूजयामासुः सर्वे स्वपरसैनिकाः ॥२०॥

tad adbhutaṁ mahat karma
pradyumnasya mahātmanaḥ
dṛṣṭvā taṁ pūjayām āsuḥ
sarve sva-para-sainikāḥ

tat—that; *adbhutam*—amazing; *mahat*—mighty; *karma*—feat; *pradyumnasya*—of Pradyumna; *mahā-ātmanaḥ*—the great personality; *dṛṣṭvā*—seeing; *tam*—Him; *pūjayām āsuḥ*—honored; *sarve*—all; *sva*—of His own side; *para*—and of the enemy side; *sainikāḥ*—the soldiers.

TRANSLATION

When they saw the glorious Pradyumna perform that amazing and mighty feat, all the soldiers on both sides praised Him.

TEXT 21

बहुरूपैकरूपं तद्दृश्यते न च दृश्यते ।
मायामयं मयकृतं दुर्विभाव्यं परैरभूत् ॥२१॥

bahu-rūpaika-rūpaṁ tad
dṛśyate na ca dṛśyate
māyā-mayaṁ maya-kṛtaṁ
durvibhāvyaṁ parair abhūt

bahu—with many; *rūpa*—forms; *eka*—with one; *rūpam*—form; *tat*—that (Saubha airship); *dṛśyate*—is seen; *na*—not; *ca*—and; *dṛśyate*—is seen; *māyā-mayam*—magical; *maya*—by Maya Dānava; *kṛtam*—made; *durvibhāvyam*—impossible to find; *paraiḥ*—by the enemy (the Yādavas); *abhūt*—it became.

TRANSLATION

At one moment the magic airship built by Maya Dānava appeared in many identical forms, and the next moment it was again only one. Sometimes it was visible, and sometimes not. Thus Śālva's opponents could never be sure where it was.

TEXT 22

क्वचिद् भूमौ क्वचिद्व्योम्नि गिरिमूर्ध्नि जले क्वचित् ।
अलातचक्रवद् भ्राम्यत्सौभं तद्दुरवस्थितम् ॥२२॥

kvacid bhūmau kvacid vyomni
giri-mūrdhni jale kvacit
alāta-cakra-vad bhrāmyat
saubhaṁ tad duravasthitam

kvacit—at one moment; *bhūmau*—on the earth; *kvacit*—at one moment; *vyomni*—in the sky; *giri*—of a mountain; *mūrdhni*—on the top; *jale*—in the water; *kvacit*—at one moment; *alāta-cakra*—a whirling firebrand; *vat*—like; *bhrāmyat*—wandering; *saubham*—Saubha; *tat*—that; *duravasthitam*—never remaining in one place.

TRANSLATION

From one moment to the next the Saubha airship appeared on the earth, in the sky, on a mountain peak or in the water. Like a whirling, flaming baton, it never remained in any one place.

TEXT 23

यत्र यत्रोपलक्ष्येत ससौभः सहसैनिकः ।
शाल्वस्ततस्ततोऽमुञ्चञ् छरान् सात्वतयूथपाः ॥२३॥

yatra yatropalakṣyeta
sa-saubhaḥ saha-sainikaḥ
śālvas tatas tato 'muñcañ
charān sātvata-yūthapāḥ

yatra yatra—wherever; *upalakṣyeta*—would appear; *sa-saubhaḥ*—with Saubha; *saha-sainikaḥ*—with his soldiers; *śālvaḥ*—Śālva; *tataḥ tataḥ*—in each of those locations; *amuñcan*—they released; *śarān*—their arrows; *sātvata*—of the Yadus; *yūtha-pāḥ*—the chiefs of the army.

TRANSLATION

Wherever Śālva would appear with his Saubha ship and his army, there the Yadu commanders would shoot their arrows.

TEXT 24

शरैरग्न्यर्कसंस्पर्शैराशीविषदुरासदैः ।
पीड्यमानपुरानीकः शाल्वोऽमुह्यत्परेरितैः ॥२४॥

śarair agny-arka-saṁsparśair
āśī-viṣa-durāsadaiḥ
pīḍyamāna-purānīkaḥ
śālvo 'muhyat pareritaiḥ

śaraiḥ—by the arrows; *agni*—like fire; *arka*—and like the sun; *saṁsparśaiḥ*—whose contact; *āśī*—of a snake; *viṣa*—like the poison; *durāsadaiḥ*—intolerable; *pīḍyamāna*—distressed; *pura*—whose aerial city; *anīkaḥ*—and whose army; *śālvaḥ*—Śālva; *amuhyat*—became bewildered; *para*—by the enemy; *īritaiḥ*—shot.

TRANSLATION

Śālva became bewildered upon seeing his army and aerial city thus harassed by his enemy's arrows, which struck like fire and the sun and were as intolerable as snake venom.

PURPORT

Śrīla Śrīdhara Svāmī explains that the arrows of the Yadu commanders burned like fire, struck simultaneously from all sides like the sun's rays, and, like snake venom, were lethal by a single touch.

TEXT 25

शाल्वानीकपशस्त्रौघैर्वृष्णिवीरा भृशार्दिताः ।
न तत्यजू रणं स्वं स्वं लोकद्वयजिगीषवः ॥२५॥

śālvānīkapa-śastraughair
vṛṣṇi-vīrā bhṛśārditāḥ
na tatyajū raṇaṁ svaṁ svaṁ
loka-dvaya-jigīṣavaḥ

śālva—of Śālva; *anīka-pa*—of the leaders of the army; *śastra*—of weapons; *oghaiḥ*—by floods; *vṛṣṇi-vīrāḥ*—the heroes of the Vṛṣṇi clan; *bhṛśa*—extremely; *arditāḥ*—pained; *na tatyajuḥ*—they did not abandon; *raṇam*—the places on the battlefield; *svam svam*—each their own; *loka*—the worlds; *dvaya*—two; *jigīṣavaḥ*—wishing to conquer.

TRANSLATION

Because the heroes of the Vṛṣṇi clan were eager for victory in this world and the next, they did not abandon their assigned posts on the battlefield, even though the downpour of weapons hurled by Śālva's commanders tormented them.

PURPORT

Śrīla Prabhupāda writes, "The heroes of the Yadu dynasty were determined to either die on the battlefield or gain victory. They were confident of the fact that if they would die in the fighting they would attain a heavenly planet, and if they would come out victorious they would enjoy the world."

TEXT 26

शाल्वामात्यो द्युमान्नाम प्रद्युम्नं प्राक् प्रपीडितः ।
आसाद्य गदया मौर्व्या व्याहत्य व्यनदद् बली ॥२६॥

śālvāmātyo dyumān nāma
pradyumnaṁ prāk prapīḍitaḥ
āsādya gadayā maurvyā
vyāhatya vyanadad balī

śālva-amātyaḥ—Śālva's minister; *dyumān nāma*—named Dyumān; *pradyumnam*—Pradyumna; *prāk*—previously; *prapīḍitaḥ*—hurt; *āsādya*—confronting; *gadayā*—with his club; *maurvyā*—made of carbonized iron; *vyāhatya*—striking; *vyanadat*—roared; *balī*—powerful.

TRANSLATION

Śālva's minister Dyumān, previously wounded by Śrī Pradyumna, now ran up to Him and, roaring loudly, struck Him with his club of black steel.

TEXT 27

प्रद्युम्नं गदया शीर्णवक्षःस्थलमरिंदमम् ।
अपोवाह रणात्सूतो धर्मविद्दारुकात्मजः ॥२७॥

pradyumnaṁ gadayā śīrṇa-
vakṣaḥ-sthalam ariṁ-damam
apovāha raṇāt sūto
dharma-vid dārukātmajaḥ

pradyumnam—Pradyumna; *gadayā*—by the club; *śīrṇa*—shattered; *vakṣaḥ-sthalam*—whose chest; *arim*—of enemies; *damam*—the subduer; *apovāha*—removed; *raṇāt*—from the battlefield; *sūtaḥ*—His chariot driver; *dharma*—of his religious duty; *vit*—the expert knower; *dāruka-ātmajaḥ*—the son of Dāruka (Lord Kṛṣṇa's driver).

TRANSLATION

Pradyumna's driver, the son of Dāruka, thought that his valiant master's chest had been shattered by the club. Knowing well his religious duty, he removed Pradyumna from the battlefield.

PURPORT

Śrīla Viśvanātha Cakravartī explains that actually Lord Pradyumna has a *sac-cid-ānanda* body, an eternal, spiritual form that can never be wounded by mundane weapons. Dāruka's son, however, was a great devotee of the Lord, and out of intense love he feared for the safety of his master and thus removed Him from the battlefield.

Śrīla Prabhupāda writes, "The name of Śālva's commander-in-chief was Dyumān. He was very powerful, and although bitten by twenty-five of Pradyumna's arrows, he suddenly attacked Pradyumna with his fierce club and struck Him so strongly that Pradyumna became unconscious. Immediately there was a roaring, 'Now He is dead! Now He is dead!' The force of the club on Pradyumna's chest was very severe, enough to tear asunder the chest of an ordinary man."

TEXT 28

लब्धसंज्ञो मुहूर्तेन कार्ष्णिः सारथिमब्रवीत् ।
अहो असाध्विदं सूत यद् रणान्मेऽपसर्पणम् ॥२८॥

labdha-saṁjño muhūrtena
kārṣṇiḥ sārathim abravīt
aho asādhv idaṁ sūta
yad raṇān me 'pasarpaṇam

labdha—attaining; *saṁjñaḥ*—consciousness; *muhūrtena*—in a moment; *kārṣṇiḥ*—the son of Lord Kṛṣṇa; *sārathim*—to His chariot driver; *abravīt*—said; *aho*—ah; *asādhu*—improper; *idam*—this; *sūta*—O driver; *yat*—which; *raṇāt*—from the battlefield; *me*—My; *apasarpaṇam*—being taken away.

TRANSLATION

Quickly regaining consciousness, Lord Kṛṣṇa's son Pradyumna said to His charioteer, "O driver, this is abominable—for Me to have been removed from the battlefield!

TEXT 29

न यदूनां कुले जातः श्रूयते रणविच्युतः ।
विना मत् क्लीबचित्तेन सूतेन प्राप्तकिल्बिषात् ॥२९॥

na yadūnāṁ kule jātaḥ
śrūyate raṇa-vicyutaḥ
vinā mat klība-cittena
sūtena prāpta-kilbiṣāt

na—not; *yadūnām*—of the Yadus; *kule*—in the family; *jātaḥ*—one who was born; *śrūyate*—is heard of; *raṇa*—the battlefield; *vicyutaḥ*—who abandoned; *vinā*—except for; *mat*—Me; *klība*—like that of a eunuch; *cittena*—whose mentality; *sūtena*—because of the driver; *prāpta*—gotten; *kilbiṣāt*—stain.

TRANSLATION

"Except for Me, no one born in the Yadu dynasty has ever been known to abandon the battlefield. My reputation has now been stained by a driver who thinks like a eunuch.

TEXT 30

किं नु वक्ष्येऽभिसंगम्य पितरौ रामकेशवौ ।
युद्धात्सम्यगपक्रान्तः पृष्टस्तत्रात्मनः क्षमम् ॥३०॥

kiṁ nu vakṣye 'bhisaṅgamya
pitarau rāma-keśavau
yuddhāt samyag apakrāntaḥ
pṛṣṭas tatrātmanaḥ kṣamam

kim—what; *nu*—then; *vakṣye*—will I say; *abhisaṅgamya*—meeting; *pitarau*—with My fathers; *rāma-keśavau*—Balarāma and Kṛṣṇa; *yuddhāt*—from the battle; *samyak*—altogether; *apakrāntaḥ*—fled; *pṛṣṭaḥ*—questioned; *tatra*—in that case; *ātmanaḥ*—for My self; *kṣamam*—fitting.

TRANSLATION

"What will I say to My fathers, Rāma and Keśava, when I return to Them after having simply fled the battle? What can I tell Them that will befit My honor?

PURPORT

Śrī Pradyumna here uses the word *pitarau*, "fathers," loosely. Lord Balarāma was of course His uncle.

TEXT 31

व्यक्तं मे कथयिष्यन्ति हसन्त्यो भ्रातृजामयः ।
क्लैब्यं कथं कथं वीर तवान्यैः कथ्यतां मृधे ॥३१॥

vyaktaṁ me kathayiṣyanti
hasantyo bhrātṛ-jāmayaḥ
klaibyaṁ kathaṁ kathaṁ vīra
tavānyaiḥ kathyatāṁ mṛdhe

vyaktam—certainly; *me*—My; *kathayiṣyanti*—will speak of; *hasantyaḥ*—laughing; *bhrātṛ-jāmayaḥ*—My brothers' wives; *klaibyam*—unmanliness; *katham*—how; *katham*—how; *vīra*—O hero; *tava*—Your; *anyaiḥ*—by Your enemies; *kathyatām*—tell us; *mṛdhe*—in battle.

TRANSLATION

"Certainly My sisters-in-law will laugh at Me and say, 'O hero, tell us how in the world Your enemies turned You into such a coward in battle.'"

TEXT 32

सारथिरुवाच
धर्मं विजानतायुष्मन् कृतमेतन्मया विभो ।
सूतः कृच्छ्रगतं रक्षेद् रथिनं सारथिं रथी ॥३२॥

sārathir uvāca
dharmaṁ vijānatāyuṣman
kṛtam etan mayā vibho
sūtaḥ kṛcchra-gataṁ rakṣed
rathinaṁ sārathiṁ rathī

sārathiḥ uvāca—the driver said; *dharmam*—prescribed duty; *vijānatā*—by one who properly understood; *āyuḥ-man*—O long-lived one; *kṛtam*—done; *etat*—this; *mayā*—by me; *vibho*—O my Lord; *sūtaḥ*—a driver; *kṛcchra*—into difficulty; *gatam*—gone; *rakṣet*—should protect; *rathinam*—the master of the chariot; *sārathim*—his charioteer; *rathī*—the chariot owner.

TRANSLATION

The driver replied: O long-lived one, I have done this knowing full well my prescribed duty. O my Lord, the chariot driver must protect the master of the chariot when he is in danger, and the master must also protect his driver.

TEXT 33

एतद्विदित्वा तु भवान्मयापोवाहितो रणात् ।
उपसृष्टः परेणेति मूर्च्छितो गदया हतः ॥३३॥

etad viditvā tu bhavān
mayāpovāhito raṇāt
upasṛṣṭaḥ pareṇeti
mūrcchito gadayā hataḥ

etat—this; *viditvā*—knowing; *tu*—indeed; *bhavān*—You; *mayā*—by me; *apovāhitaḥ*—removed; *raṇāt*—from the battlefield; *upasṛṣṭaḥ*—hurt;

pareṇa—by the enemy; *iti*—thus thinking; *mūrcchitaḥ*—unconscious; *gadayā*—by his club; *hataḥ*—struck.

TRANSLATION

With this rule in mind, I removed You from the battlefield, since You had been struck unconscious by Your enemy's club and I thought You were seriously injured.

Thus end the purports of the humble servants of His Divine Grace A. C. Bhaktivedanta Swami Prabhupāda to the Tenth Canto, Seventy-sixth Chapter, of the Śrīmad-Bhāgavatam, *entitled "The Battle Between Śālva and the Vṛṣṇis."*

CHAPTER SEVENTY-SEVEN

Lord Kṛṣṇa Slays the Demon Śālva

This chapter describes how Lord Śrī Kṛṣṇa disposed of Śālva, the master of deception, and destroyed his airship Saubha.

Having been removed from the battlefield, Pradyumna was extremely ashamed, and He ordered His driver to take His chariot once again into the presence of Dyumān. As Pradyumna fought with Dyumān, other Yadu heroes like Gada, Sātyaki, and Sāmba began to create havoc among Śālva's army. The battle continued in this way for twenty-seven days and nights.

When Lord Kṛṣṇa returned to Dvārakā, He found it under siege. At once He ordered Dāruka to drive Him onto the battlefield. Suddenly Śālva noticed the Lord and threw his spear at Kṛṣṇa's charioteer, but the Lord shattered the weapon into hundreds of pieces and pierced Śālva and his Saubha vehicle with numerous arrows. Śālva responded by shooting an arrow that struck Kṛṣṇa's left arm. Amazingly, the Lord dropped the Śārṅga bow He was holding in His left hand. The demigods watching the battle cried out in alarm upon seeing the bow fall, while Śālva took the opportunity to insult Kṛṣṇa.

Lord Kṛṣṇa then struck Śālva with His club, but the demon, vomiting blood, disappeared. A moment later a man came before Lord Kṛṣṇa and, after offering Him obeisances, introduced himself as a messenger from mother Devakī. The man informed the Lord that His father, Vasudeva, had been kidnapped by Śālva. Upon hearing this, Lord Kṛṣṇa seemed to lament like an ordinary man. Śālva then led forward someone who looked just like Vasudeva, decapitated him and took the head with him into his Saubha airship. Lord Śrī Kṛṣṇa, however, could understand the magic tricks of Śālva. Thus He pierced Śālva with a shower of arrows and struck the Saubha vehicle with His club, demolishing it. Śālva descended from his airplane and rushed toward Lord Kṛṣṇa to attack Him, but the Lord took up His Sudarśana disc and severed Śālva's head from his body.

With the killing of Śālva, the demigods in the sky played kettledrums in jubilation. The demon Dantavakra then took a vow to avenge his friend Śālva's death.

TEXT 1

श्रीशुक उवाच
स उपस्पृश्य सलिलं दंशितो धृतकार्मुकः ।
नय मां द्युमतः पार्श्वं वीरस्येत्याह सारथिम् ॥१॥

śrī-śuka uvāca
sa upaspṛśya salilaṁ
daṁśito dhṛta-kārmukaḥ
naya māṁ dyumataḥ pārśvaṁ
vīrasyety āha sārathim

śrī-śukaḥ uvāca—Śukadeva Gosvāmī said; *saḥ*—He (Pradyumna); *upaspṛśya*—touching; *salilam*—water; *daṁśitaḥ*—fastening His armor; *dhṛta*—taking up; *kārmukaḥ*—His bow; *naya*—take; *mām*—Me; *dyumataḥ*—of Dyumān; *pārśvam*—to the side; *vīrasya*—of the hero; *iti*—thus; *āha*—He spoke; *sārathim*—to His driver.

TRANSLATION

Śukadeva Gosvāmī said: After refreshing Himself with water, putting on His armor and picking up His bow, Lord Pradyumna told His driver, "Take Me back to where the hero Dyumān is standing."

PURPORT

Pradyumna was eager to rectify the discrepancy of His having left the battlefield when His chariot driver carried Him away unconscious.

TEXT 2

विधमन्तं स्वसैन्यानि द्युमन्तं रुक्मिणीसुतः ।
प्रतिहत्य प्रत्यविध्यान्नाराचैरष्टभिः स्मयन् ॥२॥

vidhamantaṁ sva-sainyāni
dyumantaṁ rukmiṇī-sutaḥ
pratihatya pratyavidhyān
nārācair aṣṭabhiḥ smayan

vidhamantam—smashing; *sva*—His; *sainyāni*—soldiers; *dyumantam*—Dyumān; *rukmiṇī-sutaḥ*—the son of Rukmiṇī (Pradyumna); *pratihatya*—counterattacking; *pratyavidhyāt*—He struck back; *nārācaiḥ*—with special arrows made of iron; *aṣṭabhiḥ*—eight; *smayan*—while smiling.

TRANSLATION

In Pradyumna's absence, Dyumān had been devastating His army, but now Pradyumna counterattacked Dyumān and, smiling, pierced him with eight *nārāca* arrows.

PURPORT

Śrīla Viśvanātha Cakravartī comments that Pradyumna challenged Dyumān, saying "Now see if you can strike Me!" After saying this and allowing Dyumān to shoot his weapons, Pradyumna released His own deadly arrows.

TEXT 3

चतुर्भिश्चतुरो वाहान् सूतमेकेन चाहनत् ।
द्वाभ्यां धनुश्च केतुं च शरेणान्येन वै शिरः ॥३॥

caturbhiś caturo vāhān
sūtam ekena cāhanat
dvābhyāṁ dhanuś ca ketuṁ ca
śareṇānyena vai śiraḥ

caturbhiḥ—with four (arrows); *caturaḥ*—four; *vāhān*—carriers; *sūtam*—the driver; *ekena*—with one; *ca*—and; *ahanat*—He struck; *dvābhyām*—with two; *dhanuḥ*—the bow; *ca*—and; *ketum*—the flag; *ca*—and; *śareṇa*—with an arrow; *anyena*—another; *vai*—indeed; *śiraḥ*—the head.

TRANSLATION

With four of these arrows He struck Dyumān's four horses, with one arrow, his driver, with two more arrows, his bow and chariot flag, and with the last arrow, Dyumān's head.

TEXT 4

गदसात्यकिसाम्बाद्या जघ्नुः सौभपतेर्बलम् ।
पेतुः समुद्रे सौभेयाः सर्वे सञ्छिन्नकन्धराः ॥४॥

gada-sātyaki-sāmbādyā
jaghnuḥ saubha-pater balam
petuḥ samudre saubheyāḥ
sarve sañchinna-kandharāḥ

gada-sātyaki-sāmba-ādyāḥ—Gada, Sātyaki, Sāmba and others; *jaghnuḥ*—they killed; *saubha-pateḥ*—of the master of Saubha (Śālva); *balam*—the army; *petuḥ*—they fell; *samudre*—into the ocean; *saubheyāḥ*—those who were standing inside Saubha; *sarve*—all; *sañchinna*—cut through; *kandharāḥ*—whose necks.

TRANSLATION

Gada, Sātyaki, Sāmba and others began killing Śālva's army, and thus all the soldiers inside the airship began falling into the ocean, their necks severed.

TEXT 5

एवं यदूनां शाल्वानां निघ्नतामितरेतरम् ।
युद्धं त्रिनवरात्रं तदभूत्तुमुलमुल्बणम् ॥५॥

evaṁ yadūnāṁ śālvānāṁ
nighnatām itaretaram
yuddhaṁ tri-nava-rātraṁ tad
abhūt tumulam ulbaṇam

evam—thus; *yadūnām*—of the Yadus; *śālvānām*—and the followers of Śālva; *nighnatām*—striking; *itara-itaram*—one another; *yuddham*—fight; *tri*—three times; *nava*—nine; *rātram*—for nights; *tat*—that; *abhūt*—was; *tumulam*—tumultuous; *ulbaṇam*—fearsome.

TRANSLATION

As the Yadus and Śālva's followers thus went on attacking one another, the tumultuous, fearsome battle continued for twenty-seven days and nights.

TEXTS 6–7

इन्द्रप्रस्थं गतः कृष्ण आहूतो धर्मसूनुना ।
राजसूयेऽथ निवृत्ते शिशुपाले च संस्थिते ॥६॥
कुरुवृद्धाननुज्ञाप्य मुनींश्च ससुतां पृथाम् ।
निमित्तान्यतिघोराणि पश्यन् द्वारवतीं ययौ ॥७॥

indraprasthaṁ gataḥ kṛṣṇa
āhūto dharma-sūnunā
rājasūye 'tha nivṛtte
śiśupāle ca saṁsthite

kuru-vṛddhān anujñāpya
munīṁś ca sa-sutāṁ pṛthām
nimittāny ati-ghorāṇi
paśyan dvāravatīṁ yayau

indraprastham—to Indraprastha, the capital of the Pāṇḍavas; *gataḥ*—gone; *kṛṣṇaḥ*—Lord Kṛṣṇa; *āhūtaḥ*—called; *dharma-sūnunā*—by the son of Yamarāja, religion personified (King Yudhiṣṭhira); *rājasūye*—the Rājasūya sacrifice; *atha*—then; *nivṛtte*—when it was complete; *śiśupāle*—Śiśupāla; *ca*—and; *saṁsthite*—when he had been killed; *kuru-vṛddhān*—of the elders of the Kuru dynasty; *anujñāpya*—taking leave; *munīn*—of the sages; *ca*—and; *sa*—with; *sutām*—her sons (the Pāṇḍavas); *pṛthām*—of Queen Kuntī; *nimittāni*—bad omens; *ati*—very; *ghorāṇi*—terrible; *paśyan*—seeing; *dvāravatīm*—to Dvārakā; *yayau*—He went.

TRANSLATION

Invited by Yudhiṣṭhira, the son of Dharma, Lord Kṛṣṇa had gone to Indraprastha. Now that the Rājasūya sacrifice had been

completed and Śiśupāla killed, the Lord began to see inauspicious omens. So He took leave of the Kuru elders and the great sages, and also of Pṛthā and her sons, and returned to Dvārakā.

TEXT 8

आह चाहमिहायात आर्यमिश्राभिसंगतः ।
राजन्याश्चैद्यपक्षीया नूनं हन्युः पुरीं मम ॥८॥

āha cāham ihāyāta
ārya-miśrābhisaṅgataḥ
rājanyāś caidya-pakṣīyā
nūnaṁ hanyuḥ purīṁ mama

āha—He said; *ca*—and; *aham*—I; *iha*—to this place (Indraprastha); *āyātaḥ*—having come; *ārya*—by My elder (brother Balarāma); *miśra*—the distinguished personality; *abhisaṅgataḥ*—accompanied; *rājanyāḥ*—kings; *caidya-pakṣīyāḥ*—siding with Caidya (Śiśupāla); *nūnam*—certainly; *hanyuḥ*—must be attacking; *purīm*—city; *mama*—My.

TRANSLATION

The Lord said to Himself: Because I have come here with My respected elder brother, kings partial to Śiśupāla may well be attacking My capital city.

TEXT 9

वीक्ष्य तत्कदनं स्वानां निरूप्य पुररक्षणम् ।
सौभं च शाल्वराजं च दारुकं प्राह केशवः ॥९॥

vīkṣya tat kadanaṁ svānāṁ
nirūpya pura-rakṣaṇam
saubhaṁ ca śālva-rājaṁ ca
dārukaṁ prāha keśavaḥ

vīkṣya—seeing; *tat*—that; *kadanam*—destruction; *svānām*—of His own men; *nirūpya*—arranging; *pura*—of the city; *rakṣaṇam*—for protection; *saubham*—the vehicle Saubha; *ca*—and; *śālva-rājam*—the King of the Śālva province; *ca*—and; *dārukam*—to Dāruka, His chariot driver; *prāha*—spoke; *keśavaḥ*—Lord Kṛṣṇa.

TRANSLATION

[Śukadeva Gosvāmī continued:] After He arrived at Dvārakā and saw how His people were threatened with destruction, and also saw Śālva and his Saubha airship, Lord Keśava arranged for the city's defense and then addressed Dāruka as follows.

PURPORT

Lord Kṛṣṇa placed Śrī Balarāma in a strategic position to guard the city, and He also appointed a special guard for Śrī Rukmiṇī and the other queens inside the palaces. According to Śrīla Viśvanātha Cakravartī, by a secret route special soldiers conveyed the queens to safety inside Dvārakā.

TEXT 10

रथं प्रापय मे सूत शाल्वस्यान्तिकमाशु वै ।
सम्भ्रमस्ते न कर्तव्यो मायावी सौभराडयम् ॥१०॥

ratham prāpaya me sūta
śālvasyāntikam āśu vai
sambhramas te na kartavyo
māyāvī saubha-rāḍ ayam

ratham—chariot; *prāpaya*—bring; *me*—My; *sūta*—O driver; *śālvasya*—of Śālva; *antikam*—into the proximity; *āśu*—quickly; *vai*—indeed; *sambhramaḥ*—bewilderment; *te*—by you; *na kartavyaḥ*—should not be experienced; *māyā-vī*—a great magician; *saubha-rāṭ*—lord of Saubha; *ayam*—this.

TRANSLATION

[Lord Kṛṣṇa said:] O driver, quickly take My chariot near Śālva. This lord of Saubha is a powerful magician; don't let him bewilder you.

TEXT 11

इत्युक्तश्चोदयामास रथमास्थाय दारुकः ।
विशन्तं ददृशुः सर्वे स्वे परे चारुणानुजम् ॥११॥

ity uktaś codayām āsa
ratham āsthāya dārukaḥ
viśantaṁ dadṛśuḥ sarve
sve pare cāruṇānujam

iti—thus; *uktaḥ*—told; *codayām āsa*—he drove forward; *ratham*—the chariot; *āsthāya*—taking control of it; *dārukaḥ*—Dāruka; *viśantam*—entering; *dadṛśuḥ*—saw; *sarve*—everyone; *sve*—His own men; *pare*—the opposite party; *ca*—also; *aruṇa-anujam*—the younger brother of Aruṇa (Garuḍa, on Lord Kṛṣṇa's flag).

TRANSLATION

Thus ordered, Dāruka took command of the Lord's chariot and drove forth. As the chariot entered the battlefield, everyone there, both friend and foe, caught sight of the emblem of Garuḍa.

TEXT 12

शाल्वश्च कृष्णमालक्ष्य हतप्रायबलेश्वरः ।
प्राहरत्कृष्णसूताय शक्तिं भीमरवां मृधे ॥१२॥

śālvaś ca kṛṣṇam ālokya
hata-prāya-baleśvaraḥ
prāharat kṛṣṇa-sūtāya
śaktiṁ bhīma-ravāṁ mṛdhe

śālvaḥ—Śālva; *ca*—and; *kṛṣṇam*—Lord Kṛṣṇa; *ālokya*—seeing; *hata*—destroyed; *prāya*—virtually; *bala*—of an army; *īśvaraḥ*—the master; *prāharat*—he cast; *kṛṣṇa-sūtāya*—at Kṛṣṇa's chariot driver; *śaktim*—his spear; *bhīma*—frightening; *ravām*—whose roaring sound; *mṛdhe*—on the battlefield.

TRANSLATION

When Śālva, the master of a decimated army, saw Lord Kṛṣṇa approaching, he hurled his spear at the Lord's charioteer. The spear roared frighteningly as it flew across the battlefield.

TEXT 13

तामापतन्तीं नभसि महोल्कामिव रंहसा ।
भासयन्तीं दिशः शौरिः सायकैः शतधाच्छिनत् ॥१३॥

tām āpatantīṁ nabhasi
maholkām iva raṁhasā
bhāsayantīṁ diśaḥ śauriḥ
sāyakaiḥ śatadhācchinat

tām—that; *āpatantīm*—flying toward; *nabhasi*—in the sky; *mahā*—great; *ulkām*—a meteor; *iva*—like; *raṁhasā*—swiftly; *bhāsayantīm*—illuminating; *diśaḥ*—the directions; *śauriḥ*—Lord Kṛṣṇa; *sāyakaiḥ*—with His arrows; *śatadhā*—in hundreds of pieces; *acchinat*—cut.

TRANSLATION

Śālva's hurtling spear lit up the whole sky like a mighty meteor, but Lord Śauri tore the great weapon into hundreds of pieces with His arrows.

TEXT 14

तं च षोडशभिर्विद्ध्वा बाणैः सौभं च खे भ्रमत् ।
अविध्यच्छरसन्दोहैः खं सूर्य इव रश्मिभिः ॥१४॥

taṁ ca ṣoḍaśabhir viddhvā
bāṇaiḥ saubhaṁ ca khe bhramat
avidhyac chara-sandohaiḥ
khaṁ sūrya iva raśmibhiḥ

tam—him, Śālva; *ca*—and; *ṣoḍaśabhiḥ*—with sixteen; *viddhvā*—piercing; *bāṇaiḥ*—arrows; *saubham*—Saubha; *ca*—also; *khe*—in the sky; *bhramat*—wandering; *avidhyat*—He struck; *śara*—of arrows; *sandohaiḥ*—with torrents; *kham*—the sky; *sūryaḥ*—the sun; *iva*—as; *raśmibhiḥ*—with its rays.

TRANSLATION

Lord Kṛṣṇa then pierced Śālva with sixteen arrows and struck the Saubha airship with a deluge of arrows as it darted about the sky. Firing His arrows, the Lord appeared like the sun flooding the heavens with its rays.

TEXT 15

शाल्वः शौरेस्तु दोः सव्यं सशार्ङ्गं शार्ङ्गधन्वनः ।
बिभेद न्यपतद्धस्ताच्छार्ङ्गमासीत्तदद्भुतम् ॥१५॥

śālvaḥ śaures tu doḥ savyaṁ
sa-śārṅgaṁ śārṅga-dhanvanaḥ
bibheda nyapatad dhastāc
chārṅgam āsīt tad adbhutam

śālvaḥ—Śālva; *saureḥ*—of Lord Kṛṣṇa; *tu*—but; *doḥ*—the arm; *savyam*—left; *sa*—with; *śārṅgam*—the Lord's bow, called Śārṅga; *śārṅga-dhanvanaḥ*—of Him who is called Śārṅga-dhanvā; *bibheda*—struck; *nyapatat*—fell; *hastāt*—from His hand; *śārṅgam*—the Śārṅga bow; *āsīt*—was; *tat*—this; *adbhutam*—amazing.

TRANSLATION

Śālva then managed to strike Lord Kṛṣṇa's left arm, which held His bow Śārṅga, and, amazingly, Śārṅga fell from His hand.

TEXT 16

हाहाकारो महानासीद् भूतानां तत्र पश्यताम् ।
निनद्य सौभराडुच्चैरिदमाह जनार्दनम् ॥१६॥

hāhā-kāro mahān āsīd
bhūtānāṁ tatra paśyatām
ninadya saubha-rāḍ uccair
idam āha janārdanam

hāhā-kāraḥ—a cry of dismay; *mahān*—great; *āsīt*—arose; *bhūtānām*—among the living beings; *tatra*—there; *paśyatām*—who were witnessing; *ninadya*—roaring; *saubha-rāṭ*—the lord of Saubha; *uccaiḥ*—loudly; *idam*—this; *āha*—said; *janārdanam*—to Lord Kṛṣṇa.

TRANSLATION

Those who witnessed this all cried out in dismay. Then the master of Saubha roared loudly and addressed Lord Janārdana.

TEXTS 17–18

यत्त्वया मूढ नः सख्युर्भ्रातुर्भार्या हृतेक्षताम् ।
प्रमत्तः स सभामध्ये त्वया व्यापादितः सखा ॥१७॥
तं त्वाद्य निशितैर्बाणैरपराजितमानिनम् ।
नयाम्यपुनरावृत्तिं यदि तिष्ठेर्ममाग्रतः ॥१८॥

yat tvayā mūḍha naḥ sakhyur
bhrātur bhāryā hṛtekṣatām
pramattaḥ sa sabhā-madhye
tvayā vyāpāditaḥ sakhā

taṁ tvādya niśitair bāṇair
aparājita-māninam
nayāmy apunar-āvṛttiṁ
yadi tiṣṭher mamāgrataḥ

yat—since; *tvayā*—by You; *mūḍha*—O fool; *naḥ*—our; *sakhyuḥ*—of the friend (Śiśupāla); *bhrātuḥ*—of (Your) brother (or more exactly, cousin); *bhāryā*—the bride; *hṛtā*—taken away; *īkṣatām*—as (we) looked on; *pramattaḥ*—inattentive; *saḥ*—he, Śiśupāla; *sabhā*—the assembly (of the Rājasūya sacrifice); *madhye*—within; *tvayā*—by You; *vyāpāditaḥ*—killed; *sakhā*—my friend; *tam tvā*—You Yourself; *adya*—today; *niśitaiḥ*—sharp; *bāṇaiḥ*—with arrows; *aparājita*—invincible; *māninam*—who presume Yourself; *nayāmi*—I will send; *apunaḥ-āvṛttim*—to the realm of no return; *yadi*—if; *tiṣṭheḥ*—You will stand; *mama*—of me; *agrataḥ*—in front.

TRANSLATION

[Śālva said:] You fool! Because in our presence You kidnapped the bride of our friend Śiśupāla, Your own cousin, and because You later murdered him in the sacred assembly while he was inattentive, today with my sharp arrows I will send You to the land of no return! Though You think Yourself invincible, I will kill You now if You dare stand before me.

TEXT 19

श्रीभगवानुवाच
वृथा त्वं कत्थसे मन्द न पश्यस्यन्तिकेऽन्तकम् ।
पौरुषं दर्शयन्ति स्म शूरा न बहुभाषिणः ॥१९॥

śrī-bhagavān uvāca
vṛthā tvaṁ katthase manda
na paśyasy antike 'ntakam
pauruṣaṁ darśayanti sma
śūrā na bahu-bhāṣiṇaḥ

śrī-bhagavān uvāca—the Supreme Lord said; *vṛthā*—in vain; *tvam*—you; *katthase*—boast; *manda*—O dull one; *na paśyasi*—you do not see; *antike*—near; *antakam*—death; *pauruṣam*—their prowess; *darśayanti*—demonstrate; *sma*—indeed; *śūrāḥ*—heroes; *na*—not; *bahu*—much; *bhāṣiṇaḥ*—speaking.

TRANSLATION

The Supreme Lord said: O dullard, you boast in vain, since you fail to see death standing near you. Real heroes do not talk much but rather show their prowess in action.

TEXT 20

इत्युक्त्वा भगवाञ् छाल्वं गदया भीमवेगया ।
तताड जत्रौ संरब्धः स चकम्पे वमन्नसृक् ॥२०॥

ity uktvā bhagavāñ chālvaṁ
gadayā bhīma-vegayā
tatāḍa jatrau saṁrabdhaḥ
sa cakampe vamann asṛk

iti—thus; *uktvā*—speaking; *bhagavān*—the Lord; *śālvam*—Śālva; *gadayā*—with His club; *bhīma*—fearsome; *vegayā*—whose force and speed; *tatāḍa*—struck; *jatrau*—on the collarbone; *saṁrabdhaḥ*—infuriated; *saḥ*—he; *cakampe*—trembled; *vaman*—vomiting; *asṛk*—blood.

TRANSLATION

Having said this, the furious Lord swung His club with frightening power and speed and hit Śālva on the collarbone, making him tremble and vomit blood.

TEXT 21

गदायां सन्निवृत्तायां शाल्वस्त्वन्तरधीयत ।
ततो मुहूर्त आगत्य पुरुषः शिरसाच्युतम् ।
देवक्या प्रहितोऽस्मीति नत्वा प्राह वचो रुदन् ॥२१॥

gadāyām sannivṛttāyāṁ
śālvas tv antaradhīyata
tato muhūrta āgatya
puruṣaḥ śirasācyutam
devakyā prahito 'smīti
natvā prāha vaco rudan

gadāyām—the club; *sannivṛttāyām*—when it was withdrawn; *śālvaḥ*—Śālva; *tu*—but; *antaradhīyata*—disappeared; *tataḥ*—then; *muhūrte*—after a moment; *āgatya*—coming; *puruṣaḥ*—a man; *śirasā*—with his head; *acyutam*—to Lord Kṛṣṇa; *devakyā*—by mother Devakī; *prahitaḥ*—sent; *asmi*—I am; *iti*—so saying; *natvā*—bowing down; *prāha*—he spoke; *vacaḥ*—these words; *rudan*—crying.

TRANSLATION

But as soon as Lord Acyuta withdrew His club, Śālva disappeared from sight, and a moment later a man approached the Lord. Bowing his head down to Him, he announced, "Devakī has sent me," and, sobbing, spoke the following words.

TEXT 22

कृष्ण कृष्ण महाबाहो पिता ते पितृवत्सल ।
बद्ध्वापनीतः शाल्वेन सौनिकेन यथा पशुः ॥२२॥

kṛṣṇa kṛṣṇa mahā-bāho
pitā te pitṛ-vatsala
baddhvāpanītaḥ śālvena
saunikena yathā paśuḥ

kṛṣṇa kṛṣṇa—O Kṛṣṇa, Kṛṣṇa; *mahā-bāho*—O mighty-armed one; *pitā*—father; *te*—Your; *pitṛ*—to Your parents; *vatsala*—O You who are so affectionate; *baddhvā*—being captured; *apanītaḥ*—taken away; *śālvena*—by Śālva; *saunikena*—by a butcher; *yathā*—as; *paśuḥ*—a domestic animal.

TRANSLATION

[The man said:] O Kṛṣṇa, Kṛṣṇa, might-armed one, who are so affectionate to Your parents! Śālva has seized Your father and taken him away, as a butcher leads an animal to slaughter.

TEXT 23

निशम्य विप्रियं कृष्णो मानुषीं प्रकृतिं गतः ।
विमनस्को घृणी स्नेहाद् बभाषे प्राकृतो यथा ॥२३॥

niśamya vipriyaṁ kṛṣṇo
mānuṣīṁ prakṛtiṁ gataḥ
vimanasko ghṛṇī snehād
babhāṣe prākṛto yathā

niśamya—hearing; *vipriyam*—disturbing words; *kṛṣṇaḥ*—Lord Kṛṣṇa; *mānuṣīm*—humanlike; *prakṛtim*—a nature; *gataḥ*—having assumed; *vimanaskaḥ*—unhappy; *ghṛṇī*—compassionate; *snehāt*—out of love; *babhāṣe*—He spoke; *prākṛtaḥ*—an ordinary person; *yathā*—like.

TRANSLATION

When He heard this disturbing news, Lord Kṛṣṇa, who was playing the role of a mortal man, showed sorrow and compassion, and out of love for His parents He spoke the following words like an ordinary conditioned soul.

TEXT 24

कथं राममसम्भ्रान्तं जित्वाजेयं सुरासुरैः ।
शाल्वेनाल्पीयसा नीतः पिता मे बलवान् विधिः ॥२४॥

kathaṁ rāmam asambhrāntaṁ
jitvājeyaṁ surāsuraiḥ
śālvenālpīyasā nītaḥ
pitā me balavān vidhiḥ

katham—how; *rāmam*—Lord Balarāma; *asambhrāntam*—never confused; *jitvā*—defeating; *ajeyam*—undefeatable; *sura*—by demigods; *asuraiḥ*—and demons; *śālvena*—by Śālva; *alpīyasā*—very small; *nītaḥ*—taken; *pitā*—father; *me*—My; *bala-vān*—powerful; *vidhiḥ*—fate.

TRANSLATION

[Lord Kṛṣṇa said:] Balarāma is ever vigilant, and no demigod or demon can defeat Him. So how could this insignificant Śālva defeat Him and abduct My father? Indeed, fate is all-powerful!

TEXT 25

इति ब्रुवाणे गोविन्दे सौभराट् प्रत्युपस्थितः ।
वसुदेवमिवानीय कृष्णं चेदमुवाच सः ॥२५॥

iti bruvāṇe govinde
saubha-rāṭ pratyupasthitaḥ
vasudevam ivānīya
kṛṣṇaṁ cedam uvāca saḥ

iti—thus; *bruvāṇe*—saying; *govinde*—Lord Kṛṣṇa; *saubha-rāṭ*—the master of Saubha (Śālva); *pratyupasthitaḥ*—came forward; *vasudevam*—Vasudeva, Lord Kṛṣṇa's father; *iva*—as if; *ānīya*—leading; *kṛṣṇam*—to Lord Kṛṣṇa; *ca*—and; *idam*—this; *uvāca*—said; *saḥ*—he.

TRANSLATION

After Govinda spoke these words, the master of Saubha again appeared, apparently leading Vasudeva before the Lord. Śālva then spoke as follows.

TEXT 26

एष ते जनिता तातो यदर्थमिह जीवसि ।
वधिष्ये वीक्षतस्तेऽमुमीशश्चेत्पाहि बालिश ॥२६॥

eṣa te janitā tāto
yad-artham iha jīvasi
vadhiṣye vīkṣatas te 'mum
īśaś cet pāhi bāliśa

eṣaḥ—this; *te*—Your; *janitā*—father who begot You; *tātaḥ*—dear; *yat-artham*—for whose sake; *iha*—in this world; *jīvasi*—You live; *vadhiṣye*—I shall kill; *vīkṣataḥ te*—as You witness; *amum*—him; *īśaḥ*—able; *cet*—if; *pāhi*—save him; *bāliśa*—O childish one.

TRANSLATION

[Śālva said:] Here is Your dear father, who begot You and for whose sake You are living in this world. I shall now kill him before Your very eyes. Save him if You can, weakling!

TEXT 27

एवं निर्भर्त्स्य मायावी खड्गेनानकदुन्दुभेः ।
उत्कृत्य शिर आदाय खस्थं सौभं समाविशत् ॥२७॥

evaṁ nirbhartsya māyāvī
khaḍgenānakadundubheḥ
utkṛtya śira ādāya
kha-sthaṁ saubhaṁ samāviśat

evam—thus; *nirbhartsya*—mocking; *māyā-vī*—the magician; *khaḍgena*—with his sword; *ānakadundubheḥ*—of Śri Vasudeva; *utkṛtya*—cutting off; *śiraḥ*—the head; *ādāya*—taking it; *kha*—in the sky; *stham*—situated; *saubham*—Saubha; *samāviśat*—he entered.

TRANSLATION

After he had mocked the Lord in this way, the magician Śālva appeared to cut off Vasudeva's head with his sword. Taking the head with him, he entered the Saubha vehicle, which was hovering in the sky.

TEXT 28

ततो मुहूर्तं प्रकृतावुपप्लुतः
स्वबोध आस्ते स्वजनानुषंगतः ।
महानुभावस्तदबुध्यदासुरीं
मायां स शाल्वप्रसृतां मयोदिताम् ॥२८॥

tato muhūrtaṁ prakṛtāv upaplutaḥ
sva-bodha āste sva-janānuṣaṅgataḥ

mahānubhāvas tad abudhyad āsurīṁ
māyāṁ sa śālva-prasṛtāṁ mayoditām

tataḥ—then; *muhūrtam*—for a moment; *prakṛtau*—in ordinary (human) nature; *upaplutaḥ*—absorbed; *sva-bodhaḥ*—(although) fully self-cognizant; *āste*—He remained; *sva-jana*—for His dear ones; *anuṣaṅgataḥ*—due to His affection; *mahā-anubhāvaḥ*—the possessor of great powers of perception; *tat*—that; *abudhyat*—recognized; *āsurīm*—demoniac; *māyām*—the illusory magic; *saḥ*—He; *śālva*—by Śālva; *prasṛtām*—utilized; *maya*—by Maya Dānava; *uditām*—developed.

TRANSLATION

By nature Lord Kṛṣṇa is full in knowledge, and He possesses unlimited powers of perception. Yet for a moment, out of great affection for His loved ones, He remained absorbed in the mood of an ordinary human being. He soon recalled, however, that this was all a demoniac illusion engineered by Maya Dānava and employed by Śālva.

TEXT 29

न तत्र दूतं न पितु: कलेवरं
प्रबुद्ध आजौ समपश्यदच्युत: ।
स्वाप्नं यथा चाम्बरचारिणं रिपुं
सौभस्थमालोक्य निहन्तुमुद्यत: ॥२९॥

na tatra dūtaṁ na pituḥ kalevaraṁ
prabuddha ājau samapaśyad acyutaḥ
svāpnaṁ yathā cāmbara-cāriṇaṁ ripuṁ
saubha-sthaṁ ālokya nihantum udyataḥ

na—not; *tatra*—there; *dūtam*—the messenger; *na*—nor; *pituḥ*—of His father; *kalevaram*—the body; *prabuddhaḥ*—alert; *ājau*—on the battlefield; *samapaśyat*—saw; *acyutaḥ*—Lord Kṛṣṇa; *svāpnam*—in a dream; *yathā*—like; *ca*—and; *ambara*—in the sky; *cāriṇam*—moving; *ripum*—His enemy (Śālva); *saubha-stham*—sitting in the Saubha plane; *ālokya*—seeing; *nihantum*—to kill him; *udyataḥ*—He prepared.

TRANSLATION

Now alert to the actual situation, Lord Acyuta saw before Him on the battlefield neither the messenger nor His father's body. It was as if He had awakened from a dream. Seeing His enemy flying above Him in his Saubha plane, the Lord then prepared to kill him.

TEXT 30

एवं वदन्ति राजर्षे ऋषयः के च नान्विताः ।
यत्स्ववाचो विरुध्येत नूनं ते न स्मरन्त्युत ॥३०॥

evaṁ vadanti rājarṣe
ṛṣayaḥ ke ca nānvitāḥ
yat sva-vāco virudhyeta
nūnaṁ te na smaranty uta

evam—so; *vadanti*—say; *rāja-ṛṣe*—O sage among kings (Parīkṣit); *ṛṣayaḥ*—sages; *ke ca*—some; *na*—not; *anvitāḥ*—reasoning correctly; *yat*—since; *sva*—their own; *vācaḥ*—words; *virudhyeta*—are contradicted; *nūnam*—for certain; *te*—they; *na smaranti*—do not remember; *uta*—indeed.

TRANSLATION

Such is the account given by some sages, O wise King, but those who speak in this illogical way are contradicting themselves, having forgotten their own previous statements.

PURPORT

If someone thinks that Lord Kṛṣṇa was actually bewildered by Śālva's magic and that the Lord was subjected to ordinary mundane lamentation, such an opinion is illogical and contradictory, since it is well known that Lord Kṛṣṇa is the Supreme Personality of Godhead, transcendental and absolute. This will be further explained in the following verses.

TEXT 31

क्व शोकमोहौ स्नेहो वा भयं वा येऽज्ञसम्भवाः ।
क्व चाखण्डितविज्ञानज्ञानैश्वर्यस्त्वखण्डितः ॥३१॥

kva śoka-mohau sneho vā
bhayaṁ vā ye 'jña-sambhavāḥ
kva cākhaṇḍita-vijñāna-
jñānaiśvaryas tv akhaṇḍitaḥ

kva—where; *śoka*—lamentation; *mohau*—and bewilderment; *snehaḥ*—material affection; *vā*—or; *bhayam*—fear; *vā*—or; *ye*—those which; *ajña*—out of ignorance; *sambhavāḥ*—born; *kva ca*—and where, on the other hand; *akhaṇḍita*—infinite; *vijñāna*—whose perception; *jñāna*—knowledge; *aiśvaryaḥ*—and power; *tu*—but; *akhaṇḍitaḥ*—the infinite Supreme Lord.

TRANSLATION

How can lamentation, bewilderment, material affection or fear, all born out of ignorance, be ascribed to the infinite Supreme Lord, whose perception, knowledge and power are all similarly infinite?

PURPORT

Śrīla Prabhupāda writes, "Lamentation, aggrievement and bewilderment are characteristics of conditioned souls, but how can such things affect the person of the Supreme, who is full of knowledge, power and all opulence? Actually, it is not at all possible that Lord Kṛṣṇa was misled by the mystic jugglery of Śālva. He was displaying His pastime of playing the role of a human being."

All the great *Bhāgavatam* commentators conclude that grief, illusion, attachment and fear, which arise out of ignorance of the soul, can never be present in the transcendental dramatic pastimes enacted by the Lord. Śrīla Jīva Gosvāmī gives many examples from Kṛṣṇa's pastimes to illustrate this point. For instance, when the cowherd boys entered the mouth of Aghāsura, Lord Kṛṣṇa was apparently astonished. Similarly, when Brahmā took away Lord Kṛṣṇa's cowherd boyfriends and calves, the Lord at first began to look for them as if He did not know where they were. Thus the Lord plays the part of an ordinary human being so as to relish transcendental pastimes with His devotees. One should never think the Personality of Godhead is an ordinary person, as Śukadeva Gosvāmī explains in this and the following verse.

TEXT 32

यत्पादसेवोर्जितयात्मविद्यया
हिन्वन्त्यनाद्यात्मविपर्ययग्रहम् ।
लभन्त आत्मीयमनन्तमैश्वरं
कुतो नु मोहः परमस्य सद्गतेः ॥३२॥

yat-pāda-sevorjitayātma-vidyayā
hinvanty anādyātma-viparyaya-graham
labhanta ātmīyam anantam aiśvaraṁ
kuto nu mohaḥ paramasya sad-gateḥ

yat—whose; *pāda*—of the feet; *sevā*—by service; *ūrjitayā*—made strong; *ātma-vidyayā*—by self-realization; *hinvanti*—they dispel; *anādi*—beginningless; *ātma*—of the self; *viparyaya-graham*—the misidentification; *labhante*—they attain; *ātmīyam*—in a personal relationship with Him; *anantam*—eternal; *aiśvaram*—glory; *kutaḥ*—how; *nu*—indeed; *mohaḥ*—bewilderment; *paramasya*—for the Supreme; *sat*—of saintly devotees; *gateḥ*—the destination.

TRANSLATION

By virtue of self-realization fortified by service rendered to His feet, devotees of the Lord dispel the bodily concept of life, which has bewildered the soul since time immemorial. Thus they attain eternal glory in His personal association. How, then, can that Supreme Truth, the destination of all genuine saints, be subject to illusion?

PURPORT

As a result of fasting the body becomes weak, and one thinks, "I am emaciated." Similarly, sometimes a conditioned soul thinks, "I am happy" or "I am unhappy"—ideas based on the bodily concept of life. Simply by serving the lotus feet of Lord Kṛṣṇa, however, devotees become free from this bodily concept of life. So how could such illusion possibly affect the Supreme Personality of Godhead at any time?

TEXT 33

तं शस्त्रपूगैः प्रहरन्तमोजसा
शाल्वं शरैः शौरिरमोघविक्रमः ।
विद्ध्वाच्छिनद्वर्म धनुः शिरोमणिं
सौभं च शत्रोर्गदया रुरोज ह ॥३३॥

taṁ śastra-pūgaiḥ praharantam ojasā
śālvaṁ śaraiḥ śaurir amogha-vikramaḥ
viddhvācchinad varma dhanuḥ śiro-maṇiṁ
saubhaṁ ca śatror gadayā ruroja ha

tam—Him; *śastra*—of weapons; *pūgaiḥ*—with torrents; *praharantam*—attacking; *ojasā*—with great force; *śālvam*—Śālva; *śaraiḥ*—with His arrows; *śauriḥ*—Lord Kṛṣṇa; *amogha*—never exhibited in vain; *vikramaḥ*—whose prowess; *viddhvā*—piercing; *acchinat*—He broke; *varma*—the armor; *dhanuḥ*—the bow; *śiraḥ*—on the head; *maṇim*—the jewel; *saubham*—the Saubha vehicle; *ca*—and; *śatroḥ*—of His enemy; *gadayā*—with His club; *ruroja*—He broke; *ha*—indeed.

TRANSLATION

While Śālva continued to hurl torrents of weapons at Him with great force, Lord Kṛṣṇa, whose prowess never fails, shot His arrows at Śālva, wounding him and shattering his armor, bow and crest jewel. Then with His club the Lord smashed His enemy's Saubha airship.

PURPORT

Śrīla Prabhupāda writes, "When Śālva thought that Kṛṣṇa had been bewildered by his mystic representations, he became encouraged and began to attack the Lord with greater strength and energy by showering volumes of arrows upon Him. But the enthusiasm of Śālva can be compared to the speedy march of flies into a fire. Lord Kṛṣṇa, by hurling His arrows with unfathomable strength, injured Śālva, whose armor, bow and jeweled helmet all scattered into pieces. With a crashing blow from Kṛṣṇa's club, Śālva's wonderful airplane burst into pieces and fell into the sea."

The fact that Śālva's insignificant mystic power could not bewilder Lord Kṛṣṇa is here emphatically demonstrated.

TEXT 34

तत्कृष्णहस्तेरितया विचूर्णितं
पपात तोये गदया सहस्रधा ।
विसृज्य तद् भूतलमास्थितो गदाम्
उद्यम्य शाल्वोऽच्युतमभ्यगाद् द्रुतम् ॥३४॥

tat kṛṣṇa-hasteritayā vicūrṇitaṁ
papāta toye gadayā sahasradhā
visṛjya tad bhū-talam āsthito gadām
udyamya śālvo 'cyutam abhyagād drutam

tat—that (Saubha); *kṛṣṇa-hasta*—by Lord Kṛṣṇa's hand; *īritayā*—wielded; *vicūrṇitam*—shattered; *papāta*—it fell; *toye*—into the water; *gadayā*—by the club; *sahasradhā*—into thousands of pieces; *visṛjya*—abandoning; *tat*—it; *bhū-talam*—on the ground; *āsthitaḥ*—standing; *gadām*—his club; *udyamya*—taking up; *śālvaḥ*—Śālva; *acyutam*—Lord Kṛṣṇa; *abhyagāt*—attacked; *drutam*—swiftly.

TRANSLATION

Shattered into thousands of pieces by Lord Kṛṣṇa's club, the Saubha airship plummeted into the water. Śālva abandoned it, stationed himself on the ground, took up his club and rushed toward Lord Acyuta.

TEXT 35

आधावतः सगदं तस्य बाहुं
भल्लेन छित्त्वाथ रथांगमद्भुतम् ।

वधाय शाल्वस्य लयार्कसन्निभं
बिभ्रद् बभौ सार्क इवोदयाचलः ॥३५॥

ādhāvataḥ sa-gadaṁ tasya bāhuṁ
bhallena chittvātha rathāṅgam adbhutam
vadhāya śālvasya layārka-sannibhaṁ
bibhrad babhau sārka ivodayācalaḥ

ādhāvataḥ—running toward Him; *sa-gadam*—carrying his club; *tasya*—his; *bāhum*—arm; *bhallena*—with a special kind of arrow; *chittvā*—severing; *atha*—then; *ratha-aṅgam*—His disc weapon; *adbhutam*—wonderful; *vadhāya*—for the killing; *śālvasya*—of Śālva; *laya*—at the time of universal annihilation; *arka*—the sun; *sannibham*—exactly resembling; *bibhrat*—holding; *babhau*—He shone; *sa-arkaḥ*—together with the sun; *iva*—as if; *udaya*—of the sunrise; *acalaḥ*—the mountain.

TRANSLATION

As Śālva rushed at Him, the Lord shot a *bhalla* dart and cut off his arm that held the club. Having finally decided to kill Śālva, Kṛṣṇa then raised His Sudarśana disc weapon, which resembled the sun at the time of universal annihilation. The brilliantly shining Lord appeared like the easternmost mountain bearing the rising sun.

TEXT 36

जहार तेनैव शिरः सकुण्डलं
किरीटयुक्तं पुरुमायिनो हरिः ।
वज्रेण वृत्रस्य यथा पुरन्दरो
बभूव हाहेति वचस्तदा नृणाम् ॥३६॥

jahāra tenaiva śiraḥ sa-kuṇḍalaṁ
kirīṭa-yuktaṁ puru-māyino hariḥ
vajreṇa vṛtrasya yathā purandaro
babhūva hāheti vacas tadā nṛṇām

jahāra—He removed; *tena*—with it; *eva*—indeed; *śiraḥ*—the head; *sa*—with; *kuṇḍalam*—earrings; *kirīṭa*—crown; *yuktam*—wearing; *puru*—vast; *māyinaḥ*—of the possessor of magical powers; *hariḥ*—Lord Kṛṣṇa; *vajreṇa*—with his thunderbolt weapon; *vṛtrasya*—of Vṛtrāsura; *yathā*—as; *purandaraḥ*—Lord Indra; *babhūva*—there arose; *hā-hā iti*—"alas, alas"; *vacaḥ*—voices; *tadā*—then; *nṛṇām*—of (Śālva's) men.

TRANSLATION

Employing His disc, Lord Hari removed that great magician's head with its earrings and crown, just as Purandara had used his thunderbolt to cut off Vṛtra's head. Seeing this, all of Śālva's followers cried out, "Alas, alas!"

TEXT 37

तस्मिन्निपतिते पापे सौभे च गदया हते ।
नेदुर्दुन्दुभयो राजन् दिवि देवगणेरिताः ।
सखीनामपचितिं कुर्वन् दन्तवक्रो रुषाभ्यगात् ॥३७॥

tasmin nipatite pāpe
saubhe ca gadayā hate
nedur dundubhayo rājan
divi deva-gaṇeritāḥ
sakhīnām apacitiṁ kurvan
dantavakro ruṣābhyagāt

tasmin—he; *nipatite*—having fallen; *pāpe*—sinful; *saubhe*—the Saubha vehicle; *ca*—and; *gadayā*—by the club; *hate*—being destroyed; *neduḥ*—there resounded; *dundubhayaḥ*—kettledrums; *rājan*—O King (Parīkṣit); *divi*—in the sky; *deva-gaṇa*—by groups of demigods; *īritāḥ*—played; *sakhīnām*—for his friends; *apacitim*—revenge; *kurvan*—intending to carry out; *dantavakraḥ*—Dantavakra; *ruṣā*—angrily; *abhyagāt*—ran forward.

TRANSLATION

With the sinful Śālva now dead and his Saubha airship destroyed, the heavens resounded with kettledrums played by groups of demigods. Then Dantavakra, wanting to avenge the death of his friends, furiously attacked the Lord.

Thus end the purports of the humble servants of His Divine Grace A. C. Bhaktivedanta Swami Prabhupāda to the Tenth Canto, Seventy-seventh Chapter, of the Śrīmad-Bhāgavatam, *entitled "Lord Kṛṣṇa Slays the Demon Śālva."*

CHAPTER SEVENTY-EIGHT

The Killing of Dantavakra, Vidūratha and Romaharṣaṇa

This chapter relates how Lord Kṛṣṇa killed Dantavakra and Vidūratha, visited Vṛndāvana, and then returned to Dvārakā. It also describes how Lord Baladeva killed the offensive Romaharṣaṇa Sūta.

Intent upon avenging the death of his friend Śālva, Dantavakra appeared on the battlefield with club in hand. Lord Kṛṣṇa took up His own club and came before him. Dantavakra then insulted the Lord with harsh words and struck Him a terrific blow on the head. Without budging in the slightest, Lord Kṛṣṇa bludgeoned Dantavakra's chest, shattering his heart. Dantavakra had a brother named Vidūratha, and he became distraught at Dantavakra's death. Taking up his sword, Vidūratha confronted Śrī Kṛṣṇa, but the Lord cut off Vidūratha's head with His Sudarśana disc. Lord Kṛṣṇa then visited Vṛndāvana for two months, and finally He returned to Dvārakā.

When Lord Baladeva heard that the Pāṇḍavas and Kauravas were about to go to war, in order to remain neutral He left Dvārakā on the pretext of going on pilgrimage. The Lord bathed in sacred places such as Prabhāsa, Tritakūpa and Viśāla, and eventually He came to the holy Naimiṣāraṇya forest, where great sages were performing an extended fire sacrifice. While being worshiped by the assembled sages and offered a seat of honor, the Lord noticed that Romaharṣaṇa Sūta, sitting on the speaker's seat, had failed to stand in deference to Him. Greatly angered by this offense, Lord Balarāma killed Romaharṣaṇa by touching him with the tip of a blade of *kuśa* grass.

The assembled sages were disturbed by what Lord Baladeva had done, and they said to Him, "You have unknowingly killed a *brāhmaṇa*. Therefore, even though You are above the Vedic injunctions, we request You to set a perfect example for the general populace by atoning for this sin." Then Śrī Baladeva, following the Vedic maxim that "one's son takes birth as one's own self," granted to Romaharṣaṇa's son Ugraśravā the position of speaker of the *Purāṇas,* and in accordance with the sages' desires He promised Ugraśravā a long life with unfailing sensory capacity.

Wanting to do something more for the sages, Lord Baladeva promised to kill a demon named Balvala, who had been polluting their sacrificial arena. Finally, on the sages' advice, He agreed to go on a year-long pilgrimage of all the holy places in India.

TEXTS 1–2

श्रीशुक उवाच
शिशुपालस्य शाल्वस्य पौण्ड्रकस्यापि दुर्मतिः ।
परलोकगतानां च कुर्वन् पारोक्ष्यसौहृदम् ॥१॥
एकः पदातिः संक्रुद्धो गदापाणिः प्रकम्पयन् ।
पद्भ्यामिमां महाराज महासत्त्वो व्यदृश्यत ॥२॥

śrī-śuka uvāca
śiśupālasya śālvasya
pauṇḍrakasyāpi durmatiḥ
para-loka-gatānāṁ ca
kurvan pārokṣya-sauhṛdam

ekaḥ padātiḥ saṅkruddho
gadā-pāṇiḥ prakampayan
padbhyām imāṁ mahā-rāja
mahā-sattvo vyadṛśyata

śrī-śukaḥ uvāca—Śukadeva Gosvāmī said; *śiśupālasya*—for Śiśupāla; *śālvasya*—Śālva; *pauṇḍrakasya*—Pauṇḍraka; *api*—also; *durmatiḥ*—evil-hearted (Dantavakra); *para-loka*—to the next world; *gatānām*—who had gone; *ca*—and; *kurvan*—doing; *pārokṣya*—for those who have passed away; *sauhṛdam*—act of friendship; *ekaḥ*—alone; *padātiḥ*—on foot; *saṅkruddhaḥ*—infuriated; *gadā*—a club; *pāṇiḥ*—in his hand; *prakampayan*—making tremble; *padbhyām*—with his feet; *imām*—this (earth); *mahā-rāja*—O great King (Parīkṣit); *mahā*—great; *sattvaḥ*—whose physical power; *vyadṛśyata*—was seen.

TRANSLATION

Śukadeva Gosvāmī said: Acting out of friendship for Śiśupāla, Śālva and Pauṇḍraka, who had all passed on to the next world, the

wicked Dantavakra appeared on the battlefield in a great rage, O King. All alone, on foot and wielding a club in his hand, the mighty warrior shook the earth with his footsteps.

TEXT 3

तं तथायान्तमालोक्य गदामादाय सत्वरः ।
अवप्लुत्य रथात्कृष्णः सिन्धुं वेलेव प्रत्यधात् ॥३॥

taṁ tathāyāntam ālokya
gadām ādāya satvaraḥ
avaplutya rathāt kṛṣṇaḥ
sindhuṁ veleva pratyadhāt

tam—him; *tathā*—in this way; *āyāntam*—approaching; *ālokya*—seeing; *gadām*—His club; *ādāya*—taking; *satvaraḥ*—quickly; *avaplutya*—leaping down; *rathāt*—from His chariot; *kṛṣṇaḥ*—Lord Kṛṣṇa; *sindhum*—the sea; *velā*—the shore; *iva*—as; *pratyadhāt*—checked.

TRANSLATION

Seeing Dantavakra approach, Lord Kṛṣṇa quickly picked up His club, jumped down from His chariot and stopped His advancing opponent just as the shore holds back the ocean.

PURPORT

Śrīla Prabhupāda writes, "When Kṛṣṇa appeared before Dantavakra, his heroic march was immediately stopped, just as the great furious waves of the ocean are stopped by the beach."

TEXT 4

गदामुद्यम्य कारूषो मुकुन्दं प्राह दुर्मदः ।
दिष्ट्या दिष्ट्या भवानद्य मम दृष्टिपथं गतः ॥४॥

gadām udyamya kārūṣo
mukundaṁ prāha durmadaḥ

diṣṭyā diṣṭyā bhavān adya
mama dṛṣṭi-pathaṁ gataḥ

gadām—his club; *udyamya*—wielding; *kārūṣaḥ*—the King of Karūṣa (Dantavakra); *mukundam*—to Lord Kṛṣṇa; *prāha*—said; *durmadaḥ*—intoxicated by foolish pride; *diṣṭyā*—by good fortune; *diṣṭyā*—by good fortune; *bhavān*—You; *adya*—today; *mama*—my; *dṛṣṭi*—of the sight; *patham*—into the path; *gataḥ*—come.

TRANSLATION

Raising his club, the reckless King of Karūṣa said to Lord Mukunda, "What luck! What luck—to have You come before me today!

PURPORT

Śrīla Śrīdhara Svāmī explains that after having waited for three lifetimes, Dantavakra, formerly a gatekeeper in Vaikuṇṭha, could now return to the spiritual world. Therefore the transcendental meaning of his statement is: "How fortunate! How fortunate I am that today I can return to my constitutional position in the spiritual world!"

In the next verse, Dantavakra will refer to Kṛṣṇa as *mātuleya,* a maternal cousin. Dantavakra's mother, Śrutaśravā, was the sister of Kṛṣṇa's father, Vasudeva.

TEXT 5

त्वं मातुलेयो नः कृष्ण मित्रध्रुङ् मां जिघांससि ।
अतस्त्वां गदया मन्द हनिष्ये वज्रकल्पया ॥५॥

tvaṁ mātuleyo naḥ kṛṣṇa
mitra-dhruṅ māṁ jighāṁsasi
atas tvāṁ gadayā manda
haniṣye vajra-kalpayā

tvam—You; *mātuleyaḥ*—maternal cousin; *naḥ*—our; *kṛṣṇa*—O Kṛṣṇa; *mitra*—to my friends; *dhruk*—who have committed violence; *mām*—me; *jighāṁsasi*—You wish to kill; *ataḥ*—therefore; *tvām*—You;

gadayā—with my club; *manda*—O fool; *haniṣye*—I will kill; *vajra-kalpayā*—like a thunderbolt.

TRANSLATION

"You are our maternal cousin, Kṛṣṇa, but You committed violence against my friends, and now You want to kill me also. Therefore, fool, I will kill You with my thunderbolt club.

PURPORT

The *ācāryas* have given the following alternate grammatical division of the third line of this verse: *atas tvāṁ gadayā amanda,* in which case Dantavakra says, "My dear Lord Kṛṣṇa, You are *amanda* [not foolish], and therefore with Your powerful club You will now send me back home, back to Godhead." This is the inner meaning of this verse.

TEXT 6

तर्ह्यानृण्यमुपैम्यज्ञ मित्राणां मित्रवत्सलः ।
बन्धुरूपमरिं हत्वा व्याधिं देहचरं यथा ॥६॥

tarhy ānṛṇyam upaimy ajña
mitrāṇāṁ mitra-vatsalaḥ
bandhu-rūpam ariṁ hatvā
vyādhiṁ deha-caraṁ yathā

tarhi—then; *ānṛṇyam*—payment of my debt; *upaimi*—I will achieve; *ajña*—O unintelligent one; *mitrāṇām*—to my friends; *mitra-vatsalaḥ*—who am affectionate to my friends; *bandhu*—of a family member; *rūpam*—in the form; *arim*—the enemy; *hatvā*—having killed; *vyādhim*—a disease; *deha-caram*—in one's body; *yathā*—like.

TRANSLATION

"Then, O unintelligent one, I who am obliged to my friends will have repaid my debt to them by killing You, my enemy disguised as a relative, who are like a disease within my body."

PURPORT

According to the *ācāryas,* the word *ajña* indicates that in comparison to Lord Kṛṣṇa, no one is more intelligent. Further, the word *bandhu-rūpam* indicates that Lord Kṛṣṇa is actually everyone's true friend, and *vyādhim* indicates that Lord Kṛṣṇa is the Supersoul, the object of meditation within the heart, who takes away our mental distress. Furthermore, the *ācāryas* translate the word *hatvā* as *jñātvā;* in other words, by knowing Kṛṣṇa properly one can actually liberate all of one's friends.

TEXT 7

एवं रूक्षैस्तुदन् वाक्यैः कृष्णं तोत्रैरिव द्विपम् ।
गदयाताडयन्मूर्ध्नि सिंहवद्व्यनदच्च सः ॥७॥

evaṁ rūkṣais tudan vākyaiḥ
kṛṣṇaṁ totrair iva dvipam
gadayātāḍayan mūrdhni
siṁha-vad vyanadac ca saḥ

evam—thus; *rūkṣaiḥ*—harsh; *tudan*—harassing; *vākyaiḥ*—with words; *kṛṣṇam*—Lord Kṛṣṇa; *totraiḥ*—with goads; *iva*—as if; *dvipam*—an elephant; *gadayā*—with his club; *atāḍayat*—he struck Him; *mūrdhni*—on the head; *siṁha-vat*—like a lion; *vyanadat*—roared; *ca*—and; *saḥ*—he.

TRANSLATION

Thus trying to harass Lord Kṛṣṇa with harsh words, as one might prick an elephant with sharp goads, Dantavakra struck the Lord on the head with his club and roared like a lion.

TEXT 8

गदयाभिहतोऽप्याजौ न चचाल यदूद्वहः ।
कृष्णोऽपि तमहन् गुर्व्या कौमोदक्या स्तनान्तरे ॥८॥

gadayābhihato 'py ājau
na cacāla yadūdvahaḥ
kṛṣṇo 'pi tam ahan gurvyā
kaumodakyā stanāntare

gadayā—by the club; *abhihataḥ*—hit; *api*—although; *ājau*—on the battlefield; *na cacāla*—did not move; *yadu-udvahaḥ*—the deliverer of the Yadus; *kṛṣṇaḥ*—Lord Kṛṣṇa; *api*—and; *tam*—him, Dantavakra; *ahan*—struck; *gurvyā*—heavy; *kaumodakyā*—with His club, named Kaumodakī; *stana-antare*—in the middle of his chest.

TRANSLATION

Although hit by Dantavakra's club, Lord Kṛṣṇa, the deliverer of the Yadus, did not budge from His place on the battlefield. Rather, with His massive Kaumodakī club the Lord struck Dantavakra in the middle of his chest.

TEXT 9

गदानिर्भिन्नहृदय उद्वमन् रुधिरं मुखात् ।
प्रसार्य केशबाह्वङ्घ्रीन् धरण्यां न्यपतद्व्यसुः ॥९॥

gadā-nirbhinna-hṛdaya
udvaman rudhiraṁ mukhāt
prasārya keśa-bāhv-aṅghrīn
dharaṇyāṁ nyapatad vyasuḥ

gadā—by the club; *nirbhinna*—broken to pieces; *hṛdayaḥ*—his heart; *udvaman*—vomiting; *rudhiram*—blood; *mukhāt*—from his mouth; *prasārya*—thrusting outward; *keśa*—his hair; *bāhu*—arms; *aṅghrīn*—and legs; *dharaṇyām*—on the ground; *nyapatat*—he fell; *vyasuḥ*—lifeless.

TRANSLATION

His heart shattered by the club's blow, Dantavakra vomited blood and fell lifeless to the ground, his hair disheveled and his arms and legs sprawling.

TEXT 10

ततः सूक्ष्मतरं ज्योतिः कृष्णमाविशदद्भुतम् ।
पश्यतां सर्वभूतानां यथा चैद्यवधे नृप ॥१०॥

tataḥ sūkṣmataraṁ jyotiḥ
kṛṣṇam āviśad adbhutam
paśyatāṁ sarva-bhūtānāṁ
yathā caidya-vadhe nṛpa

tataḥ—then; *sūkṣma-taram*—very subtle; *jyotiḥ*—a light; *kṛṣṇam*—Lord Kṛṣṇa; *āviśat*—entered; *adbhutam*—amazing; *paśyatām*—as they watched; *sarva*—all; *bhūtānām*—living beings; *yathā*—just as; *caidya-vadhe*—when Śiśupāla was killed; *nṛpa*—O King (Parīkṣit).

TRANSLATION

A most subtle and wondrous spark of light then [rose from the demon's body and] entered Lord Kṛṣṇa while everyone looked on, O King, just as when Śiśupāla was killed.

TEXT 11

विदूरथस्तु तद्भ्राता भ्रातृशोकपरिप्लुतः ।
आगच्छदसिचर्माभ्यामुच्छ्वसंस्तज्जिघांसया ॥११॥

vidūrathas tu tad-bhrātā
bhrātṛ-śoka-pariplutaḥ
āgacchad asi-carmābhyām
ucchvasaṁs taj-jighāṁsayā

vidūrathaḥ—Vidūratha; *tu*—but; *tat*—his, Dantavakra's; *bhrātā*—brother; *bhrātṛ*—for his brother; *śoka*—in sorrow; *pariplutaḥ*—submerged; *āgacchat*—came forward; *asi*—with sword; *carmābhyām*—and shield; *ucchvasan*—breathing heavily; *tat*—Him, Lord Kṛṣṇa; *jighāṁsayā*—wanting to kill.

TRANSLATION

But then Dantavakra's brother Vidūratha, immersed in sorrow over his brother's death, came forward breathing heavily, sword and shield in hand. He wanted to kill the Lord.

TEXT 12

तस्य चापततः कृष्णश्चक्रेण क्षुरनेमिना ।
शिरो जहार राजेन्द्र सकिरीटं सकुण्डलम् ॥१२॥

tasya cāpatataḥ kṛṣṇaś
cakreṇa kṣura-neminā
śiro jahāra rājendra
sa-kirīṭaṁ sa-kuṇḍalam

tasya—of him; *ca*—and; *āpatataḥ*—who was attacking; *kṛṣṇaḥ*—Lord Kṛṣṇa; *cakreṇa*—with His Sudarśana disc; *kṣura*—like a razor; *neminā*—whose edge; *śiraḥ*—the head; *jahāra*—removed; *rāja-indra*—O best of kings; *sa*—with; *kirīṭam*—helmet; *sa*—with; *kuṇḍalam*—earrings.

TRANSLATION

O best of kings, as Vidūratha fell upon Him, Lord Kṛṣṇa used His razor-edged Sudarśana disc to remove his head, complete with its helmet and earrings.

TEXTS 13–15

एवं सौभं च शाल्वं च दन्तवक्रं सहानुजम् ।
हत्वा दुर्विषहानन्यैरीडितः सुरमानवैः ॥१३॥
मुनिभिः सिद्धगन्धर्वैर्विद्याधरमहोरगैः ।
अप्सरोभिः पितृगणैर्यक्षैः किन्नरचारणैः ॥१४॥
उपगीयमानविजयः कुसुमैरभिवर्षितः ।
वृतश्च वृष्णिप्रवरैर्विवेशालंकृतां पुरीम् ॥१५॥

evaṁ saubhaṁ ca śālvaṁ ca
dantavakraṁ sahānujam
hatvā durviṣahān anyair
īḍitaḥ sura-mānavaiḥ

munibhiḥ siddha-gandharvair
vidyādhara-mahoragaiḥ
apsarobhiḥ pitṛ-gaṇair
yakṣaiḥ kinnara-cāraṇaiḥ

upagīyamāna-vijayaḥ
kusumair abhivarṣitaḥ
vṛtaś ca vṛṣṇi-pravarair
viveśālaṅkṛtāṁ purīm

evam—thus; *saubham*—the vehicle Saubha; *ca*—and; *śālvam*—Śālva; *ca*—and; *dantavakram*—Dantavakra; *saha*—together with; *anujam*—his younger brother, Vidūratha; *hatvā*—having killed; *durviṣahān*—insurmountable; *anyaiḥ*—by others; *īḍitaḥ*—praised; *sura*—by demigods; *mānavaiḥ*—and men; *munibhiḥ*—by sages; *siddha*—by perfected mystics; *gandharvaiḥ*—and by heavenly singers; *vidyādhara*—by residents of the Vidyādhara planet; *mahā-uragaiḥ*—and celestial serpents; *apsarobhiḥ*—by dancing girls of heaven; *pitṛ-gaṇaiḥ*—by elevated forefathers; *yakṣaiḥ*—Yakṣas; *kinnara-cāraṇaiḥ*—and by Kinnaras and Cāraṇas; *upagīyamāna*—being chanted; *vijayaḥ*—whose victory; *kusumaiḥ*—with flowers; *abhivarṣitaḥ*—rained upon; *vṛtaḥ*—surrounded; *ca*—and; *vṛṣṇi-pravaraiḥ*—by the most eminent of the Vṛṣṇis; *viveśa*—He entered; *alaṅkṛtām*—decorated; *purīm*—His capital, Dvārakā.

TRANSLATION

Having thus destroyed Śālva and his Saubha airship, along with Dantavakra and his younger brother, all of whom were invincible before any other opponent, the Lord was praised by demigods, human beings and great sages, by Siddhas, Gandharvas, Vidyādharas and Mahoragas, and also by Apsarās, Pitās, Yakṣas, Kinnaras and Cāraṇas. As they sang His glories and showered Him with flowers, the Supreme Lord entered His festively decorated capital city in the company of the most eminent Vṛṣṇis.

TEXT 16

एवं योगेश्वरः कृष्णो भगवान् जगदीश्वरः ।
ईयते पशुदृष्टीनां निर्जितो जयतीति सः ॥१६॥

evaṁ yogeśvaraḥ kṛṣṇo
bhagavān jagad-īśvaraḥ
īyate paśu-dṛṣṭīnām
nirjito jayatīti saḥ

evam—in this fashion; *yoga*—of mystic *yoga; īśvaraḥ*—the Lord; *kṛṣṇaḥ*—Kṛṣṇa; *bhagavān*—the Personality of Godhead; *jagat*—of the universe; *īśvaraḥ*—the Lord; *īyate*—seems; *paśu*—like animals; *dṛṣṭī-nām*—to those whose sight; *nirjitaḥ*—defeated; *jayati*—is victorious; *iti*—as if; *saḥ*—He.

TRANSLATION

Thus Lord Kṛṣṇa, the Supreme Personality of Godhead, the master all mystic power and Lord of the universe, is ever victorious. Only those of beastly vision think He sometimes suffers defeat.

PURPORT

Śrīla Viśvanātha Cakravartī gives the following elaborate commentary on this section of *Śrīmad-Bhāgavatam:*

Concerning the killing of Dantavakra, the *Uttara-khaṇḍa* (279) of the *Padma Purāṇa* contains further details in the following prose passage: *atha śiśupālaṁ nihataṁ śrutvā dantavakraḥ kṛṣṇena saha yoddhuṁ mathurām ājagāma. kṛṣṇas tu tac chrutvā ratham āruhya mathurām āyayau.* "Then, hearing that Śiśupāla had been killed, Dantavakra went to Mathurā to fight against Kṛṣṇa. When Kṛṣṇa, moreover, heard of this, He mounted His chariot and went to Mathurā."

Tayor dantavakra-vāsudevayor aho-rātraṁ mathurā-dvāri saṅgrāmaḥ samavartata. kṛṣṇas tu gadayā taṁ jaghāna. sa tu cūrṇita-sarvāṅgo vajra-nirbhinno mahīdhara iva gatāsur avani-tale nipapāta. so 'pi hareḥ sārūpyeṇa yogi-gamyaṁ nityānanda-sukha-daṁ śāśvataṁ paramaṁ padam avāpa: "Between the two of them—Dantavakra and Lord Vāsudeva—there then began a battle at the gate of Mathurā that lasted all day and night. Finally Kṛṣṇa struck Dantavakra with His club, at which point Dantavakra fell lifeless to the ground, all his limbs smashed like a mountain shattered by a lightning bolt. Dantavakra achieved the liberation of gaining a form equal to the Lord's, and thus he also achieved the Lord's eternal, supreme abode, attainable by perfect *yogīs,* which bestows the happiness of everlasting spiritual bliss."

Itthaṁ jaya-vijayau sanakādi-śāpa-vyājena kevalaṁ bhagavato līlārthaṁ saṁsṛtāv avatīrya janma-traye 'pi tenaiva nihatau janma-trayāvasāne muktim avāptau: "So it was that Jaya and Vijaya—apparently because of being cursed by Sanaka and his brothers but actually to facilitate the Supreme Lord's pastimes—descended to this material world and in three consecutive lifetimes were killed by the Lord Himself. Then, at the completion of these three lifetimes, they attained liberation."

In this passage of the *Padma Purāṇa* the words *kṛṣṇas tu tac chrutvā,* "when Kṛṣṇa heard of this," indicate that the Lord heard from Nārada, who travels as swiftly as the mind, that Dantavakra had gone to Mathurā. Therefore immediately after killing Śālva, without first entering Dvārakā, the Lord reached the vicinity of Mathurā in a single moment on His chariot, which also moves as swiftly as the mind, and there He saw Dantavakra. Thus it is that even today, by the gate of Mathurā facing the direction of Dvārakā, there is a village known in the vernacular as Datihā, a name derived from the Sanskrit *dantavakra-hā,* "killer of Dantavakra." This village was founded by Kṛṣṇa's great-grandson Vajra.

In the same section of the *Padma Purāṇa,* these statements follow: *kṛṣṇo 'pi taṁ hatvā yamunām uttīrya nanda-vrajaṁ gatvā sotkaṇṭhau pitarāv abhivādyāśvāsya tābhyāṁ sāśru-sekam āliṅgitaḥ sakala-gopa-vṛddhān praṇamya bahu-vastrābharaṇādibhis tatra-sthān santarpayām āsa.* "And after killing him [Vidūratha], Kṛṣṇa crossed the Yamunā and went to the cowherd village of Nanda, where He honored and consoled His aggrieved parents. They drenched Him with tears and embraced Him, and then the Lord offered obeisances to the elder cowherd men and gratified all the residents with abundant gifts of clothing, ornaments and so on."

kālindyāḥ puline ramye
puṇya-vṛkṣa-samācite
gopa-nārībhir aniśaṁ
krīḍayām āsa keśavaḥ

ramya-keli-sukhenaiva
gopa-veśa-dharaḥ prabhuḥ
bahu-prema-rasenātra
māsa-dvayam uvāsa ha

"Lord Keśava sported continuously with the cowherd women on the Kālindī's charming bank, which was filled with pious trees. Thus the Supreme Lord, assuming the appearance of a cowherd, resided there for two months, enjoying the pleasure of intimate pastimes in various moods of loving reciprocation."

Atha tatra-sthā nanda-gopādayaḥ sarve janāḥ putra-dārādi-sahitā vāsu-deva-prasādena divya-rūpa-dharā vimānam ārūḍhāḥ paramaṁ vaikuṇṭha-lokam avāpuḥ. kṛṣṇas tu nanda-gopa-vrajaukasāṁ sarveṣāṁ nirāmayaṁ sva-padaṁ dattvā divi deva-gaṇaiḥ saṁstūyamāno dvāravatīṁ viveśa: "Then, by Lord Vāsudeva's grace, Nanda and all the other residents of that place, together with their children and wives, assumed their eternal, spiritual forms, boarded a celestial airplane and ascended to the supreme Vaikuṇṭha planet [Goloka Vṛndāvana]. Lord Kṛṣṇa, however, after bestowing on Nanda Gopa and all the other inhabitants of Vraja His own transcendental abode, which is free of all disease, traveled through the sky and returned to Dvārakā as demigods chanted His praises."

Śrīla Rūpa Gosvāmī comments as follows on this passage in his *Laghu-bhāgavatāmṛta* (1.488-89):

vrajeśāder aṁśa-bhūtā
ye droṇādyā avātaran
kṛṣṇas tān eva vaikuṇṭhe
prāhiṇod iti sāmpratam

preṣṭhebhyo 'pi priyatamair
janair gokula-vāsibhiḥ
vṛndāraṇye sadaivāsau
vihāraṁ kurute hariḥ

"Since Droṇa and other demigods had previously descended to earth to merge as partial expansions into the King of Vraja and other devotees of Vṛndāvana, at this time it was these demigod expansions whom Lord Kṛṣṇa sent off to Vaikuṇṭha. Lord Hari is perpetually enjoying pastimes in Vṛndāvana with His intimate devotees, the residents of Gokula, who are dearer to Him than even His most dear other devotees."

In the passage of the *Padma Purāṇa,* the word *putra* in the phrase *nanda-gopādayaḥ sarve janāḥ putra-dārādi-sahitāḥ* ("Nanda Gopa and the others, together with their children and wives") refers to such sons as Kṛṣṇa, Śrīdāmā and Subala, while the word *dāra* refers to such wives as Śrī Yaśodā and Kīrtidā, the mother of Rādhārāṇī. The phrase *sarve janāḥ* ("all the people") refers to everyone living in the district of Vraja. Thus they all went to the topmost Vaikuṇṭha planet, Goloka. The phrase *divya-rūpa-dharāḥ* indicates that in Goloka they engage in pastimes appropriate to demigods, not those suited to humans, as in Gokula. Just as during Lord Rāmacandra's incarnation the residents of Ayodhyā were transported to Vaikuṇṭha in their selfsame bodies, so in this incarnation of Kṛṣṇa the residents of Vraja attained to Goloka in theirs.

Lord Kṛṣṇa's journey from Dvārakā to Vraja is confirmed by the following passage of *Śrīmad-Bhāgavatam* (1.11.9): *yarhy ambujākṣāpasasāra bho bhavān kurūn madhūn vātha suhṛd-didṛkṣayā/ tatrābda-koṭi-pratimaḥ kṣaṇo bhavet.* "O lotus-eyed Lord, whenever You go away to Mathurā, Vṛndāvana or Hastināpura to meet Your friends and relatives, every moment of Your absence seems like a million years." Lord Kṛṣṇa had been harboring a desire to go see His friends and relatives in Vraja ever since Lord Baladeva had gone there, but His mother, father and other elders in Dvārakā had refused to give Him permission. Now, however, after the killing of Śālva, when Kṛṣṇa heard from Nārada that Dantavakra had gone to Mathurā, no one could object to the Lord's going there immediately without first entering Dvārakā. And after killing Dantavakra, He would have the opportunity to meet with His friends and relatives living in Vraja.

Thinking like this, and also remembering Uddhava's allusion to the *gopīs* in the words *gāyanti te viśada-karma* (*Bhāg.* 10.71.9), He went to Vraja, dispelling the feelings of separation of the inhabitants. For two months Lord Kṛṣṇa enjoyed in Vṛndāvana just as before, previous to His leaving there to kill Kaṁsa in Mathurā. Then, at the end of two months, He withdrew His Vraja pastimes from mundane eyes by taking the demigod portions of His parents and other relatives and friends to Vaikuṇṭha. Thus, in one complete plenary manifestation He went to Goloka in the spiritual world, in another He remained perpetually enjoying in Vraja while invisible to material eyes, and in yet another He mounted His chariot and returned alone to Dvārakā. The people of Śaurasena province thought that after killing Dantavakra Kṛṣṇa had paid a visit to His parents and other dear ones and now was returning to Dvārakā. The people of Vraja, on the other hand, could not understand where He had suddenly disappeared to, and so they were totally astonished.

Furthermore, Śukadeva considered that Parīkṣit Mahārāja might think, "How is it that the same Kṛṣṇa who caused the cowherds to attain Vaikuṇṭha in their selfsame bodies also caused the residents of Dvārakā to attain such an inauspicious condition in the course of His *mauṣala-līlā*?" Thus the King might consider the arrangement unfair because of his own affinity for the Yadus. That is why Śukadeva Gosvāmī did not allow him to hear this pastime, which, as mentioned above, is related in the *Uttara-khaṇḍa* of *Śrī Padma Purāṇa.*

In *Śrī Vaiṣṇava-toṣaṇī,* Sanātana Gosvāmī's commentary on the Tenth Canto, we find the following sequential list of pastimes: First was the journey on the occasion of the solar eclipse, then the Rājasūya assembly, then the gambling match and attempted disrobing of Draupadī, then the Pāṇḍavas' exile to the forest, then the killing of Śālva and Dantavakra, then Kṛṣṇa's visit to Vṛndāvana, and finally the winding up of the Vṛndāvana pastimes.

TEXT 17

श्रुत्वा युद्धोद्यमं रामः कुरूणां सह पाण्डवैः ।
तीर्थाभिषेकव्याजेन मध्यस्थः प्रययौ किल ॥१७॥

śrutvā yuddhodyamaṁ rāmaḥ
kurūṇāṁ saha pāṇḍavaiḥ
tīrthābhiṣeka-vyājena
madhya-sthaḥ prayayau kila

śrutvā—hearing; *yuddha*—for battle; *udyamam*—the preparations; *rāmaḥ*—Lord Balarāma; *kurūṇām*—of the Kurus; *saha*—with; *pāṇḍavaiḥ*—the Pāṇḍavas; *tīrtha*—in holy places; *abhiṣeka*—of bathing; *vyājena*—on the pretext; *madhya-sthaḥ*—neutral; *prayayau*—He departed; *kila*—indeed.

TRANSLATION

Lord Balarāma then heard that the Kurus were preparing for war with the Pāṇḍavas. Being neutral, He departed on the pretext of going to bathe in holy places.

PURPORT

Both Duryodhana and Yudhiṣṭhira were dear to Lord Balarāma, and so to avoid an awkward situation He departed. Furthermore, after killing the demon Vidūratha, Lord Kṛṣṇa put aside His weapons, but Lord Balarāma still had to kill Romaharṣaṇa and Balvala to finish relieving the earth of her burden of demons.

TEXT 18

स्नात्वा प्रभासे सन्तर्प्य देवर्षिपितृमानवान् ।
सरस्वतीं प्रतिस्रोतं ययौ ब्राह्मणसंवृतः ॥१८॥

snātvā prabhāse santarpya
devarṣi-pitṛ-mānavān
sarasvatīṁ prati-srotaṁ
yayau brāhmaṇa-saṁvṛtaḥ

snātvā—having bathed; *prabhāse*—at Prabhāsa; *santarpya*—and having honored; *deva*—the demigods; *ṛṣi*—sages; *pitṛ*—forefathers; *mānavān*—and human beings; *sarasvatīm*—to the river Sarasvatī; *prati-srotam*—which flows toward the sea; *yayau*—He went; *brāhmaṇa-saṁvṛtaḥ*—surrounded by *brāhmaṇas.*

TRANSLATION

After bathing at Prabhāsa and honoring the demigods, sages, forefathers and prominent human beings, He went in the company of *brāhmaṇas* to the portion of the Sarasvatī that flows westward into the sea.

TEXTS 19–20

पृथूदकं बिन्दुसरस्त्रितकूपं सुदर्शनम् ।
विशालं ब्रह्मतीर्थं च चक्रं प्राचीं सरस्वतीम् ॥१९॥

यमुनामनु यान्येव गंगामनु च भारत ।
जगाम नैमिषं यत्र ऋषयः सत्रमासते ॥२०॥

pṛthūdakaṁ bindu-saras
tritakūpaṁ sudarśanam
viśālaṁ brahma-tīrthaṁ ca
cakraṁ prācīṁ sarasvatīm

yamunām anu yāny eva
gaṅgām anu ca bhārata
jagāma naimiṣaṁ yatra
ṛṣayaḥ satram āsate

pṛthu—broad; *udakam*—whose water; *bindu-saraḥ*—the lake Bindu-sarovara; *trita-kūpam sudarśanam*—the pilgrimage places known as Tritakūpa and Sudarśana; *viśālam brahma-tīrtham ca*—Viśāla and Brahma-tīrtha; *cakram*—Cakra-tīrtha; *prācīm*—flowing east; *sarasvatīm*—the Sarasvatī River; *yamunām*—the Yamunā River; *anu*—along; *yāni*—which; *eva*—all; *gaṅgām*—the Ganges; *anu*—along; *ca*—also; *bhārata*—O descendant of Bharata (Parīkṣit Mahārāja); *jagāma*—He visited; *naimiṣam*—the Naimiṣa forest; *yatra*—where; *ṛṣayaḥ*—great sages; *satram*—an elaborate sacrifice; *āsate*—were performing.

TRANSLATION

Lord Balarāma visited the broad Bindu-saras Lake, Tritakūpa, Sudarśana, Viśāla, Brahma-tīrtha, Cakra-tīrtha and the eastward-flowing Sarasvatī. He also went to all the holy places along the Yamunā and the Ganges, O Bhārata, and then He came to the Naimiṣa forest, where great sages were performing an elaborate sacrifice.

TEXT 21

तमागतमभिप्रेत्य मुनयो दीर्घसत्रिणः ।
अभिनन्द्य यथान्यायं प्रणम्योत्थाय चार्चयन् ॥२१॥

tam āgatam abhipretya
munayo dīrgha-satriṇaḥ

abhinandya yathā-nyāyaṁ
praṇamyotthāya cārcayan

tam—Him; *āgatam*—arrived; *abhipretya*—recognizing; *munayaḥ*—the sages; *dīrgha*—for a long time; *satriṇaḥ*—who had been engaged in the sacrificial performance; *abhinandya*—greeting; *yathā*—as; *nyāyam*—correct; *praṇamya*—bowing down; *utthāya*—having stood up; *ca*—and; *ārcayan*—they worshiped.

TRANSLATION

Recognizing the Lord upon His arrival, the sages, who had been engaged in their sacrificial rituals for a long time, greeted Him properly by standing up, bowing down and worshiping Him.

TEXT 22

सोऽर्चितः सपरीवारः कृतासनपरिग्रहः ।
रोमहर्षणमासीनं महर्षेः शिष्यमैक्षत ॥२२॥

so 'rcitaḥ sa-parīvāraḥ
kṛtāsana-parigrahaḥ
romaharṣaṇam āsīnaṁ
maharṣeḥ śiṣyam aikṣata

saḥ—He; *arcitaḥ*—worshiped; *sa*—together with; *parīvāraḥ*—His entourage; *kṛta*—having done; *āsana*—of a seat; *parigrahaḥ*—acceptance; *romaharṣaṇam*—Romaharṣaṇa Sūta; *āsīnam*—seated; *mahā-ṛṣeḥ*—of the greatest of sages, Vyāsadeva; *śiṣyam*—the disciple; *aikṣata*—saw.

TRANSLATION

After being thus worshiped along with His entourage, the Lord accepted a seat of honor. Then He noticed that Romaharṣaṇa, Vyāsadeva's disciple, had remained seated.

TEXT 23

अप्रत्युत्थायिनं सूतमकृतप्रह्वणाञ्जलिम् ।
अध्यासीनं च तान् विप्रांश्चुकोपोद्वीक्ष्य माधवः ॥२३॥

apratyutthāyinaṁ sūtam
akṛta-prahvaṇāñjalim
adhyāsīnaṁ ca tān viprāṁś
cukopodvīkṣya mādhavaḥ

apratyutthāyinam—who had failed to stand up; *sūtam*—the son of a mixed marriage between a *kṣatriya* father and *brāhmaṇa* mother; *akṛta*—who had not done; *prahvaṇa*—bowing down; *añjalim*—and joining of palms; *adhyāsīnam*—sitting higher; *ca*—and; *tān*—than those; *viprān*—learned *brāhmaṇas; cukopa*—became angry; *udvīkṣya*—seeing; *mādhavaḥ*—Lord Balarāma.

TRANSLATION

Lord Balarāma became extremely angry upon seeing how this member of the *sūta* caste had failed to stand up, bow down or join his palms, and also how he was sitting above all the learned *brāhmaṇas.*

PURPORT

Romaharṣaṇa had failed to greet Lord Balarāma in any of the standard ways for welcoming a superior personality. Also, despite being of a lower caste, he sat in a seat above the assembly of exalted *brāhmaṇas.*

TEXT 24

यस्मादसाविमान् विप्रानध्यास्ते प्रतिलोमजः ।
धर्मपालांस्तथैवास्मान् वधमर्हति दुर्मतिः ॥२४॥

yasmād asāv imān viprān
adhyāste pratiloma-jaḥ
dharma-pālāṁs tathaivāsmān
vadham arhati durmatiḥ

yasmāt—because; *asau*—he; *imān*—than these; *viprān*—*brāhmaṇas; adhyāste*—is sitting higher; *pratiloma-jaḥ*—born from an improperly mixed marriage; *dharma*—of the principles of religion; *pālān*—the protector; *tathā eva*—also; *asmān*—Myself; *vadham*—death; *arhati*—he deserves; *durmatiḥ*—foolish.

TRANSLATION

[Lord Balarāma said:] Because this fool born from an improperly mixed marriage sits above all these *brāhmaṇas* and even above Me, the protector of religion, he deserves to die.

TEXTS 25–26

ऋषेर्भगवतो भूत्वा शिष्योऽधीत्य बहूनि च ।
सेतिहासपुराणानि धर्मशास्त्राणि सर्वशः ॥२५॥
अदान्तस्याविनीतस्य वृथा पण्डितमानिनः ।
न गुणाय भवन्ति स्म नटस्येवाजितात्मनः ॥२६॥

ṛṣer bhagavato bhūtvā
śiṣyo 'dhītya bahūni ca
setihāsa-purāṇāni
dharma-śāstrāṇi sarvaśaḥ

adāntasyāvinītasya
vṛthā paṇḍita-māninaḥ
na guṇāya bhavanti sma
naṭasyevājitātmanaḥ

ṛṣeḥ—of the sage (Vyāsadeva); *bhagavataḥ*—the incarnation of Godhead; *bhūtvā*—becoming; *śiṣyaḥ*—a disciple; *adhītya*—studying; *bahūni*—many; *ca*—and; *sa*—together with; *itihāsa*—epic histories; *purāṇāni*—and *Purāṇas; dharma-śāstrāṇi*—the scriptures describing the religious duties of man; *sarvaśaḥ*—fully; *adāntasya*—for him who is not self-controlled; *avinītasya*—not humble; *vṛthā*—vainly; *paṇḍita*—a scholarly authority; *māninaḥ*—thinking himself; *na guṇāya*—not leading to good qualities; *bhavanti sma*—they have become; *naṭasya*—of a stage performer; *iva*—like; *ajita*—unconquered; *ātmanaḥ*—whose mind.

TRANSLATION

Although he is a disciple of the divine sage Vyāsa and has thoroughly learned many scriptures from him, including the law-books of religious duties and the epic histories and *Purāṇas*, all this study has not produced good qualities in him. Rather, his study of the scriptures is like an actor's studying his part, for he is not self-controlled or humble and vainly presumes himself a scholarly authority, though he has failed to conquer his own mind.

PURPORT

One might argue that Romaharṣaṇa committed an innocent mistake when he failed to recognize Lord Balarāma, but such an argument is refuted here by Lord Balarāma's strong criticism.

TEXT 27

एतदर्थो हि लोकेऽस्मिन्नवतारो मया कृतः ।
वध्या मे धर्मध्वजिनस्ते हि पातकिनोऽधिकाः ॥२७॥

etad-artho hi loke 'sminn
avatāro mayā kṛtaḥ
vadhyā me dharma-dhvajinas
te hi pātakino 'dhikāḥ

etat—for this; *arthaḥ*—purpose; *hi*—indeed; *loke*—into the world; *asmin*—this; *avatāraḥ*—descent; *mayā*—by Me; *kṛtaḥ*—done; *vadhyāḥ*—to be killed; *me*—by Me; *dharma-dhvajinaḥ*—those who pose as religious; *te*—they; *hi*—indeed; *pātakinaḥ*—sinful; *adhikāḥ*—most.

TRANSLATION

The very purpose of My descent into this world is to kill such hypocrites who pretend to be religious. Indeed, they are the most sinful rascals.

PURPORT

Lord Balarāma was not prepared to overlook Romaharṣaṇa's offense. The Lord had descended specifically to eliminate those who claim to be great religious leaders but do not even respect the Supreme Personality of Godhead.

TEXT 28

एतावदुक्त्वा भगवान्निवृत्तोऽसद्वधादपि ।
भावित्वात्तं कुशाग्रेण करस्थेनाहनत्प्रभुः ॥२८॥

etāvad uktvā bhagavān
nivṛtto 'sad-vadhād api
bhāvitvāt taṁ kuśāgreṇa
kara-sthenāhanat prabhuḥ

etāvat—this much; *uktvā*—saying; *bhagavān*—the Personality of Godhead; *nivṛttaḥ*—stopped; *asat*—the impious; *vadhāt*—from killing; *api*—although; *bhāvitvāt*—because it was inevitable; *tam*—him, Romaharṣaṇa; *kuśa*—of *kuśa* grass; *agreṇa*—with the tip of a blade; *kara*—in His hand; *sthena*—held; *ahanat*—killed; *prabhuḥ*—the Lord.

TRANSLATION

[Śukadeva Gosvāmī continued:] Although Lord Balarāma had stopped killing the impious, Romaharṣaṇa's death was inevitable. Thus, having spoken, the Lord killed him by picking up a blade of *kuśa* grass and touching him with its tip.

PURPORT

Śrīla Prabhupāda writes, "Lord Balarāma had avoided taking part in the Battle of Kurukṣetra, and yet because of His position, the reestablishment of religious principles was His prime duty. Considering these points, He killed Romaharṣaṇa Sūta simply by striking him with a *kuśa* straw, which was nothing but a blade of grass. If someone questions how Lord Balarāma could kill Romaharṣaṇa Sūta simply by striking him with a blade of *kuśa* grass, the answer is given in the *Śrīmad-Bhāgavatam* by the use of the word *prabhu* (master). The Lord's position is always transcendental, and because He is omnipotent He can act as He likes without being obliged to follow the material laws and principles. Thus it was possible for Him to kill Romaharṣaṇa Sūta simply by striking him with a blade of *kuśa* grass."

TEXT 29

हाहेतिवादिनः सर्वे मुनयः खिन्नमानसाः ।
ऊचुः संकर्षणं देवमधर्मस्ते कृतः प्रभो ॥२९॥

hāheti-vādinaḥ sarve
munayaḥ khinna-mānasāḥ
ūcuḥ saṅkarṣaṇaṁ devam
adharmas te kṛtaḥ prabho

hā-hā—"alas, alas"; *iti*—thus; *vādinaḥ*—saying; *sarve*—all; *munayaḥ*—the sages; *khinna*—disturbed; *mānasāḥ*—whose minds; *ūcuḥ*—they told; *saṅkarṣaṇam*—Balarāma; *devam*—the Supreme Lord; *adharmaḥ*—an irreligious act; *te*—by You; *kṛtaḥ*—done; *prabho*—O master.

TRANSLATION

All the sages cried out, "Alas, alas!" in great distress. They told Lord Saṅkarṣaṇa, "O master, You have committed an irreligious act!

TEXT 30

अस्य ब्रह्मासनं दत्तमस्माभिर्यदुनन्दन ।
आयुश्चात्माक्लमं तावद्यावत्सत्रं समाप्यते ॥३०॥

asya brahmāsanaṁ dattam
asmābhir yadu-nandana
āyuś cātmāklamaṁ tāvad
yāvat satraṁ samāpyate

asya—his; *brahma-āsanam*—the spiritual master's seat; *dattam*—given; *asmābhiḥ*—by us; *yadu-nandana*—O darling of the Yadus; *āyuḥ*—

long life; *ca*—and; *ātma*—bodily; *aklamam*—freedom from trouble; *tāvat*—for that long; *yāvat*—until; *satram*—the sacrifice; *samāpyate*—is completed.

TRANSLATION

"O favorite of the Yadus, we gave him the seat of the spiritual master and promised him long life and freedom from physical pain for as long as this sacrifice continues.

PURPORT

Although Romaharṣaṇa was not a *brāhmaṇa,* having been born of a mixed marriage, he was invested with that status by the assembled sages and thus given the *brahmāsana,* the seat of the chief officiating priest.

TEXTS 31–32

अजानतैवाचरितस्त्वया ब्रह्मवधो यथा ।
योगेश्वरस्य भवतो नाम्नायोऽपि नियामकः ॥३१॥
यद्येतद्ब्रह्महत्यायाः पावनं लोकपावन ।
चरिष्यति भवाल्ँलोकसंग्रहोऽनन्यचोदितः ॥३२॥

ajānataivācaritas
tvayā brahma-vadho yathā
yogeśvarasya bhavato
nāmnāyo 'pi niyāmakaḥ

yady etad-brahma-hatyāyāḥ
pāvanaṁ loka-pāvana
cariṣyati bhavāl̐ loka-
saṅgraho 'nanya-coditaḥ

ajānatā—not knowing; *eva*—only; *ācaritaḥ*—done; *tvayā*—by You; *brahma*—of a *brāhmaṇa; vadhaḥ*—the killing; *yathā*—actually; *yoga*—of mystic power; *īśvarasya*—for the Lord; *bhavataḥ*—Yourself; *na*—not; *āmnāyaḥ*—scriptural injunction; *api*—even; *niyāmakaḥ*—regulator; *yadi*—if; *etat*—for this; *brahma*—of a *brāhmaṇa; hatyāyāḥ*—killing;

pāvanam—purifying atonement; *loka*—of the world; *pāvana*—O purifier; *cariṣyati*—executes; *bhavān*—Your good self; *loka-saṅgrahaḥ*—benefit for the people in general; *ananya*—by no one else; *coditaḥ*—impelled.

TRANSLATION

"You have unknowingly killed a *brāhmaṇa*. Of course, even the injunctions of revealed scripture cannot dictate to You, the Lord of all mystic power. But if by Your own free will You nonetheless carry out the prescribed purification for this slaying of a *brāhmaṇa*, O purifier of the whole world, people in general will greatly benefit by Your example."

TEXT 33

श्रीभगवानुवाच
चरिष्ये वधनिर्वेशं लोकानुग्रहकाम्यया ।
नियमः प्रथमे कल्पे यावान् स तु विधीयताम् ॥३३॥

śrī-bhagavān uvāca
cariṣye vadha-nirveśaṁ
lokānugraha-kāmyayā
niyamaḥ prathame kalpe
yāvān sa tu vidhīyatām

śrī-bhagavān uvāca—the Supreme Lord said; *cariṣye*—I will execute; *vadha*—for the killing; *nirveśam*—atonement; *loka*—for the people in general; *anugraha*—compassion; *kāmyayā*—desiring to show; *niyamaḥ*—the regulative injunction; *prathame*—in the primary; *kalpe*—ritual; *yāvān*—as much; *saḥ*—that; *tu*—indeed; *vidhīyatām*—please prescribe.

TRANSLATION

The Personality of Godhead said: I will certainly perform the atonement for this killing, since I wish to show compassion to the people in general. Please, therefore, prescribe for Me whatever ritual is to be done first.

TEXT 34

दीर्घमायुर्बतैतस्य सत्त्वमिन्द्रियमेव च ।
आशासितं यत्तद् ब्रूते साधये योगमायया ॥३४॥

dīrgham āyur bataitasya
sattvam indriyam eva ca
āśāsitaṁ yat tad brūte
sādhaye yoga-māyayā

dīrgham—long; *āyuḥ*—life span; *bata*—oh; *etasya*—for him; *sattvam*—strength; *indriyam*—sensory power; *eva ca*—also; *āśāsitam*—promised; *yat*—which; *tat*—that; *brūte*—please say; *sādhaye*—I shall make happen; *yoga-māyayā*—by My mystic power.

TRANSLATION

O sages, just say the word, and by My mystic power I shall restore everything you promised him—long life, strength and sensory power.

TEXT 35

ऋषय ऊचुः

अस्त्रस्य तव वीर्यस्य मृत्योरस्माकमेव च ।
यथा भवेद्वचः सत्यं तथा राम विधीयताम् ॥३५॥

ṛṣaya ūcuḥ
astrasya tava vīryasya
mṛtyor asmākam eva ca
yathā bhaved vacaḥ satyaṁ
tathā rāma vidhīyatām

ṛṣayaḥ ūcuḥ—the sages said; *astrasya*—of the weapon (the blade of *kuśa* grass); *tava*—Your; *vīryasya*—potency; *mṛtyoḥ*—of the death; *asmākam*—our; *eva ca*—also; *yathā*—so that; *bhavet*—may remain; *vacaḥ*—the words; *satyam*—true; *tathā*—thus; *rāma*—O Rāma; *vidhīyatām*—please arrange.

TRANSLATION

The sages said: Please see to it, O Rāma, that Your power and that of Your *kuśa* weapon, as well as our promise and Romaharṣaṇa's death, all remain intact.

TEXT 36

श्रीभगवानुवाच
आत्मा वै पुत्र उत्पन्न इति वेदानुशासनम् ।
तस्मादस्य भवेद्वक्ता आयुरिन्द्रियसत्त्ववान् ॥३६॥

śrī-bhagavān uvāca
ātmā vai putra utpanna
iti vedānuśāsanam
tasmād asya bhaved vaktā
āyur-indriya-sattva-vān

śrī-bhagavān uvāca—the Supreme Lord said; *ātmā*—one's self; *vai*—indeed; *putraḥ*—the son; *utpannaḥ*—born; *iti*—thus; *veda-anuśāsanam*—the instruction of the *Vedas;* *tasmāt*—therefore; *asya*—his (son); *bhavet*—should be; *vaktā*—the speaker; *āyuḥ*—long life; *indriya*—strong senses; *sattva*—and physical power; *vān*—possessing.

TRANSLATION

The Supreme Lord said: The *Vedas* instruct us that one's own self takes birth again as one's son. Thus let Romaharṣaṇa's son become the speaker of the *Purāṇas,* and let him be endowed with long life, strong senses and stamina.

PURPORT

Śrīla Śrīdhara Svāmī quotes the following Vedic verse to illustrate the principle enunciated here by Lord Balarāma:

aṅgād aṅgāt sambhavasi
hṛdayād abhijāyase
ātmā vai putra-nāmāsi
sañjīva śaradaḥ śatam

"You have taken birth from my various limbs and have arisen from my very heart. You are my own self in the form of my son. May you live through a hundred autumns." This verse appears in the *Śatapatha Brāhmaṇa* (14.9.8.4) and the *Bṛhad-āraṇyaka Upaniṣad* (6.4.8).

TEXT 37

किं वः कामो मुनिश्रेष्ठा ब्रूताहं करवाण्यथ ।
अजानतस्त्वपचितिं यथा मे चिन्त्यतां बुधाः ॥३७॥

kiṁ vaḥ kāmo muni-śreṣṭhā
brūtāhaṁ karavāṇy atha
ajānatas tv apacitiṁ
yathā me cintyatāṁ budhāḥ

kim—what; *vaḥ*—your; *kāmaḥ*—desire; *muni*—of sages; *śreṣṭhāḥ*—O best; *brūta*—please say; *aham*—I; *karavāṇi*—shall do it; *atha*—and then; *ajānataḥ*—who does not know; *tu*—indeed; *apacitim*—the atonement; *yathā*—properly; *me*—for Me; *cintyatām*—please think of; *budhāḥ*—O intelligent ones.

TRANSLATION

Please tell Me your desire, O best of sages, and I shall certainly fulfill it. And, O wise souls, please carefully determine My proper atonement, since I do not know what it might be.

PURPORT

Lord Balarāma here sets a perfect example for people in general by humbly submitting Himself before the qualified *brāhmaṇas*.

TEXT 38

ऋषय ऊचुः

इल्वलस्य सुतो घोरो बल्वलो नाम दानवः ।
स दूषयति नः सत्रमेत्य पर्वणि पर्वणि ॥३८॥

ṛṣaya ūcuḥ
ilvalasya suto ghoro
balvalo nāma dānavaḥ
sa dūṣayati naḥ satram
etya parvaṇi parvaṇi

ṛṣayaḥ ūcuḥ—the sages said; *ilvalasya*—of Ilvala; *sutaḥ*—the son; *ghoraḥ*—fearsome; *balvalaḥ nāma*—named Balvala; *dānavaḥ*—demon; *saḥ*—he; *dūṣayati*—contaminates; *naḥ*—our; *satram*—sacrifice: *etya*—coming; *parvaṇi parvaṇi*—on each new-moon day.

TRANSLATION

The sages said: A fearsome demon named Balvala, the son of Ilvala, comes here every new-moon day and contaminates our sacrifice.

PURPORT

First the sages tell Lord Balarāma the favor they would like Him to do for them.

TEXT 39

तं पापं जहि दाशार्ह तन्नः शुश्रूषणं परम् ।
पूयशोणितविन्मूत्रसुरामांसाभिवर्षिणम् ॥३९॥

taṁ pāpaṁ jahi dāśārha
tan naḥ śuśrūṣaṇaṁ param
pūya-śoṇita-vin-mūtra-
surā-māṁsābhivarṣiṇam

tam—that; *pāpam*—sinful person; *jahi*—please kill; *dāśārha*—O descendant of Daśārha; *tat*—that; *naḥ*—to us; *śuśrūṣaṇam*—service; *param*—best; *pūya*—pus; *śoṇita*—blood; *vit*—feces; *mūtra*—urine; *surā*—wine; *māṁsa*—and meat; *abhivarṣiṇam*—who pours down.

TRANSLATION

O descendant of Daśārha, please kill that sinful demon, who pours down pus, blood, feces, urine, wine and meat upon us. This is the best service You can do for us.

TEXT 40

ततश्च भारतं वर्षं परीत्य सुसमाहितः ।
चरित्वा द्वादशमासांस्तीर्थस्नायी विशुध्यसि ॥४०॥

tataś ca bhāratam̐ varṣam̐
parītya su-samāhitaḥ
caritvā dvādaśa-māsām̐s
tīrtha-snāyī viśudhyasi

tataḥ—then; *ca*—and; *bhāratam varṣam*—the land of Bhārata (India); *parītya*—circumambulating; *su-samāhitaḥ*—in a serious mood; *caritvā*—performing penances; *dvādaśa*—twelve; *māsān*—months; *tīrtha*—at holy places of pilgrimage; *snāyī*—bathing; *viśudhyasi*—You will be purified.

TRANSLATION

Thereafter, for twelve months, You should circumambulate the land of Bhārata in a mood of serious meditation, executing austerities and bathing at various holy pilgrimage sites. In this way You will become purified.

PURPORT

Śrīla Jīva Gosvāmī points out that the word *viśudhyasi* means that Lord Balarāma would achieve spotless fame by setting such a perfect example for the people in general.

Śrīla Prabhupāda writes, "The *brāhmaṇas* could understand the purpose of the Lord, and thus they suggested that He atone in a manner which would be beneficial for them."

Thus end the purports of the humble servants of His Divine Grace A. C. Bhaktivedanta Swami Prabhupāda to the Tenth Canto, Seventy-eighth Chapter, of the Śrīmad-Bhāgavatam, *entitled "The Killing of Dantavakra, Vidūratha and Romaharṣaṇa."*

CHAPTER SEVENTY-NINE

Lord Balarāma Goes on Pilgrimage

This chapter describes how Lord Baladeva satisfied the *brāhmaṇas* by killing Balvala, bathed at various holy pilgrimage sites and attempted to dissuade Bhīmasena and Duryodhana from fighting.

At the sacrificial arena of the sages at Naimiṣāraṇya forest, a harsh wind began to blow on the new-moon day, spreading the obnoxious smell of pus and obscuring everything with dust. The demon Balvala then appeared there with a trident in his hand, his massive body pitch black and his face very frightening. Lord Baladeva caught the demon with His plow and then struck him a ferocious blow on the head with His club, killing him. The sages chanted Lord Baladeva's glories and presented Him with lavish gifts.

Lord Balarāma then began His pilgrimage, during which He visited many holy *tīrthas.* When He heard news of the battle between the Kurus and Pāṇḍavas, the Lord went to Kurukṣetra to try to stop the duel between Bhīma and Duryodhana. But He could not dissuade them from fighting, so deep was their enmity. Understanding that the fight was the arrangement of fate, Lord Baladeva left the battlefield and returned to Dvārakā.

Some time later, Balarāma again went to the Naimiṣāraṇya forest, where the sages performed a number of fire sacrifices on His behalf. Lord Baladeva reciprocated by granting the sages transcendental knowledge and revealing to them His eternal identity.

TEXT 1

श्रीशुक उवाच
ततः पर्वण्युपावृत्ते प्रचण्डः पांशुवर्षणः ।
भीमो वायुरभूद् राजन् पूयगन्धस्तु सर्वशः ॥१॥

śrī-śuka uvāca
tataḥ parvaṇy upāvṛtte
pracaṇḍaḥ pāṁśu-varṣaṇaḥ

bhīmo vāyur abhūd rājan
pūya-gandhas tu sarvaśaḥ

śrī-śukaḥ uvāca—Śukadeva Gosvāmī said; *tataḥ*—then; *parvaṇi*—the new-moon day; *upāvṛtte*—when it came; *pracaṇḍaḥ*—fierce; *pāṁśu*—dust; *varṣaṇaḥ*—raining; *bhīmaḥ*—frightening; *vāyuḥ*—a wind; *abhūt*—arose; *rājan*—O King (Parīkṣit); *pūya*—of pus; *gandhaḥ*—the smell; *tu*—and; *sarvaśaḥ*—all over.

TRANSLATION

Śukadeva Gosvāmī said: Then, on the new-moon day, O King, a fierce and frightening wind arose, scattering dust all about and spreading the smell of pus everywhere.

TEXT 2

ततोऽमेध्यमयं वर्षं बल्वलेन विनिर्मितम् ।
अभवद्यज्ञशालायां सोऽन्वदृश्यत शूलधृक् ॥२॥

tato 'medhya-mayaṁ varṣaṁ
balvalena vinirmitam
abhavad yajña-śālāyāṁ
so 'nvadṛśyata śūla-dhṛk

tataḥ—then; *amedhya*—abominable things; *mayam*—full of; *varṣam*—a rain; *balvalena*—by Balvala; *vinirmitam*—produced; *abhavat*—occurred; *yajña*—of the sacrifice; *śālāyām*—upon the arena; *saḥ*—he, Balvala; *anvadṛśyata*—appeared after this; *śūla*—a trident; *dhṛk*—carrying.

TRANSLATION

Next, onto the sacrificial arena came a downpour of abominable things sent by Balvala, after which the demon himself appeared, trident in hand.

TEXTS 3–4

तं विलोक्य बृहत्कायं भिन्नाञ्जनचयोपमम् ।
तप्तताम्रशिखाश्मश्रुं दंष्ट्रोग्रभ्रुकुटीमुखम् ॥३॥
सस्मार मूषलं रामः परसैन्यविदारणम् ।
हलं च दैत्यदमनं ते तूर्णमुपतस्थतुः ॥४॥

taṁ vilokya bṛhat-kāyaṁ
bhinnāñjana-cayopamam
tapta-tāmra-śikhā-śmaśruṁ
daṁṣṭrogra-bhru-kuṭī-mukham

sasmāra mūṣalaṁ rāmaḥ
para-sainya-vidāraṇam
halaṁ ca daitya-damanaṁ
te tūrṇam upatasthatuḥ

tam—him; *vilokya*—seeing; *bṛhat*—immense; *kāyam*—whose body; *bhinna*—broken; *añjana*—of black eye-makeup; *caya*—a pile; *upamam*—resembling; *tapta*—burning; *tāmra*—(colored like) copper; *śikhā*—whose topknot; *śmaśrum*—and beard; *daṁṣṭrā*—with its teeth; *ugra*—fearsome; *bhru*—of eyebrows; *kuṭī*—with furrows; *mukham*—whose face; *sasmāra*—remembered; *mūṣalam*—His club; *rāmaḥ*—Lord Balarāma; *para*—opposing; *sainya*—armies; *vidāraṇam*—which tears asunder; *halam*—His plow; *ca*—and; *daitya*—demons; *damanam*—which subdues; *te*—they; *tūrṇam*—at once; *upatasthatuḥ*—presented themselves.

TRANSLATION

The immense demon resembled a mass of black carbon. His topknot and beard were like molten copper, and his face had horrible fangs and furrowed eyebrows. Upon seeing him, Lord Balarāma thought of His club, which tears to pieces His enemies' armies, and His plow weapon, which punishes the demons. Thus summoned, His two weapons appeared before Him at once.

TEXT 5

तमाकृष्य हलाग्रेण बल्वलं गगनेचरम् ।
मूषलेनाहनत्क्रुद्धो मूर्ध्नि ब्रह्मद्रुहं बलः ॥५॥

tam ākṛṣya halāgreṇa
balvalaṁ gagane-caram
mūṣalenāhanat kruddho
mūrdhni brahma-druhaṁ balaḥ

tam—him; *ākṛṣya*—pulling toward Him; *hala*—of His plow; *agreṇa*—with the front end; *balvalam*—Balvala; *gagane*—in the sky; *caram*—who was moving; *mūṣalena*—with His club; *ahanat*—struck; *kruddhaḥ*—angry; *mūrdhni*—on the head; *brahma*—of *brāhmaṇas; druham*—the harasser; *balaḥ*—Lord Balarāma.

TRANSLATION

With the tip of His plow Lord Balarāma caught hold of the demon Balvala as he flew through the sky, and with His club the Lord angrily struck that harasser of *brāhmaṇas* on the head.

TEXT 6

सोऽपतद् भुवि निर्भिन्नललाटोऽसृक् समुत्सृजन् ।
मुञ्चन्नार्तस्वरं शैलो यथा वज्रहतोऽरुणः ॥६॥

so 'patad bhuvi nirbhinna-
lalāṭo 'sṛk samutsṛjan
muñcann ārta-svaraṁ śailo
yathā vajra-hato 'ruṇaḥ

saḥ—he, Balvala; *apatat*—fell; *bhuvi*—to the ground; *nirbhinna*—cracked open; *lalāṭaḥ*—his forehead; *asṛk*—blood; *samutsṛjan*—gushing; *muñcan*—releasing; *ārta*—of agony; *svaram*—a sound; *śailaḥ*—a mountain; *yathā*—like; *vajra*—by a lightning bolt; *hataḥ*—struck; *aruṇaḥ*—reddish.

TRANSLATION

Balvala cried out in agony and fell to the ground, his forehead cracked open and gushing blood. He resembled a red mountain struck by a lightning bolt.

PURPORT

According to the *ācāryas,* the demon appeared reddish with blood, like a mountain red with oxide.

TEXT 7

संस्तुत्य मुनयो रामं प्रयुज्यावितथाशिषः ।
अभ्यषिञ्चन्महाभागा वृत्रघ्नं विबुधा यथा ॥७॥

saṁstutya munayo rāmaṁ
prayujyāvitathāśiṣaḥ
abhyaṣiñcan mahā-bhāgā
vṛtra-ghnaṁ vibudhā yathā

saṁstutya—sincerely praising; *munayaḥ*—the sages; *rāmam*—Lord Balarāma; *prayujya*—awarding; *avitatha*—infallible; *āśiṣaḥ*—benedictions; *abhyaṣiñcan*—ceremoniously bathed; *mahā-bhāgāḥ*—the great personalities; *vṛtra*—of Vṛtrāsura; *ghnam*—the killer (Lord Indra); *vibudhāḥ*—the demigods; *yathā*—as.

TRANSLATION

The exalted sages honored Lord Rāma with sincere prayers and awarded Him infallible blessings. Then they performed His ritual bath, just as the demigods had formally bathed Indra when he killed Vṛtra.

TEXT 8

वैजयन्तीं ददुर्मालां श्रीधामाम्लानपंकजाम् ।
रामाय वाससी दिव्ये दिव्यान्याभरणानि च ॥८॥

vaijayantīṁ dadur mālāṁ
śrī-dhāmāmlāna-paṅkajām
rāmāya vāsasī divye
divyāny ābharaṇāni ca

vaijayantīm—named Vaijayantī; *daduḥ*—they gave; *mālām*—the flower garland; *śrī*—of the goddess of fortune; *dhāma*—the abode; *amlāna*—unfading; *paṅkajām*—made of lotus flowers; *rāmāya*—to Lord Balarāma; *vāsasī*—a pair of (upper and lower) garments; *divye*—divine; *divyāni*—divine; *ābharaṇāni*—jewelry; *ca*—and.

TRANSLATION

They gave Lord Balarāma a Vaijayantī garland of unfading lotuses in which resided the goddess of fortune, and they also gave Him a set of divine garments and jewelry.

TEXT 9

अथ तैरभ्यनुज्ञातः कौशिकीमेत्य ब्राह्मणैः ।
स्नात्वा सरोवरमगाद्यतः सरयूरास्रवत् ॥९॥

atha tair abhyanujñātaḥ
kauśikīm etya brāhmaṇaiḥ
snātvā sarovaram agād
yataḥ sarayūr āsravat

atha—then; *taiḥ*—by them; *abhyanujñātaḥ*—given leave; *kauśikīm*—to the Kauśikī River; *etya*—coming; *brāhmaṇaiḥ*—with *brāhmaṇas; snātvā*—bathing; *sarovaram*—to the lake; *agāt*—went; *yataḥ*—from which; *sarayūḥ*—the Sarayū River; *āsravat*—flows out.

TRANSLATION

Then, given leave by the sages, the Lord went with a contingent of *brāhmaṇas* to the Kauśikī River, where He bathed. From there He went to the lake from which flows the river Sarayū.

TEXT 10

अनुस्रोतेन सरयूं प्रयागमुपगम्य सः ।
स्नात्वा सन्तर्प्य देवादीन् जगाम पुलहाश्रमम् ॥१०॥

anu-srotena sarayūṁ
prayāgam upagamya saḥ
snātvā santarpya devādīn
jagāma pulahāśramam

anu—following; *srotena*—its current; *sarayūm*—along the Sarayū; *prayāgam*—to Prayāga; *upagamya*—coming; *saḥ*—He; *snātvā*—bathing; *santarpya*—propitiating; *deva-ādīn*—the demigods and so on; *jagāma*—He went; *pulaha-āśramam*—to the hermitage of Pulaha Ṛṣi.

TRANSLATION

The Lord followed the course of the Sarayū until He came to Prayāga, where He bathed and then performed rituals to propitiate the demigods and other living beings. Next He went to the *āśrama* of Pulaha Ṛṣi.

PURPORT

Pulahāśrama is also known as Hari-kṣetra.

TEXTS 11–15

गोमतीं गण्डकीं स्नात्वा विपाशां शोण आप्लुतः ।
गयां गत्वा पितॄनिष्ट्वा गंगासागरसंगमे ॥११॥
उपस्पृश्य महेन्द्राद्रौ रामं दृष्ट्वाभिवाद्य च ।
सप्तगोदावरीं वेणां पम्पां भीमरथीं ततः ॥१२॥
स्कन्दं दृष्ट्वा ययौ रामः श्रीशैलं गिरिशालयम् ।
द्रविडेषु महापुण्यं दृष्ट्वाद्रिं वेंकटं प्रभुः ॥१३॥
कामकोष्णीं पुरीं काञ्चीं कावेरीं च सरिद्वराम् ।
श्रीरंगाख्यं महापुण्यं यत्र सन्निहितो हरिः ॥१४॥

ऋषभाद्रिं हरेः क्षेत्रं दक्षिणां मथुरां तथा ।
सामुद्रं सेतुमगमत्महापातकनाशनम् ॥१५॥

gomatīṁ gaṇḍakīṁ snātvā
vipāśāṁ śoṇa āplutaḥ
gayāṁ gatvā pitṝn iṣṭvā
gaṅgā-sāgara-saṅgame

upaspṛśya mahendrādrau
rāmaṁ dṛṣṭvābhivādya ca
sapta-godāvarīṁ veṇāṁ
pampāṁ bhīmarathīṁ tataḥ

skandaṁ dṛṣṭvā yayau rāmaḥ
śrī-śailaṁ giriśālayam
draviḍeṣu mahā-puṇyaṁ
dṛṣṭvādriṁ veṅkaṭaṁ prabhuḥ

kāma-koṣṇīṁ purīṁ kāñcīṁ
kāverīṁ ca sarid-varām
śrī-raṅgākhyaṁ mahā-puṇyaṁ
yatra sannihito hariḥ

ṛṣabhādriṁ hareḥ kṣetraṁ
dakṣiṇāṁ mathurāṁ tathā
sāmudraṁ setum agamat
mahā-pātaka-nāśanam

gomatīm—at the Gomatī River; *gaṇḍakīm*—the Gaṇḍakī River; *snātvā*—bathing; *vipāśām*—at the Vipāśā River; *śoṇe*—in the Śoṇa River; *āplutaḥ*—having immersed Himself; *gayām*—to Gayā; *gatvā*—going; *pitṝn*—His forefathers; *iṣṭvā*—worshiping; *gaṅgā*—of the Ganges; *sāgara*—and the ocean; *saṅgame*—at the confluence; *upaspṛśya*—touching water (bathing); *mahā-indra-adrau*—at the Mahendra Mountain; *rāmam*—Lord Paraśurāma; *dṛṣṭvā*—seeing; *abhivādya*—honoring; *ca*—and; *sapta-godāvarīm*—(going) to the convergence of the seven Godāvarīs; *veṇām*—the Veṇā River; *pampām*—the Pampā River; *bhīma-rathīm*—and the Bhīmarathī River; *tataḥ*—then; *skandam*—Lord Skanda

(Kārttikeya); *dṛṣṭvā*—seeing; *yayau*—went; *rāmaḥ*—Lord Balarāma; *śrī-śailam*—to Śrī-śaila; *giri-śa*—of Lord Śiva; *ālayam*—the residence; *draviḍeṣu*—in the southern provinces; *mahā*—most; *puṇyam*—pious; *dṛṣṭvā*—seeing; *adrim*—the hill; *veṅkaṭam*—known as Veṅkaṭa (the abode of Lord Bālajī); *prabhuḥ*—the Supreme Lord; *kāma-koṣṇīm*—to Kāmakoṣṇī; *purīm kāñcīm*—to Kāñcīpuram; *kāverīm*—to the Kāverī; *ca*—and; *sarit*—of rivers; *varām*—the greatest; *śrī-raṅga-ākhyam*—known as Śrī-raṅga; *mahā-puṇyam*—most pious place; *yatra*—where; *sannihitaḥ*—manifested; *hariḥ*—Lord Kṛṣṇa (in the form of Raṅganātha); *ṛṣabha-adrim*—the Ṛṣabha Mountain; *hareḥ*—of Lord Viṣṇu; *kṣetram*—the place; *dakṣiṇām mathurām*—the southern Mathurā (Madurai, the abode of Goddess Mīnākṣī); *tathā*—also; *sāmudram*—on the ocean; *setum*—to the bridge (Setubandha); *agamat*—He went; *mahā*—the greatest; *pātaka*—sins; *nāśanam*—which destroys.

TRANSLATION

Lord Balarāma bathed in the Gomatī, Gaṇḍakī and Vipāśā rivers, and also immersed Himself in the Śoṇa. He went to Gayā, where He worshiped His forefathers, and to the mouth of the Ganges, where He performed purifying ablutions. At Mount Mahendra He saw Lord Paraśurāma and offered Him prayers, and then He bathed in the seven branches of the Godāvarī River, and also in the rivers Veṇā, Pampā and Bhīmarathī. Then Lord Balarāma met Lord Skanda and visited Śrī-śaila, the abode of Lord Giriśa. In the southern provinces known as Draviḍa-deśa the Supreme Lord saw the sacred Veṅkaṭa Hill, as well as the cities of Kāmakoṣṇī and Kāñcī, the exalted Kāverī River and the most holy Śrī-raṅga, where Lord Kṛṣṇa has manifested Himself. From there He went to Ṛṣabha Mountain, where Lord Kṛṣṇa also lives, and to the southern Mathurā. Then He came to Setubandha, where the most grievous sins are destroyed.

PURPORT

Usually one goes to Gayā to worship deceased forefathers. But as Śrīla Viśvanātha Cakravartī explains, although Lord Balarāma's father and grandfather were still alive, it was on His father's order that He carefully worshiped His forefathers at Gayā. Drawing insight from the *Vaiṣṇava-toṣaṇī*, the *ācārya* further explains that although Lord Balarāma was in the immediate proximity of Jagannātha Purī, He did not go there, since He wanted to avoid the embarrassment of having to worship Himself among the forms of Śrī Kṛṣṇa, Balabhadra and Subhadrā.

TEXTS 16–17

तत्रायुतमदाद्धेनूर्ब्राह्मणेभ्यो हलायुधः ।
कृतमालां ताम्रपर्णीं मलयं च कुलाचलम् ॥१६॥
तत्रागस्त्यं समासीनं नमस्कृत्याभिवाद्य च ।
योजितस्तेन चाशीर्भिरनुज्ञातो गतोऽर्णवम् ।
दक्षिणं तत्र कन्याख्यां दुर्गां देवीं ददर्श सः ॥१७॥

tatrāyutam adād dhenūr
brāhmaṇebhyo halāyudhaḥ
kṛtamālāṁ tāmraparṇīṁ
malayaṁ ca kulācalam

tatrāgastyaṁ samāsīnaṁ
namaskṛtyābhivādya ca
yojitas tena cāśīrbhir
anujñāto gato 'rṇavam
dakṣiṇaṁ tatra kanyākhyāṁ
durgāṁ devīṁ dadarśa saḥ

tatra—there (at Setubandha, known also as Rāmeśvaram); *ayutam*—ten thousand; *adāt*—He gave away; *dhenūḥ*—cows; *brāhmaṇebhyaḥ*—to *brāhmaṇas; hala-āyudhaḥ*—Lord Balarāma, whose weapon is the plow; *kṛtamālām*—to the Kṛtamālā River; *tāmraparṇīm*—the Tāmraparṇī River; *malayam*—Malaya; *ca*—and; *kula-acalam*—the principal mountain range; *tatra*—there; *agastyam*—to Agastya Ṛṣi; *samāsīnam*—sitting (in meditation); *namaskṛtya*—bowing down; *abhivādya*—glorifying; *ca*—and; *yojitaḥ*—granted; *tena*—by him; *ca*—and; *āśīrbhiḥ*—blessings; *anujñātaḥ*—given permission to leave; *gataḥ*—He went; *arṇavam*—to the ocean; *dakṣiṇam*—southern; *tatra*—there; *kanyā-ākhyām*—known as Kanyā-kumārī; *durgām devīm*—Goddess Durgā; *dadarśa*—saw; *saḥ*—He.

TRANSLATION

There at Setubandha [Rāmeśvaram] Lord Halāyudha gave *brāhmaṇas* ten thousand cows in charity. He then visited the Kṛtamālā and Tāmraparṇī rivers and the great Malaya Mountains. In the Malaya range Lord Balarāma found Agastya Ṛṣi sitting in meditation. After bowing down to the sage, the Lord offered him prayers and then received blessings from him. Taking leave from Agastya, He proceeded to the shore of the southern ocean, where He saw Goddess Durgā in her form of Kanyā-kumārī.

TEXT 18

ततः फाल्गुनमासाद्य पञ्चाप्सरसमुत्तमम् ।
विष्णुः सन्निहितो यत्र स्नात्वास्पर्शद् गवायुतम् ॥१८॥

tataḥ phālgunam āsādya
pañcāpsarasam uttamam
viṣṇuḥ sannihito yatra
snātvāsparśad gavāyutam

tataḥ—then; *phālgunam*—Phālguna; *āsādya*—reaching; *pañca-apsarasam*—the lake of the five Apsarās; *uttamam*—exalted; *viṣṇuḥ*—the Supreme Lord, Viṣṇu; *sannihitaḥ*—manifested; *yatra*—wherein; *snātvā*—bathing; *asparśat*—He touched (as part of the ritual in giving as charity); *gava*—cows; *ayutam*—ten thousand.

TRANSLATION

Next He went to Phālguna-tīrtha and bathed in the sacred Pañcāpsarā Lake, where Lord Viṣṇu had directly manifested Himself. At this place He gave away another ten thousand cows.

TEXTS 19–21

ततोऽभिव्रज्य भगवान् केरलांस्तु त्रिगर्तकान् ।
गोकर्णाख्यं शिवक्षेत्रं सान्निध्यं यत्र धूर्जटेः ॥१९॥

आर्यां द्वैपायनीं दृष्ट्वा शूर्पारकमगाद् बलः ।
तापीं पयोष्णीं निर्विन्ध्यामुपस्पृश्याथ दण्डकम् ॥२०॥
प्रविश्य रेवामगमद्यत्र माहिष्मती पुरी ।
मनुतीर्थमुपस्पृश्य प्रभासं पुनरागमत् ॥२१॥

tato 'bhivrajya bhagavān
keralāṁs tu trigartakān
gokarṇākhyaṁ śiva-kṣetraṁ
sānnidhyaṁ yatra dhūrjaṭeḥ

āryāṁ dvaipāyanīṁ dṛṣṭvā
śūrpārakam agād balaḥ
tāpīṁ payoṣṇīṁ nirvindhyām
upaspṛśyātha daṇḍakam

praviśya revām agamad
yatra māhiṣmatī purī
manu-tīrtham upaspṛśya
prabhāsaṁ punar āgamat

tataḥ—then; *abhivrajya*—traveling; *bhagavān*—the Supreme Lord; *keralān*—through the kingdom of Kerala; *tu*—and; *trigartakān*—Trigarta; *gokarṇa-ākhyam*—named Gokarṇa (on the coast of the Arabian Sea in northern Karnataka); *śiva-kṣetram*—the place sacred to Lord Śiva; *sānnidhyam*—manifestation; *yatra*—where; *dhūrjaṭeḥ*—of Lord Śiva; *āryām*—the honored goddess (Pāravatī, wife of Lord Śiva); *dvaipa*—on an island (off the coast near Gokarṇa); *ayanīm*—who resides; *dṛṣṭvā*—seeing; *śūrpārakam*—to the holy district of Śūrpāraka; *agāt*—went; *balaḥ*—Lord Balarāma; *tāpīm payoṣṇīm nirvindhyām*—to the Tāpī, Payoṣṇī and Nirvindhyā rivers; *upaspṛśya*—touching water; *atha*—next; *daṇḍakam*—the Daṇḍaka forest; *praviśya*—entering; *revām*—to the Revā River; *agamat*—He went; *yatra*—where; *māhiṣmatī purī*—the city of Māhiṣmatī; *manu-tīrtham*—to Manu-tīrtha; *upaspṛśya*—touching water; *prabhāsam*—to Prabhāsa; *punaḥ*—again; *āgamat*—He came.

TRANSLATION

The Supreme Lord then traveled through the kingdoms of Kerala and Trigarta, visiting Lord Śiva's sacred city of Gokarṇa,

where Lord Dhūrjaṭi [Śiva] directly manifests himself. After also visiting Goddess Pārvatī, who dwells on an island, Lord Balarāma went to the holy district of Śūrpāraka and bathed in the Tāpī, Payoṣṇī and Nirvindhyā rivers. He next entered the Daṇḍaka forest and went to the river Revā, along which the city of Māhiṣmatī is found. Then He bathed at Manu-tīrtha and finally returned to Prabhāsa.

TEXT 22

श्रुत्वा द्विजैः कथ्यमानं कुरुपाण्डवसंयुगे ।
सर्वराजन्यनिधनं भारं मेने हृतं भुवः ॥२२॥

śrutvā dvijaiḥ kathyamānaṁ
kuru-pāṇḍava-saṁyuge
sarva-rājanya-nidhanaṁ
bhāraṁ mene hṛtaṁ bhuvaḥ

śrutvā—hearing; *dvijaiḥ*—by *brāhmaṇas; kathyamānam*—being related; *kuru-pāṇḍava*—between the Kurus and the Pāṇḍavas; *saṁyuge*—in the battle; *sarva*—of all; *rājanya*—kings; *nidhanam*—the annihilation; *bhāram*—the burden; *mene*—He thought; *hṛtam*—removed; *bhuvaḥ*—of the earth.

TRANSLATION

The Lord heard from some *brāhmaṇas* how all the kings involved in the battle between the Kurus and Pāṇḍavas had been killed. From this He concluded that the earth was now relieved of her burden.

TEXT 23

स भीमदुर्योधनयोर्गदाभ्यां युध्यतोर्मृधे ।
वारयिष्यन् विनशनं जगाम यदुनन्दनः ॥२३॥

sa bhīma-duryodhanayor
gadābhyāṁ yudhyator mṛdhe

vārayiṣyan vinaśanaṁ
jagāma yadu-nandanaḥ

saḥ—He, Lord Balarāma; *bhīma-duryodhanayoḥ*—Bhīma and Duryodhana; *gadābhyām*—with clubs; *yudhyatoḥ*—who were fighting; *mṛdhe*—on the battlefield; *vārayiṣyan*—intending to stop; *vinaśanam*—to the battlefield; *jagāma*—went; *yadu*—of the Yadus; *nandanaḥ*—the beloved son (Lord Balarāma).

TRANSLATION

Wanting to stop the club fight then raging between Bhīma and Duryodhana on the battlefield, Lord Balarāma went to Kurukṣetra.

TEXT 24

युधिष्ठिरस्तु तं दृष्ट्वा यमौ कृष्णार्जुनावपि ।
अभिवाद्याभवंस्तुष्णीं किं विवक्षुरिहागतः ॥२४॥

yudhiṣṭhiras tu taṁ dṛṣṭvā
yamau kṛṣṇārjunāv api
abhivādyābhavaṁs tuṣṇīṁ
kiṁ vivakṣur ihāgataḥ

yudhiṣṭhiraḥ—King Yudhiṣṭhira; *tu*—but; *tam*—Him, Lord Balarāma; *dṛṣṭvā*—seeing; *yamau*—the twin brothers, Nakula and Sahadeva; *kṛṣṇa-arjunau*—Lord Kṛṣṇa and Arjuna; *api*—also; *abhivādya*—offering obeisances; *abhavan*—they were; *tuṣṇīm*—silent; *kim*—what; *vivakṣuḥ*—intending to say; *iha*—here; *āgataḥ*—has come.

TRANSLATION

When Yudhiṣṭhira, Lord Kṛṣṇa, Arjuna and the twin brothers Nakula and Sahadeva saw Lord Balarāma, they offered Him respectful obeisances but said nothing, thinking "What has He come here to tell us?"

PURPORT

Śrīla Prabhupāda writes, "The reason why they were silent was that Lord Balarāma was somewhat affectionate toward Duryodhana, and Duryodhana had learned from Balarāmajī the art of fighting with a club. Thus, when the fighting was going on, King Yudhiṣṭhira and the others thought that Balarāma might have come there to say something in favor of Duryodhana, and therefore they remained silent."

TEXT 25

गदापाणी उभौ दृष्ट्वा संरब्धौ विजयैषिणौ ।
मण्डलानि विचित्राणि चरन्ताविदमब्रवीत् ॥२५॥

gadā-pāṇī ubhau dṛṣṭvā
saṁrabdhau vijayaiṣiṇau
maṇḍalāni vicitrāṇi
carantāv idam abravīt

gadā—with clubs; *pāṇī*—in their hands; *ubhau*—both of them, Duryodhana and Bhīma; *dṛṣṭvā*—seeing; *saṁrabdhau*—furious; *vijaya*—victory; *eṣiṇau*—striving for; *maṇḍalāni*—circles; *vicitrāṇi*—artistic; *carantau*—moving in; *idam*—this; *abravīt*—He said.

TRANSLATION

Lord Balarāma found Duryodhana and Bhīma with clubs in their hands, each furiously striving for victory over the other as they circled about skillfully. The Lord addressed them as follows.

TEXT 26

युवां तुल्यबलौ वीरौ हे राजन् हे वृकोदर ।
एकं प्राणाधिकं मन्ये उतैकं शिक्षयाधिकम् ॥२६॥

yuvāṁ tulya-balau vīrau
he rājan he vṛkodara
ekaṁ prāṇādhikaṁ manye
utaikaṁ śikṣayādhikam

yuvām—you two; *tulya*—equal; *balau*—in prowess; *vīrau*—warriors; *he rājan*—O King (Duryodhana); *he vṛkodara*—O Bhīma; *ekam*—one;

prāṇa—in terms of vital force; *adhikam*—greater; *manye*—I consider; *uta*—on the other hand; *ekam*—one; *śikṣayā*—in terms of training; *adhikam*—greater.

TRANSLATION

[Lord Balarāma said:] King Duryodhana! And Bhīma! Listen! You two warriors are equal in fighting prowess. I know that one of you has greater physical power, while the other is better trained in technique.

PURPORT

Bhīma was physically more powerful, but Duryodhana was more advanced in terms of technique.

TEXT 27

तस्मादेकतरस्येह युवयोः समवीर्ययोः ।
न लक्ष्यते जयोऽन्यो वा विरमत्वफलो रणः ॥२७॥

tasmād ekatarasyeha
yuvayoḥ sama-vīryayoḥ
na lakṣyate jayo 'nyo vā
viramatv aphalo raṇaḥ

tasmāt—therefore; *ekatarasya*—of either of the two; *iha*—here; *yuvayoḥ*—of you; *sama*—equal; *vīryayoḥ*—whose prowess; *na lakṣyate*—cannot be seen; *jayaḥ*—victory; *anyaḥ*—the opposite (defeat); *vā*—or; *viramatu*—it should stop; *aphalaḥ*—fruitless; *raṇaḥ*—the battle.

TRANSLATION

Since you are so evenly matched in fighting prowess, I do not see how either of you can win or lose this duel. Therefore please stop this useless battle.

TEXT 28

न तद्वाक्यं जगृहतुर्बद्धवैरौ नृपार्थवत् ।
अनुस्मरन्तावन्योन्यं दुरुक्तं दुष्कृतानि च ॥२८॥

na tad-vākyaṁ jagṛhatur
baddha-vairau nṛpārthavat
anusmarantāv anyonyaṁ
duruktaṁ duṣkṛtāni ca

na—not; *tat*—His; *vākyam*—words; *jagṛhatuḥ*—the two of them accepted; *baddha*—fixed; *vairau*—whose enmity; *nṛpa*—O King (Parīkṣit); *artha-vat*—sensible; *anusmarantau*—continuing to remember; *anyonyam*—about each other; *duruktam*—the harsh words; *duṣkṛtāni*—the misdeeds; *ca*—also.

TRANSLATION

[Śukadeva Gosvāmī continued:] They did not accept Lord Balarāma's request, O King, although it was logical, for their mutual enmity was irrevocable. Each of them constantly remembered the insults and injuries he had suffered from the other.

TEXT 29

दिष्टं तदनुमन्वानो रामो द्वारवतीं ययौ ।
उग्रसेनादिभिः प्रीतैर्ज्ञातिभिः समुपागतः ॥२९॥

diṣṭaṁ tad anumanvāno
rāmo dvāravatīṁ yayau
ugrasenādibhiḥ prītair
jñātibhiḥ samupāgataḥ

diṣṭam—fate; *tat*—that; *anumanvānaḥ*—deciding; *rāmaḥ*—Lord Balarāma; *dvāravatīm*—to Dvārakā; *yayau*—went; *ugrasena-ādibhiḥ*—headed by Ugrasena; *prītaiḥ*—delighted; *jñātibhiḥ*—by His family members; *samupāgataḥ*—greeted.

TRANSLATION

Concluding that the battle was the arrangement of fate, Lord Balarāma went back to Dvārakā. There He was greeted by Ugrasena and His other relatives, who were all delighted to see Him.

PURPORT

Śrīla Viśvanātha Cakravartī explains that the word *diṣṭam,* "fate," indicates that the battle between Bhīma and Duryodhana had been enjoined by Lord Kṛṣṇa and set into motion by Him.

TEXT 30

तं पुनर्नैमिषं प्राप्तमृषयोऽयाजयन्मुदा ।
क्रत्वंगं क्रतुभिः सर्वैर्निवृत्ताखिलविग्रहम् ॥३०॥

taṁ punar naimiṣaṁ prāptam
ṛṣayo 'yājayan mudā
kratv-aṅgaṁ kratubhiḥ sarvair
nivṛttākhila-vigraham

tam—Him, Lord Balarāma; *punaḥ*—again; *naimiṣam*—at Naimiṣāraṇya; *prāptam*—arrived; *ṛṣayaḥ*—the sages; *ayājayan*—engaged in performing Vedic sacrifices; *mudā*—with pleasure; *kratu*—of all sacrifices; *aṅgam*—the embodiment; *kratubhiḥ*—with ritualistic performances; *sarvaiḥ*—all varieties; *nivṛtta*—who had renounced; *akhila*—all; *vigraham*—warfare.

TRANSLATION

Later Lord Balarāma returned to Naimiṣāraṇya, where the sages joyfully engaged Him, the embodiment of all sacrifice, in performing various kinds of Vedic sacrifice. Lord Balarāma was now retired from warfare.

PURPORT

Śrīla Prabhupāda writes, "[When Lord Balarāma] went to the holy place of pilgrimage at Naimiṣāraṇya,... the sages, saintly persons and *brāhmaṇas* all received Him standing. They understood that Lord Balarāma, although a *kṣatriya,* was now retired from the fighting business. The *brāhmaṇas* and the sages, who were always for peace and tranquillity, were very pleased at this. All of them embraced Balarāma with great affection and induced Him to perform various kinds of sacrifices in that sacred spot of Naimiṣāraṇya. Actually Lord Balarāma had no business performing the sacrifices recommended for ordinary human beings; He is the Supreme Personality of Godhead, and therefore He Himself is the enjoyer of all such sacrifices. As such, His exemplary action in performing sacrifices was only to give a lesson to the common man, to show how one should abide by the injunctions of the *Vedas.*"

TEXT 31

तेभ्यो विशुद्धं विज्ञानं भगवान् व्यतरद्विभुः ।
येनैवात्मन्यदो विश्वमात्मानं विश्वगं विदुः ॥३१॥

tebhyo viśuddhaṁ vijñānaṁ
bhagavān vyatarad vibhuḥ
yenaivātmany ado viśvam
ātmānaṁ viśva-gaṁ viduḥ

tebhyaḥ—upon them; *viśuddham*—perfectly pure; *vijñānam*—divine knowledge; *bhagavān*—the Supreme Lord; *vyatarat*—bestowed; *vibhuḥ*—the Almighty; *yena*—by which; *eva*—indeed; *ātmani*—within Himself, the Supreme Lord; *adaḥ*—this; *viśvam*—universe; *ātmānam*—Himself; *viśva-gam*—pervading the universe; *viduḥ*—they could perceive.

TRANSLATION

The all-powerful Lord Balarāma bestowed upon the sages pure spiritual knowledge, by which they could see the whole universe within Him and also see Him pervading everything.

TEXT 32

स्वपत्यावभृथस्नातो ज्ञातिबन्धुसुहृद्वृतः ।
रेजे स्वज्योत्स्नयेवेन्दुः सुवासाः सुष्ठ्वलंकृतः ॥३२॥

sva-patyāvabhṛtha-snāto
jñāti-bandhu-suhṛd-vṛtaḥ
reje sva-jyotsnayevenduḥ
su-vāsāḥ suṣṭhv alaṅkṛtaḥ

sva—together with His; *patyā*—wife; *avabhṛtha*—with the *avabhṛtha* ritual, which marks the end of sacrificial initiation; *snātaḥ*—having bathed; *jñāti*—by His immediate family members; *bandhu*—other relatives; *suhṛt*—and friends; *vṛtaḥ*—surrounded; *reje*—He appeared splendid; *sva-jyotsnayā*—with its own rays; *iva*—as; *induḥ*—the moon; *su*—well; *vāsāḥ*—dressed; *suṣṭhu*—nicely; *alaṅkṛtaḥ*—adorned.

TRANSLATION

After executing with His wife the *avabhṛtha* ablutions, the beautifully dressed and ornamented Lord Balarāma, encircled by His immediate family and other relatives and friends, looked as splendid as the moon surrounded by its effulgent rays.

PURPORT

Śrīla Prabhupāda beautifully describes this scene as follows: "Lord Balarāma then took the *avabhṛtha* bath, which is accepted after finishing sacrificial performances. After taking His bath, He dressed Himself in new silken garments and decorated Himself with beautiful jewelry amidst His relatives and friends. He appeared to be a shining full moon amidst the luminaries in the sky."

TEXT 33

ईदृग्विधान्यसंख्यानि बलस्य बलशालिनः ।
अनन्तस्याप्रमेयस्य मायामर्त्यस्य सन्ति हि ॥३३॥

īdṛg-vidhāny asaṅkhyāni
balasya bala-śālinaḥ

anantasyāprameyasya
māyā-martyasya santi hi

īdṛk-vidhāni—of this sort; *asaṅkhyāni*—uncountable; *balasya*—of Lord Balarāma; *bala-śālinaḥ*—mighty; *anantasya*—unlimited; *aprameya-sya*—immeasurable; *māyā*—by His illusory energy; *martyasya*—who appears as if a mortal; *santi*—there are; *hi*—indeed.

TRANSLATION

Countless other such pastimes were performed by mighty Balarāma, the unlimited and immeasurable Supreme Lord, whose mystic Yogamāyā power makes Him appear to be a human being.

TEXT 34

योऽनुस्मरेत रामस्य कर्माण्यद्भुतकर्मणः ।
सायं प्रातरनन्तस्य विष्णोः स दयितो भवेत् ॥३४॥

yo 'nusmareta rāmasya
karmāṇy adbhuta-karmaṇaḥ
sāyaṁ prātar anantasya
viṣṇoḥ sa dayito bhavet

yaḥ—whoever; *anusmareta*—regularly remembers; *rāmasya*—of Lord Balarāma; *karmāṇi*—the activities; *adbhuta*—amazing; *karmaṇaḥ*—all of whose activities; *sāyam*—at dusk; *prātaḥ*—at dawn; *anantasya*—who is unlimited; *viṣṇoḥ*—to the Supreme Lord, Viṣṇu; *saḥ*—he; *dayitaḥ*—dear; *bhavet*—becomes.

TRANSLATION

All the activities of the unlimited Lord Balarāma are amazing. Anyone who regularly remembers them at dawn and dusk will become very dear to the Supreme Personality of Godhead, Śrī Viṣṇu.

PURPORT

Śrīla Prabhupāda writes, "Lord Balarāma is the original Viṣṇu; therefore anyone remembering these pastimes of Lord Balarāma in the morning and evening will certainly become a great devotee of the Supreme Personality of Godhead, and thus his life will become successful in all respects."

Thus end the purports of the humble servants of His Divine Grace A. C. Bhaktivedanta Swami Prabhupāda to the Tenth Canto, Seventy-ninth Chapter, of the Śrīmad-Bhāgavatam, *entitled "Lord Balarāma Goes on Pilgrimage."*

CHAPTER EIGHTY

The Brāhmaṇa Sudāmā Visits Lord Kṛṣṇa in Dvārakā

This chapter relates how Lord Kṛṣṇa worshiped His *brāhmaṇa* friend Sudāmā, who came to His palace seeking charity, and how the two of them discussed the pastimes they had shared while living at the home of their spiritual master, Sāndīpani Muni.

The *brāhmaṇa* Sudāmā, a personal friend of Lord Kṛṣṇa's, was completely free of material desires. He maintained himself and his wife with whatever came of its own accord, and thus they were poverty-stricken. One day Sudāmā's wife, unable to find any food to prepare for her husband, went to him and asked that he visit his friend Kṛṣṇa in Dvārakā and beg some charity. Sudāmā was reluctant, but when she persisted he agreed to go, reflecting that an opportunity to see the Lord was extremely auspicious. His wife begged a few handfuls of flattened rice as a gift for Śrī Kṛṣṇa, and Sudāmā set off for Dvārakā.

As Sudāmā approached the palace of Lord Kṛṣṇa's principal wife, Rukmiṇī-devī, the Lord saw him from a distance. Kṛṣṇa immediately rose from His seat on Rukmiṇī's bed and embraced His friend with great joy. Then He sat Sudāmā down on the bed, washed his feet with His own hands and sprinkled the wash water on His head. After this He presented him with various gifts and worshiped him with incense, lamps and so on. Meanwhile, Rukmiṇī fanned the shabbily dressed *brāhmaṇa* with a yak-tail whisk. All of this astonished the residents of the palace.

Lord Śrī Kṛṣṇa then took the hand of His friend, and the two of them reminisced about the things they had done together long ago, while living in the school of their spiritual master. Sudāmā pointed out that Kṛṣṇa engages in the pastime of acquiring an education only to set an example for human society.

TEXT 1

श्रीराजोवाच
भगवन् यानि चान्यानि मुकुन्दस्य महात्मनः ।
वीर्याण्यनन्तवीर्यस्य श्रोतुमिच्छामि हे प्रभो ॥१॥

śrī-rājovāca
bhagavan yāni cānyāni
mukundasya mahātmanaḥ
vīryāṇy ananta-vīryasya
śrotum icchāmi he prabho

śrī-rājā uvāca—the King (Parīkṣit) said; *bhagavan*—my lord (Śukadeva Gosvāmī); *yāni*—which; *ca*—and; *anyāni*—others; *mukundasya*—of Lord Kṛṣṇa; *mahā-ātmanaḥ*—the Supreme Soul; *vīryāṇi*—valorous deeds; *ananta*—unlimited; *vīryasya*—whose valor; *śrotum*—to hear; *icchāmi*—I wish; *he prabho*—O master.

TRANSLATION

King Parīkṣit said: My lord, O master, I wish to hear about other valorous deeds performed by the Supreme Personality of Godhead, Mukunda, whose valor is unlimited.

TEXT 2

को नु श्रुत्वासकृद् ब्रह्मन्नुत्तमःश्लोकसत्कथाः ।
विरमेत विशेषज्ञो विषण्णः काममार्गणैः ॥२॥

ko nu śrutvāsakṛd brahmann
uttamaḥśloka-sat-kathāḥ
virameta viśeṣa-jño
viṣaṇṇaḥ kāma-mārgaṇaiḥ

kaḥ—who; *nu*—indeed; *śrutvā*—having heard; *asakṛt*—repeatedly; *brahman*—O *brāhmaṇa; uttamaḥ-śloka*—of Lord Kṛṣṇa; *sat*—transcendental; *kathāḥ*—topics; *virameta*—can desist; *viśeṣa*—the essence (of life); *jñaḥ*—who knows; *viṣaṇṇaḥ*—disgusted; *kāma*—for material desire; *mārgaṇaiḥ*—with seeking.

TRANSLATION

O *brāhmaṇa,* how could anyone who knows the essence of life and is disgusted with endeavoring for sense gratification give up the transcendental topics of Lord Uttamaḥśloka after hearing them repeatedly?

PURPORT

Śrīla Viśvanātha Cakravartī comments herein that we see many persons who, even after hearing the topics of the Lord repeatedly, give up their spiritual dedication. The *ācārya* replies that the word *viśeṣa-jña* is therefore significant here. Those who have actually understood the essence of life do not give up Kṛṣṇa consciousness. A further qualification is to be *viṣaṇṇaḥ kāma-mārgaṇaiḥ,* disgusted with material sense gratification. These two qualities are complementary. One who has experienced the real taste of Kṛṣṇa consciousness automatically becomes disgusted with the inferior taste of material pleasure. Such a genuine hearer of the topics of Kṛṣṇa cannot give up hearing about the Lord's fascinating pastimes.

TEXT 3

सा वाग् यया तस्य गुणान् गृणीते
करौ च तत्कर्मकरौ मनश्च ।
स्मरेद्वसन्तं स्थिरजंगमेषु
शृणोति तत्पुण्यकथाः स कर्णः ॥३॥

sā vāg yayā tasya guṇān gṛṇīte
karau ca tat-karma-karau manaś ca
smared vasantaṁ sthira-jaṅgameṣu
śṛṇoti tat-puṇya-kathāḥ sa karṇaḥ

sā—that (is); *vāk*—power of speech; *yayā*—by which; *tasya*—His; *guṇān*—qualities; *gṛṇīte*—one describes; *karau*—pair of hands; *ca*—and; *tat*—His; *karma*—work; *karau*—doing; *manaḥ*—mind; *ca*—and; *smaret*—remembers; *vasantam*—dwelling; *sthira*—within the unmoving; *jaṅgameṣu*—and moving; *śṛṇoti*—hears; *tat*—His; *puṇya*—sanctifying; *kathāḥ*—topics; *saḥ*—that (is); *karṇaḥ*—an ear.

TRANSLATION

Actual speech is that which describes the qualities of the Lord, real hands are those that work for Him, a true mind is that which

always remembers Him dwelling within everything moving and nonmoving, and actual ears are those that listen to sanctifying topics about Him.

PURPORT

While continuing from the previous verse to glorify the sense of hearing dedicated to the Lord, King Parīkṣit mentions the other senses also, so that we gain a complete picture of Kṛṣṇa consciousness. Here he declares that without any connection to Kṛṣṇa, the Supreme Lord, all the organs of the body become useless. A similar statement is made by Śaunaka Ṛṣi in the Second Canto, Third Chapter, verses 20 to 24.

Śrīla Viśvanātha Cakravartī mentions that the senses should work together in Kṛṣṇa consciousness. In other words, whatever the eyes or the ears experience, the mind should simply remember Kṛṣṇa, who is within all things.

TEXT 4

शिरस्तु तस्योभयलिंगमानमेत्
तदेव यत्पश्यति तद्धि चक्षुः ।
अंगानि विष्णोरथ तज्जनानां
पादोदकं यानि भजन्ति नित्यम् ॥४॥

śiras tu tasyobhaya-liṅgam ānamet
tad eva yat paśyati tad dhi cakṣuḥ
aṅgāni viṣṇor atha taj-janānāṁ
pādodakaṁ yāni bhajanti nityam

śiraḥ—head; *tu*—and; *tasya*—of Him; *ubhaya*—both; *liṅgam*—to the manifestations; *ānamet*—bows down; *tat*—that; *eva*—only; *yat*—which; *paśyati*—sees; *tat*—that; *hi*—indeed; *cakṣuḥ*—eye; *aṅgāni*—limbs; *viṣṇoḥ*—of Lord Viṣṇu; *atha*—or; *tat*—His; *janānām*—of the devotees; *pāda-udakam*—the water which has washed the feet; *yāni*—which; *bhajanti*—honor; *nityam*—regularly.

TRANSLATION

An actual head is one that bows down to the Lord in His manifestations among the moving and nonmoving creatures, real eyes are those that see only the Lord, and actual limbs are those which regularly honor the water that has bathed the Lord's feet or those of His devotees.

TEXT 5

सूत उवाच
विष्णुरातेन सम्पृष्टो भगवान् बादरायणिः ।
वासुदेवे भगवति निमग्नहृदयोऽब्रवीत् ॥५॥

sūta uvāca
viṣṇu-rātena sampṛṣṭo
bhagavān bādarāyaṇiḥ
vāsudeve bhagavati
nimagna-hṛdayo 'bravīt

sūtaḥ uvāca—Sūta Gosvāmī said; *viṣṇu-rātena*—by Viṣṇurāta (Mahārāja Parīkṣit); *sampṛṣṭaḥ*—well questioned; *bhagavān*—the powerful sage; *bādarāyaṇiḥ*—Śukadeva; *vāsudeve*—in Lord Vāsudeva; *bhagavati*—the Supreme Personality of Godhead; *nimagna*—fully absorbed; *hṛdayaḥ*—his heart; *abravīt*—he spoke.

TRANSLATION

Sūta Gosvāmī said: Thus questioned by King Viṣṇurāta, the powerful sage Bādarāyaṇi replied, his heart fully absorbed in meditation on the Supreme Personality of Godhead, Vāsudeva.

TEXT 6

श्रीशुक उवाच
कृष्णस्यासीत्सखा कश्चिद् ब्राह्मणो ब्रह्मवित्तमः ।
विरक्त इन्द्रियार्थेषु प्रशान्तात्मा जितेन्द्रियः ॥६॥

śrī-śuka uvāca
kṛṣṇasyāsīt sakhā kaścid
brāhmaṇo brahma-vittamaḥ
virakta indriyārtheṣu
praśāntātmā jitendriyaḥ

śrī-śukaḥ uvāca—Śukadeva Gosvāmī said; *kṛṣṇasya*—of Lord Kṛṣṇa; *āsīt*—there was; *sakhā*—friend (named Sudāmā); *kaścit*—a certain; *brāhmaṇaḥ*—*brāhmaṇa; brahma*—in the *Vedas; vit-tamaḥ*—most learned; *viraktaḥ*—detached; *indriya-artheṣu*—from the objects of sense enjoyment; *praśānta*—peaceful; *ātmā*—whose mind; *jita*—conquered; *indriyaḥ*—whose senses.

TRANSLATION

Śukadeva Gosvāmī said: Lord Kṛṣṇa had a certain *brāhmaṇa* friend [named Sudāmā] who was most learned in Vedic knowledge and detached from all sense enjoyment. Furthermore, his mind was peaceful and his senses subdued.

TEXT 7

यदृच्छयोपपन्नेन वर्तमानो गृहाश्रमी ।
तस्य भार्या कुचैलस्य क्षुत्क्षामा च तथाविधा ॥७॥

yadṛcchayopapannena
vartamāno gṛhāśramī
tasya bhāryā ku-cailasya
kṣut-kṣāmā ca tathā-vidhā

yadṛcchayā—of its own accord; *upapannena*—by what was obtained; *vartamānaḥ*—existing; *gṛha-āśramī*—in the household order of life; *tasya*—of him; *bhāryā*—the wife; *ku-cailasya*—who was poorly dressed; *kṣut*—from hunger; *kṣāmā*—emaciated; *ca*—and; *tathā-vidhā*—similarly.

TRANSLATION

Living as a householder, he maintained himself with whatever came of its own accord. The wife of that poorly dressed *brāhmaṇa* suffered along with him and was emaciated from hunger.

PURPORT

Sudāmā's chaste wife was also poorly dressed, and whatever food she obtained she gave to her husband. Thus she remained fatigued from hunger.

TEXT 8

पतिव्रता पतिं प्राह म्लायता वदनेन सा ।
दरिद्रं सीदमाना वै वेपमानाभिगम्य च ॥८॥

pati-vratā patiṁ prāha
mlāyatā vadanena sā
daridraṁ sīdamānā vai
vepamānābhigamya ca

pati-vratā—faithful to her husband; *patim*—to her husband; *prāha*—she said; *mlāyatā*—drying up; *vadanena*—with her face; *sā*—she; *daridram*—poor; *sīdamānā*—distressed; *vai*—indeed; *vepamānā*—trembling; *abhigamya*—approaching; *ca*—and.

TRANSLATION

The chaste wife of the poverty-stricken *brāhmaṇa* once approached him, her face dried up because of her distress. Trembling with fear, she spoke as follows.

PURPORT

According to Śrīdhara Svāmī, the chaste lady was especially unhappy because she could not obtain food to feed her husband. Further, she was fearful to approach her husband because she knew that he did not want to beg for anything other than devotion to the Supreme Lord.

TEXT 9

ननु ब्रह्मन् भगवतः सखा साक्षाच्छ्रियः पतिः ।
ब्रह्मण्यश्च शरण्यश्च भगवान् सात्वतर्षभः ॥९॥

nanu brahman bhagavataḥ
sakhā sākṣāc chriyaḥ patiḥ
brahmaṇyaś ca śaraṇyaś ca
bhagavān sātvatarṣabhaḥ

nanu—indeed; *brahman*—O *brāhmaṇa; bhagavataḥ*—of your exalted self; *sakhā*—the friend; *sākṣāt*—directly; *śriyaḥ*—of the supreme goddess of fortune; *patiḥ*—the husband; *brahmaṇyaḥ*—compassionate to *brāhmaṇas; ca*—and; *śaraṇyaḥ*—willing to give shelter; *ca*—and; *bhagavān*—the Supreme Lord; *sātvata*—of the Yādavas; *ṛṣabhaḥ*—the best.

TRANSLATION

[Sudāmā's wife said:] O *brāhmaṇa*, isn't it true that the husband of the goddess of fortune is the personal friend of your exalted self? That greatest of Yādavas, the Supreme Lord Kṛṣṇa, is compassionate to *brāhmaṇas* and very willing to grant them His shelter.

PURPORT

Śrīla Viśvanātha Cakravartī explains in his commentary how the *brāhmaṇa's* wife anticipated every possible objection her husband might make to her request that he go to Lord Kṛṣṇa to beg charity. If the *brāhmaṇa* might say, "How could the husband of the goddess of fortune befriend a fallen soul like myself?" she replies by saying that Lord Kṛṣṇa is *brahmaṇya*, very favorably disposed toward the *brāhmaṇas*. If Sudāmā might claim to have no real devotion for the Lord, she replies by saying that he is a great and wise personality who would surely obtain the shelter and mercy of the Lord. If the *brāhmaṇa* might object that Lord Kṛṣṇa is equally disposed to all the countless unhappy conditioned souls suffering the fruits of their own *karma*, she replies that Lord Kṛṣṇa is especially the Lord of the devotees, and thus even if He Himself did not grant Sudāmā His mercy, certainly the devotees engaged in serving the Lord would mercifully give him some charity. Since the Lord protects the Sātvatas, the members of the Yadu dynasty, what difficulty would there be for Him to protect a humble *brāhmaṇa* like Sudāmā, and what fault would there be in His doing so?

TEXT 10

तमुपैहि महाभाग साधूनां च परायणम् ।
दास्यति द्रविणं भूरि सीदते ते कुटुम्बिने ॥१०॥

tam upaihi mahā-bhāga
sādhūnāṁ ca parāyaṇam
dāsyati draviṇaṁ bhūri
sīdate te kuṭumbine

tam—Him; *upaihi*—approach; *mahā-bhāga*—O fortunate one; *sādhūnām*—of saintly devotees; *ca*—and; *para-ayaṇam*—the ultimate shelter; *dāsyati*—He will give; *draviṇam*—wealth; *bhūri*—plentiful; *sīdate*—suffering; *te*—to you; *kuṭumbine*—who are maintaining a family.

TRANSLATION

O fortunate one, please approach Him, the real shelter of all saints. He will certainly give abundant wealth to such a suffering householder as you.

TEXT 11

आस्तेऽधुना द्वारवत्यां भोजवृष्ण्यन्धकेश्वरः ।
स्मरतः पादकमलमात्मानमपि यच्छति ।
किं न्वर्थकामान् भजतो नात्यभीष्टान् जगद्गुरुः ॥११॥

āste 'dhunā dvāravatyām
bhoja-vṛṣṇy-andhakeśvaraḥ
smarataḥ pāda-kamalam
ātmānam api yacchati
kiṁ nv artha-kāmān bhajato
nāty-abhīṣṭān jagad-guruḥ

āste—is present; *adhunā*—now; *dvāravatyām*—at Dvārakā; *bhoja-vṛṣṇi-andhaka*—of the Bhojas, Vṛṣṇis and Andhakas; *īśvaraḥ*—the Lord; *smarataḥ*—to one who remembers; *pāda-kamalam*—His lotus feet;

ātmānam—Himself; *api*—even; *yacchati*—He gives; *kim nu*—what then to speak of; *artha*—economic success; *kāmān*—and sense gratification; *bhajataḥ*—to one who worships Him; *na*—not; *ati*—very much; *abhīṣṭān*—desirable; *jagat*—of the whole universe; *guruḥ*—the spiritual master.

TRANSLATION

Lord Kṛṣṇa is now the ruler of the Bhojas, Vṛṣṇis and Andhakas and is staying at Dvārakā. Since He gives even His own self to anyone who simply remembers His lotus feet, what doubt is there that He, the spiritual master of the universe, will bestow upon His sincere worshiper prosperity and material enjoyment, which are not even very desirable?

PURPORT

The *brāhmaṇa's* wife here implies that since Lord Kṛṣṇa is the ruler of the Bhojas, Vṛṣṇis and Andhakas, if these opulent rulers merely acknowledge Sudāmā as a personal friend of Kṛṣṇa's, they could give him everything he required.

In this connection Śrīla Viśvanātha Cakravartī comments that since Lord Kṛṣṇa had at this point put aside His weapons, He no longer traveled outside His own capital of Dvārakā. Thus Śrīla Prabhupāda writes in *Kṛṣṇa, the Supreme Personality of Godhead:* "[The *brāhmaṇa's* wife said:] 'I have heard that He never leaves His capital city, Dvārakā. He is living there without outside engagements.'"

As mentioned here, material wealth and sense gratification are not very desirable. The reason for this is that in the long run they give no real satisfaction. Still, Sudāmā's wife thought, even if Sudāmā went to Dvārakā and simply remained silent before the Lord, He would certainly give him abundant wealth, as well as shelter at His lotus feet, which was Sudāmā's real objective.

TEXTS 12–13

स एवं भार्यया विप्रो बहुशः प्रार्थितो मुहुः ।
अयं हि परमो लाभ उत्तमःश्लोकदर्शनम् ॥१२॥

इति सञ्चिन्त्य मनसा गमनाय मतिं दधे ।
अप्यस्त्युपायनं किञ्चिद् गृहे कल्याणि दीयताम् ॥१३॥

sa evaṁ bhāryayā vipro
bahuśaḥ prārthito muhuḥ
ayaṁ hi paramo lābha
uttamaḥśloka-darśanam

iti sañcintya manasā
gamanāya matiṁ dadhe
apy asty upāyanaṁ kiñcid
gṛhe kalyāṇi dīyatām

saḥ—he; *evam*—in this way; *bhāryayā*—by his wife; *vipraḥ*—the *brāhmaṇa; bahuśaḥ*—profusely; *prārthitaḥ*—entreated; *muhuḥ*—over and over; *ayam*—this; *hi*—indeed; *paramaḥ*—the supreme; *lābhaḥ*—gain; *uttamaḥ-śloka*—of Lord Kṛṣṇa; *darśanam*—the sight; *iti*—so; *sañcintya*—thinking; *manasā*—within his mind; *gamanāya*—to go; *matim dadhe*—he made his decision; *api*—whether; *asti*—there is; *upāyanam*—gift; *kiñcit*—some; *gṛhe*—in the house; *kalyāṇi*—my good woman; *dīyatām*—please give.

TRANSLATION

[Śukadeva Gosvāmī continued:] When his wife thus repeatedly implored him in various ways, the *brāhmaṇa* thought to himself, "To see Lord Kṛṣṇa is indeed the greatest achievement in life." Thus he decided to go, but first he told her, "My good wife, if there is anything in the house I can bring as a gift, please give it to me."

PURPORT

Sudāmā was naturally humble, and thus although at first he was dissatisfied with his wife's proposal, finally he settled his mind and decided to go. Now the last detail was that he had to take a gift for his friend.

TEXT 14

याचित्वा चतुरो मुष्टीन् विप्रान् पृथुकतण्डुलान् ।
चैलखण्डेन तान् बद्ध्वा भर्त्रे प्रादादुपायनम् ॥१४॥

yācitvā caturo muṣṭīn
viprān pṛthuka-taṇḍulān
caila-khaṇḍena tān baddhvā
bhartre prādād upāyanam

yācitvā—begging; *caturaḥ*—four: *muṣṭīn*—fistfuls; *viprān*—from the (neighboring) *brāhmaṇas; pṛthuka-taṇḍulān*—flat rice; *caila*—of cloth; *khaṇḍena*—with a ripped piece; *tān*—them; *baddhvā*—tying up; *bhartre*—to her husband; *prādāt*—she gave; *upāyanam*—gift.

TRANSLATION

Sudāmā's wife begged four handfuls of flat rice from neighboring *brāhmaṇas*, tied up the rice in a torn piece of cloth and gave it to her husband as a present for Lord Kṛṣṇa.

TEXT 15

स तानादाय विप्राग्र्यः प्रययौ द्वारकां किल ।
कृष्णसन्दर्शनं मह्यं कथं स्यादिति चिन्तयन् ॥१५॥

sa tān ādāya viprāgryaḥ
prayayau dvārakāṁ kila
kṛṣṇa-sandarśanaṁ mahyaṁ
kathaṁ syād iti cintayan

saḥ—he; *tān*—them; *ādāya*—taking; *vipra-agryaḥ*—the best of *brāhmaṇas; prayayau*—went; *dvārakām*—to Dvārakā; *kila*—indeed; *kṛṣṇa-sandarśanam*—the audience of Lord Kṛṣṇa; *mahyam*—for me; *katham*—how; *syāt*—will it happen; *iti*—thus; *cintayan*—thinking.

TRANSLATION

Taking the flat rice, the saintly *brāhmaṇa* set off for Dvārakā, all the while wondering "How will I be able to have Kṛṣṇa's audience?"

PURPORT

Among other things, Sudāmā assumed that the gatekeepers would stop him.

TEXTS 16–17

त्रीणि गुल्मान्यतीयाय तिस्रः कक्षाश्च सद्विजः ।
विप्रोऽगम्यान्धकवृष्णीनां गृहेष्वच्युतधर्मिणाम् ॥१६॥
गृहं द्व्यष्टसहस्राणां महिषीणां हरेर्द्विजः ।
विवेशैकतमं श्रीमद् ब्रह्मानन्दं गतो यथा ॥१७॥

trīṇi gulmāny atīyāya
tisraḥ kakṣāś ca sa-dvijaḥ
vipro 'gamyāndhaka-vṛṣṇīnāṁ
gṛheṣv acyuta-dharmiṇām

gṛhaṁ dvy-aṣṭa-sahasrāṇāṁ
mahiṣīṇāṁ harer dvijaḥ
viveśaikatamaṁ śrīmad
brahmānandaṁ gato yathā

trīṇi—three; *gulmāni*—contingents of guards; *atīyāya*—passing; *tisraḥ*—three; *kakṣāḥ*—gateways; *ca*—and; *sa-dvijaḥ*—accompanied by *brāhmaṇas; vipraḥ*—the learned *brāhmaṇa; agamya*—impassable; *andhaka-vṛṣṇīnām*—of the Andhakas and Vṛṣṇis; *gṛheṣu*—between the houses; *acyuta*—Lord Kṛṣṇa; *dharmiṇām*—who follow faithfully; *gṛham*—residence; *dvi*—two; *aṣṭa*—times eight; *sahasrāṇām*—thousands; *mahiṣīṇām*—of the queens; *hareḥ*—of Lord Kṛṣṇa; *dvijaḥ*—the *brāhmaṇa; viveśa*—entered; *ekatamam*—one of them; *śrī-mat*—opulent; *brahma-ānandam*—the bliss of impersonal liberation; *gataḥ*—attaining; *yathā*—as if.

TRANSLATION

The learned *brāhmaṇa,* joined by some local *brāhmaṇas,* passed three guard stations and went through three gateways, and then he walked by the homes of Lord Kṛṣṇa's faithful devotees, the Andhakas and Vṛṣṇis, which ordinarily no one could do. He then entered one of the opulent palaces belonging to Lord Hari's sixteen thousand queens, and when he did so he felt as if he were attaining the bliss of liberation.

PURPORT

When the saintly *brāhmaṇa* entered the precincts of Lord Kṛṣṇa's palaces and then actually entered one of the palaces, he completely forgot everything else, and thus his state of mind is compared to that of one who has just achieved the bliss of spiritual liberation. Śrīla Viśvanātha Cakravartī quotes from the *Padma Purāṇa, Uttara-khaṇḍa,* wherein we learn that the *brāhmaṇa* actually entered the palace of Rukmiṇī: *sa tu rukmiṇy-antaḥ-pura-dvāri kṣaṇaṁ tūṣṇīṁ sthitaḥ.* "He stood for a moment in silence at the doorway of Queen Rukmiṇī's palace."

TEXT 18

तं विलोक्याच्युतो दूरात्प्रियापर्यंकमास्थितः ।
सहसोत्थाय चाभ्येत्य दोर्भ्यां पर्यग्रहीन्मुदा ॥१८॥

taṁ vilokyācyuto dūrāt
priyā-paryaṅkam āsthitaḥ
sahasotthāya cābhyetya
dorbhyāṁ paryagrahīn mudā

tam—him; *vilokya*—seeing; *acyutaḥ*—Lord Kṛṣṇa; *dūrāt*—at a distance; *priyā*—of His beloved consort; *paryaṅkam*—on the bed; *āsthitaḥ*—seated; *sahasā*—immediately; *utthāya*—rising; *ca*—and; *abhyetya*—coming forward; *dorbhyām*—in His arms; *paryagrahīt*—embraced; *mudā*—with pleasure.

TRANSLATION

At that time Lord Acyuta was seated on His consort's bed. Spotting the *brāhmaṇa* at some distance, the Lord immediately stood up, went forward to meet him and with great pleasure embraced him.

TEXT 19

सख्युः प्रियस्य विप्रर्षेरंगसंगातिनिर्वृतः ।
प्रीतो व्यमुञ्चदब्बिन्दून्नेत्राभ्यां पुष्करेक्षणः ॥१९॥

sakhyuḥ priyasya viprarṣer
aṅga-saṅgāti-nirvṛtaḥ
prīto vyamuñcad ab-bindūn
netrābhyāṁ puṣkarekṣaṇaḥ

sakhyuḥ—of His friend; *priyasya*—dear; *vipra-ṛṣeḥ*—the sagacious *brāhmaṇa; aṅga*—of the body; *saṅga*—by the contact; *ati*—extremely; *nirvṛtaḥ*—ecstatic; *prītaḥ*—affectionate; *vyamuñcat*—He released; *ap*—of water; *bindūn*—drops; *netrābhyām*—from His eyes; *puṣkara-īkṣaṇaḥ*—the lotus-eyed Personality of Godhead.

TRANSLATION

The lotus-eyed Supreme Lord felt intense ecstasy upon touching the body of His dear friend, the wise *brāhmaṇa*, and thus He shed tears of love.

TEXTS 20–22

अथोपवेश्य पर्यंके स्वयं सख्युः समर्हणम् ।
उपहृत्यावनिज्यास्य पादौ पादावनेजनीः ॥२०॥
अग्रहीच्छिरसा राजन् भगवाल्ँलोकपावनः ।
व्यलिम्पद्दिव्यगन्धेन चन्दनागुरुकुंकुमैः ॥२१॥
धूपैः सुरभिभिर्मित्रं प्रदीपावलिभिर्मुदा ।
अर्चित्वावेद्य ताम्बूलं गां च स्वागतमब्रवीत् ॥२२॥

athopaveśya paryaṅke
svayaṁ sakhyuḥ samarhaṇam
upahṛtyāvanijyāsya
pādau pādāvanejanīḥ

agrahīc chirasā rājan
bhagavāl̐ loka-pāvanaḥ
vyalimpad divya-gandhena
candanāguru-kuṅkumaiḥ

dhūpaiḥ surabhibhir mitraṁ
pradīpāvalibhir mudā
arcitvāvedya tāmbūlaṁ
gāṁ ca svāgatam abravīt

atha—then; *upaveśya*—having him sit; *paryaṅke*—on the bed; *svayam*—Himself; *sakhyuḥ*—for His friend; *samarhaṇam*—items of worship; *upahṛtya*—bringing forward; *avanijya*—washing; *asya*—his; *pādau*—feet; *pāda-avanejanīḥ*—the water which had washed his feet; *agrahīt*—He took; *śirasā*—on His head; *rājan*—O King (Parīkṣit); *bhagavān*—the Supreme Lord; *loka*—of all worlds; *pāvanaḥ*—the purifier; *vyalimpat*—He anointed him; *divya*—divine; *gandhena*—whose fragrance; *candana*—with sandalwood paste; *aguru*—aloe-wood paste; *kuṅkumaiḥ*—and vermilion; *dhūpaiḥ*—with incense; *surabhibhiḥ*—aromatic; *mitram*—His friend; *pradīpa*—of lamps; *avalibhiḥ*—with rows; *mudā*—gladly; *arcitvā*—worshiping; *āvedya*—offering as refreshment; *tāmbūlam*—betel nut; *gām*—a cow; *ca*—and; *su-āgatam*—welcome; *abravīt*—He spoke.

TRANSLATION

Lord Kṛṣṇa seated His friend Sudāmā upon the bed. Then the Lord, who purifies the whole world, personally offered him various tokens of respect and washed his feet, O King, after which He sprinkled the water on His own head. He anointed him with divinely fragrant sandalwood, *aguru* and *kuṅkuma* pastes and happily worshiped him with aromatic incense and arrays of lamps. After finally offering him betel nut and the gift of a cow, He welcomed him with pleasing words.

TEXT 23

कुचैलं मलिनं क्षामं द्विजं धमनिसन्ततम् ।
देवी पर्यचरत्साक्षाच्चामरव्यजनेन वै ॥२३॥

ku-cailaṁ malinaṁ kṣāmaṁ
dvijaṁ dhamani-santatam
devī paryacarat sākṣāc
cāmara-vyajanena vai

ku—poor; *cailam*—whose dress; *malinam*—dirty; *kṣāmam*—emaciated; *dvijam*—the *brāhmaṇa; dhamani-santatam*—his veins visible; *devī*—the goddess of fortune; *paryacarat*—served; *sākṣāt*—personally; *cāmara*—with a yak-tail fan; *vyajanena*—by fanning; *vai*—indeed.

TRANSLATION

By fanning him with her *cāmara*, the divine goddess of fortune personally served that poor *brāhmaṇa*, whose clothing was torn and dirty and who was so thin that veins were visible all over his body.

TEXT 24

अन्तःपुरजनो दृष्ट्वा कृष्णेनामलकीर्तिना ।
विस्मितोऽभूदतिप्रीत्या अवधूतं सभाजितम् ॥२४॥

antaḥ-pura-jano dṛṣṭvā
kṛṣṇenāmala-kīrtinā
vismito 'bhūd ati-prītyā
avadhūtaṁ sabhājitam

antaḥ-pura—of the royal palace; *janaḥ*—the people; *dṛṣṭvā*—seeing; *kṛṣṇena*—by Lord Kṛṣṇa; *amala*—spotless; *kīrtinā*—whose fame; *vismitaḥ*—amazed; *abhūt*—they became; *ati*—intense; *prītyā*—with loving affection; *avadhūtam*—the unkempt *brāhmaṇa; sabhājitam*—honored.

TRANSLATION

The people in the royal palace were astonished to see Kṛṣṇa, the Lord of spotless glory, so lovingly honor this shabbily dressed *brāhmaṇa*.

TEXTS 25–26

किमनेन कृतं पुण्यमवधूतेन भिक्षुणा ।
श्रिया हीनेन लोकेऽस्मिन् गर्हितेनाधमेन च ॥२५॥
योऽसौ त्रिलोकगुरुणा श्रीनिवासेन सम्भृतः ।
पर्यंकस्थां श्रियं हित्वा परिष्वक्तोऽग्रजो यथा ॥२६॥

kim anena kṛtaṁ puṇyam
avadhūtena bhikṣuṇā
śriyā hīnena loke 'smin
garhitenādhamena ca

yo 'sau tri-loka-guruṇā
śrī-nivāsena sambhṛtaḥ
paryaṅka-sthāṁ śriyaṁ hitvā
pariṣvakto 'gra-jo yathā

kim—what; *anena*—by him; *kṛtam*—was done; *puṇyam*—pious activity; *avadhūtena*—unwashed; *bhikṣuṇā*—by the mendicant; *śriyā*—of prosperity; *hīnena*—who is deprived; *loke*—in the world; *asmin*—this; *garhitena*—condemned; *adhamena*—lowly; *ca*—and; *yaḥ*—who; *asau*—himself; *tri*—three; *loka*—of the planetary systems of the universe; *guruṇā*—by the spiritual master; *śrī*—of Lakṣmī, the supreme goddess of fortune; *nivāsena*—the abode; *sambhṛtaḥ*—served reverentially; *paryaṅka*—on her bed; *sthām*—seated; *śriyam*—the goddess of fortune; *hitvā*—leaving aside; *pariṣvaktaḥ*—embraced; *agra-jaḥ*—an elder brother; *yathā*—as.

TRANSLATION

[The residents of the palace said:] What pious acts has this unkempt, impoverished *brāhmaṇa* performed? People regard

him as lowly and contemptible, yet the spiritual master of the three worlds, the abode of Goddess Śrī, is serving him reverently. Leaving the goddess of fortune sitting on her bed, the Lord has embraced this *brāhmaṇa* as if he were an older brother.

TEXT 27

कथयां चक्रतुर्गाथाः पूर्वा गुरुकुले सतोः ।
आत्मनोर्ललिता राजन् करौ गृह्य परस्परम् ॥२७॥

kathayāṁ cakratur gāthāḥ
pūrvā guru-kule satoḥ
ātmanor lalitā rājan
karau gṛhya parasparam

kathayām cakratuḥ—they discussed; *gāthāḥ*—topics; *pūrvāḥ*—of the past; *guru-kule*—in the school of their spiritual master; *satoḥ*—who used to reside; *ātmanoḥ*—of themselves; *lalitāḥ*—charming; *rājan*—O King (Parīkṣit); *karau*—hands; *gṛhya*—taking hold of; *parasparam*—each other's.

TRANSLATION

[Śukadeva Gosvāmī continued:] Taking each other's hands, O King, Kṛṣṇa and Sudāmā talked pleasantly about how they once lived together in the school of their *guru*.

TEXT 28

श्रीभगवानुवाच
अपि ब्रह्मन् गुरुकुलाद् भवता लब्धदक्षिणात् ।
समावृत्तेन धर्मज्ञ भार्योढा सदृशी न वा ॥२८॥

śrī-bhagavān uvāca
api brahman guru-kulād
bhavatā labdha-dakṣiṇāt
samāvṛttena dharma-jña
bhāryoḍhā sadṛśī na vā

śrī-bhagavān uvāca—the Supreme Lord said; *api*—whether; *brahman*—O *brāhmaṇa; guru-kulāt*—from the spiritual master's school; *bhavatā*—by your good self; *labdha*—having received; *dakṣiṇāt*—remuneration; *samāvṛttena*—returned; *dharma*—of religious principles; *jña*—O knower; *bhāryā*—a wife; *ūḍhā*—married; *sadṛśī*—suitable; *na*—not; *vā*—or.

TRANSLATION

The Supreme Lord said: My dear *brāhmaṇa,* you know well the ways of *dharma.* After you offered the gift of remuneration to our *guru* and returned home from his school, did you marry a compatible wife or not?

PURPORT

Among civilized human beings, the question of *āśrama,* or spiritual order, is significant. In other words, every human being must execute prescibed duties as a celibate student, a married man or woman, a retired person or a renunciant. Since Lord Kṛṣṇa could see that the *brāhmaṇa* was poorly dressed, He inquired if His friend had been properly married and was executing the duties of household life. Since he was not dressed as a renunciant, he would be without a suitable *āśrama* unless he were properly married.

TEXT 29

प्रायो गृहेषु ते चित्तमकामविहितं तथा ।
नैवातिप्रीयसे विद्वन् धनेषु विदितं हि मे ॥२९॥

prāyo gṛheṣu te cittam
akāma-vihitaṁ tathā
naivāti-prīyase vidvan
dhaneṣu viditaṁ hi me

prāyaḥ—for the most part; *gṛheṣu*—in household affairs; *te*—your; *cittam*—mind; *akāma-vihitam*—uninfluenced by material desires; *tathā*—also; *na*—not; *eva*—indeed; *ati*—very much; *prīyase*—you take pleasure; *vidvan*—O wise one; *dhaneṣu*—in the pursuit of material wealth; *viditam*—it is known; *hi*—indeed; *me*—by Me.

TRANSLATION

Even though you are mostly involved in household affairs, your mind is not affected by material desires. Nor, O learned one, do you take much pleasure in the pursuit of material wealth. This I am well aware of.

PURPORT

Lord Kṛṣṇa here reveals that in fact He was well aware of His friend's situation. Sudāmā was actually learned and spiritually advanced, and therefore he was not interested in ordinary sense gratification, as is the common man.

TEXT 30

केचित्कुर्वन्ति कर्माणि कामैरहतचेतसः ।
त्यजन्तः प्रकृतीर्दैवीर्यथाहं लोकसंग्रहम् ॥३०॥

kecit kurvanti karmāṇi
kāmair ahata-cetasaḥ
tyajantaḥ prakṛtīr daivīr
yathāhaṁ loka-saṅgraham

kecit—some people; *kurvanti*—execute; *karmāṇi*—worldly duties; *kāmaiḥ*—by desires; *ahata*—undisturbed; *cetasaḥ*—whose minds; *tyajantaḥ*—giving up; *prakṛtīḥ*—propensities; *daivīḥ*—created by the Supreme Lord's material energy; *yathā*—as; *aham*—I; *loka-saṅgraham*—to instruct the people in general.

TRANSLATION

Having renounced all material propensities, which spring from the Lord's illusory energy, some people execute worldly duties with their minds undisturbed by mundane desires. They act as I do, to instruct the general populace.

TEXT 31

कच्चिद् गुरुकुले वासं ब्रह्मन् स्मरसि नौ यतः ।
द्विजो विज्ञाय विज्ञेयं तमसः पारमश्नुते ॥३१॥

kaccid guru-kule vāsaṁ
brahman smarasi nau yataḥ
dvijo vijñāya vijñeyaṁ
tamasaḥ pāram aśnute

kaccit—whether; *guru-kule*—in the spiritual master's school; *vāsam*—residence; *brahman*—O *brāhmaṇa; smarasi*—you remember; *nau*—our; *yataḥ*—from which (spiritual master); *dvijaḥ*—a twice-born person; *vijñāya*—understanding; *vijñeyam*—what needs to be known; *tamasaḥ*—of ignorance; *pāram*—the transcending; *aśnute*—experiences.

TRANSLATION

My dear *brāhmaṇa*, do you remember how we lived together in our spiritual master's school? When a twice-born student has learned from his *guru* all that is to be learned, he can enjoy spiritual life, which lies beyond all ignorance.

TEXT 32

स वै सत्कर्मणां साक्षाद् द्विजातेरिह सम्भवः ।
आद्योऽङ्ग यत्राश्रमिणां यथाहं ज्ञानदो गुरुः ॥३२॥

sa vai sat-karmaṇāṁ sākṣād
dvijāter iha sambhavaḥ
ādyo 'ṅga yatrāśramiṇāṁ
yathāhaṁ jñāna-do guruḥ

saḥ—he; *vai*—indeed; *sat*—sanctified; *karmaṇām*—of duties; *sākṣāt*—directly; *dvi-jāteḥ*—of one who has been twice born; *iha*—in this material life; *sambhavaḥ*—birth; *ādyaḥ*—first; *aṅga*—My dear friend; *yatra*—through whom; *āśramiṇām*—for the members of all the spiritual orders of society; *yathā*—as; *aham*—Myself; *jñāna*—of divine knowledge; *daḥ*—the bestower; *guruḥ*—spiritual master.

TRANSLATION

My dear friend, he who gives a person his physical birth is his first spiritual master, and he who initiates him as a twice-born

brāhmaṇa and engages him in religious duties is indeed more directly his spiritual master. But the person who bestows transcendental knowledge upon the members of all the spiritual orders of society is one's ultimate spiritual master. Indeed, he is as good as My own self.

TEXT 33

नन्वर्थकोविदा ब्रह्मन् वर्णाश्रमवतामिह ।
ये मया गुरुणा वाचा तरन्त्यञ्जो भवार्णवम् ॥३३॥

nanv artha-kovidā brahman
varṇāśrama-vatām iha
ye mayā guruṇā vācā
taranty añjo bhavārṇavam

nanu—certainly; *artha*—of their true welfare; *kovidāḥ*—expert knowers; *brahman*—O *brāhmaṇa; varṇāśrama-vatām*—among those engaged in the *varṇāśrama* system; *iha*—in this world; *ye*—who; *mayā*—by Me; *guruṇā*—as the spiritual master; *vācā*—through his words; *taranti*—cross beyond; *añjaḥ*—easily; *bhava*—of material life; *arṇavam*—the ocean.

TRANSLATION

Certainly, O _brāhmaṇa,_ of all the followers of the _varṇāśrama_ system, those who take advantage of the words I speak in My form as the spiritual master and thus easily cross over the ocean of material existence best understand their own true welfare.

PURPORT

One's father is a natural object of reverence, as is a religious leader who initiates one into sacred ceremonies and instructs one in general wisdom. But ultimately the bona fide spiritual master, learned in the transcendental science and thus able to take one across the ocean of birth and death to the spiritual world—such a *guru* is most deserving of worship and respect, for he is the direct representative of the Supreme Personality of Godhead, as stated here.

TEXT 34

नाहमिज्याप्रजातिभ्यां तपसोपशमेन वा ।
तुष्येयं सर्वभूतात्मा गुरुशुश्रूषया यथा ॥३४॥

nāham ijyā-prajātibhyāṁ
tapasopaśamena vā
tuṣyeyaṁ sarva-bhūtātmā
guru-śuśrūṣayā yathā

na—not; *aham*—I; *ijyā*—by ritual worship; *prajātibhyām*—the higher birth of *brāhmaṇa* initiation; *tapasā*—by austerity; *upaśamena*—by self-control; *vā*—or; *tuṣyeyam*—can be satisfied; *sarva*—of all; *bhūta*—beings; *ātmā*—the Soul; *guru*—to one's spiritual master; *śuśrūṣayā*—by faithful service; *yathā*—as.

TRANSLATION

I, the Soul of all beings, am not as satisfied by ritual worship, brahminical initiation, penances or self-discipline as I am by faithful service rendered to one's spiritual master.

PURPORT

The word *prajāti* here indicates either begetting good children or the second birth obtained by ritual initiation into Vedic culture. Although both of these are praiseworthy, Lord Kṛṣṇa here states that faithful service rendered to a bona fide spiritual master is still higher.

TEXTS 35–36

अपि नः स्मर्यते ब्रह्मन् वृत्तं निवसतां गुरौ ।
गुरुदारैश्चोदितानामिन्धनानयने क्वचित् ॥३५॥
प्रविष्टानां महारण्यमपर्तौ सुमहद् द्विज ।
वातवर्षमभूद् तीव्रं निष्ठुराः स्तनयित्नवः ॥३६॥

api naḥ smaryate brahman
vṛttaṁ nivasatāṁ gurau
guru-dārais coditānām
indhanānayane kvacit

praviṣṭānāṁ mahāraṇyam
apartau su-mahad dvija
vāta-varṣam abhūt tīvraṁ
niṣṭhurāḥ stanayitnavaḥ

api—whether; *naḥ*—of us; *smaryate*—are remembered; *brahman*—O *brāhmaṇa; vṛttam*—what we did; *nivasatām*—who were living; *gurau*—with our spiritual master; *guru*—of our *guru; dāraiḥ*—by the wife; *coditānām*—who were sent; *indhana*—firewood; *anayane*—for fetching; *kvacit*—once; *praviṣṭānām*—having entered; *mahā-araṇyam*—the large forest; *apa-ṛtau*—unseasonal; *su-mahat*—very great; *dvija*—O twice-born one; *vāta*—wind; *varṣam*—and rain; *abhūt*—arose; *tīvram*—fierce; *niṣṭhurāḥ*—harsh; *stanayitnavaḥ*—thundering.

TRANSLATION

O *brāhmaṇa*, do you remember what happened to us while we were living with our spiritual master? Once our *guru's* wife sent us to fetch firewood, and after we entered the vast forest, O twice-born one, an unseasonal storm arose, with fierce wind and rain and harsh thunder.

PURPORT

Śrīla Viśvanātha Cakravartī explains that this storm arose during winter and was therefore unseasonal.

TEXT 37

सूर्यश्चास्तं गतस्तावत्तमसा चावृता दिशः ।
निम्नं कूलं जलमयं न प्राज्ञायत किञ्चन ॥३७॥

sūryaś cāstaṁ gatas tāvat
tamasā cāvṛtā diśaḥ
nimnaṁ kūlaṁ jala-mayaṁ
na prājñāyata kiñcana

sūryaḥ—the sun; *ca*—and; *astam gataḥ*—having set; *tāvat*—thereupon; *tamasā*—by darkness; *ca*—and; *āvṛtāḥ*—covered; *diśaḥ*—all the directions; *nimnam*—low; *kūlam*—high land; *jala-mayam*—with water all around; *na prājñāyata*—could not be recognized; *kiñcana*—any.

TRANSLATION

Then, as the sun set, the forest was covered by darkness in every direction, and with all the flooding we could not distinguish high land from low.

TEXT 38

वयं भृशं तत्र महानिलाम्बुभिर्
निहन्यमाना मुहुरम्बुसम्प्लवे ।
दिशोऽविदन्तोऽथ परस्परं वने
गृहीतहस्ताः परिबभ्रिमातुराः ॥३८॥

vayaṁ bhṛśaṁ tatra mahānilāmbubhir
nihanyamānā muhur ambu-samplave
diśo 'vidanto 'tha parasparaṁ vane
gṛhīta-hastāḥ paribabhrimāturāḥ

vayam—we; *bhṛśam*—thoroughly; *tatra*—there; *mahā*—great; *anila*—by the wind; *ambubhiḥ*—and water; *nihanyamānāḥ*—beset; *muhuḥ*—continuously; *ambu-samplave*—in the flooding; *diśaḥ*—the directions; *avidantaḥ*—unable to discern; *atha*—then; *parasparam*—each other's; *vane*—in the forest; *gṛhīta*—holding; *hastāḥ*—hands; *paribabhrima*—we wandered; *āturāḥ*—distressed.

TRANSLATION

Constantly besieged by the powerful wind and rain, we lost our way amidst the flooding waters. We simply held each other's hands and, in great distress, wandered aimlessly about the forest.

PURPORT

Śrīla Śrīdhara Svāmī points out that the verb *paribabhrima* may be understood to be the prefix *pari* with either the verb *bhṛ* or *bhram*. In the case of *bhram*, it indicates that Kṛṣṇa and Sudāmā wandered all about, and in the case of *bhṛ*, which means "to carry," it indicates that as the two young boys wandered about, they continued to carry the firewood they had secured for their spiritual master.

TEXT 39

एतद्विदित्वा उदिते रवौ सान्दीपनिर्गुरुः ।
अन्वेषमाणो नः शिष्यानाचार्योऽपश्यदातुरान् ॥३९॥

etad viditvā udite
ravau sāndīpanir guruḥ
anveṣamāṇo naḥ śiṣyān
ācāryo 'paśyad āturān

etat—this; *viditvā*—knowing; *udite*—when it rose; *ravau*—the sun; *sāndīpaniḥ*—Sāndīpani; *guruḥ*—our spiritual master; *anveṣamāṇaḥ*—searching; *naḥ*—for us; *śiṣyān*—his disciples; *ācāryaḥ*—our teacher; *apaśyat*—saw; *āturān*—who were distressed.

TRANSLATION

Our *guru*, Sāndīpani, understanding our predicament, set out after sunrise to search for us, his disciples, and found us in distress.

TEXT 40

अहो हे पुत्रका यूयमस्मदर्थेऽतिदुःखिताः ।
आत्मा वै प्राणिनां प्रेष्ठस्तमनादृत्य मत्पराः ॥४०॥

aho he putrakā yūyam
asmad-arthe 'ti-duḥkhitāḥ
ātmā vai prāṇināṁ preṣṭhas
tam anādṛtya mat-parāḥ

aho—ah; *he putrakāḥ*—O children; *yūyam*—you; *asmat*—our; *arthe*—for the sake; *ati*—extremely; *duḥkhitāḥ*—have suffered; *ātmā*—the body; *vai*—indeed; *prāṇinām*—for all living beings; *preṣṭhaḥ*—the most dear; *tam*—that; *anādṛtya*—disregarding; *mat*—to me; *parāḥ*—dedicated.

TRANSLATION

[Sāndīpani said:] O my children, you have suffered so much for my sake! The body is most dear to every living creature, but you are so dedicated to me that you completely disregarded your own comfort.

TEXT 41

एतदेव हि सच्छिष्यैः कर्तव्यं गुरुनिष्कृतम् ।
यद्वै विशुद्धभावेन सर्वार्थात्मार्पणं गुरौ ॥४१॥

etad eva hi sac-chiṣyaiḥ
kartavyaṁ guru-niṣkṛtam
yad vai viśuddha-bhāvena
sarvārthātmārpaṇaṁ gurau

etat—this; *eva*—alone; *hi*—certainly; *sat*—true; *śiṣyaiḥ*—by disciples; *kartavyam*—to be done; *guru*—to the spiritual master; *niṣkṛtam*—repayment of one's debt; *yat*—which; *vai*—indeed; *viśuddha*—completely pure; *bhāvena*—with an attitude; *sarva*—of all; *artha*—assets; *ātmā*—and one's body; *arpaṇam*—the offering; *gurau*—to one's spiritual master.

TRANSLATION

This indeed is the duty of all true disciples: to repay the debt to their spiritual master by offering him, with pure hearts, their wealth and even their very lives.

PURPORT

One engages one's body to realize one's purposes. The body is also the basis of the material conception of "I," while one's fortune is the basis of the conception of "mine." Thus by offering everything to the spiritual master, one realizes one's self to be an eternal servant of the Lord. The spiritual master does not exploit the disciple but rather engages him fully in Kṛṣṇa consciousness for the disciple's eternal benefit.

TEXT 42

तुष्टोऽहं भो द्विजश्रेष्ठाः सत्याः सन्तु मनोरथाः ।
छन्दांस्ययातयामानि भवन्त्विह परत्र च ॥४२॥

tuṣṭo 'haṁ bho dvija-śreṣṭhāḥ
satyāḥ santu manorathāḥ
chandāṁsy ayāta-yāmāni
bhavantv iha paratra ca

tuṣṭaḥ—satisfied; *aham*—I am; *bho*—my dear ones; *dvija*—of *brāhmaṇas; śreṣṭhāḥ*—O best; *satyāḥ*—fulfilled; *santu*—may they be; *manaḥ-rathāḥ*—your desires; *chandāṁsi*—Vedic *mantras; ayāta-yāmāni*—never growing old; *bhavantu*—may they be; *iha*—in this world; *paratra*—in the next world; *ca*—and.

TRANSLATION

You boys are first-class *brāhmaṇas,* and I am satisfied with you. May all your desires be fulfilled, and may the Vedic *mantras* you have learned never lose their meaning for you, in this world or the next.

PURPORT

Cooked food left sitting for three hours is called *yāta-yāma,* indicating that it has lost its taste, and similarly if a devotee does not remain fixed in

Kṛṣṇa consciousness, the transcendental knowledge that once inspired him on the spiritual path will lose its "taste," or meaning, for him. Thus Sāndīpani Muni blesses his disciples that the Vedic *mantras,* which reveal the Absolute Truth, will never lose their meaning for them but will remain ever fresh in their minds.

TEXT 43

इत्थंविधान्यनेकानि वसतां गुरुवेश्मनि ।
गुरोरनुग्रहेणैव पुमान् पूर्णः प्रशान्तये ॥४३॥

itthaṁ-vidhāny anekāni
vasatāṁ guru-veśmani
guror anugraheṇaiva
pumān pūrṇaḥ praśāntaye

ittham-vidhāni—like this; *anekāni*—many things; *vasatām*—by us who were living; *guru*—of our spiritual master; *veśmani*—in the home; *guroḥ*—of the spiritual master; *anugraheṇa*—by the mercy; *eva*—simply; *pumān*—a person; *pūrṇaḥ*—fulfilled; *praśāntaye*—for attaining total peace.

TRANSLATION

[Lord Kṛṣṇa continued:] We had many similar experiences while living in our spiritual master's home. Simply by the grace of the spiritual master a person can fulfill life's purpose and attain eternal peace.

TEXT 44

श्रीब्राह्मण उवाच
किमस्माभिरनिर्वृत्तं देवदेव जगद्गुरो ।
भवता सत्यकामेन येषां वासो गुरोरभूत् ॥४४॥

śrī-brāhmaṇa uvāca
kim asmābhir anirvṛttaṁ
deva-deva jagad-guro

bhavatā satya-kāmena
yeṣāṁ vāso guror abhūt

śrī-brāhmaṇaḥ uvāca—the *brāhmaṇa* said; *kim*—what; *asmābhiḥ*—by us; *anirvṛttam*—not achieved; *deva-deva*—O Lord of lords; *jagat*—of the universe; *guro*—O spiritual master; *bhavatā*—with You; *satya*—fulfilled; *kāmena*—all whose desires; *yeṣām*—whose; *vāsaḥ*—residence; *guroḥ*—at the home of the spiritual master; *abhūt*—was.

TRANSLATION

The *brāhmaṇa* said: What could I possibly have failed to achieve, O Lord of lords, O universal teacher, since I was able to personally live with You, whose every desire is fulfilled, at the home of our spiritual master?

PURPORT

Sudāmā Brāhmaṇa wisely understands his extraordinary good fortune of having lived with Śrī Kṛṣṇa at the residence of their spiritual master. Thus whatever external difficulties they experienced were actually an expression of the Lord's mercy, to teach the importance of service to the spiritual master.

Śrīla Prabhupāda renders the learned *brāhmaṇa's* feelings as follows: "[Sudāmā said:] 'My dear Kṛṣṇa, You are the Supreme Lord and the supreme spiritual master of everyone, and since I was fortunate enough to live with You in the house of our *guru,* I think I have nothing more to do in the matter of prescribed Vedic duties.'"

TEXT 45

यस्य च्छन्दोमयं ब्रह्म देह आवपनं विभो ।
श्रेयसां तस्य गुरुषु वासोऽत्यन्तविडम्बनम् ॥४५॥

yasya cchando-mayaṁ brahma
deha āvapanaṁ vibho
śreyasāṁ tasya guruṣu
vāso 'tyanta-viḍambanam

yasya—whose; *chandaḥ*—the *Vedas; mayam*—consisting of; *brahma*—the Absolute Truth; *dehe*—within the body; *āvapanam*—the sowing field; *vibho*—O almighty Lord; *śreyasām*—of auspicious goals; *tasya*—His; *guruṣu*—with spiritual masters; *vāsaḥ*—residence; *atyanta*—extreme; *viḍambanam*—pretense.

TRANSLATION

O almighty Lord, Your body comprises the Absolute Truth in the form of the *Vedas* and is thus the source of all auspicious goals of life. That You took up residence at the school of a spiritual master is simply one of Your pastimes in which You play the role of a human being.

Thus end the purports of the humble servants of His Divine Grace A. C. Bhaktivedanta Swami Prabhupāda to the Tenth Canto, Eightieth Chapter, of the Śrīmad-Bhāgavatam, *entitled "The* Brāhmaṇa *Sudāmā Visits Lord Kṛṣṇa in Dvārakā."*

CHAPTER EIGHTY-ONE

The Lord Blesses Sudāmā Brāhmaṇa

This chapter describes how Lord Kṛṣṇa ate a morsel of the flat rice brought by His friend Sudāmā and bestowed upon him wealth greater than that of the King of heaven.

In the course of His loving talks with His friend Sudāmā, Lord Kṛṣṇa said, "My dear *brāhmaṇa*, have you brought any gift for Me from home? I regard as very significant even the smallest offering from My loving devotee." But the poor *brāhmaṇa* was ashamed to present Kṛṣṇa with his meager gift of flat rice. However, since Lord Kṛṣṇa is the Supersoul dwelling in all hearts, He knew why Sudāmā had come to visit Him. So He grabbed the bundle of flat rice Sudāmā was hiding and ate a handful of it with great pleasure. He was about to eat a second morsel when Rukmiṇī-devī stopped Him.

Feeling as if he had gone back to Godhead, Sudāmā spent that night comfortably in Lord Kṛṣṇa's palace, and the next morning he set off for home. As he passed along the highway, he thought of how fortunate he was to have been so honored by Śrī Kṛṣṇa. Absorbed in this meditation, Sudāmā arrived at the place where his home used to be—and he was struck with great wonder. Instead of his broken-down hovel, he saw a series of opulent palaces. While he stood astonished, a group of beautiful men and women came forward to greet him with singing and music. The *brāhmaṇa's* wife, wonderfully adorned with celestial jewelry, came out of the palace and welcomed him with great love and reverence. Sudāmā entered his home together with her, thinking that this extraordinary transformation must have been due to the Supreme Lord's mercy on him.

From then on Sudāmā lived his life amidst lavish wealth, yet he maintained his mood of detachment and constantly chanted the glories of Lord Kṛṣṇa. In a short time he broke off all bonds of bodily attachment and attained to the kingdom of God.

TEXTS 1–2

श्रीशुक उवाच
स इत्थं द्विजमुख्येन सह संकथयन् हरिः ।
सर्वभूतमनोऽभिज्ञः स्मयमान उवाच तम् ॥१॥
ब्रह्मण्यो ब्राह्मणं कृष्णो भगवान् प्रहसन् प्रियम् ।
प्रेम्णा निरीक्षणेनैव प्रेक्षन् खलु सतां गतिः ॥२॥

śrī-śuka uvāca
sa ittham dvija-mukhyena
saha saṅkathayan hariḥ
sarva-bhūta-mano-'bhijñaḥ
smayamāna uvāca tam

brahmaṇyo brāhmaṇaṁ kṛṣṇo
bhagavān prahasan priyam
premṇā nirīkṣaṇenaiva
prekṣan khaḷu satāṁ gatiḥ

śrī-śukaḥ uvāca—Śukadeva Gosvāmī said; *saḥ*—He; *ittham*—in this manner; *dvija*—of *brāhmaṇas; mukhyena*—with the best; *saha*—together; *saṅkathayan*—conversing; *hariḥ*—Lord Hari; *sarva*—of all; *bhūta*—living beings; *manaḥ*—the minds; *abhijñaḥ*—who knows perfectly; *smayamānaḥ*—smiling; *uvāca*—said; *tam*—to him; *brahmaṇyaḥ*—devoted to the *brāhmaṇas; brāhmaṇam*—to the *brāhmaṇa; kṛṣṇaḥ*—Lord Kṛṣṇa; *bhagavān*—the Supreme Personality of Godhead; *prahasan*—laughing; *priyam*—at His dear friend; *premṇā*—lovingly; *nirīkṣaṇena*—with a glance; *eva*—indeed; *prekṣan*—looking; *khalu*—indeed; *satām*—of the saintly devotees; *gatiḥ*—the goal.

TRANSLATION

[Śukadeva Gosvāmī said:] Lord Hari, Kṛṣṇa, perfectly knows the hearts of all living beings, and He is especially devoted to the *brāhmaṇas*. While the Supreme Lord, the goal of all saintly persons, conversed in this way with the best of the twice-born, He laughed and spoke the following words to that dear friend of His, the *brāhmaṇa* Sudāmā, all the while smiling and looking upon him with affection.

PURPORT

According to Śrīla Śrīdhara Svāmī, the words *sarva-bhūta-mano-'bhijña* indicate that since Lord Kṛṣṇa knows the minds of everyone, He could tell at once that His friend Sudāmā had brought some flat rice for Him and was ashamed to present it. According to Śrīla Viśvanātha Cakravartī's further explanation of this verse, Lord Kṛṣṇa smiled at this moment, thinking "Yes, I am going to make you show what you brought for Me." His smile then turned to laughter as He thought, "How long are you going to keep this precious gift hidden in your cloth?"

Kṛṣṇa glanced toward the bundle hidden inside His friend's garment, telling Sudāmā by His loving glance, "The veins showing through your emaciated skin and your ragged clothes astonish everyone present, but these symptoms of poverty will last only until tomorrow morning."

Although Lord Kṛṣṇa is Bhagavān, the supreme, independent Lord, He is always pleased to reciprocate with those who are *priya*, His cherished servants. As the indulgent patron of the *brāhmaṇa* class, He especially enjoys favoring *brāhmaṇas* who are additionally qualified by unconditional devotion to Him.

TEXT 3

श्रीभगवानुवाच
किमुपायनमानीतं ब्रह्मन्मे भवता गृहात् ।
अण्वप्युपाहृतं भक्तैः प्रेम्णा भूर्येव मे भवेत् ।
भूर्यप्यभक्तोपहृतं न मे तोषाय कल्पते ॥३॥

śrī-bhagavān uvāca
kim upāyanam ānītaṁ
brahman me bhavatā gṛhāt
aṇv apy upāhṛtaṁ bhaktaiḥ
premṇā bhūry eva me bhavet
bhūry apy abhaktopahṛtaṁ
na me toṣāya kalpate

śrī-bhagavān uvāca—the Supreme Lord said; *kim*—what; *upāyanam*—gift; *ānītam*—brought; *brahman*—O *brāhmaṇa; me*—for Me; *bhavatā*—by you; *gṛhāt*—from your home; *aṇu*—infinitesimal; *api*—even; *upāhṛtam*—thing offered; *bhaktaiḥ*—by devotees; *premṇā*—in pure love;

bhūri—immense; *eva*—indeed; *me*—for Me; *bhavet*—it becomes; *bhūri*—huge; *api*—even; *abhakta*—by nondevotees; *upahṛtam*—presented; *na*—not; *me*—My; *toṣāya*—for the satisfaction; *kalpate*—is competent.

TRANSLATION

The Supreme Lord said: O *brāhmaṇa,* what gift have you brought Me from home? I regard as great even the smallest gift offered by My devotees in pure love, but even great offerings presented by nondevotees do not please Me.

TEXT 4

पत्रं पुष्पं फलं तोयं यो मे भक्त्या प्रयच्छति ।
तदहं भक्त्युपहृतमश्नामि प्रयतात्मनः ॥४॥

patraṁ puṣpaṁ phalaṁ toyaṁ
yo me bhaktyā prayacchati
tad ahaṁ bhakty-upahṛtam
aśnāmi prayatātmanaḥ

patram—a leaf; *puṣpam*—a flower; *phalam*—a fruit; *toyam*—water; *yaḥ*—whoever; *me*—unto Me; *bhaktyā*—with devotion; *prayacchati*—offers; *tat*—that; *aham*—I; *bhakti-upahṛtam*—offered in devotion; *aśnāmi*—accept; *prayata-ātmanaḥ*—from one in pure consciousness.

TRANSLATION

If one offers Me with love and devotion a leaf, a flower, a fruit or water, I will accept it.

PURPORT

These famous words are also spoken by the Lord in *Bhagavad-gītā* (9.26); the translation and word meanings here are taken from Śrīla Prabhupāda's *Bhagavad-gītā As It Is.*

In the context of the current episode of Sudāmā's visit to Dvārakā, Śrīla Viśvanātha Cakravartī has kindly continued his explanation of Lord Kṛṣṇa's statements: This verse is a reply to Sudāmā's anxiety that his bringing such an unfit offering was ill-considered. The use of the words *bhaktyā prayacchati* and *bhakty-upahṛtam* may seem redundant, since they both mean "offered with devotion," but *bhaktyā* can indicate how the Lord reciprocates the devotional mood of whoever offers Him something with love. In other words, Lord Kṛṣṇa here declares that His reciprocation in a pure loving exchange is not dependent on the external quality of what is offered. Kṛṣṇa says, "Something may or may not be impressive and pleasing in its own right, but when My devotee offers it to Me in devotion, with the expectation that I will enjoy it, it gives Me great pleasure; in this regard I make no discrimination." The verb *aśnāmi*, "I eat," implies that Lord Kṛṣṇa eats even a flower, which is supposed to be smelled, bewildered as He is by the ecstatic love He feels for His devotee.

Someone might then question the Lord, "So, will You refuse an offering made to You by a devotee of some other deity?" The Lord answers, "Yes, I will refuse to eat it." This the Lord states by the phrase *prayatātmanaḥ*, implying "Only by devotional service to Me can one become pure in heart."

TEXT 5

इत्युक्तोऽपि द्विजस्तस्मै व्रीडितः पतये श्रियः ।
पृथुकप्रसृतिं राजन्न प्रायच्छदवाङ्मुखः ॥५॥

ity ukto 'pi dvijas tasmai
vrīḍitaḥ pataye śriyaḥ
pṛthuka-prasṛtiṁ rājan
na prāyacchad avāṅ-mukhaḥ

iti—thus; *uktaḥ*—addressed; *api*—although; *dvijaḥ*—the *brāhmaṇa; tasmai*—to Him; *vrīḍitaḥ*—embarrassed; *pataye*—to the husband; *śriyaḥ*—of the goddess of fortune; *pṛthuka*—of flat rice; *prasṛtim*—the palmfuls; *rājan*—O King (Parīkṣit); *na prāyacchat*—did not offer; *avāk*—bowed down; *mukhaḥ*—whose head.

TRANSLATION

[Śukadeva Gosvāmī continued:] Even after being addressed in this way, O King, the *brāhmaṇa* felt too embarrassed to offer his

palmfuls of flat rice to the husband of the goddess of fortune. He simply kept his head bowed in shame.

PURPORT

According to Ācārya Viśvanātha Cakravartī, the description here of Kṛṣṇa as "the husband of the goddess of fortune" implies that Sudāmā questioned himself, "How can the Lord of Śrī eat this hard, stale rice?" By bowing his head, the *brāhmaṇa* revealed his meditation: "My dear master, please do not make me ashamed. Even if You request it from me repeatedly, I will not give this to You. I have made up my mind." But the Lord countered with His own thought: "The intention you had fixed in your mind while coming here must not be frustrated, for you are My devotee."

TEXTS 6–7

सर्वभूतात्मदृक् साक्षात्तस्यागमनकारणम् ।
विज्ञायाचिन्तयन्नायं श्रीकामो माभजत्पुरा ॥६॥
पत्न्याः पतिव्रतायास्तु सखा प्रियचिकीर्षया ।
प्राप्तो मामस्य दास्यामि सम्पदोऽमर्त्यदुर्लभाः ॥७॥

sarva-bhūtātma-dṛk sākṣāt
tasyāgamana-kāraṇam
vijñāyācintayan nāyaṁ
śrī-kāmo mābhajat purā

patnyāḥ pati-vratāyās tu
sakhā priya-cikīrṣayā
prāpto mām asya dāsyāmi
sampado 'martya-durlabhāḥ

sarva—of all; *bhūta*—living beings; *ātma*—of the hearts; *dṛk*—the witness; *sākṣāt*—direct; *tasya*—his (Sudāmā's); *āgamana*—for the coming; *kāraṇam*—the reason; *vijñāya*—understanding fully; *acintayat*—He thought; *na*—not; *ayam*—he; *śrī*—of opulence; *kāmaḥ*—desirous; *mā*—Me; *abhajat*—worshiped; *purā*—in the past; *patnyāḥ*—of his wife; *pati*—to her husband; *vratāyāḥ*—chastely devoted; *tu*—however; *sakhā*—My friend; *priya*—the satisfaction; *cikīrṣayā*—with the desire of securing; *prāptaḥ*—now come; *mām*—to Me; *asya*—to him; *dāsyāmi*—I will give; *sampadaḥ*—riches; *amartya*—by the demigods; *durlabhāḥ*—unobtainable.

TRANSLATION

Being the direct witness in the hearts of all living beings, Lord Kṛṣṇa fully understood why Sudāmā had come to see Him. Thus He thought, "In the past My friend has never worshiped Me out of a desire for material opulence, but now he comes to Me to satisfy his chaste and devoted wife. I will give him riches that even the immortal demigods cannot obtain."

PURPORT

Śrīla Viśvanātha Cakravartī comments that the Lord momentarily wondered, "How has it come about, despite My omniscience, that this devotee of Mine has fallen into such poverty?" Then, quickly understanding the situation, He spoke to Himself the words related in this verse.

But someone may point out that Sudāmā should not have been so poverty-stricken, since appropriate enjoyment comes as a by-product of service to God even for a devotee who has no ulterior motives. This is confirmed in *Bhagavad-gītā* (9.22):

ananyāś cintayanto māṁ
ye janāḥ paryupāsate
teṣāṁ nityābhiyuktānāṁ
yoga-kṣemaṁ vahāmy aham

"But those who always worship Me with exclusive devotion, meditating on My transcendental form—to them I carry what they lack, and I preserve what they have."

In response to this point, a distinction must be made between two kinds of renounced devotees: one kind is inimical to sense gratification, and the other is indifferent to it. The Supreme Lord does not force sense gratification upon the devotee who is extremely averse to worldly enjoyments. This is seen among such great renouncers as Jaḍa Bharata. On the other hand, the Lord may give limitless wealth and power to a devotee who is neither repelled nor attracted by material things, such as Prahlāda Mahārāja. Up to this point in his life, Sudāmā Brāhmaṇa was totally averse to sense gratification, but now, out of compassion for his faithful wife—and also because he hankered to have Kṛṣṇa's audience—he went to beg from the Lord.

TEXT 8

इत्थं विचिन्त्य वसनाच्चीरबद्धान् द्विजन्मनः ।
स्वयं जहार किमिदमिति पृथुकतण्डुलान् ॥८॥

ittham vicintya vasanāc
cīra-baddhān dvi-janmanaḥ
svayaṁ jahāra kim idam
iti pṛthuka-taṇḍulān

ittham—in this manner; *vicintya*—thinking; *vasanāt*—from the garment; *cīra*—in a strip of cloth; *baddhān*—tied up; *dvi-janmanaḥ*—of the twice-born *brāhmaṇa; svayam*—Himself; *jahāra*—He took hold of; *kim*—what; *idam*—this; *iti*—so saying; *pṛthuka-taṇḍulān*—the grains of flat rice.

TRANSLATION

Thinking like this, the Lord snatched from the *brāhmaṇa's* garment the grains of flat rice tied up in an old piece of cloth and exclaimed, "What is this?

TEXT 9

नन्वेतदुपनीतं मे परमप्रीणनं सखे ।
तर्पयन्त्यंग मां विश्वमेते पृथुकतण्डुलाः ॥९॥

nanv etad upanītaṁ me
parama-prīṇanaṁ sakhe
tarpayanty aṅga māṁ viśvam
ete pṛthuka-taṇḍulāḥ

nanu—whether; *etat*—this; *upanītam*—brought; *me*—for Me; *parama*—supreme; *prīṇanam*—giving satisfaction; *sakhe*—O friend; *tarpayanti*—ingratiate; *aṅga*—My dear; *mām*—Me; *viśvam*—(who am) the whole universe; *ete*—these; *pṛthuka-taṇḍulāḥ*—grains of flat rice.

TRANSLATION

"My friend, have You brought this for Me? It gives Me extreme pleasure. Indeed, these few grains of flat rice will satisfy not only Me but also the entire universe."

PURPORT

Śrīla Prabhupāda writes in *Kṛṣṇa, the Supreme Personality of Godhead:* "It is understood from this statement that Kṛṣṇa, being the original source of everything, is the root of the entire creation. As watering the root of a tree immediately distributes water to every part of the tree, so an offering made to Kṛṣṇa, or any action done for Kṛṣṇa, is to be considered the highest welfare work for everyone, because the benefit of such an offering is distributed throughout the creation. Love for Kṛṣṇa becomes distributed to all living entities."

TEXT 10

इति मुष्टिं सकृज्जग्ध्वा द्वितीयं जग्धुमाददे ।
तावच्छ्रीर्जगृहे हस्तं तत्परा परमेष्ठिनः ॥१०॥

iti muṣṭiṁ sakṛj jagdhvā
dvitīyāṁ jagdhum ādade
tāvac chrīr jagṛhe hastaṁ
tat-parā parameṣṭhinaḥ

iti—thus speaking; *muṣṭim*—a handful; *sakṛt*—one time; *jagdhvā*—eating; *dvitīyām*—a second; *jagdhum*—to eat; *ādade*—He took; *tāvat*—thereupon; *śrīḥ*—the goddess of fortune (Rukmiṇī-devī); *jagṛhe*—seized; *hastam*—the hand; *tat*—to Him; *parā*—devoted; *parame-sthinaḥ*—of the Supreme Lord.

TRANSLATION

After saying this, the Supreme Lord ate one palmful and was about to eat a second when the devoted goddess Rukmiṇī took hold of His hand.

PURPORT

Queen Rukmiṇī took hold of Kṛṣṇa's hand to prevent Him from eating any more of the flat rice. According to Śrīpāda Śrīdhara Svāmī, with this gesture she meant to tell the Lord, "This much of Your grace is sufficient to assure anyone vast riches, which are merely the play of my glance. But please do not force me to surrender myself to this *brāhmaṇa,* as will happen if You eat one more handful."

Śrīla Viśvanātha Cakravartī explains that by taking hold of the Lord's hand Rukmiṇī implied, "If You eat all of this wonderful treat Your friend brought from his house, what will I have left for my friends, co-wives, servants and myself? There will not be enough left to distribute even one grain to each of us." And to her maidservant companions she said by her gesture, "This hard rice will upset my Lord's tender stomach."

Śrīla Prabhupāda comments that "when food is offered to Lord Kṛṣṇa with love and devotion and He is pleased and accepts it from the devotee, Rukmiṇī-devī, the goddess of fortune, becomes so greatly obliged to the devotee that she has to personally go to the devotee's home to turn it into the most opulent home in the world. If one feeds Nārāyaṇa sumptuously, the goddess of fortune, Lakṣmī, automatically becomes a guest in one's house, which means that one's home becomes opulent."

TEXT 11

एतावतालं विश्वात्मन् सर्वसम्पत्समृद्धये ।
अस्मिन् लोकेऽथ वामुष्मिन् पुंसस्त्वत्तोषकारणम् ॥११॥

etāvatālaṁ viśvātman
sarva-sampat-samṛddhaye
asmin loke 'tha vāmuṣmin
puṁsas tvat-toṣa-kāraṇam

etāvatā—this much; *alam*—enough; *viśva*—of the universe; *ātman*—O Soul; *sarva*—of all; *sampat*—opulent assets; *samṛddhaye*—for the prospering; *asmin*—in this; *loke*—world; *atha vā*—or else; *amuṣmin*—in the next; *puṁsaḥ*—for a person; *tvat*—Your; *toṣa*—satisfaction; *kāraṇam*—having as its cause.

TRANSLATION

[Queen Rukmiṇī said:] This is more than enough, O Soul of the universe, to secure him an abundance of all kinds of wealth in this world and the next. After all, one's prosperity depends simply on Your satisfaction.

TEXT 12

ब्राह्मणस्तां तु रजनीमुषित्वाच्युतमन्दिरे ।
भुक्त्वा पीत्वा सुखं मेने आत्मानं स्वर्गतं यथा ॥१२॥

brāhmaṇas tāṁ tu rajanīm
uṣitvācyuta-mandire
bhuktvā pītvā sukhaṁ mene
ātmānaṁ svar-gataṁ yathā

brāhmaṇaḥ—the *brāhmaṇa; tām*—that; *tu*—and; *rajanīm*—night; *uṣitvā*—residing; *acyuta*—of Lord Kṛṣṇa; *mandire*—in the palace; *bhuktvā*—eating; *pītvā*—drinking; *sukham*—to his satisfaction; *mene*—he thought; *ātmānam*—himself; *svaḥ*—the spiritual world; *gatam*—having attained; *yathā*—as if.

TRANSLATION

[Śukadeva Gosvāmī continued:] The *brāhmaṇa* spent that night in Lord Acyuta's palace after eating and drinking to his full satisfaction. He felt as if he had gone to the spiritual world.

TEXT 13

श्वोभूते विश्वभावेन स्वसुखेनाभिवन्दितः ।
जगाम स्वालयं तात पथ्यनुव्रज्य नन्दितः ॥१३॥

śvo-bhūte viśva-bhāvena
sva-sukhenābhivanditaḥ
jagāma svālayaṁ tāta
pathy anuvrajya nanditaḥ

śvaḥ-bhūte—on the following day; *viśva*—of the universe; *bhāvena*—by the maintainer; *sva*—within Himself; *sukhena*—who experiences happiness; *abhivanditaḥ*—honored; *jagāma*—he went; *sva*—to his own; *ālayam*—residence; *tāta*—my dear (King Parīkṣit); *pathi*—along the path; *anuvrajya*—walking; *nanditaḥ*—delighted.

TRANSLATION

The next day, Sudāmā set off for home while being honored by Lord Kṛṣṇa, the self-satisfied maintainer of the universe. The *brāhmaṇa* felt greatly delighted, my dear King, as he walked along the road.

PURPORT

We are here reminded that Lord Kṛṣṇa maintains the supply of desirable objects for the whole universe. Therefore it is to be understood that He was about to manifest for Sudāmā opulence greater than Indra's. Being *sva-sukha*, perfectly complete in His own bliss, the Lord has an unlimited capacity for bestowing gifts.

According to Śrīla Bhaktisiddhānta Sarasvatī Ṭhākura, the word *abhivanditaḥ* indicates that Śrī Kṛṣṇa accompanied Sudāmā on the road for a short distance and finally parted with the *brāhmaṇa* after bowing down to him and speaking some respectful words.

TEXT 14

स चालब्ध्वा धनं कृष्णान्न तु याचितवान् स्वयम् ।
स्वगृहान् व्रीडितोऽगच्छन्महद्दर्शननिर्वृतः ॥१४॥

sa cālabdhvā dhanaṁ kṛṣṇān
na tu yācitavān svayam
sva-gṛhān vrīḍito 'gacchan
mahad-darśana-nirvṛtaḥ

saḥ—he; *ca*—and; *alabdhvā*—not having obtained; *dhanam*—wealth; *kṛṣṇāt*—from Lord Kṛṣṇa; *na*—not; *tu*—however; *yācitavān*—did beg; *svayam*—on his own initiative; *sva*—to his; *gṛhān*—home; *vrīḍitaḥ*—embarrassed; *agacchat*—he went; *mahat*—of the Supreme Lord; *darśana*—by the audience; *nirvṛtaḥ*—made joyful.

TRANSLATION

Although he had apparently received no wealth from Lord Kṛṣṇa, Sudāmā was too shy to beg for it on his own. He simply returned home, feeling perfectly satisfied to have had the Supreme Lord's audience.

TEXT 15

अहो ब्रह्मण्यदेवस्य दृष्टा ब्रह्मण्यता मया ।
यद्दरिद्रतमो लक्ष्मीमाश्लिष्टो बिभ्रतोरसि ॥१५॥

aho brahmaṇya-devasya
dṛṣṭā brahmaṇyatā mayā
yad daridratamo lakṣmīm
āśliṣṭo bibhratorasi

aho—ah; *brahmaṇya*—who is dedicated to *brāhmaṇas; devasya*—of the Supreme Lord; *dṛṣṭā*—seen; *brahmaṇyatā*—the devotion to *brāhmaṇas; mayā*—by me; *yat*—inasmuch; *daridra-tamaḥ*—the poorest person; *lakṣmīm*—the goddess of fortune; *āśliṣṭaḥ*—embraced; *bibhratā*—by Him who carries; *urasi*—on His chest.

TRANSLATION

[Sudāmā thought:] Lord Kṛṣṇa is known to be devoted to the *brāhmaṇas*, and now I have personally seen this devotion. Indeed, He who carries the goddess of fortune on His chest has embraced the poorest beggar.

TEXT 16

क्वाहं दरिद्रः पापीयान् क्व कृष्णः श्रीनिकेतनः ।
ब्रह्मबन्धुरिति स्माहं बाहुभ्यां परिरम्भितः ॥१६॥

kvāhaṁ daridraḥ pāpīyān
kva kṛṣṇaḥ śrī-niketanaḥ
brahma-bandhur iti smāhaṁ
bāhubhyāṁ parirambhitaḥ

kva—who am; *aham*—I; *daridraḥ*—poor; *pāpīyān*—sinful; *kva*—who is; *kṛṣṇaḥ*—Kṛṣṇa, the Supreme Personality of Godhead; *śrī-niketanaḥ*—the transcendental form of all opulence; *brahma-bandhuḥ*—the friend of a *brāhmaṇa*, not fit even to be called a *brāhmaṇa; iti*—thus; *sma*—certainly; *aham*—I; *bāhubhyām*—by the arms; *parirambhitaḥ*—embraced.

TRANSLATION

Who am I? A sinful, poor friend of a *brāhmaṇa*. And who is Kṛṣṇa? The Supreme Personality of Godhead, full in six opulences. Nonetheless, He has embraced me with His two arms.

PURPORT

This translation is from Śrīla Prabhupāda's English rendering of *Caitanya-caritāmṛta* (*Madhya* 7.143).

Sudāmā was so humble that he considered his poverty to be his own fault, a result of sin. Such a mentality is in accord with the saying, *dāridrya-doṣo guṇa-rāśi-nāśī:* "The discrepency of being poor ruins heaps of good qualities."

TEXT 17

निवासितः प्रियाजुष्टे पर्यंके भ्रातरो यथा ।
महिष्या वीजितः श्रान्तो बालव्यजनहस्तया ॥१७॥

nivāsitaḥ priyā-juṣṭe
paryaṅke bhrātaro yathā
mahiṣyā vījitaḥ śrānto
bāla-vyajana-hastayā

nivāsitaḥ—seated; *priyā*—by His beloved; *juṣṭe*—used; *paryaṅke*—on the bed; *bhrātaraḥ*—brothers; *yathā*—just as; *mahiṣyā*—by His queen;

vījitaḥ—fanned; *śrāntaḥ*—tired; *bāla*—of (yak-tail) hair; *vyajana*—a fan; *hastayā*—in whose hand.

TRANSLATION

He treated me just like one of His brothers, making me sit on the bed of His beloved consort. And because I was fatigued, His queen personally fanned me with a yak-tail *cāmara*.

TEXT 18

शुश्रूषया परमया पादसंवाहनादिभिः ।
पूजितो देवदेवेन विप्रदेवेन देववत् ॥१८॥

śuśrūṣayā paramayā
pāda-saṁvāhanādibhiḥ
pūjito deva-devena
vipra-devena deva-vat

śuśrūṣayā—with service; *paramayā*—sincere; *pāda*—of the feet; *saṁvāhana*—massaging; *ādibhiḥ*—and so on; *pūjitaḥ*—worshiped; *deva-devena*—by the Lord of all the demigods; *vipra-devena*—by the Lord of the *brāhmaṇas; deva*—a demigod; *vat*—like.

TRANSLATION

Although He is the Lord of all demigods and the object of worship for all *brāhmaṇas*, He worshiped me as if I were a demigod myself, massaging my feet and rendering other humble services.

TEXT 19

स्वर्गापवर्गयोः पुंसां रसायां भुवि सम्पदाम् ।
सर्वासामपि सिद्धीनां मूलं तच्चरणार्चनम् ॥१९॥

svargāpavargayoḥ puṁsāṁ
rasāyāṁ bhuvi sampadām

sarvāsām api siddhīnāṁ
mūlaṁ tac-caraṇārcanam

svarga—of heaven; *apavargayoḥ*—and of ultimate liberation; *puṁsām*—for all men; *rasāyām*—in the subterranean regions; *bhuvi*—and on the earth; *sampadām*—of opulences; *sarvāsām*—all; *api*—also; *siddhīnām*—of mystic perfections; *mūlam*—the root cause; *tat*—His; *caraṇa*—of the feet; *arcanam*—the worship.

TRANSLATION

Devotional service to His lotus feet is the root cause of all the perfections a person can find in heaven, in liberation, in the subterranean regions and on earth.

TEXT 20

अधनोऽयं धनं प्राप्य माद्यन्नुच्चैर्न मां स्मरेत् ।
इति कारुणिको नूनं धनं मेऽभूरि नाददात् ॥२०॥

adhano 'yaṁ dhanaṁ prāpya
mādyann uccair na māṁ smaret
iti kāruṇiko nūnaṁ
dhanaṁ me 'bhūri nādadāt

adhanaḥ—poor person; *ayam*—this; *dhanam*—riches; *prāpya*—obtaining; *mādyan*—delighting; *uccaiḥ*—excessively; *na*—not; *mām*—Me; *smaret*—will remember; *iti*—thus thinking; *kāruṇikaḥ*—compassionate; *nūnam*—indeed; *dhanam*—wealth; *me*—to me; *abhūri*—slight; *na ādadāt*—He did not give.

TRANSLATION

Thinking "If this poor wretch suddenly becomes rich, he will forget Me in his intoxicating happiness," the compassionate Lord did not grant me even a little wealth.

PURPORT

Sudāmā's statement that Lord Kṛṣṇa bestowed on him "not even a little wealth" may also be taken to mean that instead of giving him wealth that was *abhūri,* "slight," the Lord in fact gave him the immense treasure of His association. This alternate meaning has been suggested by Śrīla Viśvanātha Cakravartī.

TEXTS 21–23

इति तच्चिन्तयन्नन्तः प्राप्तो निजगृहान्तिकम् ।
सूर्यानलेन्दुसंकाशैर्विमानैः सर्वतो वृतम् ॥२१॥
विचित्रोपवनोद्यानैः कूजद्द्विजकुलाकुलैः ।
प्रोत्फुल्लकुमुदाम्भोजकह्लारोत्पलवारिभिः ॥२२॥
जुष्टं स्वलंकृतैः पुम्भिः स्त्रीभिश्च हरिणाक्षिभिः ।
किमिदं कस्य वा स्थानं कथं तदिदमित्यभूत् ॥२३॥

iti tac cintayann antaḥ
prāpto nija-gṛhāntikam
sūryānalendu-saṅkāśair
vimānaiḥ sarvato vṛtam

vicitropavanodyānaiḥ
kūjad-dvija-kulākulaiḥ
protphulla-kumudāmbhoja-
kahlārotpala-vāribhiḥ

juṣṭaṁ sv-alaṅkṛtaiḥ pumbhiḥ
strībhiś ca hariṇākṣibhiḥ
kim idaṁ kasya vā sthānaṁ
kathaṁ tad idam ity abhūt

iti—thus; *tat*—this; *cintayan*—thinking; *antaḥ*—inwardly; *prāptaḥ*—arrived; *nija*—his; *gṛha*—of the home; *antikam*—at the vicinity; *sūrya*—the sun; *anala*—fire; *indu*—and the moon; *saṅkāśaiḥ*—rivaling;

vimānaiḥ—with celestial palaces; *sarvataḥ*—on all sides; *vṛtam*—surrounded; *vicitra*—wonderful; *upavana*—with courtyards; *udyānaiḥ*—and gardens; *kūjat*—cooing; *dvija*—of birds; *kula*—with hordes; *ākulaiḥ*—swarming; *protphulla*—fully bloomed; *kumuda*—having night-blooming lotuses; *ambhoja*—day-blooming lotuses; *kahlāra*—white lotuses; *utpala*—and water lilies; *vāribhiḥ*—with reservoirs of water; *juṣṭam*—adorned; *su*—well; *alaṅkṛtaiḥ*—ornamented; *pumbhiḥ*—with men; *strībhiḥ*—with women; *ca*—and; *hariṇā*—like those of she-deer; *akṣibhiḥ*—whose eyes; *kim*—what; *idam*—this; *kasya*—whose; *vā*—or; *sthānam*—place; *katham*—how; *tat*—it; *idam*—this; *iti*—so; *abhūt*—has become.

TRANSLATION

[Śukadeva Gosvāmī continued:] Thinking thus to himself, Sudāmā finally came to the place where his home stood. But that place was now crowded on all sides with towering, celestial palaces rivaling the combined brilliance of the sun, fire and the moon. There were splendorous courtyards and gardens, each filled with flocks of cooing birds and beautified by ponds in which *kumuda, ambhoja, kahlāra* and *utpala* lotuses grew. Finely attired men and doe-eyed women stood in attendance. Sudāmā wondered, "What is all this? Whose property is it? How has this all come about?"

PURPORT

Śrīla Śrīdhara Svāmī gives the sequence of the *brāhmaṇa's* thoughts: First, seeing a great, unfamiliar effulgence, he thought, "What is this?" Then, noting the palaces, he asked himself, "Whose place is this?" And recognizing it as his own, he wondered, "How has it become so transformed?"

TEXT 24

एवं मीमांसमानं तं नरा नार्योऽमरप्रभाः ।
प्रत्यगृह्णन्महाभागं गीतवाद्येन भूयसा ॥२४॥

evaṁ mīmāṁsamānaṁ taṁ
narā nāryo 'mara-prabhāḥ

pratyagṛhṇan mahā-bhāgaṁ
gīta-vādyena bhūyasā

evam—thus; *mīmāṁsamānam*—who was deeply pondering; *tam*—him; *narāḥ*—the men; *nāryaḥ*—and women; *amara*—like the demigods'; *prabhāḥ*—whose effulgent complexions; *pratyagṛhṇan*—greeted; *mahā-bhāgam*—most fortunate; *gīta*—with singing; *vādyena*—and instrumental accompaniment; *bhūyasā*—loud.

TRANSLATION

As he continued to ponder in this way, the beautiful men- and maidservants, as effulgent as demigods, came forward to greet their greatly fortunate master with loud song and instrumental music.

PURPORT

As explained by Ācārya Viśvanātha Cakravartī, the word *pratyagṛhṇan* ("they acknowledged in turn") indicates that first Sudāmā accepted the servants within his mind, deciding "My Lord must want me to have them," and in response to the visible change in his attitude, they approached him as their master.

TEXT 25

पतिमागतमाकर्ण्य पत्न्युद्धर्षातिसम्भ्रमा ।
निश्चक्राम गृहात्तूर्णं रूपिणी श्रीरिवालयात् ॥२५॥

patim āgatam ākarṇya
patny uddharṣāti-sambhramā
niścakrāma gṛhāt tūrṇaṁ
rūpiṇī śrīr ivālayāt

patim—her husband; *āgatam*—come; *ākarṇya*—hearing; *patnī*—his wife; *uddharṣā*—jubilant; *ati*—extremely; *sambhramā*—excited; *niś-cakrāma*—she came out; *gṛhāt*—from the house; *tūrṇam*—quickly; *rūpiṇī*—manifesting her personal form; *śrīḥ*—the goddess of fortune; *iva*—as if; *ālayāt*—from her abode.

TRANSLATION

When she heard that her husband had arrived, the *brāhmaṇa's* wife quickly came out of the house in a jubilant flurry. She resembled the goddess of fortune herself emerging from her divine abode.

PURPORT

Śrīla Śrīdhara Svāmī points out that since Lord Kṛṣṇa had turned Sudāmā's home into a heavenly abode, everyone living there now possessed beautiful bodies and attire appropriate to the residents of heaven. Śrīla Viśvanātha Cakravartī adds this insight: The night before, Sudāmā's poor, emaciated wife had been sleeping in rags under a crumbling roof, but when she woke in the moring she found herself and her house wonderfully changed. Only for a moment was she confused; she then realized that this opulence was the Lord's gift to her husband, who must be on his way home. Thus she prepared to greet him.

TEXT 26

पतिव्रता पतिं दृष्ट्वा प्रेमोत्कण्ठाश्रुलोचना ।
मीलिताक्ष्यनमद् बुद्ध्या मनसा परिषस्वजे ॥२६॥

pati-vratā patiṁ dṛṣṭvā
premotkaṇṭhāśru-locanā
mīlitākṣy anamad buddhyā
manasā pariṣasvaje

pati-vratā—devoted to her husband; *patim*—her husband; *dṛṣṭvā*—seeing; *prema*—of love; *utkaṇṭha*—with the eagerness; *aśru*—tearful; *locanā*—whose eyes; *mīlita*—holding closed; *akṣī*—her eyes; *anamat*—she bowed down; *buddhyā*—with thoughtful reflection; *manasā*—with her heart; *pariṣasvaje*—she embraced.

TRANSLATION

When the chaste lady saw her husband, her eyes filled with tears of love and eagerness. As she held her eyes closed, she solemnly bowed down to him, and in her heart she embraced him.

TEXT 27

पत्नीं वीक्ष्य विस्फुरन्तीं देवीं वैमानिकीमिव ।
दासीनां निष्ककण्ठीनां मध्ये भान्तीं स विस्मितः ॥२७॥

patnīṁ vīkṣya visphurantīṁ
devīṁ vaimānikīm iva
dāsīnāṁ niṣka-kaṇṭhīnāṁ
madhye bhāntīṁ sa vismitaḥ

patnīm—his wife; *vīkṣya*—seeing; *visphurantīm*—appearing effulgent; *devīm*—a demigoddess; *vaimānikīm*—come in a heavenly airplane; *iva*—as if; *dāsīnām*—of maidservants; *niṣka*—lockets; *kaṇṭhīnām*—on whose necks; *madhye*—in the midst; *bhāntīm*—shining; *saḥ*—he; *vismitaḥ*—amazed.

TRANSLATION

Sudāmā was amazed to see his wife. Shining forth in the midst of maidservants adorned with jeweled lockets, she looked as effulgent as a demigoddess in her celestial airplane.

PURPORT

Śrīla Viśvanātha Cakravartī explains that up to now the Supreme Lord had kept the *brāhmaṇa* in his wretched state so that his wife could recognize him.

TEXT 28

प्रीतः स्वयं तया युक्तः प्रविष्टो निजमन्दिरम् ।
मणिस्तम्भशतोपेतं महेन्द्रभवनं यथा ॥२८॥

prītaḥ svayaṁ tayā yuktaḥ
praviṣṭo nija-mandiram
maṇi-stambha-śatopetaṁ
mahendra-bhavanaṁ yathā

prītaḥ—pleased; *svayam*—himself; *tayā*—by her; *yuktaḥ*—joined; *praviṣṭaḥ*—having entered; *nija*—his; *mandiram*—home; *maṇi*—with gems; *stambha*—columns; *śata*—hundreds; *upetam*—having; *mahā-indra*—of great Indra, the King of heaven; *bhavanam*—the palace; *yathā*—like.

TRANSLATION

With pleasure he took his wife with him and entered his house, where there were hundreds of gem-studded pillars, just as in the palace of Lord Mahendra.

PURPORT

Śrīla Viśvanātha Cakravartī comments that Sudāmā was simply astonished at the sight of his wife. As he wondered, "Who is this demigod's wife who has approached such a fallen soul as me?" the maidservants informed him, "This is indeed your wife." At that very moment Sudāmā's body became young and beautiful, bedecked in fine clothing and jewelry. The word *prītaḥ* here indicates that these changes gave him considerable pleasure.

The famous "Thousand Names of Viṣṇu" hymn of the *Mahābhārata* immortalizes Sudāmā's sudden opulence in the following phrase: *śrīdāmā-raṅka-bhaktārtha-bhūmy-ānītendra-vaibhavaḥ*. "Lord Viṣṇu is also known as He who brought Indra's opulence to this earth for the benefit of His pitiful devotee Śrīdāmā [Sudāmā]."

TEXTS 29–32

पय:फेननिभा: शय्या दान्ता रुक्मपरिच्छदा: ।
पर्यंका हेमदण्डानि चामरव्यजनानि च ॥२९॥
आसनानि च हैमानि मृदूपस्तरणानि च ।
मुक्तादामविलम्बीनि वितानानि द्युमन्ति च ॥३०॥
स्वच्छस्फटिककुडयेषु महामारकतेषु च ।
रत्नदीपान् भ्राजमानान् ललना रत्नसंयुता: ॥३१॥
विलोक्य ब्राह्मणस्तत्र समृद्धी: सर्वसम्पदाम् ।
तर्कयामास निर्व्यग्र: स्वसमृद्धिमहैतुकीम् ॥३२॥

payaḥ-phena-nibhāḥ śayyā
dāntā rukma-paricchadāḥ
paryaṅkā hema-daṇḍāni
cāmara-vyajanāni ca

āsanāni ca haimāni
mṛdūpastaraṇāni ca
muktādāma-vilambīni
vitānāni dyumanti ca

svaccha-sphaṭika-kuḍyeṣu
mahā-mārakateṣu ca
ratna-dīpān bhrājamānān
lalanā ratna-saṁyutāḥ

vilokya brāhmaṇas tatra
samṛddhīḥ sarva-sampadām
tarkayām āsa nirvyagraḥ
sva-samṛddhim ahaitukīm

payaḥ—of milk; *phena*—the foam; *nibhāḥ*—resembling; *śayyāḥ*—beds; *dāntāḥ*—made of elephant tusks; *rukma*—golden; *paricchadāḥ*—whose ornamentation; *paryaṅkāḥ*—couches; *hema*—of gold; *daṇḍāni*—whose legs; *cāmara-vyajanāni*—yak-tail fans; *ca*—and; *āsanāni*—chairs; *ca*—and; *haimāni*—golden; *mṛdu*—soft; *upastaraṇāni*—cushions; *ca*—and; *muktā-dāma*—with strings of pearls; *vilambīni*—hanging; *vitānāni*—canopies; *dyumanti*—gleaming; *ca*—and; *svaccha*—clear; *sphaṭika*—of crystal glass; *kuḍyeṣu*—upon the walls; *mahā-mārakateṣu*—with precious emeralds; *ca*—also; *ratna*—jeweled; *dīpān*—lamps; *bhrājamānān*—shining; *lalanāḥ*—women; *ratna*—with jewels; *saṁyutāḥ*—decorated; *vilokya*—seeing; *brāhmaṇaḥ*—the *brāhmaṇa; tatra*—there; *samṛddhīḥ*—the flourishing; *sarva*—all; *sampadām*—of opulences; *tarkayām āsa*—he conjectured; *nirvyagraḥ*—free from agitation; *sva*—his own; *samṛddhim*—about the prosperity; *ahaitukīm*—unexpected.

TRANSLATION

In Sudāmā's home were beds as soft and white as the foam of milk, with bedsteads made of ivory and ornamented with gold.

There were also couches with golden legs, as well as royal *cāmara* fans, golden thrones, soft cushions and gleaming canopies hung with strings of pearls. Upon the walls of sparkling crystal glass, inlaid with precious emeralds, shone jeweled lamps, and the women in the palace were all adorned with precious gems. As he viewed this luxurious opulence of all varieties, the *brāhmaṇa* calmly reasoned to himself about his unexpected prosperity.

TEXT 33

नूनं बतैतन्मम दुर्भगस्य
शश्वद्दरिद्रस्य समृद्धिहेतुः ।
महाविभूतेरवलोकतोऽन्यो
नैवोपपद्येत यदूत्तमस्य ॥३३॥

nūnaṁ bataitan mama durbhagasya
śaśvad daridrasya samṛddhi-hetuḥ
mahā-vibhūter avalokato 'nyo
naivopapadyeta yadūttamasya

nūnam bata—certainly; *etat*—of this same person; *mama*—myself; *durbhagasya*—who am unfortunate; *śaśvat*—always; *daridrasya*—poverty-stricken; *samṛddhi*—of the prosperity; *hetuḥ*—cause; *mahā-vibhūteḥ*—of Him who possesses the greatest opulences; *avalokataḥ*—than the glance; *anyaḥ*—other; *na*—not; *eva*—indeed; *upapadyeta*—is to be found; *yadu-uttamasya*—of the best of the Yadus.

TRANSLATION

[Sudāmā thought:] I have always been poor. Certainly the only possible way that such an unfortunate person as myself could become suddenly rich is that Lord Kṛṣṇa, the supremely opulent chief of the Yadu dynasty, has glanced upon Me.

TEXT 34

नन्वब्रुवाणो दिशते समक्षं
याचिष्णवे भूर्यपि भूरिभोजः ।

पर्जन्यवत्तत्स्वयमीक्षमाणो
दाशार्हकाणामृषभः सखा मे ॥३४॥

nanv abruvāṇo diśate samakṣaṁ
yāciṣṇave bhūry api bhūri-bhojaḥ
parjanya-vat tat svayam īkṣamāṇo
dāśārhakāṇām ṛṣabhaḥ sakhā me

nanu—after all; *abruvāṇaḥ*—not speaking; *diśate*—He has given; *samakṣam*—in His presence; *yāciṣṇave*—to him who was intending to beg; *bhūri*—plentiful (wealth); *api*—even; *bhūri*—of plentiful (wealth); *bhojaḥ*—the enjoyer; *parjanya-vat*—like a cloud; *tat*—that; *svayam*—Himself; *īkṣamāṇaḥ*—seeing; *dāśārhakāṇām*—of the descendants of King Daśārha; *ṛṣabhaḥ*—the most exalted; *sakhā*—friend; *me*—my.

TRANSLATION

After all, my friend Kṛṣṇa, the most exalted of the Dāśārhas and the enjoyer of unlimited wealth, noticed that I secretly intended to beg from Him. Thus even though He said nothing about it when I stood before Him, He actually bestowed upon me the most abundant riches. In this way He acted just like a merciful rain cloud.

PURPORT

Śrī Kṛṣṇa is *bhūri-bhoja,* the unlimited enjoyer. He did not tell Sudāmā how He was going to fulfill his unspoken request because, according to Śrīla Viśvanātha Cakravartī, He was thinking at the time, "My dear friend has given Me these grains of rice, which are greater than all the treasures I own. Even though in his own house he had no such gift to bring Me, he took the trouble of begging it from a neighbor. Therefore it is only proper that I give him something more valuable than all My possessions. But nothing is equal to or greater than what I possess, so all I can do is give him such meager things as the treasures of Indra, Brahmā and other demigods." Embarrassed at being unable to properly reciprocate His devotee's offering, Lord Kṛṣṇa bestowed His favor on the *brāhmaṇa* silently. The Lord acted just like a magnanimous rain cloud, which provides the necessities of life for everyone near and far but feels ashamed that its rain is too insignificant a gift to give in return for the abundant offerings that farmers make to it. Out of shame the cloud may wait until nighttime, when the farmers are asleep, before watering their fields.

The chiefs of the Dāśārha clan, with whom Lord Kṛṣṇa is identified in this verse, were especially renowned for their generosity.

TEXT 35

किञ्चित्करोत्युर्वपि यत्स्वदत्तं
सुहृत्कृतं फल्ग्वपि भूरिकारी ।
मयोपनीतं पृथुकैकमुष्टिं
प्रत्यग्रहीत्प्रीतियुतो महात्मा ॥३५॥

kiñcit karoty urv api yat sva-dattaṁ
suhṛt-kṛtaṁ phalgv api bhūri-kārī
mayopanītaṁ pṛthukaika-muṣṭiṁ
pratyagrahīt prīti-yuto mahātmā

kiñcit—insignificant; *karoti*—He makes; *uru*—great; *api*—even; *yat*—which; *sva*—by Himself; *dattam*—given; *suhṛt*—by a well-wishing friend; *kṛtam*—done; *phalgu*—meager; *api*—even; *bhūri*—great; *kārī*—making; *mayā*—by me; *upanītam*—brought; *pṛthuka*—of flat rice; *eka*—one; *muṣṭim*—palmful; *pratyagrahīt*—He accepted; *prīti-yutaḥ*—with pleasure; *mahā-ātmā*—the Supreme Soul.

TRANSLATION

The Lord considers even His greatest benedictions to be insignificant, while He magnifies even a small service rendered to Him by His well-wishing devotee. Thus with pleasure the Supreme Soul accepted a single palmful of the flat rice I brought Him.

TEXT 36

तस्यैव मे सौहृदसख्यमैत्री-
दास्यं पुनर्जन्मनि जन्मनि स्यात् ।

महानुभावेन गुणालयेन
विषज्जतस्तत्पुरुषप्रसंगः ॥३६॥

tasyaiva me sauhṛda-sakhya-maitrī-
dāsyaṁ punar janmani janmani syāt
mahānubhāvena guṇālayena
viṣajjatas tat-puruṣa-prasaṅgaḥ

tasya—for Him; *eva*—indeed; *me*—my; *sauhṛda*—love; *sakhya*—friendship; *maitrī*—sympathy; *dāsyam*—and servitude; *punaḥ*—repeatedly; *janmani janmani*—life after life; *syāt*—may be; *mahā-anubhāvena*—with the supremely compassionate Lord; *guṇa*—of transcendental qualities; *ālayena*—the reservoir; *viṣajjataḥ*—who becomes thoroughly attached; *tat*—His; *puruṣa*—of the devotees; *prasaṅgaḥ*—the valuable association.

TRANSLATION

The Lord is the supremely compassionate reservoir of all transcendental qualities. Life after life may I serve Him with love, friendship and sympathy, and may I cultivate such firm attachment for Him by the precious association of His devotees.

PURPORT

As explained by Śrīla Viśvanātha Cakravartī, *sauhṛdam* here signifies affection toward Him who is so compassionate to His devotees, *sakhyam* is affinity manifested in the desire to live in His company, *maitrī* is the attitude of intimate comradeship, and *dāsyam* is the urge to do service.

TEXT 37

भक्ताय चित्रा भगवान् हि सम्पदो
राज्यं विभूतीर्न समर्थयत्यजः ।
अदीर्घबोधाय विचक्षणः स्वयं
पश्यन्निपातं धनिनां मदोद्भवम् ॥३७॥

bhaktāya citrā bhagavān hi sampado
rājyaṁ vibhūtīr na samarthayaty ajaḥ
adīrgha-bodhāya vicakṣaṇaḥ svayaṁ
paśyan nipātaṁ dhaninām madodbhavam

bhaktāya—to His devotee; *citrāḥ*—wonderful; *bhagavān*—the Supreme Lord; *hi*—indeed; *sampadaḥ*—opulences; *rājyam*—kingdom; *vibhūtīḥ*—material assets; *na samarthayati*—does not bestow; *ajaḥ*—unborn; *adīrgha*—short; *bodhāya*—whose understanding; *vicakṣaṇaḥ*—wise; *svayam*—Himself; *paśyan*—seeing; *nipātam*—the downfall; *dhaninām*—of the wealthy; *mada*—of the intoxication of pride; *udbhavam*—the rise.

TRANSLATION

To a devotee who lacks spiritual insight, the Supreme Lord will not grant the wonderful opulences of this world—kingly power and material assets. Indeed, in His infinite wisdom the unborn Lord well knows how the intoxication of pride can cause the downfall of the wealthy.

PURPORT

As explained by Śrīla Viśvanātha Cakravartī, the humble *brāhmaṇa* Sudāmā considered himself unworthy of the Supreme Lord's most rare and valuable benediction, pure devotional service. He reasoned that if he had any true devotion, the Lord would have granted him perfect, unflinching devotion rather than the material riches and servants he had received. Lord Kṛṣṇa would have protected a more serious devotee by denying him such distractions. The Lord will give a sincere but less intelligent devotee not as much material wealth as he desires, but only what will promote his devotional progress. Sudāmā thought, "A great saint like Prahlāda Mahārāja can avoid becoming contaminated by immeasurable wealth, power and fame, but I must always be wary of temptation in my new situation."

We may understand that this humble attitude assured Sudāmā Vipra final success in his execution of *bhakti-yoga* by the standard process of hearing and repeating the glories of Lord Kṛṣṇa.

TEXT 38

इत्थं व्यवसितो बुद्‌ध्या भक्तोऽतीव जनार्दने ।
विषयान् जायया त्यक्ष्यन् बुभुजे नातिलम्पटः ॥३८॥

itthaṁ vyavasito buddhyā
bhakto 'tīva janārdane
viṣayān jāyayā tyakṣyan
bubhuje nāti-lampaṭaḥ

ittham—in this way; *vyavasitaḥ*—fixing his determination; *buddhyā*—with intelligence; *bhaktaḥ*—devoted; *atīva*—absolutely; *janārdane*—to Lord Kṛṣṇa, the shelter of all living beings; *viṣayān*—the objects of sense gratification; *jāyayā*—with his wife; *tyakṣyan*—wanting to renounce; *bubhuje*—he enjoyed; *na*—not; *ati*—avaricious.

TRANSLATION

[Śukadeva Gosvāmī continued:] Thus firmly fixing his determination by means of his spiritual intelligence, Sudāmā remained absolutely devoted to Lord Kṛṣṇa, the shelter of all living beings. Free from avarice, he enjoyed, together with his wife, the sense pleasures that had been bestowed upon him, always with the idea of eventually renouncing all sense gratification.

TEXT 39

तस्य वै देवदेवस्य हरेर्यज्ञपतेः प्रभोः ।
ब्राह्मणाः प्रभवो दैवं न तेभ्यो विद्यते परम् ॥३९॥

tasya vai deva-devasya
harer yajña-pateḥ prabhoḥ
brāhmaṇāḥ prabhavo daivaṁ
na tebhyo vidyate param

tasya—of Him; *vai*—even; *deva-devasya*—of the Lord of lords; *hareḥ*—Kṛṣṇa; *yajña*—of Vedic sacrifice; *pateḥ*—the controller;

prabhoḥ—the supreme master; *brāhmaṇāḥ*—the *brāhmaṇas; prabhavaḥ*—masters; *daivam*—deity; *na*—not; *tebhyaḥ*—than them; *vidyate*—exists; *param*—greater.

TRANSLATION

Lord Hari is the God of all gods, the master of all sacrifices, and the supreme ruler. But He accepts the saintly *brāhmaṇas* as His masters, and so there exists no deity higher than them.

PURPORT

Śrīla Viśvanātha Cakravartī points out that even though Śrī Kṛṣṇa is the supreme ruler of creation, He accepts the *brāhmaṇas* as His masters; even though He is the God of all gods, the *brāhmaṇas* are His deities; and even though He is the Lord of all sacrifices, He performs sacrifices to worship them.

TEXT 40

एवं स विप्रो भगवत्सुहृत्तदा
दृष्ट्वा स्वभृत्यैरजितं पराजितम् ।
तद्ध्यानवेगोद्ग्रथितात्मबन्धनस्
तद्धाम लेभेऽचिरतः सतां गतिम् ॥४०॥

evaṁ sa vipro bhagavat-suhṛt tadā
dṛṣṭvā sva-bhṛtyair ajitaṁ parājitam
tad-dhyāna-vegodgrathitātma-bandhanas
tad-dhāma lebhe 'cirataḥ satāṁ gatim

evam—thus; *saḥ*—he; *vipraḥ*—the *brāhmaṇa; bhagavat*—of the Supreme Lord; *suhṛt*—the friend; *tadā*—then; *dṛṣṭvā*—seeing; *sva*—His own; *bhṛtyaiḥ*—by the servants; *ajitam*—unconquerable; *parājitam*—conquered; *tat*—upon Him; *dhyāna*—of his meditation; *vega*—by the momentum; *udgrathita*—untied; *ātma*—of the self; *bandhanaḥ*—his bondage; *tat*—His; *dhāma*—abode; *lebhe*—he attained; *aciratah*—in a short time; *satām*—of great saints; *gatim*—the destination.

TRANSLATION

Thus seeing how the unconquerable Supreme Lord is nonetheless conquered by His own servants, the Lord's dear *brāhmaṇa* friend felt the remaining knots of material attachment within his heart being cut by the force of his constant meditation on the Lord. In a short time he attained Lord Kṛṣṇa's supreme abode, the destination of great saints.

PURPORT

Sudāmā's earthly fortune has been described, and now Śukadeva Gosvāmī describes the treasure the *brāhmaṇa* enjoyed in the next world. Śrī Jīva Gosvāmī mentions that Sudāmā's last trace of illusion lay in the subtle pride of being a renounced *brāhmaṇa*. This trace was also destroyed by his contemplating the Supreme Lord's submission to His devotees.

TEXT 41

एतद् ब्रह्मण्यदेवस्य श्रुत्वा ब्रह्मण्यतां नरः ।
लब्धभावो भगवति कर्मबन्धाद्विमुच्यते ॥४१॥

etad brahmaṇya-devasya
śrutvā brahmaṇyatāṁ naraḥ
labdha-bhāvo bhagavati
karma-bandhād vimucyate

etat—this; *brahmaṇya-devasya*—of the Supreme Lord, who especially favors the *brāhmaṇas; śrutvā*—hearing; *brahmaṇyatām*—of the kindness toward *brāhmaṇas; naraḥ*—a man; *labdha*—obtaining; *bhāvaḥ*—love; *bhagavati*—for the Lord; *karma*—of material work; *bandhāt*—from the bondage; *vimucyate*—becomes freed.

TRANSLATION

The Lord always shows *brāhmaṇas* special favor. Anyone who hears this account of the Supreme Lord's kindness to *brāhmaṇas*

will come to develop love for the Lord and thus become freed from the bondage of material work.

PURPORT

In the introduction to the chapter of *Kṛṣṇa, the Supreme Personality of Godhead* that describes this pastime, His Divine Grace Śrīla Prabhupāda comments, "Lord Kṛṣṇa, the Supreme Personality of Godhead, the Supersoul of all living entities, knows very well everyone's heart. He is especially inclined to the *brāhmaṇa* devotees. Lord Kṛṣṇa is also called *brahmaṇya-deva,* which means that He is worshiped by the *brāhmaṇas.* Therefore it is understood that a devotee who is fully surrendered unto the Supreme Personality of Godhead has already acquired the position of a *brāhmaṇa.* Without becoming a *brāhmaṇa,* one cannot approach the Supreme Brahman, Lord Kṛṣṇa. Kṛṣṇa is especially concerned with vanquishing the distress of His devotees, and He is the only shelter of His devotees."

Thus end the purports of the humble servants of His Divine Grace A. C. Bhaktivedanta Swami Prabhupāda to the Tenth Canto, Eighty-first Chapter, of the Śrīmad-Bhāgavatam, *entitled "The Lord Blesses Sudāmā* Brāhmaṇa."

CHAPTER EIGHTY-TWO

Kṛṣṇa and Balarāma Meet the Inhabitants of Vṛndāvana

This chapter describes how the Yādavas and many other kings met at Kurukṣetra during a solar eclipse and discussed topics concerning Lord Kṛṣṇa. It also relates how Kṛṣṇa met Nanda Mahārāja and the other residents of Vṛndāvana at Kurukṣetra and gave them great joy.

Hearing that a total eclipse of the sun was soon to occur, people from all over Bhārata-varṣa, including the Yādavas, converged at Kurukṣetra to earn special pious credit. After the Yadus had bathed and performed other obligatory rituals, they noticed that kings of Matsya, Uśīnara and other places had also come, as well as Nanda Mahārāja and the cowherd community of Vraja, who were always feeling the intense anxiety of separation from Kṛṣṇa. The Yādavas, overjoyed to see all these old friends, embraced them one by one as they shed tears of happiness. Their wives also embraced one another with great pleasure.

When Queen Kuntī saw her brother Vasudeva and other members of her family, she put aside her sorrow. Yet still she said to Vasudeva, "O brother, I am so unfortunate, because all of you forgot me during my tribulations. Alas, even one's relatives forget a person whom Providence no longer favors."

Vasudeva replied, "My dear sister, everyone is merely a plaything of fate. We Yādavas were so harassed by Kaṁsa that we were forced to scatter and take shelter in foreign lands. So there was no way for us to keep in touch with you."

The kings present were struck with wonder upon beholding Lord Śrī Kṛṣṇa and His wives, and they began to glorify the Yādavas for having gotten the Lord's personal association. Seeing Nanda Mahārāja, the Yādavas were delighted, and each of them embraced him tightly. Vasudeva also embraced Nanda with great joy and remembered how, when Vasudeva was tormented by Kaṁsa, Nanda had taken his sons, Kṛṣṇa and Balarāma, under his protection. Balarāma and Kṛṣṇa embraced and bowed down to mother Yaśodā, but Their throats choked up with emotion and they could say nothing to her. Nanda and Yaśodā lifted their two sons onto their laps and embraced Them, and in this way they relieved the distress of separation. Rohiṇī and Devakī both embraced Yaśodā and, remembering the great friendship she had shown them, told her that the kindness she had done by raising and supporting Kṛṣṇa and Balarāma could not be repaid even with the wealth of Indra.

Then the Supreme Lord approached the young cowherd girls in a secluded place. He consoled them by pointing out that He is all-pervasive, being the source of all energies, and thus He implied that they could never be separated from Him. Having been at long last reunited with Kṛṣṇa, the *gopīs* prayed simply to have His lotus feet manifested in their hearts.

TEXT 1

श्रीशुक उवाच
अथैकदा द्वारवत्यां वसतो रामकृष्णयोः ।
सूर्योपरागः सुमहानासीत्कल्पक्षये यथा ॥१॥

śrī-śuka uvāca
athaikadā dvāravatyāṁ
vasato rāma-kṛṣṇayoḥ
sūryoparāgaḥ su-mahān
āsīt kalpa-kṣaye yathā

śrī-śukaḥ uvāca—Śukadeva Gosvāmī said; *atha*—then; *ekadā*—on one occasion; *dvāravatyām*—in Dvārakā; *vasatoḥ*—while They were living; *rāma-kṛṣṇayoḥ*—Balarāma and Kṛṣṇa; *sūrya*—of the sun; *uparāgaḥ*—an eclipse; *su-mahān*—very great; *āsīt*—there was; *kalpa*—of Lord Brahmā's day; *kṣaye*—at the end; *yathā*—as if.

TRANSLATION

Śukadeva Gosvāmī said: Once, while Balarāma and Kṛṣṇa were living in Dvārakā, there occurred a great eclipse of the sun, just as if the end of Lord Brahmā's day had come.

PURPORT

As Śrīla Viśvanātha Cakravartī Ṭhākura points out, the words *atha* and *ekadā* are commonly used in Sanskrit literature to introduce a new topic.

Here they especially indicate that the reunion of the Yadus and Vṛṣṇis at Kurukṣetra is being narrated out of chronological sequence.

Śrīla Sanātana Gosvāmī explains in his *Vaiṣṇava-toṣaṇī* commentary that the events of this eighty-second chapter occur after Lord Baladeva's visit to Vraja (Chapter 65) and before Mahārāja Yudhiṣṭhira's Rājasūya sacrifice (Chapter 74). This must be so, the *ācārya* reasons, since during the eclipse at Kurukṣetra all the Kurus, including Dhṛtarāṣṭra, Yudhiṣṭhira, Bhīṣma and Droṇa, met in friendship and happily shared the company of Śrī Kṛṣṇa. At the Rājasūya-yajña, on the other hand, Duryodhana's jealousy against the Pāṇḍavas became irrevocably inflamed. Soon after this, Duryodhana challenged Yudhiṣṭhira and his brothers to the gambling match, in which he cheated them of their kingdom and exiled them to the forest. Right after the Pāṇḍavas' return from exile, the great Battle of Kurukṣetra took place, during which Bhīṣma and Droṇa were killed. So it is not logically possible for the solar eclipse at Kurukṣetra to have happened after the Rājasūya sacrifice.

TEXT 2

तं ज्ञात्वा मनुजा राजन् पुरस्तादेव सर्वतः ।
समन्तपञ्चकं क्षेत्रं ययुः श्रेयोविधित्सया ॥२॥

taṁ jñātvā manujā rājan
purastād eva sarvataḥ
samanta-pañcakaṁ kṣetraṁ
yayuḥ śreyo-vidhitsayā

tam—that; *jñātvā*—knowing; *manujāḥ*—people; *rājan*—O King (Parīkṣit); *purastāt*—beforehand; *eva*—even; *sarvataḥ*—from everywhere; *samanta-pañcakam*—named Samanta-pañcaka (within the sacred district of Kurukṣetra); *kṣetram*—to the field; *yayuḥ*—went; *śreyaḥ*—benefit; *vidhitsayā*—wishing to create.

TRANSLATION

Knowing of this eclipse in advance, O King, many people went to the holy place known as Samanta-pañcaka in order to earn pious credit.

PURPORT

Vedic astronomers of five thousand years ago could predict eclipses of the sun and moon just as well as our modern astronomers can. The knowledge of the ancient astronomers went much further, however, since they understood the karmic influences of such events. Solar and lunar eclipses are generally very inauspicious, with certain rare exceptions. But just as the otherwise inauspicious Ekādaśī day becomes beneficial when used for the glorification of Lord Hari, so the time of an eclipse is also advantageous for fasting and worship.

The holy pilgrimage site known as Samanta-pañcaka is located at Kurukṣetra, the "sacred ground of the Kurus," where the Kuru kings' predecessors performed many Vedic sacrifices. The Kurus were thus advised by learned *brāhmaṇas* that this would be the best place for them to observe vows during the eclipse. Long before their time, Lord Paraśurāma had done penance at Kurukṣetra to atone for his killings. Samanta-pañcaka, the five ponds he dug there, were still present at the end of Dvāpara-yuga, as they are even today.

TEXTS 3–6

निःक्षत्रियां महीं कुर्वन् रामः शस्त्रभृतां वरः ।
नृपाणां रुधिरौघेण यत्र चक्रे महाह्रदान् ॥३॥
ईजे च भगवान् रामो यत्रास्पृष्टोऽपि कर्मणा ।
लोकं संग्राहयन्नीशो यथान्योऽघापनुत्तये ॥४॥
महत्यां तीर्थयात्रायां तत्रागन् भारतीः प्रजाः ।
वृष्णयश्च तथाक्रूरवसुदेवाहुकादयः ॥५॥
ययुर्भारत तत्क्षेत्रं स्वमघं क्षपयिष्णवः ।
गदप्रद्युम्नसाम्बाद्याः सुचन्द्रशुकसारणैः ।
आस्तेऽनिरुद्धो रक्षायां कृतवर्मा च यूथपः ॥६॥

niḥkṣatriyāṁ mahīṁ kurvan
rāmaḥ śastra-bhṛtāṁ varaḥ
nṛpāṇāṁ rudhiraugheṇa
yatra cakre mahā-hradān

ïje ca bhagavān rāmo
yatrāspṛṣṭo 'pi karmaṇā
lokaṁ saṅgrāhayann īśo
yathānyo 'ghāpanuttaye

mahatyāṁ tīrtha-yātrāyāṁ
tatrāgan bhāratīḥ prajāḥ
vṛṣṇayaś ca tathākrūra-
vasudevāhukādayaḥ

yayur bhārata tat kṣetraṁ
svam aghaṁ kṣapayiṣṇavaḥ
gada-pradyumna-sāmbādyāḥ
sucandra-śuka-sāraṇaiḥ
āste 'niruddho rakṣāyāṁ
kṛtavarmā ca yūtha-paḥ

niḥkṣatriyām—rid of kings; *mahīm*—the earth; *kurvan*—having made; *rāmaḥ*—Lord Paraśurāma; *śastra*—of weapons; *bhṛtām*—of the holders; *varaḥ*—the greatest; *nṛpāṇām*—of kings; *rudhira*—of the blood; *oghena*—with the floods; *yatra*—where; *cakre*—he made; *mahā*—great; *hradān*—lakes; *ïje*—worshiped; *ca*—and; *bhagavān*—the Supreme Lord; *rāmaḥ*—Paraśurāma; *yatra*—where; *aspṛṣṭaḥ*—untouched; *api*—even though; *karmaṇā*—by material work and its reactions; *lokam*—the world in general; *saṅgrāhayan*—instructing; *īśaḥ*—the Lord; *yathā*—as if; *anyaḥ*—another person; *agha*—sins; *apanuttaye*—in order to dispel; *mahatyām*—mighty; *tīrtha-yātrāyām*—on the occasion of the holy pilgrimage; *tatra*—there; *āgan*—came; *bhāratīḥ*—of Bhārata-varṣa; *prajāḥ*—people; *vṛṣṇayaḥ*—members of the Vṛṣṇi clan; *ca*—and; *tathā*—also; *akrūra-vasudeva-āhuka-ādayaḥ*—Akrūra, Vasudeva, Āhuka (Ugrasena) and others; *yayuḥ*—went; *bhārata*—O descendant of Bharata (Parikṣit); *tat*—that; *kṣetram*—to the holy place; *svam*—their own; *agham*—sins; *kṣapayiṣṇavaḥ*—desirous of eradicating; *gada-pradyumna-sāmba-ādyāḥ*—Gada, Pradyumna, Sāmba and others; *sucandra-śuka-sāraṇaiḥ*—with Sucandra, Śuka and Sāraṇa; *āste*—remained; *aniruddhaḥ*—Aniruddha; *rakṣāyām*—for guarding; *kṛtavarmā*—Kṛtavarmā; *ca*—and; *yūtha-paḥ*—leader of the army.

TRANSLATION

After ridding the earth of kings, Lord Paraśurāma, the foremost of warriors, created huge lakes from the kings' blood at Samanta-pañcaka. Although he is never tainted by karmic reactions, Lord Paraśurāma performed sacrifices there to instruct people in general; thus he acted like an ordinary person trying to free himself of sins. From all parts of Bhārata-varṣa a great number of people now came to that Samanta-pañcaka on pilgrimage. O descendant of Bharata, among those arriving at the holy place were many Vṛṣṇis, such as Gada, Pradyumna and Sāmba, hoping to be relieved of their sins; Akrūra, Vasudeva, Āhuka and other kings also went there. Aniruddha remained in Dvārakā with Sucandra, Śuka and Sāraṇa to guard the city, together with Kṛtavarmā, the commander of their armed forces.

PURPORT

According to Śrīla Viśvanātha Cakravartī, Śrī Kṛṣṇa's grandson Aniruddha remained in Dvārakā to protect the city because He is originally Lord Viṣṇu's manifestation as the guardian of the spritual planet Śvetadvīpa.

TEXTS 7–8

ते रथैर्देवधिष्ण्याभैर्हयैश्च तरलप्लवैः ।
गजैर्नदद्भिरभ्राभैर्नृभिर्विद्याधरद्युभिः ॥७॥
व्यरोचन्त महातेजाः पथि काञ्चनमालिनः ।
दिव्यस्रग्वस्त्रसन्नाहाः कलत्रैः खेचरा इव ॥८॥

te rathair deva-dhiṣṇyābhair
hayaiś ca tarala-plavaiḥ
gajair nadadbhir abhrābhair
nṛbhir vidyādhara-dyubhiḥ

vyarocanta mahā-tejāḥ
pathi kāñcana-mālinaḥ
divya-srag-vastra-sannāhāḥ
kalatraiḥ khe-carā iva

te—they; *rathaiḥ*—with (soldiers riding) chariots; *deva*—of demigods; *dhiṣṇya*—the airplanes; *ābhaiḥ*—resembling; *hayaiḥ*—horses; *ca*—and; *tarala*—(like) waves; *plavaiḥ*—whose movement; *gajaiḥ*—elephants; *nadadbhiḥ*—bellowing; *abhra*—clouds; *ābhaiḥ*—resembling; *nṛbhiḥ*—and foot soldiers; *vidyādhara*—(like) Vidyādhara demigods; *dyubhiḥ*—effulgent; *vyarocanta*—(the Yādava princes) appeared resplendent; *mahā*—very; *tejāḥ*—powerful; *pathi*—on the road; *kāñcana*—gold; *mālinaḥ*—having necklaces; *divya*—divine; *srak*—having flower garlands; *vastra*—dress; *sannāhāḥ*—and armor; *kalatraiḥ*—with their wives; *khe-carāḥ*—demigods who fly in the sky; *iva*—as if.

TRANSLATION

The mighty Yādavas passed with great majesty along the road. They were attended by their soldiers, who rode on chariots rivaling the airplanes of heaven, on horses moving with a rhythmic gait, and on bellowing elephants as huge as clouds. Also with them were many infantrymen as effulgent as celestial Vidyādharas. The Yādavas were so divinely dressed—being adorned with gold necklaces and flower garlands and wearing fine armor—that as they proceeded along the road with their wives they seemed to be demigods flying through the sky.

TEXT 9

तत्र स्नात्वा महाभागा उपोष्य सुसमाहिताः ।
ब्राह्मणेभ्यो ददुर्धेनूर्वासःस्रग्रुक्ममालिनीः ॥९॥

tatra snātvā mahā-bhāgā
upoṣya su-samāhitāḥ
brāhmaṇebhyo dadur dhenūr
vāsaḥ-srag-rukma-mālinīḥ

tatra—there; *snātvā*—bathing; *mahā-bhāgāḥ*—the greatly pious (Yādavas); *upoṣya*—fasting; *su-samāhitāḥ*—with careful attention; *brāhmaṇebhyaḥ*—to *brāhmaṇas;* *daduḥ*—they gave; *dhenūḥ*—cows; *vāsaḥ*—with garments; *srak*—flower garlands; *rukma*—gold; *mālinīḥ*—and necklaces.

TRANSLATION

At Samanta-pañcaka, the saintly Yādavas bathed and then observed a fast with careful attention. Afterward they presented *brāhmaṇas* with cows bedecked with garments, flower garlands and gold necklaces.

TEXT 10

रामह्रदेषु विधिवत्पुनराप्लुत्य वृष्णयः ।
ददुः स्वन्नं द्विजाग्र्येभ्यः कृष्णे नो भक्तिरस्त्विति ॥१०॥

rāma-hradeṣu vidhi-vat
punar āplutya vṛṣṇayaḥ
daduḥ sv-annaṁ dvijāgryebhyaḥ
kṛṣṇe no bhaktir astv iti

rāma—of Lord Paraśurāma; *hradeṣu*—in the lakes; *vidhi-vat*—in accordance with scriptural injunctions; *punaḥ*—again; *āplutya*—taking a bath; *vṛṣṇayaḥ*—the Vṛṣṇis; *daduḥ*—gave; *su*—fine; *annam*—food; *dvija*—to *brāhmaṇas; agryebhyaḥ*—excellent; *kṛṣṇe*—to Kṛṣṇa; *naḥ*—our; *bhaktiḥ*—devotion; *astu*—may there be; *iti*—thus.

TRANSLATION

In accordance with scriptural injunctions, the descendants of Vṛṣṇi then bathed once more in Lord Paraśurāma's lakes and fed first-class *brāhmaṇas* with sumptuous food. All the while they prayed, "May we be granted devotion to Lord Kṛṣṇa."

PURPORT

This second bath marked the end of their fasting, on the following day.

TEXT 11

स्वयं च तदनुज्ञाता वृष्णयः कृष्णदेवताः ।
भुक्त्वोपविविशुः कामं स्निग्धच्छायाङ्घ्रिपाङ्घ्रिषु ॥११॥

svayaṁ ca tad-anujñātā
vṛṣṇayaḥ kṛṣṇa-devatāḥ
bhuktvopaviviśuḥ kāmaṁ
snigdha-cchāyāṅghripāṅghriṣu

svayam—themselves; *ca*—and; *tat*—by Him (Lord Kṛṣṇa); *anujñātāḥ*—given permission; *vṛṣṇayaḥ*—the Vṛṣṇis; *kṛṣṇa*—Lord Kṛṣṇa; *devatāḥ*—whose exclusive Deity; *bhuktvā*—eating; *upaviviśuḥ*—sat down; *kāmam*—at will; *snigdha*—cool; *chāyā*—whose shade; *aṅghripa*—of trees; *aṅghriṣu*—at the feet.

TRANSLATION

Then, with the permission of Lord Kṛṣṇa, their sole object of worship, the Vṛṣṇis ate breakfast and sat down at their leisure beneath trees that gave cooling shade.

TEXTS 12–13

तत्रागतांस्ते ददृशुः सुहृत्सम्बन्धिनो नृपान् ।
मत्स्योशीनरकौशल्यविदर्भकुरुसृञ्जयान् ॥१२॥
काम्बोजकैकयान्मद्रान् कुन्तीनानर्तकेरलान् ।
अन्यांश्चैवात्मपक्षीयान् परांश्च शतशो नृप ।
नन्दादीन् सुहृदो गोपान् गोपीश्चोत्कण्ठिताश्चिरम् ॥१३॥

tatrāgatāṁs te dadṛśuḥ
suhṛt-sambandhino nṛpān
matsyośīnara-kauśalya-
vidarbha-kuru-sṛñjayān

kāmboja-kaikayān madrān
kuntīn ānarta-keralān
anyāṁś caivātma-pakṣīyān
parāṁś ca śataśo nṛpa
nandādīn suhṛdo gopān
gopīś cotkaṇṭhitāś ciram

tatra—there; *āgatān*—arrived; *te*—they (the Yādavas); *dadṛśuḥ*—saw; *suhṛt*—friends; *sambandhinaḥ*—and relatives; *nṛpān*—kings; *matsya-uśīnara-kauśalya-vidarbha-kuru-sṛñjayān*—the Matsyas, Uśīnaras, Kauśalyas, Vidarbhas, Kurus and Sṛñjayas; *kāmboja-kaikayān*—the Kāmbojas and Kaikayas; *madrān*—the Madras; *kuntīn*—the Kuntīs; *ānarta-keralān*—the Ānartas and Keralas; *anyān*—others; *ca eva*—also; *ātma-pakṣīyān*—of their own party; *parān*—adversaries; *ca*—and; *śataśaḥ*—by the hundreds; *nṛpa*—O King (Parīkṣit); *nanda-ādīn*—headed by Nanda Mahārāja; *suhṛdaḥ*—their dear friends; *gopān*—the cowherd men; *gopīḥ*—the cowherd women; *ca*—and; *utkaṇṭhitāḥ*—in anxiety; *ciram*—for a long time.

TRANSLATION

The Yādavas saw that many of the kings who had arrived were old friends and relatives—the Matsyas, Uśīnaras, Kauśalyas, Vidarbhas, Kurus, Sṛñjayas, Kāmbojas, Kaikayas, Madras, Kuntīs and the kings of Ānarta and Kerala. They also saw many hundreds of other kings, both allies and adversaries. In addition, my dear King Parīkṣit, they saw their dear friends Nanda Mahārāja and the cowherd men and women, who had been suffering in anxiety for so long.

TEXT 14

अन्योन्यसन्दर्शनहर्षरंहसा
प्रोत्फुल्लहृद्वक्त्रसरोरुहश्रियः ।
आश्लिष्य गाढं नयनैः स्रवज्जला
हृष्यत्त्वचो रुद्धगिरो ययुर्मुदम् ॥१४॥

anyonya-sandarśana-harṣa-raṁhasā
protphulla-hṛd-vaktra-saroruha-śriyaḥ
āśliṣya gāḍhaṁ nayanaiḥ sravaj-jalā
hṛṣyat-tvaco ruddha-giro yayur mudam

anyonya—of each other; *sandarśana*—from the seeing; *harṣa*—of the joy; *raṁhasā*—by the impulse; *protphulla*—blooming; *hṛt*—of their hearts; *vaktra*—and faces; *saroruha*—of the lotuses; *śriyaḥ*—whose beauty; *āśliṣya*—embracing; *gāḍham*—tightly; *nayanaiḥ*—from their eyes; *sravat*—pouring; *jalāḥ*—water (tears); *hṛṣyat*—erupting with hair standing on end; *tvacaḥ*—whose skin; *ruddha*—choked; *giraḥ*—whose speech; *yayuḥ*—they experienced; *mudam*—delight.

TRANSLATION

As the great joy of seeing one another made the lotuses of their hearts and faces bloom with fresh beauty, the men embraced one another enthusiastically. With tears pouring from their eyes, the hair on their bodies standing on end and their voices choked up, they all felt intense bliss.

TEXT 15

स्त्रियश्च संवीक्ष्य मिथोऽतिसौहृद-
स्मितामलापांगदृशोऽभिरेभिरे ।
स्तनैः स्तनान् कुंकुमपंकरूषितान्
निहत्य दोर्भिः प्रणयाश्रुलोचनाः ॥१५॥

striyaś ca saṁvīkṣya mitho 'ti-sauhṛda-
smitāmalāpāṅga-dṛśo 'bhirebhire
stanaiḥ stanān kuṅkuma-paṅka-rūṣitān
nihatya dorbhiḥ praṇayāśru-locanāḥ

striyaḥ—the women; *ca*—and; *saṁvīkṣya*—seeing; *mithaḥ*—one another; *ati*—extreme; *sauhṛda*—with friendly affection; *smita*—smiling; *amala*—pure; *apāṅga*—exhibiting glances; *dṛśaḥ*—whose eyes; *abhirebhire*—they embraced; *stanaiḥ*—with breasts; *stanān*—breasts; *kuṅkuma*—of saffron; *paṅka*—with paste; *rūṣitān*—smeared; *nihatya*—pressing; *dorbhiḥ*—with their arms; *praṇaya*—of love; *aśru*—tears; *locanāḥ*—in whose eyes.

TRANSLATION

The women glanced at one another with pure smiles of loving friendship. And when they embraced, their breasts, smeared with saffron paste, pressed against one another as their eyes filled with tears of affection.

TEXT 16

ततोऽभिवाद्य ते वृद्धान् यविष्ठैरभिवादिताः ।
स्वागतं कुशलं पृष्ट्वा चक्रुः कृष्णकथा मिथः ॥१६॥

tato 'bhivādya te vṛddhān
yaviṣṭhair abhivāditāḥ
sv-āgataṁ kuśalaṁ pṛṣṭvā
cakruḥ kṛṣṇa-kathā mithaḥ

tataḥ—then; *abhivādya*—offering obeisances; *te*—they; *vṛddhān*—to their elders; *yaviṣṭhaiḥ*—by their younger relatives; *abhivāditāḥ*—offered obeisances; *su-āgatam*—comfortable arrival; *kuśalam*—and well-being; *pṛṣṭvā*—inquiring about; *cakruḥ*—they made; *kṛṣṇa*—about Kṛṣṇa; *kathāḥ*—conversation; *mithaḥ*—among one another.

TRANSLATION

They all then offered obeisances to their elders and received respect in turn from their younger relatives. After inquiring from one another about the comfort of their trip and their well-being, they proceeded to talk about Kṛṣṇa.

PURPORT

These are the special dealings of Vaiṣṇavas. Even the family entanglements that delude ordinary conditioned souls are no encumbrance for those whose family members are all pure devotees of the Lord. Impersonalists have no capacity for appreciating these intimate dealings, since their philosophy condemns as illusory any kind of personal, emotional existence. When followers of impersonalism pretend to understand the loving relationships of Kṛṣṇa and His devotees, they only create havoc for themselves and whoever listens to them.

TEXT 17

पृथा भ्रातॄन् स्वसॄर्वीक्ष्य तत्पुत्रान् पितरावपि ।
भ्रातृपत्नीर्मुकुन्दं च जहौ संकथया शुचः ॥१७॥

pṛthā bhrātṝn svasṝr vīkṣya
tat-putrān pitarāv api
bhrātṛ-patnīr mukundaṁ ca
jahau saṅkathayā śucaḥ

pṛthā—Kuntī; *bhrātṝn*—her brothers; *svasṝḥ*—and sisters; *vīkṣya*—seeing; *tat*—their; *putrān*—children; *pitarau*—her parents; *api*—also; *bhrātṛ*—of her brothers; *patnīḥ*—the wives; *mukundam*—Lord Kṛṣṇa; *ca*—also; *jahau*—she gave up; *saṅkathayā*—while talking; *śucaḥ*—her sorrow.

TRANSLATION

Queen Kuntī met with her brothers and sisters and their children, and also with her parents, her brothers' wives and Lord Mukunda. While talking with them she forgot her sorrow.

PURPORT

Even the constant anxiety of a pure devotee, apparently just the opposite of the impersonalists' *śānti,* can be an exalted manifestation of love of God, as exemplified by Śrīmatī Kuntīdevī, the aunt of Lord Kṛṣṇa and mother of the Pāṇḍavas.

TEXT 18

कुन्त्युवाच
आर्य भ्रातरहं मन्ये आत्मानमकृताशिषम् ।
यद्वा आपत्सु मद्वार्तां नानुस्मरथ सत्तमाः ॥१८॥

kunty uvāca
ārya bhrātar ahaṁ manye
ātmānam akṛtāśiṣam
yad vā āpatsu mad-vārtāṁ
nānusmaratha sattamāḥ

kuntī uvāca—Queen Kuntī said; *ārya*—O respectable one; *bhrātaḥ*—O brother; *aham*—I; *manye*—think; *ātmānam*—myself; *akṛta*—having failed to achieve; *āśiṣam*—my desires; *yat*—since; *vai*—indeed; *āpatsu*—in times of danger; *mat*—to me; *vārtām*—what occurred; *na anusmaratha*—all of you do not remember; *sat-tamāḥ*—most saintly.

TRANSLATION

Queen Kuntī said: My dear, respectable brother, I feel that my desires have been frustrated, because although all of you are most saintly, you forgot me during my calamities.

PURPORT

Here Queen Kuntī addresses her brother Vasudeva.

TEXT 19

सुहृदो ज्ञातयः पुत्रा भ्रातरः पितरावपि ।
नानुस्मरन्ति स्वजनं यस्य दैवमदक्षिणम् ॥१९॥

suhṛdo jñātayaḥ putrā
bhrātaraḥ pitarāv api
nānusmaranti sva-janaṁ
yasya daivam adakṣiṇam

suhṛdaḥ—friends; *jñātayaḥ*—and relatives; *putrāḥ*—sons; *bhrātaraḥ*—brothers; *pitarau*—parents; *api*—even; *na anusmaranti*—do not remember; *sva-janam*—a dear one; *yasya*—whose; *daivam*—Providence; *adakṣiṇam*—unfavorable.

TRANSLATION

Friends and family members—even children, brothers and parents—forget a dear one whom Providence no longer favors.

PURPORT

Śrīla Śrīdhara Svāmī and Viśvanātha Cakravartī Ṭhākura both comment that Kuntī does not blame her relatives for her suffering. Thus she calls them "most saintly persons" and alludes here to her own bad fortune as the cause of her unhappiness.

TEXT 20

श्रीवसुदेव उवाच
अम्ब मास्मानसूयेथा दैवक्रीडनकान्नरान् ।
ईशस्य हि वशे लोकः कुरुते कार्यतेऽथ वा ॥२०॥

śrī-vasudeva uvāca
amba māsmān asūyethā
daiva-krīḍanakān narān
īśasya hi vaśe lokaḥ
kurute kāryate 'tha vā

śrī-vasudevaḥ uvāca—Śrī Vasudeva said; *amba*—my dear sister; *mā*—please do not; *asmān*—with us; *asūyethāḥ*—be angry; *daiva*—of fate; *krīḍanakān*—the playthings; *narān*—men; *īśasya*—of the Supreme Lord; *hi*—indeed; *vaśe*—under the control; *lokaḥ*—a person; *kurute*—acts on his own; *kāryate*—is made to act by others; *atha vā*—or else.

TRANSLATION

Śrī Vasudeva said: Dear sister, please do not be angry with us. We are only ordinary men, playthings of fate. Indeed, whether a person acts on his own or is forced by others, he is always under the Supreme Lord's control.

TEXT 21

कंसप्रतापिताः सर्वे वयं याता दिशं दिशम् ।
एतर्ह्येव पुनः स्थानं दैवेनासादिताः स्वसः ॥२१॥

kaṁsa-pratāpitāḥ sarve
vayaṁ yātā diśaṁ diśam
etarhy eva punaḥ sthānaṁ
daivenāsāditāḥ svasaḥ

kaṁsa—by Kaṁsa; *pratāpitāḥ*—severely troubled; *sarve*—all; *vayam*—we; *yātāḥ*—went away; *diśam diśam*—in various directions; *etarhi eva*—just now; *punaḥ*—again; *sthānam*—to our proper places; *daivena*—by Providence; *āsāditāḥ*—brought; *svasaḥ*—O sister.

TRANSLATION

Harassed by Kaṁsa, we all fled in various directions, but by the grace of Providence we have now finally been able to return to our homes, my dear sister.

TEXT 22

श्रीशुक उवाच
वसुदेवोग्रसेनाद्यैर्यदुभिस्तेऽर्चिता नृपाः ।
आसन्नच्युतसन्दर्शपरमानन्दनिर्वृताः ॥२२॥

śrī-śuka uvāca
vasudevograsenādyair
yadubhis te 'rcitā nṛpāḥ
āsann acyuta-sandarśa-
paramānanda-nirvṛtāḥ

śrī-śukaḥ uvāca—Śrī Śukadeva Gosvāmī said; *vasudeva-ugrasena-ādyaiḥ*—headed by Vasudeva and Ugrasena; *yadubhiḥ*—by the Yādavas; *te*—they; *arcitāḥ*—honored; *nṛpāḥ*—the kings; *āsan*—became; *acyuta*—of Lord Kṛṣṇa; *sandarśa*—by the seeing; *parama*—supreme; *ānanda*—in ecstasy; *nirvṛtāḥ*—pacified.

TRANSLATION

Śukadeva Gosvāmī said: Vasudeva, Ugrasena and the other Yadus honored the various kings, who became supremely blissful and content upon seeing Lord Acyuta.

TEXTS 23–26

भीष्मो द्रोणोऽम्बिकापुत्रो गान्धारी ससुता तथा ।
सदाराः पाण्डवाः कुन्ती सञ्जयो विदुरः कृपः ॥२३॥
कुन्तीभोजो विराटश्च भीष्मको नग्नजिन्महान् ।
पुरुजिद् द्रुपदः शल्यो धृष्टकेतुः स काशिराट् ॥२४॥
दमघोषो विशालाक्षो मैथिलो मद्रकेकयौ ।
युधामन्युः सुशर्मा च ससुता बाह्लिकादयः ॥२५॥

राजानो ये च राजेन्द्र युधिष्ठिरमनुव्रताः ।
श्रीनिकेतं वपुः शौरेः सस्त्रीकं वीक्ष्य विस्मिताः ॥२६॥

bhīṣmo droṇo 'mbikā-putro
gāndhārī sa-sutā tathā
sa-dārāḥ pāṇḍavāḥ kuntī
sañjayo viduraḥ kṛpaḥ

kuntībhojo virāṭaś ca
bhīṣmako nagnajin mahān
purujid drupadaḥ śalyo
dhṛṣṭaketuḥ sa kāśi-rāṭ

damaghoṣo viśālākṣo
maithilo madra-kekayau
yudhāmanyuḥ suśarmā ca
sa-sutā bāhlikādayaḥ

rājāno ye ca rājendra
yudhiṣṭhiram anuvratāḥ
śrī-niketaṁ vapuḥ śaureḥ
sa-strīkaṁ vīkṣya vismitāḥ

bhīṣmaḥ droṇaḥ ambikā-putraḥ—Bhīṣma, Droṇa and the son of Ambikā (Dhṛtarāṣṭra); *gāndhārī*—Gāndhārī; *sa*—together with; *sutāḥ*—her sons; *tathā*—also; *sa-dārāḥ*—with their wives; *pāṇḍavāḥ*—the sons of Pāṇḍu; *kuntī*—Kuntī; *sañjayaḥ viduraḥ kṛpaḥ*—Sañjaya, Vidura and Kṛpa; *kuntībhojaḥ virāṭaḥ ca*—Kuntībhoja and Virāṭa; *bhīṣmakaḥ*—Bhīṣmaka; *nagnajit*—Nagnajit; *mahān*—the great; *purujit drupadaḥ śalyaḥ*—Purujit, Drupada and Śalya; *dhṛṣṭaketuḥ*—Dhṛṣṭaketu; *saḥ*—he; *kāśi-rāṭ*—the King of Kāśī; *damaghoṣaḥ viśālākṣaḥ*—Damaghoṣa and Viśālākṣa; *maithilaḥ*—the King of Mithilā; *madra-kekayau*—the kings of Madra and Kekaya; *yudhāmanyuḥ suśarmā ca*—Yudhāmanyu and Suśarmā; *sa-sutāḥ*—with their sons; *bāhlika-ādayaḥ*—Bāhlika and others; *rājānaḥ*—kings; *ye*—who; *ca*—and; *rāja-indra*—O best of kings (Parīkṣit); *yudhiṣṭhiram*—Mahārāja Yudhiṣṭhira; *anuvratāḥ*—following; *śrī*—of opulence and beauty; *niketam*—the abode; *vapuḥ*—the personal form; *śaureḥ*—of Lord Kṛṣṇa; *sa-strīkam*—along with His wives; *vīkṣya*—seeing; *vismitāḥ*—amazed.

TRANSLATION

All the royalty present, including Bhīṣma, Droṇa, Dhṛtarāṣṭra, Gāndhārī and her sons, the Pāṇḍavas and their wives, Kuntī, Sañjaya, Vidura, Kṛpācārya, Kuntībhoja, Virāṭa, Bhīṣmaka, the great Nagnajit, Purujit, Drupada, Śalya, Dhṛṣṭaketu, Kāśirāja, Damaghoṣa, Viśālākṣa, Maithila, Madra, Kekaya, Yudhāmanyu, Suśarmā, Bāhlika with his associates and their sons, and the many other kings subservient to Mahārāja Yudhiṣṭhira—all of them, O best of kings, were simply amazed to see the transcendental form of Lord Kṛṣṇa, the abode of all opulence and beauty, standing before them with His consorts.

PURPORT

All these kings were now followers of Yudhiṣṭhira because he had subjugated each of them to earn the privilege of performing the Rājasūya sacrifice. The Vedic injunctions state that a *kṣatriya* who wants to execute the Rājasūya for elevation to heaven must first send out a "victory horse" to roam freely; any other king whose territory this horse enters must either voluntarily submit or face the *kṣatriya* or his representatives in battle.

TEXT 27

अथ ते रामकृष्णाभ्यां सम्यक् प्राप्तसमर्हणाः ।
प्रशशंसुर्मुदा युक्ता वृष्णीन् कृष्णपरिग्रहान् ॥२७॥

atha te rāma-kṛṣṇābhyāṁ
samyak prāpta-samarhaṇāḥ
praśaśaṁsur mudā yuktā
vṛṣṇīn kṛṣṇa-parigrahān

atha—then; *te*—they; *rāma-kṛṣṇābhyām*—by Balarāma and Kṛṣṇa; *samyak*—properly; *prāpta*—having received; *samarhaṇāḥ*—appropriate tokens of honor; *praśaśaṁsuḥ*—enthusiastically praised; *mudā*—with joy; *yuktāḥ*—filled; *vṛṣṇīn*—the Vṛṣṇis; *kṛṣṇa*—of Lord Kṛṣṇa; *parigrahān*—the personal associates.

TRANSLATION

After Lord Balarāma and Lord Kṛṣṇa had liberally honored them, with great joy and enthusiasm these kings began to praise the members of the Vṛṣṇi clan, Śrī Kṛṣṇa's personal associates.

TEXT 28

अहो भोजपते यूयं जन्मभाजो नृणामिह ।
यत्पश्यथासकृत्कृष्णं दुर्दर्शमपि योगिनाम् ॥२८॥

aho bhoja-pate yūyaṁ
janma-bhājo nṛṇām iha
yat paśyathāsakṛt kṛṣṇaṁ
durdarśam api yoginām

aho—ah; *bhoja-pate*—O master of the Bhojas, Ugrasena; *yūyam*—you; *janma-bhājaḥ*—having taken a worthwhile birth; *nṛṇām*—among men; *iha*—in this world; *yat*—because; *paśyatha*—you see; *asakṛt*—repeatedly; *kṛṣṇam*—Lord Kṛṣṇa; *durdarśam*—rarely seen; *api*—even; *yoginām*—by great mystics.

TRANSLATION

[The kings said:] O King of the Bhojas, you alone among men have achieved a truly exalted birth, for you continually behold Lord Kṛṣṇa, who is rarely visible even to great *yogīs*.

TEXTS 29–30

यद्विश्रुतिः श्रुतिनुतेदमलं पुनाति
पादावनेजनपयश्च वचश्च शास्त्रम् ।
भूः कालभर्जितभगापि यदङ्घ्रिपद्म-
स्पर्शोत्थशक्तिरभिवर्षति नोऽखिलार्थान् ॥२९॥
तद्दर्शनस्पर्शनानुपथप्रजल्प-
शय्यासनाशनसयौनसपिण्डबन्धः ।

येषां गृहे निरयवर्त्मनि वर्ततां वः
स्वर्गापवर्गविरमः स्वयमास विष्णुः ॥३०॥

yad-viśrutiḥ śruti-nutedam alaṁ punāti
pādāvanejana-payaś ca vacaś ca śāstram
bhūḥ kāla-bharjita-bhagāpi yad-aṅghri-padma-
sparśottha-śaktir abhivarṣati no 'khilārthān

tad-darśana-sparśanānupatha-prajalpa-
śayyāsanāśana-sayauna-sapiṇḍa-bandhaḥ
yeṣāṁ gṛhe niraya-vartmani vartatāṁ vaḥ
svargāpavarga-viramaḥ svayam āsa viṣṇuḥ

yat—whose; *viśrutiḥ*—fame; *śruti*—by the *Vedas; nutā*—vibrated; *idam*—this (universe); *alam*—thoroughly; *punāti*—purifies; *pāda*—whose feet; *avanejana*—washing; *payaḥ*—the water; *ca*—and; *vacaḥ*—words; *ca*—and; *śāstram*—the revealed scriptures; *bhūḥ*—the earth; *kāla*—by time; *bharjita*—ravaged; *bhagā*—whose good fortune; *api*—even; *yat*—whose; *aṅghri*—of the feet; *padma*—lotuslike; *sparśa*—by the touch; *uttha*—wakened; *śaktiḥ*—whose energy; *abhivarṣati*—abundantly rains; *naḥ*—upon us; *akhila*—all; *arthān*—objects of desire; *tat*—Him; *darśana*—with seeing; *sparśana*—touching; *anupatha*—walking alongside; *prajalpa*—conversing with; *śayyā*—lying down to take rest; *āsana*—sitting; *aśana*—eating; *sa-yauna*—in relationships through marriage; *sa-piṇḍa*—and in blood relationships; *bandhaḥ*—connections; *yeṣām*—in whose; *gṛhe*—family life; *niraya*—of hell; *vartmani*—upon the path; *vartatām*—who travel; *vaḥ*—your; *svarga*—of (desire for attaining) heaven; *apavarga*—and liberation; *viramaḥ*—the (cause of) cessation; *svayam*—in person; *āsa*—has been present; *viṣṇuḥ*—the Supreme Lord Viṣṇu.

TRANSLATION

His fame, as broadcast by the *Vedas*, the water that has washed His feet, and the words He speaks in the form of the revealed scriptures—these thoroughly purify this universe. Although the earth's good fortune was ravaged by time, the touch of His lotus feet has revitalized her, and thus she is raining down on us the fulfillment of all our desires. The same Lord Viṣṇu who makes one

forget the goals of heaven and liberation has now entered into marital and blood relationships with you, who otherwise travel on the hellish path of family life. Indeed, in these relationships you see and touch Him directly, walk beside Him, converse with Him, and together with Him lie down to rest, sit at ease and take your meals.

PURPORT

All Vedic *mantras* glorify Lord Viṣṇu; this truth is supported with elaborate evidence by learned *ācāryas* like Rāmānuja, in his *Vedārtha-saṅgraha,* and Madhva, in his *Ṛg-veda-bhāṣya.* The words Viṣṇu Himself speaks, such as the *Bhagavad-gītā,* are the confidential essence of all scripture. In His manifestation as Vyāsadeva, the Supreme Lord composed both the *Vedānta-sūtras* and *Mahābhārata,* and this *Mahābhārata* includes Śrī Kṛṣṇa's personal statement: *vedaiś ca sarvair aham eva vedyo/ vedānta-kṛd veda-vid eva cāham.* "By all the *Vedas,* I am to be known. Indeed, I am the compiler of *Vedānta,* and I am the knower of the *Vedas.*" (*Bhagavad-gītā* 15.15)

When Lord Viṣṇu appeared before Bali Mahārāja to beg three steps of land, the Lord's second step pierced the shells of the universe. The water of the transcendental river Virajā, lying just outside the universal egg, thus seeped inside, washing Lord Vāmana's foot and flowing down to become the Ganges River. Because of the sanctity of its origin, the Ganges is generally considered the most holy of rivers. But even more potent is the water of the Yamunā, where Lord Viṣṇu in His original form of Govinda played with His intimate companions.

In these two verses the assembled kings praise the special merit of Lord Kṛṣṇa's Yadu clan. Not only do they see Kṛṣṇa, but they are also directly connected with Him by dual bonds of marital and blood relationships. Śrīla Viśvanātha Cakravartī suggests that the word *bandha,* beside its more obvious meaning of "relation," can also be understood in the sense of "capture," expressing that the love the Yadus feel for the Lord obliges Him always to stay with them.

TEXT 31

श्रीशुक उवाच
नन्दस्तत्र यदून् प्राप्तान् ज्ञात्वा कृष्णपुरोगमान् ।
तत्रागमद्वृतो गोपैरनःस्थार्थैर्दिदृक्षया ॥३१॥

śrī-śuka uvāca
nandas tatra yadūn prāptān
jñātvā kṛṣṇa-purogamān
tatrāgamad vṛto gopair
anaḥ-sthārthair didṛkṣayā

śrī-śukaḥ uvāca—Śukadeva Gosvāmī said; *nandaḥ*—Nanda Mahārāja; *tatra*—there; *yadūn*—the Yadus; *prāptān*—arrived; *jñātvā*—finding out; *kṛṣṇa*—Lord Kṛṣṇa; *puraḥ-gamān*—keeping in front; *tatra*—there; *agamat*—he went; *vṛtaḥ*—accompanied; *gopaiḥ*—by the cowherds; *anaḥ*—on their wagons; *stha*—placed; *arthaiḥ*—whose possessions; *didṛkṣayā*—wanting to see.

TRANSLATION

Śukadeva Gosvāmī said: When Nanda Mahārāja learned that the Yadus had arrived, led by Kṛṣṇa, he immediately went to see them. The cowherds accompanied him, their various possessions loaded on their wagons.

PURPORT

The cowherds of Vraja were planning to stay at Kurukṣetra for some days, so they came equipped with adequate provisions, especially milk products and other foods for the pleasure of Kṛṣṇa and Balarāma.

TEXT 32

तं दृष्ट्वा वृष्णयो हृष्टास्तन्वः प्राणमिवोत्थिताः ।
परिषस्वजिरे गाढं चिरदर्शनकातराः ॥३२॥

taṁ dṛṣṭvā vṛṣṇayo hṛṣṭās
tanvaḥ prāṇam ivotthitāḥ
pariṣasvajire gāḍhaṁ
cira-darśana-kātarāḥ

tam—him, Nanda; *dṛṣṭvā*—seeing; *vṛṣṇayaḥ*—the Vṛṣṇis; *hṛṣṭāḥ*—delighted; *tanvaḥ*—living bodies; *prāṇam*—their vital air; *iva*—as if; *utthitāḥ*—rising; *pariṣasvajire*—they embraced him; *gāḍham*—firmly; *cira*—after a long time; *darśana*—in seeing; *kātarāḥ*—agitated.

TRANSLATION

Seeing Nanda, the Vṛṣṇis were delighted and stood up like dead bodies coming back to life. Having felt much distress at not seeing him for so long, they held him in a tight embrace.

TEXT 33

वसुदेवः परिष्वज्य सम्प्रीतः प्रेमविह्वलः ।
स्मरन् कंसकृतान् क्लेशान् पुत्रन्यासं च गोकुले ॥३३॥

vasudevaḥ pariṣvajya
samprītaḥ prema-vihvalaḥ
smaran kaṁsa-kṛtān kleśān
putra-nyāsaṁ ca gokule

vasudevaḥ—Vasudeva; *pariṣvajya*—embracing (Nanda Mahārāja); *samprītaḥ*—overjoyed; *prema*—due to love; *vihvalaḥ*—beside himself; *smaran*—remembering; *kaṁsa-kṛtān*—created by Kaṁsa; *kleśān*—the troubles; *putra*—of his sons; *nyāsam*—the leaving; *ca*—and; *gokule*—in Gokula.

TRANSLATION

Vasudeva embraced Nanda Mahārāja with great joy. Beside himself with ecstatic love, Vasudeva remembered the troubles Kaṁsa had caused him, forcing him to leave his sons in Gokula for Their safety.

TEXT 34

कृष्णरामौ परिष्वज्य पितरावभिवाद्य च ।
न किञ्चनोचतुः प्रेम्णा साश्रुकण्ठौ कुरूद्वह ॥३४॥

kṛṣṇa-rāmau pariṣvajya
pitarāv abhivādya ca
na kiñcanocatuḥ premṇā
sāśru-kaṇṭhau kurūdvaha

kṛṣṇa-rāmau—Kṛṣṇa and Balarāma; *pariṣvajya*—embracing; *pitarau*—Their parents; *abhivādya*—offering respects; *ca*—and; *na kiñcana*—nothing; *ūcatuḥ*—said; *premṇā*—with love; *sa-aśru*—full of tears; *kaṇṭhau*—whose throats; *kuru-udvaha*—O most heroic of the Kurus.

TRANSLATION

O hero of the Kurus, Kṛṣṇa and Balarāma embraced Their foster parents and bowed down to them, but Their throats were so choked up with tears of love that the two Lords could say nothing.

PURPORT

After a long separation, a respectful child should first offer obeisances to his parents. Nanda and Yaśodā gave their sons no opportunity for this, however, for as soon as they saw Them they embraced Them. Only then could Kṛṣṇa and Balarāma offer Their proper respects.

TEXT 35

तावात्मासनमारोप्य बाहुभ्यां परिरभ्य च ।
यशोदा च महाभागा सुतौ विजहतुः शुचः ॥३५॥

tāv ātmāsanam āropya
bāhubhyāṁ parirabhya ca
yaśodā ca mahā-bhāgā
sutau vijahatuḥ śucaḥ

tau—the two of Them; *ātma-āsanam*—onto their laps; *āropya*—raising; *bāhubhyām*—with their arms; *parirabhya*—embracing; *ca*—and; *yaśodā*—mother Yaśodā; *ca*—also; *mahā-bhāgā*—saintly; *sutau*—their sons; *vijahatuḥ*—they gave up; *śucaḥ*—their sorrow.

TRANSLATION

Raising their two sons onto their laps and holding Them in their arms, Nanda and saintly mother Yaśodā forgot their sorrow.

PURPORT

Śrīla Viśvanātha Cakravartī explains that after the initial embraces and obeisances, Vasudeva led Nanda and Yaśodā into his tent as they held the hands of Kṛṣṇa and Balarāma. Following them inside were Rohiṇī, other women and men of Vraja, and a number of attendants. Inside, Nanda and Yaśodā took the two boys on their laps. Despite having heard the glories of the two Lords of Dvārakā, and despite seeing these opulences now before their eyes, Nanda and Yaśodā looked upon Them as if They were still their eight-year-old children.

TEXT 36

रोहिणी देवकी चाथ परिष्वज्य व्रजेश्वरीम् ।
स्मरन्त्यौ तत्कृतां मैत्रीं बाष्पकण्ठ्यौ समूचतुः ॥३६॥

rohiṇī devakī cātha
pariṣvajya vrajeśvarīm
smarantyau tat-kṛtāṁ maitrīṁ
bāṣpa-kaṇṭhyau samūcatuḥ

rohiṇī—Rohiṇī; *devakī*—Devakī; *ca*—and; *atha*—next; *pariṣvajya*—embracing; *vraja-īśvarīm*—the Queen of Vraja (Yaśodā); *smarantyau*—remembering; *tat*—by her; *kṛtām*—done; *maitrīm*—friendship; *bāṣpa*—tears; *kaṇṭhyau*—in whose throats; *samūcatuḥ*—they addressed her.

TRANSLATION

Then Rohiṇī and Devakī both embraced the Queen of Vraja, remembering the faithful friendship she had shown them. Their throats choking with tears, they addressed her as follows.

PURPORT

At this time, according to Śrīla Viśvanātha Cakravartī, Śrī Vasudeva invited Nanda outside to meet Ugrasena and the other elder Yadus. Taking this opportunity, Rohiṇī and Devakī talked with Queen Yaśodā.

TEXT 37

का विस्मरेत वां मैत्रीमनिवृत्तां व्रजेश्वरि ।
अवाप्याप्यैन्द्रमैश्वर्यं यस्या नेह प्रतिक्रिया ॥३७॥

kā vismareta vāṁ maitrīm
anivṛttāṁ vrajeśvari
avāpyāpy aindram aiśvaryaṁ
yasyā neha pratikriyā

kā—what woman; *vismareta*—can forget; *vām*—of you two (Yaśodā and Nanda); *maitrīm*—the friendship; *anivṛttām*—unceasing; *vraja-īśvari*—O Queen of Vraja; *avāpya*—obtaining; *api*—even; *aindram*—of Indra; *aiśvaryam*—opulence; *yasyāḥ*—for which; *na*—not; *iha*—in this world; *prati-kriyā*—repayment.

TRANSLATION

[Rohiṇī and Devakī said:] What woman could forget the unceasing friendship you and Nanda have shown us, dear Queen of Vraja? There is no way to repay you in this world, even with the wealth of Indra.

TEXT 38

एतावदृष्टपितरौ युवयोः स्म पित्रोः
सम्प्रीणनाभ्युदयपोषणपालनानि ।
प्राप्योषतुर्भवति पक्ष्म ह यद्वदक्ष्णोर्
न्यस्तावकुत्र च भयौ न सतां परः स्वः ॥३८॥

etav adṛṣṭa-pitarau yuvayoḥ sma pitroḥ
samprīṇanābhyudaya-poṣaṇa-pālanāni
prāpyoṣatur bhavati pakṣma ha yadvad akṣṇor
nyastāv akutra ca bhayau na satāṁ paraḥ svaḥ

etau—these two; *adṛṣṭa*—not having seen; *pitarau*—Their parents; *yuvayoḥ*—of you two; *sma*—indeed; *pitroḥ*—the parents; *samprīṇana*—

coddling; *abhyudaya*—bringing up; *poṣaṇa*—nourishment; *pālanāni*—and protection; *prāpya*—receiving; *ūṣatuḥ*—They resided; *bhavati*—my good lady; *pakṣma*—eyelids; *ha*—indeed; *yadvat*—just as; *akṣṇoḥ*—of the eyes; *nyastau*—place in custody; *akutra*—nowhere; *ca*—and; *bhayau*—whose fear; *na*—not; *satām*—for saintly persons; *paraḥ*—other; *svaḥ*—own.

TRANSLATION

Before these two boys had ever seen Their real parents, you acted as Their parents and gave Them all affectionate care, training, nourishment and protection. They were never afraid, good lady, because you protected Them just as eyelids protect the eyes. Indeed, saintly persons like you never discriminate between outsiders and their own kin.

PURPORT

As Śrīla Viśvanātha Cakravartī explains, Kṛṣṇa and Balarāma had not seen Their parents for two reasons: because of Their exile in Vraja, and also because They are never actually born and therefore have no parents.

Śrīla Viśvanātha Cakravartī also describes what Devakī thought before speaking this verse: "Alas, because for so long these two sons of mine had you, Yaśodā, as Their guardian and mother, and because They were immersed in such a vast ocean of ecstatic loving dealings with you, now that you are once more before Them They are too distracted to even notice me. Also, you are behaving as if insane and blind with love for Them, showing millions of times more maternal affection than I possess. Thus you simply keep staring at us, your friends, without recognizing us. So let me bring you back to reality on the pretext of some affectionate words."

Then, when Devakī failed to get any response from Yaśodā even after addressing her, Rohiṇī said, "My dear Devakī, it's impossible just now to rouse her out of this ecstatic trance. We are crying in the wilderness, and her two sons are no less bound up in the ropes of affection for her than she is for Them. So let us now go outside to meet with Pṛthā, Draupadī and the others."

TEXT 39

श्रीशुक उवाच
गोप्यश्च कृष्णमुपलभ्य चिरादभीष्टं
यत्प्रेक्षणे दृशिषु पक्ष्मकृतं शपन्ति ।
दृग्भिर्हृदीकृतमलं परिरभ्य सर्वास्
तद्भावमापुरपि नित्ययुजां दुरापम् ॥३९॥

śrī-śuka uvāca
gopyaś ca kṛṣṇam upalabhya cirād abhīṣṭaṁ
yat-prekṣaṇe dṛśiṣu pakṣma-kṛtaṁ śapanti
dṛgbhir hṛdī-kṛtam alaṁ parirabhya sarvās
tad-bhāvam āpur api nitya-yujāṁ durāpam

śrī-śukaḥ uvāca—Śukadeva Gosvāmī said; *gopyaḥ*—the young cowherd women; *ca*—and; *kṛṣṇam*—Kṛṣṇa; *upalabhya*—sighting; *cirāt*—after a long time; *abhīṣṭam*—their object of desire; *yat*—whom; *prekṣaṇe*—while seeing; *dṛśiṣu*—on their eyes; *pakṣma*—of lids; *kṛtam*—the maker; *śapanti*—they would curse; *dṛgbhiḥ*—with their eyes; *hṛdī-kṛtam*—taken into their hearts; *alam*—to their satisfaction; *parirabhya*—embracing; *sarvāḥ*—all of them; *tat*—in Him; *bhāvam*—ecstatic absorption; *āpuḥ*—attained; *api*—even though; *nitya*—constantly; *yujām*—for those who engage in yogic discipline; *durāpam*—difficult to attain.

TRANSLATION

Śukadeva Gosvāmī said: While gazing at their beloved Kṛṣṇa, the young *gopīs* used to condemn the creator of their eyelids, [which would momentarily block their vision of Him]. Now, seeing Kṛṣṇa again after such a long separation, with their eyes they took Him into their hearts, and there they embraced Him to their full satisfaction. In this way they became totally absorbed in ecstatic meditation on Him, although those who constantly practice mystic *yoga* find such absorption difficult to achieve.

PURPORT

According to Śrīla Viśvanātha Cakravartī, just then Lord Balarāma saw the *gopīs* standing a short distance away. Seeing them trembling with eagerness to meet Kṛṣṇa, and apparently ready to give up their lives if they could not, He tactfully decided to get up and involve Himself elsewhere. Then the *gopīs* attained the state described in the current verse. In referring to the *gopīs'* intolerant disrespect of Lord Brahmā, "the creator of eyelids," Śukadeva Gosvāmī is giving vent to his own subtle jealousy of the *gopīs'* favored position.

Śrīla Jīva Gosvāmī offers an alternate understanding of the phrase *nitya-yujām*, which may mean "even of the Lord's principal queens, who tend to be proud of their constant association with Him."

In *Kṛṣṇa, the Supreme Personality of Godhead*, Śrīla Prabhupāda writes, "Because they had been separated from Kṛṣṇa for so many years, the *gopīs*, having come along with Nanda Mahārāja and mother Yaśodā, felt intense ecstasy in seeing Kṛṣṇa. No one can even imagine how anxious the *gopīs* were to see Kṛṣṇa again. As soon as Kṛṣṇa became visible to them, they took Him inside their hearts through their eyes and embraced Him to their full satisfaction. Even though they were embracing Kṛṣṇa only mentally, they became so ecstatic and overwhelmed with joy that for the time being they completely forgot themselves. The ecstatic trance which they achieved simply by mentally embracing Kṛṣṇa is impossible to achieve even for great *yogīs* constantly engaged in meditation on the Supreme Personality of Godhead. Kṛṣṇa could understand that the *gopīs* were rapt in ecstasy by embracing Him in their minds, and therefore, since He is present in everyone's heart, He also reciprocated the embracing from within."

TEXT 40

भगवांस्तास्तथाभूता विविक्त उपसंगतः ।
आश्लिष्यानामयं पृष्ट्वा प्रहसन्निदमब्रवीत् ॥४०॥

bhagavāṁs tās tathā-bhūtā
vivikta upasaṅgataḥ
āśliṣyānāmayaṁ pṛṣṭvā
prahasann idam abravīt

bhagavān—the Supreme Lord; *tāḥ*—them; *tathā-bhūtāḥ*—being in such a state; *vivikte*—in a secluded place; *upasaṅgataḥ*—going up to; *āśliṣya*—embracing; *anāmayam*—health; *pṛṣṭvā*—asking about; *prahasan*—laughed; *idam*—this; *abravīt*—said.

TRANSLATION

The Supreme Lord approached the *gopīs* in a secluded place as they stood in their ecstatic trance. After embracing each of them and inquiring about their well-being, He laughed and spoke as follows.

PURPORT

Śrīla Viśvanātha Cakravartī comments that Kṛṣṇa expanded Himself by His *vibhūti-śakti* to embrace each of the *gopīs* individually, thus waking each of them from her trance. He inquired, "Are you now relieved of your pain of separation?" and laughed to help lighten their spirits.

TEXT 41

अपि स्मरथ नः सख्यः स्वानामर्थचिकीर्षया ।
गतांश्चिरायिताञ् छत्रुपक्षक्षपणचेतसः ॥४१॥

api smaratha naḥ sakhyaḥ
svānām artha-cikīrṣayā
gatāṁś cirāyitāñ chatru-
pakṣa-kṣapaṇa-cetasaḥ

api—whether; *smaratha*—you remember; *naḥ*—Us; *sakhyaḥ*—girlfriends; *svānām*—of dear ones; *artha*—the purposes; *cikīrṣayā*—with the desire of executing; *gatān*—gone away; *cirāyitān*—having remained long; *śatru*—of Our enemies; *pakṣa*—the party; *kṣapaṇa*—to destroy; *cetasaḥ*—whose intent.

TRANSLATION

[Lord Kṛṣṇa said:] My dear girlfriends, do you still remember Me? It was for My relatives' sake that I stayed away so long, intent on destroying My enemies.

TEXT 42

अप्यवध्यायथास्मान् स्विदकृतज्ञाविशंकया ।
नूनं भूतानि भगवान् युनक्ति वियुनक्ति च ॥४२॥

apy avadhyāyathāsmān svid
akṛta-jñāviśaṅkayā
nūnaṁ bhūtāni bhagavān
yunakti viyunakti ca

api—also; *avadhyāyatha*—you hold in contempt; *asmān*—Us; *svit*—perhaps; *akṛta-jña*—as being ungrateful; *āviśaṅkayā*—with the suspicion; *nūnam*—indeed; *bhūtāni*—living beings; *bhagavān*—the Supreme Lord; *yunakti*—joins; *viyunakti*—separates; *ca*—and.

TRANSLATION

Do you perhaps think I'm ungrateful and thus hold Me in contempt? After all, it is the Supreme Lord who brings living beings together and then separates them.

PURPORT

Śrīla Viśvanātha Cakravartī reveals the *gopīs'* thoughts: "We are not like You, who, with Your heart shattered by remembering us day and night, gave up all sense enjoyment in Your distress of separation. Rather, we have not remembered You at all; in fact, we have been quite happy without You." In response, Kṛṣṇa here asks whether they resent His ingratitude.

TEXT 43

वायुर्यथा घनानीकं तृणं तूलं रजांसि च ।
संयोज्याक्षिपते भूयस्तथा भूतानि भूतकृत् ॥४३॥

vāyur yathā ghanānīkaṁ
tṛṇaṁ tūlaṁ rajāṁsi ca
saṁyojyākṣipate bhūyas
tathā bhūtāni bhūta-kṛt

vāyuḥ—the wind; *yathā*—as; *ghana*—of clouds; *anīkam*—groups; *tṛṇam*—grass; *tūlam*—cotton; *rajāṁsi*—dust; *ca*—and; *saṁyojya*—bringing together; *ākṣipate*—throws apart; *bhūyaḥ*—once again; *tathā*—so; *bhūtāni*—living beings; *bhūta*—of living beings; *kṛt*—the creator.

TRANSLATION

Just as the wind brings together masses of clouds, blades of grass, wisps of cotton and particles of dust, only to scatter them all again, so the creator deals with His created beings in the same way.

TEXT 44

मयि भक्तिर्हि भूतानाममृतत्वाय कल्पते ।
दिष्टया यदासीन्मत्स्नेहो भवतीनां मदापनः ॥४४॥

mayi bhaktir hi bhūtānām
amṛtatvāya kalpate
diṣṭyā yad āsīn mat-sneho
bhavatīnāṁ mad-āpanaḥ

mayi—to Me; *bhaktiḥ*—devotional service; *hi*—indeed; *bhūtānām*—for living beings; *amṛtatvāya*—to immortality; *kalpate*—leads; *diṣṭyā*—by good fortune; *yat*—which; *āsīt*—has developed; *mat*—for Me; *snehaḥ*—the love; *bhavatīnām*—on the part of your good selves; *mat*—Me; *āpanaḥ*—which is the cause of obtaining.

TRANSLATION

Rendering devotional service to Me qualifies any living being for eternal life. But by your good fortune you have developed a special loving attitude toward Me, by which you have obtained Me.

PURPORT

According to Śrīla Viśvanātha Cakravartī, the *gopīs* then replied, "But that Supreme Lord You are blaming is none other than Yourself, O most clever of speakers. Everyone in the world knows this! Why should we be ignorant of this fact?" "All right," Lord Kṛṣṇa then told them, "if this is true, I must be God, but still I am conquered by your loving affection."

TEXT 45

अहं हि सर्वभूतानामादिरन्तोऽन्तरं बहिः ।
भौतिकानां यथा खं वार्भूर्वायुर्ज्योतिरंगनाः ॥४५॥

ahaṁ hi sarva-bhūtānām
ādir anto 'ntaraṁ bahiḥ
bhautikānāṁ yathā khaṁ vār
bhūr vāyur jyotir aṅganāḥ

aham—I; *hi*—indeed; *sarva*—all; *bhūtānām*—of created beings; *ādiḥ*—the beginning; *antaḥ*—the end; *antaram*—inside; *bahiḥ*—outside; *bhautikānām*—of material things; *yathā*—as; *kham*—ether; *vāḥ*—water; *bhūḥ*—earth; *vāyuḥ*—air; *jyotiḥ*—and fire; *aṅganāḥ*—O ladies.

TRANSLATION

Dear ladies, I am the beginning and end of all created beings and exist both within and without them, just as the elements ether, water, earth, air and fire are the beginning and end of all material objects and exist both within and without them.

PURPORT

According to Śrīla Śrīdhara Svāmī and Śrīla Viśvanātha Cakravartī, Lord Kṛṣṇa implies the following idea in this verse: "If you know that I am the Supreme Lord, there should be no question of your suffering any separation from Me, since I pervade all existence. Your unhappiness must be due to a lack of discrimination. Therefore please take this instruction from Me, which will remove your ignorance.

"But the truth of the matter is that you *gopīs* were in your previous lives great masters of *yoga,* and thus you must already know this science of *jñāna-yoga*. Furthermore, whether I try to teach this to you in person or through My representative, such as Uddhava, it will not produce the desired result. *Jñāna-yoga* simply causes suffering for those who are fully immersed in pure love of Godhead."

TEXT 46

एवं ह्येतानि भूतानि भूतेष्वात्मात्मना ततः ।
उभयं मय्यथ परे पश्यताभातमक्षरे ॥४६॥

evaṁ hy etāni bhūtāni
bhūteṣv ātmātmanā tataḥ
ubhayaṁ mayy atha pare
paśyatābhātam akṣare

evam—in this manner; *hi*—indeed; *etāni*—these; *bhūtāni*—material entities; *bhūteṣu*—within the elements of creation; *ātmā*—the self; *ātmanā*—in its own true identity; *tataḥ*—pervasive; *ubhayam*—both; *mayi*—within Me; *atha*—that is to say; *pare*—within the Supreme Truth; *paśyata*—you should see; *ābhātam*—manifested; *akṣare*—within the imperishable.

TRANSLATION

In this way all created things reside within the basic elements of creation, while the spirit souls pervade the creation, remaining in their own true identity. You should see both of these—the material creation and the self—as manifest within Me, the imperishable Supreme Truth.

PURPORT

One should properly understand the relationships among the material objects of this world, the elements comprising their basic substance, the individual spirit souls and the one Supreme Soul. The various objects of material enjoyment, such as pots, rivers and mountains, are manufactured from the basic material elements—earth, water, fire and so on. These elements pervade material things as their cause, while the spirit souls pervade them in their special role as their enjoyer (*svātmanā*). And ultimately, the material elements, their products and the living entities are all manifested within and pervaded by the imperishable, perfectly complete Supreme Soul, Kṛṣṇa.

A *jñānī* with realization of these facts should feel no separation from the Lord in any situation, but the *gopīs* of Vraja are much more elevated in their Kṛṣṇa consciousness than ordinary *jñānīs*. Because of their intense love for Kṛṣṇa in His most humanlike, all-attractive aspect as a young cowherd boy, Kṛṣṇa's internal potency, Yogamāyā, covered their knowledge of His majestic aspects, such as His all-pervasiveness. Thus the *gopīs* were able to relish the intense ecstasy caused by their love in separation from Him. Only in jest is Śrī Kṛṣṇa ascribing to them a lack of spiritual discrimination.

TEXT 47

श्रीशुक उवाच
अध्यात्मशिक्षया गोप्य एवं कृष्णेन शिक्षिताः ।
तदनुस्मरणध्वस्तजीवकोशास्तमध्यगन् ॥४७॥

śrī-śuka uvāca
adhyātma-śikṣayā gopya
evaṁ kṛṣṇena śikṣitāḥ
tad-anusmaraṇa-dhvasta-
jīva-kośās tam adhyagan

śrī-śukaḥ uvāca—Śukadeva Gosvāmī said; *adhyātma*—about the soul; *śikṣayā*—with instruction; *gopyaḥ*—the *gopīs; evam*—thus; *kṛṣṇena*—by Kṛṣṇa; *śikṣitāḥ*—taught; *tat*—on Him; *anusmaraṇa*—by constant meditation; *dhvasta*—eradicated; *jīva-kośāḥ*—the subtle covering of the soul (false ego); *tam*—Him; *adhyagan*—they came to understand.

TRANSLATION

Śukadeva Gosvāmī said: Having thus been instructed by Kṛṣṇa in spiritual matters, the *gopīs* were freed of all tinges of false ego because of their incessant meditation upon Him. And with their deepening absorption in Him, they came to understand Him fully.

PURPORT

Śrila Prabhupāda renders this passage as follows in *Kṛṣṇa:* "The *gopīs*, having been instructed by Kṛṣṇa in this philosophy of simultaneous oneness and difference, remained always in Kṛṣṇa consciousness and thus became liberated from all material contamination. The consciousness of the living entity who falsely presents himself as the enjoyer of the material world is called *jīva-kośa,* which means imprisonment by the false ego. Not only the *gopīs* but anyone who follows these instructions of Kṛṣṇa becomes immediately freed from the *jīva-kośa* imprisonment. A person in full Kṛṣṇa consciousness is always liberated from false egoism; he utilizes everything for Kṛṣṇa's service and is not at any time separated from Kṛṣṇa."

TEXT 48

आहुश्च ते नलिननाभ पदारविन्दं
योगेश्वरैर्हृदि विचिन्त्यमगाधबोधैः ।
संसारकूपपतितोत्तरणावलम्बं
गेहं जुषामपि मनस्युदियात्सदा नः ॥४८॥

āhuś ca te nalina-nābha padāravindaṁ
yogeśvarair hṛdi vicintyam agādha-bodhaiḥ
saṁsāra-kūpa-patitottaraṇāvalambaṁ
gehaṁ juṣām api manasy udiyāt sadā naḥ

āhuḥ—the *gopīs* said; *ca*—and; *te*—Your; *nalina-nābha*—O Lord, whose navel is just like a lotus flower; *pada-aravindam*—lotus feet; *yoga-īśvaraiḥ*—by the great mystic *yogīs; hṛdi*—within the heart; *vicintyam*—to be meditated upon; *agādha-bodhaiḥ*—who were highly learned philosophers; *saṁsāra-kūpa*—the dark well of material existence; *patita*—of those fallen; *uttaraṇa*—of deliverers; *avalambam*—the only shelter; *geham*—family affairs; *juṣām*—of those engaged; *api*—though; *manasi*—in the minds; *udiyāt*—let be awakened; *sadā*—always; *naḥ*—our.

TRANSLATION

The *gopīs* spoke thus: Dear Lord, whose navel is just like a lotus flower, Your lotus feet are the only shelter for those who have fallen into the deep well of material existence. Your feet are worshiped and meditated upon by great mystic *yogīs* and highly learned philosophers. We wish that these lotus feet may also be awakened within our hearts, although we are only ordinary persons engaged in household affairs.

PURPORT

The translation and word meanings for this verse are taken from Śrīla Prabhupāda's English rendering of *Śrī Caitanya-caritāmṛta* (*Madhya* 1.81), where this verse is quoted.

Revealing the jealous mood in which the *gopīs* spoke these deceptively reverential words, Śrīla Viśvanātha Cakravartī gives their statements as follows: "O Supreme Lord, O directly manifest Supersoul, O crest jewel of instructors in definitive knowledge, You were aware of our excessive attachment to home, property and family. Therefore You previously had Uddhava instruct us in the knowledge that dispels ignorance, and now You have done so Yourself. In this way You have purified our hearts of contamination, and as a result we understand Your pure love for us, free from any motivation other than assuring our liberation. But we are only unintelligent cowherd women; how can this knowledge remain fixed in our hearts? We cannot even meditate steadily on Your feet, the focus of realization for great souls like Lord Brahmā. Please be merciful to us and somehow make it possible for us to concentrate on You, even a little. We are still suffering the reactions of our own fruitive work, so how can we meditate on You, the goal of great *yogīs*? Such *yogīs* are immeasurably wise, but we are mere feeble-minded women. Please do something to get us out of this deep well of material life."

Pure devotees are never motivated by a desire for material elevation or spiritual liberation. And even if the Lord offers them such benedictions, the devotees often refuse to accept them. As stated by Lord Kṛṣṇa in the Eleventh Canto of *Śrīmad-Bhāgavatam* (11.20.34),

na kiñcit sādhavo dhīrā
bhaktā hy ekāntino mama
vāñchanty api mayā dattaṁ
kaivalyam apunar-bhavam

"Because My devotees possess saintly behavior and deep intelligence, they completely dedicate themselves to Me and do not desire anything besides Me. Indeed, even if I offer them liberation from birth and death, they do not accept it." It is quite appropriate, therefore, that the *gopīs* respond with a trace of jealous anger to Lord Kṛṣṇa's attempt at teaching them *jñāna-yoga*.

Thus, according to Śrīla Viśvanātha Cakravartī Ṭhākura, the words the *gopīs* speak in this verse may be interpreted as follows: "O sun who directly destroys the darkness of ignorance, we are scorched by the sun-rays of this philosophical knowledge. We are *cakora* birds who can subsist only on the moonlight radiating from Your beautiful face. Please come back to Vṛndāvana with us, and in this way bring us back to life."

And if He says, "Then come to Dvārakā; there we will enjoy together," they reply that Śrī Vṛndāvana is their home, and they are too attached to it for them to take up residence anywhere else. Only there, the *gopīs* imply, can Kṛṣṇa attract them by wearing peacock feathers in His turban and playing enchanting music with His flute. Only by His appearing again in Vṛndāvana can the *gopīs* be saved, not by any other kind of meditation on Him or theoretical knowledge of the self.

Thus end the purports of the humble servants of His Divine Grace A. C. Bhaktivedanta Swami Prabhupāda to the Tenth Canto, Eighty-second Chapter, of the Śrīmad-Bhāgavatam, *entitled "Kṛṣṇa and Balarāma Meet the Inhabitants of Vṛndāvana."*

CHAPTER EIGHTY-THREE

Draupadī Meets the Queens of Kṛṣṇa

This chapter relates a conversation between Draupadī and Lord Kṛṣṇa's foremost queens, in which each of them describes how the Lord married her.

Lord Śrī Kṛṣṇa returned from His meeting with the *gopīs* and asked King Yudhiṣṭhira and His other relatives whether they were well. They replied, "My Lord, anyone who has just once imbibed through his ears the honey of Your pastimes can never know misfortune."

Then Draupadī inquired from Lord Kṛṣṇa's wives how the Lord had come to marry them. Queen Rukmiṇī spoke first: "Many kings, headed by Jarāsandha, were intent on giving me in marriage to Śiśupāla. Thus at my wedding they all stood with bows in hand, ready to support Śiśupāla against any opponents. But Śrī Kṛṣṇa came and forcibly took me away, as a lion takes his prey from amidst goats and sheep."

Queen Satyabhāmā said, "When my uncle Prasena was killed, my father, Satrājit, falsely accused Lord Kṛṣṇa of murder. To clear His name, Kṛṣṇa defeated Jāmbavān, recovered the Syamantaka jewel and returned it to Satrājit. Repentant, my father presented the Lord with both the jewel and myself."

Queen Jāmbavatī said, "When Śrī Kṛṣṇa entered my father's cave in search of the Syamantaka jewel, at first my father, Jāmbavān, did not uderstand who He was. So my father fought with Him for twenty-seven days and nights. Finally, Jāmbavān understood that Kṛṣṇa was none other than Lord Rāmacandra, his worshipable Lord. Thus he gave Kṛṣṇa the Syamantaka jewel, along with me."

Queen Kālindī said, "To obtain Kṛṣṇa as my husband, I performed severe austerities. Then one day Lord Kṛṣṇa came to me in the company of Arjuna, and at that time the Lord agreed to marry me."

Queen Mitravindā said, "Śrī Kṛṣṇa came to my *svayaṁ-vara* ceremony, where He defeated all the opposing kings and took me away to His city of Dvārakā."

Queen Satyā said, "My father stipulated that to win my hand, a prospective suitor would have to subdue and tie up seven powerful bulls. Accepting this challenge, Lord Kṛṣṇa playfully subdued them, defeated all His rival suitors and married me."

Queen Bhadrā said, "My father invited his nephew Kṛṣṇa, to whom I had already given my heart, and offered me to Him as His bride. The dowry was an entire military division and a retinue of my female companions."

Queen Lakṣmaṇā said to Draupadī, "At my *svayaṁ-vara,* as at yours, a fish-target was fastened near the ceiling. But in my case the fish was concealed on all sides, and only its relfection could be seen in a pot of water below. Several kings tried to hit the fish with an arrow but failed. Arjuna then made his attempt. He concentrated on the reflection of the fish in the water and took careful aim, but when he released his arrow it only grazed the target. Then Śrī Kṛṣṇa fixed His arrow on the bow and shot it straight through the target, knocking it to the ground. I placed the victory necklaçe on Śrī Kṛṣṇa's neck, but the kings who had failed raised a violent protest. Lord Kṛṣṇa valiantly fought them, cutting off the heads, arms and legs of many and sending the rest fleeing for their lives. Then the Lord took me to Dvārakā for our lavish wedding."

Rohiṇī-devī, representing all the other queens, explained that they were daughters of the kings defeated by Bhaumāsura. The demon had held them captive, but when Lord Kṛṣṇa killed him He had released them and married them all.

TEXT 1

श्रीशुक उवाच
तथानुगृह्य भगवान् गोपीनां स गुरुर्गतिः ।
युधिष्ठिरमथापृच्छत्सर्वांश्च सुहृदोऽव्ययम् ॥१॥

śrī-śuka uvāca
tathānugṛhya bhagavān
gopīnāṁ sa gurur gatiḥ
yudhiṣṭhiram athāpṛcchat
sarvāṁś ca suhṛdo 'vyayam

śrī-śukaḥ uvāca—Śukadeva Gosvāmī said; *tathā*—in this way; *anugṛhya*—showing favor; *bhagavān*—the Supreme Lord; *gopīnām*—of the young cowherd women; *saḥ*—He; *guruḥ*—their spiritual master;

gatiḥ—and goal; *yudhiṣṭhiram*—from Yudhiṣṭhira; *atha*—then; *apṛcchat*—He inquired; *sarvān*—all; *ca*—and; *su-hṛdaḥ*—His well-wishing relatives; *avyayam*—welfare.

TRANSLATION

Śukadeva Gosvāmī said: Thus Lord Kṛṣṇa, the spiritual master of the *gopīs* and the very purpose of their life, showed them His mercy. He then met with Yudhiṣṭhira and all His other relatives and inquired from them about their welfare.

PURPORT

The words *gurur gatiḥ* have been translated here in their usual sense: "spiritual master and goal." Śrīla Viśvanātha Cakravartī, however, points out an additional meaning: While Lord Kṛṣṇa is the goal for all *sādhus* in general, for the *gopīs* specifically He is that goal which is *guru*, "predominant," in the sense of completely eclipsing the significance of all other possible goals.

TEXT 2

त एवं लोकनाथेन परिपृष्टाः सुसत्कृताः ।
प्रत्यूचुर्हृष्टमनसस्तत्पादेक्षाहतांहसः ॥२॥

ta evaṁ loka-nāthena
paripṛṣṭāḥ su-sat-kṛtāḥ
pratyūcur hṛṣṭa-manasas
tat-pādekṣā-hatāṁhasaḥ

te—they (Yudhiṣṭhira and Lord Kṛṣṇa's other relatives); *evam*—thus; *loka*—of the universe; *nāthena*—by the Lord; *paripṛṣṭāḥ*—questioned; *su*—very much; *sat-kṛtāḥ*—honored; *pratyūcuḥ*—replied; *hṛṣṭa*—joyful; *manasaḥ*—whose minds; *tat*—His; *pāda*—the feet; *īkṣā*—by seeing; *hata*—destroyed; *aṁhasaḥ*—whose sins.

TRANSLATION

Feeling greatly honored, King Yudhiṣṭhira and the others, freed of all sinful reactions by seeing the feet of the Lord of the universe, gladly answered His inquiries.

TEXT 3

कुतोऽशिवं त्वच्चरणाम्बुजासवं
महन्मनस्तो मुखनिःसृतं क्वचित् ।
पिबन्ति ये कर्णपुटैरलं प्रभो
देहंभृतां देहकृदस्मृतिच्छिदम् ॥३॥

kuto 'śivaṁ tvac-caraṇāmbujāsavaṁ
mahan-manasto mukha-niḥsṛtaṁ kvacit
pibanti ye karṇa-puṭair alaṁ prabho
dehaṁ-bhṛtāṁ deha-kṛd-asmṛti-cchidam

kutaḥ—from where; *aśivam*—inauspiciousness; *tvat*—Your; *caraṇa*—of the feet; *ambuja*—lotuslike; *āsavam*—the intoxicating nectar; *mahat*—of great souls; *manastaḥ*—from the minds; *mukha*—through their mouths; *niḥsṛtam*—poured out; *kvacit*—at any time; *pibanti*—drink; *ye*—who; *karṇa*—of their ears; *puṭaiḥ*—with the drinking cups; *alam*—as much as they wish; *prabho*—O master; *deham*—material bodies; *bhṛtām*—for those who possess; *deha*—of bodies; *kṛt*—about the creator; *asmṛti*—of forgetfulness; *chidam*—the eradicator.

TRANSLATION

[Lord Kṛṣṇa's relatives said:] O master, how can misfortune arise for those who have even once freely drunk the nectar coming from Your lotus feet? This intoxicating liquor pours into the drinking cups of their ears, having flowed from the minds of great devotees through their mouths. It destroys the embodied souls' forgetfulness of the creator of their bodily existence.

TEXT 4

हि त्वात्मधामविधुतात्मकृतत्र्यवस्थाम्
आनन्दसम्प्लवमखण्डमकुण्ठबोधम् ।
कालोपसृष्टनिगमावन आत्तयोग-
मायाकृतिं परमहंसगतिं नताः स्म ॥४॥

hi tvātma-dhāma-vidhutātma-kṛta-try-avasthām
ānanda-samplavam akhaṇḍam akuṇṭha-bodham
kālopasṛṣṭa-nigamāvana ātta-yoga-
māyākṛtiṁ paramahaṁsa-gatiṁ natāḥ sma

hi—indeed; *tvā*—to You; *ātma*—of Your personal form; *dhāma*—by the illumination; *vidhuta*—dispelled; *ātma*—by material consciousness; *kṛta*—created; *tri*—three; *avasthām*—the material conditions; *ānanda*—in ecstasy; *samplavam*—(within whom is) the total immersion; *akhaṇḍam*—unlimited; *akuṇṭha*—unrestricted; *bodham*—whose knowledge; *kāla*—by time; *upasṛṣṭa*—endangered; *nigama*—of the *Vedas; avane*—for the protection; *ātta*—having assumed; *yoga-māyā*—by Your divine power of illusion; *ākṛtim*—this form; *parama-haṁsa*—of perfect saints; *gatim*—the goal; *natāḥ sma*—(we) have bowed down.

TRANSLATION

The radiance of Your personal form dispels the threefold effects of material consciousness, and by Your grace we become immersed in total happiness. Your knowledge is indivisible and unrestricted. By Your Yogamāyā potency You have assumed this human form for protecting the *Vedas,* which had been threatened by time. We bow down to You, the final destination of perfect saints.

PURPORT

Simply by the effulgent light emanating from the beautiful form of Lord Kṛṣṇa, one's intelligence is purified of all material contamination, and thus the soul's various entanglements in the modes of goodness, passion and ignorance are dispelled. "How then," the Lord's relatives imply, "can we ever suffer misfortune? We are always immersed in absolute happiness." This is their answer to His inquiry about their welfare.

TEXT 5

श्रीऋषिरुवाच
इत्युत्तमःश्लोकशिखामणिं जनेष्व्
अभिष्टुवत्स्वन्धककौरवस्त्रियः ।

समेत्य गोविन्दकथा मिथोऽगृणंस्
त्रिलोकगीताः शृणु वर्णयामि ते ॥५॥

śrī-ṛṣir uvāca
ity uttamaḥ-śloka-śikhā-maṇiṁ janeṣv
abhiṣṭuvatsv andhaka-kaurava-striyaḥ
sametya govinda-kathā mitho 'gṛṇaṁs
tri-loka-gītāḥ śṛṇu varṇayāmi te

śrī-ṛṣiḥ uvāca—the great sage, Śukadeva, said; *iti*—thus; *uttamaḥ-śloka*—of great personalities who are glorified in choice poetry; *śikhā-maṇim*—the crest jewel (Lord Kṛṣṇa); *janeṣu*—His devotees; *abhiṣṭuvatsu*—while they were glorifying; *andhaka-kaurava*—of the Andhaka and Kaurava clans; *striyaḥ*—the women; *sametya*—meeting; *govinda-kathāḥ*—topics of Lord Govinda; *mithaḥ*—among one another; *agṛṇan*—spoke; *tri*—three; *loka*—in the worlds; *gītāḥ*—sung; *śṛṇu*—please hear; *varṇayāmi*—I will describe; *te*—to you (Parīkṣit Mahārāja).

TRANSLATION

The great sage Śukadeva Gosvāmī said: As Yudhiṣṭhira and the others were thus praising Lord Kṛṣṇa, the crest jewel of all sublimely glorified personalities, the women of the Andhaka and Kaurava clans met with one another and began discussing topics about Govinda that are sung throughout the three worlds. Please listen as I relate these to you.

TEXTS 6–7

श्रीद्रौपद्युवाच
हे वैदर्भ्यच्युतो भद्रे हे जाम्बवति कौशले ।
हे सत्यभामे कालिन्दि शैब्ये रोहिणि लक्ष्मणे ॥६॥
हे कृष्णपत्न्य एतन्नो ब्रूते वो भगवान् स्वयम् ।
उपयेमे यथा लोकमनुकुर्वन् स्वमायया ॥७॥

śrī-draupady uvāca
he vaidarbhy acyuto bhadre
he jāmbavati kauśale

he satyabhāme kālindi
śaibye rohiṇi lakṣmaṇe

he kṛṣṇa-patnya etan no
brūte vo bhagavān svayam
upayeme yathā lokam
anukurvan sva-māyayā

śrī-draupadī uvāca—Śrī Draupadī said; *he vaidarbhi*—O daughter of Vaidarbha (Rukmiṇī); *acyutaḥ*—Lord Kṛṣṇa; *bhadre*—O Bhadrā; *he jāmbavati*—O daughter of Jāmbavān; *kauśale*—O Nāgnajitī; *he satyabhāme*—O Satyabhāmā; *kālindi*—O Kālindī; *śaibye*—O Mitravindā; *rohiṇi*—O Rohiṇī (one of the sixteen thousand queens married after the killing of Narakāsura); *lakṣmaṇe*—O Lakṣmaṇā; *he kṛṣṇa-patnyaḥ*—O (other) wives of Kṛṣṇa; *etat*—this; *naḥ*—to us; *brūte*—please speak; *vaḥ*—you; *bhagavān*—the Supreme Lord; *svayam*—Himself; *upayeme*—married; *yathā*—how; *lokam*—ordinary society; *anukurvan*—imitating; *sva-māyayā*—by His own mystic power.

TRANSLATION

Śrī Draupadī said: O Vaidarbhī, Bhadrā and Jāmbavatī, O Kauśalā, Satyabhāmā and Kālindī, O Śaibyā, Rohiṇī, Lakṣmaṇā and other wives of Lord Kṛṣṇa, please tell me how the Supreme Lord Acyuta, imitating the ways of this world by His mystic power, came to marry each of you.

PURPORT

The Rohiṇī addressed here by Draupadī is not Lord Balarāma's mother but another Rohiṇī, the foremost of the sixteen thousand princesses Lord Kṛṣṇa rescued from the prison of Bhaumāsura. Draupadī turns to her as the representative of all sixteen thousand, and as a virtual equal to Śrī Kṛṣṇa's eight chief queens.

TEXT 8

श्रीरुक्मिण्युवाच
चैद्याय मार्पयितुमुद्यतकार्मुकेषु
राजस्वजेयभटशेखरिताङ्घ्रिरेणुः ।

निन्ये मृगेन्द्र इव भागमजावियूथात्
तच्छ्रीनिकेतचरणोऽस्तु ममार्चनाय ॥८॥

śrī-rukmiṇy uvāca
caidyāya mārpayitum udyata-kārmukeṣu
rājasv ajeya-bhaṭa-śekharitāṅghri-reṇuḥ
ninye mṛgendra iva bhāgam ajāvi-yūthāt
tac-chrī-niketa-caraṇo 'stu mamārcanāya

śrī-rukmiṇī uvāca—Śrī Rukmiṇī said; *caidyāya*—to Śiśupāla; *mā*—me; *arpayitum*—in order to offer; *udyata*—holding at the ready; *kārmukeṣu*—whose bows; *rājasu*—when the kings; *ajeya*—invincible; *bhaṭa*—of soldiers; *śekharita*—placed upon the heads; *aṅghri*—of whose feet; *reṇuḥ*—the dust; *ninye*—He took away; *mṛgendraḥ*—a lion; *iva*—as if; *bhāgam*—his share; *aja*—of goats; *avi*—and sheep; *yūthāt*—from a group; *tat*—of Him; *śrī*—of the supreme goddess of fortune; *niketa*—who is the abode; *caraṇaḥ*—the feet; *astu*—may be; *mama*—my; *arcanāya*—for the worship.

TRANSLATION

Śrī Rukmiṇī said: When all the kings held their bows at the ready to assure that I would be presented to Śiśupāla, He who puts the dust of His feet on the heads of invincible warriors took me from their midst, as a lion forcibly takes his prey from the midst of goats and sheep. May I always be allowed to worship those feet of Lord Kṛṣṇa, the abode of Goddess Śrī.

PURPORT

Lord Kṛṣṇa's pastime of kidnapping Rukmiṇī is narrated in detail in chapters 52 through 54 of the *Śrīmad-Bhāgavatam's* Tenth Canto.

TEXT 9

श्रीसत्यभामोवाच
यो मे सनाभिवधतप्तहृदा ततेन
लिप्ताभिशापमपमार्ष्टुमुपाजहार ।

जित्वर्क्षराजमथ रत्नमदात्स तेन
भीतः पितादिशत मां प्रभवेऽपि दत्ताम् ॥९॥

śrī-satyabhāmovāca
yo me sanābhi-vadha-tapta-hṛdā tatena
liptābhiśāpam apamārṣṭum upājahāra
jitvarkṣa-rājam atha ratnam adāt sa tena
bhītaḥ pitādiśata māṁ prabhave 'pi dattām

śrī-satyabhāmā uvāca—Śrī Satyabhāmā said; *yaḥ*—who; *me*—my; *sanābhi*—of my brother; *vadha*—by the killing; *tapta*—distressed; *hṛdā*—whose heart; *tatena*—by my father; *lipta*—tainted; *abhiśāpam*—with condemnation; *apamārṣṭum*—to cleanse away; *upājahāra*—He removed; *jitvā*—after defeating; *ṛkṣa-rājam*—the king of the bears, Jāmbavān; *atha*—then; *ratnam*—the jewel (Syamantaka); *adāt*—gave; *saḥ*—He; *tena*—because of this; *bhītaḥ*—afraid; *pitā*—my father; *adiśata*—offered; *mām*—me; *prabhave*—to the Lord; *api*—although; *dattām*—already given.

TRANSLATION

Śrī Satyabhāmā said: My father, his heart tormented by my brother's murder, blamed Lord Kṛṣṇa for the crime. To remove the stain on His reputation, the Lord defeated the king of the bears and took back the Syamantaka jewel, which He then returned to my father. Fearing the consequences of his offense, my father offered me to the Lord, even though I had already been promised to others.

PURPORT

As described in Chapter 56 of this canto, King Satrājit had already compromised himself by promising his daughter's hand first to Akrūra and then again to a number of other suitors. But after the return of the Syamantaka jewel, he felt impelled by his shame to offer her to Lord Kṛṣṇa instead. According to Śrīla Śrīdhara Svāmī, the word *prabhave* ("unto the Lord") answers any doubt as to the propriety of offering Kṛṣṇa a bride who had already been promised to others. It is perfectly proper to offer Him everything one owns, and improper to withhold anything from Him.

TEXT 10

श्रीजाम्बवत्युवाच
प्राज्ञाय देहकृदमुं निजनाथदैवं
सीतापतिं त्रिनवहान्यमुनाभ्ययुध्यत् ।
ज्ञात्वा परीक्षित उपाहरदर्हणं मां
पादौ प्रगृह्य मणिनाहममुष्य दासी ॥१०॥

śrī-jāmbavaty uvāca
prājñāya deha-kṛd amuṁ nija-nātha-daivaṁ
sītā-patiṁ tri-navahāny amunābhyayudhyat
jñātvā parīkṣita upāharad arhaṇaṁ māṁ
pādau pragṛhya maṇināham amuṣya dāsī

śrī-jāmbavatī uvāca—Śrī Jāmbavatī said; *prājñāya*—unaware; *deha*—of my body; *kṛt*—the maker (my father); *amum*—of Him; *nija*—his own; *nātha*—as the master; *daivam*—and worshipable Deity; *sītā*—of Goddess Sītā; *patim*—the husband; *tri*—three; *nava*—times nine; *ahāni*—for days; *amunā*—with Him; *abhyayudhyat*—he fought; *jñātvā*—recognizing; *parīkṣitaḥ*—awakened to proper understanding; *upāharat*—he presented; *arhaṇam*—as a respectful offering; *mām*—me; *pādau*—His feet; *pragṛhya*—taking hold of; *maṇinā*—with the jewel; *aham*—I; *amuṣya*—His; *dāsī*—maidservant.

TRANSLATION

Śrī Jāmbavatī said: Unaware that Lord Kṛṣṇa was none other than his own master and worshipable Deity, the husband of Goddess Sītā, my father fought with Him for twenty-seven days. When my father finally came to his senses and recognized the Lord, he took hold of His feet and presented Him with both me and the Syamantaka jewel as tokens of his reverence. I am simply the Lord's maidservant.

PURPORT

Jāmbavān had been Lord Rāmacandra's servant many thousands of years before. Śrīla Viśvanātha Cakravartī mentions that while hearing Jāmbavatī's story, the women present recognized her as the girl whom

Jāmbavān had once offered to Lord Śrī Rāma to be His wife. Since Lord Rāma had taken a vow to have only one wife, He could not accept her then, but did so when He returned in the Dvāpara-yuga as Kṛṣṇa. The other queens wanted to honor Jāmbavatī for this, but she replied humbly, "I am just the Lord's maidservant."

How Jāmbavatī and Satyabhāmā became Lord Kṛṣṇa's wives is told in Chapter 56 of the Tenth Canto.

TEXT 11

श्रीकालिन्द्युवाच
तपश्चरन्तीमाज्ञाय स्वपादस्पर्शनाशया ।
सख्योपेत्याग्रहीत्पाणिं योऽहं तद्गृहमार्जनी ॥११॥

śrī-kālindy uvāca
tapaś carantīm ājñāya
sva-pāda-sparśanāśayā
sakhyopetyāgrahīt pāṇiṁ
yo 'haṁ tad-gṛha-mārjanī

śrī-kālindī uvāca—Śrī Kālindī said; *tapaḥ*—penances; *carantīm*—executing; *ājñāya*—knowing; *sva*—His; *pāda*—of the feet; *sparśana*—for the touch; *āśayā*—with the desire; *sakhyā*—together with His friend (Arjuna); *upetya*—coming; *agrahīt*—took; *pāṇim*—my hand; *yaḥ*—who; *aham*—I; *tat*—His; *gṛha*—of the residence; *mārjanī*—the cleaner.

TRANSLATION

Śrī Kālindī said: The Lord knew I was performing severe austerities and penances with the hope of one day touching His lotus feet. So He came to me in the company of His friend and took my hand in marriage. Now I am engaged as a sweeper in His palace.

TEXT 12

श्रीमित्रविन्दोवाच
यो मां स्वयंवर उपेत्य विजित्य भूपान्
निन्ये श्वयूथगमिवात्मबलिं द्विपारिः ।

भ्रातॄंश्च मेऽपकुरुतः स्वपुरं श्रियौकस्
तस्यास्तु मेऽनुभवमंघ्र्यवनेजनत्वम् ॥१२॥

śrī-mitravindovāca
yo māṁ svayaṁ-vara upetya vijitya bhū-pān
ninye śva-yūtha-gam ivātma-baliṁ dvipāriḥ
bhrātṝṁś ca me 'pakurutaḥ sva-puraṁ śriyaukas
tasyāstu me 'nu-bhavam aṅghry-avanejanatvam

śrī-mitravindā uvāca—Śrī Mitravindā said; *yaḥ*—who; *mām*—me; *svayaṁ-vare*—during my *svayaṁ-vara* (the ceremony in which a princess chooses a husband from a number of eligible suitors); *upetya*—coming forward; *vijitya*—after defeating; *bhū-pān*—kings; *ninye*—took; *śva*—of dogs; *yūtha*—into a group; *gam*—gone; *iva*—as if; *ātma*—own; *balim*—share; *dvipa-ariḥ*—a lion ("enemy of elephants"); *bhrātṝn*—brothers; *ca*—and; *me*—my; *apakurutaḥ*—who were insulting Him; *sva*—to His; *puram*—capital city; *śrī*—of the goddess of fortune; *okaḥ*—the residence; *tasya*—His; *astu*—may be; *me*—for me; *anu-bhavam*—life after life; *aṅghri*—the feet; *avanejanatvam*—the status of washing.

TRANSLATION

Śrī Mitravindā said: At my *svayaṁ-vara* ceremony He came forward, defeated all the kings present—including my brothers, who dared insult Him—and took me away just as a lion removes his prey from amidst a pack of dogs. Thus Lord Kṛṣṇa, the shelter of the goddess of fortune, brought me to His capital city. May I be allowed to serve Him by washing His feet, life after life.

TEXTS 13–14

श्रीसत्योवाच
सप्तोक्षणोऽतिबलवीर्यसुतीक्ष्णशृंगान्
पित्रा कृतान् क्षितिपवीर्यपरीक्षणाय ।
तान् वीरदुर्मदहनस्तरसा निगृह्य
क्रीडन् बबन्ध ह यथा शिशवोऽजतोकान् ॥१३॥

य इत्थं वीर्यशुल्कां मां दासीभिश्चतुरर्गिणीम् ।
पथि निर्जित्य राजन्यान्निन्ये तद्दास्यमस्तु मे ॥१४॥

śrī-satyovāca
saptokṣaṇo 'ti-bala-vīrya-su-tīkṣṇa-śṛṅgān
pitrā kṛtān kṣitipa-vīrya-parīkṣaṇāya
tān vīra-durmada-hanas tarasā nigṛhya
krīḍan babandha ha yathā śiśavo 'ja-tokān

ya ittham vīrya-śulkām mām
dāsībhiś catur-aṅgiṇīm
pathi nirjitya rājanyān
ninye tad-dāsyam astu me

śrī-satyā uvāca—Śrī Satyā said; sapta—seven; ukṣaṇaḥ—bulls; ati—great; bala—whose strength; vīrya—and vitality; su—very; tīkṣṇa—sharp; śṛṅgān—whose horns; pitrā—by my father; kṛtān—made; kṣitipa—of the kings; vīrya—the prowess; parīkṣaṇāya—for testing; tān—them (the bulls); vīra—of heroes; durmada—the false pride; hanaḥ—who destroyed; tarasā—quickly; nigṛhya—subduing; krīḍan—playing; babandha ha—He tied up; yathā—as; śiśavaḥ—children; aja—of goats; tokān—the infants; yaḥ—who; ittham—in this manner; vīrya—heroism; śulkām—whose price; mām—me; dāsībhiḥ—with maidservants; catuḥ-aṅgiṇīm—protected by an army of four divisions (chariots, horses, elephants and infantry); pathi—along the road; nirjitya—defeating; rājanyān—the kings; ninye—He took me away; tat—to Him; dāsyam—servitude; astu—may there be; me—my.

TRANSLATION

Śrī Satyā said: My father arranged for seven extremely powerful and vigorous bulls with deadly sharp horns to test the prowess of the kings who desired my hand in marriage. Although these bulls destroyed the false pride of many heroes, Lord Kṛṣṇa subdued them effortlessly, tying them up in the same way that children playfully tie up a goat's kids. He thus purchased me with His valor. Then He took me away with my maidservants and a full army of four divisions, defeating all the kings who opposed Him along the road. May I be granted the privilege of serving that Lord.

TEXTS 15–16

श्रीभद्रोवाच
पिता मे मातुलेयाय स्वयमाहूय दत्तवान् ।
कृष्णे कृष्णाय तच्चित्तामक्षौहिण्या सखीजनैः ॥१५॥
अस्य मे पादसंस्पर्शो भवेज्जन्मनि जन्मनि ।
कर्मभिर्भ्राम्यमाणाया येन तच्छ्रेय आत्मनः ॥१६॥

śrī-bhadrovāca
pitā me mātuleyāya
svayam āhūya dattavān
kṛṣṇe kṛṣṇāya tac-cittām
akṣauhiṇyā sakhī-janaiḥ

asya me pāda-saṁsparśo
bhavej janmani janmani
karmabhir bhrāmyamāṇāyā
yena tac chreya ātmanaḥ

śrī-bhadrā uvāca—Śrī Bhadrā said; *pitā*—father; *me*—my; *mātuleyāya*—to my maternal cousin; *svayam*—of his own accord; *āhūya*—inviting; *dattavān*—gave; *kṛṣṇe*—O Kṛṣṇā (Draupadī); *kṛṣṇāya*—to Lord Kṛṣṇa; *tat*—absorbed in whom; *cittām*—whose heart; *akṣauhiṇyā*—with an *akṣauhiṇī* military guard; *sakhī-janaiḥ*—and with my female companions; *asya*—His; *me*—for me; *pāda*—of the feet; *saṁsparśaḥ*—the touch; *bhavet*—may it be; *janmani janmani*—in one life after another; *karmabhiḥ*—due to the reactions of material activities; *bhrāmyamāṇāyāḥ*—who will be wandering; *yena*—by which; *tat*—that; *śreyaḥ*—ultimate perfection; *ātmanaḥ*—of myself.

TRANSLATION

Śrī Bhadrā said: My dear Draupadī, of his own free will my father invited his nephew Kṛṣṇa, to whom I had already dedicated my heart, and offered me to Him as His bride. My father presented me to the Lord with an *akṣauhiṇī* military guard and a retinue of my female companions. My ultimate perfection is this: to always be

allowed to touch Lord Kṛṣṇa's lotus feet as I wander from life to life, bound by my *karma*.

PURPORT

With the word *ātmanaḥ,* Queen Bhadrā speaks not only for herself but for all living entities as well. The soul's perfection (*śreya ātmanaḥ*) is devotional service to Lord Kṛṣṇa, both in this world and beyond, in liberation.

Śrīla Jīva Gosvāmī comments that although in civilized society it is normally considered disrespectful to publicly speak the name of one's *guru* or husband, Lord Kṛṣṇa's name is unique: the mere utterance of the name Kṛṣṇa is commendable as the highest expression of reverence for God. As the *Śvetāśvatara Upaniṣad* (4.19) states, *yasya nāma mahad yaśaḥ:* "The holy name of the Lord is supremely glorious."

TEXT 17

श्रीलक्ष्मणोवाच

ममापि राज्ञ्यच्युतजन्मकर्म
श्रुत्वा मुहुर्नारदगीतमास ह ।
चित्तं मुकुन्दे किल पद्महस्तया
वृतः सुसम्मृश्य विहाय लोकपान् ॥१७॥

śrī-lakṣmaṇovāca
mamāpi rājñy acyuta-janma-karma
śrutvā muhur nārada-gītam āsa ha
cittaṁ mukunde kila padma-hastayā
vṛtaḥ su-sammṛśya vihāya loka-pān

śrī-lakṣmaṇā uvāca—Śrī Lakṣmaṇā said; *mama*—my; *api*—also; *rājñi*—O Queen; *acyuta*—of Lord Kṛṣṇa; *janma*—about the births; *karma*—and activities; *śrutvā*—hearing; *muhuḥ*—repeatedly; *nārada*—by Nārada Muni; *gītam*—chanted; *āsa ha*—became; *cittam*—my heart; *mukunde*—(fixed) upon Mukunda; *kila*—indeed; *padma-hastayā*—by the supreme goddess of fortune, who holds a lotus in her hand; *vṛtaḥ*—chosen; *su*—carefully; *sammṛśya*—considering; *vihāya*—rejecting; *loka*—of planets; *pān*—the rulers.

TRANSLATION

Śrī Lakṣmaṇā said: O Queen, I repeatedly heard Nārada Muni glorify the appearances and activities of Acyuta, and thus my heart also became attached to that Lord, Mukunda. Indeed, even Goddess Padmahastā chose Him as her husband after careful consideration, rejecting the great demigods who rule various planets.

TEXT 18

ज्ञात्वा मम मतं साध्वि पिता दुहितृवत्सलः ।
बृहत्सेन इति ख्यातस्तत्रोपायमचीकरत् ॥१८॥

jñātvā mama mataṁ sādhvi
pitā duhitṛ-vatsalaḥ
bṛhatsena iti khyātas
tatropāyam acīkarat

jñātvā—knowing; *mama*—my; *matam*—mentality; *sādhvi*—O saintly lady; *pitā*—my father; *duhitṛ*—to his daughter; *vatsalaḥ*—affectionate; *bṛhatsenaḥ iti khyātaḥ*—known as Bṛhatsena; *tatra*—toward this end; *upāyam*—a means; *acīkarat*—arranged.

TRANSLATION

My father, Bṛhatsena, was by nature compassionate to his daughter, and knowing how I felt, O saintly lady, he arranged to fulfill my desire.

TEXT 19

यथा स्वयंवरे राज्ञि मत्स्यः पार्थेप्सया कृतः ।
अयं तु बहिराच्छन्नो दृश्यते स जले परम् ॥१९॥

yathā svayaṁ-vare rājñi
matsyaḥ pārthepsayā kṛtaḥ
ayaṁ tu bahir ācchanno
dṛśyate sa jale param

yathā—just as; *svayaṁ-vare*—in (your) *svayaṁ-vara* ceremony; *rājñi*—O Queen; *matsyaḥ*—a fish; *pārtha*—Arjuna; *īpsayā*—with the desire of obtaining; *kṛtaḥ*—made (into a target); *ayam*—this (fish); *tu*—however; *bahiḥ*—outwardly; *ācchannaḥ*—covered; *dṛśyate*—was seen; *saḥ*—it; *jale*—in water; *param*—only.

TRANSLATION

Just as a fish was used as a target in your *svayaṁ-vara* ceremony, O Queen, to assure that you would obtain Arjuna as your husband, so a fish was also used in my ceremony. In my case, however, it was concealed on all sides, and only its reflection could be seen in a pot of water below.

PURPORT

Arjuna is famous as the most expert bowman. Why, then, could he not hit the fish target at Śrīmatī Lakṣmaṇā's *svayaṁ-vara* ceremony just as he had done once before to win Draupadī? Śrīla Śrīdhara Svāmī explains: The target at Draupadī's *svayaṁ-vara* had been covered only partially, so that a marksman could see it if he looked straight up the pillar on which it was placed. To shoot Lakṣmaṇa's target, however, it was necessary to aim by looking up and down at the same time, an impossible feat for any mortal. Therefore only Kṛṣṇa could strike the target.

TEXT 20

श्रुत्वैतत्सर्वतो भूपा आययुर्मत्पितुः पुरम् ।
सर्वास्त्रशस्त्रतत्त्वज्ञाः सोपाध्यायाः सहस्रशः ॥२०॥

śrutvaitat sarvato bhū-pā
āyayur mat-pituḥ puram
sarvāstra-śastra-tattva-jñāḥ
sopādhyāyāḥ sahasraśaḥ

śrutvā—hearing; *etat*—of this; *sarvataḥ*—from everywhere; *bhū-pāḥ*—kings; *āyayuḥ*—came; *mat*—my; *pituḥ*—of the father; *puram*—to the city; *sarva*—all; *astra*—concerning weapons shot as arrows; *śastra*—and other weapons; *tattva*—of the science; *jñāḥ*—expert knowers; *sa*—along with; *upādhyāyāḥ*—their teachers; *sahasraśaḥ*—by the thousands.

TRANSLATION

Hearing of this, thousands of kings expert in shooting arrows and in wielding other weapons converged from all directions on my father's city, accompanied by their military teachers.

TEXT 21

पित्रा सम्पूजिताः सर्वे यथावीर्यं यथावयः ।
आददुः सशरं चापं वेद्धुं पर्षदि मद्धियः ॥२१॥

pitrā sampūjitāḥ sarve
yathā-vīryaṁ yathā-vayaḥ
ādaduḥ sa-śaraṁ cāpaṁ
veddhuṁ parṣadi mad-dhiyaḥ

pitrā—by my father; *sampūjitāḥ*—fully honored; *sarve*—all of them; *yathā*—according to; *vīryam*—strength; *yathā*—according to; *vayaḥ*—age; *ādaduḥ*—they took up; *sa*—with; *śaram*—arrows; *cāpam*—the bow; *veddhum*—to pierce (the target); *parṣadi*—in the assembly; *mat*—(fixed) upon me; *dhiyaḥ*—whose minds.

TRANSLATION

My father properly honored each king according to his strength and seniority. Then those whose minds were fixed on me took up the bow and arrow and one by one tried to pierce the target in the midst of the assembly.

PURPORT

According to the *ācāryas,* only those kings who were extremely intent on winning the hand of the princess even dared try to shoot the target.

TEXT 22

**आदाय व्यसृजन् केचित्सज्यं कर्तुमनीश्वराः ।
आकोष्ठं ज्यां समुत्कृष्य पेतुरेकेऽमुनाहताः ॥२२॥**

ādāya vyasṛjan kecit
sajyaṁ kartum anīśvarāḥ
ā-koṣṭhaṁ jyāṁ samutkṛṣya
petur eke 'munāhatāḥ

ādāya—after picking up; *vyasṛjan*—let go; *kecit*—some of them; *sajyam*—strung; *kartum*—to make it; *anīśvarāḥ*—unable; *ā-koṣṭham*—up to the tip (of the bow); *jyām*—the bowstring; *samutkṛṣya*—having pulled; *petuḥ*—fell down; *eke*—some; *amunā*—by it (the bow); *hatāḥ*—hit.

TRANSLATION

Some of them picked up the bow but could not string it, and so they threw it aside in frustration. Some managed to pull the bowstring toward the tip of the bow, only to have the bow spring back and knock them to the ground.

TEXT 23

**सज्यं कृत्वापरे वीरा मागधाम्बष्ठचेदिपाः ।
भीमो दुर्योधनः कर्णो नाविदंस्तदवस्थितिम् ॥२३॥**

sajyaṁ kṛtvāpare vīrā
māgadhāmbaṣṭha-cedipāḥ
bhīmo duryodhanaḥ karṇo
nāvidaṁs tad-avasthitim

sajyam—strung; *kṛtvā*—making (the bow); *apare*—other; *vīrāḥ*—heroes; *māgadha*—the King of Magadha (Jarāsandha); *ambaṣṭha*—the King of Ambaṣṭha; *cedi-pāḥ*—the ruler of Cedi (Śiśupāla); *bhīmaḥ duryodhanaḥ karṇaḥ*—Bhīma, Duryodhana and Karṇa; *na avidan*—they could not find; *tad*—of it (the target); *avasthitim*—the location.

TRANSLATION

A few heroes—namely Jarāsandha, Śiśupāla, Bhīma, Duryodhana, Karṇa and the King of Ambaṣṭha—succeeded in stringing the bow, but none of them could find the target.

PURPORT

These kings were very strong physically, but they were not skillful enough to find the target.

TEXT 24

मत्स्याभासं जले वीक्ष्य ज्ञात्वा च तदवस्थितिम् ।
पार्थो यत्तोऽसृजद् बाणं नाच्छिनत्पस्पृशे परम् ॥२४॥

matsyābhāsaṁ jale vīkṣya
jñātvā ca tad-avasthitim
pārtho yatto 'sṛjad bāṇaṁ
nācchinat paspṛśe param

matsya—of the fish; *ābhāsam*—the reflection; *jale*—in the water; *vīkṣya*—looking at; *jñātvā*—knowing; *ca*—and; *tat*—its; *avasthitim*—location; *pārthaḥ*—Arjuna; *yattaḥ*—taking careful aim; *asṛjat*—shot; *bāṇam*—the arrow; *na acchinat*—he did not pierce it; *paspṛśe*—he touched it; *param*—only.

TRANSLATION

Then Arjuna looked at the reflection of the fish in the water and determined its position. When he carefully shot his arrow at it, however, he did not pierce the target but merely grazed it.

PURPORT

According to the explanation of Śrīla Śrīdhara Svāmī, Arjuna was more expert a marksman than the other kings, but his physical strength was not adequate to the task of shooting it with perfect accuracy.

TEXTS 25–26

राजन्येषु निवृत्तेषु भग्नमानेषु मानिषु ।
भगवान् धनुरादाय सज्यं कृत्वाथ लीलया ॥२५॥
तस्मिन् सन्धाय विशिखं मत्स्यं वीक्ष्य सकृज्जले ।
छित्त्वेषुणापातयत्तं सूर्ये चाभिजिति स्थिते ॥२६॥

rājanyeṣu nivṛtteṣu
bhagna-māneṣu māniṣu
bhagavān dhanur ādāya
sajyaṁ kṛtvātha līlayā

tasmin sandhāya viśikhaṁ
matsyaṁ vīkṣya sakṛj jale
chittveṣuṇāpātayat taṁ
sūrye cābhijiti sthite

rājanyeṣu—when the kings; *nivṛtteṣu*—had given up; *bhagna*—defeated; *māneṣu*—whose pride; *māniṣu*—proud; *bhagavān*—the Supreme Lord; *dhanuḥ*—the bow; *ādāya*—taking up; *sajyam kṛtvā*—stringing it; *atha*—then; *līlayā*—as play; *tasmin*—onto it; *sandhāya*—fixing; *viśikham*—the arrow; *matsyam*—the fish; *vīkṣya*—looking at; *sakṛt*—only once; *jale*—in the water; *chittvā*—piercing; *iṣuṇā*—with the arrow; *apātayat*—He made fall; *tam*—it; *sūrye*—when the sun; *ca*—and; *abhijite*—in the constellation Abhijit; *sthite*—situated.

TRANSLATION

After all the arrogant kings had given up, their pride broken, the Supreme Personality of Godhead picked up the bow, easily strung it and then fixed His arrow upon it. As the sun stood in the constellation Abhijit, He looked at the fish in the water only once and then pierced it with the arrow, knocking it to the ground.

PURPORT

Each day the sun passes once through the lunar constellation Abhijit, marking the period most auspicious for victory. As pointed out by Śrīla

Viśvanātha Cakravartī, on this particular day the *muhūrta* of Abhijit coincided with high noon, further emphasizing Lord Kṛṣṇa's greatness by making the target all the more difficult to see.

TEXT 27

दिवि दुन्दुभयो नेदुर्जयशब्दयुता भुवि ।
देवाश्च कुसुमासारान्मुमुचुर्हर्षविह्वलाः ॥२७॥

divi dundubhayo nedur
jaya-śabda-yutā bhuvi
devāś ca kusumāsārān
mumucur harṣa-vihvalāḥ

divi—in the sky; *dundubhayaḥ*—kettledrums; *neduḥ*—resounded; *jaya*—"victory"; *śabda*—the sound; *yutāḥ*—together with; *bhuvi*—on the earth; *devāḥ*—demigods; *ca*—and; *kusuma*—of flowers; *āsārān*—torrents; *mumucuḥ*—released; *harṣa*—with joy; *vihvalāḥ*—overwhelmed.

TRANSLATION

Kettledrums resounded in the sky, and on the earth people shouted "*Jaya! Jaya!*" Overjoyed, demigods showered flowers.

TEXT 28

तद् रंगमाविशमहं कलनूपुराभ्यां
पद्भ्यां प्रगृह्य कनकोज्ज्वलरत्नमालाम् ।
नूत्ने निवीय परिधाय च कौशिकाग्र्ये
सव्रीडहासवदना कवरीधृतस्रक् ॥२८॥

tad raṅgam āviśam ahaṁ kala-nūpurābhyāṁ
padbhyāṁ pragṛhya kanakojjvala-ratna-mālām
nūtne nivīya paridhāya ca kauśikāgrye
sa-vrīḍa-hāsa-vadanā kavarī-dhṛta-srak

tat—then; *raṅgam*—the arena; *āviśam*—entered; *aham*—I; *kala*—gently sounding; *nūpurābhyām*—having ankle bells; *padbhyām*—with feet; *pragṛhya*—holding; *kanaka*—of gold; *ujjvala*—brilliant; *ratna*—with jewels; *mālām*—a necklace; *nūtne*—new; *nivīya*—having tied with a belt; *paridhāya*—wearing; *ca*—and; *kauśika*—a pair of silk garments; *agrye*—excellent; *sa-vrīḍa*—shy; *hāsa*—with a smile; *vadanā*—my face; *kavarī*—on the locks of my hair; *dhṛta*—carrying; *srak*—a wreath of flowers.

TRANSLATION

Just then I walked onto the ceremonial ground, the ankle bells on my feet gently tinkling. I was wearing new garments of the finest silk, tied with a belt, and I carried a brilliant necklace fashioned of gold and jewels. There was a shy smile on my face and a wreath of flowers in my hair.

PURPORT

Śrīla Śrīdhara Svāmī states that Śrī Lakṣmaṇā was so excited by remembering how she obtained the Supreme Lord that she forgot her natural shyness and went on to describe her own triumph.

TEXT 29

उन्नीय वक्त्रमुरुकुन्तलकुण्डलत्विड्-
गण्डस्थलं शिशिरहासकटाक्षमोक्षैः ।
राज्ञो निरीक्ष्य परितः शनकैर्मुरारेर्
अंसेऽनुरक्तहृदया निदधे स्वमालाम् ॥२९॥

unnīya vaktram uru-kuntala-kuṇḍala-tviḍ-
gaṇḍa-sthalaṁ śiśira-hāsa-kaṭākṣa-mokṣaiḥ
rājño nirīkṣya paritaḥ śanakair murārer
aṁse 'nurakta-hṛdayā nidadhe sva-mālām

unnīya—lifting; *vaktram*—my face; *uru*—abundant; *kuntala*—with locks of hair; *kuṇḍala*—of earrings; *tviṭ*—and with the effulgenee; *gaṇḍa-sthalam*—whose cheeks; *śiśira*—cooling; *hāsa*—with a smile; *kaṭa-akṣa*—of sidelong glances; *mokṣaiḥ*—and with the casting; *rājñaḥ*—the kings; *nirīkṣya*—looking at; *paritaḥ*—all around; *śanakaiḥ*—slowly; *murāreḥ*—of Kṛṣṇa; *aṁse*—upon the shoulder; *anurakta*—attracted; *hṛdayā*—whose heart; *nidadhe*—I placed; *sva*—my; *mālām*—necklace.

TRANSLATION

I lifted my face, which was encircled by my abundant locks and effulgent from the glow of my earrings reflected from my cheeks. Smiling coolly, I glanced about. Then, looking around at all the kings, I slowly placed the necklace on the shoulder of Murāri, who had captured my heart.

TEXT 30

तावन्मृदंगपटहाः शंखभेर्यानकादयः ।
निनेदुर्नटनर्तक्यो ननृतुर्गायका जगुः ॥३०॥

tāvan mṛdaṅga-paṭahāḥ
śaṅkha-bhery-ānakādayaḥ
ninedur naṭa-nartakyo
nanṛtur gāyakā jaguḥ

tāvat—just then; *mṛdaṅga-paṭahāḥ*—*mṛdaṅga* and *paṭaha* drums; *śaṅkha*—conchshells; *bherī*—kettledrums; *ānaka*—large military drums; *ādayaḥ*—and so on; *ninedūḥ*—resounded; *naṭa*—male dancers; *nartakyaḥ*—and female dancers; *nanṛtuḥ*—danced; *gāyakāḥ*—singers; *jaguḥ*—sang.

TRANSLATION

Just then there were loud sounds of conchshells and *mṛdaṅga*, *paṭaha*, *bherī* and *ānaka* drums, as well as other instruments. Men and women began to dance, and singers began to sing.

TEXT 31

एवं वृते भगवति मयेशे नृपयूथपाः ।
न सेहिरे याज्ञसेनि स्पर्धन्तो हृच्छयातुराः ॥३१॥

evaṁ vṛte bhagavati
mayeśe nṛpa-yūthapāḥ
na sehire yājñaseni
spardhanto hṛc-chayāturāḥ

evam—thus; *vṛte*—being chosen; *bhagavati*—the Personality of Godhead; *mayā*—by me; *īśe*—the Lord; *nṛpa*—of kings; *yūtha-pāḥ*—the leaders; *na sehire*—could not tolerate it; *yājñaseni*—O Draupadī; *spardhantaḥ*—becoming quarrelsome; *hṛt-śaya*—by lust; *āturāḥ*—distressed.

TRANSLATION

The leading kings there could not tolerate my having chosen the Supreme Personality of Godhead, O Draupadī. Burning with lust, they became quarrelsome.

PURPORT

Śrīla Śrīdhara Svāmī comments that the contamination of lust led the kings to quarrel foolishly with the Lord even after seeing His supreme power.

TEXT 32

मां तावद् रथमारोप्य हयरत्नचतुष्टयम् ।
शार्ङ्गमुद्यम्य सन्नद्धस्तस्थावाजौ चतुर्भुजः ॥३२॥

māṁ tāvad ratham āropya
haya-ratna-catuṣṭayam
śārṅgam udyamya sannaddhas
tasthāv ājau catur-bhujaḥ

mām—me; *tāvat*—at that point; *ratham*—on the chariot; *āropya*—lifting; *haya*—of horses; *ratna*—gems; *catuṣṭayam*—having four; *śārṅgam*—His bow, named Śārṅga; *udyamya*—readying; *sannaddhaḥ*—putting on His armor; *tasthau*—He stood; *ājau*—on the battleground; *catuḥ*—four; *bhujaḥ*—with arms.

TRANSLATION

The Lord then placed me on His chariot, drawn by four most excellent horses. Donning His armor and readying His bow Śārṅga, He stood on the chariot, and there on the battleground He manifested His four arms.

PURPORT

With two of His four arms, according to Śrīla Viśvanātha Cakravartī, Lord Kṛṣṇa embraced His bride, and with the other two He held His bow and arrows.

TEXT 33

दारुकश्चोदयामास काञ्चनोपस्करं रथम् ।
मिषतां भूभुजां राज्ञि मृगाणां मृगराडिव ॥३३॥

dārukaś codayām āsa
kāñcanopaskaraṁ ratham
miṣatāṁ bhū-bhujāṁ rājñi
mṛgāṇāṁ mṛga-rāḍ iva

dārukaḥ—Dāruka (Lord Kṛṣṇa's chariot driver); *codayām āsa*—drove; *kāñcana*—golden; *upaskaram*—whose trimmings; *ratham*—the chariot; *miṣatām*—as they watched; *bhū-bhujām*—the kings; *rājñi*—O Queen; *mṛgāṇām*—animals; *mṛga-rāṭ*—the king of animals, the lion; *iva*—as if.

TRANSLATION

Dāruka drove the Lord's gold-trimmed chariot as the kings looked on, O Queen, like small animals helplessly watching a lion.

TEXT 34

तेऽन्वसज्जन्त राजन्या निषेद्धुं पथि केचन ।
संयत्ता उद्धृतेष्वासा ग्रामसिंहा यथा हरिम् ॥३४॥

te 'nvasajjanta rājanyā
niṣeddhuṁ pathi kecana
saṁyattā uddhṛteṣv-āsā
grāma-siṁhā yathā harim

te—they; *anvasajjanta*—followed from behind; *rājanyāḥ*—the kings; *niṣeddhum*—to check Him; *pathi*—on the path; *kecana*—some of them; *saṁyattāḥ*—ready; *uddhṛta*—raised; *iṣu-āsāḥ*—whose bows; *grāma-siṁhā*—"lions of the village" (dogs); *yathā*—as; *harim*—a lion.

TRANSLATION

The kings pursued the Lord like village dogs chasing a lion. Some kings, raising their bows, stationed themselves on the road to stop Him as He passed by.

TEXT 35

ते शार्ङ्गच्युतबाणौघैः कृत्तबाह्वङ्घ्रिकन्धराः ।
निपेतुः प्रधने केचिदेके सन्त्यज्य दुद्रुवुः ॥३५॥

te śārṅga-cyuta-bāṇaughaiḥ
kṛtta-bāhv-aṅghri-kandharāḥ
nipetuḥ pradhane kecid
eke santyajya dudruvuḥ

te—they; *śārṅga*—from Lord Kṛṣṇa's bow; *cyuta*—shot; *bāṇa*—of arrows; *oghaiḥ*—by the floods; *kṛtta*—severed; *bāhu*—whose arms; *aṅghri*—legs; *kandharāḥ*—and necks; *nipetuḥ*—fell; *pradhane*—on the battlefield; *kecit*—some; *eke*—some; *santyajya*—giving up; *dudruvuḥ*—fled.

TRANSLATION

These warriors were deluged by arrows shot from the Lord's bow, Śārṅga. Some of the kings fell on the battlefield with severed arms, legs and necks; the rest gave up the fight and fled.

TEXT 36

ततः पुरीं यदुपतिरत्यलंकृतां
रविच्छदध्वजपटचित्रतोरणां ।
कुशस्थलीं दिवि भुवि चाभिसंस्तुतां
समाविशत्तरणिरिव स्वकेतनम् ॥३६॥

tataḥ purīṁ yadu-patir aty-alaṅkṛtāṁ
ravi-cchada-dhvaja-paṭa-citra-toraṇām
kuśasthalīṁ divi bhuvi cābhisaṁstutāṁ
samāviśat taraṇir iva sva-ketanam

tataḥ—then; *purīm*—His city; *yadu-patiḥ*—the Lord of the Yadus; *ati*—profusely; *alaṅkṛtām*—decorated; *ravi*—the sun; *chada*—blocking; *dhvaja*—upon flagpoles; *paṭa*—with banners; *citra*—wonderful; *toraṇām*—and with archways; *kuśasthalīm*—Dvārakā; *divi*—in heaven; *bhuvi*—on the earth; *ca*—and; *abhisaṁstutām*—glorified; *samāviśat*—He entered; *taraṇiḥ*—the sun; *iva*—as if; *sva*—his own; *ketanam*—abode.

TRANSLATION

The Lord of the Yadus then entered His capital city, Kuśasthalī [Dvārakā], which is glorified in heaven and on earth. The city was elaborately decorated with flagpoles carrying banners that blocked the sun, and also with splendid archways. As Lord Kṛṣṇa entered, He appeared like the sun-god entering his abode.

PURPORT

The abode of the sun is in the western mountains, where he sets each evening.

TEXT 37

पिता मे पूजयामास सुहृत्सम्बन्धिबान्धवान् ।
महार्हवासोऽलंकारैः शय्यासनपरिच्छदैः ॥३७॥

pitā me pūjayām āsa
suhṛt-sambandhi-bāndhavān
mahārha-vāso-'laṅkāraiḥ
śayyāsana-paricchadaiḥ

pitā—father; *me*—my; *pūjayām āsa*—worshiped; *suhṛt*—his friends; *sambandhi*—immediate relations; *bāndhavān*—and other family members; *mahā*—very; *arha*—valuable; *vāsaḥ*—with clothing; *alaṅkāraiḥ*—and jewelry; *śayyā*—with beds; *āsana*—thrones; *paricchadaiḥ*—and other furniture.

TRANSLATION

My father honored his friends, family and in-laws with priceless clothing and jewelry and with royal beds, thrones and other furnishings.

TEXT 38

दासीभिः सर्वसम्पद्भिर्भटेभरथवाजिभिः ।
आयुधानि महार्हाणि ददौ पूर्णस्य भक्तितः ॥३८॥

dāsībhiḥ sarva-sampadbhir
bhaṭebha-ratha-vājibhiḥ
āyudhāni mahārhāṇi
dadau pūrṇasya bhaktitaḥ

dāsībhiḥ—along with maidservants; *sarva*—all; *sampadbhiḥ*—endowed with riches; *bhaṭa*—with infantry soldiers; *ibha*—soldiers riding elephants; *ratha*—soldiers riding chariots; *vājibhiḥ*—and soldiers riding horses; *āyudhāni*—weapons; *mahā-arhāṇi*—extremely valuable; *dadau*—he gave; *pūrṇasya*—to the perfectly complete Lord; *bhaktitaḥ*—out of devotion.

TRANSLATION

With devotion he presented the perfectly complete Lord with a number of maidservants bedecked with precious ornaments.

Accompanying these maidservants were guards walking on foot and others riding elephants, chariots and horses. He also gave the Lord extremely valuable weapons.

PURPORT

The Supreme Lord is *pūrṇa,* perfect and complete in Himself. He requires nothing for His satisfaction. Knowing this, a pure devotee makes offerings to the Lord only out of love, *bhaktitaḥ,* with no expectation of material profit. And on His part, the Lord happily accepts even a small gift of flowers, *tulasī* leaves and water when it has been offered in love.

TEXT 39

आत्मारामस्य तस्येमा वयं वै गृहदासिकाः ।
सर्वसंगनिवृत्त्याद्धा तपसा च बभूविम ॥३९॥

ātmārāmasya tasyemā
vayaṁ vai gṛha-dāsikāḥ
sarva-saṅga-nivṛttyāddhā
tapasā ca babhūvima

ātma-ārāmasya—of the self-satisfied; *tasya*—Him; *imāḥ*—these; *vayam*—we; *vai*—indeed; *gṛha*—in the home; *dāsikāḥ*—maidservants; *sarva*—all; *saṅga*—of material association; *nivṛttyā*—by the cessation; *addhā*—directly; *tapasā*—by austerity; *ca*—and; *babhūvima*—have become.

TRANSLATION

Thus, by renouncing all material association and practicing austere penances, we queens have all become personal maidservants of the self-satisfied Supreme Lord.

PURPORT

In the opinion of Śrīla Viśvanātha Cakravartī, Śrīmatī Lakṣmaṇā became embarrassed when she realized that she had been talking about herself, and so she spoke this verse praising her co-wives. In her humility

Lakṣmaṇā claimed that Kṛṣṇa's queens, unlike ordinary wives, could not bring their husband under control, and thus they could relate to Him only as servile housekeepers. In fact, however, since the Lord's queens are direct expansions of His internal pleasure potency (*hlādinī-śakti*), they fully controlled Him with their love.

TEXT 40

महिष्य ऊचुः
भौमं निहत्य सगणं युधि तेन रुद्धा
ज्ञात्वाथ नः क्षितिजये जितराजकन्याः ।
निर्मुच्य संसृतिविमोक्षमनुस्मरन्तीः
पादाम्बुजं परिणिनाय य आप्तकामः ॥४०॥

mahiṣya ūcuḥ
bhaumaṁ nihatya sa-gaṇaṁ yudhi tena ruddhā
jñātvātha naḥ kṣiti-jaye jita-rāja-kanyāḥ
nirmucya saṁsṛti-vimokṣam anusmarantīḥ
pādāmbujaṁ pariṇināya ya āpta-kāmaḥ

mahiṣyaḥ ūcuḥ—the (other) queens said; *bhaumam*—the demon Bhauma; *nihatya*—killing; *sa*—along with; *gaṇam*—his followers; *yudhi*—in battle; *tena*—by him (Bhauma); *ruddhāḥ*—imprisoned; *jñātvā*—knowing; *atha*—then; *naḥ*—us; *kṣiti-jaye*—during (Bhauma's) conquest of the earth; *jita*—defeated; *rāja*—of kings; *kanyāḥ*—the daughters; *nirmucya*—releasing; *saṁsṛti*—from material existence; *vimokṣam*—(the source of) liberation; *anusmarantīḥ*—constantly remembering; *pāda-ambujam*—His lotus feet; *pariṇināya*—married; *yaḥ*—who; *āpta-kāmaḥ*—already fulfilled in all desires.

TRANSLATION

Rohiṇī-devī, speaking for the other queens, said: After killing Bhaumāsura and his followers, the Lord found us in the demon's prison and could understand that we were the daughters of the kings whom Bhauma had defeated during his conquest of the earth. The Lord set us free, and because we had been constantly

meditating upon His lotus feet, the source of liberation from material entanglement, He agreed to marry us, though His every desire is already fulfilled.

PURPORT

Rohiṇī-devī was one of the nine queens questioned by Draupadī in Texts 6 and 7, and thus it is assumed that she speaks here, representing the 16,099 other queens. Śrīla Prabhupāda confirms this in *Kṛṣṇa, the Supreme Personality of Godhead.*

TEXTS 41–42

न वयं साध्वि साम्राज्यं स्वाराज्यं भौज्यमप्युत ।
वैराज्यं पारमेष्ठ्यं च आनन्त्यं वा हरेः पदम् ॥४१॥
कामयामह एतस्य श्रीमत्पादरजः श्रियः ।
कुचकुंकुमगन्धाढ्यं मूर्ध्ना वोढुं गदाभृतः ॥४२॥

na vayaṁ sādhvi sāmrājyaṁ
svārājyaṁ bhaujyam apy uta
vairājyaṁ pārameṣṭhyaṁ ca
ānantyaṁ vā hareḥ padam

kāmayāmaha etasya
śrīmat-pāda-rajaḥ śriyaḥ
kuca-kuṅkuma-gandhāḍhyaṁ
mūrdhnā voḍhuṁ gadā-bhṛtaḥ

na—not; *vayam*—we; *sādhvi*—O saintly lady (Draupadī); *sām-rājyam*—rulership over the entire earth; *svā-rājyam*—the position of Lord Indra, King of heaven; *bhaujyam*—unlimited powers of enjoyment; *api uta*—even; *vairājyam*—mystic power; *pārameṣṭhyam*—the position of Lord Brahmā, creator of the universe; *ca*—and; *ānantyam*—immortality; *vā*—or; *hareḥ*—of the Supreme Lord; *padam*—the abode; *kāmayāmahe*—we desire; *etasya*—His; *śrī-mat*—divine; *pāda*—of the feet; *rajaḥ*—the dust; *śriyaḥ*—of the goddess of fortune; *kuca*—from the breast; *kuṅkuma*—of the cosmetic powder; *gandha*—by the fragrance;

āḍhyam—enriched; *mūrdhnā*—on our heads; *voḍhum*—to carry; *gadā-bhṛtaḥ*—of Lord Kṛṣṇa, the wielder of the club.

TRANSLATION

O saintly lady, we do not desire dominion over the earth, the sovereignty of the King of heaven, unlimited facility for enjoyment, mystic power, the position of Lord Brahmā, immortality or even attainment of the kingdom of God. We simply desire to carry on our heads the glorious dust of Lord Kṛṣṇa's feet, enriched by the fragrance of *kuṅkuma* from His consort's bosom.

PURPORT

The verb *rāj* means "to rule," and from it are derived the words *sāmrājyam,* meaning "rulership over the entire earth," and *svārājyam,* meaning "rulership over heaven." *Bhaujyam* comes from the verb *bhuj,* "to enjoy," and thus refers to the capacity of enjoying whatever one desires. *Virāṭ* is explained by Śrīla Viśvanātha Cakravartī as representing the phrase *vividhaṁ virājate* ("one enjoys many kinds of opulence") and specifically indicating the eight mystic perfections of *aṇimā* and so on.

An alternative explanation of these terms is given by Śrīla Śrīdhara Svāmī, who says that according to the *Bahv-ṛca Brāhmaṇa,* these four terms designate the power of sovereignty over each of the four cardinal directions: *sāmrājya* for the East, *bhaujya* for the South, *svārājya* for the West, and *vairājya* for the North.

Lord Kṛṣṇa's queens clearly state that they do not desire any of these powers, or even the position of Brahmā, liberation or entrance into the kingdom of God. They simply want the dust from Śrī Kṛṣṇa's feet, which Goddess Śrī herself worships. Śrīla Viśvanātha Cakravartī tells us that the goddess of fortune mentioned here is not Lakṣmī, the consort of Nārāyaṇa. After all, the *ācārya* explains, Goddess Lakṣmī could not attain the direct association of Kṛṣṇa even after performing extended austerities, as Uddhava states: *nāyaṁ śriyo 'ṅga u nitānta-rateḥ prasādaḥ* (*Bhāg.* 10.47.60). Rather, the Śrī referred to here is the supreme goddess of fortune identified by the *Bṛhad-gautamīya-tantra:*

devī kṛṣṇa-mayī proktā
rādhikā para-devatā

sarva-lakṣmī-mayī sarva-
kāntiḥ sammohinī parā

"The transcendental goddess Śrīmatī Rādhārāṇī is the direct counterpart of Lord Śrī Kṛṣṇa. She is the central figure for all the goddesses of fortune. She possesses all the attractiveness to attract the all-attractive Personality of Godhead. She is the primeval internal potency of the Lord."

TEXT 43

व्रजस्त्रियो यद्वाञ्छन्ति पुलिन्द्यस्तृणवीरुधः ।
गावश्चारयतो गोपाः पादस्पर्शं महात्मनः ॥४३॥

vraja-striyo yad vāñchanti
pulindyas tṛṇa-vīrudhaḥ
gāvaś cārayato gopāḥ
pāda-sparśaṁ mahātmanaḥ

vraja—of Vraja; *striyaḥ*—the women; *yat*—as; *vāñchanti*—they desire; *pulindyaḥ*—the women of the aborigine Pulinda tribe in Vraja; *tṛṇa*—from the grass; *vīrudhaḥ*—and plants; *gāvaḥ*—the cows; *cārayataḥ*—who is grazing; *gopāḥ*—the cowherd boys; *pāda*—of the feet; *sparśam*—the touch; *mahā-ātmanaḥ*—of the Supreme Soul.

TRANSLATION

We desire the same contact with the Supreme Lord's feet that the young women of Vraja, the cowherd boys and even the aborigine Pulinda women desire—the touch of the dust He leaves on the plants and grass as He tends His cows.

PURPORT

Śrīla Viśvanātha Cakravartī reminds us of the jealous rivalry that always existed between the queens of Dvārakā and the *gopīs* of Vraja. The *gopīs* considered the sophisticated women of Dvārakā the most serious threat to their hold on Śrī Kṛṣṇa, confessing their anxiety to Uddhava: *kasmāt kṛṣṇa ihāyāti prāpta-rājyo hatāhitaḥ/ narendra-kanyā udvāhya.*

"Why should Kṛṣṇa come back here after winning a kingdom, killing His enemies and marrying the daughters of kings?" (*Bhāg.* 10.47.45)

Rukmiṇī and her seven chief co-wives considered themselves so fortunate in their relationship with Kṛṣṇa as He appeared in Dvārakā that they did not especially desire to see Him as He is in Vṛndāvana. But the sixteen thousand lesser queens, after hearing Uddhava describe Śrī Rādhā's superexcellent qualities, became attracted to touch the dust that falls from Kṛṣṇa's feet onto the grass and plants of Vṛndāvana. Śrīla Viśvanātha Cakravartī indicates that some commentators give this as the reason why, after the *mauṣala-līlā,* these sixteen thousand queens were stolen from Arjuna on the road by Lord Kṛṣṇa Himself in the disguise of sixteen thousand cowherds, who then took them away to Gokula.

Thus end the purports of the humble servants of His Divine Grace A. C. Bhaktivedanta Swami Prabhupāda to the Tenth Canto, Eighty-third Chapter, of the Śrīmad-Bhāgavatam, *entitled "Draupadī Meets the Queens of Kṛṣṇa."*

CHAPTER EIGHTY-FOUR

The Sages' Teachings at Kurukṣetra

This chapter describes the arrival of great sages at Kurukṣetra to observe the auspicious occasion of a solar eclipse, the sages' glorification of Lord Kṛṣṇa, and Vasudeva's enthusiastic performance of sacrifices.

On the occasion of a solar eclipse at Kurukṣetra, exalted ladies like Kuntī, Draupadī and Subhadrā got the chance to associate with Lord Kṛṣṇa's queens. Seeing how much the Lord's consorts loved their husband, the ladies were struck with wonder. As the women talked among themselves, and the men did likewise, great sages headed by Nārada and Vyāsadeva arrived there, desiring to see Lord Kṛṣṇa. The various kings and other leading personalities who were sitting at their leisure, including the Pāṇḍavas, Kṛṣṇa and Balarāma, stood up as soon as they saw the sages. The leaders all bowed down to the great souls, inquired about their well-being and worshiped them by offering them sitting places, water and so on. Lord Kṛṣṇa then said, "Now our lives are successful, for we have obtained the goal of life: the audience of great sages and *yoga* masters, which even demigods only rarely obtain. The water at a holy place of pilgrimage and the deity forms of the gods can purify one only after a long time, but saintly sages purify just by being seen. Those who identify themselves with their bodies and neglect to honor transcendental sages like you are no better than asses."

After hearing Lord Kṛṣṇa speak these words in the mood of a mere mortal, the sages remained silent for some time, bewildered. Then they said, "How amazing our Lord is! He covers His true identity with human-like activities and pretends to be subject to superior control. Surely He has spoken in this way only to enlighten the general populace. Such behavior of His is indeed inconceivable." The sages continued to glorify the Lord as the Supreme Personality of Godhead, the Supersoul, and the friend and worshiper of the *brāhmaṇas.*

After the sages had praised Him, Lord Kṛṣṇa offered them His obeisances, and they begged His permission to return to their hermitages. But just then Vasudeva came forward, bowed to the sages and asked, "What activities can one perform to be freed from the bondage of fruitive work?" The sages replied, "By worshiping the Supreme Lord, Hari, through the performance of Vedic sacrifices, you will become free from the bondage of fruitive work." Vasudeva then requested the sages to act as his priests, and he arranged for Vedic sacrifices to be performed with superexcellent paraphernalia. Afterward, Vasudeva presented the priests with valuable gifts of cows and jewelry, and also with marriageable *brāhmaṇa* girls. He then performed the ritual bath marking the end of the sacrifice and fed everyone sumptuously, even the village dogs. Next he gave ample gifts to his relatives, the various kings and others, who all took Śrī Kṛṣṇa's leave and returned to their own homes.

Unable to depart because of his intense affection for his relatives, Nanda Mahārāja remained at Kurukṣetra for three months, served with reverence by the Yādavas. On one occasion, Vasudeva began to describe the deep friendship Nanda had shown him, shedding tears openly. At the end of three months, Nanda left for Mathurā with the fond farewells of all the Yādavas. When the Yādavas finally saw that the rainy season was about to begin, they returned to Dvārakā, where they related all that had happened at Kurukṣetra to the residents of their capital.

TEXT 1

श्रीशुक उवाच
श्रुत्वा पृथा सुबलपुत्र्यथ याज्ञसेनी
माधव्यथ क्षितिपपत्न्य उत स्वगोप्यः ।
कृष्णेऽखिलात्मनि हरौ प्रणयानुबन्धं
सर्वा विसिस्म्युरलमश्रुकलाकुलाक्ष्यः ॥१॥

śrī-śuka uvāca
śrutvā pṛthā subala-putry atha yājñasenī
mādhavy atha kṣitipa-patnya uta sva-gopyaḥ
kṛṣṇe 'khilātmani harau praṇayānubandhaṁ
sarvā visismyur alam aśru-kalākulākṣyaḥ

śrī-śukaḥ uvāca—Śukadeva Gosvāmī said; *śrutvā*—hearing; *pṛthā*—Kuntī; *subala-putrī*—Gāndhārī, the daughter of King Subala; *atha*—and; *yājñasenī*—Draupadī; *mādhavī*—Subhadrā; *atha*—and; *kṣiti-pa*—of the kings; *patnyaḥ*—the wives; *uta*—also; *sva*—(Lord Kṛṣṇa's) own;

gopyaḥ—*gopīs; kṛṣṇe*—to Kṛṣṇa; *akhila*—of all; *ātmani*—the Soul; *harau*—the Supreme Lord Hari; *praṇaya*—loving; *anubandham*—attachment; *sarvāḥ*—all of them; *visismyuḥ*—became amazed; *alam*—greatly; *aśru-kala*—with tears; *ākula*—filling; *akṣyaḥ*—whose eyes.

TRANSLATION

Śukadeva Gosvāmī said: Pṛthā, Gāndhārī, Draupadī, Subhadrā, the wives of other kings and the Lord's cowherd girlfriends were all amazed to hear of the queens' deep love for Lord Kṛṣṇa, the Supreme Personality of Godhead and Soul of all beings, and their eyes filled with tears.

PURPORT

Draupadī is the chief hearer in this assembly of exalted women, since, as explained by Śrīla Śrīdhara Svāmī, she had asked the question that Lord Kṛṣṇa's queens answered by relating their respective stories. Since Gāndhārī and the other ladies named here were not even mentioned in the previous chapter as having been present, Ācārya Śrīdhara concludes that they must have heard the queens' narrations only secondhand. Indeed, Draupadī would never have spoken so freely in the presence of Pṛthā and Gāndhārī, her elders, or before the *gopīs,* whose attitude toward the queens of Dvārakā was not particularly sympathetic. Even though the *gopīs* joined in shedding tears, it was more because of their being reminded of Śrī Kṛṣṇa's pastimes than because of any loving affinity between them and the queens.

We should remember, of course, that there is always perfect harmony on the spiritual platform. Apparent conflict between pure devotees is nothing like mundane envy and strife. The jealousy of the *gopīs* was more show than substance, being exhibited by them as an ecstatic symptom of their overflowing love for Kṛṣṇa. Śrīla Śrīdhara Svāmipāda further analyzes the phrase *sva-gopyaḥ* as implying that these *gopīs* were the queens' *sva-svarūpa,* the original prototypes of whom the queens were specific expansions.

TEXTS 2–5

इति सम्भाषमाणासु स्त्रीभिः स्त्रीषु नृभिर्नृषु ।
आययुर्मुनयस्तत्र कृष्णरामदिदृक्षया ॥२॥

द्वैपायनो नारदश्च च्यवनो देवलोऽसितः ।
विश्वामित्रः शतानन्दो भरद्वाजोऽथ गौतमः ॥३॥
रामः सशिष्यो भगवान् वसिष्ठो गालवो भृगुः ।
पुलस्त्यः कश्यपोऽत्रिश्च मार्कण्डेयो बृहस्पतिः ॥४॥
द्वितस्त्रितश्चैकतश्च ब्रह्मपुत्रास्तथाङ्गिराः ।
अगस्त्यो याज्ञवल्क्यश्च वामदेवादयोऽपरे ॥५॥

iti sambhāṣamāṇāsu
strībhiḥ strīṣu nṛbhir nṛṣu
āyayur munayas tatra
kṛṣṇa-rāma-didṛkṣayā

dvaipāyano nāradaś ca
cyavano devalo 'sitaḥ
viśvāmitraḥ śatānando
bharadvājo 'tha gautamaḥ

rāmaḥ sa-śiṣyo bhagavān
vasiṣṭho gālavo bhṛguḥ
pulastyaḥ kaśyapo 'triś ca
mārkaṇḍeyo bṛhaspatiḥ

dvitas tritaś caikataś ca
brahma-putrās tathāṅgirāḥ
agastyo yājñavalkyaś ca
vāmadevādayo 'pare

iti—thus; *sambhāṣamāṇāsu*—as they were conversing; *strībhiḥ*—with women; *strīṣu*—women; *nṛbhiḥ*—with men; *nṛṣu*—men; *āyayuḥ*—arrived; *munayaḥ*—great sages; *tatra*—at that place; *kṛṣṇa-rāma*—Lord Kṛṣṇa and Lord Balarāma; *didṛkṣayā*—with the desire to see; *dvaipāyanaḥ*—Dvaipāyana Vedavyāsa; *nāradaḥ*—Nārada; *ca*—and; *cyavanaḥ devalaḥ asitaḥ*—Cyavana, Devala and Asita; *viśvāmitraḥ śatānandaḥ*—Viśvāmitra and Śatānanda; *bharadvājaḥ atha gautamaḥ*—Bharadvāja and Gautama; *rāmaḥ*—Paraśurāma; *sa*—with; *śiṣyaḥ*—his disciples; *bhagavān*—the incarnation of the Supreme Lord; *vasiṣṭhaḥ gālavaḥ bhṛguḥ*—Vasiṣṭha, Gālava and Bhṛgu; *pulastyaḥ kaśyapaḥ atriḥ ca*—Pulastya, Kaśyapa and Atri; *mārkaṇḍeyaḥ bṛhaspatiḥ*—Mārkaṇḍeya and Bṛhaspati; *dvitaḥ tritaḥ ca ekataḥ ca*—Dvita, Trita and Ekata; *brahma-putrāḥ*—sons of Lord Brahmā (Sanaka, Sanat, Sananda and Sanātana); *tathā*—and also; *aṅgirāḥ*—Aṅgirā; *agastyaḥ yājñavalkyaḥ ca*—Agastya and Yājñavalkya; *vāmadeva-ādayaḥ*—led by Vāmadeva; *apare*—others.

TRANSLATION

As the women thus talked among themselves and the men among themselves, a number of great sages arrived there, all of them eager to see Lord Kṛṣṇa and Lord Balarāma. They included Dvaipāyana, Nārada, Cyavana, Devala and Asita, Viśvāmitra, Śatānanda, Bharadvāja and Gautama, Lord Paraśurāma and his disciples, Vasiṣṭha, Gālava, Bhṛgu, Pulastya and Kaśyapa, Atri, Mārkaṇḍeya and Bṛhaspati, Dvita, Trita, Ekata and the four Kumāras, and Aṅgirā, Agastya, Yājñavalkya and Vāmadeva.

TEXT 6

तान् दृष्ट्वा सहसोत्थाय प्रागासीना नृपादयः ।
पाण्डवाः कृष्णरामौ च प्रणेमुर्विश्ववन्दितान् ॥६॥

tān dṛṣṭvā sahasotthāya
prāg āsīnā nṛpādayaḥ
pāṇḍavāḥ kṛṣṇa-rāmau ca
praṇemur viśva-vanditān

tān—them; *dṛṣṭvā*—seeing; *sahasā*—immediately; *utthāya*—standing up; *prāk*—until now; *āsīnāḥ*—seated; *nṛpa-ādayaḥ*—the kings and others; *pāṇḍavāḥ*—the Pāṇḍavas; *kṛṣṇa-rāmau*—Kṛṣṇa and Balarāma; *ca*—also; *praṇemuḥ*—bowed down; *viśva*—by the whole universe; *vanditān*—to them who are honored.

TRANSLATION

As soon as they saw the sages approaching, the kings and other gentlemen who had been seated immediately stood up, including

the Pāṇḍava brothers and Kṛṣṇa and Balarāma. They all then bowed down to the sages, who are honored throughout the universe.

TEXT 7

तानानर्चुर्यथा सर्वे सहरामोऽच्युतोऽर्चयत् ।
स्वागतासनपाद्यार्घ्यमाल्यधूपानुलेपनैः ॥७॥

tān ānarcur yathā sarve
saha-rāmo 'cyuto 'rcayat
svāgatāsana-pādyārghya-
mālya-dhūpānulepanaiḥ

tān—them; *ānarcuḥ*—they worshiped; *yathā*—properly; *sarve*—all of them; *saha-rāma*—including Lord Balarāma; *acyutaḥ*—and Lord Kṛṣṇa; *arcayat*—worshiped them; *sv-āgata*—with greetings; *āsana*—sitting places; *pādya*—water to wash the feet; *arghya*—water to drink; *mālya*—flower garlands; *dhūpa*—incense; *anulepanaiḥ*—and sandalwood paste.

TRANSLATION

Lord Kṛṣṇa, Lord Balarāma and the other kings and leaders properly worshiped the sages by offering them words of greeting, sitting places, water for washing their feet, drinking water, flower garlands, incense and sandalwood paste.

TEXT 8

उवाच सुखमासीनान् भगवान् धर्मगुप्तनुः ।
सदसस्तस्य महतो यतवाचोऽनुशृण्वतः ॥८॥

uvāca sukham āsīnān
bhagavān dharma-gup-tanuḥ
sadasas tasya mahato
yata-vāco 'nuśṛṇvataḥ

uvāca—said; *sukham*—comfortably; *āsīnān*—to them who were seated; *bhagavān*—the Supreme Lord; *dharma*—of religion; *gup*—the means of protection; *tanuḥ*—whose body; *sadasaḥ*—in the assembly; *tasya*—that; *mahataḥ*—to the great souls; *yata*—subdued; *vācaḥ*—whose speech; *anuśṛṇvataḥ*—as they listened carefully.

TRANSLATION

After the sages were comfortably seated, the Supreme Lord Kṛṣṇa, whose transcendental body protects religious principles, addressed them in the midst of that great assembly. Everyone listened silently with rapt attention.

TEXT 9

श्रीभगवानुवाच
अहो वयं जन्मभृतो लब्धं कार्त्स्न्येन तत्फलम् ।
देवानामपि दुष्प्रापं यद्योगेश्वरदर्शनम् ॥९॥

śrī-bhagavān uvāca
aho vayaṁ janma-bhṛto
labdhaṁ kārtsnyena tat-phalam
devānām api duṣprāpaṁ
yad yogeśvara-darśanam

śrī-bhagavān uvāca—the Supreme Lord said; *aho*—ah; *vayam*—we; *janma-bhṛtaḥ*—having taken birth successfully; *labdham*—obtained; *kārtsnyena*—altogether; *tat*—of it (one's birth); *phalam*—the fruit; *devānām*—for demigods; *api*—even; *duṣprāpam*—rarely obtained; *yat*—which; *yoga-īśvara*—of masters of *yoga; darśanam*—the sight.

TRANSLATION

The Supreme Lord said: Now our lives are indeed successful, for we have obtained life's ultimate goal: the audience of great *yoga* masters, which even demigods only rarely obtain.

PURPORT

Despite the great privileges the demigods enjoy as administrators of the universe, they rarely see such sages as Nārada and Vyāsadeva. How much rarer, then, must it be for earthly kings and mere cowherds to see them. Here Lord Kṛṣṇa, identifying Himself with all the kings and others who had assembled at Samanta-pañcaka, speaks on their behalf.

TEXT 10

किं स्वल्पतपसां नृणामर्चायां देवचक्षुषाम् ।
दर्शनस्पर्शनप्रश्नप्रह्वपादार्चनादिकम् ॥१०॥

kiṁ svalpa-tapasāṁ nṝṇām
arcāyāṁ deva-cakṣuṣām
darśana-sparśana-praśna-
prahva-pādārcanādikam

kim—whether; *su-alpa*—very meager; *tapasām*—whose austerities; *nṝṇām*—for human beings; *arcāyām*—in the Deity in the temple; *deva*—God; *cakṣuṣām*—whose perception; *darśana*—seeing; *sparśana*—touching; *praśna*—asking questions; *prahva*—bowing down; *pāda-arcana*—worshiping the feet; *ādikam*—and so on.

TRANSLATION

How is it that people who are not very austere and who recognize God only in His Deity form in the temple can now see you, touch you, inquire from you, bow down to you, worship your feet and serve you in other ways?

TEXT 11

न ह्यम्मयानि तीर्थानि न देवा मृच्छिलामयाः ।
ते पुनन्त्युरुकालेन दर्शनादेव साधवः ॥११॥

na hy am-mayāni tīrthāni
na devā mṛc-chilā-mayāḥ

te punanty uru-kālena
darśanād eva sādhavaḥ

na—not; *hi*—indeed; *ap*—of water; *mayāni*—composed; *tīrthāni*—holy places; *na*—not; *devāḥ*—deities; *mṛt*—of earth; *śilā*—and stone; *mayāḥ*—composed; *te*—they; *punanti*—purify; *uru-kālena*—after a long time; *darśanāt*—by being seen; *eva*—only; *sādhavaḥ*—saints.

TRANSLATION

Mere bodies of water are not the real sacred places of pilgrimage, nor are mere images of earth and stone the true worshipable deities. These purify one only after a long time, but saintly sages purify one immediately upon being seen.

PURPORT

Because the Personality of Godhead is absolute—the Supreme Spirit—any representation of Him, whether manifested in stone, paint, sound or any other authorized medium, is nondifferent from His original form in the topmost spiritual planet, Goloka Vṛndāvana. But ordinary demigods are not absolute, being infinitesimal spirit souls, and thus representations of the demigods are not identical with them. Worship of demigods or ritual bathing in a sanctified place gives only limited benefit to those who lack transcendental faith in the Supreme Lord.

On the other hand, great Vaiṣṇava saints like Vyāsadeva, Nārada and the four Kumāras are always absorbed in Kṛṣṇa consciousness, and thus they are veritable moving *tīrthas*, places of pilgrimage. Even a moment's association with them, especially by hearing their glorification of the Lord, can deliver one from all material entanglement. As King Yudhiṣṭhira said to Vidura,

bhavad-vidhā bhāgavatās
tīrtha-bhūtāḥ svayaṁ vibho
tīrthī-kurvanti tīrthāni
svāntaḥ-sthena gadābhṛtā

"My Lord, devotees like your good self are verily holy places personified. Because you carry the Personality of Godhead within your heart, you turn all places into places of pilgrimage." (*Bhāg.* 1.13.10)

TEXT 12

नाग्निर्न सूर्यो न च चन्द्रतारका
न भूर्जलं खं श्वसनोऽथ वाङ् मनः ।
उपासिता भेदकृतो हरन्त्यघं
विपश्चितो घ्नन्ति मुहूर्तसेवया ॥१२॥

nāgnir na sūryo na ca candra-tārakā
na bhūr jalaṁ khaṁ śvasano 'tha vāṅ manaḥ
upāsitā bheda-kṛto haranty aghaṁ
vipaścito ghnanti muhūrta-sevayā

na—not; *agniḥ*—fire; *na*—not; *sūryaḥ*—the sun; *na*—not; *ca*—and; *candra*—the moon; *tārakāḥ*—and stars; *na*—not; *bhūḥ*—earth; *jalam*—water; *kham*—ether; *śvasanaḥ*—breath; *atha*—or; *vāk*—speech; *manaḥ*—and the mind; *upāsitāḥ*—worshiped; *bheda*—differences (between himself and other living beings); *kṛtaḥ*—of one who creates; *haranti*—they take away; *agham*—the sins; *vipaścitaḥ*—wise men; *ghnanti*—destroy; *muhūrta*—for a span of minutes; *sevayā*—by service.

TRANSLATION

Neither the demigods controlling fire, the sun, the moon and the stars nor those in charge of earth, water, ether, air, speech and mind actually remove the sins of their worshipers, who continue to see in terms of dualities. But wise sages destroy one's sins when respectfully served for even a few moments.

PURPORT

An immature devotee of the Supreme Lord may accept only the Deity of the Lord as divine and see everything else as material—even the Lord's confidential servants. Nonetheless, because he recognizes Lord Viṣṇu's supreme position, such a devotee is better situated than materialistic worshipers of the demigods, and he thus deserves a degree of respect.

Association with advanced sages, either directly or by hearing their instructions, is recommended in this verse for one who wishes to advance beyond the lowest stages of devotional life. A neophyte devotee may be free from the more obvious sins of violence against innocent creatures and against his own body and mind, but until he becomes very advanced on the devotional path, he must always contend with the subtler contaminations of false pride, disrespect toward respectable Vaiṣṇavas and lack of compassion for suffering creatures. The best remedy for these symptoms of immaturity is to hear from and honor pure Vaiṣṇavas and to assist them in working to deliver the fallen, conditioned souls.

TEXT 13

यस्यात्मबुद्धिः कुणपे त्रिधातुके
स्वधीः कलत्रादिषु भौम इज्यधीः ।
यत्तीर्थबुद्धिः सलिले न कर्हिचिज्
जनेष्वभिज्ञेषु स एव गोखरः ॥१३॥

yasyātma-buddhiḥ kuṇape tri-dhātuke
sva-dhīḥ kalatrādiṣu bhauma ijya-dhīḥ
yat-tīrtha-buddhiḥ salile na karhicij
janeṣv abhijñeṣu sa eva go-kharaḥ

yasya—whose; *ātma*—as his self; *buddhiḥ*—idea; *kuṇape*—in a corpse-like body; *tri-dhātuke*—made of three basic elements; *sva*—as his own; *dhīḥ*—idea; *kalatra-ādiṣu*—in wife and so on; *bhaume*—in earth; *ijya*—as worshipable; *dhīḥ*—idea; *yat*—whose; *tīrtha*—as a place of pilgrimage; *buddhiḥ*—idea; *salile*—in water; *na karhicit*—never; *janeṣu*—in men; *abhijñeṣu*—wise; *saḥ*—he; *eva*—indeed; *gaḥ*—a cow; *kharaḥ*—or an ass.

TRANSLATION

One who identifies his self as the inert body composed of mucus, bile and air, who assumes his wife and family are permanently his own, who thinks an earthen image or the land of his birth is worshipable, or who sees a place of pilgrimage as merely the water there, but who never identifies himself with, feels kinship with, worships or even visits those who are wise in spiritual truth—such a person is no better than a cow or an ass.

PURPORT

True intelligence is shown by one's freedom from false identification of the self. As stated in the *Bṛhaspati-saṁhitā,*

ajñāta-bhagavad-dharmā
mantra-vijñāna-saṁvidaḥ
narās te go-kharā jñeyā
api bhū-pāla-vanditāḥ

"Men who do not know the principles of devotional service to the Supreme Lord should be known as cows and asses, even if they are expert in technically analyzing Vedic *mantras* and are adored by world leaders."

An imperfect Vaiṣṇava advancing toward the second-class platform identifies himself with the sages who have established the true spiritual path, even while he still may have some inferior material attachments to body, family and so on. Such a devotee of the Lord is not a foolish cow or stubborn ass like the majority of materialists. But most excellent is the Vaiṣṇava who has gained the special mercy of the Lord and broken free from the bondage of illusory attachments altogether.

According to Śrīla Viśvanātha Cakravartī, the words *bhauma ijya-dhīḥ,* "who thinks an image made of earth is worshipable," refer not to the Deity form of the Supreme Lord in His temple but to deities of demigods, and the words *yat-tīrtha-buddhiḥ salile,* "who sees a place of pilgrimage as merely the water there," refer not to sacred rivers like the Ganges or Yamunā but to lesser rivers.

TEXT 14

श्रीशुक उवाच
निशम्येत्थं भगवतः कृष्णस्याकुण्ठमेधसः ।
वचो दुरन्वयं विप्रास्तूष्णीमासन् भ्रमद्धियः ॥१४॥

śrī-śuka uvāca
niśamyetthaṁ bhagavataḥ
kṛṣṇasyākuṇṭha-medhasaḥ
vaco duranvayaṁ viprās
tūṣṇīm āsan bhramad-dhiyaḥ

śrī-śukaḥ uvāca—Śukadeva Gosvāmī said; *niśamya*—hearing; *ittham*—such; *bhagavataḥ*—of the Supreme Lord; *kṛṣṇasya*—Kṛṣṇa; *akuṇṭha*—unrestricted; *medhasaḥ*—whose wisdom; *vacaḥ*—the words; *duranvayam*—difficult to comprehend; *viprāḥ*—the learned *brāhmaṇas; tūṣṇīm*—silent; *āsan*—were; *bhramat*—unsteady; *dhiyaḥ*—their minds.

TRANSLATION

Śukadeva Gosvāmī said: Hearing such unfathomable words from the unlimitedly wise Lord Kṛṣṇa, the learned *brāhmaṇas* remained silent, their minds bewildered.

TEXT 15

चिरं विमृश्य मुनय ईश्वरस्येशितव्यताम् ।
जनसंग्रह इत्यूचुः स्मयन्तस्तं जगद्गुरुम् ॥१५॥

ciraṁ vimṛśya munaya
īśvarasyeśitavyatām
jana-saṅgraha ity ūcuḥ
smayantas taṁ jagad-gurum

ciram—for some time; *vimṛśya*—thinking; *munayaḥ*—the sages; *īśvarasya*—of the supreme controller; *īśitavyatām*—the status of being controlled; *jana-saṅgrahaḥ*—the enlightenment of the people in general; *iti*—thus (concluding); *ūcuḥ*—they said; *smayantaḥ*—smiling; *tam*—to Him; *jagat*—of the universe; *gurum*—the spiritual master.

TRANSLATION

For some time the sages pondered the Supreme Lord's behavior, which resembled that of a subordinate living being. They concluded that He was acting this way to instruct the people in general. Thus they smiled and spoke to Him, the spiritual master of the universe.

PURPORT

Śrīla Śrīdhara Svāmī explains the word *īśitavyatā* as referring to one's not being a controller, or in other words, to being under the law of *karma*, obliged to work and experience the results of one's work. While addressing the sages, Lord Kṛṣṇa accepted the role of a subordinate living being to emphasize the importance of hearing and serving saintly Vaiṣṇavas. The Personality of Godhead is also the supreme teacher of spiritual surrender.

TEXT 16

श्रीमुनय ऊचुः
यन्मायया तत्त्वविदुत्तमा वयं
विमोहिता विश्वसृजामधीश्वराः ।
यदीशितव्यायति गूढ ईहया
अहो विचित्रं भगवद्विचेष्टितम् ॥१६॥

śrī-munaya ūcuḥ
yan-māyayā tattva-vid-uttamā vayaṁ
vimohitā viśva-sṛjām adhīśvarāḥ
yad īśitavyāyati gūḍha īhayā
aho vicitraṁ bhagavad-viceṣṭitam

śrī-munayaḥ ūcuḥ—the great sages said; *yat*—whose; *māyayā*—by the power of illusion; *tattva*—of the truth; *vit*—knowers; *uttamāḥ*—best; *vayam*—we; *vimohitāḥ*—confused; *viśva*—of the universe; *sṛjām*—of creators; *adhīśvarāḥ*—chief; *yat*—the fact that; *īśitavyāyati*—(the Supreme Lord) pretends to be subject to higher control; *gūḍhaḥ*—hidden; *īhayā*—by His activities; *aho*—ah; *vicitram*—amazing; *bhagavat*—of the Supreme Lord; *viceṣṭitam*—the activity.

TRANSLATION

The great sages said: Your power of illusion has totally bewildered us, the most exalted knowers of the truth and leaders among the universal creators. Ah, how amazing is the behavior of the Supreme Lord! He covers Himself with His humanlike activities and pretends to be subject to superior control.

PURPORT

The sages have characterized the Lord's statements as inscrutable (*duranvayam*). How this is so is stated here: His words and activities bewilder even the most learned when He plays at subordinating Himself to His own servants.

TEXT 17

अनीह एतद् बहुधैक आत्मना
सृजत्यवत्यत्ति न बध्यते यथा ।
भौमैर्हि भूमिर्बहुनामरूपिणी
अहो विभूम्नश्चरितं विडम्बनम् ॥१७॥

anīha etad bahudhaika ātmanā
sṛjaty avaty atti na badhyate yathā
bhaumair hi bhūmir bahu-nāma-rūpiṇī
aho vibhūmnaś caritaṁ viḍambanam

anīhaḥ—exerting no endeavor; *etat*—this (universe); *bahudhā*—manifold; *ekaḥ*—alone; *ātmanā*—by Himself; *sṛjati*—He creates; *avati*—maintains; *atti*—annihilates; *na badhyate*—is not bound up; *yathā*—as; *bhaumaiḥ*—by the transformations of earth; *hi*—indeed; *bhūmiḥ*—earth; *bahu*—many; *nāma-rūpiṇī*—having names and forms; *aho*—ah; *vibhūmnaḥ*—of the almighty Lord; *caritam*—the activities; *viḍambanam*—a pretense.

TRANSLATION

Indeed, the humanlike pastimes of the Almighty are simply a pretense! Effortlessly, He alone sends forth from His Self this variegated creation, maintains it and then swallows it up again, all without becoming entangled, just as the element earth takes on many names and forms in its various transformations.

PURPORT

The one Supreme expands Himself as many without diminishing His completeness. He does this effortlessly, without depending on anyone or anything else. This mystic process of the Lord's self-expansion is incomprehensible to all but Himself, but the example of the substance earth and its manifold products bears enough resemblance to provide some idea. The same example is also presented in an often-cited passage of the *Chāndogya Upaniṣad* (6.1), *vācārambhaṇaṁ vikāro nāmadheyaṁ mṛttikety eva satyam:* "Earth's transformations are merely verbal creations of the process of naming; the substance earth itself is alone real."

Śrīla Śrīdhara Svāmī suggests that this verse of *Śrīmad-Bhāgavatam* answers a possible objection on the part of Lord Kṛṣṇa: "How can I create, maintain and destroy the universe if I am Vasudeva's son?" The answer is given by the words *aho vibhūmnaś caritaṁ viḍambanam:* "You are the perfectly complete whole, and Your birth and pastimes are only an imitation of ordinary persons' activities in the material world. You simply pretend to be under higher control."

TEXT 18

अथापि काले स्वजनाभिगुप्तये
बिभर्षि सत्त्वं खलनिग्रहाय च ।
स्वलीलया वेदपथं सनातनं
वर्णाश्रमात्मा पुरुषः परो भवान् ॥१८॥

athāpi kāle sva-janābhiguptaye
bibharṣi sattvaṁ khala-nigrahāya ca
sva-līlayā veda-pathaṁ sanātanaṁ
varṇāśramātmā puruṣaḥ paro bhavān

atha api—nonetheless; *kāle*—at the correct time; *sva-jana*—of Your devotees; *abhiguptaye*—for the protection; *bibharṣi*—You assume; *sattvam*—the mode of goodness; *khala*—of the wicked; *nigrahāya*—for the punishment; *ca*—and; *sva*—Your; *līlayā*—by the pastimes; *veda-patham*—the path of the *Vedas;* *sanātanam*—eternal; *varṇa-āśrama*—of the divine system of occupational and spiritual divisions of society; *ātmā*—the Soul; *puruṣaḥ*—the Personality of Godhead; *paraḥ*—Supreme; *bhavān*—Your good self.

TRANSLATION

Nonetheless, at suitable times You assume the pure mode of goodness to protect Your devotees and punish the wicked. Thus You, the Soul of the *varṇāśrama* social order, the Supreme Personality of Godhead, maintain the eternal path of the *Vedas* by enjoying Your pleasure pastimes.

PURPORT

This verse describes the Lord's enlightening people in general (*jana-saṅgraha*) and His imitation of worldly behavior. Because the Personality of Godhead remains always perfect, the body He manifests when He comes to this world is not touched by material goodness; rather, it is a manifestation of the pure goodness known as *viśuddha-sattva*, the same spiritual substance that constitutes His original form.

TEXT 19

ब्रह्म ते हृदयं शुक्लं तपःस्वाध्यायसंयमैः ।
यत्रोपलब्धं सद्‌व्यक्तमव्यक्तं च ततः परम् ॥१९॥

brahma te hṛdayaṁ śuklaṁ
tapaḥ-svādhyāya-saṁyamaiḥ
yatropalabdhaṁ sad vyaktam
avyaktaṁ ca tataḥ param

brahma—the *Vedas; te*—Your; *hṛdayam*—heart; *śuklam*—pure; *tapaḥ*—by austerities; *svādhyāya*—study; *saṁyamaiḥ*—and self-control; *yatra*—in which; *upalabdham*—perceived; *sat*—pure spiritual existence; *vyaktam*—the manifest (products of material creation); *avyaktam*—the unmanifest (subtle causes of creation); *ca*—and; *tataḥ*—to that; *param*—transcendental.

TRANSLATION

The *Vedas* are Your spotless heart, and through them one can perceive—by means of austerity, study and self-control—the

manifest, the unmanifest and the pure existence transcendental to both.

PURPORT

Vyakta, "the manifest," consists of the visible things of this world, and *avyakta* consists of the subtle, underlying causes of cosmic creation. The *Vedas* point toward the transcendental realm of Brahman, which lies beyond all material cause and effect.

TEXT 20

तस्माद् ब्रह्मकुलं ब्रह्मन् शास्त्रयोनेस्त्वमात्मनः ।
सभाजयसि सद्धाम तद् ब्रह्मण्याग्रणीर्भवान् ॥२०॥

tasmād brahma-kulaṁ brahman
śāstra-yones tvam ātmanaḥ
sabhājayasi sad dhāma
tad brahmaṇyāgraṇīr bhavān

tasmāt—therefore; *brahma*—of *brāhmaṇas; kulam*—to the community; *brahman*—O Absolute Truth; *śāstra*—the revealed scriptures; *yoneḥ*—whose means of realization; *tvam*—You; *ātmanaḥ*—of Yourself; *sabhājayasi*—show honor; *sat*—perfect; *dhāma*—the abode; *tat*—consequently; *brahmaṇya*—of those who respect brahminical culture; *agraṇīḥ*—the leader; *bhavān*—You.

TRANSLATION

Therefore, O Supreme Brahman, You honor the members of the brahminical community, for they are the perfect agents by which one can realize You through the evidence of the *Vedas.* For that very reason You are the foremost worshiper of the *brāhmaṇas.*

TEXT 21

अद्य नो जन्मसाफल्यं विद्यायास्तपसो दृशः ।
त्वया संगम्य सद्गत्या यदन्तः श्रेयसां परः ॥२१॥

adya no janma-sāphalyaṁ
vidyāyās tapaso dṛśaḥ
tvayā saṅgamya sad-gatyā
yad antaḥ śreyasāṁ paraḥ

adya—today; *naḥ*—our; *janma*—of the birth; *sāphalyam*—fruition; *vidyāyāḥ*—of the education; *tapasaḥ*—of the austerities; *dṛśaḥ*—of the power of sight; *tvayā*—with You; *saṅgamya*—obtaining association; *sat*—of saintly persons; *gatyā*—who are the goal; *yat*—because; *antaḥ*—the limit; *śreyasām*—of benefits; *paraḥ*—ultimate.

TRANSLATION

Today our birth, education, austerity and vision have all become perfect because we have been able to associate with You, the goal of all saintly persons. Indeed, You Yourself are the ultimate, supreme blessing.

PURPORT

The sages here contrast their respect for the Lord with His reciprocal worship of them. Lord Kṛṣṇa honors *brāhmaṇas* as a means of instructing less intelligent men, whereas He is in fact absolutely independent. The *brāhmaṇas* who worship Him, on the other hand, benefit themselves more than they can imagine.

TEXT 22

नमस्तस्मै भगवते कृष्णायाकुण्ठमेधसे ।
स्वयोगमाययाच्छन्नमहिम्ने परमात्मने ॥२२॥

namas tasmai bhagavate
kṛṣṇāyākuṇṭha-medhase
sva-yogamāyayācchanna-
mahimne paramātmane

namaḥ—obeisances; *tasmai*—to Him; *bhagavate*—the Supreme Lord; *kṛṣṇāya*—Kṛṣṇa; *akuṇṭha*—unrestricted; *medhase*—whose wisdom; *sva*—

His own; *yoga-māyayā*—by the internal illusory potency; *ācchanna*—covered; *mahimne*—whose glories; *parama-ātmane*—the Supersoul.

TRANSLATION

Let us offer obeisances unto that Supreme Personality of Godhead, Lord Kṛṣṇa, the infinitely intelligent Supersoul, who has disguised His greatness through His mystic Yogamāyā.

PURPORT

Apart from any future profit to be obtained from worshiping the Supreme Lord, it is every person's most essential obligation to bow down to Him as an acknowledgement of one's dependence and servitude. Lord Kṛṣṇa recomends,

man-manā bhava mad-bhakto
mad-yājī māṁ namaskuru
mām evaiṣyasi yuktvaivam
ātmānaṁ mat-parāyaṇaḥ

"Engage your mind always in thinking of Me, become My devotee, offer obeisances to Me and worship Me. Being completely absorbed in Me, surely you will come to Me." (Bg. 9.34)

TEXT 23

न यं विदन्त्यमी भूपा एकारामाश्च वृष्णयः ।
मायाजवनिकाच्छन्नमात्मानं कालमीश्वरम् ॥२३॥

na yaṁ vidanty amī bhū-pā
ekārāmāś ca vṛṣṇayaḥ
māyā-javanikācchannam
ātmānaṁ kālam īśvaram

na—not; *yam*—whom; *vidanti*—know; *amī*—these; *bhū-pāḥ*—kings; *eka*—together; *ārāmāḥ*—who enjoy; *ca*—and; *vṛṣṇayaḥ*—the Vṛṣṇis;

māyā—of the divine power of illusion; *javanikā*—by the curtain; *ācchannam*—covered; *ātmānam*—the Supreme Soul; *kālam*—time; *īśvaram*—the supreme controller.

TRANSLATION

Neither these kings nor even the Vṛṣṇis, who enjoy Your intimate association, know You as the Soul of all existence, the force of time and the supreme controller. For them You are covered by the curtain of Māyā.

PURPORT

Śrīla Viśvanātha Cakravartī explains that Lord Kṛṣṇa's family, the Vṛṣṇis, were too familiar with Him to realize that He is the Supersoul residing in the heart of every created being. And those kings at Kurukṣetra who were not devotees of Kṛṣṇa could not recognize Him as time, the annihilator of everything. Devotees and nondevotees are both covered by Māyā, but in different ways. For the materialists Māyā is illusion, but for the Vaiṣṇavas she acts as Yogamāyā, the internal potency who covers their awareness of the Supreme Lord's majesty and engages them in His eternal pleasure pastimes.

TEXTS 24–25

यथा शयानः पुरुष आत्मानं गुणतत्त्वदृक् ।
नाममात्रेन्द्रियाभातं न वेद रहितं परम् ॥२४॥
एवं त्वा नाममात्रेषु विषयेष्विन्द्रियेहया ।
मायया विभ्रमच्चित्तो न वेद स्मृत्युपप्लवात् ॥२५॥

yathā śayānaḥ puruṣa
ātmānaṁ guṇa-tattva-dṛk
nāma-mātrendriyābhātaṁ
na veda rahitaṁ param

evaṁ tvā nāma-mātreṣu
viṣayeṣv indriyehayā
māyayā vibhramac-citto
na veda smṛty-upaplavāt

yathā—as; *śayānaḥ*—sleeping; *puruṣaḥ*—a person; *ātmānam*—himself; *guṇa*—secondary; *tattva*—of reality; *dṛk*—whose vision; *nāma*—with names; *mātra*—and forms; *indriya*—through his mind; *ābhātam*—manifest; *na veda*—he does not know; *rahitam*—separate; *param*—rather; *evam*—similarly; *tvā*—You; *nāma-mātreṣu*—having names and forms; *viṣayeṣu*—in objects of material perception; *indriya*—of the senses; *īhayā*—by the activity; *māyayā*—because of the influence of Your illusory energy; *vibhramat*—becoming bewildered; *cittaḥ*—whose consciousness; *na veda*—one does not know; *smṛti*—of his memory; *upaplavāt*—due to the disruption.

TRANSLATION

A sleeping person imagines an alternative reality for himself and, seeing himself as having various names and forms, forgets his waking identity, which is distinct from the dream. Similarly, the senses of one whose consciousness is bewildered by illusion perceive only the names and forms of material objects. Thus such a person loses his memory and cannot know You.

PURPORT

Just as a person's dream is a secondary reality created from the stock of his memories and desires, so this universe exists as the inferior creation of the Supreme Lord, in no real way separate from Him. And just as the person who awakens from sleep experiences the higher reality of his waking life, so the Supreme Lord also has His distinct, higher reality beyond everything we know of this world. In His own words,

mayā tatam idaṁ sarvaṁ
jagad avyakta-mūrtinā
mat-sthāni sarva-bhūtāni
na cāhaṁ teṣv avasthitaḥ

na ca mat-sthāni bhūtāni
paśya me yogam aiśvaram
bhūta-bhṛn na ca bhūta-stho
mamātmā bhūta-bhāvanaḥ

"By Me, in My unmanifested form, this entire universe is pervaded. All beings are in Me, but I am not in them. And yet everything that is created does not rest in Me. Behold My mystic opulence! Although I am the maintainer of all living entities and although I am everything, I am not part of this cosmic manifestation, for My Self is the very source of creation." (Bg. 9.4-5)

TEXT 26

तस्याद्य ते ददृशिमाङ्घ्रिमघौघमर्ष-
तीर्थास्पदं हृदि कृतं सुविपक्वयोगैः ।
उत्सिक्तभक्त्युपहताशयजीवकोशा
आपुर्भवद्गतिमथानुगृहाण भक्तान् ॥२६॥

tasyādya te dadṛśimāṅghrim aghaugha-marṣa-
tīrthāspadaṁ hṛdi kṛtaṁ su-vipakva-yogaiḥ
utsikta-bhakty-upahatāśaya-jīva-kośā
āpur bhavad-gatim athānugṛhāṇa bhaktān

tasya—His; *adya*—today; *te*—Your; *dadṛśima*—we have seen; *aṅghrim*—the feet; *agha*—of sins; *ogha*—floods; *marṣa*—which undo; *tīrtha*—of the holy pilgrimage site (the Ganges); *āspadam*—the source; *hṛdi*—in the heart; *kṛtam*—placed; *su*—well; *vipakva*—matured; *yogaiḥ*—by those whose practice of *yoga; utsikta*—fully developed; *bhakti*—by devotional service; *upahata*—destroyed; *āśaya*—the material mentality; *jīva*—of the individual soul; *kośāḥ*—whose external covering; *āpuḥ*—they attained; *bhavat*—Your; *gatim*—destination; *atha*—therefore; *anugṛhāṇa*—please show mercy; *bhaktān*—to Your devotees.

TRANSLATION

Today we have directly seen Your feet, the source of the holy Ganges, which washes away volumes of sins. Perfected *yogīs* can at best meditate upon Your feet within their hearts. But only those who render You wholehearted devotional service and in this way vanquish the soul's covering—the material mind—attain You as their final destination. Therefore kindly show mercy to us, Your devotees.

PURPORT

The holy river Ganges has the power to destroy all sorts of sinful reactions because she originates at the Lord's lotus feet and thus contains the dust of His feet. Explaining this verse, Śrīla Śrīdhara Svāmī says, "If the Lord might advise the sages that they need not concern themselves with devotional practices because they are already far advanced in spiritual knowledge and austerity, they hereby respectfully decline such a suggestion, pointing out that only those *yogīs* who have destroyed their material mind and ego by surrendering to Kṛṣṇa in pure devotional service can attain full perfection. They conclude by praying to the Lord that He favor them in the most merciful way by making them His devotees."

TEXT 27

श्रीशुक उवाच
इत्यनुज्ञाप्य दाशार्हं धृतराष्ट्रं युधिष्ठिरम् ।
राजर्षे स्वाश्रमान् गन्तुं मुनयो दधिरे मनः ॥२७॥

śrī-śuka uvāca
ity anujñāpya dāśārhaṁ
dhṛtarāṣṭraṁ yudhiṣṭhiram
rājarṣe svāśramān gantuṁ
munayo dadhire manaḥ

śrī-śukaḥ uvāca—Śukadeva Gosvāmī said; *iti*—thus speaking; *anujñāpya*—taking permission to leave; *dāśārham*—of Lord Kṛṣṇa, the descendant of Mahārāja Daśārha; *dhṛtarāṣṭram*—of Dhṛtarāṣṭra; *yudhiṣṭhiram*—of Yudhiṣṭhira; *rāja*—among kings; *ṛṣe*—O sage; *sva*—their own; *āśramān*—to the hermitages; *gantum*—to going; *munayaḥ*—the sages; *dadhire*—turned; *manaḥ*—their minds.

TRANSLATION

Śukadeva Gosvāmī said: Having thus spoken, O wise king, the sages then took leave of Lord Dāśārha, Dhṛtarāṣṭra and Yudhiṣṭhira and prepared to depart for their *āśramas*.

TEXT 28

तद्वीक्ष्य तानुपव्रज्य वसुदेवो महायशाः ।
प्रणम्य चोपसंगृह्य बभाषेदं सुयन्त्रितः ॥२८॥

tad vīkṣya tān upavrajya
vasudevo mahā-yaśāḥ
praṇamya copasaṅgṛhya
babhāṣedaṁ su-yantritaḥ

tat—this; *vīkṣya*—seeing; *tān*—them; *upavrajya*—approaching; *vasudevaḥ*—Vasudeva; *mahā*—great; *yaśāḥ*—whose fame; *praṇamya*—bowing down; *ca*—and; *upasaṅgṛhya*—taking hold of their feet; *babhāṣa*—he said; *idam*—this; *su*—very; *yantritaḥ*—carefully composed.

TRANSLATION

Seeing that they were about to leave, the renowned Vasudeva approached the sages. After bowing down to them and touching their feet, he spoke to them with carefully chosen words.

TEXT 29

श्रीवसुदेव उवाच

नमो वः सर्वदेवेभ्य ऋषयः श्रोतुमर्हथ ।
कर्मणा कर्मनिर्हारो यथा स्यान्नस्तदुच्यताम् ॥२९॥

śrī-vasudeva uvāca
namo vaḥ sarva-devebhya
ṛṣayaḥ śrotum arhatha
karmaṇā karma-nirhāro
yathā syān nas tad ucyatām

śrī-vasudevaḥ uvāca—Śrī Vasudeva said; *namaḥ*—obeisances; *vaḥ*—to you; *sarva*—all; *devebhyaḥ*—(who comprise) the demigods; *ṛṣayaḥ*—O sages; *śrotum arhatha*—please listen; *karmaṇā*—by material work; *karma*—of (previous) work; *nirhāraḥ*—the purging; *yathā*—how; *syāt*—there may be; *naḥ*—to us; *tat*—that; *ucyatām*—please say.

TRANSLATION

Śrī Vasudeva said: Obeisances to you, the residence of all the demigods. Please hear me, O sages. Kindly tell us how the reactions of one's work can be counteracted by further work.

PURPORT

Here Vasudeva addresses the sages as "the residence of all the demigods." His statement is confirmed in the authoritative *śruti-mantras,* which declare, *yāvatīr vai devatās tāḥ sarvā veda-vidi brāhmaṇe vasanti:* "Whatever demigods exist, all reside in a *brāhmaṇa* who knows the *Veda.*"

TEXT 30

श्रीनारद उवाच
नातिचित्रमिदं विप्रा वसुदेवो बुभुत्सया ।
कृष्णं मत्वार्भकं यन्नः पृच्छति श्रेय आत्मनः ॥३०॥

śrī-nārada uvāca
nāti-citram idaṁ viprā
vasudevo bubhutsayā
kṛṣṇaṁ matvārbhakaṁ yan naḥ
pṛcchati śreya ātmanaḥ

śrī-nāradaḥ uvāca—Śrī Nārada said; *na*—not; *ati*—very; *citram*—wonderful; *idam*—this; *viprāḥ*—O *brāhmaṇas; vasudevaḥ*—Vasudeva; *bubhutsayā*—with the desire of learning; *kṛṣṇam*—Lord Kṛṣṇa; *matvā*—thinking; *arbhakam*—a boy; *yat*—the fact that; *naḥ*—from us; *pṛcchati*—he asks; *śreyaḥ*—about the highest good; *ātmanaḥ*—for himself.

TRANSLATION

Śrī Nārada Muni said: O *brāhmaṇas,* it is not so amazing that in his eagerness to know, Vasudeva has asked us about his ultimate benefit, for he considers Kṛṣṇa a mere boy.

PURPORT

Śrīla Jīva Gosvāmī relates Nārada's thoughts: Śrī Nārada understood how Vasudeva, in line with his mood of pretending to be an ordinary householder, asked the sages about *karma-yoga,* although he had already attained spiritual goals even great *yogīs* and *ṛṣis* cannot achieve. But Nārada was still concerned that Vasudeva might create an awkward mood by treating Lord Kṛṣṇa as a mere child in the presence of all the sages. Nārada and the other sages felt obliged to maintain their attitude of reverence toward Lord Kṛṣṇa, so how could they ignore Him and presume to answer Vasudeva themselves? To avoid this embarrassment, Nārada took this opportunity to remind everyone present of Śrī Kṛṣṇa's absolute supremacy.

TEXT 31

सन्निकर्षोऽत्र मर्त्यानामनादरणकारणम् ।
गांगं हित्वा यथान्याम्भस्तत्रत्यो याति शुद्धये ॥३१॥

sannikarṣo 'tra martyānām
anādaraṇa-kāraṇam
gāṅgaṁ hitvā yathānyāmbhas
tatratyo yāti śuddhaye

sannikarṣaḥ—proximity; *atra*—here (in this world); *martyānām*—for mortals; *anādaraṇa*—of disregard; *kāraṇam*—a cause; *gāṅgam*—(the water) of the Ganges; *hitvā*—leaving; *yathā*—as; *anya*—other; *ambhaḥ*—to water; *tatratyaḥ*—one who lives near it; *yāti*—goes; *śuddhaye*—for purification.

TRANSLATION

In this world familiarity breeds contempt. For example, one who lives on the banks of the Ganges might travel to some other body of water to be purified.

TEXT 32–33

यस्यानुभूतिः कालेन लयोत्पत्त्यादिनास्य वै ।
स्वतोऽन्यस्माच्च गुणतो न कुतश्चन रिष्यति ॥३२॥
तं क्लेशकर्मपरिपाकगुणप्रवाहैर्
अव्याहतानुभवमीश्वरमद्वितीयम् ।

प्राणादिभिः स्वविभवैरुपगूढमन्यो
मन्येत सूर्यमिव मेघहिमोपरागैः ॥३३॥

yasyānubhūtiḥ kālena
layotpatty-ādināsya vai
svato 'nyasmāc ca guṇato
na kutaścana riṣyati

taṁ kleśa-karma-paripāka-guṇa-pravāhair
avyāhatānubhavam īśvaram advitīyam
prāṇādibhiḥ sva-vibhavair upagūḍham anyo
manyeta sūryam iva megha-himoparāgaiḥ

yasya—whose; *anubhūtiḥ*—awareness; *kālena*—caused by time; *laya*—by the destruction; *utpatti*—creation; *ādinā*—and so on; *asya*—of this (universe); *vai*—indeed; *svataḥ*—on its own; *anyasmāt*—due to some other agency; *ca*—or; *guṇataḥ*—in terms of its qualities; *na*—not; *kutaścana*—for any reason; *riṣyati*—becomes disrupted; *tam*—Him; *kleśa*—by material distresses; *karma*—material activities; *paripāka*—their consequences; *guṇa*—of the modes of nature; *pravāhaiḥ*—and by the constant flow; *avyāhata*—unaffected; *anubhavam*—whose consciousness; *īśvaram*—the supreme controller; *advitīyam*—who has no second; *prāṇa*—by the vital air; *ādibhiḥ*—and other (elements of the material body); *sva*—His own; *vibhavaiḥ*—expansions; *upagūḍham*—disguised; *anyaḥ*—someone else; *manyeta*—considers; *sūryam iva*—like the sun; *megha*—by clouds; *hima*—snow; *uparāgaiḥ*—and eclipses.

TRANSLATION

The Supreme Lord's awareness is never disturbed by time, by the creation and destruction of the universe, by changes in its own qualities, or by anything else, whether self-caused or external. But although the consciousness of the Personality of Godhead, who is the supreme one without a second, is never affected by material distress, by the reactions of material work or by the constant flow of nature's modes, ordinary persons nonetheless think that the Lord is covered by His own creations of *prāṇa* and other material elements, just as one may think that the sun is covered by clouds, snow or an eclipse.

PURPORT

Things of this world are inevitably destroyed by one means or another. Time itself causes the eventual decay of every created being—a fruit, for instance, which may grow ripe but then must either rot or be eaten. Some things, like lightning, destroy themselves as soon as they are manifested, while others are destroyed suddenly by external agents, as a clay pot is by a hammer. Even in living bodies and other things whose existence continues for some time, there is a constant flux of various qualities that are destroyed and replaced by others.

In contrast to all of this, the Supreme Personality of Godhead's awareness is never disrupted by anything. Only out of ignorance could one imagine Him to be an ordinary human being subject to material conditions. Mortal beings are covered by their entanglement in fruitive activities and their consequent happiness and distress, but the Supreme Lord cannot be covered by what are in fact His own expansions. Analogously, the immense sun is the source of the relatively insignificant phenomena of clouds, snow and eclipses, and so it cannot be covered by them, though the ordinary observer may think that it is.

TEXT 34

अथोचुर्मुनयो राजन्नाभाष्यानकदुन्दुभिम् ।
सर्वेषां शृण्वतां राज्ञां तथैवाच्युतरामयोः ॥३४॥

athocur munayo rājann
ābhāṣyānakadundubhim
sarveṣāṁ śṛṇvatāṁ rājñāṁ
tathaivācyuta-rāmayoḥ

atha—then; *ūcuḥ*—said; *munayaḥ*—the sages; *rājan*—O King (Parīkṣit); *ābhāṣya*—speaking; *ānaka-dundubhim*—to Vasudeva; *sarveṣām*—all; *śṛṇvatām*—as they listened; *rājñām*—the kings; *tathā eva*—also; *acyuta-rāmayoḥ*—Kṛṣṇa and Balarāma.

TRANSLATION

[Śukadeva Gosvāmī continued:] The sages then spoke again, O King, addressing Vasudeva while all the kings, along with Lord Acyuta and Lord Rāma, listened.

TEXT 35

कर्मणा कर्मनिर्हार एष साधुनिरूपितः ।
यच्छ्रद्धया यजेद्विष्णुं सर्वयज्ञेश्वरं मखैः ॥३५॥

karmaṇā karma-nirhāra
eṣa sādhu-nirūpitaḥ
yac chraddhayā yajed viṣṇuṁ
sarva-yajñeśvaraṁ makhaiḥ

karmaṇā—by activity; *karma*—of the reactions of past actions; *nirhāraḥ*—the counteraction; *eṣaḥ*—this; *sādhu*—correctly; *nirūpitaḥ*—ascertained; *yat*—that; *śraddhayā*—with faith; *yajet*—one should worship; *viṣṇum*—Viṣṇu; *sarva*—of all; *yajña*—sacrifices; *īśvaram*—the Lord; *makhaiḥ*—by Vedic fire rituals.

TRANSLATION

[The sages said:] It has been definitely concluded that work is counteracted by further work when one executes Vedic sacrifices as a means of worshiping Viṣṇu, the Lord of all sacrifices, with sincere faith.

TEXT 36

चित्तस्योपशमोऽयं वै कविभिः शास्त्रचक्षुषा ।
दर्शितः सुगमो योगो धर्मश्चात्ममुदावहः ॥३६॥

cittasyopaśamo 'yaṁ vai
kavibhiḥ śāstra-cakṣuṣā
darśitaḥ su-gamo yogo
dharmaś cātma-mud-āvahaḥ

cittasya—of the mind; *upaśamaḥ*—the pacification; *ayam*—this; *vai*—indeed; *kavibhiḥ*—by learned scholars; *śāstra*—of scripture; *cakṣuṣā*—with the eye; *darśitaḥ*—shown; *su-gamaḥ*—easily performed; *yogaḥ*—means of attaining liberation; *dharmaḥ*—religious duty; *ca*—and; *ātma*—to the heart; *mut*—pleasure; *āvahaḥ*—which brings.

TRANSLATION

Learned authorities who see through the eye of scripture have demonstrated that this is the easiest method of subduing the agitated mind and attaining liberation, and that it is a sacred duty which brings joy to the heart.

TEXT 37

अयं स्वस्त्ययनः पन्था द्विजातेर्गृहमेधिनः ।
यच्छ्रद्धयाप्तवित्तेन शुक्लेनेज्येत पूरुषः ॥३७॥

ayaṁ svasty-ayanaḥ panthā
dvi-jāter gṛha-medhinaḥ
yac chraddhayāpta-vittena
śuklenejyeta pūruṣaḥ

ayam—this; *svasti*—auspiciousness; *ayanaḥ*—bringing; *panthā*—the path; *dvi-jāteḥ*—for one who is twice-born (being a member of one of the three higher social orders); *gṛha*—at home; *medhinaḥ*—who performs sacrifices; *yat*—that; *śraddhayā*—selflessly; *āpta*—obtained by just means; *vittena*—with his possessions; *śuklena*—untainted; *ījyeta*—one should worship; *pūruṣaḥ*—the Personality of Godhead.

TRANSLATION

This is the most auspicious path for a religious householder of the twice-born orders—to selflessly worship the Personality of Godhead with wealth honestly obtained.

PURPORT

Both Śrīdhara Svāmī and Śrī Jīva Gosvāmī here agree that the ritual *karma* of Vedic sacrifices is particularly meant for attached householders. Those who are already renounced in Kṛṣṇa consciousness, like Vasudeva himself, need only cultivate their faith in the Lord's devotees, His Deity form, His name, the remnants of His food and His teachings, as given in *Bhagavad-gītā* and *Śrīmad-Bhāgavatam.*

TEXT 38

वित्तैषणां यज्ञदानैर्गृहैर्दारसुतैषणाम् ।
आत्मलोकैषणां देव कालेन विसृजेद् बुधः ।
ग्रामे त्यक्तैषणाः सर्वे ययुर्धीरास्तपोवनम् ॥३८॥

vittaiṣaṇāṁ yajña-dānair
gṛhair dāra-sutaiṣaṇām
ātma-lokaiṣaṇāṁ deva
kālena visṛjed budhaḥ
grāme tyaktaiṣaṇāḥ sarve
yayur dhīrās tapo-vanam

vitta—for wealth; *eṣaṇām*—the desire; *yajña*—by sacrifices; *dānaiḥ*—and by charity; *gṛhaiḥ*—by engagement in household affairs; *dāra*—for wife; *suta*—and children; *eṣaṇām*—the desire; *ātma*—for oneself; *loka*—for an exalted planet (in the next life); *eṣaṇām*—the desire; *deva*—O saintly Vasudeva; *kālena*—because of time; *visṛjet*—one should renounce; *budhaḥ*—who is intelligent; *grāme*—for household life; *tyakta*—who renounced; *eṣaṇāḥ*—their desires; *sarve*—all; *yayuḥ*—they went; *dhīrāḥ*—sober sages; *tapaḥ*—of austerities; *vanam*—to the forest.

TRANSLATION

An intelligent person should learn to renounce his desire for wealth by performing sacrifices and acts of charity. He should learn to renounce his desire for wife and children by experiencing family life. And he should learn to renounce his desire for promotion to a higher planet in his next life, O saintly Vasudeva, by studying the effects of time. Self-controlled sages who have thus renounced their attachment to household life go to the forest to perform austerities.

TEXT 39

ऋणैस्त्रिभिर्द्विजो जातो देवर्षिपितॄणां प्रभो ।
यज्ञाध्ययनपुत्रैस्तान्यनिस्तीर्य त्यजन् पतेत् ॥३९॥

ṛṇais tribhir dvijo jāto
devarṣi-pitṝṇāṁ prabho
yajñādhyayana-putrais tāny
anistīrya tyajan patet

ṛṇaiḥ—with debts; *tribhiḥ*—three; *dvi-jaḥ*—a member of the twice-born classes; *jātaḥ*—is born; *deva*—to the demigods; *ṛṣi*—sages; *pitṝṇām*—and forefathers; *prabho*—O master (Vasudeva); *yajña*—by sacrifice; *adhyayana*—study of scripture; *putraiḥ*—and (begetting) children; *tāni*—these (debts); *anistīrya*—not liquidating; *tyajan*—leaving (his body); *patet*—he falls down.

TRANSLATION

Dear Prabhu, a member of the twice-born classes is born with three kinds of debts—those owed to the demigods, to the sages and to his forefathers. If he leaves his body without first liquidating these debts by performing sacrifice, studying the scriptures and begetting children, he will fall down into a hellish condition.

PURPORT

Concerning the special obligations of a *brāhmaṇa,* the *śruti* states, *jāyamāno vai brāhmaṇas tribhir ṛṇavāñ jāyate brahmacaryeṇa ṛṣibhyo yajñena devebhyaḥ prajayā pitṛbhyaḥ:* "Whenever a *brāhmaṇa* takes birth, three debts are born along with him. He can pay his debt to the sages by celibacy, his debt to the demigods by sacrifice, and his debt to his forefathers by begetting children."

TEXT 40

त्वं त्वद्य मुक्तो द्वाभ्यां वै ऋषिपित्रोर्महामते ।
यज्ञैर्देवर्णमुन्मुच्य निरृणोऽशरणो भव ॥४०॥

tvaṁ tv adya mukto dvābhyāṁ vai
ṛṣi-pitror mahā-mate
yajñair devarṇam unmucya
nirṛṇo 'śaraṇo bhava

tvam—you; *tu*—but; *adya*—now; *muktaḥ*—freed; *dvābhyām*—from two (of the debts); *vai*—certainly; *ṛṣi*—to the sages; *pitroḥ*—and to the forefathers; *mahā-mate*—O generous one; *yajñaiḥ*—by Vedic sacrifices; *deva*—to the demigods; *ṛṇam*—from the debt; *unmucya*—relieving yourself; *nirṛṇaḥ*—without debt; *aśaraṇaḥ*—without material shelter; *bhava*—become.

TRANSLATION

But you, O magnanimous soul, are already free from two of your debts—those to the sages and the forefathers. Now absolve yourself of your debt to the demigods by executing Vedic sacrifices, and in this way free yourself completely of debt and renounce all material shelter.

TEXT 41

वसुदेव भवान्नूनं भक्त्या परमया हरिम् ।
जगतामीश्वरं प्रार्चः स यद्वां पुत्रतां गतः ॥४१॥

vasudeva bhavān nūnaṁ
bhaktyā paramayā harim
jagatām īśvaraṁ prārcaḥ
sa yad vāṁ putratāṁ gataḥ

vasudeva—O Vasudeva; *bhavān*—your good self; *nūnam*—doubtlessly; *bhaktyā*—with devotion; *paramayā*—supreme; *harim*—Lord Kṛṣṇa; *jagatām*—of all the worlds; *īśvaram*—the supreme controller; *prārcaḥ*—have worshiped thoroughly; *saḥ*—He; *yat*—inasmuch; *vām*—of both of you (Vasudeva and Devakī); *putratām*—the role of son; *gataḥ*—has taken on.

TRANSLATION

O Vasudeva, without doubt you must have previously worshiped Lord Hari, the master of all worlds. Both you and your wife must have perfectly worshiped Him with supreme devotion, since He has accepted the role of your son.

PURPORT

Śrīla Viśvanātha Cakravartī paraphrases the sages' mood as follows: "We have answered you, who questioned us in the manner of ordinary discourse, in the same ordinary way. In truth, however, since you are the eternally liberated father of the Supreme Lord, neither worldly customs nor the injunctions of scripture have any authority over you."

According to Śrīla Viśvanātha Cakravartī, the very name *Vasudeva* indicates that Vasudeva manifests brilliantly (*dīvyati*) the superexcellent wealth (*vasu*) of pure devotional service. In the Eleventh Canto Nārada will again meet with Vasudeva and at that time remind him,

devarṣi-bhūtāpta-nṛṇāṁ pitṝṇāṁ
na kiṅkaro nāyam ṛṇī ca rājan
sarvātmanā yaḥ śaraṇaṁ śaraṇyaṁ
gato mukundaṁ parihṛtya kartam

"O King, one who has given up all material duties and has taken full shelter of the lotus feet of Mukunda, who offers shelter to all, is not indebted to the demigods, great sages, ordinary living beings, relatives, friends, mankind or even his forefathers who have passed away. Since all such classes of living entities are part and parcel of the Supreme Lord, one who has surrendered to the Lord's service has no need to serve such persons separately." (*Bhāg.* 11.5.41)

TEXT 42

श्रीशुक उवाच
इति तद्वचनं श्रुत्वा वसुदेवो महामनाः ।
तानृषीनृत्विजो वव्रे मूर्ध्नानम्य प्रसाद्य च ॥४२॥

śrī-śuka uvāca
iti tad-vacanaṁ śrutvā
vasudevo mahā-manāḥ
tān ṛṣīn ṛtvijo vavre
mūrdhnānamya prasādya ca

śrī-śukaḥ uvāca—Śukadeva Gosvāmī said; *iti*—thus spoken; *tat*—their; *vacanam*—words; *śrutvā*—having heard; *vasudevaḥ*—Vasudeva; *mahā-manāḥ*—generous; *tān*—them; *ṛṣīn*—the sages; *ṛtvijaḥ*—as priests; *vavre*—chose; *mūrdhnā*—with his head; *ānamya*—bowing down; *prasādya*—gratifying them; *ca*—also.

TRANSLATION

Śukadeva Gosvāmī said: After hearing these statements of the sages, generous Vasudeva bowed his head to the ground and, praising them, requested them to become his priests.

TEXT 43

त एनमृषयो राजन् वृता धर्मेण धार्मिकम् ।
तस्मिन्नयाजयन् क्षेत्रे मखैरुत्तमकल्पकैः ॥४३॥

ta enam ṛṣayo rājan
vṛtā dharmeṇa dhārmikam
tasminn ayājayan kṣetre
makhair uttama-kalpakaiḥ

te—they; *enam*—him; *ṛṣayaḥ*—the sages; *rājan*—O King (Parīkṣit); *vṛtāḥ*—chosen; *dharmeṇa*—according to religious principles; *dhārmikam*—who was religious; *tasmin*—in that; *ayājayan*—they engaged in executing sacrifices; *kṣetre*—holy field (of Kurukṣetra); *makhaiḥ*—with fire rituals; *uttama*—superexcellent; *kalpakaiḥ*—whose arrangements.

TRANSLATION

Thus requested by him, O King, the sages engaged the pious Vasudeva in performing fire sacrifices at that holy place of Kurukṣetra according to strict religious principles and with most excellent ritual arrangements.

TEXTS 44–45

तद्दीक्षायां प्रवृत्तायां वृष्णयः पुष्करस्रजः ।
स्नाताः सुवाससो राजन् राजानः सुष्ठ्वलंकृताः ॥४४॥
तन्महिष्यश्च मुदिता निष्ककण्ठ्यः सुवाससः ।
दीक्षाशालामुपाजग्मुरालिप्ता वस्तुपाणयः ॥४५॥

tad-dīkṣāyāṁ pravṛttāyāṁ
vṛṣṇayaḥ puṣkara-srajaḥ

snātāḥ su-vāsaso rājan
rājānaḥ suṣṭhv-alaṅkṛtāḥ

tan-mahiṣyaś ca muditā
niṣka-kaṇṭhyaḥ su-vāsasaḥ
dīkṣā-śālām upājagmur
āliptā vastu-pāṇayaḥ

tat—of him (Vasudeva); *dīkṣāyām*—the initiation for the sacrifice; *pravṛttāyām*—when it was about to begin; *vṛṣṇayaḥ*—the Vṛṣṇis; *puṣkara*—of lotuses; *srajaḥ*—wearing garlands; *snātāḥ*—bathed; *su-vāsasaḥ*—well dressed; *rājan*—O King; *rājānaḥ*—(other) kings; *suṣṭhu*—elaborately; *alaṅkṛtāḥ*—ornamented; *tat*—their; *mahiṣyaḥ*—queens; *ca*—and; *muditāḥ*—joyful; *niṣka*—jeweled lockets; *kaṇṭhyaḥ*—on whose necks; *su-vāsasaḥ*—well dressed; *dīkṣā*—of initiation; *śālām*—the pavilion; *upājagmuḥ*—they approached; *āliptāḥ*—anointed; *vastu*—with auspicious items; *pāṇayaḥ*—in whose hands.

TRANSLATION

When Mahārāja Vasudeva was about to be initiated for the sacrifice, O King, the Vṛṣṇis came to the initiation pavilion after bathing and putting on fine clothes and garlands of lotuses. The other kings also came, elaborately ornamented, as well as all their joyful queens, who wore jeweled lockets around their necks and were also clad in fine garments. The royal wives were anointed with sandalwood paste and carried auspicious items for the worship.

TEXT 46

नेदुर्मृदंगपटहशंखभेर्यानकादयः ।
ननृतुर्नटनर्तक्यस्तुष्टुवुः सूतमागधाः ।
जगुः सुकण्ठ्यो गन्धर्व्यः संगीतं सहभर्तृकाः ॥४६॥

nedur mṛdaṅga-paṭaha-
śaṅkha-bhery-ānakādayaḥ
nanṛtur naṭa-nartakyas
tuṣṭuvuḥ sūta-māgadhāḥ

jaguḥ su-kaṇṭhyo gandharvyaḥ
saṅgītaṁ saha-bhartṛkāḥ

neduḥ—sounded; *mṛdaṅga-paṭaha*—*mṛdaṅga* and *paṭaha* drums; *śaṅkha*—conchshells; *bherī-ānaka*—*bherī* and *ānaka* drums; *ādayaḥ*—and other instruments; *nanṛtuḥ*—danced; *naṭa-nartakyaḥ*—male and female dancers; *tuṣṭuvuḥ*—recited praise; *sūta-māgadhāḥ*—*sūta* and *māgadha* bards; *jaguḥ*—sang; *su-kaṇṭhyaḥ*—sweet-voiced; *gandharvyaḥ*—female Gandharvas; *saṅgītam*—songs; *saha*—along with; *bhartṛkāḥ*—their husbands.

TRANSLATION

Mṛdaṅgas, paṭahas, conchshells, _bherīs, ānakas_ and other instruments resounded, male and female dancers danced, and _sūtas_ and _māgadhas_ recited glorifications. Sweet-voiced Gandharvīs sang, accompanied by their husbands.

TEXT 47

तमभ्यषिञ्चन् विधिवदक्तमभ्यक्तमृत्विजः ।
पत्नीभिरष्टादशभिः सोमराजमिवोडुभिः ॥४७॥

tam abhyasiñcan vidhi-vad
aktam abhyaktam ṛtvijaḥ
patnībhir aṣṭā-daśabhiḥ
soma-rājam ivoḍubhiḥ

tam—him; *abhyasiñcan*—they sprinkled with sacred water; *vidhi-vat*—according to scriptural rules; *aktam*—his eyes decorated with mascara; *abhyaktam*—his body smeared with newly-churned butter; *ṛtvijaḥ*—the priests; *patnībhiḥ*—along with his wives; *aṣṭā-daśabhiḥ*—eighteen; *soma-rājam*—the kingly; *iva*—as if; *uḍubhiḥ*—with stars.

TRANSLATION

After Vasudeva's eyes had been decorated with black cosmetic and his body smeared with fresh butter, the priests initiated him

according to scriptural rules by sprinkling him and his eighteen wives with sacred water. Encircled by his wives, he resembled the regal moon encircled by stars.

PURPORT

Devakī was Vasudeva's principal wife, but she had several co-wives, including her six sisters. This fact is recorded in the Ninth Canto of *Śrīmad-Bhāgavatam:*

devakaś cograsenaś ca
catvāro devakātmajāḥ

devavān upadevaś ca
sudevo devavardhanaḥ
teṣāṁ svasāraḥ saptāsan
dhṛtadevādayo nṛpa

śāntidevopadevā ca
śrīdevā devarakṣitā
sahadevā devakī ca
vasudeva uvāha tāḥ

"Āhuka had two sons, named Devaka and Ugrasena. Devaka had four sons, named Devavān, Upadeva, Sudeva and Devavardhana, and he also had seven daughters, named Śāntidevā, Upadevā, Śrīdevā, Devarakṣitā, Sahadevā, Devakī and Dhṛtadevā. Dhṛtadevā was the eldest. Vasudeva, the father of Kṛṣṇa, married all these sisters." (*Bhāg.* 9.24.21-23)

Some of Vasudeva's other wives are mentioned a few verses later:

pauravī rohiṇī bhadrā
madirā rocanā ilā
devakī-pramukhāś cāsan
patnya ānakadundubheḥ

"Devakī, Pauravī, Rohiṇī, Bhadrā, Madirā, Rocanā, Ilā and others were all wives of Ānankadundubhi [Vasudeva]. Among them all, Devakī was the chief." (*Bhāg.* 9.24.45)

TEXT 48

ताभिर्दुकूलवलयैर्हारनूपुरकुण्डलैः ।
स्वलंकृताभिर्विबभौ दीक्षितोऽजिनसंवृतः ॥४८॥

tābhir dukūla-valayair
hāra-nūpura-kuṇḍalaiḥ
sv-alaṅkṛtābhir vibabhau
dīkṣito 'jina-saṁvṛtaḥ

tābhiḥ—with them; *dukūla*—with silk *sārīs; valayaiḥ*—and bangles; *hāra*—wearing necklaces; *nūpura*—ankle bells; *kuṇḍalaiḥ*—and earrings; *su*—finely; *alaṅkṛtābhiḥ*—decorated; *vibabhau*—he shone brilliantly; *dīkṣitaḥ*—having been initiated; *ajina*—by a deerskin; *saṁvṛtaḥ*—enwrapped.

TRANSLATION

Vasudeva received initiation along with his wives, who wore silk *sārīs* and were adorned with bangles, necklaces, ankle bells and earrings. With his body wrapped in a deerskin, Vasudeva shone splendidly.

TEXT 49

तस्यर्त्विजो महाराज रत्नकौशेयवाससः ।
ससदस्या विरेजुस्ते यथा वृत्रहणोऽध्वरे ॥४९॥

tasyartvijo mahā-rāja
ratna-kauśeya-vāsasaḥ
sa-sadasyā virejus te
yathā vṛtra-haṇo 'dhvare

tasya—his; *ṛtvijaḥ*—priests; *mahā-rāja*—O great king (Parīkṣit); *ratna*—with jewels; *kauśeya*—silk; *vāsasaḥ*—and garments; *sa*—along with; *sadasyāḥ*—the officiating members of the assembly; *virejuḥ*—appeared effulgent; *te*—they; *yathā*—as if; *vṛtra-haṇaḥ*—of Lord Indra, the killer of Vṛtra; *adhvare*—in the sacrifice.

TRANSLATION

My dear Mahārāja Parīkṣit, Vasudeva's priests and the officiating members of the assembly, dressed in silk *dhotīs* and jeweled ornaments, looked so effulgent that they seemed to be standing in the sacrificial arena of Indra, the killer of Vṛtra.

TEXT 50

तदा रामश्च कृष्णश्च स्वैः स्वैर्बन्धुभिरन्वितौ ।
रेजतुः स्वसुतैर्दारैर्जीवेशौ स्वविभूतिभिः ॥५०॥

tadā rāmaś ca kṛṣṇaś ca
svaiḥ svair bandhubhir anvitau
rejatuḥ sva-sutair dārair
jīveśau sva-vibhūtibhiḥ

tadā—at that time; *rāmaḥ*—Lord Balarāma; *ca*—and; *kṛṣṇaḥ*—Lord Kṛṣṇa; *ca*—also; *svaiḥ svaiḥ*—each by His own; *bandhubhiḥ*—relatives; *anvitau*—accompanied; *rejatuḥ*—appeared brilliant; *sva*—with His own; *sutaiḥ*—sons; *dāraiḥ*—and wives; *jīva*—of all living entities; *īśau*—the two Lords; *sva-vibhūtibhiḥ*—with the expansions of Their own opulences.

TRANSLATION

At that time Balarāma and Kṛṣṇa, the Lords of all living entities, shone forth with great majesty in the company of Their respective sons, wives and other family members, who were expansions of Their opulences.

TEXT 51

ईजेऽनुयज्ञं विधिना अग्निहोत्रादिलक्षणैः ।
प्राकृतैर्वैकृतैर्यज्ञैर्द्रव्यज्ञानक्रियेश्वरम् ॥५१॥

ije 'nu-yajñaṁ vidhinā
agni-hotrādi-lakṣaṇaiḥ

prākṛtair vaikṛtair yajñair
dravya-jñāna-kriyeśvaram

ije—he worshiped; *anu-yajñam*—with each kind of sacrifice; *vidhinā*—by the proper regulations; *agni-hotra*—by offering oblations into the sacred fire; *ādi*—and so on; *lakṣaṇaiḥ*—characterized; *prākṛtaiḥ*—unmodified, completely specified by *śruti* injunctions; *vaikṛtaiḥ*—modified, adjusted according to the indications of other sources; *yajñaiḥ*—with sacrifices; *dravya*—of the sacrificial paraphernalia; *jñāna*—of the knowledge of *mantras; kriyā*—and of the rituals; *īśvaram*—the Lord.

TRANSLATION

Performing various kinds of Vedic sacrifice according to the proper regulations, Vasudeva worshiped the Lord of all sacrificial paraphernalia, *mantras* and rituals. He executed both primary and secondary sacrifices, offering oblations to the sacred fire and carrying out other aspects of sacrificial worship.

PURPORT

There are numerous kinds of Vedic fire sacrifice, each of which involves several elaborate rituals. The *Brāhmaṇa* portion of the Vedic *śruti* specifies the complete step-by-step procedure of only a few prototype sacrifices, such as the Jyotiṣṭoma and Darśa-pūrṇamāsa. These are called the *prākṛta*, or original, *yajñas;* the details of other *yajñas* must be extrapolated from the patterns of these *prākṛta* injunctions according to the strict rules of the *Mīmāṁsā-śāstra*. Since other *yajñas* are thus known by derivation from the prototype sacrifices, they are called *vaikṛta*, or "changed."

TEXT 52

अथर्त्विग्भ्योऽददात्काले यथाम्नातं स दक्षिणाः ।
स्वलंकृतेभ्योऽलंकृत्य गोभूकन्या महाधनाः ॥५२॥

athartvigbhyo 'dadāt kāle
yathāmnātaṁ sa dakṣiṇāḥ

sv-alaṅkṛtebhyo 'laṅkṛtya
go-bhū-kanyā mahā-dhanāḥ

atha—then; *ṛtvigbhyaḥ*—to the priests; *adadāt*—gave; *kāle*—at the appropriate time; *yathā-āmnātam*—as stipulated in the scriptures; *saḥ*—he; *dakṣiṇāḥ*—gifts of thanks; *su-alaṅkṛtebhyaḥ*—who were richly adorned; *alaṅkṛtya*—decorating them even more elaborately; *go*—cows; *bhū*—land; *kanyāḥ*—and marriageable girls; *mahā*—greatly; *dhanāḥ*—valuable.

TRANSLATION

Then, at the appropriate time and according to scripture, Vasudeva remunerated the priests by decorating them with precious ornaments, though they were already richly adorned, and offering them valuable gifts of cows, land and marriageable girls.

TEXT 53

पत्नीसंयाजावभृथ्यैश्चरित्वा ते महर्षयः ।
सस्नू रामह्रदे विप्रा यजमानपुरःसराः ॥५३॥

patnī-saṁyājāvabhṛthyaiś
caritvā te maharṣayaḥ
sasnū rāma-hrade viprā
yajamāna-puraḥ-sarāḥ

patnī-saṁyāja—the ritual in which the sponsor of the sacrifice offers oblations together with his wife; *avabhṛthyaiḥ*—and the final rituals, known as *avabhṛthya; caritvā*—having executed; *te*—they; *mahā-ṛṣayaḥ*—the great sages; *sasnuḥ*—bathed; *rāma*—of Lord Paraśurāma; *hrade*—in the lake; *viprāḥ*—*brāhmaṇas; yajamāna*—the sponsor of the sacrifice (Vasudeva); *puraḥ-sarāḥ*—placing in front.

TRANSLATION

After supervising the *patnī-saṁyāja* and *avabhṛthya* rituals, the great *brāhmaṇa* sages bathed in Lord Paraśurāma's lake with the sponsor of the sacrifice, Vasudeva, who led them.

TEXT 54

स्नातोऽलंकारवासांसि वन्दिभ्योऽदात्तथा स्त्रियः ।
ततः स्वलंकृतो वर्णानाश्वभ्योऽन्नेन पूजयत् ॥५४॥

snāto 'laṅkāra-vāsāṁsi
vandibhyo 'dāt tathā striyaḥ
tataḥ sv-alaṅkṛto varṇān
ā-śvabhyo 'nnena pūjayat

snātaḥ—bathed; *alaṅkāra*—jewelry; *vāsāṁsi*—and clothing; *vandibhyaḥ*—to the bards; *adāt*—gave; *tathā*—also; *striyaḥ*—the women; *tataḥ*—then; *su-alaṅkṛtaḥ*—well ornamented; *varṇān*—all classes of people; *ā*—extending; *śvabhyaḥ*—to the dogs; *annena*—with food; *pūjayat*—he honored.

TRANSLATION

His sacred bath complete, Vasudeva joined with his wives in giving the jewelry and clothes they had been wearing to the professional reciters. Vasudeva then put on new garments, after which he honored all classes of people by feeding everyone, even the dogs.

TEXTS 55–56

बन्धून् सदारान् ससुतान् पारिबर्हेण भूयसा ।
विदर्भकोशलकुरून् काशिकेकयसृञ्जयान् ॥५५॥
सदस्यर्त्विक्सुरगणान्नृभूतपितृचारणान् ।
श्रीनिकेतमनुज्ञाप्य शंसन्तः प्रययुः क्रतुम् ॥५६॥

bandhūn sa-dārān sa-sutān
pāribarheṇa bhūyasā
vidarbha-kośala-kurūn
kāśi-kekaya-sṛñjayān

sadasyartvik-sura-gaṇān
nṛ-bhūta-pitṛ-cāraṇān

śrī-niketam anujñāpya
śaṁsantaḥ prayayuḥ kratum

bandhūn—his relatives; *sa-dārān*—with their wives; *sa-sutān*—with their children; *pāribarheṇa*—with gifts; *bhūyasā*—opulent; *vidarbha-kośala-kurūn*—the leaders of the Vidarbha, Kośala and Kuru clans; *kāśi-kekaya-sṛñjayān*—also the Kāśis, Kekayas and Sṛñjayas; *sadasya*—the officials of the sacrificial assembly; *ṛtvik*—the priests; *sura-gaṇān*—the various classes of demigods; *nṛ*—the humans; *bhūta*—ghostly spirits; *pitṛ*—forefathers; *cāraṇān*—and Cāraṇas, members of a class of minor demigods; *śrī-niketam*—from Lord Kṛṣṇa, the abode of the goddess of fortune; *anujñāpya*—taking leave; *śaṁsantaḥ*—praising; *prayayuḥ*—they departed; *kratum*—the sacrificial performance.

TRANSLATION

With opulent gifts he honored his relatives, including all their wives and children; the royalty of the Vidarbha, Kośala, Kuru, Kāśī, Kekaya and Sṛñjaya kingdoms; the officiating members of the assembly; and also the priests, witnessing demigods, humans, spirits, forefathers and Cāraṇas. Then, taking permission from Lord Kṛṣṇa, the shelter of the goddess of fortune, the various guests departed as they all chanted the glories of Vasudeva's sacrifice.

TEXTS 57–58

धृतराष्ट्रोऽनुजः पार्था भीष्मो द्रोणः पृथा यमौ ।
नारदो भगवान् व्यासः सुहृत्सम्बन्धिबान्धवाः ॥५७॥
बन्धून् परिष्वज्य यदून् सौहृदाक्लिन्नचेतसः ।
ययुर्विरहकृच्छ्रेण स्वदेशांश्चापरे जनाः ॥५८॥

dhṛtarāṣṭro 'nujaḥ pārthā
bhīṣmo droṇaḥ pṛthā yamau
nārado bhagavān vyāsaḥ
suhṛt-sambandhi-bāndhavāḥ

bandhūn pariṣvajya yadūn
sauhṛdāklinna-cetasaḥ
yayur viraha-kṛcchreṇa
sva-deśāṁś cāpare janāḥ

dhṛtarāṣṭraḥ—Dhṛtarāṣṭra; *anujaḥ*—(Dhṛtarāṣṭra's) younger brother (Vidura); *pārthāḥ*—the sons of Pṛthā (Yudhiṣṭhira, Bhīma and Arjuna); *bhīṣmaḥ*—Bhīṣma; *droṇaḥ*—Droṇa; *pṛthā*—Kuntī; *yamau*—the twins (Nakula and Sahadeva); *nāradaḥ*—Nārada; *bhagavān vyāsaḥ*—the Personality of Godhead Vyāsadeva; *suhṛt*—friends; *sambandhi*—immediate family members; *bāndhavāḥ*—and other relatives; *bandhūn*—their relatives and friends; *pariṣvajya*—embracing; *yadūn*—the Yadus; *sauhṛda*—out of feelings of friendship; *āklinna*—melting; *cetasaḥ*—their hearts; *yayuḥ*—they went; *viraha*—because of becoming separated; *kṛcchreṇa*—with difficulty; *sva*—to their respective; *deśān*—kingdoms; *ca*—also; *apare*—the other; *janāḥ*—people.

TRANSLATION

The Yadus were all embraced by their friends, close family members and other relatives, including Dhṛtarāṣṭra and his younger brother, Vidura; Pṛthā and her sons; Bhīṣma; Droṇa; the twins Nakula and Sahadeva; Nārada; and Vedavyāsa, the Personality of Godhead. Their hearts melting with affection, these and the other guests left for their kingdoms, their progress slowed by the pain of separation.

TEXT 59

नन्दस्तु सह गोपालैर्बृहत्या पूजयार्चितः ।
कृष्णरामोग्रसेनाद्यैर्न्यवात्सीद् बन्धुवत्सलः ॥५९॥

nandas tu saha gopālair
bṛhatyā pūjayārcitaḥ
kṛṣṇa-rāmograsenādyair
nyavātsīd bandhu-vatsalaḥ

nandaḥ—Nanda Mahārāja; *tu*—and; *saha*—together with; *gopālaiḥ*—the cowherds; *bṛhatyā*—especially opulent; *pūjayā*—with worship;

arcitaḥ—honored; *kṛṣṇa-rāma-ugrasena-ādyaiḥ*—by Kṛṣṇa, Balarāma, Ugrasena and the others; *nyavātsīt*—stayed; *bandhu*—to his relatives; *vatsalaḥ*—affectionate.

TRANSLATION

Nanda Mahārāja showed his affection for his relatives, the Yadus, by remaining with them a little longer, together with his cowherds. During his stay, Kṛṣṇa, Balarāma, Ugrasena and the others honored him with especially opulent worship.

TEXT 60

वसुदेवोऽञ्जसोत्तीर्य मनोरथमहार्णवम् ।
सुहृद्वृतः प्रीतमना नन्दमाह करे स्पृशन् ॥६०॥

vasudevo 'ñjasottīrya
manoratha-mahārṇavam
suhṛd-vṛtaḥ prīta-manā
nandam āha kare spṛśan

vasudevaḥ—Vasudeva; *añjasā*—easily; *uttīrya*—having crossed over; *manaḥ-ratha*—of his desires (to perform Vedic sacrifices); *mahā*—great; *arṇavam*—the ocean; *suhṛt*—by his well-wishers; *vṛtaḥ*—surrounded; *prīta*—pleased; *manāḥ*—in his mind; *nandam*—to Nanda; *āha*—he spoke; *kare*—his hand; *spṛśan*—touching.

TRANSLATION

Having so easily crossed over the vast ocean of his ambition, Vasudeva felt fully satisfied. In the company of his many well-wishers, he took Nanda by the hand and addressed him as follows.

TEXT 61

श्रीवसुदेव उवाच

भ्रातरीशकृतः पाशो नृणां यः स्नेहसंज्ञितः ।
तं दुस्त्यजमहं मन्ये शूराणामपि योगिनाम् ॥६१॥

śrī-vasudeva uvāca
bhrātar īśa-kṛtaḥ pāśo
nṛṇāṁ yaḥ sneha-saṁjñitaḥ
taṁ dustyajam ahaṁ manye
śūrāṇām api yoginām

śrī-vasudevaḥ uvāca—Śrī Vasudeva said; *bhrātaḥ*—O brother; *īśa*—by the Supreme Lord; *kṛtaḥ*—made; *pāśaḥ*—the noose; *nṛṇām*—of men; *yaḥ*—which; *sneha*—affection; *saṁjñitaḥ*—named; *tam*—it; *dustyajam*—difficult to free oneself from; *aham*—I; *manye*—think; *śūrāṇām*—for heroes; *api*—even; *yoginām*—and for *yogīs*.

TRANSLATION

Śrī Vasudeva said: My dear brother, God Himself has tied the knot called affection, which tightly binds human beings together. It seems to me that even great heroes and mystics find it very difficult to free themselves from it.

PURPORT

Heroic leaders of men try to transcend their petty attachments by force of will, while introspective *yogīs* pursue knowledge for the same purpose. But the Lord's illusory energy, Māyā, is much stronger than any conditioned soul. Only by taking shelter of Kṛṣṇa, the Lord of Māyā, can one become immune to her influence.

TEXT 62

अस्मास्वप्रतिकल्पेयं यत्कृताज्ञेषु सत्तमैः ।
मैत्र्यर्पिताफला चापि न निवर्तेत कर्हिचित् ॥६२॥

asmāsv apratikalpeyaṁ
yat kṛtājñeṣu sattamaiḥ
maitry arpitāphalā cāpi
na nivarteta karhicit

asmāsu—to us; *apratikalpā*—incomparable; *iyam*—this; *yat*—since; *kṛta-ajñeṣu*—who are oblivious of the mercy that has been shown them;

sat-tamaiḥ—by those who are most saintly; *maitrī*—friendship; *arpitā*—offered; *aphalā*—unreciprocated; *ca api*—even though; *na nivarteta*—it does not cease; *karhicit*—ever.

TRANSLATION

Indeed, the Supreme Lord must have created the bonds of affection, for such exalted saints as you have never stopped showing matchless friendship toward us ingrates, although it has never been properly reciprocated.

TEXT 63

प्रागकल्पाच्च कुशलं भ्रातर्वो नाचराम हि ।
अधुना श्रीमदान्धाक्षा न पश्यामः पुरः सतः ॥६३॥

prāg akalpāc ca kuśalaṁ
bhrātar vo nācarāma hi
adhunā śrī-madāndhākṣā
na paśyāmaḥ puraḥ sataḥ

prāk—previously; *akalpāt*—because of incapacity; *ca*—and; *kuśalam*—welfare; *bhrātaḥ*—O brother; *vaḥ*—your; *na ācarāma*—we did not carry out; *hi*—indeed; *adhunā*—now; *śrī*—with opulence; *mada*—due to the intoxication; *andha*—blinded; *akṣāḥ*—whose eyes; *na paśyāmaḥ*—we fail to see; *puraḥ*—in front; *sataḥ*—present.

TRANSLATION

Previously, dear brother, we did nothing to benefit you because we were unable to, yet even now that you are present before us, our eyes are so blinded by the intoxication of material good fortune that we continue to ignore you.

PURPORT

While living under the tyranny of Kaṁsa, Vasudeva was unable to do anything to help Nanda and his subjects defend themselves against the many demons sent from Mathurā to kill Kṛṣṇa and Balarāma.

TEXT 64

मा राज्यश्रीरभूत्पुंसः श्रेयस्कामस्य मानद ।
स्वजनानुत बन्धून् वा न पश्यति ययान्धदृक् ॥६४॥

mā rājya-śrīr abhūt puṁsaḥ
śreyas-kāmasya māna-da
sva-janān uta bandhūn vā
na paśyati yayāndha-dṛk

mā—may not; *rājya*—royal; *śrīḥ*—fortune; *abhūt*—arise; *puṁsaḥ*—for a person; *śreyaḥ*—the real benefit of life; *kāmasya*—who desires; *māna-da*—O giver of respect; *sva-janān*—his kinsmen; *uta*—even; *bandhūn*—his friends; *vā*—or; *na paśyati*—he does not see; *yayā*—by which (opulence); *andha*—blinded; *dṛk*—whose vision.

TRANSLATION

O most respectful one, may a person who wants the highest benefit in life never gain kingly opulence, for it leaves him blind to the needs of his own family and friends.

PURPORT

It is, of course, out of his deep humility that Vasudeva is berating himself, but his condemnation of opulence is in general valid. Earlier in this canto Nārada Muni delivered a stinging criticism of Nalakūvara and Maṇigrīva, two wealthy sons of Kuvera, the treasurer of heaven. Intoxicated by both pride and liquor, the two had failed to offer proper respects to Nārada when he happened upon them as they sported naked in the Mandākinī River with some young women. Seeing them in their shameful condition, Nārada said,

na hy anyo juṣato joṣyān
buddhi-bhraṁśo rajo-guṇaḥ
śrī-madād ābhijātyādir
yatra strī dyūtam āsavaḥ

"Among all the attractions of material enjoyment, the attraction of riches bewilders one's intelligence more than having beautiful bodily features, taking birth in an aristocratic family, and being learned. When one is uneducated but falsely puffed up by wealth, the result is that one engages his wealth in enjoying wine, women and gambling." (*Bhāg.* 10.10.8)

TEXT 65

श्रीशुक उवाच
एवं सौहृदशैथिल्यचित्त आनकदुन्दुभिः ।
रुरोद तत्कृतां मैत्रीं स्मरन्नश्रुविलोचनः ॥६५॥

śrī-śuka uvāca
evaṁ sauhṛda-śaithilya-
citta ānakadundubhiḥ
ruroda tat-kṛtāṁ maitrīṁ
smarann aśru-vilocanaḥ

śrī-śukaḥ uvāca—Śrī Śukadeva Gosvāmī said; *evam*—thus; *sauhṛda*—by intimate sympathy; *śaithilya*—made soft; *cittaḥ*—whose heart; *ānakadundubhiḥ*—Vasudeva; *ruroda*—cried; *tat*—by him (Nanda); *kṛtām*—done; *maitrīm*—the acts of friendship; *smaran*—remembering; *aśru*—tears; *vilocanaḥ*—in whose eyes.

TRANSLATION

Śrī Śukadeva Gosvāmī said: His heart softened by feelings of intimate sympathy, Vasudeva wept. His eyes brimmed with tears as he remembered the friendship Nanda had shown him.

TEXT 66

नन्दस्तु सख्युः प्रियकृत्प्रेम्णा गोविन्दरामयोः ।
अद्य श्व इति मासांस्त्रीन् यदुभिर्मानितोऽवसत् ॥६६॥

nandas tu sakhyuḥ priya-kṛt
premṇā govinda-rāmayoḥ

adya śva iti māsāṁs trīn
yadubhir mānito 'vasat

nandaḥ—Nanda; *tu*—and; *sakhyuḥ*—to his friend; *priya*—affection; *kṛt*—who showed; *premṇā*—out of his love; *govinda-rāmayoḥ*—for Kṛṣṇa and Balarāma; *adya*—(I will go later) today; *śvaḥ*—(I will go) tomorrow; *iti*—thus saying; *māsān*—months; *trīn*—three; *yadubhiḥ*—by the Yadus; *mānitaḥ*—honored; *avasat*—he remained.

TRANSLATION

And on his part, Nanda was also full of affection for his friend Vasudeva. Thus during the following days Nanda would repeatedly announce, "I will be leaving later today" and "I will be leaving tomorrow." But out of love for Kṛṣṇa and Balarāma he remained there for three more months, honored by all the Yadus.

PURPORT

After settling that he would leave first thing in the morning, Nanda would then decide, "I'll go later today," and then, when the afternoon came, he would say, "I'll just stay until tomorrow." Śrīla Viśvanātha Cakravartī suggests one possible reason for his procrastination: Nanda secretly intended to bring Kṛṣṇa back with him to Vraja but did not want to break Vasudeva's heart. Thus his indecision continued for three months.

TEXTS 67–68

ततः कामैः पूर्यमाणः सव्रजः सहबान्धवः ।
परार्ध्याभरणक्षौमनानानर्घ्यपरिच्छदैः ॥६७॥
वसुदेवोग्रसेनाभ्यां कृष्णोद्धवबलादिभिः ।
दत्तमादाय पारिबर्हं यापितो यदुभिर्ययौ ॥६८॥

tataḥ kāmaiḥ pūryamāṇaḥ
sa-vrajaḥ saha-bāndhavaḥ
parārdhyābharaṇa-kṣauma-
nānānarghya-paricchadaiḥ

vasudevograsenābhyāṁ
kṛṣṇoddhava-balādibhiḥ
dattam ādāya pāribarhaṁ
yāpito yadubhir yayau

tataḥ—then; *kāmaiḥ*—with desirable objects; *pūryamāṇaḥ*—satiated; *sa-vrajaḥ*—with the people of Vraja; *saha-bāndhavaḥ*—with his family members; *para*—extremely; *ardhya*—valuable; *ābharaṇa*—with ornaments; *kṣauma*—fine linen; *nānā*—various; *anarghya*—priceless; *paricchadaiḥ*—and household furnishings; *vasudeva-ugrasenābhyām*—by Vasudeva and Ugrasena; *kṛṣṇa-uddhava-bala-ādibhiḥ*—and by Kṛṣṇa, Uddhava, Balarāma and others; *dattam*—given; *ādāya*—taking; *pāribarham*—the gifts; *yāpitaḥ*—seen off; *yadubhiḥ*—by the Yadus; *yayau*—he departed.

TRANSLATION

Then, after Vasudeva, Ugrasena, Kṛṣṇa, Uddhava, Balarāma and others had fulfilled his desires and presented him with precious ornaments, fine linen and varieties of priceless household furnishings, Nanda Mahārāja accepted all these gifts and took his leave. Seen off by all the Yadus, he departed with his family members and the residents of Vraja.

PURPORT

According to Śrīla Viśvanātha Cakravartī, at the end of the three months Mahārāja Nanda approached Kṛṣṇa and told Him, "My dear son, for one drop of perspiration from Your divine face I am ready to give up countless lives. Let us leave now for Vraja; I cannot spend any more time here." Then he went to Vasudeva and told him, "My dear friend, please send Kṛṣṇa to Vraja," and of King Ugrasena he requested, "Please order my friend to do this. If you refuse, I will have to drown myself here in Lord Paraśurāma's lake. Just watch, if you do not believe me! We people of Vraja came to this holy place not to gain some piety on the occasion of the solar eclipse, but to get Kṛṣṇa back or die." Hearing these desperate words from Nanda, Vasudeva and the others tried to pacify him with valuable gifts.

Well-versed in the arts of diplomacy, Vasudeva consulted with his most trustworthy advisors and then satisfied Śrī Nanda by telling him, "My dearest friend, O King of Vraja, it is of course true that none of you can live without Kṛṣṇa. And how can we allow you to kill yourselves? Therefore, by all means I must send Kṛṣṇa back to Vraja. I will do so right after we accompany Him and His relatives and friends—among them many helpless women—back to Dvārakā. Then, the very next day, without trying to obstruct Him in any way, I will let Him leave for Vraja at an auspicious time of the day. This I swear to you a thousand times over. After all, how can we who came here with Kṛṣṇa go home without Him? What will people say about us? You are a great scholar in all matters, so please forgive me for making this request of you."

Next Ugrasena addressed Nanda Mahārāja: "My dear master of Vraja, I bear witness to Vasudeva's statement and take this solemn vow: I will send Kṛṣṇa back to Vraja even if I have to do it by force."

Then Lord Kṛṣṇa, joined by Uddhava and Balarāma, spoke to Nanda in private. He said, "Dear father, if I go directly to Vraja today, leaving aside all these Vṛṣṇis, they will die from the pain of separation from Me. Then many thousands of enemies more powerful than even Keśī and Ariṣṭa will come to annihilate all these kings.

"Since I am omniscient, I know what is inevitably going to happen to Me. Listen and I will describe it to you. After returning to Dvārakā, I will receive an invitation from Yudhiṣṭhira and will go to Indraprastha to participate in his Rājasūya sacrifice. There I will kill Śiśupāla, after which I will again return to Dvārakā and kill Śālva. Next I will travel to a place just south of Mathurā to save you by killing Dantavakra. I will then go back to Vraja, see all My old friends and again sit in your lap with great pleasure. Indeed, with great happiness I will spend the rest of My life with you. God has written this fate on My forehead, and it has been written on your foreheads that until the day I return you must tolerate separation from Me. Neither of our destinies can possibly be changed, so please find the courage to leave Me here for now and go home to Vraja.

"And if, in the meantime, you, My dear parents, and you, My beloved friends, are distressed by the unavoidable fate written on our foreheads, then whenever you wish to feed Me some delicacy or play some game with Me or simply see Me, just close your eyes and I will appear before you to turn your torment into sky-flowers and fulfill all your desires. I promise you this, and the young friends of Mine whose lives I saved in a forest fire can vouch for it."

Convinced by all these arguments that his son's happiness was of prime importance, Nanda accepted the gifts offered him and took his leave, accompanied by the Yadus' large army.

TEXT 69

नन्दो गोपाश्च गोप्यश्च गोविन्दचरणाम्बुजे ।
मनः क्षिप्तं पुनर्हर्तुमनीशा मथुरां ययुः ॥६९॥

nando gopāś ca gopyaś ca
govinda-caraṇāmbuje
manaḥ kṣiptaṁ punar hartum
anīśā mathurāṁ yayuḥ

nandaḥ—Nanda; *gopāḥ*—the cowherd men; *ca*—and; *gopyaḥ*—the cowherd women; *ca*—also; *govinda*—of Kṛṣṇa; *caraṇa-ambuje*—at the lotus feet; *manaḥ*—their minds; *kṣiptam*—cast; *punaḥ*—again; *hartum*—to remove; *anīśāḥ*—incapable; *mathurām*—to Mathurā; *yayuḥ*—they went.

TRANSLATION

Unable to withdraw their minds from Lord Govinda's lotus feet, where they had surrendered them, Nanda and the cowherd men and women returned to Mathurā.

TEXT 70

बन्धुषु प्रतियातेषु वृष्णयः कृष्णदेवताः ।
वीक्ष्य प्रावृषमासन्नाद् ययुर्द्वारवतीं पुनः ॥७०॥

bandhuṣu pratiyāteṣu
vṛṣṇayaḥ kṛṣṇa-devatāḥ
vīkṣya prāvṛṣam āsannād
yayur dvāravatīṁ punaḥ

bandhuṣu—their relatives; *pratiyāteṣu*—having departed; *vṛṣṇayaḥ*—the Vṛṣṇis; *kṛṣṇa-devatāḥ*—whose worshipable Deity was Kṛṣṇa;

vīkṣya—seeing; *prāvṛṣam*—the rainy season; *āsannāt*—imminent; *yayuḥ*—went; *dvāravatīm*—to Dvārakā; *punaḥ*—again.

TRANSLATION

Their relatives having thus departed, and seeing that the rainy season was approaching, the Vṛṣṇis, whose only Lord was Kṛṣṇa, went back to Dvārakā.

TEXT 71

जनेभ्यः कथयां चक्रुर्यदुदेवमहोत्सवम् ।
यदासीत्तीर्थयात्रायां सुहृत्सन्दर्शनादिकम् ॥७१॥

janebhyaḥ kathayāṁ cakrur
yadu-deva-mahotsavam
yad āsīt tīrtha-yātrāyāṁ
suhṛt-sandarśanādikam

janebhyaḥ—to the people; *kathayām cakruḥ*—they related; *yadu-deva*—of the lord of the Yadus, Vasudeva; *mahā-utsavam*—the great festivity; *yat*—what; *āsīt*—occurred; *tīrtha-yātrāyām*—during their pilgrimage; *suhṛt*—of their well-wishing friends; *sandarśana*—the seeing; *ādikam*—and so on.

TRANSLATION

They told the people of the city about the festive sacrifices performed by Vasudeva, lord of the Yadus, and about everything else that had happened during their pilgrimage, especially how they had met with all their loved ones.

Thus end the purports of the humble servants of His Divine Grace A. C. Bhaktivedanta Swami Prabhupāda to the Tenth Canto, Eighty-fourth Chapter, of the Śrīmad-Bhāgavatam, *entitled "The Sages' Teachings at Kurukṣetra."*

CHAPTER EIGHTY-FIVE

Lord Kṛṣṇa Instructs Vasudeva and Retrieves Devakī's Sons

This chapter relates how Lord Kṛṣṇa imparted divine knowledge to His father and, along with Lord Balarāma, retrieved His mother's dead sons.

Having heard the visiting sages glorify Kṛṣṇa, Vasudeva ceased to regard Him and Balarāma as his sons and began praising Their omnipotence, omnipresence and omniscience as the Supreme Personality of Godhead. After glorifying his sons, Vasudeva fell at Lord Kṛṣṇa's lotus feet and begged Him to drive away the conception that the Lord was his son. Instead, Lord Kṛṣṇa restored that conception by instructing Vasudeva in the science of Godhead, and upon hearing these instructions, Vasudeva became peaceful and free of doubt.

Then mother Devakī praised Kṛṣṇa and Balarāma, reminding Them how They had retrieved the dead son of Their spiritual master. She said, "Please fulfill my desire in the same way. Please bring back my sons who were killed by Kaṁsa so I may see them once again." Entreated in this way by Their mother, the two Lords went to the subterranean planet of Sutala, where They approached Bali Mahārāja. King Bali greeted Them respectfully, offering Them seats of honor, worshiping Them and reciting prayers. Kṛṣṇa and Balarāma then requested Bali to return Devakī's dead sons. The Lords received the boys from Bali and returned them to Devakī, who felt such a surge of affection for them that milk began spontaneously flowing from her breasts. Overjoyed, Devakī fed the children her breast-milk, and by drinking the remnants of milk once drunk by Lord Kṛṣṇa Himself, they regained their original forms as demigods and went back to heaven.

TEXT 1

श्रीबादरायणिरुवाच

अथैकदात्मजौ प्राप्तौ कृतपादाभिवन्दनौ ।
वसुदेवोऽभिनन्द्याह प्रीत्या संकर्षणाच्युतौ ॥१॥

śrī-bādarāyaṇir uvāca
athaikadātmajau prāptau
kṛta-pādābhivandanau
vasudevo 'bhinandyāha
prītyā saṅkarṣaṇācyutau

śrī-bādarāyaṇiḥ uvāca—Śrī Bādarāyaṇi (Śukadeva Gosvāmī) said; *atha*—then; *ekadā*—one day; *ātmajau*—his two sons; *prāptau*—came to him; *kṛta*—having done; *pāda*—of his feet; *abhivandanau*—honoring; *vasudevaḥ*—Vasudeva; *abhinandya*—greeting Them; *āha*—said; *prītyā*—affectionately; *saṅkarṣaṇa-acyutau*—to Balarāma and Kṛṣṇa.

TRANSLATION

Śrī Bādarāyaṇi said: One day the two sons of Vasudeva—Saṅkarṣaṇa and Acyuta—came to pay him respects, bowing down at his feet. Vasudeva greeted Them with great affection and spoke to Them.

TEXT 2

मुनीनां स वचः श्रुत्वा पुत्रयोर्धामसूचकम् ।
तद्वीर्यैर्जातविश्रम्भः परिभाष्याभ्यभाषत ॥२॥

munīnāṁ sa vacaḥ śrutvā
putrayor dhāma-sūcakam
tad-vīryair jāta-viśrambhaḥ
paribhāṣyābhyabhāṣata

munīnām—of the sages; *saḥ*—he; *vacaḥ*—the words; *śrutvā*—having heard; *putrayoḥ*—of his two sons; *dhāma*—the power; *sūcakam*—which referred to; *tat*—Their; *vīryaiḥ*—because of the valorous deeds; *jāta*—having developed; *viśrambhaḥ*—conviction; *paribhāṣya*—addressing Them by name; *abhyabhāṣata*—he told Them.

TRANSLATION

Having heard the great sages' words concerning the power of his two sons, and having seen Their valorous deeds, Vasudeva

became convinced of Their divinity. Thus, addressing Them by name, he spoke to Them as follows.

TEXT 3

कृष्ण कृष्ण महायोगिन् संकर्षण सनातन ।
जाने वामस्य यत्साक्षात्प्रधानपुरुषौ परौ ॥३॥

kṛṣṇa kṛṣṇa mahā-yogin
saṅkarṣaṇa sanātana
jāne vām asya yat sākṣāt
pradhāna-puruṣau parau

kṛṣṇa kṛṣṇa—O Kṛṣṇa, Kṛṣṇa; *mahā-yogin*—O greatest *yogī; saṅkarṣaṇa*—O Balarāma; *sanātana*—eternal; *jāne*—I know; *vām*—You two; *asya*—of this (universe); *yat*—which; *sākṣāt*—directly; *pradhāna*—the creative principle of nature; *puruṣau*—and the creating Personality of Godhead; *parau*—supreme.

TRANSLATION

[Vasudeva said:] O Kṛṣṇa, Kṛṣṇa, best of *yogīs*, O eternal Saṅkarṣaṇa! I know that You two are personally the source of universal creation and the ingredients of creation as well.

PURPORT

As taught in the Sāṅkhya doctrine of Lord Kapiladeva, *pradhāna* is the creative energy of the *puruṣa*, the Supreme Person. Thus, of these two principles, the *pradhāna* is the predominated energy, female, incapable of independent action, while the *puruṣa* is the absolutely independent, primeval creator and enjoyer. Neither Kṛṣṇa nor His brother Balarāma belong to the category of subordinate energy; rather, both of Them together are the original *puruṣa*, who is always joined by His manifold potencies of pleasure, knowledge and creative emanation.

TEXT 4

यत्र येन यतो यस्य यस्मै यद्यद्यथा यदा ।
स्यादिदं भगवान् साक्षात्प्रधानपुरुषेश्वरः ॥४॥

yatra yena yato yasya
yasmai yad yad yathā yadā
syād idaṁ bhagavān sākṣāt
pradhāna-puruṣeśvaraḥ

yatra—in which; *yena*—by which; *yataḥ*—from which; *yasya*—of which; *yasmai*—unto which; *yat yat*—whatever; *yathā*—however; *yadā*—whenever; *syāt*—comes into existence; *idam*—this (creation); *bhagavān*—the Supreme Lord; *sākṣāt*—in His personal presence; *pradhāna-puruṣa*—of nature and its creator (Mahā-Viṣṇu); *īśvaraḥ*—the predominator.

TRANSLATION

You are the Supreme Personality of Godhead, who manifest as the Lord of both nature and the creator of nature [Mahā-Viṣṇu]. Everything that comes into existence, however and whenever it does so, is created within You, by You, from You, for You and in relation to You.

PURPORT

To casual observers the known world appears to be produced by many different agents. A good indication of this conception is language itself, which traditional Sanskrit grammarians explain as reflecting the visible diversity of nature. In the standard Sanskrit grammar taught by the sage Pāṇini, the verb, expressing action, is taken to be the essential core of a sentence, and all the other words function in relation to it. Nouns, for example, are put into any of several cases to show their particular relationship to the verb in a sentence. These relationships of noun to verb are called *kārakas,* namely the relations of subject (*kartā,* "who does"), object (*karma,* "what is done"), instrument (*karaṇa,* "by which"), recipient (*sampradāna,* "for or toward which"), source (*apadāna,* "from or because of which") and location (*adhikaraṇa,* "in which"). Apart from these *kārakas,* nouns may also sometimes point to other nouns in a possessive sense, and there are also various kinds of adverbs of time, place and manner. But although language thus seems to indicate the activity of many separate agents in the manifest creation, the deeper truth is that all grammatical forms refer first of all to the Supreme Personality of Godhead. In this verse Vasudeva makes this point by glorifying his two exalted sons in terms of the different grammatical forms.

TEXT 5

**एतन्नानाविधं विश्वमात्मसृष्टमधोक्षज ।
आत्मनानुप्रविश्यात्मन् प्राणो जीवो बिभर्ष्यज ॥५॥**

etan nānā-vidhaṁ viśvam
ātma-sṛṣṭam adhokṣaja
ātmanānupraviśyātman
prāṇo jīvo bibharṣy aja

etat—this; *nānā-vidham*—variegated; *viśvam*—universe; *ātma*—from Yourself; *sṛṣṭam*—created; *adhokṣaja*—O transcendental Lord; *ātma-nā*—in Your manifestation (as the Paramātmā); *anupraviśya*—entering within; *ātman*—O Supreme Soul; *prāṇaḥ*—the principle of vitality; *jīvaḥ*—and the principle of consciousness; *bibharṣi*—You maintain; *aja*—O unborn one.

TRANSLATION

O transcendental Lord, from Yourself You created this entire variegated universe, and then You entered within it in Your personal form as the Supersoul. In this way, O unborn Supreme Soul, as the life force and consciousness of everyone, You maintain the creation.

PURPORT

When creating the material universe, the Lord expands Himself as the Paramātmā, or Supersoul, and accepts the creation as His universal body. No material body has any reason for existing without some *jīva* soul desiring it for his enjoyment, and no *jīva* can independently maintain a body without the Paramātmā accompanying him there for guidance. The Vaiṣṇava *ācāryas,* in their commentaries on the Second Canto of *Śrīmad-Bhāgavatam,* explain that even before Brahmā is born from the lotus navel of Garbhodakaśāyī Viṣṇu, he first accepts the whole material energy, the *mahat-tattva,* as his body. Thus Brahmā is the *jīva* embodied by the universe, and Viṣṇu is the Paramātmā who joins him. Brahmā must organize the specific manifestations of creation, but he cannot begin to do so until Lord Viṣṇu expands Himself again into the subtle energy of action—which is the *sūtra-tattva,* or original vital air—and also into the creative energy of consciousness, *buddhi-tattva.*

TEXT 6

प्राणादीनां विश्वसृजां शक्तयो याः परस्य ताः ।
पारतन्त्र्याद्वैसादृश्याद् द्वयोश्चेष्टैव चेष्टताम् ॥६॥

prāṇādīnāṁ viśva-sṛjāṁ
śaktayo yāḥ parasya tāḥ
pāratantryād vaisādṛśyād
dvayoś ceṣṭaiva ceṣṭatām

prāṇa—of the life air; *ādīnām*—and so on; *viśva*—of the universe; *sṛjām*—the creative factors; *śaktayaḥ*—potencies; *yāḥ*—which; *parasya*—belonging to the Supreme; *tāḥ*—they; *pāratantryāt*—because of being dependent; *vaisādṛśyāt*—because of being different; *dvayoḥ*—of both (living and nonliving manifestations in the material world); *ceṣṭā*—the activity; *eva*—merely; *ceṣṭatām*—of those entities (namely, *prāṇa* and so on) that are active.

TRANSLATION

Whatever potencies the life air and other elements of universal creation exhibit are actually all personal energies of the Supreme Lord, for both life and matter are subordinate to Him and dependent on Him, and also different from one another. Thus everything active in the material world is set into motion by the Supreme Lord.

PURPORT

Prāṇa is the vital air of life, a more subtle element than the ordinary air we can touch. And because *prāṇa* is so subtle—finer than the tangible manifestations of creation—it is sometimes considered the ultimate source of everything. But even subtle energies such as *prāṇa* depend for their functional capacity on the supremely subtle Paramātmā. That is the idea Vasudeva expresses here by the word *pāratantryāt,* "because of dependence." Just as the velocity of an arrow is derived from the strength of the bowman who shoots it, so all subordinate energies depend on the power of the Supreme Lord.

Furthermore, even when various subtle causes have been empowered with their capacity to act, they cannot act in concert without the Supersoul's coordinating direction. As Lord Brahmā states in his description of creation in the Second Canto of *Śrīmad-Bhāgavatam*,

yadaite 'saṅgatā bhāvā
bhūtendriya-mano-guṇāḥ
yadāyatana-nirmāṇe
na śekur brahma-vittama

tadā saṁhatya cānyonyaṁ
bhagavac-chakti-coditāḥ
sad-asattvam upādāya
cobhayaṁ sasṛjur hy adaḥ

"O Nārada, best of the transcendentalists, the forms of the body cannot manifest as long as these created parts, namely the elements, senses, mind and modes of nature, are not assembled. Thus when all these became assembled by the force of the energy of the Supreme Personality of Godhead, this universe certainly came into being by accepting both the primary and secondary causes of creation." (*Bhāg*. 2.5.32-33)

TEXT 7

कान्तिस्तेजः प्रभा सत्ता चन्द्राग्न्यर्कर्क्षविद्युताम् ।
यत्स्थैर्यं भूभृतां भूमेर्वृत्तिर्गन्धोऽर्थतो भवान् ॥७॥

kāntis tejaḥ prabhā sattā
candrāgny-arkarkṣa-vidyutām
yat sthairyaṁ bhū-bhṛtāṁ bhūmer
vṛttir gandho 'rthato bhavān

kāntiḥ—the attractive glow; *tejaḥ*—brilliance; *prabhā*—luminosity; *sattā*—and particular existence; *candra*—of the moon; *agni*—fire; *arka*—the sun; *ṛkṣa*—the stars; *vidyutām*—and lightning; *yat*—which; *sthairyam*—permanence; *bhū-bhṛtām*—of mountains; *bhūmeḥ*—of the earth; *vṛttiḥ*—the quality of sustaining; *gandhaḥ*—fragrance; *arthataḥ*—in truth; *bhavān*—Yourself.

TRANSLATION

The glow of the moon, the brilliance of fire, the radiance of the sun, the twinkling of the stars, the flash of lightning, the permanence of mountains and the aroma and sustaining power of the earth—all these are actually You.

PURPORT

Śrī Vasudeva, in telling Kṛṣṇa that He is the essence of the sun, moon, stars, lightning and fire, is only reiterating the opinion of scripture, both *śruti* and *smṛti.* The *Śvetāśvatara Upaniṣad* (6.14), for example, states,

na tatra sūryo bhāti na candra-tārakaṁ
nemā vidyuto bhānti kuto 'yam agniḥ
tam eva bhāntam anu bhāti sarvaṁ
tasya bhāsā sarvam idaṁ vibhāti

"There [in the spiritual sky] the sun does not shine, nor does the moon, the stars or lightning as we know them, what to speak of ordinary fire. It is by the reflection of the spiritual sky's effulgence that everything else gives light, and thus through its radiance this entire universe becomes luminous." And in *Śrīmad Bhagavad-gītā* (15.12), the Supreme Lord says,

yad āditya-gataṁ tejo
jagad bhāsayate 'khilam
yac candramasi yac cāgnau
tat tejo viddhi māmakam

"The splendor of the sun, which dissipates the darkness of this whole world, comes from Me. And the splendor of the moon and the splendor of fire also come from Me."

TEXT 8

तर्पणं प्राणनमपां देव त्वं ताश्च तद्रसः ।
ओजः सहो बलं चेष्टा गतिर्वायोस्तवेश्वर ॥८॥

tarpaṇaṁ prāṇanam apāṁ
deva tvaṁ tāś ca tad-rasaḥ
ojaḥ saho balaṁ ceṣṭā
gatir vāyos taveśvara

tarpaṇam—the capacity to generate satisfaction; *prāṇanam*—the giving of life; *apām*—of water; *deva*—O Lord; *tvam*—You; *tāḥ*—(water) itself; *ca*—and; *tat*—of it (water); *rasaḥ*—the taste; *ojaḥ*—bodily warmth and vitality, due to strength of the vital air; *sahaḥ*—mental strength; *balam*—and physical strength; *ceṣṭā*—endeavor; *gatiḥ*—and movement; *vāyoḥ*—of air; *tava*—Your; *īśvara*—O supreme controller.

TRANSLATION

My Lord, You are water, and also its taste and and its capacities to quench thirst and sustain life. You exhibit Your potencies through the manifestations of the air as bodily warmth, vitality, mental power, physical strength, endeavor and movement.

TEXT 9

दिशां त्वमवकाशोऽसि दिशः खं स्फोट आश्रयः ।
नादो वर्णस्त्वम् ॐकार आकृतीनां पृथक्कृतिः ॥९॥

diśāṁ tvam avakāśo 'si
diśaḥ khaṁ sphoṭa āśrayaḥ
nādo varṇas tvam oṁ-kāra
ākṛtīnāṁ pṛthak-kṛtiḥ

diśām—of the directions; *tvam*—You; *avakāśaḥ*—the power to accommodate; *asi*—are; *diśaḥ*—the directions; *kham*—the ether; *sphoṭaḥ*—elemental sound; *āśrayaḥ*—having (ether) as its basis; *nādaḥ*—sound in its form of unmanifest vibration; *varṇaḥ*—the primeval syllable; *tvam*—You; *oṁ-kāraḥ—om; ākṛtīnām*—of particular forms; *pṛthak-kṛtiḥ*—the cause of differentiation (namely, manifest language).

TRANSLATION

You are the directions and their accommodating capacity, the all-pervading ether and the elemental sound residing within it. You are the primeval, unmanifested form of sound; the first syllable, *om;* and audible speech, by which sound, as words, acquires particular references.

PURPORT

In accordance with the general process of creation, speech always becomes audible in stages, which proceed from subtle inner impulse to outward expression. These stages are mentioned in the *mantras* of the *Ṛg Veda* (1.164.45):

catvāri vāk-parimitā padāni
tāni vidur brāhmaṇā ye manīṣiṇaḥ
guhāyāṁ trīṇi nihitāni neṅgayanti
turīyaṁ vāco manuṣyā vadanti

"Discriminating *brāhmaṇas* know of four progressive stages of language. Three of these remain hidden within the heart as imperceptible vibrations, while the fourth stage is what people ordinarily understand as speech."

TEXT 10

इन्द्रियं त्विन्द्रियाणां त्वं देवाश्च तदनुग्रहः ।
अवबोधो भवान् बुद्धेर्जीवस्यानुस्मृतिः सती ॥१०॥

indriyaṁ tv indriyāṇāṁ tvaṁ
devāś ca tad-anugrahaḥ
avabodho bhavān buddher
jīvasyānusmṛtiḥ satī

indriyam—the power to illuminate their objects; *tu*—and; *indriyāṇām*—of the senses; *tvam*—You; *devāḥ*—the demigods (who regulate the various senses); *ca*—and; *tat*—of them (the demigods); *anugrahaḥ*—the mercy (by which one's senses can act); *avabodhaḥ*—the power of decision; *bhavān*—You; *buddheḥ*—of intelligence; *jīvasya*—of the living entity; *anusmṛtiḥ*—the power of recollection; *satī*—correct.

TRANSLATION

You are the power of the senses to reveal their objects, the senses' presiding demigods, and the sanction these demigods give for sensory activity. You are the capacity of the intelligence for decision-making, and the living being's ability to remember things accurately.

PURPORT

Śrīla Viśvanātha Cakravartī points out that whenever one of the material senses is involved with its object, the presiding demigod of that particular sense organ must give his sanction. Ācārya Viśvanātha Cakravartī explains the word *anusmṛti* in this verse in its higher sense, as one's recognition of himself as an eternal spirit soul.

TEXT 11

भूतानामसि भूतादिरिन्द्रियाणां च तैजसः ।
वैकारिको विकल्पानां प्रधानमनुशायिनम् ॥११॥

bhūtānām asi bhūtādir
indriyāṇāṁ ca taijasaḥ
vaikāriko vikalpānāṁ
pradhānam anuśāyinam

bhūtānām—of the physical elements; *asi*—You are; *bhūta-ādiḥ*—their source, false ego in the mode of ignorance; *indriyāṇām*—of the senses; *ca*—and; *taijasaḥ*—false ego in the mode of passion; *vaikārikaḥ*—false ego in the mode of goodness; *vikalpānām*—of the creative demigods; *pradhānam*—the unmanifest, total material energy; *anuśāyinam*—underlying.

TRANSLATION

You are false ego in the mode of ignorance, which is the source of the physical elements; false ego in the mode of passion, which is

the source of the bodily senses; false ego in the mode of goodness, which is the source of the demigods; and the unmanifest, total material energy, which underlies everything.

TEXT 12

नश्वरेष्विह भावेषु तदसि त्वमनश्वरम् ।
यथा द्रव्यविकारेषु द्रव्यमात्रं निरूपितम् ॥१२॥

naśvareṣv iha bhāveṣu
tad asi tvam anaśvaram
yathā dravya-vikāreṣu
dravya-mātraṁ nirūpitam

naśvareṣu—subject to destruction; *iha*—in this world; *bhāveṣu*—among entities; *tat*—that; *asi*—are; *tvam*—You; *anaśvaram*—the indestructible; *yathā*—just as; *dravya*—of a substance; *vikāreṣu*—among the transformations; *dravya-mātram*—the substance itself; *nirūpitam*—ascertained.

TRANSLATION

You are the one indestructible entity among all the destructible things of this world, like the underlying substance that is seen to remain unchanged while the things made from it undergo transformations.

TEXT 13

सत्त्वं रजस्तम इति गुणास्तद्वृत्तयश्च याः ।
त्वय्यद्धा ब्रह्मणि परे कल्पिता योगमायया ॥१३॥

sattvaṁ rajas tama iti
guṇās tad-vṛttayaś ca yāḥ
tvayy addhā brahmaṇi pare
kalpitā yoga-māyayā

sattvam rajaḥ tamaḥ iti—known as goodness, passion and ignorance; *guṇāḥ*—the modes of material nature; *tat*—their; *vṛttayaḥ*—functions; *ca*—and; *yāḥ*—which; *tvayi*—within You; *addhāḥ*—manifestly; *brahmaṇi*—within the Absolute Truth; *pare*—supreme; *kalpitāḥ*—arranged; *yoga-māyayā*—by Yogamāyā (the internal potency of the Supreme Lord that facilitates His pastimes).

TRANSLATION

The modes of material nature—namely goodness, passion and ignorance—together with all their functions, become directly manifest within You, the Supreme Absolute Truth, by the arrangement of Your Yogamāyā.

PURPORT

Vasudeva's description of how the Supreme Lord expands Himself into the products of the three material modes may possibly be misunderstood to imply that He is touched by the modes, or even that He is subject to destruction. To negate these misunderstandings, Vasudeva states here that the three modes and their products function by the arrangement of the Lord's creative energy, Yogamāyā, who is always completely under His control. Thus the Lord is never tainted in the least by any material contact.

TEXT 14

तस्मान्न सन्त्यमी भावा यर्हि त्वयि विकल्पिताः ।
त्वं चामीषु विकारेषु ह्यन्यदाव्यावहारिकः ॥१४॥

tasmān na santy amī bhāvā
yarhi tvayi vikalpitāḥ
tvaṁ cāmīṣu vikāreṣu
hy anyadāvyāvahārikaḥ

tasmāt—therefore; *na*—not; *santi*—exist; *amī*—these; *bhāvāḥ*—entities; *yarhi*—when; *tvayi*—within You; *vikalpitāḥ*—arranged; *tvam*—You; *ca*—also; *amīṣu*—within these; *vikāreṣu*—products of creation; *hi*—indeed; *anyadā*—at any other time; *avyāvahārikaḥ*—nonmaterial.

TRANSLATION

Thus these created entities, transformations of material nature, do not exist except when material nature manifests them within You, at which time You also manifest within them. But aside from such periods of creation, You stand alone as the transcendental reality.

PURPORT

When the universe is wound up at the time of its periodic annihilation, all the inert objects and bodies of living beings that hitherto were manifested by the Lord's Māyā become disconnected from His sight. Then, since He maintains no association with them during the period of universal dissolution, they in fact no longer exist. In other words, material manifestations have real, functioning existence only when the Lord turns His attention to the creation and maintenance of the material cosmos. The Lord is never "within" these objects in any material sense, but He does mercifully pervade them all as the impersonal Brahman, and as the Paramātmā He enters within every atom and also accompanies the *jīva* souls in their individual embodiments. As the Lord describes in His own words in the verses of *Bhagavad-gītā* (9.4–5):

mayā tatam idaṁ sarvam
jagad avyakta-mūrtinā
mat-sthāni sarva-bhūtāni
na cāhaṁ teṣv avasthitaḥ

na ca mat-sthāni bhūtāni
paśya me yogam aiśvaram
bhūta-bhṛn na ca bhūta-stho
mamātmā bhūta-bhāvanaḥ

"By Me, in My unmanifest form, this entire universe is pervaded. All beings are in Me, but I am not in them. And yet everything that is created does not rest in Me. Behold My mystic opulence! Although I am the maintainer of all living entities and although I am everywhere, I am not part of this cosmic manifestation, for My Self is the very source of creation."

TEXT 15

गुणप्रवाह एतस्मिन्नबुधास्त्वखिलात्मनः ।
गतिं सूक्ष्मामबोधेन संसरन्तीह कर्मभिः ॥१५॥

guṇa-pravāha etasminn
abudhās tv akhilātmanaḥ
gatiṁ sūkṣmām abodhena
saṁsarantīha karmabhiḥ

guṇa—of the material modes; *pravāhe*—in the flow; *etasmin*—this; *abudhāḥ*—those who are ignorant; *tu*—but; *akhila*—of everything; *ātmanaḥ*—of the Soul; *gatim*—the destination; *sūkṣmām*—sublime; *abodhena*—because of their lack of understanding; *saṁsaranti*—they move through the cycle of birth and death; *iha*—in this world; *karmabhiḥ*—forced by their material activities.

TRANSLATION

They are truly ignorant who, while imprisoned within the ceaseless flow of this world's material qualities, fail to know You, the Supreme Soul of all that be, as their ultimate, sublime destination. Because of their ignorance, the entanglement of material work forces such souls to wander in the cycle of birth and death.

PURPORT

A soul who forgets his true identity as a servant of God is sent to this world to be imprisoned in a succession of material bodies. Wrongly identifying himself with these bodies, such a conditioned soul suffers the consequent distress of karmic action and reaction. Vasudeva, as a compassionate Vaiṣṇava, laments for the suffering conditioned souls, whose unhappiness, the result of ignorance, can be remedied by knowledge of the principles of devotional service to Lord Kṛṣṇa.

TEXT 16

यदृच्छया नृतां प्राप्य सुकल्पामिह दुर्लभाम् ।
स्वार्थे प्रमत्तस्य वयो गतं त्वन्माययेश्वर ॥१६॥

yadṛcchayā nṛtāṁ prāpya
su-kalpām iha durlabhām
svārthe pramattasya vayo
gataṁ tvan-māyayeśvara

yadṛcchayā—somehow or other; *nṛtām*—human status; *prāpya*—obtaining; *su-kalpām*—fit; *iha*—in this life; *durlabhām*—difficult to achieve; *sva*—his own; *arthe*—about the welfare; *pramattasya*—of one who is confused; *vayaḥ*—the span of life; *gatam*—spent; *tvat*—Your; *māyayā*—by the illusory energy; *īśvara*—O Lord.

TRANSLATION

By good fortune a soul may obtain a healthy human life—an opportunity rarely achieved. But if he is nonetheless deluded about what is best for him, O Lord, Your illusory Māyā will cause him to waste his entire life.

TEXT 17

असावहं ममैवैते देहे चास्यान्वयादिषु ।
स्नेहपाशैर्निबध्नाति भवान् सर्वमिदं जगत् ॥१७॥

asāv ahaṁ mamaivaite
dehe cāsyānvayādiṣu
sneha-pāśair nibadhnāti
bhavān sarvam idaṁ jagat

asau—this; *aham*—I; *mama*—mine; *eva*—indeed; *ete*—these; *dehe*—in connection with one's body; *ca*—and; *asya*—of it; *anvaya-ādiṣu*—and in connection with progeny and other related things; *sneha*—of affection; *pāśaiḥ*—with the ropes; *nibadhnāti*—tie up; *bhavān*—You; *sarvam*—all; *idam*—this; *jagat*—world.

TRANSLATION

You keep this whole world bound up by the ropes of affection, and thus when people consider their material bodies, they think,

"This is me," and when they consider their progeny and other relations, they think, "These are mine."

TEXT 18

युवां न नः सुतौ साक्षात्प्रधानपुरुषेश्वरौ ।
भूभारक्षत्रक्षपण अवतीर्णौ तथात्थ ह ॥१८॥

yuvāṁ na naḥ sutau sākṣāt
pradhāna-puruṣeśvarau
bhū-bhāra-kṣatra-kṣapaṇa
avatīrṇau tathāttha ha

yuvām—You two; *na*—not; *naḥ*—our; *sutau*—sons; *sākṣāt*—directly; *pradhāna-puruṣa*—of nature and its creator (Mahā-Viṣṇu); *īśvarau*—the supreme controllers; *bhū*—of the earth; *bhāra*—the burden; *kṣatra*—royalty; *kṣapaṇe*—for eradicating; *avatīrṇau*—descended; *tathā*—so; *āttha*—You have said; *ha*—indeed.

TRANSLATION

You are not our sons but the very Lords of both material nature and its creator [Mahā-Viṣṇu]. As You Yourself have told us, You have descended to rid the earth of the rulers who are a heavy burden upon her.

PURPORT

According to Śrīla Viśvanātha Cakravartī, in this verse Vasudeva offers himself and his wife as excellent examples of those who are materially deluded. Although at the time of His birth in Kaṁsa's prison Lord Kṛṣṇa told Vasudeva and Devakī that His mission was to rid the earth of unwanted *kṣatriyas*, still His two parents could not avoid thinking of Him as their helpless son who needed protection from King Kaṁsa. In reality, of course, both Vasudeva and Devakī were participating in the divine pastime of the Lord's birth under the perfect direction of His internal energy; only out of transcendental humility does Vasudeva criticize himself in this way.

TEXT 19

तत्ते गतोऽस्म्यरणमद्य पदारविन्दम्
आपन्नसंसृतिभयापहमार्तबन्धो ।
एतावतालमलमिन्द्रियलालसेन
मर्त्यात्मदृक् त्वयि परे यदपत्यबुद्धिः ॥१९॥

tat te gato 'smy araṇam adya padāravindam
āpanna-saṁsṛti-bhayāpaham ārta-bandho
etāvatālam alam indriya-lālasena
martyātma-dṛk tvayi pare yad apatya-buddhiḥ

tat—therefore; *te*—Your; *gataḥ*—come; *asmi*—I am; *araṇam*—for shelter; *adya*—today; *pada-aravindam*—to the lotus feet; *āpanna*—for those who have surrendered; *saṁsṛti*—of material entanglement; *bhaya*—the fear; *apaham*—which remove; *ārta*—of the distressed; *bandho*—O friend; *etāvatā*—this much; *alam alam*—enough, enough; *indriya*—for sense enjoyment; *lālasena*—with hankering; *martya*—as mortal (the material body); *ātma*—myself; *dṛk*—whose seeing; *tvayi*—toward You; *pare*—the Supreme; *yat*—because of which (hankering); *apatya*—(of Your being my) child; *buddhiḥ*—the mentality.

TRANSLATION

Therefore, O friend of the distressed, I now approach Your lotus feet for shelter—the same lotus feet that dispel all fear of worldly existence for those who have surrendered to them. Enough! Enough with hankering for sense enjoyment, which makes me identify with this mortal body and think of You, the Supreme, as my child.

PURPORT

Śrīla Jīva Gosvāmī suggests that Vasudeva condemns himself here for thinking of trying to gain special opulences because he is the father of the Supreme Lord. Thus Vasudeva contrasts himself with Nanda, the King of Vraja, who was satisfied with pure love of God and nothing else.

TEXT 20

सूतीगृहे ननु जगाद भवानजो नौ
सञ्जज्ञे इत्यनुयुगं निजधर्मगुप्त्यै ।
नानातनूर्गगनवद्विदधज्जहासि
को वेद भूम्न उरुगाय विभूतिमायाम् ॥२०॥

sūtī-gṛhe nanu jagāda bhavān ajo nau
sañjajña ity anu-yugaṁ nija-dharma-guptyai
nānā-tanūr gagana-vad vidadhaj jahāsi
ko veda bhūmna uru-gāya vibhūti-māyām

sūtī-gṛhe—in the maternity room; *nanu*—indeed; *jagāda*—said; *bhavān*—You; *ajaḥ*—the unborn Lord; *nau*—to us; *sañjajñe*—You have taken birth; *iti*—thus; *anu-yugam*—in one age after another; *nija*—Your own; *dharma*—the principles of religion; *guptyai*—to protect; *nānā*—various; *tanūḥ*—divine bodies; *gagana-vat*—like a cloud; *vidadhat*—assuming; *jahāsi*—You make unmanifest; *kaḥ*—who; *veda*—can understand; *bhūmnaḥ*—of the all-pervading Supreme Lord; *uru-gāya*—O You who are greatly glorified; *vibhūti*—of the opulent expansions; *māyām*—the mystic, deluding potency.

TRANSLATION

Indeed, while still in the maternity room You told us that You, the unborn Lord, had already been born several times as our son in previous ages. After manifesting each of these transcendental bodies to protect Your own principles of religion, You then made them unmanifest, thus appearing and disappearing like a cloud. O supremely glorified, all-pervading Lord, who can understand the mystic, deluding potency of Your opulent expansions?

PURPORT

Lord Kṛṣṇa was first born to Vasudeva and Devakī in their previous lives as Sutapā and Pṛśni. Later they again became His parents as Kaśyapa and Aditi. This, then, was the third time He had appeared as their son.

TEXT 21

श्रीशुक उवाच
आकर्ण्येत्थं पितुर्वाक्यं भगवान् सात्वतर्षभः ।
प्रत्याह प्रश्रयानम्रः प्रहसन् श्लक्ष्णया गिरा ॥२१॥

śrī-śuka uvāca
ākarṇyetthaṁ pitur vākyaṁ
bhagavān sātvatarṣabhaḥ
pratyāha praśrayānamraḥ
prahasan ślakṣṇayā girā

śrī-śukaḥ uvāca—Śukadeva Gosvāmī said; *ākarṇya*—hearing; *ittham*—in this manner; *pituḥ*—of His father; *vākyam*—the statements; *bhagavān*—the Supreme Lord; *sātvata-ṛṣabhaḥ*—best of the Yadus; *pratyāha*—replied; *praśraya*—with humility; *ānamraḥ*—bowing (His head); *prahasan*—smiling broadly; *ślakṣṇayā*—gentle; *girā*—with a voice.

TRANSLATION

Śukadeva Gosvāmī said: Having heard His father's words, the Supreme Lord, leader of the Sātvatas, replied in a gentle voice as He bowed His head in humility and smiled.

PURPORT

Śrīla Jīva Gosvāmī describes what Lord Kṛṣṇa thought after hearing His father glorify Him: "Vasudeva has been honored with the eternal role of My father, something even demigods like Brahmā cannot aspire for. Therefore he shouldn't be absorbed in thinking of My godly aspects. Moreover, his reverence greatly embarrasses Me. It was to avoid this very situation that, after killing Kaṁsa, I made a special effort to reinforce their pure parental love for Me and Balarāma. But now, unfortunately, the statements of these sages threaten to revive some of Vasudeva's and Devakī's previous awareness of My majesty."

TEXT 22

श्रीभगवानुवाच
वचो वः समवेतार्थं तातैतदुपमन्महे ।
यन्नः पुत्रान् समुद्दिश्य तत्त्वग्राम उदाहृतः ॥२२॥

śrī-bhagavān uvāca
vaco vaḥ samavetārthaṁ
tātaitad upamanmahe
yan naḥ putrān samuddiśya
tattva-grāma udāhṛtaḥ

śrī-bhagavān uvāca—the Personality of Godhead said; *vacaḥ*—words; *vaḥ*—your; *samaveta*—appropriate; *artham*—whose meaning; *tāta*—O father; *etat*—these; *upamanmahe*—I consider; *yat*—since; *naḥ*—Us; *putrān*—your sons; *samuddiśya*—by referring to; *tattva*—of categories of fact; *grāmaḥ*—the totality; *udāhṛtaḥ*—set forth.

TRANSLATION

The Supreme Lord said: My dear father, I consider your statements appropriate, since you have explained the various categories of existence by referring to Us, your sons.

PURPORT

Posing as Vasudeva's dependent son, Lord Kṛṣṇa expresses gratitude for His father's edifying instructions.

TEXT 23

अहं यूयमसावार्य इमे च द्वारकौकसः ।
सर्वेऽप्येवं यदुश्रेष्ठ विमृग्याः सचराचरम् ॥२३॥

ahaṁ yūyam asāv ārya
ime ca dvārakaukasaḥ
sarve 'py evaṁ yadu-śreṣṭha
vimṛgyāḥ sa-carācaram

aham—I; *yūyam*—you; *asau*—He; *āryaḥ*—My respected brother (Balarāma); *ime*—these; *ca*—and; *dvārakā-okasaḥ*—inhabitants of Dvārakā; *sarve*—all; *api*—even; *evam*—in this same way; *yadu-śreṣṭha*—O best of the Yadus; *vimṛgyāḥ*—to be considered; *sd*—along with; *cara*—that which moves; *acaram*—and that which does not move.

TRANSLATION

Not only I, but also you, along with My respected brother and these residents of Dvārakā, should all be considered in this same philosophical light, O best of the Yadus. Indeed, we should include all that exists, both moving and nonmoving.

PURPORT

To protect His parents' intimate relationship with Him, Lord Kṛṣṇa stresses the oneness of all existence in this statement to His father, Vasudeva. Vasudeva had been reminded of his sons' greatness by hearing the sages gathered at Kurukṣetra. But his sense of awe was ruining his intimate parental relationship with Kṛṣṇa, and therefore Kṛṣṇa wanted to dispel it.

We should not misunderstand the "oneness" Lord Kṛṣṇa speaks of here. The subtle words of the *Upaniṣads* often mislead impersonalists into believing that all existence is ineffably one, without any variety in the ultimate issue. Some Upaniṣadic *mantras* emphasize the sameness of God and His creation, while others speak about their difference. *Tat tvam asi śvetaketo* ("You are that, O Śvetaketu"), for example, is an *abheda-vākya,* a *mantra* affirming that all things are one with God, being His dependent expansions. But the *Upaniṣads* also contain many *bheda-vākyas,* statements that affirm the unique, distinguishing qualities of the Supreme, such as this statement: *ka evānyāt kaḥ prāṇyād yady eṣa ākāśa ānando na syāt, eṣa evānandayati.* "Who would there be to activate the creation and give life to all beings if this infinite Supreme were not the original enjoyer? Indeed, He alone is the source of all pleasure." (*Taittirīya Up.* 2.7.1) By the influence of the Supreme Lord's bewildering Māyā, envious impersonalists read the *abheda-vākyas* literally and accept the *bheda-vākyas* only in a figurative way. Authoritative Vaiṣṇava commentators, on the other hand, carefully reconcile the apparent contradictions in accordance with the interpretive principles of Vedic Mīmāṁsā and the logically established conclusions of Vedānta.

TEXT 24

आत्मा ह्येकः स्वयंज्योतिर्नित्योऽन्यो निर्गुणो गुणैः ।
आत्मसृष्टैस्तत्कृतेषु भूतेषु बहुधेयते ॥२४॥

ātmā hy ekaḥ svayaṁ-jyotir
nityo 'nyo nirguṇo guṇaiḥ
ātma-sṛṣṭais tat-kṛteṣu
bhūteṣu bahudheyate

ātmā—the Supreme Soul; *hi*—indeed; *ekaḥ*—one; *svayam-jyotiḥ*—self-luminous; *nityaḥ*—eternal; *anyaḥ*—distinct (from the material energy); *nirguṇaḥ*—free from material qualities; *guṇaiḥ*—by the modes; *ātma*—from itself; *sṛṣṭaiḥ*—created; *tat*—in their; *kṛteṣu*—products; *bhūteṣu*—material entities; *bahudhā*—manifold; *īyate*—it appears.

TRANSLATION

The supreme spirit, Paramātmā, is indeed one. He is self-luminous and eternal, transcendental and devoid of material qualities. But through the agency of the very modes He has created, the one Supreme Truth manifests as many among the expansions of those modes.

TEXT 25

खं वायुर्ज्योतिरापो भूस्तत्कृतेषु यथाशयम् ।
आविस्तिरोऽल्पभूर्येको नानात्वं यात्यसावपि ॥२५॥

khaṁ vāyur jyotir āpo bhūs
tat-kṛteṣu yathāśayam
āvis-tiro-'lpa-bhūry eko
nānātvaṁ yāty asāv api

kham—ether; *vāyuḥ*—air; *jyotiḥ*—fire; *āpaḥ*—water; *bhūḥ*—earth; *tat*—their; *kṛteṣu*—in the products; *yathā-āśayam*—according to the particular locations; *āviḥ*—manifest; *tiraḥ*—unmanifest; *alpa*—small; *bhūri*—large; *ekaḥ*—one; *nānātvam*—the status of being many; *yāti*—assumes; *asau*—it; *api*—also.

TRANSLATION

The elements of ether, air, fire, water and earth become visible, invisible, minute or extensive as they manifest in various objects. Similarly, the Paramātmā, though one, appears to become many.

PURPORT

Śrīla Viśvanātha Cakravartī explains this and the previous verse as follows: The one Paramātmā appears to be many by the influence of the modes of nature that He Himself creates. How is that? Because although in truth the Paramātmā is self-illuminating, eternal, aloof from everything, and free of the modes of nature, when He appears as His manifestations He seems to be just the opposite—a multiplicity of temporary objects saturated with the modes of nature. Just as the elements of ether and so on, when manifesting in pots and other things, seem to appear and disappear, so the Paramātmā seems to appear and disappear in His various manifestations.

TEXT 26

श्रीशुक उवाच
एवं भगवता राजन् वसुदेव उदाहृतः ।
श्रुत्वा विनष्टनानाधीस्तूष्णीं प्रीतमना अभूत् ॥२६॥

śrī-śuka uvāca
evaṁ bhagavatā rājan
vasudeva udāhṛtaḥ
śrutvā vinaṣṭa-nānā-dhīs
tūṣṇīṁ prīta-manā abhūt

śrī-śukaḥ uvāca—Śukadeva Gosvāmī said; *evam*—thus; *bhagavatā*—by the Supreme Lord; *rājan*—O King (Parīkṣit); *vasudevaḥ*—Vasudeva; *udāhṛtaḥ*—spoken to; *śrutvā*—hearing; *vinaṣṭa*—destroyed; *nānā*—dualistic; *dhīḥ*—his mentality; *tūṣṇīm*—silent; *prīta*—satisfied; *manāḥ*—in his heart; *abhūt*—he was.

TRANSLATION

Śukadeva Gosvāmī said: O King, hearing these instructions spoken to him by the Supreme Lord, Vasudeva became freed from all ideas of duality. Satisfied at heart, he remained silent.

TEXTS 27–28

अथ तत्र कुरुश्रेष्ठ देवकी सर्वदेवता ।
श्रुत्वानीतं गुरोः पुत्रमात्मजाभ्यां सुविस्मिता ॥२७॥

कृष्णरामौ समाश्राव्य पुत्रान् कंसविहिंसितान् ।
स्मरन्ती कृपणं प्राह वैक्लव्यादश्रुलोचना ॥२८॥

atha tatra kuru-śreṣṭha
devakī sarva-devatā
śrutvānītaṁ guroḥ putram
ātmajābhyāṁ su-vismitā

kṛṣṇa-rāmau samāśrāvya
putrān kaṁsa-vihiṁsitān
smarantī kṛpaṇaṁ prāha
vaiklavyād aśru-locanā

atha—then; *tatra*—at that place; *kuru-śreṣṭha*—O best of the Kurus; *devakī*—mother Devakī; *sarva*—of everyone; *devatā*—the supremely worshipable goddess; *śrutvā*—having heard; *nītam*—brought back; *guroḥ*—of Their spiritual master; *putram*—the son; *ātmajābhyām*—by her two sons; *su*—very much; *vismitā*—amazed; *kṛṣṇa-rāmau*—Kṛṣṇa and Balarāma; *samāśrāvya*—clearly addressing; *putrān*—her sons; *kaṁsa-vihiṁsitān*—murdered by Kaṁsa; *smarantī*—remembering; *kṛpaṇam*—pitifully; *prāha*—she spoke; *vaiklavyāt*—due to her distraught condition; *aśru*—(filled with) tears; *locanā*—her eyes.

TRANSLATION

At that time, O best of the Kurus, the universally worshiped Devakī took the opportunity to address her two sons, Kṛṣṇa and Balarāma. Previously she had heard with astonishment that They had brought Their spiritual master's son back from death. Now, thinking of her own sons who had been murdered by Kaṁsa, she felt great sorrow, and thus with tear-filled eyes she beseeched Kṛṣṇa and Balarāma.

PURPORT

Vasudeva's love for Kṛṣṇa had been disturbed because his awareness of Kṛṣṇa's opulences conflicted with seeing Him as his son. In a different way, Devakī's love was somewhat distracted by her lamentation for her dead sons. So Kṛṣṇa arranged to relieve her of the mistaken idea that anyone else but Him was actually her son. Since Devakī is known to be worshiped by all great souls, her show of maternal affection must actually have been an effect of the Lord's Yogamāyā, who increases the pleasure of His pastimes. Thus in Text 54 Devakī will be described as *mohitā māyayā viṣṇoḥ,* "bewildered by the internal energy of Lord Viṣṇu."

TEXT 29

श्रीदेवक्युवाच
राम रामाप्रमेयात्मन् कृष्ण योगेश्वरेश्वर ।
वेदाहं वां विश्वसृजामीश्वरावादिपूरुषौ ॥२९॥

śrī-devaky uvāca
rāma rāmāprameyātman
kṛṣṇa yogeśvareśvara
vedāhaṁ vāṁ viśva-sṛjām
īśvarāv ādi-pūruṣau

śrī-devakī uvāca—Śrī Devakī said; *rāma rāma*—O Rāma, Rāma; *aprameya-ātman*—O immeasurable Supersoul; *kṛṣṇa*—O Kṛṣṇa; *yoga-īśvara*—of the masters of mystic *yoga; īśvara*—O master; *veda*—know; *aham*—I; *vām*—You both; *viśva*—of the universe; *sṛjām*—of the creators; *īśvarau*—the Lords; *ādi*—original; *pūruṣau*—the two Personalities of Godhead.

TRANSLATION

Śrī Devakī said: O Rāma, Rāma, immeasurable Supreme Soul! O Kṛṣṇa, Lord of all masters of *yoga*! I know that You are the ultimate rulers of all universal creators, the primeval Personalities of Godhead.

TEXT 30

कालविध्वस्तसत्त्वानां राज्ञामुच्छास्त्रवर्तिनाम् ।
भूमेर्भारायमाणानामवतीर्णौ किलाद्य मे ॥३०॥

kāla-vidhvasta-sattvānāṁ
rājñām ucchāstra-vartinām

bhūmer bhārāyamāṇānām
avatīrṇau kilādya me

kāla—by time; *vidhvasta*—destroyed; *sattvānām*—whose good qualities; *rājñām*—for (killing) the kings; *ut-śāstra*—outside the scope of scriptural rules; *vartinām*—who act; *bhūmeḥ*—for the earth; *bhārāyamāṇānām*—becoming a burden; *avatīrṇau*—(both of You) descended; *kila*—indeed; *adya*—now; *me*—to me.

TRANSLATION

Taking birth from me, You have now descended to this world in order to kill those kings whose good qualities have been destroyed by the present age, and who thus defy the authority of revealed scriptures and burden the earth.

TEXT 31

यस्यांशांशांशभागेन विश्वोत्पत्तिलयोदयाः ।
भवन्ति किल विश्वात्मंस्तं त्वाद्याहं गतिं गता ॥३१॥

yasyāṁśāṁśāṁśa-bhāgena
viśvotpatti-layodayāḥ
bhavanti kila viśvātmaṁs
taṁ tvādyāhaṁ gatiṁ gatā

yasya—whose; *aṁśa*—of the expansion; *aṁśa*—of the expansion; *aṁśa*—of the expansion; *bhāgena*—by a part; *viśva*—of the universe; *utpatti*—the generation; *laya*—dissolution; *udayāḥ*—and prosperity; *bhavanti*—arise; *kila*—indeed; *viśva-ātman*—O Soul of all that be; *tat*—to Him; *tvā*—Yourself; *adya*—today; *aham*—I; *gatim*—for shelter; *gatā*—come.

TRANSLATION

O Soul of all that be, the creation, maintenance and destruction of the universe are all carried out by a fraction of an expansion of an expansion of Your expansion. Today I have come to take shelter of You, the Supreme Lord.

PURPORT

Śrīla Śrīdhara Svāmī explains this verse as follows: The Lord of Vaikuṇṭha, Nārāyaṇa, is but one expansion of Śrī Kṛṣṇa. Mahā-Viṣṇu, the first creator, is Lord Nārāyaṇa's expansion. The total material energy emanates from Mahā-Viṣṇu's glance, and of that total material energy the three modes of nature are divided portions. Thus it is Śrī Kṛṣṇa, acting through His expansions, who generates, sustains and dissolves the universe.

TEXTS 32–33

चिरान्मृतसुतादाने गुरुणा किल चोदितौ ।
आनिन्यथुः पितृस्थानाद् गुरवे गुरुदक्षिणाम् ॥३२॥
तथा मे कुरुतं कामं युवां योगेश्वरेश्वरौ ।
भोजराजहतान् पुत्रान् कामये द्रष्टुमाहतान् ॥३३॥

cirān mṛta-sutādāne
guruṇā kila coditau
āninyathuḥ pitṛ-sthānād
gurave guru-dakṣiṇām

tathā me kurutaṁ kāmaṁ
yuvāṁ yogeśvareśvarau
bhoja-rāja-hatān putrān
kāmaye draṣṭum āhṛtān

cirāt—for a long time; *mṛta*—dead; *suta*—the son; *ādāne*—to return; *guruṇā*—by Your spiritual master; *kila*—it has been heard; *coditau*—ordered; *āninyathuḥ*—You brought him; *pitṛ*—of the forefathers; *sthānāt*—from the place; *gurave*—to Your spiritual master; *guru-dakṣiṇām*—as a token of thanksgiving for Your *guru's* mercy; *tathā*—in the same way; *me*—my; *kurutam*—please fulfill; *kāmam*—the desire; *yuvām*—You two; *yoga-īśvara*—of the masters of *yoga; īśvarau*—O masters; *bhoja-rāja*—by the King of Bhoja (Kaṁsa); *hatān*—killed; *putrān*—my sons; *kāmaye*—I wish; *draṣṭum*—to see; *āhṛtān*—brought back.

TRANSLATION

It is said that when Your spiritual master ordered You to retrieve his long-dead son, You brought him back from the fore-fathers' abode as a token of remuneration for Your *guru's* mercy. Please fulfill my desire in the same way, O supreme masters of all *yoga* masters. Please bring back my sons who were killed by the King of Bhoja, so that I may see them once again.

TEXT 34

ऋषिरुवाच
एवं सञ्चोदितौ मात्रा रामः कृष्णश्च भारत ।
सुतलं संविविशतुर्योगमायामुपाश्रितौ ॥३४॥

ṛṣir uvāca
evaṁ sañcoditau mātrā
rāmaḥ kṛṣṇaś ca bhārata
sutalaṁ saṁviviśatur
yoga-māyām upāśritau

ṛṣiḥ uvāca—the sage (Śrī Śukadeva) said; *evam*—thus; *sañcoditau*—urged; *mātrā*—by Their mother; *rāmaḥ*—Balarāma; *kṛṣṇaḥ*—Kṛṣṇa; *ca*—and; *bhārata*—O descendant of Bhārata (Parīkṣit); *sutalam*—the subterranean planet of Sutala, ruled by Bali Mahārāja; *saṁviviśatuḥ*—They entered; *yoga-māyāyam*—Their mystic pastime potency; *upāśritau*—utilizing.

TRANSLATION

The sage Śukadeva said: Thus entreated by Their mother, O Bhārata, Balarāma and Kṛṣṇa employed Their mystic Yogamāyā potency and entered the region of Sutala.

TEXT 35

तस्मिन् प्रविष्टावुपलभ्य दैत्यराड्
विश्वात्मदैवं सुतरां तथात्मनः ।

तद्दर्शनाह्लादपरिप्लुताशयः
सद्यः समुत्थाय ननाम सान्वयः ॥३५॥

tasmin praviṣṭāv upalabhya daitya-rāḍ
viśvātma-daivaṁ sutarāṁ tathātmanaḥ
tad-darśanāhlāda-pariplutāśayaḥ
sadyaḥ samutthāya nanāma sānvayaḥ

tasmin—there; *praviṣṭau*—(the two of Them) entered; *upalabhya*—noticing; *daitya-rāṭ*—the King of the Daityas (Bali); *viśva*—of the entire universe; *ātma*—the Soul; *daivam*—and supreme Deity; *sutarām*—especially; *tathā*—also; *ātmanaḥ*—of himself; *tat*—Them; *darśana*—due to seeing; *āhlāda*—with the joy; *paripluta*—overwhelmed; *āśayaḥ*—his heart; *sadyaḥ*—immediately; *samutthāya*—standing up; *nanāma*—he bowed down; *sa*—together with; *anvayaḥ*—his entourage.

TRANSLATION

When the King of the Daityas, Bali Mahārāja, noticed the arrival of the two Lords, his heart overflowed with joy, since he knew Them to be the Supreme Soul and worshipable Deity of the entire universe, and especially of himself. He immediately stood up and then bowed down to offer respects, along with his entire entourage.

TEXT 36

तयोः समानीय वरासनं मुदा
निविष्टयोस्तत्र महात्मनोस्तयोः ।
दधार पादाववनिज्य तज्जलं
सवृन्द आब्रह्म पुनद्यदम्बु ह ॥३६॥

tayoḥ samānīya varāsanaṁ mudā
niviṣṭayos tatra mahātmanos tayoḥ
dadhāra pādāv avanijya taj jalaṁ
sa-vṛnda ā-brahma punad yad ambu ha

tayoḥ—for Them; *samānīya*—bringing; *vara*—elevated; *āsanam*—seats; *mudā*—happily; *niviṣṭayoḥ*—who took Their seats; *tatra*—there;

mahā-ātmanoḥ—of the greatest of personalities; *tayoḥ*—of Them; *dadhāra*—he took; *pādau*—the feet; *avanijya*—washing; *tat*—that; *jalam*—water; *sa*—together with; *vṛndaḥ*—his followers; *ā-brahma*—up to Lord Brahmā; *punat*—purifying; *yat*—which; *ambu*—water; *ha*—indeed.

TRANSLATION

Bali took pleasure in offering Them elevated seats. After They sat down, he washed the feet of the two Supreme Personalities. Then he took that water, which purifies the whole world even up to Lord Brahmā, and poured it upon himself and his followers.

TEXT 37

समर्हयामास स तौ विभूतिभिर्
महार्हवस्त्राभरणानुलेपनैः ।
ताम्बूलदीपामृतभक्षणादिभिः
स्वगोत्रवित्तात्मसमर्पणेन च ॥३७॥

samarhayām āsa sa tau vibhūtibhir
mahārha-vastrābharaṇānulepanaiḥ
tāmbūla-dīpāmṛta-bhakṣaṇādibhiḥ
sva-gotra-vittātma-samarpaṇena ca

samarhayām āsa—worshiped; *saḥ*—he; *tau*—Them; *vibhūtibhiḥ*—with his riches; *mahā-arha*—greatly valuable; *vastra*—with garments; *ābharaṇa*—ornaments; *anulepanaiḥ*—and fragrant pastes; *tāmbūla*—with betel nut; *dīpa*—lamps; *amṛta*—nectarean; *bhakṣaṇa*—food; *ādibhiḥ*—and so on; *sva*—of his; *gotra*—family; *vitta*—of the wealth; *ātma*—and of himself; *samarpaṇena*—with the offering; *ca*—and.

TRANSLATION

He worshiped Them with all the riches at his disposal—priceless clothing, ornaments, fragrant sandalwood paste, betel nut, lamps, sumptuous food and so on. Thus he offered Them all his family's wealth, and also his own self.

PURPORT

Bali Mahārāja's devotional attitude is renowned as the perfect example of complete self-surrender. When Lord Viṣṇu in the guise of a young *brāhmaṇa* student approached him for charity, Bali offered all he possessed, and when he had nothing more to offer, he surrendered himself as the Supreme Lord's eternal servant.

There are nine standard processes of devotional service, and the last, *ātma-samarpaṇam*, as taught by Bali Daityarāja, is the culmination toward which every endeavor should aim. If one tries to impress the Lord with wealth, power, intelligence and so on but fails to humbly understand oneself to be His servant, one's so-called devotion is only a presumptuous show.

TEXT 38

स इन्द्रसेनो भगवत्पदाम्बुजं
बिभ्रन्मुहुः प्रेमविभिन्नया धिया ।
उवाच हानन्दजलाकुलेक्षणः
प्रहृष्टरोमा नृप गद्गदाक्षरम् ॥३८॥

sa indraseno bhagavat-padāmbujaṁ
bibhran muhuḥ prema-vibhinnayā dhiyā
uvāca hānanda-jalākulekṣaṇaḥ
prahṛṣṭa-romā nṛpa gadgadākṣaram

saḥ—he; *indra-senaḥ*—Bali, who conquered the army of Indra; *bhagavat*—of the Supreme Lords; *pada-ambujam*—the lotus feet; *bibhrat*—taking hold of; *muhuḥ*—repeatedly; *prema*—out of love; *vibhinnayā*—which was melting; *dhiyā*—from his heart; *uvāca ha*—said; *ānanda*—caused by his ecstasy; *jala*—with water (tears); *ākula*—filled; *īkṣaṇaḥ*—whose eyes; *prahṛṣṭa*—standing erect; *romā*—the hair on whose limbs; *nṛpa*—O King (Parīkṣit); *gadgada*—choking; *akṣaram*—whose syllables.

TRANSLATION

Taking hold of the Lords' lotus feet again and again, Bali, the conqueror of Indra's army, spoke from his heart, which was melting out of his intense love. O King, as tears of ecstasy filled his eyes

and the hair on his limbs stood on end, he began to speak with faltering words.

PURPORT

Śrīla Prabhupāda describes this scene as follows in *Kṛṣṇa:* "King Bali was feeling such transcendental pleasure that he repeatedly grasped the lotus feet of the Lord and kept them on his chest; and sometimes he put them on the top of his head, and in this way he was feeling transcendental bliss. Tears of love and affection began to flow down from his eyes, and all his hairs stood on end."

TEXT 39

बलिरुवाच
नमोऽनन्ताय बृहते नमः कृष्णाय वेधसे ।
सांख्ययोगवितानाय ब्रह्मणे परमात्मने ॥३९॥

balir uvāca
namo 'nantāya bṛhate
namaḥ kṛṣṇāya vedhase
sāṅkhya-yoga-vitānāya
brahmaṇe paramātmane

baliḥ uvāca—Bali said; *namaḥ*—obeisances; *anantāya*—to Ananta, the unlimited Lord; *bṛhate*—the greatest being; *namaḥ*—obeisances; *kṛṣṇāya*—to Kṛṣṇa; *vedhase*—the creator; *sāṅkhya*—of *sāṅkhya* analysis; *yoga*—and of mystic *yoga; vitānāya*—the disseminator; *brahmaṇe*—the Absolute Truth; *parama-ātmane*—the Supersoul.

TRANSLATION

King Bali said: Obeisances to the unlimited Lord, Ananta, the greatest of all beings. And obeisances to Lord Kṛṣṇa, the creator of the universe, who appears as the impersonal Absolute and the Supersoul in order to disseminate the principles of *sāṅkhya* and *yoga*.

PURPORT

Śrīla Viśvanātha Cakravartī identifies the supreme Ananta named here as Lord Balarāma, from whom expands the divine serpent Ananta Śeṣa.

Impersonal Brahman is the source of the texts belonging to the *sāṅkhya* philosophers, while the personal representation of the Lord known as Paramātmā disseminates the textbooks of *yoga*.

TEXT 40

दर्शनं वां हि भूतानां दुष्प्रापं चाप्यदुर्लभम् ।
रजस्तमःस्वभावानां यन्नः प्राप्तौ यदृच्छया ॥४०॥

darśanaṁ vāṁ hi bhūtānāṁ
duṣprāpaṁ cāpy adurlabham
rajas-tamaḥ-svabhāvānāṁ
yan naḥ prāptau yadṛcchayā

darśanam—the vision; *vām*—of You two; *hi*—indeed; *bhūtānām*—for living beings in general; *duṣprāpam*—rarely achieved; *ca api*—yet still; *adurlabham*—not difficult to obtain; *rajaḥ*—in passion; *tamaḥ*—and ignorance; *svabhāvānām*—for those whose natures; *yat*—in that; *naḥ*—by us; *prāptau*—obtained; *yadṛcchayā*—causelessly.

TRANSLATION

Seeing You Lords is a rare achievement for most living beings. But even persons like us, situated in the modes of passion and ignorance, can easily see You when You reveal Yourself by Your own sweet will.

PURPORT

By ascribing to himself the degraded status of a demoniac birth, Bali Mahārāja denied any spiritual qualification for being visited by Kṛṣṇa and Balarāma. What to speak of demons like himself, Bali thought, even advanced renunciants on the paths of *jñāna* and *yoga* fail to please the Lord when they do not give up their pride and envy.

TEXTS 41–43

दैत्यदानवगन्धर्वाः सिद्धविद्याध्रचारणाः ।
यक्षरक्षःपिशाचाश्च भूतप्रमथनायकाः ॥४१॥

विशुद्धसत्त्वधाम्न्यद्धा त्वयि शास्त्रशरीरिणि ।
नित्यं निबद्धवैरास्ते वयं चान्ये च तादृशाः ॥४२॥
केचनोद्बद्धवैरेण भक्त्या केचन कामतः ।
न तथा सत्त्वसंरब्धाः सन्निकृष्टाः सुरादयः ॥४३॥

daitya-dānava-gandharvāḥ
siddha-vidyādhra-cāraṇāḥ
yakṣa-rakṣaḥ-piśācāś ca
bhūta-pramatha-nāyakāḥ

viśuddha-sattva-dhāmny addhā
tvayi śāstra-śarīriṇi
nityaṁ nibaddha-vairās te
vayaṁ cānye ca tādṛśāḥ

kecanodbaddha-vaireṇa
bhaktyā kecana kāmataḥ
na tathā sattva-saṁrabdhāḥ
sannikṛṣṭāḥ surādayaḥ

daitya-dānava—the Daitya and Dānava demons; *gandharvāḥ*—and the Gandharvas, celestial singers; *siddha-vidyādhara-cāraṇāḥ*—the Siddha, Vidyādhara and Cāraṇa demigods; *yakṣa*—the Yakṣas (semipious spirits); *rākṣaḥ*—the Rākṣasas (man-eating spirits); *piśācāḥ*—the carnivorous Piśāca demons; *ca*—and; *bhūta*—the ghosts; *pramatha-nāyakāḥ*—and the evil Pramatha and Nāyaka spirits; *viśuddha*—perfectly pure; *sattva*—of goodness; *dhāmni*—toward the embodiment; *addhā*—direct; *tvayi*—You; *śāstra*—which comprises the revealed scriptures; *śarīriṇi*—the possessor of such a body; *nityam*—always; *nibaddha*—fixed; *vairāḥ*—in enmity; *te*—they; *vayam*—we; *ca*—also; *anye*—others; *ca*—and; *tādṛśāḥ*—like them; *kecana*—some; *udbaddha*—especially obstinate; *vaireṇa*—with hatred; *bhaktyā*—with devotion; *kecana*—some; *kāmataḥ*—rising out of lust; *na*—not; *tathā*—so; *sattva*—by the material mode of goodness; *saṁrabdhāḥ*—those who are predominated; *sannikṛṣṭāḥ*—attracted; *sura*—demigods; *ādayaḥ*—and others.

TRANSLATION

Many who had been constantly absorbed in enmity toward You ultimately became attracted to You, who are the direct embodiment of transcendental goodness and whose divine form comprises the revealed scriptures. These reformed enemies include Daityas, Dānavas, Gandharvas, Siddhas, Vidyādharas, Cāraṇas, Yakṣas, Rākṣasas, Piśācas, Bhūtas, Pramathas and Nāyakas, and also ourselves and many others like us. Some of us have become attracted to You because of exceptional hatred, while others have become attracted because of their mood of devotion based on lust. But the demigods and others infatuated by material goodness feel no such attraction for You.

PURPORT

Śrīla Jīva Gosvāmī explains this pasage as follows: The Gandharvas, Siddhas, Vidyādharas and Cāraṇas are adversaries of the Supreme Lord when they follow the lead of the Daitya and Dānava demons. The Yakṣas, Rākṣasas, Piśācas and so on tend to be inimical because they are generally covered by ignorance. There are some rascals in the pure mode of ignorance, like Śiśupāla and Pauṇḍraka, who are totally absorbed in meditation on the Lord as their enemy, and this fixed consciousness earns them liberation. Others, in a mixed condition of passion and ignorance, associate with the Lord with a desire for position and prestige; Mahārāja Bali sees himself as belonging to this category. Yet Lord Viṣṇu favored Bali by becoming his doorkeeper in the subterranean region of Sutala, just as He favored the demons by killing and liberating them, and the Gandharvas by engaging them in singing His glories. On the other hand, the Lord awards sense gratification to those demigods who are proud of their being situated in the mode of goodness; thus they become deluded and forget Him.

TEXT 44

इदमित्थमिति प्रायस्तव योगेश्वरेश्वर ।
न विदन्त्यपि योगेशा योगमायां कुतो वयम् ॥४४॥

idam ittham iti prāyas
tava yogeśvareśvara

na vidanty api yogeśā
yoga-māyāṁ kuto vayam

idam—this; *ittham*—characterized like this; *iti*—in such terms; *prāyaḥ*—for the most part; *tava*—Your; *yoga-īśvara*—of the masters of *yoga; īśvara*—O supreme master; *na vidanti*—they do not know; *api*—even; *yoga-īśāḥ*—the masters of *yoga; yoga-māyām*—Your spiritual power of delusion; *kutaḥ*—what then of; *vayam*—us.

TRANSLATION

What to speak of ourselves, O Lord of all perfect *yogīs,* even the greatest mystics do not know what Your spiritual power of delusion is or how it acts.

PURPORT

Systematic understanding of something should include knowledge of both its *svarūpa,* or essential identity, and also its *viśeṣas,* the attributes that make it different from other things. Māyā, the energy underlying all material existence, is more subtle than ordinary phenomena. Only God and His liberated devotees, therefore, can know its *svarūpa* and *viśeṣa.*

TEXT 45

तन्नः प्रसीद निरपेक्षविमृग्ययुष्मत्-
पादारविन्दधिषणान्यगृहान्धकूपात् ।
निष्क्रम्य विश्वशरणांघ्र्युपलब्धवृत्तिः
शान्तो यथैक उत सर्वसखैश्चरामि ॥४५॥

tan naḥ prasīda nirapekṣa-vimṛgya-yuṣmat-
pādāravinda-dhiṣaṇānya-gṛhāndha-kūpāt
niṣkramya viśva-śaraṇāṅghry-upalabdha-vṛttiḥ
śānto yathaika uta sarva-sakhaiś carāmi

tat—in such a way; *naḥ*—to us; *prasīda*—please be merciful; *nirapekṣa*—by those who have no material motives; *vimṛgya*—searched for; *yuṣmat*—Your; *pāda*—than the feet; *aravinda*—lotus; *dhiṣaṇa*—shelter; *anya*—other; *gṛha*—from the home; *andha*—blind; *kūpāt*—which is a well; *niṣkramya*—going out; *viśva*—to the whole world; *śaraṇa*—of those who are helpful (the trees); *aṅghri*—at the feet; *upalabdha*—obtained; *vṛttiḥ*—whose livelihood; *śāntaḥ*—peaceful; *yathā*—as; *ekaḥ*—alone; *uta*—or else; *sarva*—of everyone; *sakhaiḥ*—with the friends; *carāmi*—I may wander.

TRANSLATION

Please be merciful to me so I may get out of the blind well of family life—my false home—and find the true shelter of Your lotus feet, which selfless sages always seek. Then, either alone or in the company of great saints, who are the friends of everyone, I may wander freely, finding life's necessities at the feet of the universally charitable trees.

PURPORT

Śrīla Viśvanātha Cakravartī states that in response to Bali's prayers, Śrī Kṛṣṇa invited him to choose some benediction, and in this verse Bali submits his request. Bali begs to be relieved of the entanglement of material life so he will be free to leave home and wander in the wilderness, with only the Lord's lotus feet as his shelter. For his subsistence, Bali proposes, he will take help from the forest trees, at whose feet are fruits to eat and leaves to sleep on, for all to use as needed. And if the Lord is especially merciful to him, Bali hopes, he will not have to wander alone but will be allowed to travel in the company of Lord Kṛṣṇa's devotees.

TEXT 46

शाध्यस्मानीशितव्येश निष्पापान् कुरु नः प्रभो ।
पुमान् यच्छ्रद्धयातिष्ठंश्चोदनाया विमुच्यते ॥४६॥

śādhy asmān īśitavyeśa
niṣpāpān kuru naḥ prabho
pumān yac chraddhayātiṣṭhaṁś
codanāyā vimucyate

śādhi—please order; *asmān*—us; *īśitavya*—of those who are subject to being controlled; *īśa*—O controller; *niṣpāpān*—sinless; *kuru*—please make; *naḥ*—us; *prabho*—O master; *pumān*—a person; *yat*—which; *śraddhayā*—with faith; *ātiṣṭhan*—executing; *codanāyāḥ*—of scriptural regulation; *vimucyate*—becomes free.

TRANSLATION

O Lord of all subordinate creatures, please tell us what to do and thus free us of all sin. One who faithfully executes Your command, O master, is no longer obliged to follow the ordinary Vedic rites.

PURPORT

The *ācāryas* explain Bali's thoughts as follows. Reflecting on the possibility that his request for immediate deliverance may have been too bold, Bali Mahārāja considers that first he will need to become sufficiently purified. In any case, he thinks, Lord Kṛṣṇa and Lord Balarāma must have come to him for some specific purpose; if he can receive the Lords' order and carry it out, that will be his best opportunity for purification. Indeed, as Bali states, a devotee acting under the Personality of Godhead's instruction need no longer follow the sacrificial injunctions and prohibitions of the *Vedas.*

TEXT 47

श्रीभगवानुवाच
आसन्मरीचेः षट् पुत्रा ऊर्णायां प्रथमेऽन्तरे ।
देवाः कं जहसुर्वीक्ष्य सुतां यभितुमुद्यतम् ॥४७॥

śrī-bhagavān uvāca
āsan marīceḥ ṣaṭ putrā
ūrṇāyāṁ prathame 'ntare
devāḥ kaṁ jahasur vīkṣya
sutāṁ yabhitum udyatam

śrī-bhagavān uvāca—the Supreme Lord said; *āsan*—there were; *marīceḥ*—of Marīci; *ṣaṭ*—six; *putrāḥ*—sons; *ūrṇāyām*—born of Ūrṇā (his wife); *prathame*—in the first; *antare*—rule of Manu; *devāḥ*—demigods; *kam*—at Lord Brahmā; *jahasuḥ*—they laughed; *vīkṣya*—seeing; *sutām*—with his daughter (Sarasvatī); *yabhitum*—to copulate; *udyatam*—prepared.

TRANSLATION

The Supreme Lord said: During the age of the first Manu, the sage Marīci had six sons by his wife Ūrṇā. They were all exalted demigods, but once they laughed at Lord Brahmā when they saw him preparing to have sex with his own daughter.

TEXTS 48–49

तेनासुरीमगन् योनिमधुनावद्यकर्मणा ।
हिरण्यकशिपोर्जाता नीतास्ते योगमायया ॥४८॥
देवक्या उदरे जाता राजन् कंसविहिंसिताः ।
सा तान् शोचत्यात्मजान् स्वांस्त इमेऽध्यासतेऽन्तिके ॥४९॥

tenāsurīm agan yonim
adhunāvadya-karmaṇā
hiraṇyakaśipor jātā
nītās te yoga-māyayā

devakyā udare jātā
rājan kaṁsa-vihiṁsitāḥ
sā tān śocaty ātmajān svāṁs
ta ime 'dhyāsate 'ntike

tena—by that; *āsurīm*—demoniac; *agan*—they entered; *yonim*—a womb; *adhunā*—immediately; *avadya*—improper; *karmaṇā*—by the act; *hiraṇyakaśipoḥ*—to Hiraṇyakaśipu; *jātāḥ*—born; *nītāḥ*—brought; *te*—they; *yoga-māyayā*—by the Lord's divine power of illusion; *devakyāḥ*—of Devakī; *udare*—from the womb; *jātāḥ*—born; *rājan*—O King (Bali); *kaṁsa*—by Kaṁsa; *vihiṁsitāḥ*—murdered; *sā*—she; *tān*—for them; *śocati*—laments; *ātma-jān*—sons; *svān*—her own; *te*—they; *ime*—these same; *adhyāsate*—are living; *antike*—nearby.

TRANSLATION

Because of that improper act, they immediately entered a demoniac form of life, and thus they took birth as sons of Hiraṇyakaśipu. The goddess Yogamāyā then took them away from Hiraṇyakaśipu, and they were born again from Devakī's womb. After this, O King, Kaṁsa murdered them. Devakī still laments for them, thinking of them as her sons. These same sons of Marīci are now living here with you.

PURPORT

Ācāryas Śrīdhara Svāmī and Viśvanātha Cakravartī explain that after taking Marīci's six sons from Hiraṇyakaśipu, Lord Kṛṣṇa's Yogamāyā first made them pass through one more life as children of another great demon, Kālanemi, and then she finally transferred them to the womb of Devakī.

TEXT 50

इत एतान् प्रणेष्यामो मातृशोकापनुत्तये ।
ततः शापाद्विनिर्मुक्ता लोकं यास्यन्ति विज्वराः ॥५०॥

ita etān praṇeṣyāmo
mātṛ-śokāpanuttaye
tataḥ śāpād vinirmuktā
lokaṁ yāsyanti vijvarāḥ

itaḥ—from here; *etān*—them; *praṇeṣyāmaḥ*—We wish to take; *mātṛ*—of their mother; *śoka*—the lamentation; *apanuttaye*—in order to dispel; *tataḥ*—then; *śāpāt*—from their curse; *vinirmuktāḥ*—freed; *lokam*—to their own planet (of the demigods); *yāsyanti*—they will go; *vijvarāḥ*—relieved of their feverish condition.

TRANSLATION

We wish to take them from this place to dispel their mother's sorrow. Then, released from their curse and free from all suffering, they will return to their home in heaven.

PURPORT

As pointed out by Śrīla Prabhupāda in his purports to Chapter Two, Texts 5 and 8, of this canto, Marīci's sons were condemned for their offense against Lord Brahmā, and in addition Hiraṇyakaśipu once cursed them to be killed by their own father in a future life. This curse was fulfilled by Vasudeva's letting Kaṁsa murder them one by one.

TEXT 51

स्मरोद्गीथः परिष्वंगः पतंगः क्षुद्रभृद् घृणी ।
षडिमे मत्प्रसादेन पुनर्यास्यन्ति सद्गतिम् ॥५१॥

smarodgīthaḥ pariṣvaṅgaḥ
pataṅgaḥ kṣudrabhṛd ghṛṇī
ṣaḍ ime mat-prasādena
punar yāsyanti sad-gatim

smara-udgīthaḥ pariṣvaṅgaḥ—Smara, Udgītha and Pariṣvaṅga; *pataṅgaḥ kṣudrabhṛt ghṛṇī*—Pataṅga, Kṣudrabhṛt and Ghṛṇi; *ṣaṭ*—six; *ime*—these; *mat*—My; *prasādena*—by the grace; *punaḥ*—again; *yāsyanti*—will go; *sat*—of saintly persons; *gatim*—to the destination.

TRANSLATION

By My grace these six—Smara, Udgītha, Pariṣvaṅga, Pataṅga, Kṣudrabhṛt and Ghṛṇī—will return to the abode of pure saints.

PURPORT

These are the names the six children first had when they were sons of Marīci. The oldest, Smara, was called Kīrtimān when born again to Vasudeva, as recorded in the *Śrīmad-Bhāgavatam* (10.1.57),

kīrtimantaṁ prathama-jaṁ
kaṁsāyānakadundubhiḥ
arpayām āsa kṛcchreṇa
so 'nṛtād ati-vihvalaḥ

"Vasudeva was very much disturbed by the fear of becoming a liar by breaking his promise. Thus with great pain he delivered his firstborn son, named Kīrtimān, into the hands of Kaṁsa."

TEXT 52

इत्युक्त्वा तान् समादाय इन्द्रसेनेन पूजितौ ।
पुनर्द्वारवतीमेत्य मातुः पुत्रानयच्छताम् ॥५२॥

ity uktvā tān samādāya
indrasenena pūjitau
punar dvāravatīm etya
mātuḥ putrān ayacchatām

iti—thus; *uktvā*—speaking; *tān*—them; *samādāya*—taking; *indrasenena*—by Bali Mahārāja; *pūjitau*—both honored; *punaḥ*—once more; *dvāravatīm*—to Dvārakā; *etya*—going; *mātuḥ*—of Their mother; *putrān*—the sons; *ayacchatām*—They presented.

TRANSLATION

[Śukadeva Gosvāmī continued:] After saying this, Lord Kṛṣṇa and Lord Balarāma, having been duly worshiped by Bali Mahārāja, took the six sons and returned to Dvārakā, where They presented them to Their mother.

TEXT 53

तान् दृष्ट्वा बालकान् देवी पुत्रस्नेहस्नुतस्तनी ।
परिष्वज्यांकमारोप्य मूर्ध्न्यजिघ्रदभीक्ष्णशः ॥५३॥

tān dṛṣṭvā bālakān devī
putra-sneha-snuta-stanī
pariṣvajyāṅkam āropya
mūrdhny ajighrad abhīkṣṇaśaḥ

tān—them; *dṛṣṭvā*—seeing; *bālakān*—the boys; *devī*—the goddess (Devakī); *putra*—for her sons; *sneha*—due to her affection; *snuta*—flowing; *stanī*—whose breasts; *pariṣvajya*—embracing; *aṅkam*—on her lap; *āropya*—placing; *mūrdhni*—their heads; *ajighrat*—she smelled; *abhīkṣṇaśaḥ*—repeatedly.

TRANSLATION

When she saw her lost children, Goddess Devakī felt such affection for them that milk flowed from her breasts. She embraced them and took them onto her lap, smelling their heads again and again.

TEXT 54

अपाययत्स्तनं प्रीता सुतस्पर्शपरिस्नुतम् ।
मोहिता मायया विष्णोर्यया सृष्टिः प्रवर्तते ॥५४॥

apāyayat stanaṁ prītā
suta-sparśa-parisnutam
mohitā māyayā viṣṇor
yayā sṛṣṭiḥ pravartate

apāyayat—she let them drink; *stanam*—from her breast; *prītā*—lovingly; *suta*—of her sons; *sparśa*—because of the touch; *parisnutam*—drenched; *mohitā*—bewildered; *māyayā*—by the illusory energy; *viṣṇoḥ*—of Lord Viṣṇu; *yayā*—by which; *sṛṣṭiḥ*—creation; *pravartate*—comes into being.

TRANSLATION

Lovingly she let her sons drink from her breast, which became wet with milk just by their touch. She was entranced by the same illusory energy of Lord Viṣṇu that initiates the creation of the universe.

PURPORT

In the opinion of Śrīla Jīva Gosvāmī, the word *sṛṣṭi* can here also refer to the creative process by which Lord Viṣṇu's Yogamāyā arranges the settings and situations of His pastimes. There is indeed no question of mother Devakī being affected by the material aspect of Māyā.

TEXTS 55–56

पीत्वामृतं पयस्तस्याः पीतशेषं गदाभृतः ।
नारायणांगसंस्पर्शप्रतिलब्धात्मदर्शनाः ॥५५॥
ते नमस्कृत्य गोविन्दं देवकीं पितरं बलम् ।
मिषतां सर्वभूतानां ययुर्धाम दिवौकसाम् ॥५६॥

pītvāmṛtaṁ payas tasyāḥ
pīta-śeṣaṁ gadā-bhṛtaḥ
nārāyaṇāṅga-saṁsparśa-
pratilabdhātma-darśanāḥ

te namaskṛtya govindaṁ
devakīṁ pitaraṁ balam
miṣatāṁ sarva-bhūtānāṁ
yayur dhāma divaukasām

pītvā—having drunk; *amṛtam*—nectarean; *payaḥ*—milk; *tasyāḥ*—her; *pīta*—of what had been drunk; *śeṣam*—the remnants; *gadā-bhṛtaḥ*—of Kṛṣṇa, the wielder of the club; *nārāyaṇa*—of the Supreme Lord, Nārāyaṇa (Kṛṣṇa); *aṅga*—of the body; *saṁsparśa*—by the touch; *pratilabdha*—regained; *ātma*—of their original selves (as demigods); *darśanāḥ*—the perception; *te*—they; *namaskṛtya*—bowing down; *govindam*—to Lord Kṛṣṇa; *devakīm*—to Devakī; *pitaram*—to their father; *balam*—and to Lord Balarāma; *miṣatām*—as they looked on; *sarva*—all; *bhūtānām*—the people; *yayuḥ*—they went; *dhāma*—to the abode; *diva-okasām*—of the demigods.

TRANSLATION

By drinking her nectarean milk, the remnants of what Kṛṣṇa Himself had previously drunk, the six sons touched the transcendental body of the Lord, Nārāyaṇa, and this contact awakened them to their original identities. They bowed down to Govinda, Devakī, their father and Balarāma, and then, as everyone looked on, they left for the abode of the demigods.

PURPORT

Lord Kṛṣṇa remained as an infant with Devakī and Vasudeva for only a very short time. First the Lord appeared before them in His four-armed Viṣṇu form, and after hearing their prayers He changed Himself into an apparently ordinary infant for their pleasure. But to save Kṛṣṇa from suffering His brothers' fate, Vasudeva at once removed Him from Kaṁsa's prison. Just before Vasudeva took Him away, mother Devakī suckled Kṛṣṇa once so that He would not feel thirsty during the long trip to Nanda-vraja. This we learn from the commentary of Śrīla Viśvanātha Cakravartī Ṭhākura.

TEXT 57

तं दृष्ट्वा देवकी देवी मृतागमननिर्गमम् ।
मेने सुविस्मिता मायां कृष्णस्य रचितां नृप ॥५७॥

taṁ dṛṣṭvā devakī devī
mṛtāgamana-nirgamam
mene su-vismitā māyāṁ
kṛṣṇasya racitāṁ nṛpa

tam—this; *dṛṣṭvā*—seeing; *devakī*—Devakī; *devī*—divine; *mṛta*—of the dead (sons); *āgamana*—the return; *nirgamam*—and departure; *mene*—she thought; *su*—very much; *vismitā*—amazed; *māyām*—magic; *kṛṣṇasya*—by Kṛṣṇa; *racitām*—produced; *nṛpa*—O King (Parīkṣit).

TRANSLATION

Seeing her sons return from death and then depart again, saintly Devakī was struck with wonder, O King. She concluded that this was all simply an illusion created by Kṛṣṇa.

TEXT 58

एवंविधान्यद्भुतानि कृष्णस्य परमात्मनः ।
वीर्याण्यनन्तवीर्यस्य सन्त्यनन्तानि भारत ॥५८॥

evaṁ-vidhāny adbhutāni
kṛṣṇasya paramātmanaḥ
vīryāṇy ananta-vīryasya
santy anantāni bhārata

evam-vidhāni—like this; *adbhutāni*—amazing; *kṛṣṇasya*—of Kṛṣṇa; *parama-ātmanaḥ*—the Supreme Soul; *vīryāṇi*—feats; *ananta*—unlimited; *vīryasya*—whose valor; *santi*—there are; *anantāni*—unlimited; *bhārata*—O descendant of Bharata.

TRANSLATION

Śrī Kṛṣṇa, the Supreme Soul, the Lord of unlimited valor, performed countless pastimes just as amazing as this one, O descendant of Bharata.

TEXT 59

श्रीसूत उवाच
य इदमनुशृणोति श्रावयेद्वा मुरारेश्
चरितममृतकीर्तेर्वर्णितं व्यासपुत्रैः ।
जगदघभिदलं तद्भक्तसत्कर्णपूरं
भगवति कृतचित्तो याति तत्क्षेमधाम ॥५९॥

śrī-sūta uvāca
ya idam anuśṛṇoti śrāvayed vā murāreś
caritam amṛta-kīrter varṇitaṁ vyāsa-putraiḥ
jagad-agha-bhid alaṁ tad-bhakta-sat-karṇa-pūraṁ
bhagavati kṛta-citto yāti tat-kṣema-dhāma

śrī-sūtaḥ uvāca—Śrī Sūta said (to the sages assembled at Naimiṣāraṇya, to whom he was repeating the conversation between Śukadeva Gosvāmī and Parīkṣit Mahārāja); *yaḥ*—whoever; *idam*—this; *anuśṛṇoti*—properly hears; *śrāvayet*—causes others to hear; *vā*—or; *murāreḥ*—of Lord Kṛṣṇa, killer of the demon Mura; *caritam*—pastime; *amṛta*—deathless; *kīrteḥ*—whose glories; *varṇitam*—described; *vyāsa-putraiḥ*—by the respected son of Vyāsadeva; *jagat*—of the universe; *agha*—the sins; *bhit*—which (pastime) destroys; *alam*—totally; *tat*—His; *bhakta*—for the devotees; *sat*—transcendental; *karṇa-pūram*—ornament for the ears; *bhagavati*—on the Supreme Lord; *kṛta*—fixing; *cittaḥ*—his mind; *yāti*—he goes; *tat*—His; *kṣema*—auspicious; *dhāma*—to the personal abode.

TRANSLATION

Śrī Sūta Gosvāmī said: This pastime enacted by Lord Murāri, whose fame is eternal, totally destroys the sins of the universe and serves as the transcendental ornament for His devotees' ears. Anyone who carefully hears or narrates this pastime, as recounted by the venerable son of Vyāsa, will be able to fix his mind in meditation on the Supreme Lord and attain to the all-auspicious kingdom of God.

PURPORT

According to Śrīla Śrīdhara Svāmī, hearing the wonderful events of Lord Kṛṣṇa's life destroys sins in a manner that is perfect (*alam*) because it is easy. Anyone can easily participate in this hearing, and those who become devoted to Kṛṣṇa always enjoy wearing on their ears the ornaments of topics concerning Him. Not only those who were present at the time of their occurrence, but also Śukadeva Gosvāmī, Sūta Gosvāmī, all who have heard since and everyone in the universe who will hear in the future—all are blessed by the continuous recital of Lord Kṛṣṇa's transcendental glories.

Thus end the purports of the humble servants of His Divine Grace A. C. Bhaktivedanta Swami Prabhupāda to the Tenth Canto, Eighty-fifth Chapter, of the Śrīmad-Bhāgavatam, *entitled "Lord Kṛṣṇa Instructs Vasudeva and Retrieves Devakī's Sons."*

CHAPTER EIGHTY-SIX

Arjuna Kidnaps Subhadrā, and Kṛṣṇa Blesses His Devotees

This chapter describes how Arjuna kidnapped Subhadrā and how Lord Kṛṣṇa went to Mithilā to bless His devotees Bahulāśva and Śrutadeva.

When King Parīkṣit desired to learn about the marriage of his grandmother, Subhadrā-devī, Śrī Śukadeva Gosvāmī said, "While touring on pilgrimage, Arjuna heard that Lord Baladeva intended to give the hand of His sister Subhadrā to Duryodhana in marriage. Wanting to kidnap Subhadrā and marry her himself, Arjuna disguised himself as a renunciant and went to Dvārakā. So effective was the disguise that neither Balarāma nor any other resident of Dvārakā recognized him; rather, they all showed him the respect due a Vaiṣṇava mendicant. In this way the four months of the rainy season passed. One day Arjuna received an invitation to dine at Lord Balarāma's home. There he caught sight of Subhadrā and was immediately overwhelmed with desire for her. Subhadrā also desired to have Arjuna as her husband, and thus she glanced back at him shyly. A few days later, Subhadrā left the palace to participate in a chariot festival. Taking this opportunity, Arjuna abducted Subhadrā and defeated the Yādavas who tried to stop him. Lord Balarāma was at first greatly angered to hear of this, but when Lord Śrī Kṛṣṇa and other family members pacified Him, He became joyful and sent the bride and groom off with elaborate wedding gifts."

There was a *brāhmaṇa* devotee of Śrī Kṛṣṇa's named Śrutadeva, who lived in the city of Mithilā. By the will of Providence, he could earn only barely enough to keep himself and his family alive. Still, he was always satisfied and spent all his time executing his religious duties. King Bahulāśva was another great devotee of the Lord residing in Mithilā. A member of the dynasty in which King Janaka had appeared, Bahulāśva ruled over the whole province of Videha, yet he remained as detached from material wealth as Śrutadeva. Pleased with the devotional attitude of both these great souls, Lord Kṛṣṇa went on His chariot to Mithilā to visit them, taking along Nārada and several other learned sages. The people of

Mithilā greeted the Lord and His saintly entourage with great delight. Bearing various gifts for Kṛṣṇa, they bowed down and offered obeisances to both Him and the sages.

Bahulāśva and Śrutadeva both stepped forward and respectfully requested Śrī Kṛṣṇa to visit their homes. To satisfy both of them, the Lord expanded Himself and went to each of their homes simultaneously. They each worshiped Him suitably, offered prayers, washed His feet and then sprinkled themselves and all their family members with the wash water. Lord Kṛṣṇa then praised the sages who were with Him and glorified *brāhmaṇas* in general. He also imparted instructions to His hosts concerning devotional service. Understanding these instructions, both Śrutadeva and Bahulāśva honored the sages and Lord Śrī Kṛṣṇa with single-minded devotion. Lord Kṛṣṇa then returned to Dvārakā.

TEXT 1

श्रीराजोवाच
ब्रह्मन् वेदितुमिच्छामः स्वसारं रामकृष्णयोः ।
यथोपयेमे विजयो या ममासीत्पितामही ॥१॥

śrī-rājovāca
brahman veditum icchāmaḥ
svasāraṁ rāma-kṛṣṇayoḥ
yathopayeme vijayo
yā mamāsīt pitāmahī

śrī-rājā uvāca—the great King (Parīkṣit) said; *brahman*—O *brāhmaṇa* (Śukadeva); *veditum*—to know; *icchāmaḥ*—we wish; *svasāram*—the sister; *rāma-kṛṣṇayoḥ*—of Balarāma and Kṛṣṇa; *yathā*—how; *upayeme*—married; *vijayaḥ*—Arjuna; *yā*—she who; *mama*—my; *āsīt*—was; *pitāmahī*—the grandmother.

TRANSLATION

King Parīkṣit said: O *brāhmaṇa*, we would like to learn how Arjuna married Lord Balarāma's and Lord Kṛṣṇa's sister, who was my grandmother.

PURPORT

Parīkṣit Mahārāja turns now to the topic of the marriage of Lord Kṛṣṇa's sister, Subhadrā. In the opinion of Śrīla Śrīdhara Svāmī, King Parīkṣit's question here follows from the previous narration because Arjuna's winning the hand of Subhadrā was just as difficult a feat as Lord Kṛṣṇa's retrieving the sons of Devakī from the realm of the dead, since Lord Balarāma Himself opposed Subhadrā's marriage to Arjuna.

TEXTS 2–3

श्रीशुक उवाच
अर्जुनस्तीर्थयात्रायां पर्यटन्नवनीं प्रभुः ।
गतः प्रभासमशृणोन्मातुलेयीं स आत्मनः ॥२॥
दुर्योधनाय रामस्तां दास्यतीति न चापरे ।
तल्लिप्सुः स यतिर्भूत्वा त्रिदण्डी द्वारकामगात् ॥३॥

śrī-śuka uvāca
arjunas tīrtha-yātrāyāṁ
paryaṭann avanīṁ prabhuḥ
gataḥ prabhāsam aśṛṇon
mātuleyīṁ sa ātmanaḥ

duryodhanāya rāmas tāṁ
dāsyatīti na cāpare
tal-lipsuḥ sa yatir bhūtvā
tri-daṇḍī dvārakām agāt

śrī-śukaḥ uvāca—Śukadeva Gosvāmī said; *arjunaḥ*—Arjuna; *tīrtha*—to holy places; *yātrāyām*—while on pilgrimage; *paryaṭan*—wandering; *avanīm*—the earth; *prabhuḥ*—the great lord; *gataḥ*—having gone; *prabhāsam*—to Prabhāsa; *aśṛṇot*—heard; *mātuleyīm*—uncle's daughter; *saḥ*—he; *ātmanaḥ*—his; *duryodhanāya*—to Duryodhana; *rāmaḥ*—Lord Balarāma; *tām*—her; *dāsyati*—intends to give; *iti*—thus; *na*—not; *ca*—and; *apare*—anyone else; *tat*—her; *lipsuḥ*—desirous of obtaining; *saḥ*—he, Arjuna; *yatiḥ*—a *sannyāsī; bhūtvā*—becoming; *tri-daṇḍī*—carrying a triple staff; *dvārakām*—to Dvārakā; *agāt*—went.

TRANSLATION

Śukadeva Gosvāmī said: While traveling far and wide visiting various holy places of pilgrimage, Arjuna came to Prabhāsa. There he heard that Lord Balarāma intended to give his maternal cousin Subhadrā to Duryodhana in marriage, and that no one else approved of this plan. Arjuna wanted to marry her himself, so he disguised himself as a renunciant, complete with triple staff, and went to Dvārakā.

PURPORT

Arjuna's plan for obtaining Subhadrā as his wife may have seemed unconventional, but he was not acting without encouragement; in fact, Lord Kṛṣṇa was his prime co-conspirator. And in Dvārakā, most of the members of the royal family, especially Vasudeva, were unhappy about giving their favorite daughter to Duryodhana.

TEXT 4

तत्र वै वार्षिकान्मासानवात्सीत्स्वार्थसाधकः ।
पौरैः सभाजितोऽभीक्ष्णं रामेणाजानता च सः ॥४॥

tatra vai vārṣikān māsān
avātsīt svārtha-sādhakaḥ
pauraiḥ sabhājito 'bhīkṣṇaṁ
rāmeṇājānatā ca saḥ

tatra—there; *vai*—indeed; *vārṣikān*—of the rainy season; *māsān*—for the months; *avātsīt*—he resided; *sva*—his own; *artha*—purpose; *sādhakaḥ*—trying to achieve; *pauraiḥ*—by the people of the city; *sabhājitaḥ*—honored; *abhīkṣṇam*—constantly; *rāmeṇa*—by Lord Balarāma; *ajānatā*—who was unaware; *ca*—and; *saḥ*—he.

TRANSLATION

He stayed there during the monsoon months to fulfill his purpose. Lord Balarāma and the other residents of the city, not recognizing him, offered him all honor and hospitality.

TEXT 5

एकदा गृहमानीय आतिथ्येन निमन्त्र्य तम् ।
श्रद्धयोपहृतं भैक्ष्यं बलेन बुभुजे किल ॥५॥

ekadā gṛham ānīya
ātithyena nimantrya tam
śraddhayopahṛtaṁ bhaikṣyaṁ
balena bubhuje kila

ekadā—once; *gṛham*—to His (Balarāma's) home; *ānīya*—bringing; *ātithyena*—as a guest; *nimantrya*—inviting; *tam*—him (Arjuna); *śraddhayā*—with faith; *upahṛtam*—presented; *bhaikṣyam*—food; *balena*—by Lord Balarāma; *bubhuje*—he ate; *kila*—indeed.

TRANSLATION

One day Lord Balarāma brought him to His home as His invited dinner guest, and Arjuna ate the food the Lord respectfully offered him.

PURPORT

From the explanation of Śrīla Viśvanātha Cakravartī, it is understood that Arjuna in his *sannyāsī* role had just finished the four-month vows of the rainy season and could now again accept general invitations from householders. Thus no one would have suspected any unusual motive in his visiting Lord Balarāma at this time.

TEXT 6

सोऽपश्यत्तत्र महतीं कन्यां वीरमनोहराम् ।
प्रीत्युत्फुल्लेक्षणस्तस्यां भावक्षुब्धं मनो दधे ॥६॥

so 'paśyat tatra mahatīṁ
kanyāṁ vīra-mano-harām
prīty-utphullekṣaṇas tasyāṁ
bhāva-kṣubdhaṁ mano dadhe

saḥ—he; *apaśyat*—saw; *tatra*—there; *mahatīm*—wonderful; *kanyām*—the girl; *vīra*—to heroes; *manaḥ-harām*—enchanting; *prīti*—with happiness; *utphulla*—blossoming; *īkṣaṇaḥ*—his eyes; *tasyām*—upon her; *bhāva*—with emotion; *kṣubdham*—agitated; *manaḥ*—his mind; *dadhe*—he put.

TRANSLATION

There he saw the wonderful maiden Subhadrā, who was enchanting to heroes. His eyes opened wide with delight, and his mind became agitated and absorbed in thoughts of her.

TEXT 7

सापि तं चकमे वीक्ष्य नारीणां हृदयंगमम् ।
हसन्ती व्रीडितापांगी तन्न्यस्तहृदयेक्षणा ॥७॥

sāpi taṁ cakame vīkṣya
nārīṇāṁ hṛdayaṁ-gamam
hasantī vrīḍitāpāṅgī
tan-nyasta-hṛdayekṣaṇā

sā—she; *api*—also; *tam*—him; *cakame*—desired; *vīkṣya*—seeing; *nārīṇām*—of women; *hṛdayam-gamam*—the capturer of the hearts; *hasantī*—smiling; *vrīḍitā*—bashful; *apāṅgī*—casting sidelong glances; *tat*—upon him; *nyasta*—fixed; *hṛdaya*—her heart; *īkṣaṇā*—and eyes.

TRANSLATION

Arjuna was very attractive to women, and as soon as Subhadrā saw him, she wanted to have him as her husband. Smiling bashfully with sidelong glances, she fixed her heart and eyes upon him.

PURPORT

As soon as she saw him, Subhadrā knew that Arjuna was no *sannyāsī* but rather her destined consort. In *Kṛṣṇa, the Supreme Personality of Godhead,* His Divine Grace Śrīla Prabhupāda elaborates: "Arjuna, the grandfather of Mahārāja Parīkṣit, was himself extraordinarily beautiful, and his bodily structure was very attractive to Subhadrā. Subhadrā also decided within her mind that she would accept only Arjuna as her husband. As a simple girl, she was smiling with great pleasure, looking at Arjuna."

TEXT 8

तां परं समनुध्यायन्नन्तरं प्रेप्सुरर्जुनः ।
न लेभे शं भ्रमच्चित्तः कामेनातिबलीयसा ॥८॥

tāṁ paraṁ samanudhyāyann
antaraṁ prepsur arjunaḥ
na lebhe śaṁ bhramac-cittaḥ
kāmenāti-balīyasā

tām—on her; *param*—only; *samanudhyāyan*—meditating; *antaram*—the right opportunity; *prepsuḥ*—waiting to obtain; *arjunaḥ*—Arjuna; *na lebhe*—could not experience; *śam*—peace; *bhramat*—wavering; *cittaḥ*—his heart; *kāmena*—due to lust; *ati-balīyasā*—most strong.

TRANSLATION

Meditating only on her and waiting for the opportunity to take her away, Arjuna had no peace. His heart trembled with passionate desire.

PURPORT

Even while being honored by Lord Balarāma, Arjuna was too distracted to appreciate the Lord's gracious hospitality. Arjuna's distraction and Lord Balarāma's failure to recognize Arjuna in his disguise were both arrangements of the Supreme Lord to enjoy His transcendental pastimes.

TEXT 9

महत्यां देवयात्रायां रथस्थां दुर्गनिर्गताम् ।
जहारानुमतः पित्रोः कृष्णस्य च महारथः ॥९॥

mahatyāṁ deva-yātrāyāṁ
ratha-sthāṁ durga-nirgatām
jahārānumataḥ pitroḥ
kṛṣṇasya ca mahā-rathaḥ

mahatyām—important; *deva*—for the Supreme Lord; *yātrāyām*—during a festival; *ratha*—on a chariot; *sthām*—riding; *durga*—from the fortress; *nirgatām*—having exited; *jahāra*—he seized her; *anumataḥ*—sanctioned; *pitroḥ*—by her parents; *kṛṣṇasya*—by Kṛṣṇa; *ca*—and; *mahā-rathaḥ*—the mighty chariot warrior.

TRANSLATION

Once, on the occasion of a great temple festival in honor of the Supreme Lord, Subhadrā rode out of the fortresslike palace on a chariot, and at that time the mighty chariot warrior Arjuna took the opportunity to kidnap her. Subhadrā's parents and Kṛṣṇa had sanctioned this.

PURPORT

Śrīla Viśvanātha Cakravartī identifies this festival as the annual Ratha-yātrā for Lord Viṣṇu on the occasion of His rising from mystic sleep at the end of Cāturmāsya. Subhadrā's parents are Vasudeva and Devakī.

TEXT 10

रथस्थो धनुरादाय शूरांश्चारुन्धतो भटान् ।
विद्राव्य क्रोशतां स्वानां स्वभागं मृगराडिव ॥१०॥

ratha-stho dhanur ādāya
śūrāṁś cārundhato bhaṭān
vidrāvya krośatāṁ svānāṁ
sva-bhāgaṁ mṛga-rāḍ iva

ratha—on his chariot; *sthaḥ*—standing; *dhanuḥ*—his bow; *ādāya*—taking up; *śūrān*—the heroes; *ca*—and; *arundhataḥ*—trying to block him; *bhaṭān*—and the guards; *vidrāvya*—driving off; *krośatām*—as they shouted in anger; *svānām*—her relatives; *sva*—his own; *bhāgam*—rightful portion; *mṛga-rāṭ*—the king of animals, the lion; *iva*—just as.

TRANSLATION

Standing on his chariot, Arjuna took up his bow and drove off the valiant fighters and palace guards who tried to block his way. As her relatives shouted in anger, he took Subhadrā away just as a lion takes his prey from the midst of lesser animals.

TEXT 11

तच्छ्रुत्वा क्षुभितो रामः पर्वणीव महार्णवः ।
गृहीतपादः कृष्णेन सुहृद्भिश्चानुसान्त्वितः ॥११॥

tac chrutvā kṣubhito rāmaḥ
parvaṇīva mahārṇavaḥ
gṛhīta-pādaḥ kṛṣṇena
suhṛdbhiś cānusāntvitaḥ

tat—this; *śrutvā*—hearing; *kṣubhitaḥ*—disturbed; *rāmaḥ*—Lord Balarāma; *parvaṇi*—at the juncture of the month; *iva*—as if; *mahā-arṇavaḥ*—the ocean; *gṛhīta*—grasped; *pādaḥ*—His feet; *kṛṣṇena*—by Lord Kṛṣṇa; *suhṛdbhiḥ*—by His family members; *ca*—and; *anusāntvitaḥ*—carefully pacified.

TRANSLATION

When He heard of Subhadrā's kidnapping, Lord Balarāma became as disturbed as the ocean during the full moon, but Lord Kṛṣṇa respectfully took hold of His feet and, together with other family members, pacified Him by explaining the matter.

TEXT 12

प्राहिणोत्पारिबर्हाणि वरवध्वोर्मुदा बलः ।
महाधनोपस्करेभरथाश्वनरयोषितः ॥१२॥

prāhiṇot pāribarhāṇi
vara-vadhvor mudā balaḥ

mahā-dhanopaskarebha-
rathāśva-nara-yoṣitaḥ

prāhiṇot—He sent; *pāribarhāṇi*—as wedding gifts; *vara-vadhvoḥ*—for the groom and the bride; *mudā*—with pleasure; *balaḥ*—Lord Balarāma; *mahā-dhana*—greatly valuable; *upaskara*—presents; *ibha*—elephants; *ratha*—chariots; *aśva*—horses; *nara*—men; *yoṣitaḥ*—and women.

TRANSLATION

Lord Balarāma then happily sent the bride and groom very valuable wedding gifts consisting of elephants, chariots, horses and male and female servants.

TEXT 13

श्रीशुक उवाच
कृष्णस्यासीद् द्विजश्रेष्ठः श्रुतदेव इति श्रुतः ।
कृष्णैकभक्त्या पूर्णार्थः शान्तः कविरलम्पटः ॥१३॥

śrī-śuka uvāca
kṛṣṇasyāsīd dvija-śreṣṭhaḥ
śrutadeva iti śrutaḥ
kṛṣṇaika-bhaktyā pūrṇārthaḥ
śāntaḥ kavir alampaṭaḥ

śrī-śukaḥ uvāca—Śrī Śukadeva said; *kṛṣṇasya*—of Lord Kṛṣṇa; *āsīt*—there was; *dvija*—of *brāhmaṇas; śreṣṭhaḥ*—one of the best; *śrutadevaḥ*—Śrutadeva; *iti*—thus; *śrutaḥ*—known; *kṛṣṇa*—to Lord Kṛṣṇa; *eka*—exclusive; *bhaktyā*—by his devotion; *pūrṇa*—full; *arthaḥ*—in all goals of desire; *śāntaḥ*—peaceful; *kaviḥ*—learned and discriminating; *alam-paṭaḥ*—not desirous of sense gratification.

TRANSLATION

Śukadeva Gosvāmī continued: There was a devotee of Kṛṣṇa's known as Śrutadeva, who was a first-class *brāhmaṇa*. Perfectly satisfied by rendering unalloyed devotional service to Lord Kṛṣṇa, he was peaceful, learned and free from sense gratification.

TEXT 14

स उवास विदेहेषु मिथिलायां गृहाश्रमी ।
अनीहयागताहार्यनिर्वर्तितनिजक्रियः ॥१४॥

sa uvāsa videheṣu
mithilāyāṁ gṛhāśramī
anīhayāgatāhārya-
nirvartita-nija-kriyaḥ

saḥ—he; *uvāsa*—dwelled; *videheṣu*—in the kingdom of Videha; *mithilāyām*—in the city of Mithilā; *gṛha-āśramī*—as a member of the regulated order of family life; *anīhayā*—without endeavor; *āgata*—came to him; *āhārya*—by food and other means of sustenance; *nirvartita*—carried out; *nija*—his; *kriyaḥ*—obligations.

TRANSLATION

Living as a religious householder in the city of Mithilā, within the kingdom of Videha, he managed to fulfill his obligations while maintaining himself with whatever sustenance easily came his way.

TEXT 15

यात्रामात्रं त्वहरहर्दैवादुपनमत्युत ।
नाधिकं तावता तुष्टः क्रिया चक्रे यथोचिताः ॥१५॥

yātrā-mātraṁ tv ahar ahar
daivād upanamaty uta
nādhikaṁ tāvatā tuṣṭaḥ
kriyā cakre yathocitāḥ

yātrā-mātram—bare maintenance; *tu*—and; *ahaḥ ahaḥ*—day after day; *daivāt*—due to his fate; *upanamati*—came to him; *uta*—indeed; *na adhikam*—no more; *tāvatā*—with that much; *tuṣṭaḥ*—satisfied; *kriyāḥ*—duties; *cakre*—he did; *yathā*—as; *ucitāḥ*—appropriate.

TRANSLATION

By the will of Providence he obtained each day just what he needed for his maintenance, and no more. Satisfied with this much, he properly executed his religious duties.

PURPORT

An ideal Vaiṣṇava *brāhmaṇa,* even if encumbered by the ties of family life, should work only as hard as required to meet his obligations. Without being unnecessarily agitated for material advancement, he should devote the best part of his time and assets to his higher duties in the Supreme Lord's service. If a householder can succeed in this program despite the unavoidable difficulties of this degraded age, he can expect Lord Kṛṣṇa's personal attention, as will be seen in the case of Śrutadeva, the perfect *brāhmaṇa* of Mithilā.

TEXT 16

तथा तद्राष्ट्रपालोऽङ्ग बहुलाश्व इति श्रुतः ।
मैथिलो निरहम्मान उभावप्यच्युतप्रियौ ॥१६॥

tathā tad-rāṣṭra-pālo 'ṅga
bahulāśva iti śrutaḥ
maithilo niraham-māna
ubhāv apy acyuta-priyau

tathā—also (an advanced devotee of Kṛṣṇa); *tat*—of that; *rāṣṭra*—kingdom; *pālaḥ*—the ruler; *aṅga*—my dear (Parīkṣit); *bahulāśvaḥ iti śrutaḥ*—known as Bahulāśva; *maithilaḥ*—of the royal dynasty descending from King Mithila (Janaka); *niraham-mānaḥ*—free from false ego; *ubhau*—both of them; *api*—indeed; *acyuta-priyau*—dear to Lord Acyuta.

TRANSLATION

Similarly free from false ego was the ruler of that kingdom, my dear Parīkṣit, a descendant of the Mithila dynasty named Bahulāśva. Both these devotees were very dear to Lord Acyuta.

TEXT 17

तयोः प्रसन्नो भगवान् दारुकेणाहृतं रथम् ।
आरुह्य साकं मुनिभिर्विदेहान् प्रययौ प्रभुः ॥१७॥

tayoḥ prasanno bhagavān
dārukeṇāhṛtaṁ ratham
āruhya sākaṁ munibhir
videhān prayayau prabhuḥ

tayoḥ—with both of them; *prasannaḥ*—pleased; *bhagavān*—the Personality of Godhead; *dārukeṇa*—by Dāruka; *āhṛtam*—brought forth; *ratham*—His chariot; *āruhya*—mounting; *sākam*—together with; *munibhiḥ*—sages; *videhān*—to the Videha kingdom; *prayayau*—went; *prabhuḥ*—the Lord.

TRANSLATION

Pleased with both of them, the Supreme Personality of Godhead mounted His chariot, which Dāruka had brought, and traveled to Videha with a group of sages.

PURPORT

In his commentary on this verse, Śrīla Viśvanātha Cakravartī states that Śrutadeva and Bahulāśva were unable to travel to Dvārakā to see Lord Kṛṣṇa because both of them had vowed to regularly worship their personal Deity at home. Śrī Kṛṣṇa was very glad to go out of His way to give them both His audience, and while leaving Dvārakā He insisted that the sages who wanted to come with Him should join Him on His chariot, because otherwise they would exhaust themselves following on foot. Renowned sages would ordinarily never even consider traveling in such an opulent conveyance, but on the Lord's order they put aside their natural aversion and joined Him on His chariot.

TEXT 18

नारदो वामदेवोऽत्रिः कृष्णो रामोऽसितोऽरुणिः ।
अहं बृहस्पतिः कण्वो मैत्रेयश्च्यवनादयः ॥१८॥

nārado vāmadevo 'triḥ
kṛṣṇo rāmo 'sito 'ruṇiḥ
ahaṁ bṛhaspatiḥ kaṇvo
maitreyaś cyavanādayaḥ

nāradaḥ vāmadevaḥ atriḥ—the sages Nārada, Vāmadeva and Atri; *kṛṣṇaḥ*—Kṛṣṇa-dvaipāyana Vyāsa; *rāmaḥ*—Lord Paraśurāma; *asitaḥ aruṇiḥ*—Asita and Aruṇi; *aham*—I (Śukadeva); *bṛhaspatiḥ kaṇvaḥ*—Bṛhaspati and Kaṇva; *maitreyaḥ*—Maitreya; *cyavana*—Cyavana; *ādayaḥ*—and others.

TRANSLATION

Among these sages were Nārada, Vāmadeva, Atri, Kṛṣṇa-dvaipāyana Vyāsa, Paraśurāma, Asita, Aruṇi, myself, Bṛhaspati, Kaṇva, Maitreya and Cyavana.

TEXT 19

तत्र तत्र तमायान्तं पौरा जानपदा नृप ।
उपतस्थुः सार्घ्यहस्ता ग्रहैः सूर्यमिवोदितम् ॥१९॥

tatra tatra tam āyāntaṁ
paurā jānapadā nṛpa
upatasthuḥ sārghya-hastā
grahaiḥ sūryam ivoditam

tatra tatra—in each place; *tam*—Him; *āyāntam*—as He was coming; *paurāḥ*—city residents; *jānapadāḥ*—and village residents; *nṛpa*—O King (Parīkṣit); *upatasthuḥ*—came forward to greet Him; *sa*—with; *arghya*—water to offer as a token of respect; *hastāḥ*—in their hands; *grahaiḥ*—by the planets; *sūryam*—the sun; *iva*—as; *uditam*—risen.

TRANSLATION

In every city and town the Lord passed along the way, O King, the people came forward to worship Him with offerings of *arghya* water in their hands, as if to worship the risen sun surrounded by planets.

PURPORT

Here the sages traveling with Kṛṣṇa on His chariot are likened to planets around the sun.

TEXT 20

आनर्तधन्वकुरुजांगलकंकमत्स्य-
पाञ्चालकुन्तिमधुकेकयकोशलार्णाः ।
अन्ये च तन्मुखसरोजमुदारहास-
स्निग्धेक्षणं नृप पपुर्दृशिभिर्नृनार्यः ॥२०॥

ānarta-dhanva-kuru-jāṅgala-kaṅka-matsya-
pāñcāla-kunti-madhu-kekaya-kośalārṇāḥ
anye ca tan-mukha-sarojam udāra-hāsa-
snigdhekṣaṇaṁ nṛpa papur dṛśibhir nṛ-nāryaḥ

ānarta—the people of Ānarta (the region in which Dvārakā is situated); *dhanva*—the desert (of Gujarat and Rajasthan); *kuru-jāṅgala*—the region of the Kuru forests (the districts of Thaneswar and Kurukṣetra); *kaṅka*—Kaṅka; *matsya*—Matsya (the kingdoms of Jaipur and Aloyar); *pāñcāla*—the districts surrounding both banks of the Ganges; *kunti*—Mālava; *madhu*—Mathurā; *kekaya*—in northeast Punjab, the region between the Śatadru and Vipāśā rivers; *kośala*—the ancient kingdom of Lord Rāmacandra, stretching from the northern border of Kāśī to the Himalayas; *arṇāḥ*—and the kingdom bordering Mithilā on the east; *anye*—others; *ca*—also; *tat*—His; *mukha*—face; *sarojam*—lotus; *udāra*—generous; *hāsa*—with its smiles; *snigdha*—and affectionate; *īkṣaṇam*—glances; *nṛpa*—O King; *papuḥ*—drank; *dṛśibhiḥ*—with their eyes; *nṛ-nāryaḥ*—the men and women.

TRANSLATION

The men and women of Ānarta, Dhanva, Kuru-jāṅgala, Kaṅka, Matsya, Pāñcāla, Kunti, Madhu, Kekaya, Kośala, Arṇa and many other kingdoms drank with their eyes the nectarean beauty of Lord Kṛṣṇa's lotuslike face, which was graced with generous smiles and affectionate glances.

TEXT 21

तेभ्यः स्ववीक्षणविनष्टतमिस्रदृग्भ्यः
क्षेमं त्रिलोकगुरुरर्थदृशं च यच्छन् ।
शृण्वन् दिगन्तधवलं स्वयशोऽशुभघ्नं
गीतं सुरैर्नृभिरगाच्छनकैर्विदेहान् ॥२१॥

tebhyaḥ sva-vīkṣaṇa-vinaṣṭa-tamisra-dṛgbhyaḥ
kṣemaṁ tri-loka-gurur artha-dṛśaṁ ca yacchan
śṛṇvan dig-anta-dhavalaṁ sva-yaśo 'śubha-ghnaṁ
gītaṁ surair nṛbhir agāc chanakair videhān

tebhyaḥ—to them; *sva*—His; *vīkṣaṇa*—by the glance; *vinaṣṭa*—destroyed; *tamisra*—the darkness; *dṛgbhyaḥ*—of whose eyes; *kṣemam*—fearlessness; *tri*—three; *loka*—of the worlds; *guruḥ*—the spiritual master; *artha-dṛśam*—spiritual vision; *ca*—and; *yacchan*—bestowing; *śṛṇvan*—hearing; *dik*—of the directions; *anta*—the ends; *dhavalam*—which purify; *sva*—His; *yaśaḥ*—glories; *aśubha*—inauspiciousness; *ghnam*—which eradicate; *gītam*—sung; *suraiḥ*—by demigods; *nṛbhiḥ*—and by men; *agāt*—He came; *śanakaiḥ*—gradually; *videhān*—to the kingdom of Videha.

TRANSLATION

Simply by glancing at those who came to see Him, Lord Kṛṣṇa, the spiritual master of the three worlds, delivered them from the blindness of materialism. As He thus endowed them with fearlessness and divine vision, He heard demigods and men singing His glories, which purify the entire universe and destroy all misfortune. Gradually, He reached Videha.

PURPORT

Śrīla Jīva Gosvāmī raises the logical question of how the ordinary people along the path could even see the Lord, since not only were their eyes covered by ignorance, but the Lord's chariot was traveling faster than the wind. Supplying the answer, Śrīla Jīva indicates that Lord Kṛṣṇa's special glance of mercy empowered every one of them with the devotional purity required for entering into His association. Otherwise,

He would have remained outside the scope of their power to see, as He Himself states in His instructions to Uddhava: *bhaktyāham ekayā grāhyaḥ*. "I can be perceived only by devotion." (*Bhāg*. 11.14.21) By the grammatical rule of compound formation known as *eka-śeṣa*, the term *sva-vīkṣaṇa-vinaṣṭa-tamisra-dṛgbhyaḥ*, although in its primary sense inflected as a masculine noun, may be understood in this context as referring to both men and women.

TEXT 22

तेऽच्युतं प्राप्तमाकर्ण्य पौरा जानपदा नृप ।
अभीयुर्मुदितास्तस्मै गृहीतार्हणपाणयः ॥२२॥

te 'cyutaṁ prāptam ākarṇya
paurā jānapadā nṛpa
abhīyur muditās tasmai
gṛhītārhaṇa-pāṇayaḥ

te—they; *acyutam*—Lord Kṛṣṇa; *prāptam*—arrived; *ākarṇya*—hearing; *paurāḥ*—the people of the city; *jānapadāḥ*—and of the villages; *nṛpa*—O King; *abhīyuḥ*—came forward; *muditāḥ*—joyful; *tasmai*—to Him; *gṛhīta*—holding; *arhaṇa*—offerings to present to Him; *pāṇayaḥ*—in their hands.

TRANSLATION

Hearing that Lord Acyuta had arrived, O King, the residents of the cities and villages of Videha joyfully came forth to receive Him with offerings in their hands.

TEXT 23

दृष्ट्वा त उत्तमःश्लोकं प्रीत्युत्फुल्लाननाशयाः ।
कैर्धृताञ्जलिभिर्नेमुः श्रुतपूर्वांस्तथा मुनीन् ॥२३॥

dṛṣṭvā ta uttamaḥ-ślokaṁ
prīty-utphullānanāśayāḥ
kair dhṛtāñjalibhir nemuḥ
śruta-pūrvāṁs tathā munīn

dṛṣṭvā—seeing; *te*—they; *uttamaḥ-ślokam*—Lord Kṛṣṇa, who is praised in sublime poetry; *prīti*—with love; *utphulla*—broadly blossoming; *ānana*—their faces; *āśayāḥ*—and hearts; *kaiḥ*—on their heads; *dhṛta*—held; *añjalibhiḥ*—with joined palms; *nemuḥ*—they bowed down; *śruta*—heard of; *pūrvān*—before; *tathā*—also; *munīn*—to the sages.

TRANSLATION

As soon as the people saw Lord Uttamaḥśloka, their faces and hearts blossomed with affection. Joining their palms above their heads, they bowed down to the Lord and to the sages accompanying Him, whom they had previously only heard about.

TEXT 24

स्वानुग्रहाय सम्प्राप्तं मन्वानौ तं जगद्गुरुम् ।
मैथिलः श्रुतदेवश्च पादयोः पेततुः प्रभोः ॥२४॥

svānugrahāya samprāptaṁ
manvānau taṁ jagad-gurum
maithilaḥ śrutadevaś ca
pādayoḥ petatuḥ prabhoḥ

sva—to himself; *anugrahāya*—for showing mercy; *samprāptam*—now; *manvānau*—both thinking; *tam*—Him; *jagat*—of the universe; *gurum*—the spiritual master; *maithilaḥ*—the King of Mithilā; *śruta-devaḥ*—Śrutadeva; *ca*—and; *pādayoḥ*—at the feet; *petatuḥ*—fell; *prabhoḥ*—of the Lord.

TRANSLATION

Both the King of Mithilā and Śrutadeva fell at the Lord's feet, each thinking that the spiritual master of the universe had come there just to show him mercy.

TEXT 25

न्यमन्त्रयेतां दाशार्हमातिथ्येन सह द्विजैः ।
मैथिलः श्रुतदेवश्च युगपत्संहताञ्जली ॥२५॥

nyamantrayetāṁ dāśārham
ātithyena saha dvijaiḥ
maithilaḥ śrutadevaś ca
yugapat saṁhatāñjalī

nyamantrayetām—they both invited; *dāśārham*—Kṛṣṇa, the descendant of Daśārha; *ātithyena*—to be their guest; *saha*—along with; *dvijaiḥ*—the *brāhmaṇas; maithilaḥ*—Bahulāśva; *śrutadevaḥ*—Śrutadeva; *ca*—and; *yugapat*—simultaneously; *saṁhata*—held firmly together; *añjalī*—whose palms.

TRANSLATION

At exactly the same time, King Maithila and Śrutadeva each went forward with joined palms and invited the Lord of the Daśārhas to be his guest, along with the *brāhmaṇa* sages.

TEXT 26

भगवांस्तदभिप्रेत्य द्वयोः प्रियचिकीर्षया ।
उभयोराविशद् गेहमुभाभ्यां तदलक्षितः ॥२६॥

bhagavāṁs tad abhipretya
dvayoḥ priya-cikīrṣayā
ubhayor āviśad geham
ubhābhyāṁ tad-alakṣitaḥ

bhagavān—the Supreme Lord; *tat*—this; *abhipretya*—accepting; *dvayoḥ*—of the two of them; *priya*—the pleasing; *cikīrṣayā*—wishing to do; *ubhayoḥ*—of both; *āviśat*—He entered; *geham*—the houses; *ubhābhyām*—to both; *tat*—in that (entering of the other's house); *alakṣitaḥ*—unseen.

TRANSLATION

Wanting to please them both, the Lord accepted both their invitations. Thus He simultaneously went to both homes, and neither could see Him entering the other's house.

PURPORT

According to Śrīla Viśvanātha Cakravartī, Kṛṣṇa visited Śrutadeva and Balahulāśva at the same time by manifesting Himself in duplicate forms, along with the sages. Thus King Bahulāśva thought that Lord Kṛṣṇa had come only to his house, leaving Śrutadeva to return home disappointed, while Śrutadeva believed that just the reverse was the case.

In *Kṛṣṇa,* Śrīla Prabhupāda remarks, "That [Lord Kṛṣṇa] and His companions were present in both houses, although both the *brāhmaṇa* and the King thought He was present in his house only, is another opulence of the Supreme Personality of Godhead. This opulence is described in the revealed scriptures as *vaibhava-prakāśa.* Similarly, when Lord Kṛṣṇa married sixteen thousand wives, He also expanded Himself into sixteen thousand forms, each one of them as powerful as He Himself. Similarly, in Vṛndāvana, when Brahmā stole away Kṛṣṇa's cows, calves and cowherd boys, Kṛṣṇa expanded Himself into many new cows, calves and cowherd boys."

TEXTS 27–29

श्रान्तानप्यथ तान् दूराज्जनकः स्वगृहागतान् ।
आनीतेष्वासनाग्र्येषु सुखासीनान्महामनाः ॥२७॥
प्रवृद्धभक्त्या उद्धर्षहृदयास्राविलेक्षणः ।
नत्वा तदङ्घ्रीन् प्रक्षाल्य तदपो लोकपावनीः ॥२८॥
सकुटुम्बो वहन्मूर्ध्ना पूजयां चक्र ईश्वरान् ।
गन्धमाल्याम्बराकल्पधूपदीपार्घ्यगोवृषैः ॥२९॥

śrāntān apy atha tān dūrāj
janakaḥ sva-gṛhāgatān
ānīteṣv āsanāgryeṣu
sukhāsīnān mahā-manāḥ

pravṛddha-bhaktyā uddharṣa-
hṛdayāsrāvilekṣaṇaḥ
natvā tad-aṅghrīn prakṣālya
tad-apo loka-pāvanīḥ

sa-kuṭumbo vahan mūrdhnā
pūjayāṁ cakra īśvarān
gandha-mālyāmbarākalpa-
dhūpa-dīpārghya-go-vṛṣaiḥ

śrāntān—fatigued; *api*—indeed; *atha*—then; *tān*—them; *dūrāt*—from a distance; *janakaḥ*—King Bahulāśva, a descendant of Janaka; *sva*—to his; *gṛha*—home; *āgatān*—come; *ānīteṣu*—which were brought out; *āsana*—on seats; *agryeṣu*—excellent; *sukha*—comfortably; *āsīnān*—seated; *mahā-manāḥ*—very intelligent; *pravṛddha*—intense; *bhaktyā*—with devotion; *ut-dharṣa*—overjoyed; *hṛdaya*—whose heart; *asra*—with tears; *āvila*—clouded; *īkṣaṇaḥ*—whose eyes; *natvā*—bowing down; *tat*—their; *aṅghrīn*—feet; *prakṣālya*—washing; *tat*—from that; *apaḥ*—the water; *loka*—the whole world; *pāvanīḥ*—able to purify; *sa*—together with; *kuṭumbaḥ*—his family; *vahan*—carrying; *mūrdhnā*—on his head; *pūjayām cakre*—he worshiped; *īśvarān*—the lords; *gandha*—with fragrant (sandalwood) paste; *mālya*—flower garlands; *ambara*—clothing; *ākalpa*—jewelry; *dhūpa*—incense; *dīpa*—lamps; *arghya*—*arghya* water; *go*—cows; *vṛṣaiḥ*—and bulls.

TRANSLATION

When King Bahulāśva, a descendant of Janaka, saw Lord Kṛṣṇa approaching his house from a distance with the sages, who were somewhat fatigued from the journey, he immediately arranged to have seats of honor brought out for them. After they were all comfortably seated, the wise King, his heart overflowing with joy and his eyes clouded by tears, bowed down to them and washed their feet with intense devotion. Taking the wash water, which could purify the entire world, he sprinkled it on his head and the heads of his family members. Then he worshiped all those great lords by offering them fragrant sandalwood paste, flower garlands, fine clothing and ornaments, incense, lamps, *arghya* and cows and bulls.

PURPORT

Śrīla Prabhupāda comments, "Bahulāśva, the King of Videha, was very intelligent and was a perfect gentleman. He was astonished that so many great sages, along with the Supreme Personality of Godhead, were personally present in his home. He knew perfectly well that the conditioned soul, especially when engaged in worldly affairs, cannot be a hundred percent pure, whereas the Supreme Personality of Godhead and His pure devotees are always transcendental to worldly contamination. Therefore, when he found that the Supreme Personality of Godhead Kṛṣṇa and all the great sages were at his home, he was astonished, and he began to thank Lord Kṛṣṇa for His causeless mercy."

The word *īśvara* in this verse refers not only to the Supreme Lord but also to the exalted sages in His company; this is confirmed by Ācāryas Śrīdhara Svāmī and Viśvanātha Cakravartī.

TEXT 30

वाचा मधुरया प्रीणन्निदमाहान्नतर्पितान् ।
पादावंकगतौ विष्णोः संस्पृशञ्छनकैर्मुदा ॥३०॥

vācā madhurayā prīṇann
idam āhānna-tarpitān
pādāv aṅka-gatau viṣṇoḥ
saṁspṛśañ chanakair mudā

vācā—in a voice; *madhurayā*—gentle; *prīṇan*—trying to please them; *idam*—this; *āha*—he said; *anna*—with food; *tarpitān*—who had been gratified; *pādau*—the feet; *aṅka*—on his lap; *gatau*—situated; *viṣṇoḥ*—of Lord Kṛṣṇa; *saṁspṛśan*—massaging; *śanakaiḥ*—slowly; *mudā*—happily.

TRANSLATION

When they had eaten to their full satisfaction, for their further pleasure the King began to speak slowly and in a gentle voice as he held Lord Viṣṇu's feet in his lap and happily massaged them.

TEXT 31

श्रीबहुलाश्व उवाच

भवान् हि सर्वभूतानामात्मा साक्षी स्वदृग् विभो ।
अथ नस्त्वत्पदाम्भोजं स्मरतां दर्शनं गतः ॥३१॥

śrī-bahulāśva uvāca
bhavān hi sarva-bhūtānām
ātmā sākṣī sva-dṛg vibho
atha nas tvat-padāmbhojaṁ
smaratāṁ darśanaṁ gataḥ

śrī-bahulāśvaḥ uvāca—Śrī Bahulāśva said; *bhavān*—You; *hi*—indeed; *sarva*—of all; *bhūtānām*—created beings; *ātmā*—the Supreme Soul; *sākṣī*—the witness; *sva-dṛk*—self-illumined; *vibho*—O almighty one; *atha*—thus; *naḥ*—to us; *tvat*—Your; *pada-ambhojam*—lotus feet; *smaratām*—who are remembering; *darśanam gataḥ*—have become visible.

TRANSLATION

Śrī Bahulāśva said: O almighty Lord, You are the Soul of all created beings, their self-illumined witness, and now You are giving Your audience to us, who constantly meditate on Your lotus feet.

PURPORT

Śrīla Viśvanātha Cakravartī explains Bahulāśva's inner thoughts as follows: Bahulāśva glorifies Lord Kṛṣṇa as the inspiring Soul of all life and consciousness, thinking that even an inert dullard like himself could be awakened to devotional awareness by His mercy. He glorifies the Lord as the witness of all pious and impious actions, confident that the Lord remembers whatever little devotional service he has ever done. And he glorifies Him as self-illumined, never needing to be enlightened or informed by any external source, with the knowledge that the Lord has always been aware of Bahulāśva's long-cherished secret desire to see Him.

TEXT 32

स्ववचस्तदृतं कर्तुमस्मद्दृग्गोचरो भवान् ।
यदात्थैकान्तभक्तान्मे नानन्तः श्रीरजः प्रियः ॥३२॥

sva-vacas tad ṛtaṁ kartum
asmad-dṛg-gocaro bhavān

yad ātthaikānta-bhaktān me
nānantaḥ śrīr ajaḥ priyaḥ

sva—Your own; *vacaḥ*—statement; *tat*—that; *ṛtam*—true; *kartum*—to make; *asmat*—our; *dṛk*—to the eyes; *gocaraḥ*—accessible; *bhavān*—You; *yat*—which; *āttha*—spoke; *eka-anta*—with a single aim; *bhaktāt*—than the devotee; *me*—my; *na*—not; *anantaḥ*—Lord Ananta; *śrīḥ*—Goddess Śrī; *ajaḥ*—unborn Brahmā; *priyaḥ*—more dear.

TRANSLATION

You have said, "Neither Ananta, Goddess Śrī nor unborn Brahmā is dearer to Me than My unalloyed devotee." To prove Your own words true, You have now revealed Yourself to our eyes.

TEXT 33

को नु त्वच्चरणाम्भोजमेवंविद्विसृजेत्पुमान् ।
निष्किञ्चनानां शान्तानां मुनीनां यस्त्वमात्मदः ॥३३॥

ko nu tvac-caraṇāmbhojam
evaṁ-vid visṛjet pumān
niṣkiñcanānāṁ śāntānāṁ
munīnāṁ yas tvam ātma-daḥ

kaḥ—who; *nu*—at all; *tvat*—Your; *caraṇa-ambhojam*—lotus feet; *evam*—like this; *vit*—being in knowledge; *visṛjet*—would abandon; *pumān*—person; *niṣkiñcanānām*—for those who have no material possessions; *śāntānām*—who are peaceful; *munīnām*—sages; *yaḥ*—who; *tvam*—You; *ātma*—Yourself; *daḥ*—giving.

TRANSLATION

What person who knows this truth would ever abandon Your lotus feet, when You are ready to give Your very self to peaceful sages who call nothing their own?

TEXT 34

योऽवतीर्य यदोर्वंशे नृणां संसरतामिह ।
यशो वितेने तच्छान्त्यै त्रैलोक्यवृजिनापहम् ॥३४॥

yo 'vatīrya yador vaṁśe
nṛṇāṁ saṁsaratām iha
yaśo vitene tac-chāntyai
trai-lokya-vṛjināpaham

yaḥ—who; *avatīrya*—descending; *yadoḥ*—of Yadu; *vaṁśe*—into the dynasty; *nṛṇām*—for people; *saṁsaratām*—who are caught up in the cycle of birth and death; *iha*—in this world; *yaśaḥ*—Your fame; *vitene*—has disseminated; *tat*—of that (material existence); *śāntyai*—for the stopping; *trai-lokya*—of the three worlds; *vṛjina*—the sins; *apaham*—which removes.

TRANSLATION

Appearing in the Yadu dynasty, You have spread Your glories, which can remove all the sins of the three worlds, just to deliver those entrapped in the cycle of birth and death.

TEXT 35

नमस्तुभ्यं भगवते कृष्णायाकुण्ठमेधसे ।
नारायणाय ऋषये सुशान्तं तप ईयुषे ॥३५॥

namas tubhyaṁ bhagavate
kṛṣṇāyākuṇṭha-medhase
nārāyaṇāya ṛṣaye
su-śāntaṁ tapa īyuṣe

namaḥ—obeisances; *tubhyam*—to You; *bhagavate*—the Supreme Lord; *kṛṣṇāya*—Kṛṣṇa; *akuṇṭha*—unconstricted; *medhase*—whose intelligence; *nārāyaṇāya ṛṣaye*—to the sage Nara-Nārāyaṇa; *su-śāntam*—perfectly peaceful; *tapaḥ*—austerities; *īyuṣe*—undergoing.

TRANSLATION

Obeisances to You, the Supreme Personality of Godhead, Lord Kṛṣṇa, whose intelligence is ever unrestricted. Obeisances to the sage Nara-Nārāyaṇa, who always undergoes austerities in perfect peace.

PURPORT

Śrīla Viśvanātha Cakravartī comments that the King offered these prayers to encourage Lord Kṛṣṇa to remain at his home for some days. The King thought, "Since contact with the Supreme Lord can free anyone from misconceptions and doubts, Kṛṣṇa's presence in my home will fortify my intelligence so that I can withstand the onslaughts of material desires. In His expansion as Nara-Nārāyaṇa Ṛṣi, the Lord always resides in Badarikāśrama for the good of the whole land of Bhārata, and so He may also create good fortune for the land of Mithilā by remaining here for at least a few days. Since Lord Kṛṣṇa's propensity is toward peace and simplicity, He will certainly prefer my simple home to the excessive opulence of Dvārakā."

TEXT 36

दिनानि कतिचिद् भूमन् गृहान्नो निवस द्विजैः ।
समेतः पादरजसा पुनीहीदं निमेः कुलम् ॥३६॥

dināni katicid bhūman
gṛhān no nivasa dvijaiḥ
sametaḥ pāda-rajasā
punīhīdaṁ nimeḥ kulam

dināni—days; *katicit*—a few; *bhūman*—O omnipresent one; *gṛhān*—in the home; *naḥ*—our; *nivasa*—please dwell; *dvijaiḥ*—by the *brāhmaṇas; sametaḥ*—joined; *pāda*—of Your feet; *rajasā*—with the dust; *punīhi*—please sanctify; *idam*—this; *nimeḥ*—of King Nimi; *kulam*—the dynasty.

TRANSLATION

Please stay a few days in our house, along with these *brāhmaṇas*, O all-pervading one, and with the dust of Your feet sanctify this dynasty of Nimi.

TEXT 37

इत्युपामन्त्रितो राज्ञा भगवान् लोकभावनः ।
उवास कुर्वन् कल्याणं मिथिलानरयोषिताम् ॥३७॥

ity upāmantrito rājñā
bhagavāl̐ loka-bhāvanaḥ
uvāsa kurvan kalyāṇaṁ
mithilā-nara-yoṣitām

iti—thus; *upāmantritaḥ*—invited; *rājñā*—by the King; *bhagavān*—the Supreme Lord; *loka*—of the entire world; *bhāvanaḥ*—the maintainer; *uvāsa*—resided; *kurvan*—creating; *kalyāṇam*—good fortune; *mithilā*—of the city of Mithilā; *nara*—for the men; *yoṣitām*—and women.

TRANSLATION

[Śukadeva Gosvāmī continued:] Thus invited by the King, the Supreme Lord, sustainer of the world, consented to stay for some time to bestow good fortune on the men and women of Mithilā.

TEXT 38

श्रुतदेवोऽच्युतं प्राप्तं स्वगृहाञ् जनको यथा ।
नत्वा मुनीन् सुसंहृष्टो धुन्वन् वासो ननर्त ह ॥३८॥

śrutadevo 'cyutaṁ prāptaṁ
sva-gṛhāñ janako yathā
natvā munīn su-saṁhṛṣṭo
dhunvan vāso nanarta ha

śrutadevaḥ—Śrutadeva; *acyutam*—Lord Kṛṣṇa; *prāptam*—obtained; *sva-gṛhān*—at his house; *janakaḥ*—Bahulāśva; *yathā*—just as; *natvā*—bowing down; *munīn*—to the sages; *su*—very much; *saṁhṛṣṭaḥ*—delighted; *dhunvan*—waving; *vāsaḥ*—his cloth; *nanarta ha*—he danced.

TRANSLATION

Śrutadeva received Lord Acyuta into his home with as much enthusiasm as that shown by King Bahulāśva. After bowing down to the Lord and the sages, Śrutadeva began to dance with great joy, waving his shawl.

TEXT 39

तृणपीठबृषीष्वेतानानीतेषूपवेश्य सः ।
स्वागतेनाभिनन्द्याङ्घ्रीन् सभार्योऽवनिजे मुदा ॥३९॥

tṛṇa-pīṭha-bṛṣīṣv etān
ānīteṣūpaveśya saḥ
svāgatenābhinandyāṅghrīn
sa-bhāryo 'vanije mudā

tṛṇa—of grass; *pīṭha*—on seats; *bṛṣīṣu*—and on mats of *darbha; etān*—them; *ānīteṣu*—which were brought; *upaveśya*—making sit; *saḥ*—he; *sva-āgatena*—with words of welcome; *abhinandya*—greeting them; *aṅghrīn*—their feet; *sa-bhāryaḥ*—together with his wife; *avanije*—washed; *mudā*—with pleasure.

TRANSLATION

After bringing mats of grass and *darbha* straw and seating his guests upon them, he greeted them with words of welcome. Then he and his wife washed their feet with great pleasure.

PURPORT

To provide even this simple welcome, Śrutadeva had to go next door to his neighbors and borrow extra mats. This insight is provided by Śrīla Viśvanātha Cakravartī.

TEXT 40

तदम्भसा महाभाग आत्मानं सगृहान्वयम् ।
स्नापयां चक्र उद्धर्षो लब्धसर्वमनोरथः ॥४०॥

tad-ambhasā mahā-bhāga
ātmānaṁ sa-gṛhānvayam
snāpayāṁ cakra uddharṣo
labdha-sarva-manorathaḥ

tat—with that; *ambhasā*—water; *mahā-bhāgaḥ*—very pious; *ātmānam*—himself; *sa*—along with; *gṛha*—his house; *anvayam*—and his family; *snāpayām cakre*—he bathed; *uddharṣaḥ*—overjoyed; *labdha*—having attained; *sarva*—all; *manaḥ-rathaḥ*—desires.

TRANSLATION

With the wash water, the virtuous Śrutadeva copiously sprinkled himself, his house and his family. Overjoyed, he felt that all his desires had now been fulfilled.

TEXT 41

फलार्हणोशीरशिवामृताम्बुभिर्
मृदा सुरभ्या तुलसीकुशाम्बुजैः ।
आराधयामास यथोपपन्नया
सपर्यया सत्त्वविवर्धनान्धसा ॥४१॥

phalārhaṇośīra-śivāmṛtāmbubhir
mṛdā surabhyā tulasī-kuśāmbujaiḥ
ārādhayām āsa yathopapannayā
saparyayā sattva-vivardhanāndhasā

phala—of fruits; *arhaṇa*—with offerings; *uśīra*—with a kind of aromatic root; *śiva*—pure; *amṛta*—nectar-sweet; *ambubhiḥ*—and with water; *mṛdā*—with clay; *surabhyā*—fragrant; *tulasī*—*tulasī* leaves; *kuśa*—*kuśa* grass; *ambujaiḥ*—and lotus flowers; *ārādhayām āsa*—he worshiped them; *yathā*—as; *upapannayā*—could be obtained; *saparyayā*—with items of worship; *sattva*—the mode of goodness; *vivardhana*—which increases; *andhasā*—with food.

TRANSLATION

He worshiped them with offerings of auspicious items easily available to him, such as fruits, *uśīra* root, pure, nectarean water, fragrant clay, *tulasī* leaves, *kuśa* grass and lotus flowers. Then he offered them food that increases the mode of goodness.

TEXT 42

स तर्कयामास कुतो ममान्वभूत्
गृहान्धकूपे पतितस्य संगमः ।
यः सर्वतीर्थास्पदपादरेणुभिः
कृष्णेन चास्यात्मनिकेतभूसुरैः ॥४२॥

sa tarkayām āsa kuto mamānv abhūt
gṛhāndha-kūpe patitasya saṅgamaḥ
yaḥ sarva-tīrthāspada-pāda-reṇubhiḥ
kṛṣṇena cāsyātma-niketa-bhūsuraiḥ

saḥ—he; *tarkayām āsa*—tried to understand; *kutaḥ*—for what reason; *mama*—for me; *anu*—indeed; *abhūt*—has happened; *gṛha*—of home; *andha*—blind; *kūpe*—in the well; *patitasya*—fallen; *saṅgamaḥ*—association; *yaḥ*—which; *sarva*—of all; *tīrtha*—holy places; *āspada*—which is the shelter; *pāda*—of whose feet; *reṇubhiḥ*—the dust; *kṛṣṇena*—with Lord Kṛṣṇa; *ca*—also; *asya*—this; *ātma*—of Himself; *niketa*—who are the place of residence; *bhū-suraiḥ*—with the *brāhmaṇas.*

TRANSLATION

He wondered: How is it that I, fallen into the blind well of family life, have been able to meet Lord Kṛṣṇa? And how have I also been allowed to meet these great *brāhmaṇas,* who always carry the Lord within their hearts? Indeed, the dust of their feet is the shelter of all holy places.

TEXT 43

सूपविष्टान् कृतातिथ्यान् श्रुतदेव उपस्थितः ।
सभार्यस्वजनापत्य उवाचांघ्र्यभिमर्शनः ॥४३॥

sūpaviṣṭān kṛtātithyān
śrutadeva upasthitaḥ
sa-bhārya-svajanāpatya
uvācāṅghry-abhimarśanaḥ

su-upaviṣṭān—comfortably seated; *kṛta*—having been shown; *ātithyān*—hospitality; *śrutadevaḥ*—Śrutadeva; *upasthitaḥ*—sitting near them; *sa-bhārya*—along with his wife; *sva-jana*—relatives; *apatyaḥ*—and children; *uvāca*—he spoke; *aṅghri*—(Lord Kṛṣṇa's) feet; *abhimarśanaḥ*—massaging.

TRANSLATION

When his guests were seated comfortably, having each received a proper welcome, Śrutadeva approached them and sat down nearby with his wife, children and other dependents. Then, while massaging the Lord's feet, he addressed Kṛṣṇa and the sages.

TEXT 44

श्रुतदेव उवाच
नाद्य नो दर्शनं प्राप्तः परं परमपूरुषः ।
यर्हीदं शक्तिभिः सृष्ट्वा प्रविष्टो ह्यात्मसत्तया ॥४४॥

śrutadeva uvāca
nādya no darśanaṁ prāptaḥ
paraṁ parama-pūruṣaḥ
yarhīdaṁ śaktibhiḥ sṛṣṭvā
praviṣṭo hy ātma-sattayā

śrutadevaḥ uvāca—Śrutadeva said; *na*—not; *adya*—today; *naḥ*—by us; *darśanam*—vision; *prāptaḥ*—obtained; *param*—only; *parama*—the supreme; *pūruṣaḥ*—person; *yarhi*—when; *idam*—this (universe); *śaktibhiḥ*—with His energies; *sṛṣṭvā*—creating; *praviṣṭaḥ*—entered; *hi*—indeed; *ātma*—His own; *sattayā*—in the state of existence.

TRANSLATION

Śrutadeva said: It is not that we have attained the audience of the Supreme Person only today, for we have in fact been

associating with Him ever since He created this universe with His energies and then entered it in His transcendental form.

TEXT 45

यथा शयानः पुरुषो मनसैवात्ममायया ।
सृष्ट्वा लोकं परं स्वाप्नमनुविश्यावभासते ॥४५॥

yathā śayānaḥ puruṣo
manasaivātma-māyayā
sṛṣṭvā lokaṁ paraṁ svāpnam
anuviśyāvabhāsate

yathā—as; *śayānaḥ*—sleeping; *puruṣaḥ*—a person; *manasā*—with his mind; *eva*—alone; *ātma*—own; *māyayā*—by his imagination; *sṛṣṭvā*—creating; *lokam*—a world; *param*—separate; *svāpnam*—dream; *anuviśya*—entering; *avabhāsate*—he appears.

TRANSLATION

The Lord is like a sleeping person who creates a separate world in his imagination and then enters his own dream and sees himself within it.

PURPORT

In the illusion of his dream, a sleeping person creates an apparent world, complete with cities populated by the fictional products of his imagination. In somewhat the same way, the Lord manifests the cosmos. Of course, the creation is not illusory for the Lord, but it is for those souls who are put under the control of His Māyā potency. As her service to the Lord, Māyā deludes the conditioned souls into accepting as real her temporary, insubstantial manifestations.

TEXT 46

शृण्वतां गदतां शश्वदर्चतां त्वाभिवन्दताम् ।
नृणां संवदतामन्तर्हृदि भास्यमलात्मनाम् ॥४६॥

śṛṇvatāṁ gadatāṁ śaśvad
arcatāṁ tvābhivandatām
nṛṇāṁ saṁvadatām antar
hṛdi bhāsy amalātmanām

śṛṇvatām—for those who are hearing; *gadatām*—speaking; *śaśvat*—constantly; *arcatām*—worshiping; *tvā*—You; *abhivandatām*—offering praise; *nṛṇām*—for men; *saṁvadatām*—conversing; *antaḥ*—within; *hṛdi*—the heart; *bhāsi*—You appear; *amala*—spotless; *ātmanām*—whose minds.

TRANSLATION

You reveal Yourself within the hearts of those persons of pure consciousness who constantly hear about You, chant about You, worship You, glorify You and converse with one another about You.

TEXT 47

हृदिस्थोऽप्यतिदूरस्थः कर्मविक्षिप्तचेतसाम् ।
आत्मशक्तिभिरग्राह्योऽप्यन्त्युपेतगुणात्मनाम् ॥४७॥

hṛdi-stho 'py ati-dūra-sthaḥ
karma-vikṣipta-cetasām
ātma-śaktibhir agrāhyo
'py anty upeta-guṇātmanām

hṛdi—in the heart; *sthaḥ*—situated; *api*—although; *ati*—very; *dūra-sthaḥ*—far away; *karma*—by material activities; *vikṣipta*—disturbed; *cetasām*—for those whose minds; *ātma*—by one's own; *śaktibhiḥ*—powers; *agrāhyaḥ*—not to be taken hold of; *api*—although; *anti*—near; *upeta*—realized; *guṇa*—Your qualities; *ātmanām*—by whose hearts.

TRANSLATION

But although You reside within the heart, You are very far away from those whose minds are disturbed by their entanglement in material work. Indeed, no one can grasp You by his material

powers, for You reveal Yourself only in the hearts of those who have learned to appreciate Your transcendental qualities.

PURPORT

The all-merciful Lord is in everyone's heart. Seeing Him there, however, is possible only when one's heart is completely purified. Materialists may demand that God prove His existence by coming into view as a result of their empirical investigations, but God has no need to respond to such impudence. As Lord Kṛṣṇa states in *Bhagavad-gītā* (7.25):

nāhaṁ prakāśaḥ sarvasya
yoga-māyā-samāvṛtaḥ
mūḍho 'yaṁ nābhijānāti
loko mām ajam avyayam

"I am never manifest to the foolish and unintelligent. For them I am covered by My internal potency, and therefore they do not know that I am unborn and infallible."

TEXT 48

नमोऽस्तु तेऽध्यात्मविदां परात्मने
अनात्मने स्वात्मविभक्तमृत्यवे ।
सकारणाकारणलिंगमीयुषे
स्वमाययासंवृतरुद्धदृष्टये ॥४८॥

namo 'stu te 'dhyātma-vidāṁ parātmane
anātmane svātma-vibhakta-mṛtyave
sa-kāraṇākāraṇa-liṅgam īyuṣe
sva-māyayāsaṁvṛta-ruddha-dṛṣṭaye

namaḥ—obeisances; *astu*—may there be; *te*—unto You; *adhyātma*—the Absolute Truth; *vidām*—for those who know; *para-ātmane*—the Supreme Soul; *anātmane*—to the conditioned *jīva* soul; *sva-ātma*—from Yourself (in the form of time); *vibhakta*—who gives; *mṛtyave*—death; *sa-kāraṇa*—having a cause; *akāraṇa*—having no cause; *liṅgam*—the forms (respectively, the material form of the universe and also Your original spiritual form); *īyuṣe*—who assume; *sva-māyayā*—by Your own mystic potency; *asaṁvṛta*—uncovered; *ruddha*—and blocked; *dṛṣṭaye*—vision.

TRANSLATION

Let me offer my obeisances unto You. You are realized as the Supreme Soul by those who know the Absolute Truth, whereas in Your form of time You impose death upon the forgetful souls. You appear both in Your causeless spiritual form and in the created form of this universe, thus simultaneously uncovering the eyes of Your devotees and obstructing the vision of the nondevotees.

PURPORT

When the Lord appears before His devotees in His eternal, spiritual form, their eyes become "uncovered" in the sense that all vestiges of illusion are dispelled and they drink in the beautiful vision of the Absolute Truth, the Personality of Godhead. For the nondevotees, on the other hand, the Lord "appears" as material nature, His universal form, and in this way He covers their vision so that His spiritual, personal form remains invisible to them.

Śrīla Viśvanātha Cakravartī gives another interpretation of this verse, based on an alternative understanding of *anātmane*, a form of the word *anātmā*: Various classes of men know the Absolute Truth in different ways. The devotees of the Lord who are in the reciprocal mood of neutral admiration (*śānta-rasa*) meditate on the Supreme as possessing a divine, personal form (*ātmā* or *śrī-vigraha*) transcending all aspects of material illusion. The impersonal philosophers (*jñānīs*) conceive of Him as formless (*anātmā*). And the envious demons see Him in the form of death.

TEXT 49

स त्वं शाधि स्वभृत्यान्नः किं देव करवाम हे ।
एतदन्तो नृणां क्लेशो यद् भवानक्षिगोचरः ॥४९॥

sa tvaṁ śādhi sva-bhṛtyān naḥ
kiṁ deva karavāma he
etad-anto nṛṇāṁ kleśo
yad bhavān akṣi-gocaraḥ

saḥ—He; *tvam*—You; *śādhi*—please order; *sva*—Your; *bhṛtyān*—servants; *naḥ*—us; *kim*—what; *deva*—O Lord; *karavāma*—we should do; *he*—oh; *etat*—having this; *antaḥ*—as its end; *nṛṇām*—of humans; *kleśaḥ*—the troubles; *yat*—that; *bhavān*—Your good self; *akṣi*—to the eyes; *go-caraḥ*—visible.

TRANSLATION

O Lord, You are that Supreme Soul, and we are Your servants. How shall we serve You? My Lord, simply seeing You puts an end to all the troubles of human life.

TEXT 50

श्रीशुक उवाच
तदुक्तमित्युपाकर्ण्य भगवान् प्रणतार्तिहा ।
गृहीत्वा पाणिना पाणिं प्रहसंस्तमुवाच ह ॥५०॥

śrī-śuka uvāca
tad-uktam ity upākarṇya
bhagavān praṇatārti-hā
gṛhītvā pāṇinā pāṇiṁ
prahasaṁs tam uvāca ha

śrī-śukaḥ uvāca—Śrī Śukadeva Gosvāmī said; *tat*—by him (Śrutadeva); *uktam*—what was spoken; *iti*—thus; *upākarṇya*—hearing; *bhagavān*—the Supreme Lord; *praṇata*—of the surrendered; *ārti*—of distress; *hā*—the destroyer; *gṛhītvā*—taking; *pāṇinā*—with His hand; *pāṇim*—his hand; *prahasan*—smiling broadly; *tam*—to him; *uvāca ha*—said.

TRANSLATION

Śrī Śukadeva Gosvāmī said: After hearing Śrutadeva speak these words, the Supreme Personality of Godhead, who relieves His surrendered devotees' distress, took Śrutadeva's hand in His own and, smiling, spoke to him as follows.

PURPORT

Ācārya Viśvanātha comments that Lord Kṛṣṇa took Śrutadeva's hand and smiled as a gesture of friendship, to tell Him, "Yes, you know the truth about Me, and I also know all about you. So now I will tell you something special."

TEXT 51

श्रीभगवानुवाच
ब्रह्मंस्तेऽनुग्रहार्थाय सम्प्राप्तान् विद्ध्यमून्मुनीन् ।
सञ्चरन्ति मया लोकान् पुनन्तः पादरेणुभिः ॥५१॥

śrī-bhagavān uvāca
brahmaṁs te 'nugrahārthāya
samprāptān viddhy amūn munīn
sañcaranti mayā lokān
punantaḥ pāda-reṇubhiḥ

śrī-bhagavān uvāca—the Supreme Lord said; *brahman*—O *brāhmaṇa;* *te*—your; *anugraha*—of bestowing benedictions; *arthāya*—for the purpose; *samprāptān*—come; *viddhi*—you should know; *amūn*—these; *munīn*—sages; *sañcaranti*—they wander; *mayā*—together with Me; *lokān*—all the worlds; *punantaḥ*—purifying; *pāda*—of their feet; *reṇubhiḥ*—with the dust.

TRANSLATION

The Supreme Lord said: My dear *brāhmaṇa,* you should know that these great sages have come here just to bless you. They travel throughout the worlds with Me, purifying them with the dust of their feet.

PURPORT

Śrīla Śrīdhara Svāmī explains that Lord Kṛṣṇa thought Śrutadeva had shown too much reverence to Him and not enough to the sages, and thus He turned the *brāhmaṇa's* attention to them.

TEXT 52

देवाः क्षेत्राणि तीर्थानि दर्शनस्पर्शनार्चनैः ।
शनैः पुनन्ति कालेन तदप्यर्हत्तमेक्षया ॥५२॥

devāḥ kṣetrāṇi tīrthāni
darśana-sparśanārcanaiḥ
śanaiḥ punanti kālena
tad apy arhattamekṣayā

devāḥ—temple deities; *kṣetrāṇi*—pilgrimage sites; *tīrthāni*—and sacred rivers; *darśana*—by being seen; *sparśana*—being touched; *arcanaiḥ*—and being worshiped; *śanaiḥ*—gradually; *punanti*—purify; *kālena*—with time; *tat api*—the same; *arhat-tama*—of those (*brāhmaṇas*) who are most worshipable; *īkṣayā*—by the glance.

TRANSLATION

One can gradually become purified by seeing, touching and worshiping temple deities, places of pilgrimage and holy rivers. But one can attain the same result immediately simply by receiving the glance of exalted sages.

PURPORT

Rather than remaining in seclusion and concentrating on their own perfection, Vaiṣṇava *brāhmaṇas* of the highest order dedicate their lives to sharing the benediction of the Lord's devotional service. In the words of the sons of King Prācīnabarhi:

teṣāṁ vicaratāṁ padbhyāṁ
tīrthānāṁ pāvanecchayā
bhītasya kiṁ na roceta
tāvakānāṁ samāgamaḥ

"Dear Lord, Your personal associates, Your devotees, wander all over the world to purify even the holy places of pilgrimage. Is not such activity pleasing to those who are actually afraid of material existence?" (*Bhāg.* 4.30.37) And Prahlāda Mahārāja says,

prāyeṇa deva munayaḥ sva-vimukti-kāmā
maunaṁ caranti vijane na parārtha-niṣṭhāḥ
naitān vihāya kṛpaṇān vimumukṣa eko
nānyaṁ tvad asya śaraṇam bhramato 'nupaśye

"My dear Lord Nṛsiṁhadeva, I see that there are many saintly persons indeed, but they are interested only in their own deliverance. Not caring for the big cities and towns, they go to the Himalayas or the forest to meditate with vows of silence [*mauna-vrata*]. They are not interested in delivering others. As for me, however, I do not wish to be liberated alone, leaving aside all these poor fools and rascals. I know that without Kṛṣṇa consciousness, without taking shelter of Your lotus feet, one cannot be happy. Therefore I wish to bring them back to shelter at Your lotus feet." (*Bhāg.* 7.9.44)

TEXT 53

ब्राह्मणो जन्मना श्रेयान् सर्वेषां प्राणिनामिह ।
तपसा विद्यया तुष्टया किमु मत्कलया युतः ॥५३॥

brāhmaṇo janmanā śreyān
sarveṣāṁ prāṇinām iha
tapasā vidyayā tuṣṭyā
kim u mat-kalayā yutaḥ

brāhmaṇaḥ—a *brāhmaṇa; janmanā*—by his birth; *śreyān*—the best; *sarveṣām*—of all; *prāṇinām*—living beings; *iha*—in this world; *tapasā*—by his austerity; *vidyayā*—by his learning; *tuṣṭyā*—by his satisfaction; *kim u*—what more, then; *mat*—upon Me; *kalayā*—with loving meditation; *yutaḥ*—endowed.

TRANSLATION

By his very birth, a *brāhmaṇa* is the best of all living beings in this world, and he becomes even more exalted when he is endowed with austerity, learning and self-satisfaction, what to speak of devotion to Me.

TEXT 54

न ब्राह्मणान्मे दयितं रूपमेतच्चतुर्भुजम् ।
सर्ववेदमयो विप्रः सर्वदेवमयो ह्यहम् ॥५४॥

na brāhmaṇān me dayitaṁ
rūpam etac catur-bhujam
sarva-veda-mayo vipraḥ
sarva-deva-mayo hy aham

na—not; *brāhmaṇāt*—than a *brāhmaṇa; me*—to Me; *dayitam*—more dear; *rūpam*—personal form; *etat*—this; *catuḥ-bhujam*—four-armed; *sarva*—all; *veda*—the *Vedas; mayaḥ*—comprising; *vipraḥ*—a learned *brāhmaṇa; sarva*—all; *deva*—the demigods; *mayaḥ*—comprising; *hi*—indeed; *aham*—I.

TRANSLATION

Even My own four-armed form is no dearer to Me than a *brāhmaṇa*. Within himself a learned *brāhmaṇa* comprises all the *Vedas*, just as within Myself I comprise all the demigods.

PURPORT

It is understood from the Vedic science of epistemology, the *Nyāya-śāstra*, that knowledge of an object (*prameya*) depends on a valid means of knowing (*pramāṇa*). The Supreme Personality of Godhead can be known only by means of the *Vedas*, and thus He relies on the *brāhmaṇa* sages, who are the *Vedas* personified, to reveal Him in this world. Even though Lord Kṛṣṇa embodies all the demigods and *viṣṇu-tattva* expansions of Nārāyaṇa, He considers Himself obliged to the *brāhmaṇas*.

TEXT 55

दुष्प्रज्ञा अविदित्वैवमवजानन्त्यसूयवः ।
गुरुं मां विप्रमात्मानमर्चादाविज्यदृष्टयः ॥५५॥

duṣprajñā aviditvaivam
avajānanty asūyavaḥ
guruṁ māṁ vipram ātmānam
arcādāv ijya-dṛṣṭayaḥ

duṣprajñāḥ—those of corrupted intelligence; *aviditvā*—failing to understand; *evam*—in this way; *avajānanti*—neglect; *asūyavaḥ*—and behave enviously toward; *gurum*—their spiritual master; *mām*—Me; *vipram*—the learned *brāhmaṇa; ātmānam*—their own self; *arcā-ādau*—in the visibly manifest Deity of the Lord; *ijya*—as being worshipable; *dṛṣṭayaḥ*—whose vision.

TRANSLATION

Ignorant of this truth, foolish people neglect and enviously offend a learned *brāhmaṇa*, who, being nondifferent from Me, is their spiritual master and very self. They consider worshipable only such obvious manifestations of divinity as My Deity form.

TEXT 56

चराचरमिदं विश्वं भावा ये चास्य हेतवः ।
मद्रूपाणीति चेतस्याधत्ते विप्रो मदीक्षया ॥५६॥

carācaram idaṁ viśvaṁ
bhāvā ye cāsya hetavaḥ
mad-rūpāṇīti cetasy ā-
dhatte vipro mad-īkṣayā

cara—moving; *acaram*—and nonmoving; *idam*—this; *viśvam*—universe; *bhāvāḥ*—elemental categories; *ye*—which; *ca*—and; *asya*—its; *hetavaḥ*—sources; *mat*—My; *rūpāṇi*—forms; *iti*—such a thought; *cetasi*—within his mind; *ādhatte*—maintains; *vipraḥ*—a *brāhmaṇa; mat*—of Me; *īkṣayā*—by his perception.

TRANSLATION

Because he has realized Me, a *brāhmaṇa* is firmly fixed in the knowledge that everything moving and nonmoving in the universe, and also the primary elements of its creation, are all manifest forms expanded from Me.

TEXT 57

तस्माद् ब्रह्मऋषीनेतान् ब्रह्मन्मच्छ्रद्धयार्चय ।
एवं चेदर्चितोऽस्म्यद्धा नान्यथा भूरिभूतिभिः ॥५७॥

tasmād brahma-ṛṣīn etān
brahman mac-chraddhayārcaya
evaṁ ced arcito 'smy addhā
nānyathā bhūri-bhūtibhiḥ

tasmāt—therefore; *brahma-ṛṣīn*—*brāhmaṇa* sages; *etān*—these; *brahman*—O *brāhmaṇa* (Śrutadeva); *mat*—(as you have) for Me; *śraddhayā*—with faith; *arcaya*—just worship; *evam*—thus; *cet*—if (you do); *arcitaḥ*—worshiped; *asmi*—I will be; *addhā*—directly; *na*—not; *anyathā*—otherwise; *bhūri*—vast; *bhūtibhiḥ*—with riches.

TRANSLATION

Therefore you should worship these *brāhmaṇa* sages, O *brāhmaṇa*, with the same faith you have in Me. If you do so, you will worship Me directly, which you cannot do otherwise, even with offerings of vast riches.

TEXT 58

श्रीशुक उवाच
स इत्थं प्रभुनादिष्टः सहकृष्णान् द्विजोत्तमान् ।
आराध्यैकात्मभावेन मैथिलश्चाप सद्गतिम् ॥५८॥

śrī-śuka uvāca
sa itthaṁ prabhunādiṣṭaḥ
saha-kṛṣṇān dvijottamān
ārādhyaikātma-bhāvena
maithilaś cāpa sad-gatim

śrī-śukaḥ uvāca—Śukadeva Gosvāmī said; *saḥ*—he (Śrutadeva); *ittham*—in this manner; *prabhunā*—by his Lord; *ādiṣṭaḥ*—instructed; *saha*—accompanying; *kṛṣṇān*—Lord Kṛṣṇa; *dvija*—the *brāhmaṇas; uttamān*—most exalted; *ārādhya*—by worshiping; *eka-ātma*—single-minded; *bhāvena*—with devotion; *maithilaḥ*—the King of Mithilā; *ca*—also; *āpa*—attained; *sat*—transcendental; *gatim*—the ultimate destination.

TRANSLATION

Śrī Śuka said: So instructed by his Lord, with single-minded devotion Śrutadeva worshiped Śrī Kṛṣṇa and the topmost *brāhmaṇas* accompanying Him, and King Bahulāśva did the same. Thus both Śrutadeva and the King attained the ultimate transcendental destination.

TEXT 59

एवं स्वभक्तयो राजन् भगवान् भक्तभक्तिमान् ।
उषित्वादिश्य सन्मार्गं पुनर्द्वारवतीमगात् ॥५९॥

evaṁ sva-bhaktayo rājan
bhagavān bhakta-bhaktimān
uṣitvādiśya san-mārgaṁ
punar dvāravatīm agāt

evam—thus; *sva*—His; *bhaktayoḥ*—with the two devotees; *rājan*—O King (Parīkṣit); *bhagavān*—the Supreme Lord; *bhakta*—to His devotees; *bhakti-mān*—who is devoted; *uṣitvā*—staying; *ādiśya*—teaching; *sat*—of pure saints; *mārgam*—the path; *punaḥ*—again; *dvāravatīm*—to Dvārakā; *agāt*—He went.

TRANSLATION

O King, thus the Personality of Godhead, who is devoted to His own devotees, stayed for some time with His two great devotees Śrutadeva and Bahulāśva, teaching them the behavior of perfect saints. Then the Lord returned to Dvārakā.

PURPORT

In his narration of this pastime in *Kṛṣṇa, the Supreme Personality of Godhead,* His Divine Grace A. C. Bhaktivedanta Swami Prabhupāda concludes, "The instruction we receive from this incident is that King Bahulāśva and Śrutadeva the *brāhmaṇa* were accepted by the Lord on the same level because both were pure devotees. This is the real qualification for being recognized by the Supreme Personality of Godhead. Because it has become the fashion of this age to become falsely proud of having taken birth in the family of a *kṣatriya* or a *brāhmaṇa,* we see persons without any qualification claiming to be *brāhmaṇa* or *kṣatriya* or *vaiśya.* But as it is stated in the scriptures, *kalau śūdra-sambhava:* 'In this age of Kali, everyone is born a *śūdra.*' This is because there is no performance of the purificatory process known as *saṁskāras,* which begin from the time of the mother's pregnancy and continue up to the point of the individual's death. No one can be classified as a member of a particular caste, especially of a higher caste—*brāhmaṇa, kṣatriya* or *vaiśya*—simply by birthright. If one is not purified by the process of the seed-giving ceremony, or Garbhādhāna-saṁskāra, he is immediately classified among the *śūdras,* because only the *śūdras* do not undergo this purificatory process. Sex life without the purificatory process of Kṛṣṇa consciousness is merely the seed-giving process of the *śūdras* or the animals. But Kṛṣṇa consciousness is the highest perfection, by which everyone can come to the platform of a Vaiṣṇava. This includes having all the qualifications of a *brāhmaṇa.* The Vaiṣṇavas are trained to become freed from the four kinds of sinful activities—illicit sex, indulgence in intoxicants, gambling and eating animal foodstuffs. No one can be on the brahminical platform without having these preliminary qualifications, and without becoming a qualified *brāhmaṇa,* one cannot become a pure devotee."

Thus end the purports of the humble servants of His Divine Grace A. C. Bhaktivedanta Swami Prabhupāda to the Tenth Canto, Eighty-sixth Chapter, of the Śrīmad-Bhāgavatam, *entitled "Arjuna Kidnaps Subhadrā, and Kṛṣṇa Blesses His Devotees."*

CHAPTER EIGHTY-SEVEN

The Prayers of the Personified Vedas

This chapter presents the prayers by the personified *Vedas* glorifying the personal and impersonal aspects of Lord Nārāyaṇa.

King Parīkṣit asked Śrīla Śukadeva Gosvāmī how the *Vedas* can directly refer to the Supreme Absolute Truth, Brahman, since the *Vedas* deal with the material realm governed by the three modes of nature and Brahman is completely transcendental to these modes. In reply, Śukadeva Gosvāmī described an ancient encounter between Śrī Nārāyaṇa Ṛṣi and Nārada Muni at Badarikāśrama. Traveling to that sacred hermitage, Nārada found the Lord surrounded by exalted residents of the nearby village of Kalāpa. After bowing down to Nārāyaṇa Ṛṣi and His associates, Nārada submitted this same question to Him. In reply, Nārāyaṇa Ṛṣi related an account of how this very question had been discussed long ago among the great sages living on Janaloka. Once these sages, feeling inquisitive about the nature of the Absolute Truth, chose Sanandana Kumāra to speak on the subject. Sanandana told them how the numerous personified *Vedas*, appearing as the first emanations from the breathing of Lord Nārāyaṇa, recited prayers for His glorification just before the creation. Sanandana then proceeded to recite these elaborate prayers.

The residents of Janaloka were perfectly satisfied upon hearing Sanandana recite the prayers of the personified *Vedas*, which enlightened them about the true nature of the Supreme Absolute Truth, and they honored Sanandana with their worship. Nārada Muni was equally satisfied to hear this account from Śrī Nārāyaṇa Ṛṣi. Thus Nārada offered his obeisances to the Lord and then went to see his disciple Vedavyāsa, to whom he explained everything he had heard.

TEXT 1

श्रीपरीक्षिदुवाच

ब्रह्मन् ब्रह्मण्यनिर्देश्ये निर्गुणे गुणवृत्तयः ।
कथं चरन्ति श्रुतयः साक्षात्सदसतः परे ॥१॥

śrī-parīkṣid uvāca
brahman brahmaṇy anirdeśye
nirguṇe guṇa-vṛttayaḥ
kathaṁ caranti śrutayaḥ
sākṣāt sad-asataḥ pare

śrī-parīkṣit uvāca—Śrī Parīkṣit said; *brahman*—O *brāhmaṇa* (Śukadeva); *brahmaṇi*—in the Absolute Truth; *anirdeśye*—which cannot be described in words; *nirguṇe*—which has no qualities; *guṇa*—the qualities of material nature; *vṛttayaḥ*—whose scope of action; *katham*—how; *caranti*—function (by referring); *śrutayaḥ*—the *Vedas; sākṣāt*—directly; *sat*—to material substance; *asataḥ*—and its subtle causes; *pare*—in that which is transcendental.

TRANSLATION

Śrī Parīkṣit said: O *brāhmaṇa*, how can the *Vedas* directly describe the Supreme Absolute Truth, who cannot be described in words? The *Vedas* are limited to describing the qualities of material nature, but the Supreme is devoid of these qualities, being transcendental to all material manifestations and their causes.

PURPORT

Before beginning his commentary on this chapter, Śrīla Śrīdhara Svāmī prays:

vāg-īśā yasya vadane
lakṣmīr yasya ca vakṣasi
yasyāste hṛdaye saṁvit
taṁ nṛsiṁham ahaṁ bhaje

"I worship Lord Nṛsiṁha, within whose mouth reside the great masters of eloquence, upon whose chest resides the goddess of fortune, and within whose heart resides the divine potency of consciousness."

sampradāya-viśuddhy-arthaṁ
svīya-nirbandha-yantritaḥ

śruti-stuti-mita-vyākhyāṁ
kariṣyāmi yathā-mati

"Desiring to purify my *sampradāya* and being bound by duty, I will briefly comment on the prayers of the personified *Vedas*, to the best of my realization."

śrīmad-bhāgavataṁ pūrvaiḥ
sārataḥ sanniṣevitam
mayā tu tad-upaspṛṣṭam
ucchiṣṭam upacīyate

"Inasmuch as *Śrīmad-Bhāgavatam* has already been perfectly honored by my predecessors' explanations, I can only gather together the remnants of what they have honored."

Śrīla Viśvanātha Cakravartī offers his own invocation:

mama ratna-vaṇig-bhāvaṁ
ratnāny aparicinvataḥ
hasantu santo jihremi
na sva-svānta-vinoda-kṛt

"The saintly devotees may laugh at me for becoming a jewel merchant though I know nothing about precious jewels. But I feel no shame, for at least I may entertain them."

na me 'sti vaiduṣy api nāpi bhaktir
virakti-raktir na tathāpi laulyāt
su-durgamād eva bhavāmi veda-
stuty-artha-cintāmaṇi-rāśi-gṛdhnuḥ

"Though I have no wisdom, devotion or detachment, I am still greedy to take the philosopher's stone of the *Vedas'* prayers from the fortress in which it is being kept."

māṁ nīcatāyām aviveka-vāyuḥ
pravartate pātayituṁ balāc cet

likhāmy ataḥ svāmi-sanātana-śrī-
kṛṣṇāṅghri-bhā-stambha-kṛtāvalambaḥ

"If the wind of indiscretion—my failure to acknowledge my lowly position—threatens to knock me down, then while writing this commentary I must hold on to the effulgent pillars of the feet of Śrīdhara Svāmī, Sanātana Gosvāmī and Lord Śrī Kṛṣṇa."

praṇamya śrī-guruṁ bhūyaḥ
śrī-kṛṣṇaṁ karuṇārṇavam
loka-nāthaṁ jagac-cakṣuḥ
śrī-śukaṁ tam upāśraye

"Repeatedly bowing down to my divine spiritual master and to Lord Śrī Kṛṣṇa, the ocean of mercy, I take shelter of Śrī Śukadeva Gosvāmī, the protector of the world and its universal eye."

At the end of the preceding chapter, Śukadeva Gosvāmī told Parīkṣit Mahārāja,

evaṁ sva-bhaktayo rājan
bhagavān bhakta-bhaktimān
uṣitvādiśya san-mārgaṁ
punar dvāravatīm agāt

"Thus, O King, the Personality of Godhead, who is the devotee of His own devotees, stayed for some time with His two great devotees, teaching them how perfect saints behave. Then He returned to Dvārakā." In this verse the word *san-mārgam* can be understood in at least three ways. In the first, *sat* is taken to mean "devotee of the Supreme Lord," and thus *san-mārgam* means "the path of *bhakti-yoga,* devotional service." In the second, with *sat* meaning "a seeker of transcendental knowledge," *san-mārgam* means "the philosophical path of knowledge," which has impersonal Brahman as its object. And in the third, with *sat* referring to the transcendental sound of the *Vedas, san-mārgam* means "the process of following Vedic injunctions." Both the second and the third of these interpretations of *san-mārgam* lead to the question of how the *Vedas* can describe the Absolute Truth.

Śrīla Śrīdhara Svāmī elaborately analyzes this problem in terms of the traditional discipline of Sanskrit poetics: We should consider that words have three kinds of expressive capacities, called *śabda-vṛttis*. These are the different ways a word refers to its meaning, distinguished as *mukhya-vṛtti, lakṣaṇā-vṛtti* and *gauṇa-vṛtti*. The *śabda-vṛtti* termed *mukhya* is the primary, literal meaning of a word; this is also known as *abhidhā*, a word's "denotation," or dictionary meaning. *Mukhya-vṛtti* is further divided into two subcategories, namely *rūḍhi* and *yoga*. A primary meaning is called *rūḍhi* when it is based on conventional usage, and *yoga* when it is derived from another word's meaning by regular etymological rules.

For example, the word *go* ("cow") is an example of *rūḍhi*, since its relation with its literal meaning is purely conventional. The denotation of the word *pācaka* ("chef"), on the other hand, is a *yoga-vṛtti*, through the word's derivation from the root *pac* ("to cook") by addition of the agent suffix *-ka*.

Beside its *mukhya-vṛtti*, or primary meaning, a word can also be used in a secondary, metaphorical sense. This usage is called *lakṣaṇā*. The rule is that a word should not be understood metaphorically if its *mukhya-vṛtti* makes sense in the given context; only after the *mukhya-vṛtti* fails to convey a word's meaning may *lakṣaṇā-vṛtti* be justifiably presumed. The function of *lakṣaṇā* is technically explained in the *kāvya-śāstras* as an extended reference, pointing to something in some way related to the object of the literal meaning. Thus, the phrase *gaṅgāyāṁ ghoṣaḥ* literally means "the cowherd village in the Ganges." But that idea is absurd, so here *gaṅgāyām* should rather be understood by its *lakṣaṇā* to mean "on the bank of the Ganges," the bank being something related to the river. *Gauṇa-vṛtti* is a special kind of *lakṣaṇā*, where the meaning is extended to some idea of similarity. For example, in the statement *siṁho devadattaḥ* ("Devadatta is a lion"), heroic Devadatta is metaphorically called a lion because of his lionlike qualities. In contrast, the example of the general kind of *lakṣaṇā*, namely *gaṅgāyāṁ ghoṣaḥ*, involves a relationship not of similarity but of location.

In this first verse of the Eighty-seventh Chapter, Parīkṣit Mahārāja expresses doubt as to how the words of the *Vedas* can refer to the Absolute Truth by any of the valid kinds of *śabda-vṛtti*. He asks, *kathaṁ sākṣāt caranti:* How can the *Vedas* directly describe Brahman by *rūḍha-mukhya-vṛtti*, literal meaning based on convention? After all, the Absolute is *anirdeśya*, inaccessible to designation. And how can the *Vedas* even describe Brahman by *gauṇa-vṛtti*, metaphor based on similar qualities?

The *Vedas* are *guṇa-vṛttayaḥ,* full of qualitative descriptions, but Brahman is *nirguṇa,* without qualities. Obviously, a metaphor based on similar qualities cannot apply in the case of something that has no qualities. Furthermore, Parīkṣit Mahārāja points out that Brahman is *sad-asataḥ param,* beyond all causes and effects. Having no connection with any manifest existence, subtle or gross, the Absolute cannot be expressed by either *yoga-vṛtti,* a meaning derived etymologically, or *lakṣaṇā,* metaphor, since both require some relationship of Brahman to other entities.

Thus King Parīkṣit is puzzled as to how the words of the *Vedas* can directly describe the Absolute Truth.

TEXT 2

श्रीशुक उवाच

बुद्धीन्द्रियमनःप्राणान् जनानामसृजत्प्रभुः ।
मात्रार्थं च भवार्थं च आत्मनेऽकल्पनाय च ॥२॥

śrī-śuka uvāca
buddhīndriya-manaḥ-prāṇān
janānām asṛjat prabhuḥ
mātrārthaṁ ca bhavārthaṁ ca
ātmane 'kalpanāya ca

śrī-śukaḥ uvāca—Śukadeva Gosvāmī said; *buddhi*—material intelligence; *indriya*—senses; *manaḥ*—mind; *prāṇān*—and vital air; *janānām*—of the living entities; *asṛjat*—sent forth; *prabhuḥ*—the Supreme Lord; *mātrā*—of sense gratification; *artham*—for the sake; *ca*—and; *bhava*—of birth (and the activities that follow it); *artham*—for the sake; *ca*—and; *ātmane*—for the soul (and his attainment of happiness in his next life); *akalpanāya*—for his ultimate abandonment of material motives; *ca*—and.

TRANSLATION

Śukadeva Gosvāmī said: The Supreme Lord manifested the material intelligence, senses, mind and vital air of the living entities so that they could indulge their desires for sense gratification, take repeated births to engage in fruitive activities, become elevated in future lives and ultimately attain liberation.

PURPORT

At the dawn of creation, when the conditioned living entities lay dormant within the transcendental body of Lord Viṣṇu, He initiated the process of creation by sending forth the coverings of intelligence, mind and so on for the living entities' benefit. As stated here, Viṣṇu is the independent Lord (*prabhu*), and the living entities are His *jana*, dependents. Thus we should understand that the Lord creates the cosmos entirely for the living entities' sake; compassion is His sole motive.

By providing the living entities with gross and subtle bodies, the Supreme Lord enables them to pursue sense gratification and, in the human form, religiosity, economic development and liberation. In each body the conditioned soul utilizes his senses for enjoyment, and when he comes to the human form he must also discharge various duties assigned to him at the different stages of his life. If he faithfully discharges his duties, he earns more refined and extensive enjoyment in the future; if not, he is degraded. And when the soul eventually hankers to be freed from material life, the path of liberation is always available. Śrīla Viśvanātha Cakravartī comments that in this verse the repeated use of the word *ca* ("and") indicates the importance of all of what the Lord provides—not only the path of liberation, but also the paths of gradual elevation through religious life and appropriate sense enjoyment.

In all their endeavors the living entities depend on the Lord's mercy for success. Without intelligence, senses, mind and vital air, the living entities cannot achieve anything—neither elevation to heaven, purification through knowledge, perfection of the eightfold meditational *yoga*, nor pure devotion through following the process of *bhakti-yoga*, beginning with hearing and chanting the names of God.

How, then, if the Supreme arranges all these facilities for the conditioned souls' welfare, can He be impersonal? Far from presenting the Absolute Truth as ultimately impersonal, the *Upaniṣads* speak at great length about His personal qualities. The Absolute described by the *Upaniṣads* is free from all inferior, material qualities, and yet He is omniscient, omnipotent, the master and controller of all, the universally worshipable Lord, He who awards the results of everyone's work, and the reservoir of all eternity, knowledge and bliss. The *Muṇḍaka Upaniṣad* (1.1.9) states, *yaḥ sarva-jñaḥ sa sarva-vid yasya jñāna-mayaṁ tapaḥ:* "He who is all-knowing, from whom the potency of all knowledge comes—He is the wisest of all." In the words of the *Bṛhad-āraṇyaka Upaniṣad*

(4.4.22, 3.7.3, and 1.2.4), *sarvasya vaśī sarvasyeśānaḥ:* "He is the Lord and controller of everyone"; *yaḥ pṛthivyām tiṣṭhan pṛthivyā āntaraḥ:* "He who resides within the earth and pervades it"; and *so 'kāmayata bahu syām:* "He desired, 'I will become many.'" Similarly, the *Aitareya Upaniṣad* (3.11) states, *sa aikṣata tat tejo 'sṛjata:* "He glanced at His potency, who then manifested the creation," while the *Taittirīya Upaniṣad* (2.1.1) declares, *satyaṁ jñānam anantaṁ brahma:* "The Supreme is unlimited truth and knowledge."

The phrase *tat tvam asi,* "You are that" (*Chāndogya Up.* 6.8.7), is often cited by impersonalists as a confirmation of the absolute identity of the finite *jīva* soul with his creator. Śaṅkarācārya and his followers elevate these words to the status of one of the few *mahā-vākyas,* key phrases they say express the essential purport of Vedānta. The leading thinkers of the standard Vaiṣṇava schools of Vedānta, however, vociferously disagree with this interpretation. Ācāryas Rāmānuja, Madhva, Baladeva Vidyābhūṣaṇa and others have offered numerous alternative explanations according to a systematic study of the *Upaniṣads* and other *śrutis.*

The question Mahārāja Parīkṣit has submitted here—namely, "How can the *Vedas* directly refer to the Absolute Truth?"—has been answered as follows by Śukadeva Gosvāmī: "The Lord created intelligence and other elements for the sake of the conditioned living beings." A skeptic may object that this answer is irrelevant. But Śukadeva Gosvāmī's answer is not actually irrelevant, as Śrīla Viśvanātha Cakravartī explains. Answers to subtle questions must often be phrased indirectly. As Lord Kṛṣṇa Himself states in His instructions to Uddhava (*Bhāg.* 11.21.35), *parokṣa-vādā ṛṣayaḥ parokṣaṁ mama ca priyam:* "The Vedic seers and *mantras* deal in esoteric terms, and I also am pleased by such confidential descriptions." In the present context, the impersonalists, on whose behalf Parīkṣit Mahārāja asked his question, cannot appreciate the direct answer, so instead Śrīla Śukadeva gives an indirect reply: "You say that Brahman is indescribable by words. But if the Supreme Lord had not created the intelligence, mind and senses, then sound and the other objects of perception would all be just as indescribable as your Brahman. You would have been blind and deaf since birth, and would know nothing about physical forms and sounds, what to speak of the Absolute. So, just as the merciful Lord has given us all faculties of perception for experiencing and describing to others the sensations of sight, sound and so forth, in the same way He may give someone the receptive capacity to realize

Brahman. He may, if He chooses, create some extraordinary way for words to function—apart from their ordinary references to material substances, qualities, categories and actions—that will enable them to express the Supreme Truth. He is, after all, the almighty Lord (*prabhu*), and He can easily make the indescribable describable."

Lord Matsya assures King Satyavrata that the Absolute Truth can be known from the words of the *Vedas:*

madīyaṁ mahimānaṁ ca
paraṁ brahmeti śabditam
vetsyasy anugrahītaṁ me
sampraśnair vivṛtaṁ hṛdi

"You will be thoroughly advised and favored by Me, and because of your inquiries, everything about My glories, which are known as *paraṁ brahma,* will be manifest within your heart. Thus you will know everything about Me." (*Bhāg.* 8.24.38)

The fortunate soul who has been graced by the Supreme Lord with divine inquisitiveness will ask questions about the nature of the Absolute, and by hearing the answers given by great sages, which are recorded in the Vedic literatures, he will come to understand the Lord as He is. Thus only by the special mercy of the Supreme Person does Brahman become *śabditam,* "literally denoted by words." Otherwise, without the Lord's exceptional grace, the words of the *Vedas* cannot reveal the Absolute Truth.

Śrīla Viśvanātha Cakravartī suggests that the word *buddhi* in this verse spoken by Śukadeva Gosvāmī can indicate the *mahat-tattva,* from which evolve the various expansions of ether (such as sound), which are designated here as *indriya. Mātrārtham,* then, means "for the sake of using transcendental sound to describe Brahman," since for that precise purpose the Supreme Lord inspired *prakṛti* to evolve ether and sound.

A further understanding of the purpose of creation is spoken by the words *bhavārtham* and *ātmane kalpanāya* (if the reading *kalpanāya* instead of *akalpanāya* is taken). *Bhavārtham* means "for the good of the living entities." Worship (*kalpanam*) of the Supreme Self (*ātmane*) is the means by which the living entities can fufill the divine purpose for which they exist. Intelligence, mind and senses are meant to be used for worshiping the Supreme Lord, whether or not the living entity has yet brought them to the stage of transcendental purification.

How both purified and unpurified devotees use their intelligence, mind and senses in worshiping the Lord is described in reference to the following quote from the *Gopāla-tāpanī Upaniṣad* (*Pūrva* 12):

sat-puṇḍarīka-nayanaṁ
meghābhaṁ vaidyutāmbaram
dvi-bhujaṁ mauna-mudrāḍhyaṁ
vana-mālinam īśvaram

"The Supreme Lord, appearing in His two-armed form, had divine lotus eyes, a complexion the color of a cloud, and garments that resembled lightning. He wore a garland of forest flowers, and His beauty was enhanced by His pose of meditative silence." The transcendental intelligence and senses of the Lord's perfect devotees correctly perceive His purely spiritual beauty, and their realizations are echoed in the *Gopāla-tāpanī-śruti's* comparison of Lord Kṛṣṇa's eyes, body and clothing to a lotus, a cloud and lightning. On the other hand, devotees on the level of *sādhana,* who are in the process of becoming purified, have only barely realized the Supreme Lord's boundless spiritual beauty. Nonetheless, by hearing scriptural passages such as this one from the *Gopāla-tāpanī Upaniṣad,* they engage in contemplating Him to the best of their fledgling ability. Although the neophyte devotees have not yet learned how to fully realize the Lord or meditate steadily on even the effulgence surrounding His body, still they take pleasure in presuming, "We are meditating on our Lord." And the Supreme Lord, moved by the waves of His boundless mercy, Himself thinks, "These devotees are meditating on Me." When their devotion matures, He draws them to His feet to engage in His intimate service. Thus it is concluded that the *Vedas* have access to the personal identity of the Supreme only by His mercy.

TEXT 3

सैषा ह्युपनिषद् ब्राह्मी पूर्वेषां पूर्वजैर्धृता ।
श्रद्धया धारयेद्यस्तां क्षेमं गच्छेदकिञ्चनः ॥३॥

saiṣā hy upaniṣad brāhmī
pūrveṣāṁ pūrva-jair dhṛtā

śraddhayā dhārayed yas tāṁ
kṣemaṁ gacched akiñcanaḥ

sā eṣā—this same; *hi*—indeed; *upaniṣat*—*Upaniṣad,* confidential spiritual doctrine; *brāhmī*—related to the Absolute Truth; *pūrveṣām*—of our predecessors (such as Nārada); *pūrva-jaiḥ*—by the predecessors (such as Sanaka); *dhṛtā*—meditated upon; *śraddhayā*—with faith; *dhārayet*—meditates; *yaḥ*—whoever; *tām*—upon it; *kṣemam*—ultimate success; *gacchet*—will attain; *akiñcanaḥ*—free from material connection.

TRANSLATION

Those who came before even our ancient predecessors meditated upon this same confidential knowledge of the Absolute Truth. Indeed, anyone who faithfully concentrates on this knowledge will become free from material attachments and attain the final goal of life.

PURPORT

This confidential knowledge concerning the Absolute Truth should not be doubted, since it has been passed down through authoritative lines of learned sages from time immemorial. One who cultivates the science of the Supreme with reverence, avoiding the distractions of fruitive rituals and mental speculation, will learn to give up the false designations of material body and mundane society, and thus he will become eligible for perfection.

In the opinion of Śrīla Viśvanātha Cakravartī, the first two verses of this chapter can be considered an *Upaniṣad* on the topic of Brahman. Śukadeva Gosvāmī here disclaims authorship on the grounds that this *Upaniṣad* was spoken previously by Nārada Muni, who himself heard it from Sanaka Kumāra.

TEXT 4

अत्र ते वर्णयिष्यामि गाथां नारायणान्विताम् ।
नारदस्य च संवादमृषेर्नारायणस्य च ॥४॥

atra te varṇayiṣyāmi
gāthāṁ nārāyaṇānvitām

nāradasya ca saṁvādam
ṛṣer nārāyaṇasya ca

atra—in this connection; *te*—to you; *varṇayiṣyāmi*—I will relate; *gāthām*—an account; *nārāyaṇa-anvitām*—concerning the Supreme Lord, Nārāyaṇa; *nāradasya*—of Nārada; *ca*—and; *saṁvādam*—the conversation; *ṛṣeḥ nārāyaṇasya*—of Śrī Nārāyaṇa Ṛṣi; *ca*—and.

TRANSLATION

In this connection I will relate to you a narration concerning the Supreme Lord Nārāyaṇa. It is about a conversation that once occurred between Śrī Nārāyaṇa Ṛṣi and Nārada Muni.

PURPORT

Lord Nārāyaṇa is connected in two ways with the following narration: as its speaker and as the subject it describes.

TEXT 5

एकदा नारदो लोकान् पर्यटन् भगवत्प्रियः ।
सनातनमृषिं द्रष्टुं ययौ नारायणाश्रमम् ॥५॥

ekadā nārado lokān
paryaṭan bhagavat-priyaḥ
sanātanam ṛṣiṁ draṣṭuṁ
yayau nārāyaṇāśramam

ekadā—once; *nāradaḥ*—Nārada Muni; *lokān*—the worlds; *paryaṭan*—traveling about; *bhagavat*—of the Supreme Lord; *priyaḥ*—the beloved; *sanātanam*—primeval; *ṛṣim*—the divine sage; *draṣṭum*—to see; *yayau*—went; *nārāyaṇa-āśramam*—to the hermitage of Lord Nārāyaṇa Ṛṣi.

TRANSLATION

Once, while traveling among the various planets of the universe, the Lord's beloved devotee Nārada went to visit the primeval sage Nārāyaṇa at His *āśrama.*

TEXT 6

यो वै भारतवर्षेऽस्मिन् क्षेमाय स्वस्तये नृणाम् ।
धर्मज्ञानशमोपेतमाकल्पादास्थितस्तपः ॥६॥

yo vai bhārata-varṣe 'smin
kṣemāya svastaye nṛṇām
dharma-jñāna-śamopetam
ā-kalpād āsthitas tapaḥ

yaḥ—who; *vai*—indeed; *bhārata-varṣe*—in the holy land of Bhārata (India); *asmin*—this; *kṣemāya*—for the welfare in this life; *svastaye*—and for the welfare in the next life; *nṛṇām*—of men; *dharma*—with maintenance of religious standards; *jñāna*—spiritual knowledge; *śama*—and self-control; *upetam*—enriched; *ā-kalpāt*—from the very beginning of Lord Brahmā's day; *āsthitaḥ*—executing; *tapaḥ*—austerities.

TRANSLATION

From the very beginning of Brahmā's day Lord Nārāyaṇa Ṛṣi has been undergoing austere penances in this land of Bhārata while perfectly performing religious duties and exemplifying spiritual knowledge and self-control—all for the benefit of human beings in both this world and the next.

TEXT 7

तत्रोपविष्टमृषिभिः कलापग्रामवासिभिः ।
परीतं प्रणतोऽपृच्छदिदमेव कुरूद्वह ॥७॥

tatropaviṣṭam ṛṣibhiḥ
kalāpa-grāma-vāsibhiḥ
parītaṁ praṇato 'pṛcchad
idam eva kurūdvaha

tatra—there; *upaviṣṭam*—sitting; *ṛṣibhiḥ*—by sages; *kalāpa-grāma*—in the village Kalāpa (nearby Badarikāśrama); *vāsibhiḥ*—who resided;

parītam—surrounded; *praṇataḥ*—bowing down; *apṛcchat*—he asked; *idam eva*—this same (question); *kuru-udvaha*—O most eminent of the Kurus.

TRANSLATION

There Nārada approached Lord Nārāyaṇa Ṛṣi, who was sitting amidst sages of the village of Kalāpa. After bowing down to the Lord, O hero of the Kurus, Nārada asked Him the very same question you have asked me.

TEXT 8

तस्मै ह्यवोचद् भगवानृषीणां शृण्वतामिदम् ।
यो ब्रह्मवादः पूर्वेषां जनलोकनिवासिनाम् ॥८॥

tasmai hy avocad bhagavān
ṛṣīṇāṁ śṛṇvatām idam
yo brahma-vādaḥ pūrveṣāṁ
jana-loka-nivāsinām

tasmai—to him; *hi*—indeed; *avocat*—spoke; *bhagavān*—the Supreme Lord; *ṛṣīṇām*—the sages; *śṛṇvatām*—as they listened; *idam*—this; *yaḥ*—which; *brahma*—about the Absolute Truth; *vādaḥ*—discussion; *pūrveṣām*—ancient; *jana-loka-nivāsinām*—among the inhabitants of Janaloka.

TRANSLATION

As the sages listened, Lord Nārāyaṇa Ṛṣi related to Nārada an ancient discussion about the Absolute Truth that took place among the residents of Janaloka.

TEXT 9

श्रीभगवानुवाच

स्वायम्भुव ब्रह्मसत्रं जनलोकेऽभवत्पुरा ।
तत्रस्थानां मानसानां मुनीनाम् ऊर्ध्वरेतसाम् ॥९॥

śrī-bhagavān uvāca
svāyambhuva brahma-satraṁ
jana-loke 'bhavat purā
tatra-sthānāṁ mānasānāṁ
munīnām ūrdhva-retasām

śrī-bhagavān uvāca—the Supreme Lord said; *svāyambhuva*—O son of self-born Brahmā; *brahma*—performed by the utterance of transcendental sound; *satram*—a sacrifice; *jana-loke*—on the planet Janaloka; *abhavat*—occurred; *purā*—in the past; *tatra*—there; *sthānām*—among those who resided; *mānasānām*—born from the mind (of Brahmā); *munīnām*—sages; *ūrdhva*—(flowing) upward; *retasām*—whose semen.

TRANSLATION

The Personality of Godhead said: O son of self-born Brahmā, once long ago on Janaloka, wise sages who resided there performed a great sacrifice to the Absolute Truth by vibrating transcendental sounds. These sages, mental sons of Brahmā, were all perfect celibates.

PURPORT

Śrīla Śrīdhara Svāmī explains that the word *satram* here refers to a Vedic sacrifice in which all the participants are equally qualified to serve as priests. In this instance, each of the sages present in Janaloka could speak equally well on the topic of Brahman.

TEXT 10

श्वेतद्वीपं गतवति त्वयि द्रष्टुं तदीश्वरम् ।
ब्रह्मवादः सुसंवृत्तः श्रुतयो यत्र शेरते ।
तत्र हायमभूत्प्रश्नस्त्वं मां यमनुपृच्छसि ॥१०॥

śvetadvīpaṁ gatavati
tvayi draṣṭuṁ tad-īśvaram
brahma-vādaḥ su-saṁvṛttaḥ
śrutayo yatra śerate
tatra hāyam abhūt praśnas
tvaṁ māṁ yam anupṛcchasi

śvetadvīpam—to Śvetadvīpa; *gatavati*—having gone; *tvayi*—you (Nārada); *draṣṭum*—to see; *tat*—its; *īśvaram*—Lord (Aniruddha); *brahma*—into the nature of the Supreme; *vādaḥ*—a symposium; *su*—enthusiastically; *saṁvṛttaḥ*—ensued; *śrutayaḥ*—the *Vedas; yatra*—in whom (Lord Aniruddha, also known as Kṣīrodakaśāyī Viṣṇu); *śerate*—lay down to rest; *tatra*—about Him; *ha*—indeed; *ayam*—this; *abhūt*—arose; *praśnaḥ*—question; *tvam*—you; *mām*—of Me; *yam*—which; *anupṛcchasi*—again are asking.

TRANSLATION

At that time you happened to be visiting the Lord on Śvetadvīpa—that Supreme Lord in whom the *Vedas* lie down to rest during the period of universal annihilation. A lively discussion arose among the sages on Janaloka as to the nature of the Supreme Absolute Truth. Indeed, the same question arose then that you are asking Me now.

TEXT 11

तुल्यश्रुततपःशीलास्तुल्यस्वीयारिमध्यमाः ।
अपि चक्रुः प्रवचनमेकं शुश्रूषवोऽपरे ॥११॥

tulya-śruta-tapaḥ-śīlās
tulya-svīyāri-madhyamāḥ
api cakruḥ pravacanam
ekaṁ śuśrūṣavo 'pare

tulya—equal; *śruta*—in hearing from the *Vedas; tapaḥ*—and performance of penances; *śīlāḥ*—whose character; *tulya*—equal; *svīya*—to friends; *ari*—enemies; *madhyamāḥ*—and neutral parties; *api*—although; *cakruḥ*—they made; *pravacanam*—the speaker; *ekam*—one of them; *śuśrūṣavaḥ*—eager listeners; *apare*—the others.

TRANSLATION

Although these sages were all equally qualified in terms of Vedic study and austerity, and although they all saw friends, enemies and neutral parties equally, they chose one of their number to be the speaker, and the rest became eager listeners.

TEXTS 12–13

श्रीसनन्दन उवाच
स्वसृष्टमिदमापीय शयानं सह शक्तिभिः ।
तदन्ते बोधयां चक्रुस्तल्लिंगैः श्रुतयः परम् ॥१२॥
यथा शयानं संराजं वन्दिनस्तत्पराक्रमैः ।
प्रत्यूषेऽभेत्य सुश्लोकैर्बोधयन्त्यनुजीविनः ॥१३॥

śrī-sanandana uvāca
sva-sṛṣṭam idam āpīya
śayānaṁ saha śaktibhiḥ
tad-ante bodhayāṁ cakrus
tal-liṅgaiḥ śrutayaḥ param

yathā śayānaṁ saṁrājaṁ
vandinas tat-parākramaiḥ
pratyūṣe 'bhetya su-ślokair
bodhayanty anujīvinaḥ

śrī-sanandanaḥ—Śrī Sanandana (the exalted mind-born son of Brahmā who was chosen to reply to the sages' inquiry); *uvāca*—said; *sva*—by Himself; *sṛṣṭam*—created; *idam*—this (universe); *āpīya*—having withdrawn; *śayānam*—lying asleep; *saha*—with; *śaktibhiḥ*—His energies; *tat*—of that (period of universal dissolution); *ante*—at the end; *bodhayām cakruḥ*—they awakened Him; *tat*—His; *liṅgaiḥ*—with (descriptions of) His characteristics; *śrutayaḥ*—the *Vedas; param*—the Supreme; *yathā*—just as; *śayānam*—sleeping; *saṁrājam*—a king; *vandinaḥ*—his court poets; *tat*—his; *parākramaiḥ*—with (recitations of) the heroic deeds; *pratyūṣe*—at dawn; *abhetya*—approaching him; *su-ślokaiḥ*—poetic; *bodhayanti*—they awaken; *anujīvinaḥ*—his servants.

TRANSLATION

Śrī Sanandana replied: After the Supreme Lord withdrew the universe He had previously created, He lay for some time as if asleep, and all His energies rested dormant within Him. When the time came for the next creation, the personified *Vedas* awakened

Him by chanting His glories, just as the poets serving a king approach him at dawn and awaken him by reciting his heroic deeds.

PURPORT

At the time of creation, the *Vedas* are the first emanation from the breathing of Lord Mahā-Viṣṇu, and in personified form they serve Him by waking Him from His mystic sleep. This statement made by Sanandana implies that Sanaka and the other sages had asked him the same question that Nārada had asked Nārāyaṇa Ṛṣi and Mahārāja Parīkṣit had asked Śukadeva Gosvāmī. Sanandana refers the question back to the example of the personified *Vedas* themselves in their address to Lord Mahā-Viṣṇu. Even though the *Vedas* knew that the Lord, being omniscient, does not need to be informed of His glories, they enthusiastically took this opportunity to praise Him.

TEXT 14

श्रीश्रुतय ऊचुः

जय जय जह्यजामजित दोषगृभीतगुणां
त्वमसि यदात्मना समवरुद्धसमस्तभगः ।
अगजगदोकसामखिलशक्त्यवबोधक ते
क्वचिदजयात्मना च चरतोऽनुचरेन्निगमः ॥१४॥

śrī-śrutaya ūcuḥ
jaya jaya jahy ajām ajita doṣa-gṛbhīta-guṇāṁ
tvam asi yad ātmanā samavaruddha-samasta-bhagaḥ
aga-jagad-okasām akhila-śakty-avabodhaka te
kvacid ajayātmanā ca carato 'nucaren nigamaḥ

śrī-śrutayaḥ ūcuḥ—the *Vedas* said; *jaya jaya*—victory to You, victory to You; *jahi*—please defeat; *ajām*—the eternal illusory potency of Māyā; *ajita*—O unconquerable one; *doṣa*—to create discrepancies; *gṛbhīta*—who has assumed; *guṇām*—the qualities of matter; *tvam*—You; *asi*—are; *yat*—because; *ātmanā*—in Your original status; *samavaruddha*—complete; *samasta*—in all; *bhagaḥ*—opulences; *aga*—nonmoving; *jagat*—and moving; *okasām*—of those who possess material bodies; *akhila*—of all; *śakti*—the energies; *avabodhaka*—O You who awaken; *te*—You; *kvacit*—sometimes; *ajayā*—with Your material energy; *ātmanā*—and with Your internal, spiritual energy; *ca*—also; *carataḥ*—engaging; *anucaret*—can appreciate; *nigamaḥ*—the *Vedas*.

TRANSLATION

The *śrutis* said: Victory, victory to You, O unconquerable one! By Your very nature You are perfectly full in all opulences; therefore please defeat the eternal power of illusion, who assumes control over the modes of nature to create difficulties for conditioned souls. O You who awaken all the energies of the moving and nonmoving embodied beings, sometimes the *Vedas* can recognize You as You sport with Your material and spiritual potencies.

PURPORT

According to Śrīla Jīva Gosvāmī, the twenty-eight verses of the prayers of the personified *Vedas* (Texts 14-41) represent the opinions of each of the twenty-eight major *śrutis*. These chief *Upaniṣads* and other *śrutis* concern themselves with various approaches to the Absolute Truth, and among them those *śrutis* are supreme which emphasize pure, unalloyed devotional service to the Supreme Personality of Godhead. The *Upaniṣads* direct our attention to the Personality of Godhead by first negating what is distinct from Him and then defining some of His important characteristics.

Śrīla Viśvanātha Cakravartī interprets the first words of this prayer, *jaya jaya*, to mean "please reveal Your superexcellence." The word *jaya* is repeated out of either reverence or joy.

"How should I reveal My excellence?" the Lord might ask.

The *śrutis* answer by requesting Him to mercifully destroy the ignorance of all living beings and attract them to His lotus feet.

The Lord says, "But Māyā, who imposes ignorance on the *jīvas*, is full of good qualities [*gṛbhīta-guṇām*]. Why should I oppose her?"

"Yes," the *Vedas* answer, "but she has taken on the three modes of nature to bewilder the conditioned souls and make them falsely identify with their material bodies. Her modes of goodness, passion and ignorance, moreover, are tainted [*doṣa-gṛbhīta*] because You are not manifest in their presence."

The *śrutis* go on to address the Lord as *ajita,* implying that "only You cannot be conquered by Māyā, whereas others, like Brahmā, are defeated by their own faults."

The Lord responds, "But what proof do you have that she cannot conquer Me?"

"The proof lies in the fact that in Your original state You have already realized the perfection of all opulences."

At this point the Lord might object that merely destroying the ignorance of the *jīvas* will not suffice to bring them to His lotus feet, since the *jīva* soul, even after his ignorance is dispelled, cannot attain the Lord without engaging in devotional service. As the Lord states in His own words, *bhaktyāham ekayā grāhyaḥ:* "I am attainable only through devotional service." (*Bhāg.* 11.14.21)

To this objection the *śrutis* reply, "My Lord, O You who awaken all energies, after creating the intelligence and senses of the living entities, You inspire them to work hard and enjoy the fruits of their labor. In addition, by Your mercy You awaken their ability to pursue the progressive paths of knowledge, mystic *yoga* and devotional service, allowing them to advance toward You in Your aspects of Brahman, Paramātmā and Bhagavān, respectively. And when *jñāna, yoga* and *bhakti* mature, You empower the living beings to directly realize You in each of Your three aspects."

If the Lord were to ask for authoritative evidence to support this statement by the personified *Vedas,* they humbly reply, "We ourselves are the evidence. On some occasions—such as now, the time of creation—You consort with Your external, Māyā potency, whereas You are always present with Your internal energy. It is at times such as the present, when Your activity is outwardly manifest, that we, the *Vedas,* can recognize You in Your play."

Thus endowed with authority by their personal association with the Supreme Lord, the *śrutis* promulgate the processes of *karma, jñāna, yoga* and *bhakti* as various means for the conditioned souls to employ their intelligence, senses, mind and vitality in search of the Absolute Truth.

In many places the *Vedas* glorify the transcendental, personal qualities of the Supreme. The following verse appears in the *Śvetāśvatara Upaniṣad* (6.11), the *Gopāla-tāpanī Upaniṣad* (*Uttara* 97), and the *Brahma Upaniṣad* (4.1):

eko devaḥ sarva-bhūteṣu gūḍhaḥ
sarva-vyāpī sarva-bhūtāntarātmā
karmādhyakṣaḥ sarva-bhūtādhivāsaḥ
sākṣī cetāḥ kevalo nirguṇaś ca

"The one Supreme Lord lives hidden inside all created things. He pervades all matter and sits within the hearts of all living beings. As the indwelling Supersoul, He supervises their material activities. Thus, while having no material qualities Himself, He is the unique witness and giver of consciousness."

The Supreme's personal qualities are further described in the following quotations from the *Upaniṣads: Yaḥ sarva-jñaḥ sa sarva-vid yasya jñāna-mayaṁ tapaḥ.* "He who is all-knowing, from whom the potency of all knowledge comes—He is the wisest of all" (*Muṇḍaka Up.* 1.1.9); *sarvasya vaśī sarvasyeśānaḥ:* "He is the Lord and controller of everyone" (*Bṛhad-āraṇyaka Up.* 4.4.22); and *yaḥ pṛthivyāṁ tiṣṭhan pṛthivyā āntaro yaṁ pṛthivī na veda:* "He who resides within the earth and pervades it, whom the earth does not know." (*Bṛhad-āraṇyaka Up.* 3.7.3)

The Lord's role in creation is mentioned in many statements of the *śruti*. The *Bṛhad-āranyaka Upaniṣad* (1.2.4) states, *so 'kāmayata bahu syām:* "He desired, 'I will become many.'" The phrase *so 'kāmayata* ("He desired") here implies that the Lord's personality is eternal, for even prior to the creation the Absolute Truth experienced desire, and desire is an attribute unique to persons. The *Aitareya Upaniṣad* (3.11) similarly states, *sa aikṣata tat-tejo 'sṛjata:* "He saw, and His power sent forth the creation." Here the word *tat-tejaḥ* refers to the Lord's partial expansion Mahā-Viṣṇu, who glances upon Māyā and thus manifests the material creation. Or *tat-tejaḥ* may refer to the Lord's impersonal Brahman feature, His potency of all-pervasive, eternal existence. As described in *Śrī Brahma-saṁhitā* (5.40),

yasya prabhā prabhavato jagad-aṇḍa-koṭi-
koṭiṣv aśeṣa-vasudhādi-vibhūti-bhinnam
tad brahma niṣkalam anantam aśeṣa-bhūtaṁ
govindam ādi-puruṣaṁ tam ahaṁ bhajāmi

"I worship Govinda, the primeval Lord, who is endowed with great power. The glowing effulgence of His transcendental form is the impersonal

Brahman, which is absolute, complete and unlimited and which displays the varieties of countless planets, with their different opulences, in millions and millions of universes."

In summing up this verse, Śrīla Śrīdhara Svāmī prays,

jaya jayājita jahy aga-jaṅgamā-
vṛtim ajām upanīta-mṛṣā-guṇām
na hi bhavantam ṛte prabhavanty amī
nigama-gīta-guṇārṇavatā tava

"All glories, all glories to You, O unconquerable one! Please defeat the influence of Your eternal Māyā, who covers all moving and nonmoving creatures and who rules over the modes of illusion. Without Your influence, all these Vedic *mantras* would be powerless to sing of You as the ocean of transcendental qualities."

TEXT 15

बृहदुपलब्धमेतदवयन्त्यवशेषतया
यत उदयास्तमयौ विकृतेर्मृदि वाविकृतात् ।
अत ऋषयो दधुस्त्वयि मनोवचनाचरितं
कथमयथा भवन्ति भुवि दत्तपदानि नृणाम् ॥१५॥

bṛhad upalabdham etad avayanty avaśeṣatayā
yata udayāstam-ayau vikṛter mṛdi vāvikṛtāt
ata ṛṣayo dadhus tvayi mano-vacanācaritaṁ
katham ayathā bhavanti bhuvi datta-padāni nṛṇām

bṛhat—as the Supreme; *upalabdham*—perceived; *etat*—this (world); *avayanti*—they consider; *avaśeṣatayā*—in terms of its being the all-pervading foundation of existence; *yataḥ*—since; *udaya*—the generation; *astam-ayau*—and dissolution; *vikṛteḥ*—of a transformation; *mṛdi*—of clay; *vā*—as if; *avikṛtāt*—(the Supreme itself) not being subject to transformation; *ataḥ*—therefore; *ṛṣayaḥ*—the sages (who compiled the Vedic *mantras*); *dadhuḥ*—placed; *tvayi*—in You; *manaḥ*—their minds; *vacana*—words; *ācaritam*—and actions; *katham*—how; *ayathā*—not as they are; *bhavanti*—become; *bhuvi*—upon the ground; *datta*—placed; *padāni*—the steps; *nṛṇām*—of men.

TRANSLATION

This perceivable world is identified with the Supreme because the Supreme Brahman is the ultimate foundation of all existence, remaining unchanged as all created things are generated from it and at last dissolved into it, just as clay remains unchanged by the products made from it and again merged with it. Thus it is toward You alone that the Vedic sages direct all their thoughts, words and acts. After all, how can the footsteps of men fail to touch the earth on which they live?

PURPORT

There may be some doubt as to whether the Vedic *mantras* are unanimous when identifying the Supreme Personality of Godhead. After all, some *mantras* state, *indro yāto 'vasitasya rājā:* "Indra is the King of all moving and nonmoving beings" (*Ṛg Veda* 1.32.15), while others say, *agnir mūrdhā divaḥ:* "Agni is the chief of the heavens," and yet other *mantras* point to different deities as the Absolute. It would seem, then, that the *Vedas* present a polytheistic world view.

Answering this doubt, the *Vedas* themselves explain in this verse that there can be only one source of universal creation, called Brahman or Bṛhat, "the greatest," which is the singular truth underlying and pervading all existence. No finite deity like Indra or Agni can fulfill this unique role, nor would the *śrutis* be so ignorant as to propose such an idea. As indicated here by the word *tvayi,* Lord Viṣṇu alone is the Absolute Truth. Indra and other demigods may be glorified in various ways, but they possess only those powers Lord Śrī Viṣṇu has granted them.

The Vedic sages understand that this entire world—including Indra, Agni, and everything else perceivable by the eyes, ears and other senses—is identical with the one Supreme Truth, the Personality of Godhead, who is called Bṛhat, "the greatest," because He is *avaśeṣa,* "the ultimate substance that remains." From the Lord everything expands at creation, and into Him everything dissolves at annihilation. He exists before and after the material manifestation as the constant basis, known to philosophers as the "ingredient cause," *upādāna.* Despite the fact that countless manifestations emanate from Him, the Supreme Lord exists eternally unchanged—an idea the *śrutis* specifically emphasize here with the word *avikṛtāt.*

The words *mṛdi vā* ("as in the case of clay") allude to a famous analogy spoken by Udālaka to his son Śvetaketu in the *Chāndogya Upaniṣad* (6.4.1): *vācārambhanaṁ vikāro nāmadheyaṁ mṛttikety eva satyam.* "The objects of the material world exist merely as names, transformations defined by language, whereas the ingredient cause, like the clay from which pots are made, is the actual reality." A mass of clay is the ingredient cause of various pots, statues and so on, but the clay itself remains in its essence unchanged. Eventually, the pots and other objects will be destroyed and return to the clay from which they came. Similarly, the Supreme Lord is the total ingredient cause, yet He remains eternally untouched by transformation. This is the purport of the statement *sarvaṁ khalv idaṁ brahma:* "Everything is Brahman." (*Chāndogya Up.* 3.14.1) Wondering at this mystery, the great devotee Gajendra prayed,

namo namas te 'khila-kāraṇāya
niṣkāraṇāyādbhuta-kāraṇāya

"Obeisances again and again to You, the source of all creation. You are the inconceivable cause of all causes, and of You there is no other cause." (*Bhāg.* 8.3.15)

Prakṛti, material nature, is often considered the ingredient cause of creation, in Western science as well as in the *Vedas.* This does not contradict the higher fact of the Supreme Lord's being the final cause, since *prakṛti* is His energy, and is herself subject to change. In *Śrīmad-Bhāgavatam* (11.24.19), Lord Kṛṣṇa says,

prakṛtir yasyopādānam
ādhāraḥ puruṣaḥ paraḥ
sato 'bhivyañjakaḥ kālo
brahma tat tritayaṁ tv aham

"The material universe is real, having *prakṛti* as its original ingredient and final state. Lord Mahā-Viṣṇu is the resting place of nature, which becomes manifest by the power of time. Thus nature, the almighty Viṣṇu and time are not different from Me, the Supreme Absolute Truth." *Prakṛti,* however, undergoes transformation, while her Lord, the supreme *puruṣa,* does not. *Prakṛti* is the Personality of Godhead's external energy, but He has another energy—His internal energy—which is *svarūpa-bhūtā,* nondifferent from His very essence. The Lord's internal energy, like Himself, is never subject to material change.

Therefore the *mantras* of the *Vedas,* along with the *ṛṣis* who have received these *mantras* in meditation and transmitted them for the benefit of mankind, direct their attention primarily toward the Personality of Godhead. The Vedic sages direct the activities of their mind and words—that is to say, the inner as well as the literal meaning (*abhidhā-vṛtti*) of their utterances—first of all toward Him, and only secondarily toward separated transformations of *prakṛti,* such as Indra and other demigods.

Just as a man's footsteps, whether placed on mud, stone or bricks, cannot fail to touch the surface of the earth, so whatever the *Vedas* discuss within the realm of material generation, they relate to the Absolute Truth. Mundane literature describes limited phenomena, disregarding the relation of its subjects to the total reality, but the *Vedas* always focus their perfect vision on the Supreme. As the *Chāndogya Upaniṣad* affirms in its statements *mṛttikety eva satyam* and *sarvaṁ khalv idam brahma,* reality is understood properly when everything is seen to be dependent on Brahman, the Absolute, for its existence. Brahman alone is real, not because nothing we see in this world is real, but because Brahman is the absolute, final cause of everything. Thus the word *satyam,* as used in the phrase *mṛttikety eva satyam,* has been defined in another context as "ingredient cause" by no less an authority than Lord Kṛṣṇa Himself:

yad upādāya pūrvas tu
bhāvo vikurute param
ādir anto yadā yasya
tat satyam abhidhīyate

"A material object, itself composed of an essential ingredient, creates another material object through transformation. In this way one created object becomes the cause and basis of another created object. A particular thing may be called real in that it possesses the basic nature of another object that constitutes its cause and original state." (*Bhāg.* 11.24.18)

Explaining the word *Brahman,* Śrīla Prabhupāda writes in *Kṛṣṇa, the Supreme Personality of Godhead,* "The word *Brahman* indicates the greatest of all and the maintainer of everything. The impersonalists are attracted by the greatness of the sky, but because of their poor fund of knowledge they are not attracted by the greatness of Kṛṣṇa. In our practical life, however, we are attracted by the greatness of a person and not by the greatness of a big mountain. Actually the term *Brahman* can be applied to Kṛṣṇa only; therefcre in the *Bhagavad-gītā* Arjuna admitted that Lord Kṛṣṇa is the Parabrahman, or the supreme rest of everything.

"Kṛṣṇa is the Supreme Brahman because of His unlimited knowledge, unlimited potencies, unlimited strength, unlimited influence, unlimited beauty and unlimited renunciation. Therefore the word *Brahman* can be applied to Kṛṣṇa only. Arjuna affirms that because the impersonal Brahman is the effulgence emanating as rays of Kṛṣṇa's transcendental body, Kṛṣṇa is the Parabrahman. Everything is resting on Brahman, but Brahman itself is resting on Kṛṣṇa. Therefore Kṛṣṇa is the ultimate Brahman, or Parabrahman. The material elements are accepted as inferior energies of Kṛṣṇa because by their interaction the cosmic manifestation takes place, rests on Kṛṣṇa, and after dissolution again enters into the body of Kṛṣṇa as His subtle energy. Kṛṣṇa is therefore the cause of both manifestation and dissolution."

In summary, Śrīla Śrīdhara Svāmī prays,

druhiṇa-vahni-ravīndra-mukhāmarā
jagad idaṁ na bhavet pṛthag utthitam
bahu-mukhair api mantra-gaṇair ajas
tvam uru-mūrtir ato vinigadyase

"The demigods, headed by Śiva, Agni, Sūrya and Indra, and indeed all beings in the universe, do not come into existence independently of You. The *mantras* of the *Vedas,* though they speak from various viewpoints, all speak about You, the unborn Lord appearing in numerous forms."

TEXT 16

इति तव सूरयस्त्र्यधिपतेऽखिललोकमल-
क्षपणकथामृताब्धिमवगाह्य तपांसि जहुः ।
किमुत पुनः स्वधामविधुताशयकालगुणाः
परम भजन्ति ये पदमजस्रसुखानुभवम् ॥१६॥

iti tava sūrayas try-adhipate 'khila-loka-mala-
kṣapaṇa-kathāmṛtābdhim avagāhya tapāṁsi jahuḥ
kim uta punaḥ sva-dhāma-vidhutāśaya-kāla-guṇāḥ
parama bhajanti ye padam ajasra-sukhānubhavam

iti—thus; *tava*—Your; *sūrayaḥ*—wise saints; *tri*—of the three (planetary systems of the universe, or the three modes of nature); *adhipate*—O master; *akhila*—of all; *loka*—the worlds; *mala*—the contamination; *kṣapaṇa*—which eradicates; *kathā*—of discussions; *amṛta*—nectar; *abdhim*—into the ocean; *avagāhya*—by diving deeply; *tapāṁsi*—their troubles; *jahuḥ*—have given up; *kim uta*—what to speak; *punaḥ*—moreover; *sva*—their own; *dhāma*—by the power; *vidhuta*—dispelled; *āśaya*—of their minds; *kāla*—and of time; *guṇāḥ*—the (undesirable) qualities; *parama*—O supreme one; *bhajanti*—worship; *ye*—who; *padam*—Your true nature; *ajasra*—uninterrupted; *sukha*—of happiness; *anubhavam*—(in which there is) experience.

TRANSLATION

Therefore, O master of the three worlds, the wise get rid of all misery by diving deep into the nectarean ocean of topics about You, which washes away all the contamination of the universe. Then what to speak of those who, having by spiritual strength rid their minds of bad habits and freed themselves from time, are able to worship Your true nature, O supreme one, finding within it uninterrupted bliss?

PURPORT

According to Śrīla Jīva Gosvāmī, in the previous verse those *śrutis* whose presentation of the Supreme Truth may seem impersonal clarified their true purpose. Now, in the present verse, those who focus exclusively on the divine Personality of Godhead, who speak of His transcendental pastimes, take their turn in praising Him.

Because all the *Vedas* declare the supremacy of the Personality of Godhead as the cause of all causes, discriminating persons should take to His worship. By diving into the ocean of His glories, intelligent devotees help dispel the distress of all souls and loosen their own burning attachment to materialistic life. These advancing devotees gradually give up all material attachment and lose any interest they once had in the troublesome austerities of *karma, jñāna* and *yoga.*

Beyond these devotees are the *sūris,* connoisseurs of spiritual truth, who honor the nectarean ocean of the Supreme Lord's glories by immersing themselves fully within it. These mature devotees of the Supreme

Lord achieve unimaginable perfection. The Lord, reciprocating their sincere endeavors, empowers them to realize Him in His personal form. Remembering with rapture the Lord's intimate pastimes and entourage, they are automatically freed from the last subtle traces of mental contamination and from sensitivity to the unavoidable pains of disease and old age.

Referring to the purifying power of devotional service, the *śrutis* say, *tad yathā puṣkara-palāśa āpo na śliṣyante evam evaṁ-vidi pāpaṁ karma na śliṣyate:* "Just as water does not adhere to a lotus leaf, so sinful activities do not adhere to one who knows the truth in this way." The *Śatapatha Brāhmaṇa* (14.7.28), *Taittirīya Brāhmaṇa* (3.12.9.8), *Bṛhad-āraṇyaka Upaniṣad* (4.4.28) and *Baudhāyana-dharma-śāstra* (2.6.11.30) all concur: *na karmaṇā lipyate pāpakena.* "One thus avoids becoming tainted by sinful activity."

The *Ṛg Veda* (1.154.1) refers to the Supreme Lord's pastimes as follows: *viṣṇor nu kaṁ vīryāṇi pravocaṁ yaḥ pārthivāni vimame rajāṁsi.* "Only he may fully enunciate the heroic deeds of Lord Viṣṇu who can count all the particles of dust in the world." Many *śruti-mantras* glorify devotional service to the Lord, such as *eko vaśī sarva-go ye 'nubhajanti dhīrās/ teṣāṁ sukhaṁ śāśvataṁ netareṣām:* "He is the one omnipresent Lord and controller; only those wise souls who worship Him obtain eternal happiness, not anyone else."

In this connection Śrīla Śrīdhara Svāmī prays,

sakala-veda-gaṇerita-sad-guṇas
tvam iti sarva-manīṣi-janā ratāḥ
tvayi subhadra-guṇa-śravaṇādibhis
tava pada-smaraṇena gata-klamāḥ

"Because all the *Vedas* describe Your transcendental qualities, all thoughtful persons are attracted to hearing and chanting about Your all-auspicious qualities. Thus by remembering Your lotus feet, they are freed from material distress."

TEXT 17

दृतय इव श्वसन्त्यसुभृतो यदि तेऽनुविधा
महदहमादयोऽण्डमसृजन् यदनुग्रहतः ।

पुरुषविधोऽन्वयोऽत्र चरमोऽन्नमयादिषु यः
सदसतः परं त्वमथ यदेष्ववशेषमृतम् ॥१७॥

dṛtaya iva śvasanty asu-bhṛto yadi te 'nuvidhā
mahad-aham-ādayo 'ṇḍam asṛjan yad-anugrahataḥ
puruṣa-vidho 'nvayo 'tra caramo 'nna-mayādiṣu yaḥ
sad-asataḥ paraṁ tvam atha yad eṣv avaśeṣam ṛtam

dṛtayaḥ—bellows; *iva*—as if; *śvasanti*—they breathe; *asu-bhṛtaḥ*—alive; *yadi*—if; *te*—Your; *anuvidhāḥ*—faithful followers; *mahat*—the total material energy; *aham*—false ego; *ādayaḥ*—and the other elements of creation; *aṇḍam*—the universal egg; *asṛjan*—produced; *yat*—whose; *anugrahataḥ*—by the mercy; *puruṣa*—of the living entity; *vidhaḥ*—according to the particular forms; *anvayaḥ*—whose entrance; *atra*—among these; *caramaḥ*—the ultimate; *anna-maya-ādiṣu*—among the manifestations known as *anna-maya* and so on; *yaḥ*—who; *sat-asataḥ*—from gross and subtle matter; *param*—distinct; *tvam*—You; *atha*—and furthermore; *yat*—which; *eṣu*—among these; *avaśeṣam*—underlying; *ṛtam*—the reality.

TRANSLATION

Only if they become Your faithful followers are those who breathe actually alive; otherwise their breathing is like that of a bellows. It is by Your mercy alone that the elements, beginning with the *mahat-tattva* and false ego, created the egg of this universe. Among the manifestations known as *anna-maya* and so forth, You are the ultimate one, entering within the material coverings along with the living entity and assuming the same forms as those he takes. Distinct from the gross and subtle material manifestations, You are the reality underlying them all.

PURPORT

Life is without purpose for one who remains ignorant of his most well-wishing benefactor and thus fails to worship Him. Such a person's breathing is no better than the breathing of a blacksmith's bellows. The gift of human life is a fortunate opportunity for the conditioned soul, but by turning away from his Lord, the living being commits spiritual suicide. In the words of *Śrī Īśopaniṣad* (3),

asuryā nāma te lokā
andhena tamasāvṛtāḥ
tāṁs te pretyābhigacchanti
ye ke cātma-hano janāḥ

"The killer of the soul, whoever he may be, must enter into the planets known as the worlds of the faithless, full of darkness and ignorance." *Asuryāḥ* means "to be obtained by demons," and demons are persons who have no devotion for the Supreme Lord, Viṣṇu. This definition is stated in the *Agni Purāṇa:*

dvau bhūta-sargau loke 'smin
daiva āsura eva ca
viṣṇu-bhakti-paro daiva
āsuras tad-viparyayaḥ

"There are two kinds of created beings in this world, godly and demoniac. Those dedicated to the devotional service of Lord Viṣṇu are godly, and those opposed to such service are demoniac."

Similarly, the *Bṛhad-āraṇyaka Upaniṣad* (4.4.15) states, *na ced avedīn mahatī vinaṣṭiḥ . . . ye tad vidur amṛtās te bhavanty athetare duḥkham evopayanti:* "If one does not come to know the Supreme, he must suffer utter destruction. . . . Those who realize the Supreme become immortal, but others inevitably suffer." A person must revive his Kṛṣṇa consciousness to be relieved of the suffering caused by ignorance, but the process by which this is done need not be difficult, as Lord Kṛṣṇa assures us in *Bhagavad-gītā* (9.34):

man-manā bhava mad-bhakto
mad-yājī māṁ namaskuru
mām evaiṣyasi yuktvaivam
ātmānaṁ mat-parāyaṇaḥ

"Engage your mind in always thinking of Me, become My devotee, offer obeisances to Me and worship Me. Being completely absorbed in Me, surely you will come to Me." Despite disqualifications and weaknesses, one need only willingly become *anuvidha,* the Supreme Lord's trusting and trustworthy servant. The *Kaṭha Upaniṣad* (2.2.13) proclaims,

nityo nityānāṁ cetanaś cetanānām
eko bahūnāṁ yo vidadhāti kāmān
taṁ pīṭha-gaṁ ye 'nupaśyanti dhīrās
teṣāṁ śāntiḥ śāśvatī netareṣām

"Among all the eternal, conscious beings, there is one who supplies the needs of everyone else. The wise souls who worship Him in His abode attain everlasting peace. Others cannot."

What is alive, and what is dead? The bodies and minds of materialistic nondevotees seem to display the symptoms of life, but this appearance is deceptive. Actually, the conditioned soul has little control over his own bodily existence. Against his will, he has to excrete waste, get sick from time to time, and eventually age and die. And in his mind he unwillingly suffers anger, hankering and lamentation. Lord Kṛṣṇa describes this situation as *yantrārūḍhāni māyayā* (Bg. 18.61), riding helplessly as a passenger in a mechanical vehicle. The soul undoubtedly is alive, and irrevocably so, but in his ignorance that inner life is covered and forgotten. In its place, the automaton of the external mind and body carries out the dictates of the modes of nature, which force one to act in a way altogether irrelevant to the dormant needs of the soul. Calling out to the forgetful prisoners of illusion, the *Śvetāśvatara Upaniṣad* (2.5) urges,

śṛṇvantu viśve amṛtasya putrā
ā ye dhāmāni divyāni tasthuḥ

"All you sons of immortality, hear, you who once resided in the divine kingdom!"

So, on the one hand, what is normally viewed as living—the material body—is in actuality a dead machine being manipulated by the modes of nature. And on the other hand, what the materialist condescendingly views as inert matter meant for exploitation is in its unknown essence connected with a living intelligence vastly more potent than his own. The Vedic civilization recognizes the intelligence behind nature as belonging to demigods who preside over the various elements, and ultimately to the

Supreme Lord Himself. Matter, after all, cannot act coherently without the impulse and guidance of a living force. As Kṛṣṇa states in *Bhagavad-gītā* (9.10),

mayādhyakṣeṇa prakṛtiḥ
sūyate sa-carācaram
hetunānena kaunteya
jagad viparivartate

"This material nature, which is one of My energies, is working under My direction, O son of Kuntī, producing all moving and nonmoving beings. Under its rule this manifestation is created and annihilated again and again."

In the beginning of creation, Lord Mahā-Viṣṇu glanced at the dormant material nature, *prakṛti.* Thus awakened, the subtle *prakṛti* began to evolve into more concrete forms: first the *mahat;* then false ego in conjunction with each of *prakṛti's* three modes; and gradually the various material elements, including intelligence, mind, the senses and the five physical elements with their presiding demigods. Even after becoming separately manifested, however, the deities responsible for the various elements could not work together to produce the perceptible world until Lord Viṣṇu, by His special mercy, once more intervened. This is described in the Third Canto of *Śrīmad-Bhāgavatam* (3.5.38–39):

ete devāḥ kalā viṣṇoḥ
kāla-māyāṁśa-liṅginaḥ
nānātvāt sva-kriyānīśāḥ
procuḥ prāñjalayo vibhum

devā ūcuḥ
nanāma te deva padāravindaṁ
prapanna-tāpopaśamātapatram
yan-mūla-ketā yatayo 'ñjasoru-
saṁsāra-duḥkhaṁ bahir utkṣipanti

"The controlling deities of these physical elements are empowered expansions of Lord Viṣṇu. They are embodied by eternal time under the external energy, and they are His parts and parcels. Because they were entrusted with different functions of universal duties and were unable to perform them, they offered fascinating prayers to the Lord. The demigods said, 'O Lord, Your lotus feet are like an umbrella for the surrendered souls, protecting them from all the miseries of material existence. All the sages under that shelter throw off all material miseries. We therefore offer our respectful obeisances unto Your lotus feet.'"

Hearing the prayers of the assembled demigods of the elements, the Supreme Lord then showed His favor (*Bhāg*. 3.6.1–3):

iti tāsāṁ sva-śaktīnāṁ
satīnām asametya saḥ
prasupta-loka-tantrāṇāṁ
niśāmya gatim īśvaraḥ

kāla-saṁjñāṁ tadā devīṁ
bibhrac chaktim urukramaḥ
trayoviṁśati tattvānāṁ
gaṇaṁ yugapad āviśat

so 'nupraviṣṭo bhagavāṁś
ceṣṭā-rūpeṇa taṁ gaṇam
bhinnaṁ saṁyojayām āsa
suptaṁ karma prabodhayan

"The Lord thus heard about the suspension of the progressive creative functions of the universe due to the noncombination of His potencies, such as the *mahat-tattva*. The Supreme Powerful Lord then simultaneously entered into the twenty-three elements with the goddess Kālī, His external energy, who alone amalgamates all the different elements. Thus when the Personality of Godhead entered into the elements by His energy, all the living entities were enlivened into different activities, just as one is engaged in his work after awakening from sleep."

In *Kṛṣṇa*, Śrīla Prabhupāda explains the five levels of ego covering the self: "Within the body there are five different departments of existence, known as *anna-maya*, *prāṇa-maya*, *mano-maya*, *vijñāna-maya*, and at last *ānanda-maya*. [These are enumerated in the *Brahmānanda-vallī* of the *Taittirīya Upaniṣad*.] In the beginning of life, every living entity is food conscious. A child or an animal is satisfied only by getting nice food. This stage of consciousness, in which the goal is to eat sumptuously, is called *anna-maya. Anna* means 'food.' After this one lives in the consciousness of being alive. If one can continue his life without being attacked or destroyed, one thinks himself happy. This stage is called *prāṇa-maya,* or consciousness of one's existence. After this stage, when one is situated on the mental platform, that consciousness is called *mano-maya.* The material civilization is primarily situated in these three stages—*anna-maya, prāṇa-maya* and *mano-maya.* The first concern of civilized persons is economic development, the next concern is defense against being annihilated, and the next consciousness is mental speculation, the philosophical approach to the values of life.

"If by the evolutionary process of philosophical life one happens to reach to the platform of intellectual life and understands that he is not this material body, but is a spirit soul, one is situated in the *vijñāna-maya* stage. Then by evolution of spiritual life he comes to understand the Supreme Lord, or the Supreme Soul. When one develops his relationship with Him and executes devotional service, that stage of life is called Kṛṣṇa consciousness, the *ānanda-maya* stage. *Ānanda-maya* is the blissful life of knowledge and eternity. As it is said in the *Vedānta-sūtra, ānanda-mayo 'bhyāsāt.* The Supreme Brahman and the subordinate Brahman, or the Supreme Personality of Godhead and the living entities, are both joyful by nature. As long as the living entities are situated in the lower four stages of life—*anna-maya, prāṇa-maya, mano-maya* and *vijñāna-maya*—they are considered to be in the material condition of life, but as soon as one reaches the stage of *ānanda-maya* he becomes a liberated soul. This *ānanda-maya* stage is explained in the *Bhagavad-gītā* as the *brahma-bhūta* stage. There it is said that in the *brahma-bhūta* stage of life there is no anxiety and no hankering. This stage begins when one becomes equally disposed toward all living entities, and it then expands to the stage of Kṛṣṇa consciousness, in which one hankers to render service unto the Supreme Personality of Godhead. This hankering for advancement in devotional service is not the same as hankering for sense gratification in material existence. In other words, hankering remains in spiritual life, but it becomes purified. When our senses are purified, they become freed from all material stages, namely *anna-maya, prāṇa-maya, mano-maya* and *vijñāna-maya,* and they become situated in the highest stage—*ānanda-maya,* or blissful life in Kṛṣṇa consciousness.

"The Māyāvādī philosophers consider *ānanda-maya* to be the state of being merged in the Supreme. To them. *ānanda-maya* means that the

Supersoul and the individual soul become one. But the real fact is that oneness does not mean merging into the Supreme and losing one's own individual existence. Merging into the spiritual existence is the living entity's realization of qualitative oneness with the Supreme Lord in His eternity and knowledge aspects. But the actual *ānanda-maya* (blissful) stage is obtained when one is engaged in devotional service. That is confirmed in the *Bhagavad-gītā: mad-bhaktiṁ labhate parām.* The *brahma-bhūta ānanda-maya* stage is complete only when there is the exchange of love between the Supreme and the subordinate living entities. Unless one comes to this *ānanda-maya* stage of life, his breathing is like the breathing of a bellows in a blacksmith's shop, his duration of life is like that of a tree, and he is no better than the lower animals like the camels, hogs and dogs."

In accompanying the *jīva* within the coverings of Māyā, the Paramātmā is not bound by karmic entanglement as the *jīva* is. Rather, the Supreme Soul's connection with these coverings is like the apparent connection between the moon and some tree branches it is seen through. The Supersoul is *sad-asataḥ param,* always transcendental to the subtle and gross manifestations of *anna-maya* and so on, although He enters among them as the sanctioning witness of all activities. As their final cause, the Supersoul is in one sense identical with the manifest products of creation, but in His original identity (*svarūpa*) He remains distinct. In this second sense He is the *ānanda-maya* alone, the last of the five *kośas.* Therefore the *śrutis* address Him here as *avaśeṣam,* the residual essence. This is also expressed in the text of the *Taittirīya Upaniṣad* (2.7): *raso vai saḥ.* Within His personal essence, the Supreme Lord enjoys *rasa,* the reciprocation of the mellows of devotional service, and integral to the play of *rasas* is the participation of realized *jīvas. Raso vai saḥ, rasaṁ hy evāyaṁ labdhvānandī bhavati:* "He is the embodiment of *rasa,* and the *jīva* who realizes this *rasa* becomes fully ecstatic." Or in the words of the personified *Vedas* praying in this verse, the Supersoul is *ṛtam,* which Śrīla Viśvanātha Cakravartī interprets as here meaning "realized by great sages."

In the opinion of Śrīla Viśvanātha Cakravartī, the last word of all authoritative scripture (*sarvāntima-śruti*) is contained in the aphorism *raso vai saḥ,* which is demonstrably a reference to Lord Śrī Kṛṣṇa as the infinitely expanding embodiment of divine pleasure (*sarva-bṛhattamānanda*). The *Gopāla-tāpanī śruti* (*Uttara* 96) states, *yo 'sau jāgrat-svapna-*

suṣuptim atītya turyātīto gopālaḥ: "Lord Kṛṣṇa, the cowherd, transcends not only the material consciousness of wakefulness, dream and deep sleep, but also the fourth realm of pure, spiritual awareness." The *ānanda-maya* Supersoul is simply an aspect of the primeval Lord Govinda, as declared by Him, *viṣṭabhyāham idaṁ kṛtsnam ekāṁśena sthito jagat:* "With a single fragment of Myself I pervade and support this entire universe." (Bg. 10.42)

The *śrutis* thus tactfully assert that even among the various personal forms of Godhead, Kṛṣṇa is supreme. Understanding this, Nārada Muni will later offer obeisances to Lord Kṛṣṇa in the words *namas tasmai bhagavate kṛṣṇāyāmala-kīrtaye* (Text 46), even though He is standing in front of Lord Nārāyaṇa Ṛṣi.

Śrīla Śrīdhara Svāmī concludes his comments on this verse by praying,

nara-vapuḥ pratipādya yadi tvayi
śravaṇa-varṇana-saṁsmaraṇādibhiḥ
nara-hare na bhajanti nṛṇām idaṁ
dṛti-vad ucchvasitaṁ viphalaṁ tataḥ

"O Lord Narahari, persons who have attained this human form live uselessly, merely breathing like bellows, if they fail to worship You by hearing about You, chanting Your glories, remembering You and performing the other devotional practices."

TEXT 18

उदरमुपासते य ऋषिवर्त्मसु कूर्पदृशः
परिसरपद्धतिं हृदयमारुणयो दहरम् ।
तत उदगादनन्त तव धाम शिरः परमं
पुनरिह यत्समेत्य न पतन्ति कृतान्तमुखे ॥१८॥

udaram upāsate ya ṛṣi-vartmasu kūrpa-dṛśaḥ
pariśara-paddhatiṁ hṛdayam āruṇayo daharam
tata udagād ananta tava dhāma śiraḥ paramaṁ
punar iha yat sametya na patanti kṛtānta-mukhe

udaram—the abdomen; *upāsate*—worship; *ye*—who; *ṛṣi*—of sages; *vartmasu*—according to the standard methods; *kūrpa*—gross; *dṛśaḥ*—their vision; *parisara*—from which all the prāṇic channels emanate; *paddhatim*—the node; *hṛdayam*—the heart; *āruṇayaḥ*—the Āruṇi sages; *daharam*—subtle; *tataḥ*—thence; *udagāt*—(the soul) rises up; *ananta*—O unlimited Lord; *tava*—Your; *dhāma*—place of appearance; *śiraḥ*—to the head; *paramam*—the highest destination; *punaḥ*—again; *iha*—into this world; *yat*—which; *sametya*—reaching; *na patanti*—they do not fall down; *kṛta-anta*—of death; *mukhe*—into the mouth.

TRANSLATION

Among the followers of the methods set forth by great sages, those with less refined vision worship the Supreme as present in the region of the abdomen, while the Āruṇis worship Him as present in the heart, in the subtle center from which all the prāṇic channels emanate. From there, O unlimited Lord, these worshipers raise their consciousness upward to the top of the head, where they can perceive You directly. Then, passing through the top of the head toward the supreme destination, they reach that place from which they will never again fall to this world, into the mouth of death.

PURPORT

Here the *śrutis* who teach meditational *yoga* glorify the Personality of Godhead. The various processes of *yoga* are for the most part gradual and full of opportunities for distraction. Authentic methods of *yoga*, nonetheless, all aim at meditation on the Supersoul (Paramātmā), whose primary residence is in the region of the heart, alongside the *jīva* soul. This manifestion of Paramātmā in the heart is very subtle and difficult to perceive (*daharam*), and thus only advanced *yogīs* can realize Him there.

Neophyte meditators often practice focusing on the Supersoul's secondary presence in one of the lower centers of vital energy, such as the *mūlādhāra-cakra*, at the base of the spine, the *svādhiṣṭhāna-cakra*, in the area of the navel, or the *maṇipūra-cakra*, in the abdomen. Lord Kṛṣṇa refers to His expansion as Paramātmā in the abdominal *cakra* as follows:

ahaṁ vaiśvānaro bhūtvā
prāṇināṁ deham āsthitaḥ

prāṇāpāna-samāyuktaḥ
pacāmy annaṁ catur-vidham

"I am the fire of digestion in the bodies of all living entities, and I join with the air of life, outgoing and incoming, to digest the four kinds of food." (Bg. 15.14) Lord Vaiśvānara presides over digestion and in general bestows the capacity of mobility on animals, humans and demigods. In the judgment of the *śrutis* speaking this verse, those who limit their meditation to this form of the Lord are less intelligent, *kūrpa-dṛśaḥ,* meaning literally "having eyes clouded by dust."

The superior *yogīs* known as Āruṇis, on the other hand, worship the Supersoul in His form as the indwelling companion of the *jīva* in the heart, the Lord who endows His dependent with the power of knowledge and inspires him with all varieties of practical intelligence. And just as the physical heart is the center of blood circulation, so the subtle heart-*cakra* is the crossroads of numerous channels of *prāṇa,* called *nāḍīs,* which extend outward to all parts of the body. When these passageways have been sufficiently purified, the Āruṇi *yogīs* can leave the heart region and go upward to the *cakra* at the roof of the brain. *Yogīs* who leave their bodies through this *cakra,* the *brahma-randhra,* go directly to the kingdom of God, from which they need never return to be reborn. Thus even the unsure process of meditational *yoga* can bear the fruit of pure devotion if it is followed perfectly.

Śrīla Viśvanātha Cakravartī Ṭhākura cites several *śruti-mantras* that echo the words of this verse: *udaraṁ brahmeti śārkarākṣā upāsate hṛdayaṁ brahmety āruṇayo brahmā haivaitā ita ūrdhvaṁ tv evodasarpat tac-chiro 'śrayate.* "Those whose vision is clouded identify Brahman with the abdomen, while the Āruṇis worship Brahman in the heart. One who is truly Brahman-realized travels upward from the heart to take shelter of the Lord who is manifested at the top of the head."

śataṁ caikā ca hṛdayasya nāḍyas
tāsāṁ mūrdhānam abhiniḥsṛtaikā
tayordhvam āyann amṛtatvam eti
viśvaṅṅ anyā utkramaṇe bhavanti

"There are one hundred and one subtle prāṇic channels emanating from the heart. One of these—the *suṣumṇā*—extends to the top of the head. By passing up through this channel, one transcends death. The other channels lead in all directions, to various kinds of rebirth." (*Chāndogya Up.* 8.6.6)

The *Upaniṣads* refer repeatedly to the indwelling Paramātmā. *Śrī Śvetāśvatara Upaniṣad* (3.12-13) describes Him as follows:

mahān prabhur vai puruṣaḥ
sattvasyaiṣa pravartakaḥ
su-nirmalāṁ imāṁ prāptim
īśāno jyotir avyayaḥ

aṅguṣṭha-mātraḥ puruṣo 'ntar-ātmā
sadā janānāṁ hṛdaye sanniviṣṭaḥ
hṛdā manīṣā manasābhikḷpto
ya etad vidur amṛtās te bhavanti

"The Supreme Personality of Godhead becomes the Puruṣa to initiate the expansion of this cosmos. He is the pefectly pure goal that *yogīs* strive to reach, the effulgent and infallible ultimate controller. Measuring the size of a thumb, the Puruṣa is always present as the Supersoul within the hearts of all living beings. By exercising proper intelligence, one can realize Him within the heart; those who learn this method will gain immortality."

In conclusion, Śrila Śrīdhara Svāmi prays,

udarādiṣu yaḥ puṁsāṁ
cintito muni-vartmabhiḥ
hanti mṛtyu-bhayaṁ devo
hṛd-gataṁ tam upāsmahe

"Let us worship the Supreme Lord, who resides in the heart. When mortal beings think of Him by the standard procedures established by great sages, meditating upon Him in His expansions in the abdomen and other regions of the body, the Lord reciprocates by destroying all fear of death."

TEXT 19

स्वकृतविचित्रयोनिषु विशन्निव हेतुतया
तरतमतश्चकास्स्यनलवत्स्वकृतानुकृतिः ।

अथ वितथास्वमूष्ववितथं तव धाम समं
विरजधियोऽनुयन्त्यभिविपण्यव एकरसम् ॥१९॥

sva-kṛta-vicitra-yoniṣu viśann iva hetutayā
taratamataś cakāssy anala-vat sva-kṛtānukṛtiḥ
atha vitathāsv amūṣv avitathaṁ tava dhāma samaṁ
viraja-dhiyo 'nuyanty abhivipaṇyava eka-rasam

sva—by Yourself; *kṛta*—created; *vicitra*—variegated; *yoniṣu*—within the species of life; *viśan*—entering; *iva*—apparently; *hetutayā*—as their motivation; *taratamataḥ*—according to hierarchies; *cakāssi*—You become visible; *anala-vat*—like fire; *sva*—Your own; *kṛta*—creation; *anukṛtiḥ*—imitating; *atha*—therefore; *vitathāsu*—unreal; *amūṣu*—among these (various species); *avitatham*—not unreal; *tava*—Your; *dhāma*—manifestation; *samam*—undifferentiated; *viraja*—spotless; *dhiyaḥ*—whose minds; *anuyanti*—understand; *abhivipaṇyavaḥ*—those who are free from all material entanglements (*paṇa*); *eka-rasam*—unchanging.

TRANSLATION

Apparently entering among the variegated species of living beings You have created, You inspire them to act, manifesting Yourself according to their higher and lower positions, just as fire manifests differently according to the shape of what it burns. Therefore those of spotless intelligence, who are altogether free from material attachments, realize Your undifferentiated, unchanging Self to be the permanent reality among all these impermanent life forms.

PURPORT

Hearing these prayers of the personified *Vedas*, in which the *śrutis* describe the Supersoul as entering countless varieties of material bodies, a critic may question how the Supreme can do this without becoming limited. Indeed, proponents of Advaita philosophy see no essential distinction between the Supreme Soul and His creation. In the impersonalists' conception, the Absolute has inexplicably gotten itself entrapped by illusion and has thus become first a personal God and then the demigods, humans, animals, plants and finally matter. Śaṅkarācārya and his followers take great pains to cite Vedic evidence to support this theory of how illusion is imposed on the Absolute. But speaking for themselves, the *Vedas* here answer this objection and refuse to lend their authority to Māyāvāda impersonalism.

The process of creation is technically called *sṛṣṭi,* "sending forth." The Supreme Lord sends forth His variegated energies, and these partake of His nature while remaining distinct from Him. This fact is expressed in the true Vedic philosophy of *acintya-bhedābheda,* the inconceivable, simultaneous oneness and difference of the Supreme Lord and His energies. Thus although each of the multitude of individual souls is a distinct entity, all souls consist of the same spiritual substance as the Supreme. Since they partake of the Supreme Lord's spiritual essence, the *jīvas* are unborn and eternal, just as He is. Lord Kṛṣṇa, speaking to Arjuna on the Battlefield of Kurukṣetra, confirms this:

na tv evāhaṁ jātu nāsaṁ
na tvaṁ neme janādhipāḥ
na caiva na bhaviṣyāmaḥ
sarve vayam ataḥ param

"Never was there a time when I did not exist, nor you, nor all these kings; nor in the future shall any of us cease to be." (Bg. 2.12) Material creation is a special arrangement for those *jīvas* who choose to separate themselves from the Supreme Lord's service, and thus the creation involves producing an imitation world where they can try to be independent.

After creating the many species of material life, the Supreme Lord expands into His own creation as the Supersoul in order to provide the intelligence and inspiration every living being needs for his day-to-day existence. As stated in the *Taittirīya Upaniṣad* (2.6.2), *tat sṛṣṭvā tad evānuprāviśat:* "After creating this world, He then entered within it." The Lord enters the material world, however, without forming any binding connection to it; this the *śrutis* here declare by the phrase *viśann iva,* "only seeming to enter." *Taratamataś cakāssi* means that the Paramātmā enters the body of every living being, from the great demigod Brahmā down to the insignificant germ, and exhibits differing degrees of His potency according to each soul's capacity for enlightenment. *Anala-*

vat sva-kṛtānukṛtiḥ: Just as fire ignited in several objects burns according to the different forms of those objects, so the Supreme Soul, entering the bodies of all living creatures, illuminates the consciousness of each conditioned soul according to his individual capacity.

Even in the midst of material creation and destruction, the Lord of all creatures remains eternally unchanged, as expressed here by the word *eka-rasam*. In other words, the Lord eternally maintains His personal form of immeasurable, unalloyed spiritual pleasure. The rare living beings who completely (*abhitas*) disengage themselves from material dealings, or *paṇa* (thereby becoming *abhivipaṇyavaḥ*), come to know the Supreme Lord as He is. Every intelligent person should follow the example of these great souls and beg from them the chance to also be engaged in the Supreme Lord's devotional service.

This prayer is recited by *śrutis* whose mood is similar to that expressed in the following *mantra* of the *Śvetāśvatara Upaniṣad* (6.11):

eko devaḥ sarva-bhūteṣu gūḍhaḥ
sarva-vyāpī sarva-bhūtāntarātmā
karmādhyakṣaḥ sarva-bhūtādhivāsaḥ
sākṣī cetā kevalo nirguṇaś ca

"The one Supreme Lord lives hidden inside all created things. He pervades all matter and sits within the hearts of all living beings. As the indwelling Supersoul, He supervises their material activities. Thus, while having no material qualities Himself, He is the unique witness and giver of consciousness."

Śrīla Śrīdhara Svāmī submits his own prayer:

sva-nirmiteṣu kāryeṣu
tāratamya-vivarjitam
sarvānusyūta-san-mātraṁ
bhagavantaṁ bhajāmahe

"Let us worship the Supreme Lord, who enters the products of His own creation yet remains aloof from their superior and inferior material gradations. He is the pure, undifferentiated existence pervading everything."

TEXT 20

स्वकृतपुरेष्वमीष्वबहिरन्तरसंवरणं
तव पुरुषं वदन्त्यखिलशक्तिधृतोऽंशकृतम् ।
इति नृगतिं विविच्य कवयो निगमावपनं
भवत उपासतेऽङ्घ्रिमभवं भुवि विश्वसिताः ॥२०॥

sva-kṛta-pureṣv amīṣv abahir-antara-saṁvaraṇaṁ
tava puruṣaṁ vadanty akhila-śakti-dhṛto 'ṁśa-kṛtam
iti nṛ-gatiṁ vivicya kavayo nigamāvapanaṁ
bhavata upāsate 'ṅghrim abhavaṁ bhuvi viśvasitāḥ

sva—by himself; *kṛta*—created; *pureṣu*—in the bodies; *amīṣu*—these; *abahiḥ*—not externally; *antara*—or internally; *saṁvaraṇam*—whose factual envelopment; *tava*—Your; *puruṣam*—living entity; *vadanti*—(the *Vedas*) say; *akhila*—of all; *śakti*—energies; *dhṛtaḥ*—of the possessor; *aṁśa*—as the expansion; *kṛtam*—manifested; *iti*—in this manner; *nṛ*—of the living entity; *gatim*—the status; *vivicya*—ascertaining; *kavayaḥ*—learned sages; *nigama*—of the *Vedas; āvapanam*—the field in which all offerings are sown; *bhavataḥ*—Your; *upāsate*—they worship; *aṅghrim*—the feet; *abhavam*—which cause the cessation of material existence; *bhuvi*—on the earth; *viśvasitāḥ*—having developed faith.

TRANSLATION

The individual living entity, while inhabiting the material bodies he has created for himself by his *karma*, actually remains uncovered by either gross or subtle matter. This is so because, as the *Vedas* describe, he is part and parcel of You, the possessor of all potencies. Having determined this to be the status of the living entity, learned sages become imbued with faith and worship Your lotus feet, to which all Vedic sacrifices in this world are offered, and which are the source of liberation.

PURPORT

Not only does the Supreme Lord remain totally uncontaminated when He resides within the material bodies of the conditioned souls, but even the infinitesimal *jīva* souls are never directly touched by the coverings of ignorance and lust they acquire while passing through repeated cycles of birth and death. Thus the *Taittirīya Upaniṣad* (3.10.5) proclaims, *sa yaś cāyaṁ puruṣe yaś cāsāv āditye sa ekaḥ:* "The soul of the embodied living being is one with Him who stands within the sun." Similarly, the *Chāndogya Upaniṣad* (6.8.7) teaches, *tat tvam asi:* "You are nondifferent from that Supreme Truth."

In this prayer, the personified *Vedas* refer to the finite enjoyer of material bodies (the *jīva* soul) as an expansion of the transcendental reservoir of all potencies, the Supreme Lord. The term *aṁśa-kṛtam,* "made as His portion," must be properly understood, however, in this context. The *jīva* is not created at any time, nor is he the same kind of expansion of the Lord as the omnipotent *viṣṇu-tattva* expansions. The Supreme Soul is the proper object of all worship, and the subordinate *jīva* soul is meant to be His worshiper. The Supreme Lord enacts His pastimes by showing Himself in innumerable aspects of His personality, whereas the *jīva* is forced to change bodies whenever his accumulated karmic reactions so dictate. According to *Śrī Nārada Pañcarātra,*

yat taṭa-sthaṁ tu cid-rūpaṁ
sva-saṁvedyād vinirgatam
rañjitaṁ guṇa-rāgeṇa
sa jīva iti kathyate

"The marginal potency, who is spiritual by nature, who emanates from the self-cognizant *saṁvit* energy, and who becomes tainted by his attachment to the modes of material nature, is called the *jīva.*"

Although the *jīva* soul is also an expansion of Lord Kṛṣṇa, he is distinguished from Kṛṣṇa's independent Viṣṇu expansions by his constitutional position on the margin between spirit and matter. As the *Mahā-varāha Purāṇa* explains,

svāṁśaś cātha vibhinnāṁśa
iti dvidhā śa iṣyate
aṁśino yat tu sāmarthyaṁ
yat-svarūpaṁ yathā sthitiḥ

tad eva nāṇu-mātro 'pi
bhedaṁ svāṁśāṁśinoḥ kvacit

vibhinnāṁśo 'lpa-śaktiḥ syāt
kiñcit sāmarthya-mātra-yuk

"The Supreme Lord is known in two ways: in terms of His plenary expansions and His separated expansions. Between the plenary expansions and Their source of expansion there is never any essential difference in terms of either Their capabilities, forms or situations. The separated expansions, on the other hand, possess only minute potency, being endowed only to a small extent with the Lord's powers."

The conditioned soul in this world appears as if covered by matter, internally as well as externally. Externally, gross matter surrounds him in the forms of his body and environment, while internally desire and aversion impinge upon his consciousness. But from the transcendental perspective of realized sages, both kinds of material covering are insubstantial. By logically eliminating all material identities, which are misconceptions based on the soul's gross and subtle coverings, a thoughtful person can determine that the soul is nothing material. Rather, he is a pure spark of divine spirit, a servant of the Supreme Godhead. Understanding this, one should worship the Supreme Lord's lotus feet; such worship is the fully bloomed flower of the tree of Vedic rituals. One's realization of the splendor of the Lord's lotus feet, gradually nourished by the offering of Vedic sacrifices, automatically bears the fruits of liberation from material existence and irrevocable faith in the Lord's mercy. One can accomplish all this while still living in the material world. As Lord Kṛṣṇa states in the *Gopāla-tāpanī Upaniṣad* (*Uttara* 47),

mathurā-maṇḍale yas tu
jambūdvīpe sthito 'tha vā
yo 'rcayet pratimāṁ prati
sa me priyataro bhuvi

"One who worships Me in My Deity form while living in the district of Mathurā or, indeed, anywhere in Jambūdvīpa, becomes most dear to Me in this world."

Śrīla Śrīdhara Svāmī prays,

tvad-aṁśasya mameśāna
tvan-māyā-kṛta-bandhanam

tvad-aṅghri-sevām ādiśya
parānanda nivartaya

"My Lord, please free me, Your partial expansion, from the bondage created by Your Māyā. Please do this, O abode of supreme bliss, by directing me to the service of Your feet."

TEXT 21

दुरवगमात्मतत्त्वनिगमाय तवात्ततनोश्
चरितमहामृताब्धिपरिवर्तपरिश्रमणाः ।
न परिलषन्ति केचिदपवर्गमपीश्वर ते
चरणसरोजहंसकुलसंगविसृष्टगृहाः ॥२१॥

duravagamātma-tattva-nigamāya tavātta-tanoś
carita-mahāmṛtābdhi-parivarta-pariśramaṇāḥ
na parilaṣanti kecid apavargam apīśvara te
caraṇa-saroja-haṁsa-kula-saṅga-visṛṣṭa-gṛhāḥ

duravagama—difficult to understand; *ātma*—of the self; *tattva*—the truth; *nigamāya*—in order to propagate; *tava*—of You; *ātta*—who have assumed; *tanoḥ*—Your personal forms; *carita*—of the pastimes; *mahā*—vast; *amṛta*—of nectar; *abdhi*—in the ocean; *parivarta*—by diving; *pariśramaṇāḥ*—who have been relieved of fatigue; *na parilaṣanti*—do not wish for; *kecit*—a few persons; *apavargam*—liberation; *api*—even; *īśvara*—O Lord; *te*—Your; *caraṇa*—at the feet; *saroja*—lotus; *haṁsa*—of swans; *kula*—with the community; *saṅga*—because of association; *visṛṣṭa*—abandoned; *gṛhāḥ*—whose homes.

TRANSLATION

My Lord, some fortunate souls have gotten relief from the fatigue of material life by diving into the vast nectar ocean of Your pastimes, which You enact when You manifest Your personal forms to propagate the unfathomable science of the self. These rare souls, indifferent even to liberation, renounce the happiness

of home and family because of their association with devotees who are like flocks of swans enjoying at the lotus of Your feet.

PURPORT

Ritualistic *brāhmaṇas* (*smārtas*) and impersonalists (Māyāvādīs) always try to relegate the process of *bhakti-yoga* to a relative or minor role. They say that devotion to the Personality of Godhead is for sentimental persons who lack the maturity to observe strict rituals or pursue the rigorous culture of knowledge.

In this verse, however, the personified *Vedas* most emphatically declare the superexcellence of devotional service, clearly identifying it with *ātma-tattva,* the science of the self that impersonalists so proudly claim as their own domain. Śrīla Jīva Gosvāmī here defines *ātma-tattva* as the confidential mystery of the Supreme Lord's personal forms, qualities and pastimes. He also gives a second meaning for the phrase *ātta-tanoḥ*. Instead of meaning "who assumes various bodies," the phrase can also mean "He who attracts everyone to His transcendental body."

The pastimes of Lord Kṛṣṇa and His various expansions and incarnations are an unfathomable ocean of enjoyment. When a person comes to the point of complete exhaustion in his materialistic pursuits—whether he has been searching after material success or some impersonal notion of spiritual annihilation—he can gain relief by submerging himself in this nectar. As Śrīla Rūpa Gosvāmī explains in his textbook on the science of *bhakti-yoga, Śrī Bhakti-rasāmṛta-sindhu* (rendered into English by Śrīla Prabhupāda as *The Nectar of Devotion*), one who tastes even a single drop of this vast ocean will forever lose all desire for anything else.

Giving an alternative interpretation of the word *pariśramaṇāḥ*, Śrīla Viśvanātha Cakravartī comments that although the devotees of the Lord become fatigued after repeatedly diving into the endless waves and undercurrents in the ocean of the Lord's pleasure pastimes, these devotees never desire any happiness other than the Lord's service, even the happiness of liberation. Rather, their very fatigue becomes pleasure for them, just as the fatigue produced by sex indulgence is pleasurable to those addicted to sex. The Supreme Lord's pure devotees become enthused by hearing the charming narrations of His pastimes and feel impelled to dance, sing, shout out loud, kick their heels together, faint, sob and run about like madmen. Thus they become too absorbed in ecstasy to notice any bodily discomfort.

Pure Vaiṣṇavas do not want even liberation, what to speak of other desirable goals, such as an exalted position as ruler of the heavenly planets. This degree of exclusive dedication is admittedly only rarely achieved in this world, as the *śrutis* speaking this verse indicate by the word *kecit* ("a few"). Not only do pure devotees abandon their hankering for future gain, but they also lose all their attraction for what they already possess—the common comforts of home and family life. The association of saintly Vaiṣṇavas—the disciplic succession of masters, disciples and granddisciples—becomes for them their real family, filled with swanlike personalities like Śrī Śukadeva Gosvāmī. These great personalities always drink the sweet nectar of service to the Supreme Lord's lotus feet.

Many *mantras* of the *Upaniṣads* and other *śrutis* openly declare devotional service to be superior to liberation itself. In the words of the *Nṛsiṁha-pūrva-tāpanī Upaniṣad, yaṁ sarve vedā namanti mumukṣavo brahma-vādinaś ca:* "To Him all the *Vedas,* all seekers of liberation and all students of the Absolute Truth offer their obeisances." Commenting on this *mantra,* Śrī Śaṅkarācārya admits, *muktā api līlayā vigrahaṁ kṛtvā bhajanti:* "Even liberated souls take pleasure in establishing the Supreme Lord's Deity and worshiping Him." The great rival of Ācārya Śaṅkara, Śrīla Madhvācārya Ānandatīrtha, cites his own favorite *śruti-mantras* in this regard, such as *muktā hy etam upāsate, muktānām api bhaktir hi paramānanda-rūpiṇī:* "Even those who are liberated worship Him, and even for them devotional service is the embodiment of supreme bliss"; and *amṛtasya dhārā bahudhā dohamānaṁ/ caraṇaṁ no loke su-dhitāṁ dadhātu/ oṁ tat sat:* "May His feet, which bountifully pour forth floods of nectar, bestow wisdom upon us who are living in this world."

In summary, Śrīla Śrīdhara Svāmī prays,

tvat-kathāmṛta-pāthodhau
viharanto mahā-mudaḥ
kurvanti kṛtinaḥ kecic
catur-vargaṁ tṛṇopamam

"Those rare, fortunate souls who derive great delight by sporting in the nectar ocean of topics about You consider the four great goals of life [religiosity, economic development, sense gratification and liberation] to be no more important than a blade of grass."

TEXT 22

त्वदनुपथं कुलायमिदमात्मसुहृत्प्रियवच्
चरति तथोन्मुखे त्वयि हिते प्रिय आत्मनि च ।
न बत रमन्त्यहो असदुपासनयात्महनो
यदनुशया भ्रमन्त्युरुभये कुशरीरभृतः ॥२२॥

tvad-anupathaṁ kulāyam idam ātma-suhṛt-priya-vac
carati tathonmukhe tvayi hite priya ātmani ca
na bata ramanty aho asad-upāsanayātma-hano
yad-anuśayā bhramanty uru-bhaye ku-śarīra-bhṛtaḥ

tvat—You; *anupatham*—useful for serving; *kulāyam*—body; *idam*—this; *ātma*—self; *suhṛt*—friend; *priya*—and beloved; *vat*—as; *carati*—acts; *tathā*—nevertheless; *unmukhe*—who are favorably disposed; *tvayi*—in You; *hite*—who are helpful; *priye*—who are affectionate; *ātmani*—who are their very Self; *ca*—and; *na*—not; *bata*—alas; *ramanti*—they take pleasure; *aho*—ah; *asat*—of the unreal; *upāsanayā*—by worship; *ātma*—themselves; *hanaḥ*—killing; *yat*—in which (worship of the unreal); *anuśayāḥ*—whose persistent desires; *bhramanti*—they wander; *uru*—greatly; *bhaye*—in the fearful (material existence); *ku*—degraded; *śarīra*—bodies; *bhṛtaḥ*—carrying.

TRANSLATION

When this human body is used for Your devotional service, it acts as one's self, friend and beloved. But unfortunately, although You always show mercy to the conditioned souls and affectionately help them in every way, and although You are their true Self, people in general fail to delight in You. Instead they commit spiritual suicide by worshiping illusion. Alas, because they persistently hope for success in their devotion to the unreal, they continue to wander about this greatly fearful world, assuming various degraded bodies.

PURPORT

The *Vedas* have strong words for those who choose to remain in illusion rather than serve the all-merciful Personality of Godhead. The *Bṛhad-āraṇyaka Upaniṣad* (4.3.15) states, *ārāmam asya paśyanti na taṁ paśyati kaścana. na taṁ vidātha ya imā jajānānyad yuṣmākam antaraṁ babhūva. nīhāreṇa prāvṛtā jalpyā cāsu-tṛpa uktha-śāsaś caranti:* "Everyone can see the place where the Lord manifested Himself in this world for His own pleasure, but still no one sees Him. None of you know Him who generated all these living beings, and thus there is a great difference between your vision and His. Covered by the fog of illusion, you performers of Vedic rituals indulge in useless talk and live only to gratify your senses."

The Supreme Lord pervades this universe, as He says in the *Bhagavad-gītā* (9.4), *mayā tatam idaṁ sarvaṁ jagat*. Nothing in this world, not even the most insignificant clay pot or shred of cloth, is devoid of the presence of the Personality of Godhead. But because He keeps Himself invisible to envious eyes (*avyakta-mūrtinā*), materialists are misled by His material energy and think that the source of material creation is a combination of atoms and physical forces.

Displaying their compassion for such foolish materialists, the personified *Vedas* advise them in this prayer to remember the real purpose for which they exist: to serve the Lord, their greatest well-wisher, with loving devotion. The human body is the ideal facility for reviving one's spiritual consciousness; its organs—ears, tongue, eyes and so on—are quite suitable for hearing about the Lord, chanting His glories, worshiping Him and performing all the other essential aspects of devotional service.

One's material body is destined to remain intact for only a short time, and so it is called *kulāyam*, subject to "dissolving into the earth" (*kau līyate*). Nonetheless, if properly utilized it can be one's best friend. When one is immersed in material consciousness, however, the body becomes a false friend, distracting the bewildered living entity from his true self-interest. Persons too much infatuated with their own bodies and those of their spouses, children, pets and so on are in fact misdirecting their devotion to the worship of illusion, *asad-upāsanā*. In this way, as the *śrutis* state here, such people commit spiritual suicide, insuring future punishment for failing to carry out the higher responsibilities of human existence. As the *Īśopaniṣad* (3) declares,

asuryā nāma te lokā
andhena tamasāvṛtāḥ

tāṁs te pretyābhigacchanti
ye ke cātma-hano janāḥ

"The killer of the soul, whoever he may be, must enter into the planets known as the worlds of the faithless, full of darkness and ignorance."

Those who are overly attached to sense gratification, or who worship the impermanent in the form of false, materialistic scriptures and philosophies, maintain desires that carry them into more degraded bodies in each successive life. Since they are entrapped in the perpetually rotating cycle of *saṁsāra*, their only hope for salvation is getting a chance to hear the merciful instructions spoken by the Supreme Lord's devotees.

Śrīla Śrīdhara Svāmī prays,

tvayy ātmani jagan-nāthe
man-mano ramatām iha
kadā mamedṛśaṁ janma
mānuṣaṁ sambhaviṣyati

"When will I receive a human birth in which my mind may take pleasure in You, who are the Supreme Soul and Lord of the universe?"

TEXT 23

निभृतमरुन्मनोऽक्षदृढयोगयुजो हृदि यन्
मुनयो उपासते तदरयोऽपि ययुः स्मरणात् ।
स्त्रिय उरगेन्द्रभोगभुजदण्डविषक्तधियो
वयमपि ते समाः समदृशोऽङ्घ्रिसरोजसुधाः ॥२३॥

nibhṛta-marun-mano-'kṣa-dṛḍha-yoga-yujo hṛdi yan
munaya upāsate tad arayo 'pi yayuḥ smaraṇāt
striya uragendra-bhoga-bhuja-daṇḍa-viṣakta-dhiyo
vayam api te samāḥ sama-dṛśo 'ṅghri-saroja-sudhāḥ

nibhṛta—brought under control; *marut*—with breathing; *manaḥ*—mind; *akṣa*—and senses; *dṛḍha-yoga*—in steadfast *yoga;* *yujaḥ*—engaged; *hṛdi*—in the heart; *yat*—which; *munayaḥ*—sages; *upāsate*—worship; *tat*—that; *arayaḥ*—enemies; *api*—also; *yayuḥ*—attained;

smaraṇāt—by remembering; *striyaḥ*—women; *uraga-indra*—of lordly serpents; *bhoga*—(like) the bodies; *bhuja*—whose arms; *daṇḍa*—rodlike; *viṣakta*—attracted; *dhiyaḥ*—whose minds; *vayam*—we; *api*—also; *te*—to You; *samāḥ*—equal; *sama*—equal; *dṛśaḥ*—whose vision; *aṅghri*—of the feet; *saroja*—lotuslike; *sudhāḥ*—(relishing) the nectar.

TRANSLATION

Simply by constantly thinking of Him, the enemies of the Lord attained the same Supreme Truth whom sages fixed in *yoga* worship by controlling their breath, mind and senses. Similarly, we *śrutis*, who generally see You as all-pervading, will achieve the same nectar from Your lotus feet that Your consorts are able to relish because of their loving attraction to Your mighty, serpentine arms, for You look upon us and Your consorts in the same way.

PURPORT

According to Ācārya Śrī Jīva Gosvāmī, the few *śrutis*—such as the *Gopāla-tāpanī Upaniṣad*—who identify the cowherd boy Kṛṣṇa with absolute Brahman in its highest aspect had so far been patiently waiting for their turn to speak. But after hearing the other *śrutis* offer prayers openly glorifying the Lord's personality, these intimate *śrutis* could no longer contain themselves, and so they spoke out of turn in this verse.

Followers of the path of mystic *yoga* subdue their senses and minds by practicing breath control and severe austerities. If they succeed in thoroughly purifying themselves by this regimen, they may eventually begin to realize the Paramātmā, the personal form of Brahman within the heart. And if they continue this meditation without deviation for a long time, they may in the end come to the point of true God consciousness. But the same objective achieved in this difficult and uncertain way was also attained by the demons who were killed by Lord Kṛṣṇa during His pastimes on the earth. Obsessed with enmity toward Him, demons like Kaṁsa and Śiśupāla quickly obtained the perfection of liberation simply by His killing them.

Speaking for themselves, however, the personified *Vedas* here state that they would prefer to develop love of Godhead by learning to emulate the favorable surrender of Lord Kṛṣṇa's confidential devotees, especially the young *gopīs* of Vraja. Though they appeared to be simple women attracted conjugally to the Lord's physical beauty and strength, the goddesses of Vraja exhibited the highest perfection of meditation. The *śrutis* wish to become just like them.

In this regard, Lord Brahmā relates the following historical account in the supplement to the *Bṛhad-vāmana Purāṇa:*

brahmānanda-mayo loko
vyāpī vaikuṇṭha-saṁjñitaḥ
tal-loka-vāsī tatra-sthaiḥ
stuto vedaiḥ parāt-paraḥ

"The infinite world of spiritual bliss is called Vaikuṇṭha. There the Supreme Truth lives, being glorified by the personified *Vedas,* who are also present there."

ciraṁ stutvā tatas tuṣṭaḥ
parokṣaṁ prāha tān girā
tuṣṭo 'smi brūta bho prājñā
varaṁ yaṁ manasepsitam

"Once, after the *Vedas* had elaborately praised Him, the Lord felt especially satisfied and spoke to them in a voice whose source remained invisible: 'My dear sages, I am very satisfied with you. Please ask of Me some benediction that you secretly desire.'"

śrutaya ūcuḥ
yathā tal-loka-vāsinyaḥ
kāma-tattvena gopikāḥ
bhajanti ramaṇaṁ matvā
cikīrṣājani nas tathā

"The *śrutis* replied, 'We have developed the desire to become like the cowherd women of the mortal world who, inspired by lust, worship You in the mood of a lover.'"

śrī-bhagavān uvāca
durlabho durghaṭaś caiva
yuṣmākaṁ sa manorathaḥ

mayānumoditaḥ samyak
satyo bhavitum arhati

"'The Lord then said, 'This desire of Yours is difficult to fulfill. Indeed, it is almost impossible. But since I am sanctioning it, your wish must inevitably come true.'"

āgāmini viriñcau tu
jāte sṛṣṭy-artham udite
kalpaṁ sārasvataṁ prāpya
vraje gopyo bhaviṣyatha

"'When the next Brahmā takes birth to faithfully execute his duties of creation, and when the day of his life called the Sārasvata-kalpa arrives, you will all appear in Vraja as *gopīs.*'"

pṛthivyāṁ bhārate kṣetre
māthure mama maṇḍale
vṛndāvane bhaviṣyāmi
preyān vo rāsa-maṇḍale

"'On the earth, in the land of Bhārata, in My own district of Mathurā, in the forest of Vṛndāvana, I will become your beloved in the circle of the *rāsa* dance.'"

jāra-dharmeṇa su-snehaṁ
su-dṛḍhaṁ sarvato 'dhikam
mayi samprāpya sarve 'pi
kṛta-kṛtyā bhaviṣyatha

"'Thus obtaining Me as your paramour, you will all gain the most exalted and steadfast pure love for Me, and in this way you will fulfill all your ambitions.'"

brahmovāca
śrutvaitac cintayantyas tā
rūpaṁ bhagavataś ciram
ukta-kālaṁ samāsādya
gopyo bhūtvā hariṁ gatāḥ

"Lord Brahmā said: After hearing these words, the *śrutis* meditated on the Personality of Godhead's beauty for a long time. When the designated time ultimately arrived, they became *gopīs* and obtained the association of Kṛṣṇa."

A similar account can be found in the *Sṛṣṭi-khaṇḍa* of the *Padma Purāṇa,* which describes how the Gāyatri *mantra* also became a *gopī.*

Regarding the development of *bhakti,* Lord Kṛṣṇa further states in the *Gopāla-tāpanī Upaniṣad* (*Uttara* 4), *apūtaḥ pūto bhavati yaṁ māṁ smṛtvā, avratī vratī bhavati yaṁ māṁ smṛtvā, niṣkāmaḥ sa-kāmo bhavati yaṁ māṁ smṛtvā, aśrotrī śrotrī bhavati yaṁ māṁ smṛtvā:* "By remembering Me, one who is impure becomes pure. By remembering Me, one who follows no vows becomes a strict follower of vows. By remembering Me, one who is desireless develops desires [to serve Me]. By remembering Me, one who has studied no Vedic *mantras* becomes an expert knower of the *Vedas.*"

The *Bṛhad-āraṇyaka Upaniṣad* (4.5.6) refers to the gradual steps in the process of becoming Kṛṣṇa conscious: *ātmā vā are draṣṭavyaḥ śrotavyo mantavyo nididhyāsitavyaḥ.* "It is the Self which must be observed, heard about, thought of and meditated upon with fixed concentration." The idea here is that one should realize the Supreme Self as directly visible in His full personality by the following means: First one should hear the instructions of a qualified representative of the Paramātmā and take the words of such a spiritual master into one's heart by offering him humble service and striving in all ways to please him. One should then ponder the divine message of the spiritual master continuously, with the aim of dispelling all one's doubts and misconceptions. Then one can proceed to meditate on the Supreme Lord's lotus feet with total conviction and determination.

So-called *jñānīs* may think that the *Upaniṣads* praise *nirviśeṣa* (impersonal) realization of the Supreme as more complete and final than *sa-viśeṣa* (personal) worship of the Supreme Godhead. All honest Vaiṣṇavas, however, join in adhering to the devotional service of the Supreme Lord, always meditating with pleasure on His infinitely wonderful, variegated spiritual qualities. In the words of the *śruti-mantras, yam evaiṣa vṛṇute tena labhyas/ tasyaiṣa ātmā vivṛṇute tanūṁ svām:* "To that person whom the Supreme Soul chooses, He becomes attainable. To that person the Supreme Soul reveals His personal form." (*Kaṭha Up.* 1.2.23 and *Muṇḍaka Up.* 3.2.3)

Śrīla Śrīdhara Svāmī concludes with the prayer,

caraṇa-smaraṇaṁ premṇā
tava deva su-durlabham
yathā kathañcid nṛ-hare
mama bhūyād ahar-niśam

"O Lord, loving remembrance of Your lotus feet is very rarely achieved. Please, O Nṛhari, somehow arrange for me to have that remembrance day and night."

TEXT 24

क इह नु वेद बतावरजन्मलयोऽग्रसरं
यत उदगादृषिर्यमनु देवगणा उभये ।
तर्हि न सन्न चासदुभयं न च कालजवः
किमपि न तत्र शास्त्रमवकृष्य शयीत यदा ॥२४॥

ka iha nu veda batāvara-janma-layo 'gra-saraṁ
yata udagād ṛṣir yam anu deva-gaṇā ubhaye
tarhi na san na cāsad ubhayaṁ na ca kāla-javaḥ
kim api na tatra śāstram avakṛṣya śayīta yadā

kaḥ—who; *iha*—in this world; *nu*—indeed; *veda*—knows; *bata*—ah; *avara*—recent; *janma*—whose birth; *layaḥ*—and annihilation; *agra-saram*—who came first; *yataḥ*—from whom; *udagāt*—arose; *ṛṣiḥ*—the learned sage, Brahmā; *yam anu*—following whom (Brahmā); *deva-gaṇāḥ*—the groups of demigods; *ubhaye*—both (those who control the senses and those who live in the regions above the heavenly planets); *tarhi*—at that time; *na*—no; *sat*—gross matter; *na*—no; *ca*—also; *asat*—subtle matter; *ubhayam*—that which is comprised of both (namely, the material bodies); *na ca*—nor; *kāla*—of time; *javaḥ*—the flow; *kim api na*—none at all; *tatra*—there; *śāstram*—authoritative scripture; *ava-kṛṣya*—withdrawing; *śayīta*—(the Supreme Lord) lies down; *yadā*—when.

TRANSLATION

Everyone in this world has recently been born and will soon die. So how can anyone here know Him who existed prior to

everything else and who gave rise to the first learned sage, Brahmā, and all subsequent demigods, both lesser and greater? When He lies down and withdraws everything within Himself, nothing else remains—no gross or subtle matter or bodies composed of these, no force of time or revealed scripture.

PURPORT

Here the *śrutis* express the difficulty of knowing the Supreme. Devotional service, or *bhakti-yoga*, as described in these prayers of the personified *Vedas*, is the surest and easiest path to knowledge of the Lord and to liberation. In comparison, the philosophic search for knowledge, known as *jñāna-yoga*, is very difficult, favored though it is by those who are disgusted with material life but still unwilling to surrender to the Lord. As long as the finite soul remains envious of the Lord's supremacy, the Lord does not reveal Himself. As He states in *Bhagavad-gītā* (9.25),

nāhaṁ prakāśaḥ sarvasya
yoga-māyā-samāvṛtaḥ
mūḍho 'yaṁ nābhijānāti
loko mām ajam avyayam

"I am never manifest to the foolish and unintelligent. For them I am covered by My internal potency, and therefore they do not know that I am unborn and infallible." And in the words of Lord Brahmā,

panthās tu koṭi-śata-vatsara-sampragamyo
vāyor athāpi manaso muni-puṅgavānām
so 'py asti yat-prapada-sīmny avicintya-tattve
govindam ādi-puruṣaṁ tam ahaṁ bhajāmi

"I worship Govinda, the primeval Lord, only the tip of the toe of whose lotus feet is approached by the *yogīs*, who aspire after the transcendental and betake themselves to *prāṇāyāma* by drilling the respiration; or by the *jñānīs*, who search out the undifferentiated Brahman by the process of elimination of the mundane, extending over thousands of millions of years." (*Brahma-saṁhitā* 5.34)

Brahmā, the first-born living being in this universe, is also the foremost sage. He is born from Lord Nārāyaṇa, and from him appear the hosts of demigods, including both the controllers of earthly activities and the rulers of heaven. All these powerful and intelligent beings are relatively recent productions of the Lord's creative energy. As the first speaker of the *Vedas,* Lord Brahmā should know their purport at least as well as any other authority, but even he knows the Personality of Godhead only to a limited extent. As *Śrīmad-Bhāgavatam* states (1.3.35), *veda-guhyāni hṛt-pateḥ:* "The Lord of the heart hides Himself deep within the confidential recesses of the Vedic sound." If Brahmā and the demigods born from him cannot easily know the Supreme Lord, how then can mere mortals expect success in their independent pursuit of knowledge?

As long as this creation lasts, living beings face many obstacles on the path of knowledge. Because of identifying themselves with their material coverings, consisting of body, mind and ego, they acquire all sorts of prejudices and misconceptions. Even if they have the divine scripture to guide them and the opportunity to execute the prescribed methods of *karma, jñāna* and *yoga,* the conditioned souls have but little power for gaining knowledge of the Absolute. And when the time of annihilation comes, the Vedic scriptures and their regulative injunctions become unmanifest, leaving the dormant *jīvas* completely in darkness. Therefore we should abandon our futile endeavors for knowledge without devotion and simply surrender ourselves to the Supreme Lord's mercy, heeding the advice of Lord Brahmā:

jñāne prayāsam udapāsya namanta eva
jīvanti san-mukharitāṁ bhavadīya-vārtām
sthāne sthitāḥ śruti-gatāṁ tanu-vāṅ-manobhiḥ
ye prāyaśo 'jita jito 'py asi tais tri-lokyām

"Those who, even while remaining situated in their established social positions, throw away the process of speculative knowledge and with their body, words and mind offer all respects to descriptions of Your personality and activities, dedicating their lives to these narrations, which are vibrated by You personally and by Your pure devotees, certainly conquer Your Lordship, although You are otherwise unconquerable by anyone within the three worlds." (*Bhāg.* 10.14.3)

In this regard, the *Taittirīya Upaniṣad* (2.4.1) refers to the Supreme as *yato vāco nivartante aprāpya manasā saha,* "where words cease, and where the mind cannot reach." The *Īśopaniṣad* (4) states,

anejad ekaṁ manaso javīyo
naitad devā āpnuvan pūrvam arśat
tad dhāvato 'nyān atyeti tiṣṭhat
tasmin apo mātariśvā dadhāti

"Although fixed in His abode, the Personality of Godhead is more swift than the mind and can overcome all others running. The powerful demigods cannot approach Him. Although in one place, He controls those who supply the air and rain. He surpasses all in excellence." And in the *Ṛg Veda* (3.54.5) we find this *mantra:*

ko 'ddhā veda ka iha pravocat
kuta āyātāḥ kuta iyaṁ visṛṣṭiḥ
arvāg devā visarjanenā-
thā ko veda yata ā babhūva

"Who in this world actually knows, and who can explain, whence this creation has come? The demigods, after all, are younger than the creation. Who, then, can tell whence this world has come into being?"

Śrīla Śrīdhara Svāmī thus prays,

kvāhaṁ buddhy-ādi-saṁruddhaḥ
kva ca bhūman mahas tava
dīna-bandho dayā-sindho
bhaktiṁ me nṛ-hare diśa

"What am I, a being entrapped by the material coverings of worldly intelligence and so on? And what are Your glories by comparison, O almighty one? O friend of the fallen, O ocean of mercy, Lord Nṛhari, please bless me with Your devotional service."

TEXT 25

जनिमसतः सतो मृतिमुतात्मनि ये च भिदां
विपणमृतं स्मरन्त्युपदिशन्ति त आरुपितैः ।
त्रिगुणमयः पुमानिति भिदा यदबोधकृता
त्वयि न ततः परत्र स भवेदवबोधरसे ॥२५॥

janim asataḥ sato mṛtim utātmani ye ca bhidāṁ
vipaṇam ṛtaṁ smaranty upadiśanti ta ārupitaiḥ
tri-guṇa-mayaḥ pumān iti bhidā yad abodha-kṛtā
tvayi na tataḥ paratra sa bhaved avabodha-rase

janim—creation; *asataḥ*—of the manifest world (from atoms); *sataḥ*—of that which is eternal; *mṛtim*—destruction; *uta*—also; *ātmani*—in the soul; *ye*—who; *ca*—and; *bhidām*—duality; *vipaṇam*—mundane business; *ṛtam*—real; *smaranti*—declare authoritatively; *upadiśanti*—teach; *te*—they; *ārupitaiḥ*—in terms of illusions imposed on reality; *tri*—three; *guṇa*—of the material modes; *mayaḥ*—composed; *pumān*—the living entity; *iti*—thus; *bhidā*—dualistic conception; *yat*—which; *abodha*—by ignorance; *kṛtā*—created; *tvayi*—in You; *na*—not; *tataḥ*—to such; *paratra*—transcendental; *saḥ*—that (ignorance); *bhavet*—can exist; *avabodha*—total consciousness; *rase*—whose composition.

TRANSLATION

Supposed authorities who declare that matter is the origin of existence, that the permanent qualities of the soul can be destroyed, that the self is compounded of separate aspects of spirit and matter, or that material transactions constitute reality—all such authorities base their teachings on mistaken ideas that hide the truth. The dualistic conception that the living entity is produced from the three modes of nature is simply a product of ignorance. Such a conception has no real basis in You, for You are transcendental to all illusion and always enjoy perfect, total awareness.

PURPORT

The true position of the Supreme Personality is a sublime mystery, as is also the dependent position of the *jīva* soul. Most thinkers are mistaken in one way or another about these truths, since there are countless varieties of false designation that can cover the soul and create illusion. Foolish conditioned souls submit to obvious delusions, but the illusory power of Māyā can easily subvert the intelligence of even the most sophisticated philosophers and mystics. Thus there are always divergent schools of thought propounding conflicting theories concerning basic principles of truth.

In traditional Indian philosophy, the followers of Vaiśeṣika, Nyāya, Sāṅkhya, Yoga and Mīmāṁsā philosophies all have their own erroneous ideas, which the personified *Vedas* point out in this prayer. The Vaiśeṣikas say that the visible universe is created from an original stock of atoms (*janim asataḥ*). As Kaṇāda Ṛṣi's *Vaiśeṣika-sūtras* (7.1.20) state, *nityaṁ parimaṇḍalam:* "That which is of the smallest size, the atom, is eternal." Kaṇāda and his followers also postulate eternality for other, nonatomic entities, including the souls who become embodied, and even a Supreme Soul. But in Vaiśeṣika cosmology the souls and the Supersoul play only token roles in the atomic production of the universe. Śrīla Kṛṣṇa-dvaipāyana Vedavyāsa criticizes this position in his *Vedānta-sūtras* (2.2.12): *ubhayathāpi na karmātas tad-abhāvaḥ.* According to this *sūtra,* one cannot claim that, at the time of creation, atoms first combine together because they are impelled by some karmic impulse adhering in the atoms themselves, since atoms by themselves, in their primeval state before combining into complex objects, have no ethical responsibility that might lead them to acquire pious and sinful reactions. Nor can the initial combination of atoms be explained as a result of the residual *karma* of the living entities who lie dormant prior to creation, since these reactions are each *jīva's* own and cannot be transferred from them even to other *jīvas,* what to speak of inert atoms.

Alternatively, the phrase *janim asataḥ* can be taken to allude to the Yoga philosophy of Patañjali Ṛṣi, inasmuch as his *Yoga-sūtras* teach one how to achieve the transcendental status of Brahmanhood by a mechanical process of exercise and meditation. Patañjali's *yoga* method is here called *asat* because it ignores the essential aspect of devotion—surrender to the will of the Supreme Person. As Lord Kṛṣṇa states in *Bhagavad-gītā* (17.28),

aśraddhayā hutaṁ dattaṁ
tapas taptaṁ kṛtaṁ ca yat
asad ity ucyate pārtha
na ca tat pretya no iha

"Anything done as sacrifice, charity or penance without faith in the Supreme, O son of Pṛthā, is impermanent. It is called *asat* and is useless both in this life and in the next."

The *Yoga-sūtras* acknowledge the Personality of Godhead in an oblique way, but only as a helper whom the advancing *yogī* can utilize. *Īśvara-praṇidhānād vā*: "Devotional meditation on God is yet another means of achieving concentration." (*Yoga-sūtra* 1.23) In contrast, Bādarāyaṇa Vedavyāsa's philosophy of Vedānta emphasizes devotional service not only as the primary means to liberation but also as identical with liberation itself. *Ā-prāyaṇāt tatrāpi hi dṛṣṭam:* "Worship of the Lord continues up to the point of liberation, and indeed goes on in the liberated state also, as the *Vedas* reveal." (*Vedānta-sūtra* 4.1.12)

Gautama Ṛṣi, in his *Nyāya-sūtras,* proposes that one can attain liberation by negating both illusion and unhappiness: *duḥkha-janma-pravṛtti-doṣa-mithyā-jñānānām uttarottarāpāye tad-anantarābhāvād apavargaḥ.* "By successively dispelling false conceptions, bad character, entangling action, rebirth and misery—the disappearance of one of these allowing the disappearance of the next—one can achieve final liberation." (*Nyāya-sūtra* 1.1.2) But since Nyāya philosophers believe that awareness is not an essential quality of the soul, they teach that a liberated soul has no consciousness. The Nyāya idea of liberation thus puts the soul in the condition of a dead stone. This attempt by the Nyāya philosophers to kill the soul's innate consciousness is here called *sato mṛtim* by the personified *Vedas.* But the *Vedānta-sūtra* (2.3.17) unequivocally states, *jño 'ta eva:* "The *jīva* soul is always a knower."

Although the soul is in truth both conscious and active, the proponents of Sāṅkhya philosophy wrongly separate these two functions of the living force (*ātmani ye ca bhidām*), ascribing consciousness to the soul (*puruṣa*) and activity to material nature (*prakṛti*). According to the *Sāṅkhya-kārikā* (19-20),

tasmāc ca viparyāsāt
siddhaṁ sākṣitvaṁ puruṣasya
kaivalyaṁ mādhya-sthyaṁ
draṣṭṛtvam akartṛ-bhāvaś ca

"Thus, since the apparent differences between *puruṣas* are only superficial (being due to the various modes of nature that cover them), the *puruṣa's* true status is proven to be that of a witness, characterized by his separateness, his passive indifference, his status of being an observer, and his inactivity."

tasmāt tat-saṁyogād
acetanaṁ cetanā-vad iva liṅgam
guṇa-kartṛtve 'pi tathā
karteva bhavaty udāsīnaḥ

"Thus, by contact with the soul, the unconscious subtle body seems to be conscious, while the soul appears to be the doer although he is aloof from the activity of nature's modes."

Śrīla Vyāsadeva refutes this idea in the section of the *Vedānta-sūtra* (2.3.31-39) that begins, *kartā śāstrārtha-vattvāt:* "The *jīva* soul must be a performer of actions, because the injunctions of scripture must have some purpose." Ācārya Baladeva Vidyābhūṣaṇa, in his *Govinda-bhāṣya,* explains: "The *jīva,* not the modes of nature, is the doer. Why? Because the injunctions of scripture must have some purpose (*śāstrārtha-vattvāt*). For example, such scriptural injunctions as *svarga-kāmo yajeta* ('One who desires to attain to heaven should perform ritual sacrifice') and *ātmānam eva lokam upāsīta* (*Bṛhad-āraṇyaka Up.* 1.4.15: 'One should worship with the aim of attaining the spiritual kingdom') are meaningful only if a conscious doer exists. If the modes of nature were the doer, these statements would serve no purpose. After all, scriptural injunctions engage the living entity in performing prescribed actions by convincing him that he can act to bring about certain enjoyable results. Such a mentality cannot be aroused in the inert modes of nature."

Jaimini Ṛṣi, in his *Pūrva-mīmāṁsā-sūtras,* presents material work and its results as the whole of reality (*vipaṇam ṛtam*). He and later proponents of Karma-mīmāṁsā philosophy teach that material existence is endless—that there is no liberation. For them the cycle of *karma* is perpetual, and the best one can aim for is higher birth among the demigods. Therefore, they say, the whole purpose of the *Vedas* is to engage human beings in rituals for creating good *karma,* and consequently the mature soul's prime responsibility is to ascertain the exact meaning of the *Vedas'* sacrificial injunctions and to execute them. *Codanā-lakṣaṇo 'rtho dharmaḥ:* "Duty is that which is indicated by the injunctions of the *Vedas.*" (*Pūrva-mīmāṁsā-sūtra* 1.1.2)

The *Vedānta-sūtra,* however—especially in the fourth chapter, which deals with life's ultimate goal—elaborately describes the soul's potential for achieving liberation from birth and death, while it subordinates ritual sacrifice to the role of helping one become qualified to receive spiritual knowledge. As stated there (*Vedānta-sūtra* 4.1.16), *agnihotrādi tu tat-kāryāyaiva tad-darśanāt:* "The Agnihotra and other Vedic sacrifices are meant only for producing knowledge, as the statements of the *Vedas* show." And the very last words of the *Vedānta-sūtra* (4.4.22) proclaim, *anāvṛttiḥ śabdāt:* "The liberated soul never returns to this world, as promised by the revealed scripture."

Thus the fallacious conclusions of the speculative philosophers prove that even great scholars and sages are often bewildered by the misuse of their own God-given intelligence. As the *Kaṭha Upaniṣad* (1.2.5) says,

avidyāyām antare vartamānāḥ
svayaṁ dhīrāḥ paṇḍitam-manyamānāḥ
jaṅghanyamānāḥ pariyanti mūḍhā
andhenaiva nīyamānā yathāndhāḥ

"Caught in the grip of ignorance, self-proclaimed experts consider themselves learned authorities. They wander about this world befooled, like the blind leading the blind."

Of the six orthodox philosophies of Vedic tradition—Sāṅkhya, Yoga, Nyāya, Vaiśeṣika, Mīmāṁsā and Vedānta—only the Vedānta of Bādarāyaṇa Vyāsa is free of error, and even that only as properly explained by the bona fide Vaiṣṇava *ācāryas.* Each of the six schools, nonetheless, makes some practical contribution to Vedic education: atheistic Sāṅkhya explains the evolution of natural elements from subtle to gross, Patañjali's *yoga* describes the eightfold method of meditation, Nyāya sets forth the techniques of logic, Vaiśeṣika considers the basic metaphysical categories of reality, and Mīmāṁsā establishes the standard tools of scriptural interpretation. Apart from these six, there are also the more deviant philosophies of the Buddhists, Jains and Cārvākas, whose theories of voidism and materialism deny the spiritual integrity of the eternal soul.

Ultimately, the only perfectly reliable source of knowledge is God Himself. The Personality of Godhead is *avabodha-rasa,* the infinite reservoir of unfailing vision. To those who depend on Him with absolute conviction, He grants the divine eye of knowledge. Others, following their own speculative theories, must grope for the truth through the obscuring curtain of Māyā. Śrīla Śrīdhara Svāmī prays,

mithyā-tarka-sukarkaśerita-mahā-vādāndhakārāntara-
bhrāmyan-manda-mater amanda-mahimaṁs tvad-jñāna-vartmāsphuṭam
śrīman mādhava vāmana tri-nayana śrī-śaṅkara śrī-pate
govindeti mudā vadan madhu-pate muktaḥ kadā syām aham

"For the bewildered soul wandering within the darkness of those exalted philosophies promoted by the harsh methods of false logic, the path of true knowledge of You, O Lord of magnificent glory, remains invisible. O Lord of Madhu, husband of the goddess of fortune, when will I become liberated by joyfully chanting Your names—Mādhava, Vāmana, Trinayana, Śrī Śaṅkara, Śrīpati and Govinda?"

TEXT 26

सदिव मनस्त्रिवृत्त्वयि विभात्यसदामनुजात्
सदभिमृशन्त्यशेषमिदमात्मतयात्मविदः ।
न हि विकृतिं त्यजन्ति कनकस्य तदात्मतया
स्वकृतमनुप्रविष्टमिदमात्मतयावसितम् ॥२६॥

sad iva manas tri-vṛt tvayi vibhāty asad ā-manujāt
sad abhimṛśanty aśeṣam idam ātmatayātma-vidaḥ
na hi vikṛtiṁ tyajanti kanakasya tad-ātmatayā
sva-kṛtam anupraviṣṭam idam ātmatayāvasitam

sat—real; *iva*—as if; *manaḥ*—the mind (and its manifestations); *tri-vṛt*—threefold (by the modes of material nature); *tvayi*—in You; *vibhāti*—appears; *asat*—unreal; *ā-manujāt*—extending to the human beings; *sat*—as real; *abhimṛśanti*—they consider; *aśeṣam*—entire; *idam*—this (world); *ātmatayā*—as nondifferent from the Self; *ātma-vidaḥ*—the knowers of the Self; *na*—not; *hi*—indeed; *vikṛtim*—the transformations; *tyajanti*—reject; *kanakasya*—of gold; *tat-ātmatayā*—inasmuch as they are nondifferent from it; *sva*—by Himself; *kṛtam*—created; *anupraviṣṭam*—and entered; *idam*—this; *ātmatayā*—as nondifferent from Himself; *avasitam*—ascertained.

TRANSLATION

The three modes of material nature comprise everything in this world—from the simplest phenomena to the complex human body. Although these phenomena appear real, they are only a false reflection of the spiritual reality, being a superimposition of the mind upon You. Still, those who know the Supreme Self consider the entire material creation to be real inasmuch as it is nondifferent from the Self. Just as things made of gold are indeed not to be rejected, since their substance is actual gold, so this world is undoubtedly nondifferent from the Lord who created it and then entered within it.

PURPORT

In one sense the visible world is real (*sat*), while in another it is not (*asat*). The substance of this universe is solid fact, being the Lord's external energy, but the forms that Māyā imposes on this substance are only temporary. And because material forms are temporary manifestations, those who consider them permanent are in illusion. Impersonalistic scholars, however, misinterpret this division of *sat* and *asat;* denying commonsense reality, they declare that not only material form but also material substance is unreal, and they confuse their own spiritual essence with that of the Absolute Whole. A Māyāvādī philosopher would take the words spoken by the personified *Vedas* in the preceding prayer—*tri-guṇa-mayaḥ pumān iti bhidā*—as negating any distinction between the Paramātmā and the *jīva* soul. He would claim that since the *jīva's* material embodiment is an ephemeral display of the three modes of nature, when the *jīva's* ignorance is destroyed by knowledge, he becomes the Paramātmā, the Supreme Soul; bondage, liberation and the manifest world are all unreal creations of ignorance. In response to such ideas, the *Vedas* here clarify the factual relationship between *sat* and *asat.*

In the *śruti* literature we find this statement: *asato 'dhimano 'sṛjyata, manaḥ prajāpatim asṛjat, prajāpatiḥ prajā asṛjat, tad vā idaṁ manasy eva paramaṁ pratiṣṭhitaṁ yad idaṁ kiṁ ca.* "The supreme mind was originally created from *asat.* This mind created Prajāpati, and Prajāpati created all living beings. Thus mind alone is the ultimate foundation of everything that exists in this world." Although impersonalists might misread this to mean that all manifest existence is based on the unreality of illusion (*asat*), the apparently contrary use of the word *asat* in this passage actually refers to the original cause, the Supreme Godhead, because He is transcendental to material existence (*sat*). The logic of the *Vedānta-sūtra* (2.1.17) corroborates this interpretation while denying the wrong interpretation of the impersonalists: *asad-vyapadeśān neti cen na dharmāntareṇa vākya-śeṣāt.* "If one objects that the material world and its source cannot be of one substance because the world has been called unreal, we reply, 'No, because the statement that Brahman is *asat* makes sense in terms of His having qualities distinct from those of the creation.'" Thus the *Taittirīya Upaniṣad* (2.7.1) declares, *asad vā idam agra āsīt:* "In the beginning of this creation, only *asat* was present."

In the opinion of Śrīla Jīva Gosvāmī, the word *adhimanaḥ* in the passage quoted above refers to the ruler of the aggregate mind of the universe, Lord Aniruddha, who appears as a plenary expansion of Śrī Nārāyaṇa when the latter desires to create. Prajāpati is Brahmā, the father of all other created beings. This is described in the *Mahā-nārāyaṇa Upaniṣad* (1.4): *atha punar eva nārāyaṇaḥ so 'nyaṁ kāmaṁ manasā dhyāyet. tasya dhyānāntaḥ-sthasya lalanāt svedo 'patat. tā imā pratatāpa tāsu tejo hiraṇ-mayam aṇḍaṁ tatra brahmā catur-mukho 'jāyata.* "Then Lord Nārāyaṇa meditated upon another desire of His, and as He pondered, a drop of perspiration fell from His forehead. All the material creations evolved from the fermentation of this drop. Therein the fiery, golden egg of the universe appeared, and within that globe four-headed Brahmā took his birth."

When a particular object is manufactured, it appears as a transformation of its ingredient cause, as in the case of jewelry made from gold. Persons who want gold will not reject gold earrings or necklaces, since these items are still gold, despite their modification. True *jñānīs* see in this mundane example an analogy to the different-yet-nondifferent relationship of the Puruṣa and His emanations, both material and spiritual. Thus this transcendental knowledge frees them from the bondage of illusion, for they can then see the Lord throughout His creation.

Śrīla Śrīdhara Svāmī prays,

yat sattvataḥ sadā bhāti
jagad etad asat svataḥ
sad-ābhāsam asaty asmin
bhagavantaṁ bhajāma tam

"Let us worship the Supreme Personality of Godhead, by virtue of whose substantial existence this created world seems to exist perpetually, although it is essentially insubstantial. As the Supersoul, He constitutes the representation of the real within this unreality."

TEXT 27

तव परि ये चरन्त्यखिलसत्त्वनिकेततया
त उत पदाक्रमन्त्यविगणय्य शिरो निरृतेः ।
परिवयसे पशूनिव गिरा विबुधानपि तांस्
त्वयि कृतसौहृदाः खलु पुनन्ति न ये विमुखाः ॥२७॥

tava pari ye caranty akhila-sattva-niketatayā
ta uta padākramanty aviganayya śiro nirṛteḥ
parivayase paśūn iva girā vibudhān api tāṁs
tvayi kṛta-sauhṛdāḥ khalu punanti na ye vimukhāḥ

tava—You; *pari ye caranti*—who worship; *akhila*—of all; *sattva*—created entities; *niketatayā*—as the shelter; *te*—they; *uta*—simply; *padā*—with their feet; *ākramanti*—step upon; *aviganayya*—disregarding; *śiraḥ*—the head; *nirṛteḥ*—of Death; *parivayase*—You tie up; *paśūn iva*—like animals; *girā*—with Your words (of the *Vedas*); *vibudhān*—wise; *api*—even; *tān*—them; *tvayi*—to whom; *kṛta*—those who have made; *sauhṛdāḥ*—friendship; *khalu*—indeed; *punanti*—purify; *na*—not; *ye*—who; *vimukhāḥ*—inimical.

TRANSLATION

The devotees who worship You as the shelter of all beings disregard Death and place their feet on his head. But with the words of the *Vedas* You bind the nondevotees like animals, though they be vastly learned scholars. It is Your affectionate devotees who can purify themselves and others, not those who are inimical to You.

PURPORT

The personified *Vedas* have now set aside the erroneous philosophies of several contending schools: the *asad-utpatti-vāda* of the Vaiśeṣikas, who presume a material source of creation; the *sad-vināśa-vāda* of the Naiyāyikas, who would deprive the liberated soul of consciousness; the *saguṇatva-bheda-vāda* of the Sāṅkhyas, who isolate the soul from all his apparent qualities; the *vipaṇa-vāda* of the Mīmāṁsakas, who condemn the soul to eternal involvment in the mundane commerce of *karma;* and the *vivarta-vāda* of the Māyāvādīs, who denigrate the soul's real life in this world as a hallucination. Having rejected all these ideas, the personified *Vedas* now present the philosophy of devotional service, *paricaryā-vāda.*

The Vaiṣṇavas who accept this philosophy teach that the *jīva* soul is an atomic particle of spiritual personality who possesses minute knowledge, is not independent and has no material qualities. Being minute, he is prone to come under the control of the material energy, where he suffers the pains of material life. He can end his suffering and regain the shelter of the Supreme Lord's divine, internal energy only by rendering devotional service to the Lord, not by engaging in fruitive work, mental speculation or any other process.

As Lord Kṛṣṇa says in His own words,

bhaktyāham ekayā grāhyaḥ
śraddhayātmā priyaḥ satām
bhaktiḥ punāti man-niṣṭhā
śva-pākān api sambhavāt

"Only by practicing unalloyed devotional service with full faith in Me can one obtain Me, the Supreme Personality of Godhead. I am naturally dear to My devotees, who take Me as the only goal of their loving service. By engaging in such pure devotional service, even the dog-eaters can purify themselves from the contamination of their low birth." (*Bhāg.* 11.14.21)

Devotees of the Personality of Godhead worship Him as the shelter (*niketa*) of everything that exists (*akhila-sattva*). Moreover, these Vaiṣṇava devotees themselves can be called *akhila-sattva-niketa* in the sense that their abode and shelter is the philosophic truth of the reality (*sattvam*) of both the material and spiritual worlds. Thus Śrīpāda Madhvācārya, in his *Vedānta-sūtra-bhāṣya,* quotes the *śruti-mantra: satyaṁ hy evedaṁ viśvam asṛjata.* "He created this world as real." And the Seventh Canto of *Śrīmad-Bhāgavatam* (7.1.11) refers to the Supreme Lord as *pradhāna-pumbhyāṁ naradeva satya-kṛt,* "the creator of a real universe of matter and living entities."

Śrīla Viśvanātha Cakravartī Ṭhākura points out yet another, more confidential, meaning of *akhila-sattva-niketa:* that the Supreme Lord's personal abodes are in no way *khila,* or imperfect, and so are called Vaikuṇṭha, the realms free of anxiety and restriction. Vaiṣṇavas whose devotional service the Lord has kindly accepted are so sure of His protection that they no longer fear death, which becomes for them just another easy step on the way back to their eternal home.

But are only devotees of the Supreme Lord eligible for liberation from the fear of death? Why are all other mystics and learned scholars disqualified? Here the *śrutis* answer: "Anyone who is *vimukha,* who has not turned his face toward the Lord with hopeful expectation of His mercy, is bound up in illusion by the same words of the *Vedas* that enlighten the surrendered devotees." The *Vedas* themselves warn, *tasya vāk-tantir nāmāni dāmāni. tasyedaṁ vācā tantyā nāmabhir dāmabhiḥ sarvaṁ sitam:* "The threads of this transcendental sound form a string of sacred names, but also a set of binding ropes. With the rope of their injunctions, the *Vedas* tie up this entire world, leaving all beings fettered by false designations."

The reality of the soul and Supersoul is *aparokṣa,* perceivable, but only to one with transcendental vision. Philosophers whose hearts are impure mistakenly presume that this truth is instead *parokṣa,* that it can only be speculated upon and never experienced directly. The knowledge of such thinkers may help them dispel certain doubts and misconceptions about the lesser aspects of reality, but it is useless for transcending material illusion and approaching the Absolute Truth. As a general rule, only the devotees who faithfully render loving service unto the Supreme Lord up to the point of complete purification receive His grace in the form of *aparokṣa-jñāna,* direct realization of His greatness and wonderful compassion. The Personality of Godhead is of course free to award His mercy even to the undeserving, as He does when He personally kills offensive demons, but He is much less inclined to bless Māyāvādīs and other atheistic philosophers.

One should not think, however, that the devotees of Viṣṇu are ignorant because they may not be expert in philosophic analysis and argument. The soul's perfect realization is to be gained not through his own efforts at mental speculation but by receiving the Lord's favor. This we hear from Vedic authority (*Kaṭha Upaniṣad* 2.2.23 and *Muṇḍaka Upaniṣad* 3.2.3):

nāyam ātmā pravacanena labhyo
na medhayā na bahunā śrutena

yam evaiṣa vṛṇute tena labhyas
tasyaiṣa ātmā vivṛṇute tanūṁ svām

"This Supreme Self cannot be reached by argumentation, or by applying one's independent brain power, or by studying many scriptures. Rather, he alone can achieve the Self whom the Self chooses to favor. To that person the Self reveals His own true, personal form."

Elsewhere the *śruti* describes the devotee's success: *dehānte devaḥ paraṁ brahma tārakaṁ vyacaṣṭe.* "At the end of this body's life, the sanctified soul perceives the Supreme Lord just as clearly as if seeing the stars in the sky." And in its last statement, the *Śvetāśvatara Upaniṣad* (6.23) offers this encouragement to aspiring Vaiṣṇavas:

yasya deve parā bhaktir
yathā deve tathā gurau
tasyaite kathitā hy arthāḥ
prakāśante mahātmanaḥ

"Unto those great souls who have implicit faith in both the Lord and the spiritual master, all the imports of Vedic knowledge are automatically revealed."

In this regard Śrīla Jīva Gosvāmī cites other verses of *Śrī Śvetāśvatara Upaniṣad* (4.7-8 and 4.13):

juṣṭaṁ yadā paśyaty anyam īśam
asya mahimānam iti vīta-śokaḥ

ṛco 'kṣare pare vyoman
yasmin devā adhi viśve niṣeduḥ
yas taṁ veda kim ṛcā kariṣyati
ya it tad vidus ta ime samāsate

"The Supreme Lord is He who is referred to by the *mantras* of the *Ṛg Veda,* who resides in the topmost, eternal sky, and who elevates His saintly devotees to share that same position. One who has developed pure love for Him and realizes His uniqueness then appreciates His glories and is freed from sorrow. What further good can the *Ṛg mantras* bestow on one who knows that Supreme Lord? All who come to know Him achieve the supreme destination."

yo vedānām adhipo
yasmiḻ lokā adhiśritāḥ
ya īśo 'sya dvipadaś catuṣpadas
tasmai devāya haviṣā vidhema

"To Him who is the master of all the *Vedas,* in whom all planets rest, who is the Lord of all known creatures, both the two-legged and the four-legged—to Him, the Personality of Godhead, we offer our worship with oblations of ghee."

Referring to those who desire liberation, Śrīla Śrīdhara Svāmī prays,

tapantu tāpaiḥ prapatantu parvatād
aṭantu tīrthāni paṭhantu cāgamān
yajantu yāgair vivadantu vādair
hariṁ vinā naiva mṛtiṁ taranti

"Let them suffer austerities, throw themselves from mountaintops, travel to holy places, study the scriptures, worship with fire sacrifices and argue various philosophies, but without Lord Hari they will never cross beyond death."

TEXT 28

त्वमकरणः स्वराडखिलकारकशक्तिधरस्
तव बलिमुद्वहन्ति समदन्त्यजयानिमिषाः ।
वर्षभुजोऽखिलक्षितिपतेरिव विश्वसृजो
विदधति यत्र ये त्वधिकृता भवतश्चकिताः ॥२८॥

tvam akaraṇaḥ sva-rāḍ akhila-kāraka-śakti-dharas
tava balim udvahanti samadanty ajayānimiṣāḥ
varṣa-bhujo 'khila-kṣiti-pater iva viśva-sṛjo
vidadhati yatra ye tv adhikṛtā bhavataś cakitāḥ

tvam—You; *akaraṇaḥ*—devoid of material senses; *sva-rāṭ*—self-effulgent; *akhila*—of all; *kāraka*—sensory functions; *śakti*—of the potencies; *dharaḥ*—the maintainer; *tava*—Your; *balim*—tribute; *udvahanti*—carry; *samadanti*—and partake of; *ajayā*—along with material nature; *animiṣāḥ*—the demigods; *varṣa*—of districts of a kingdom; *bhujaḥ*—the rulers; *akhila*—entire; *kṣiti*—of the land; *pateḥ*—of the lord; *iva*—as if; *viśva*—of the universe; *sṛjaḥ*—the creators; *vidadhati*—execute; *yatra*—in which; *ye*—they; *tu*—indeed; *adhikṛtā*—assigned; *bhavataḥ*—of You; *cakitāḥ*—afraid.

TRANSLATION

Though You have no material senses, You are the self-effulgent sustainer of everyone's sensory powers. The demigods and material nature herself offer You tribute, while also enjoying the tribute offered them by their worshipers, just as subordinate rulers of various districts in a kingdom offer tribute to their lord, the ultimate proprietor of the land, while also enjoying the tribute paid them by their own subjects. In this way the universal creators faithfully execute their assigned services out of fear of You.

PURPORT

All intelligent living beings should acknowledge the sovereignty of the Lord and willingly engage in devotional service to Him. Such is the consensus of the personified *Vedas.* But Lord Nārāyaṇa, while hearing these prayers, may have reasonably asked, "Since I also have a bodily form with sense organs and limbs, am I not just another doer and enjoyer? Especially since as the Supersoul in every being's heart I supervise countless organs and limbs, how am I not implicated in the sum total of everyone's sense gratification?" "No," the assembled *śrutis* here rejoin, "You have no material senses, yet You are the absolute controller of all." As expressed in the *Śvetāśvatara Upaniṣad* (3.18),

apāṇi-pādo javano grahītā
paśyaty acakṣuḥ sa śṛṇoty akarṇaḥ
sa vetti vedyaṁ na ca tasya vettā
tam āhur agryaṁ puruṣaṁ purāṇam

"He has no feet or hands, yet He is the swiftest runner and can grasp anything. Though without eyes or ears, He sees and hears. Nobody knows Him, yet He is the knower and the object of knowledge. Sages describe Him as the supreme, original Personality of Godhead."

The hands, feet, eyes and ears of the Supreme Person are not like those of an ordinary, conditioned soul, which are derived from false ego, a material substance. Rather, the Lord's transcendentally beautiful features are direct manifestations of His internal nature. Thus, unlike the soul and body of conditioned living beings, the Lord and His bodily form are identical in all respects. Moreover, His lotus hands, lotus feet, lotus eyes and other limbs are not restricted in their functions. Śrī Brahmā, the Lord's first creature, glorifies Him on this account:

aṅgāni yasya sakalendriya-vṛttimanti
paśyanti pānti kalayanti ciraṁ jaganti
ānanda-cinmaya-sad-ujjvala-vigrahasya
govindam ādi-puruṣaṁ tam ahaṁ bhajāmi

"I worship Govinda, the primeval Lord, whose transcendental form is full of bliss, truth and substantiality and thus emanates the most dazzling splendor. Each of the limbs of that transcendental figure possesses in itself the full-fledged functions of all the organs, and He eternally sees, maintains and manifests the infinite universes, both spiritual and material." (*Brahma-saṁhitā* 5.32)

Śrīla Viśvanātha Cakravartī gives an alternative explanation of the phrase *akhila-śakti-dhara:* The power that the Supreme Lord maintains within Himself is *akhila,* free from the limitations of all that is *khila,* or inferior and insignificant. He energizes the living being's senses, as described by the *Kena Upaniṣad* (1.2): *śrotrasya śrotraṁ manaso mano yad vāco ha vācam.* "He is the ear's ear, the mind's mind, and the voice's capacity of speech." And the *Śvetāśvatara Upaniṣad* (6.8) declares,

na tasya kāryaṁ karaṇaṁ ca vidyate
na tat-samaś cābhyadhikaś ca dṛśyate
parāsya śaktir vividhaiva śrūyate
svābhāvikī jñāna-bala-kriyā ca

"He has no material work to perform, nor any material senses with which to perform it. No one can be found who is equal to or greater than Him. From the *Vedas* we hear how that Supreme Lord possesses multifarious energies—the potencies of knowledge, strength and action—each of which acts autonomously."

Indra and the other demigods who rule over mortal beings are themselves servants of the Personality of Godhead, as are their superiors—

Brahmā and his sons, the secondary creators. All of these great gods and sages worship the Supreme Lord by performing their respective services of managing the universe and providing religious guidance for mankind.

The powerful controllers of the universe submit themselves in fearful reverence to the supreme controller, Lord Śrī Viṣṇu. As the *Taittirīya Upaniṣad* (2.8.1) states,

bhīṣāsmād vātaḥ pavate
bhīṣād eti sūryaḥ
bhīṣāsmād agniś cendraś ca
mṛtyur dhāvati pañcamaḥ

"Out of fear of Him, the wind blows. Out fear of Him, the sun moves and Agni and Indra execute their duties. And death, the fifth of their number, races along out of fear of Him."

Śrīla Śrīdhara Svāmī prays,

anindriyo 'pi yo devaḥ
sarva-kāraka-śakti-dhṛk
sarva-jñaḥ sarva-kartā ca
sarva-sevyaṁ namāmi tam

"The Supreme Lord has no material senses, yet He controls every living entity's sensory functions. He is the knower of everything, the ultimate performer of all action, and everyone's proper object of devotional service. I offer my obeisances to Him."

TEXT 29

स्थिरचरजातयः स्युरजयोत्थनिमित्तयुजो
विहर उदीक्षया यदि परस्य विमुक्त ततः ।
न हि परमस्य कश्चिदपरो न परश्च भवेद्
वियत इवापदस्य तव शून्यतुलां दधतः ॥२९॥

sthira-cara-jātayaḥ syur ajayottha-nimitta-yujo
vihara udīkṣayā yadi parasya vimukta tataḥ

na hi paramasya kaścid aparo na paraś ca bhaved
viyata ivāpadasya tava śūnya-tulāṁ dadhataḥ

sthira—stationary; *cara*—and moving; *jātayaḥ*—species of life; *syuḥ*—become manifest; *ajayā*—with the material energy; *uttha*—awakened; *nimitta*—their motivations for activity (and the subtle bodies activated by such); *yujaḥ*—assuming; *viharaḥ*—sport; *udīkṣayā*—by Your brief glance; *yadi*—if; *parasya*—of Him who is aloof; *vimukta*—O eternally liberated one; *tataḥ*—from her; *na*—not; *hi*—indeed; *paramasya*—for the supreme; *kaścit*—anyone; *aparaḥ*—not foreign; *na*—nor; *paraḥ*—foreign; *ca*—also; *bhavet*—can be; *viyataḥ*—for the ethereal sky; *iva*—as if; *apadasya*—which has no perceptible qualities; *tava*—for You; *śūnya*—to a void; *tulām*—a resemblance; *dadhataḥ*—who take on.

TRANSLATION

O eternally liberated, transcendental Lord, Your material energy causes the various moving and nonmoving species of life to appear by activating their material desires, but only when and if You sport with her by briefly glancing at her. You, the Supreme Personality of Godhead, see no one as an intimate friend and no one as a stranger, just as the ethereal sky has no connection with perceptible qualities. In this sense You resemble a void.

PURPORT

Not only are living beings totally dependent on the all-powerful, independent Lord for their maintenance and welfare, but even the very fact of their embodied existence is due only to His exceptional mercy. The Personality of Godhead has no interest in material affairs, since He has nothing to gain from the petty pleasures of this world and is altogether free from any contamination of envy or lust. He is exclusively involved in confidential, loving pastimes with His pure devotees in the internal realm of His spiritual energies. Therefore the only reason He ever turns to the business of material creation is to help draw lost souls back into this inner circle of eternal enjoyment.

To attempt a life separate from the Lord, rebellious souls must be provided with suitable bodies and an illusory environment in which to act out their fantasies of independence. The merciful Lord agrees to let them learn in their own way, and so He glances at Mahā-Māyā, His energy of material creation. Simply by this glance, she is awakened and makes all required arrangements on His behalf. She and her helpers manufacture countless varieties of gross and subtle bodies of demigods, humans, animals and so on, along with countless situations in heavenly and hellish worlds—all just to give the conditioned souls the exact facilities they desire and deserve.

While the uninformed may blame God for the suffering of His creatures, a sincere student of the Vedic literature will come to appreciate the Supreme Lord's equal concern for each soul. Since He has nothing to lose or gain, there is no reason for Him to distinguish between friends and opponents. We may choose to oppose Him and make all endeavors to forget Him, but He never forgets us, nor does He ever stop providing us with all our necessities, along with His unseen guidance.

Śrīla Śrīdhara Svāmī prays,

tvad-īkṣaṇa-vaśa-kṣobha-
māyā-bodhita-karmabhiḥ
jātān saṁsarataḥ khinnān
nṛ-hare pāhi naḥ pitaḥ

"O Father, O Lord appearing as half man, half lion, please save those who have been born into the endless cycle of birth and death. These souls are distressed by their karmic entanglement, which Māyā awakened when Your glance excited her to activity."

TEXT 30

अपरिमिता ध्रुवास्तनुभृतो यदि सर्वगतास्
तर्हि न शास्यतेति नियमो ध्रुव नेतरथा ।
अजनि च यन्मयं तदविमुच्य नियन्तृ भवेत्
सममनुजानतां यदमतं मतदुष्टतया ॥३०॥

aparimitā dhruvās tanu-bhṛto yadi sarva-gatās
tarhi na śāsyateti niyamo dhruva netarathā
ajani ca yan-mayaṁ tad avimucya niyantṛ bhavet
samam anujānatāṁ yad amataṁ mata-duṣṭatayā

aparimitāḥ—countless; *dhruvāḥ*—permanent; *tanu-bhṛtaḥ*—the embodied living entities; *yadi*—if; *sarva-gatāḥ*—omnipresent; *tarhi*—then; *na*—not; *śāsyatā*—sovereignty; *iti*—such; *niyamaḥ*—rule; *dhruva*—O unchanging one; *na*—not; *itarathā*—otherwise; *ajani*—was generated; *ca*—and; *yat-mayam*—from whose substance; *tat*—from that; *avimucya*—not separating itself; *niyantṛ*—regulator; *bhavet*—must be; *samam*—equally present; *anujānatām*—of those who supposedly know; *yat*—which; *amatam*—misunderstood; *mata*—of what is known; *duṣṭatayā*—because of the imperfection.

TRANSLATION

If the countless living entities were all-pervading and possessed forms that never changed, You could not possibly be their absolute ruler, O immutable one. But since they are Your localized expansions and their forms are subject to change, You do control them. Indeed, that which supplies the ingredients for the generation of something is necessarily its controller because a product never exists apart from its ingredient cause. It is simply illusion for someone to think that he knows the Supreme Lord, who is equally present in each of His expansions, since whatever knowledge one gains by material means must be imperfect.

PURPORT

Because the conditioned soul cannot directly understand the Supreme, the *Vedas* commonly refer to that Supreme Truth in such impersonal terms as Brahman and *oṁ tat sat*. If an ordinary scholar presumes to know the confidential meaning of these symbolic references, he should be rejected as an imposter. In the words of *Śrī Kena Upaniṣad* (2.1), *yadi manyase su-vedeti dabhram evāpi nūnaṁ tvaṁ vettha brahmaṇo rūpaṁ, yad asya tvaṁ yad asya deveṣu:* "If you think you know Brahman well, then your knowledge is very meager. If you think you can identify Brahman's form from among the demigods, indeed you know but little." And again,

yasyāmataṁ tasya mataṁ
mataṁ yasya na veda saḥ
avijñātaṁ vijānatāṁ
vijñātam avijānatām

"Whoever denies having any opinion of his own about the Supreme Truth is correct in his opinion, whereas one who has his own opinion about the Supreme does not know Him. He is unknown to those who claim to know Him, and can only be known by those who do not claim to know Him." (*Kena Up.* 2.3)

Ācārya Śrīdhara Svāmī gives the following explanation of this verse: Many philosophers have studied the mysteries of life from various perspectives and have formed widely differing theories. The Advaita Māyāvādīs, for example, propose that there is only one living being and one power of illusion (*avidyā*) that covers him, producing the appearance of plurality. But this hypothesis leads to the absurd conclusion that when any one living being becomes liberated, everyone obtains liberation. If, on the other hand, there are many *avidyās* to cover the one living being, each *avidyā* will cover only some part of him, and we would have to talk about his becoming partly liberated at particular times while his other parts remain in bondage. This is also obviously absurd. Thus the plurality of living beings is an unavoidable conclusion.

Furthermore, there are other theoreticians, namely the proponents of Nyāya and Vaiśeṣika, who claim that the *jīva* soul is infinite in size. If souls were infinitesimal, these scholars argue, they would not pervade their own bodies, whereas if they were of medium size they would be divisible into parts and thus could not be eternal, at least according to the axioms of Nyāya-Vaiśeṣika metaphysics. But if the numerous eternal *jīva* souls are each infinitely large, how could they be covered by any power of bondage, whether belonging to *avidyā* or to the Supreme Lord Himself? According to this theory, there can be no illusion for the soul, no limitations from which to be liberated. The infinite souls must eternally remain as they are, without change. This would mean that the souls would all be equal to God, since He would have no scope for controlling these all-pervading, unchanging rivals.

The Vedic *śruti-mantras,* which affirm unequivocally the mastery of the Lord over the individual souls, cannot be validly contradicted. A true philosopher must accept the statements of *śruti* as reliable authority on all matters they touch. Certainly in numerous places the Vedic literatures contrast the Supreme Lord's perpetual, unchanging oneness with the ever-changing embodiments of living beings caught up in the cycle of birth and death.

Śrīla Śrīdhara Svāmī prays,

antar-yantā sarva-lokasya gītaḥ
śrutyā yuktyā caivam evāvaseyaḥ
yaḥ sarva-jñaḥ sarva-śaktir nṛsiṁhaḥ
śrīmantaṁ taṁ cetasaivāvalambe

"In my heart I take shelter of Him who is glorified as the inner controller of all the worlds, and whom the *Vedas* ascertain in truth through logical reasoning. He is Nṛsiṁha, the omniscient and omnipotent Lord of the goddess of fortune."

TEXT 31

न घटत उद्भवः प्रकृतिपूरुषयोरजयोर्
उभययुजा भवन्त्यसुभृतो जलबुद्बुदवत् ।
त्वयि त इमे ततो विविधनामगुणैः परमे
सरित इवार्णवे मधुनि लिल्युरशेषरसाः ॥३१॥

na ghaṭata udbhavaḥ prakṛti-pūruṣayor ajayor
ubhaya-yujā bhavanty asu-bhṛto jala-budbuda-vat
tvayi ta ime tato vividha-nāma-guṇaiḥ parame
sarita ivārṇave madhuni lilyur aśeṣa-rasāḥ

na ghaṭate—does not happen; *udbhavaḥ*—the generation; *prakṛti*—of material nature; *pūruṣayoḥ*—and of the soul who is her enjoyer; *ajayoḥ*—who are unborn; *ubhaya*—of both; *yujā*—by the combination; *bhavanti*—come into being; *asu-bhṛtaḥ*—living bodies; *jala*—on water; *budbuda*—bubbles; *vat*—like; *tvayi*—in You; *te ime*—these (living beings); *tataḥ*—therefore; *vividha*—various; *nāma*—with names; *guṇaiḥ*—and qualities; *parame*—in the Supreme; *saritaḥ*—rivers; *iva*—as; *arṇave*—within the ocean; *madhuni*—in honey; *lilyuḥ*—become merged; *aśeṣa*—all; *rasāḥ*—flavors.

TRANSLATION

Neither material nature nor the soul who tries to enjoy her are ever born, yet living bodies come into being when these two combine, just as bubbles form where water meets the air. And just as rivers merge into the ocean or the nectar from many different

flowers blends into honey, so all these conditioned beings eventually merge back into You, the Supreme, along with their various names and qualities.

PURPORT

Without proper spiritual guidance, one may misunderstand the *Vedas'* description of the living entities emanating from the Lord to mean that they have come into being in this process and will eventually pass again into nonexistence. But if the living entities were to thus have only temporary existence, then when one of them would die his remaining *karma* would simply vanish without being used up, and when a soul would be born he would appear with unaccountable *karma* he had done nothing to earn. Furthermore, a living being's liberation would amount to the total eradication of his identity and being.

The truth is, however, that the soul's essence is one with Brahman's, just as the small portion of space contained within the walls of a clay pot is one in essence with the all-expanding sky. And like the making and breaking of a pot, the "birth" of an individual soul consists of his first becoming covered by a material body, and his "death," or liberation, consists of the destruction of his gross and subtle bodies once and for all. Certainly such "birth" and "death" take place only by the mercy of the Supreme Lord.

The combination of material nature and her controller that produces the numerous conditioned beings in material creation is likened here to the combination of water and air that produces countless bubbles of foam on the surface of the sea. Just as the efficient cause, air, impels the ingredient cause, water, to form itself into bubbles, so by His glance the Supreme Puruṣa inspires *prakṛti* to transform herself into the array of material elements and the innumerable material forms manifest from those elements. *Prakṛti* thus serves as the *upādāna-kāraṇa,* or ingredient cause, of creation. In the ultimate issue, however, since she is also an expansion of the Supreme Lord, it is the Lord alone who is the ingredient cause as well as the efficient cause. This is as stated in the *Taittirīya Upaniṣad* (2.2.1), *tasmād vā etasmād ātmana ākāśaḥ sambhūtaḥ:* "From this Supreme Soul the ether evolved," and *so 'kāmayata bahu syāṁ prajāyeya:* "He desired, 'Let Me become many by expanding into progeny.'"

The individual *jīva* souls are not created when "born" from the Supreme Lord and *prakṛti,* nor are they destroyed when they "merge" back into the Lord, rejoining Him in the pleasure pastimes of His eternal kingdom. And in the same way as the infinitesimal *jīvas* can appear to undergo birth and death without any factual change, the Supreme Lord can send forth and withdraw His emanations without Himself undergoing any transformation. Thus the *Bṛhad-āraṇyaka Upaniṣad* (4.5.14) affirms, *avināśi vāre 'yam ātmā:* "This *ātmā* is indeed indestructible"—a statement that can be applied to both the Supreme Soul and the subordinate *jīva* soul.

As explained by Śrīla Śrīdhara Svāmī, the dissolution of the living being's material condition occurs in two ways, partial and complete. Partial dissolution occurs when the soul experiences dreamless sleep, when he leaves his body and when all souls reenter the body of Mahā-Viṣṇu at the time of universal annihilation. These different types of dissolution are like the mixing of nectar brought by bees from different kinds of flowers. The different flavors of nectar represent the dormant individual karmic reactions of each living entity, which still exist but cannot easily be distinguished from one another. In contrast, the ultimate dissolution of the soul's material condition is his liberation from *saṁsāra*, which is like the flowing of rivers into the ocean. As the waters from different rivers merge together after entering the ocean and become indistinguishable from one another, so the false material designations of the *jīvas* are given up at the time of liberation, and all the liberated *jīvas* once again become equally situated as servants of the Supreme Lord.

The *Upaniṣads* describe these dissolutions as follows: *yathā saumya madhu madhu-kṛto nistiṣṭhanti nānātyayānāṁ vṛkṣāṇāṁ rasān samavahāram ekatāṁ saṅgayanti. te yathā tatra na vivekaṁ labhante amuṣyāhaṁ vṛkṣasya raso 'smy amuṣyāhaṁ raso 'smīty evam eva khalu saumyemāḥ sarvāḥ prajāḥ sati sampadya na viduḥ sati sampadyāmahe:* "My dear boy, this [partial dissolution] resembles what happens when honeybees collect honey by extracting the nectar from the flowers of various kinds of trees and merge it all into a single mixture. Just as the mixed nectars cannot distinguish, 'I am the juice of such-and-such a flower,' or 'I am the juice of another flower,' so, dear boy, when all these living entities merge together they cannot consciously think, 'Now we have merged together.'" (*Chāndogya Up.* 6.9.1-2)

yathā nadyaḥ syandamānāḥ samudre
'staṁ gacchanti nāma-rūpe vihāya

tathā vidvān nāma-rūpād vimuktaḥ
parāt-paraṁ puruṣam upaiti divyam

"As rivers flow to their dissolution in the sea, giving up their names and forms at their destination, so the wise man who becomes free from material names and forms attains to the Supreme Absolute, the wonderful Personality of Godhead." (*Muṇḍaka Up.* 3.2.8)

Śrīla Śrīdhara Svāmī prays,

yasminn udyad-vilayam api yad bhāti viśvaṁ layādau
jīvopetaṁ guru-karuṇayā kevalātmāvabodhe
atyantāntaṁ vrajati sahasā sindhu-vat sindhu-madhye
madhye cittaṁ tri-bhuvana-guruṁ bhāvaye taṁ nṛ-siṁham

"The Supreme Lord is self-effulgently omniscient. By His great mercy, this universe, which is subject to repeated creation and destruction, remains present within Him after merging back into Him along with the living entities at the time of cosmic dissolution. This total withdrawal of the universal manifestation occurs suddenly, like the flowing of a river into the ocean. Within the core of my heart I meditate upon that master of the three worlds, Lord Nṛsiṁha."

TEXT 32

नृषु तव मायया भ्रमममीष्ववगत्य भृशं
त्वयि सुधियोऽभवे दधति भावमनुप्रभवम् ।
कथमनुवर्ततां भवभयं तव यद् भ्रुकुटिः
सृजति मुहुस्त्रिनेमिरभवच्छरणेषु भयम् ॥३२॥

nṛṣu tava mayayā bhramam amīṣv avagatya bhṛśaṁ
tvayi su-dhiyo 'bhave dadhati bhāvam anuprabhavam
katham anuvartatāṁ bhava-bhayaṁ tava yad bhru-kuṭiḥ
sṛjati muhus tri-nemir abhavac-charaṇeṣu bhayam

nṛṣu—among humans; *tava*—Your; *māyayā*—by the illusory energy; *bhramam*—bewilderment; *amīṣu*—among these; *avagatya*—understanding; *bhṛśam*—fervent; *tvayi*—unto You; *su-dhiyaḥ*—those who are wise;

abhave—unto the source of liberation; *dadhati*—render; *bhāvam*—loving service; *anuprabhavam*—potent; *katham*—how; *anuvartatām*—for those who follow You faithfully; *bhava*—of material life; *bhayam*—fear; *tava*—Your; *yat*—since; *bhru*—of the eyebrows; *kuṭiḥ*—the furrowing; *sṛjati*—creates; *muhuḥ*—repeatedly; *tri-nemiḥ*—three-rimmed (in the three phases of time, namely past, present and future); *a*—not; *bhavat*—from You; *śaraṇeṣu*—for those who take shelter; *bhayam*—fear.

TRANSLATION

The wise souls who understand how Your Māyā deludes all human beings render potent loving service to You, who are the source of liberation from birth and death. How, indeed, can fear of material life affect Your faithful servants? On the other hand, Your furrowing eyebrows—the triple-rimmed wheel of time—repeatedly terrify those who refuse to take shelter of You.

PURPORT

The *Vedas* reveal their most cherished secret—devotional service to the Personality of Godhead—only to those who are tired of material illusion, which is based on a false sense of independence from the Lord. The *Vājasaneyī-saṁhitā* (32.11) of the *White Yajur Veda* contains the following *mantra:*

parītya bhūtāni parītya lokān
parītya sarvāḥ pradiśo diśaś ca
upasthāya prathama-jāmṛtasyā-
tmanātmānam abhisaṁviveśa

"After passing beyond all the species of life, all the planetary systems and all the limits of space in all directions, one approaches the original Soul of immortality. Then one receives the opportunity to enter permanently into His domain and worship Him with personal service."

The proponents of various contending materialistic philosophies may consider themselves very wise, but they are in fact all deluded by the Supreme Lord's Māyā. Vaiṣṇavas recognize this pattern of general delusion and submit themselves to the Supreme Lord in the devotional moods of servitude, friendship and so on. Instead of the heat and strife of philosophical quarrel, the pure Vaiṣṇavas experience only delight at every moment, because the object of their love is He who brings an end to material entanglement. And the devotees of Lord Viṣṇu enjoy constant pleasure not only in this life but in future lives. In whatever births they take, they enjoy loving reciprocations with the Lord. Thus the sincere Vaiṣṇava prays,

nātha yoni-sahasreṣu
yeṣu yeṣu bhramāmy aham
tatra tatrācyutā bhaktir
acyutāstu dṛḍhā tvayi

"Wherever I may wander, O master, among thousands of species of life, in each situation may I have firmly fixed devotion to You, O Acyuta." (*Viṣṇu Purāṇa*)

Some philosophers will question how the Vaiṣṇavas can overcome their material entrapment without thorough analytic knowledge of the entities *tvam* ("you," the *jīva*) and *tat* ("that," the Supreme), and without developing a sufficient hatred of material life. The personified *Vedas* here answer that there is no chance of material illusion continuing to act on devotees of the Lord because even in the earliest stages of devotional service all fear and attachment are removed by the Lord's grace.

Time is the root cause of all fear in this world. Indeed, with its three divisions of past, present and future it creates terror at the prospect of impending disease, death and hellish suffering—but only for those who have failed to obtain shelter at the feet of the Supreme Lord. As the Lord Himself says in the *Rāmāyaṇa* (*Laṅkā-khaṇḍa* 18.33),

sakṛd eva prapanno yas
tavāsmīti ca yācate
abhayaṁ sarvadā tasmai
dadāmy etad vrataṁ mama

"To whomever even once surrenders to Me, pleading 'I am Yours,' I give eternal fearlessness. This is my solemn vow." Furthermore, in the

Bhagavad-gītā (7.14) the Lord says,

daivī hy eṣā guṇa-mayī
mama māyā duratyayā
mām eva ye prapadyante
māyām etāṁ taranti te

"This divine energy of Mine, consisting of the three modes of material nature, is difficult to overcome. But those who have surrendered unto Me can easily cross beyond it."

Vaiṣṇavas do not like to waste their time in prolonged and fruitless wrangling over dry philosophic subjects. They would rather worship the Personality of Godhead than quarrel with philosophical adversaries. The Vaiṣṇavas' understanding concurs with the essential message of revealed scripture. These devotees' conception of the Supreme Absolute Truth as the infinite ocean of personality and loving pastimes in His worshipable forms of Kṛṣṇa, Rāma and other divine manifestations, and their conception of themselves as His eternal servants, amount to the perfect conclusion of Vedānta philosophy in terms of the entities *tat* and *tvam*.

The Personality of Godhead and His emanations, such as the *jīva* souls, are simultaneously different and nondifferent, just like the sun and its expanding rays. There are more *jīvas* than anyone can count, and each of them is eternally alive with consciousness, as the *śrutis* confirm: *nityo nityānāṁ cetanaś cetanānām*. (*Kaṭha Up*. 5.13 and *Śvetāśvatara Up*. 6.13) When they are sent forth from the body of Mahā-Viṣṇu at the beginning of material creation, the *jīvas* are all equal in the sense that they are all atomic particles of the Lord's marginal energy. But according to their differing conditions, they divide into four groups: Some are covered by ignorance, which obscures their vision like a cloud. Others become liberated from ignorance through a combination of knowledge and devotion. A third group of souls become endowed with pure devotion, with a slight mixture of desire for speculative knowledge and fruitive activity. Those souls attain purified bodies composed of perfect knowledge and bliss with which they can engage in the Lord's service. Finally, there are those who are devoid of any connection with ignorance; these are the Lord's eternal associates.

The marginal position of the *jīva* soul is described in the *Nārada Pañcarātra:*

yat taṭa-sthaṁ tu cid-rūpaṁ
sva-saṁvedyād vinirgatam
rañjitaṁ guṇa-rāgeṇa
sa jīva iti kathyate

"The *taṭa-stha* potency should be understood as emanating from the Lord's *saṁvit* [knowledge] energy. This emanation, called the *jīva,* becomes conditioned by the qualities of material nature." Because the minute *jīva* lives within the margin between the Lord's external, illusory potency, Māyā, and His internal, spiritual potency, *cit,* the *jīva* is called *taṭa-stha,* "marginal." When he earns liberation by cultivating devotion to the Lord, however, he comes completely under the shelter of the Lord's internal potency, and at that time he is no longer tainted by the modes of material nature. Lord Kṛṣṇa confirms this in *Bhagavad-gītā* (14.26):

māṁ ca yo 'vyabhicāreṇa
bhakti-yogena sevate
sa guṇān samatītyaitān
brahma-bhūyāya kalpate

"One who engages in full devotional service, unfailing in all circumstances, at once transcends the modes of material nature and thus comes to the level of Brahman."

The object of the soul's worship is realized in three aspects: Brahman, Paramātmā and Bhagavān. Impersonal Brahman is like the radiant effulgence of the sun; the Supersoul, or Paramātmā, is like the sun globe; and the Personality of Godhead, Bhagavān, is like the presiding deity within the sun, complemented by his elaborate entourage and paraphernalia. Or, to cite another analogy, travelers approaching a city from a distance cannot at first distinguish its features but rather see something vaguely shining ahead of them. As they come closer, they may discern a few of the taller buildings. Then, when they are sufficiently close, they will see the city as it is—a bustling metropolis with many citizens, residences, public buildings, highways and parks. In the same way, persons inclined to impersonal meditation may at best gain some realization of the Supreme Lord's effulgence (Brahman), those who approach closer can learn to see Him as the Lord in the heart (Paramātmā), and those who come very close can know Him in His full personality (Bhagavān).

In summary, Śrīla Śrīdhara Svāmī prays,

saṁsāra-cakra-krakacair vidīrṇam
udīrṇa-nānā-bhava-tāpa-taptam
kathañcid āpannam iha prapannaṁ
tvam uddhara śrī-nṛhare nṛ-lokam

"O Śrī Nṛhari, please deliver those human beings who have suffered all kinds of torments and been ripped apart by the sharp edge of *saṁsāra's* wheel, but who have now somehow found You and are surrendering themselves unto You."

TEXT 33

विजितहृषीकवायुभिरदान्तमनस्तुरगं
य इह यतन्ति यन्तुमतिलोलमुपायखिदः ।
व्यसनशतान्विताः समवहाय गुरोश्चरणं
वणिज इवाज सन्त्यकृतकर्णधरा जलधौ ॥३३॥

vijita-hṛṣīka-vāyubhir adānta-manas tura-gaṁ
ya iha yatanti yantum ati-lolam upāya-khidaḥ
vyasana-śatānvitāḥ samavahāya guroś caraṇaṁ
vaṇija ivāja santy akṛta-karṇa-dharā jaladhau

vijita—conquered; *hṛṣīka*—with senses; *vāyubhiḥ*—and vital air; *adānta*—not brought under control; *manaḥ*—the mind; *tura-gam*—(which is like) a horse; *ye*—those who; *iha*—in this world; *yatanti*—endeavor; *yantum*—to regulate; *ati*—very; *lolam*—unsteady; *upāya*—by their various methods of cultivation; *khidaḥ*—distressed; *vyasana*—disturbances; *śata*—by hundreds; *anvitāḥ*—joined; *samavahāya*—abandoning; *guroḥ*—of the spiritual master; *caraṇam*—the feet; *vaṇijaḥ*—merchants; *iva*—as if; *aja*—O unborn one; *santi*—they are; *akṛta*—having not taken; *karṇa-dharāḥ*—a helmsman; *jala-dhau*—on the ocean.

TRANSLATION

The mind is like an impetuous horse that even persons who have regulated their senses and breath cannot control. Those in this world who try to tame the uncontrolled mind, but who abandon the feet of their spritual master, encounter hundreds of

obstacles in their cultivation of various distressful practices. O unborn Lord, they are like merchants on a boat in the ocean who have failed to employ a helmsman.

PURPORT

To become qualified to attain love of Godhead, the mature fruit of liberation, one must first subdue the rebellious material mind. Though difficult, this can be achieved when a person replaces his addictions to sense gratification with a taste for the higher pleasures of spiritual life. But only by the favor of the representative of Godhead, the spiritual master, can one gain this higher taste.

The spiritual master opens the eyes of the disciple to the wonders of the transcendental realm, as indicated in the Gāyatrī prayers by the seed *mantra* of divine knowledge, *aiṁ*.

The *Muṇḍaka Upaniṣad* (1.2.12) states,

tad-vijñānārthaṁ sa gurum evābhigacchet
samit-pāṇiḥ śrotriyaṁ brahma-niṣṭham

"To understand these things properly, one must humbly approach, with firewood in hand, a spiritual master who is learned in the *Vedas* and firmly devoted to the Absolute Truth." And the *Kaṭha Upaniṣad* (2.9) declares,

naiṣā tarkeṇa matir āpaneyā
proktānyenaiva su-jñānāya preṣṭha

"This realization, my dear boy, cannot be acquired by logic. It must be spoken by an exceptionally qualified spiritual master to a knowledgeable disciple."

Non-Vaiṣṇavas often disregard the importance of surrendering to a spiritual master who stands in an authorized line of disciplic succession. Relying instead on their own abilities, proud *yogīs* and *jñānīs* exhibit their apparent success to impress the world, but their glory is but temporary:

yuñjānānām abhaktānāṁ
prāṇāyāmādibhir manaḥ
akṣīṇa-vāsanaṁ rājan
dṛśyate punar utthitam

"The minds of nondevotees who engage in such practices as *prāṇāyāma* are not fully cleansed of material desires. Thus, O King, material desires are again seen to arise in their minds." (*Bhāg.* 10.51.60)

On the other hand, a humble, steadfast devotee of Lord Viṣṇu and of the Vaiṣṇavas is assured of easy victory over the stubborn mind. He need not concern himself with performing the eightfold system of *yoga* or taking other such measures to keep his mind steady. *Sarvaṁ caitad gurau bhaktyā puruṣo hy añjasā jayet:* "A person can easily obtain all these goals simply by being devoted to his spiritual master." Otherwise, a nondevotee may conquer his senses and vital air and still fail to tame his mind, which will continue to run wild like an unbroken horse. He will suffer unending anxiety over the troublesome execution of various spiritual practices, and in the end he will remain just as lost in the vast material ocean as he ever was. The analogy given here is very appropriate: A group of merchants who hastily enter upon a sea voyage with expectations of great profit, but who fail to hire a competent helmsman for their boat, will simply experience great difficulty.

The *Bhāgavatam* declares the importance of the bona fide spiritual master in many places, such as this verse from the Eleventh Canto (20.17):

nṛ-deham ādyam su-labhaṁ su-durlabhaṁ
plavaṁ su-kalpaṁ guru-karṇa-dhāram
mayānukūlena nabhasvateritaṁ
pumān bhavābdhiṁ na taret sa ātma-hā

"The human body, which can award all benefit in life, is automatically obtained by the laws of nature, although it is a very rare achievement. This human body can be compared to a perfectly constructed boat having the spiritual master as the captain and the instructions of the Personality of Godhead as favorable winds impelling it on its course. Considering all these advantages, a human being who does not utilize his human life to cross the ocean of material existence must be considered the killer of his own soul." Therefore the first business of one who takes human life seriously is to find out a spiritual master who can guide him in Kṛṣṇa consciousness.

Śrīla Śrīdhara Svāmī prays,

yadā parānanda-guro bhavat-pade
padaṁ mano me bhagaval labheta

tadā nirastākhila-sādhana-śramaḥ
śrayeya saukhyaṁ bhavataḥ kṛpātaḥ

"O transcendentally blissful *guru,* when my mind finally achieves a place at your lotus feet, all the tiresome labor of my spiritual practices will be finished, and by your mercy I will experience the greatest happiness."

TEXT 34

स्वजनसुतात्मदारधनधामधरासुरथैस्
त्वयि सति किं नृणां श्रयत आत्मनि सर्वरसे ।
इति सदजानतां मिथुनतो रतये चरतां
सुखयति को न्विह स्वविहते स्वनिरस्तभगे ॥३४॥

svajana-sutātma-dāra-dhana-dhāma-dharāsu-rathais
tvayi sati kiṁ nṛṇāṁ śrayata ātmani sarva-rase
iti sad ajānatāṁ mithunato rataye caratāṁ
sukhayati ko nv iha sva-vihate sva-nirasta-bhage

svajana—with servants; *suta*—children; *ātma*—body; *dāra*—wife; *dhana*—money; *dhāma*—home; *dharā*—land; *asu*—vitality; *rathaiḥ*—and vehicles; *tvayi*—when You; *sati*—have become; *kim*—what (use); *nṛṇām*—for human beings; *śrayataḥ*—who are taking shelter; *ātmani*—their very Self; *sarva-rase*—the embodiment of all pleasures; *iti*—thus; *sat*—the truth; *ajānatām*—for those who fail to appreciate; *mithunataḥ*—from sexual combinations; *rataye*—for sensual indulgence; *caratām*—carrying on; *sukhayati*—gives happiness; *kaḥ*—what; *nu*—at all; *iha*—in this (world); *sva*—by its very nature; *vihate*—which is subject to destruction; *sva*—by its very nature; *nirasta*—which is devoid; *bhage*—of any essence.

TRANSLATION

To those persons who take shelter of You, You reveal Yourself as the Supersoul, the embodiment of all transcendental pleasure. What further use have such devotees for their servants, children or bodies, their wives, money or houses, their land, good health or conveyances? And for those who fail to appreciate the truth about

You and go on pursuing the pleasures of sex, what could there be in this entire world—a place inherently doomed to destruction and devoid of significance—that could give them real happiness?

PURPORT

Devotional service to Lord Viṣṇu is considered pure when one's sole desire is to please the Lord. Situated in that perfect consciousness, a Vaiṣṇava has no further interest in wordly gains and is thus excused from any obligation to perform ritual sacrifices and follow austere practices of *yoga.* As the *Muṇḍaka Upaniṣad* (1.2.12) states,

parīkṣya lokān karma-citān brāhmaṇo
nirvedam āyān nāsty akṛtaḥ kṛtena

"When a *brāhmaṇa* recognizes that elevation to the heavenly planets is merely another accumulation of *karma,* he becomes renounced and is no longer corrupted by his actions." The *Bṛhad-āraṇyaka* (4.4.9) and *Kaṭha* (6.14) *Upaniṣads* confirm,

yadā sarve pramucyante
kāmā ye 'sya hṛdi śritāḥ
atha martyo 'mṛto bhavaty
atra brahma samaśnute

"When a person completely gives up all the sinful desires he is harboring in his heart, he exchanges mortality for eternal spiritual life and attains real pleasure in the Absolute Truth." And the *Gopāla-tāpanī Upaniṣad* (*Pūrva* 15) concludes, *bhaktir asya bhajanaṁ tad ihāmutropādhi-nairāsyen-āmuṣmin manaḥ-kalpanam etad eva naiṣkarmyam.* "Devotional service is the process of worshiping the Supreme Lord. It consists of fixing one's mind upon Him by becoming disinterested in all material designations, both in this life and the next. This, indeed, is true renunciation."

The items the *śrutis* mention here are all measures of worldly success: *svajanāḥ,* servants; *ātmā,* a beautiful body; *sutāḥ,* children to be proud of; *dārāḥ,* an attractive and competent spouse; *dhanam,* financial assets; *dhāma,* a prestigious residence; *dharā,* holdings of land; *asavaḥ,* health and strength; and *rathāḥ,* cars and other vehicles that display one's status. But one who has begun to experience the ecstasy of devotional service loses all attraction for these things, since he finds real satisfaction in the Supreme Lord, the reservoir of all pleasure, who enjoys by sharing His own pleasures with His servitors.

We are each free to choose the course of our life: we can either dedicate our body, mind, words, talents and wealth to the glory of God, or else we can ignore Him and struggle instead for our personal happiness. The second path leads to a life of slavery to sex and ambition, in which the soul never feels real satisfaction but instead suffers continually. Vaiṣṇavas are distressed to see materialists suffering in this way, and so they always strive to enlighten them.

Śrīla Śrīdhara Svāmī prays,

bhajato hi bhavān sākṣāt
paramānanda-cid-dhanaḥ
ātmaiva kim ataḥ kṛtyaṁ
tuccha-dāra-sutādibhiḥ

"For those who worship You, You become their very Self, their spiritual treasure of topmost bliss. What further use have they for mundane wives, children and so forth?"

TEXT 35

भुवि पुरुपुण्यतीर्थसदनान्यृषयो विमदास्
त उत भवत्पदाम्बुजहृदोऽघभिदङ्घ्रिजलाः ।
दधति सकृन्मनस्त्वयि य आत्मनि नित्यसुखे
न पुनरुपासते पुरुषसारहरावसथान् ॥३५॥

bhuvi puru-puṇya-tīrtha-sadanāny ṛṣayo vimadās
ta uta bhavat-padāmbuja-hṛdo 'gha-bhid-aṅghri-jalāḥ
dadhati sakṛn manas tvayi ya ātmani nitya-sukhe
na punar upāsate puruṣa-sāra-harāvasathān

bhuvi—on the earth; *puru*—greatly; *puṇya*—pious; *tīrtha*—places of pilgrimage; *sadanāni*—and personal abodes of the Supreme Lord; *ṛṣayaḥ*—sages; *vimadāḥ*—free from false pride; *te*—they; *uta*—indeed; *bhavat*—Your; *pada*—feet; *ambuja*—lotus; *hṛdaḥ*—in whose hearts;

agha—sins; *bhit*—which destroys; *aṅghri*—(having bathed) whose feet; *jalāḥ*—the water; *dadhati*—turn; *sakṛt*—even once; *manaḥ*—their minds; *tvayi*—toward You; *ye*—who; *ātmani*—toward the Supreme Soul; *nitya*—always; *sukhe*—who is happy; *na punaḥ*—never again; *upāsate*—they worship; *puruṣa*—of a man; *sāra*—the essential qualities; *hara*—which steal way; *āvasathān*—their muṇdane homes.

TRANSLATION

Sages free from false pride live on this earth by frequenting the sacred pilgrimage sites and those places where the Supreme Lord displayed His pastimes. Because such devotees keep Your lotus feet within their hearts, the water that washes their feet destroys all sins. Anyone who even once turns his mind toward You, the ever-blissful Soul of all existence, no longer dedicates himself to serving family life at home, which simply robs a man of his good qualities.

PURPORT

The qualification of an aspiring sage is that he has learned about the Absolute Truth from standard authorities and developed a sober mood of renunciation. To develop his capacity for discriminating the important from the unimportant, such a person often wanders from one holy site to another, taking advantage of the association of great souls who frequent or reside in these places. If, in the course of his travels, the aspiring sage can begin to realize the Supreme Lord's lotus feet in the core of his heart, he will be released from the illusion of false ego and from the painful bondage of lust, envy and greed. Though he may still go to places of pilgrimage to bathe away his sins, the now purified sage has the power to sanctify others with the water that washes his feet and with the realized instructions he imparts. Such a sage is described by the *Muṇḍaka Upaniṣad* (2.2.9)

bhidyate hṛdaya-granthiś
chidyante sarva-saṁśayāḥ
kṣīyante cāsya karmāṇi
tasmin dṛṣṭe parāvare

"The knot in the heart is pierced, all misgivings are cut to pieces, and the chain of fruitive actions is terminated when one sees the Supreme Lord everywhere, within all superior and inferior beings." To sages who have reached this stage, the *Muṇḍaka Upaniṣad* (3.2.11) thus pays homage: *namaḥ paramarṣibhyaḥ, namaḥ paramarṣibhyaḥ*. "Obeisances to the topmost sages, obeisances to the topmost sages!"

Putting aside the affectionate company of wives, children, friends and followers, saintly Vaiṣṇavas travel to the holy *dhāmas* where the Supreme Lord's worship can be most successfuly prosecuted—places such as Vṛndāvana, Māyāpura and Jagannātha Purī, or anywhere else where sincere devotees of Lord Viṣṇu congregate. Even those Vaiṣṇavas who have not taken *sannyāsa* and still live at home or in their *guru's āśrama,* but who have once tasted just a drop of the sublime pleasure of devotional service, will also have little inclination to meditate on the pleasures of a materialistic family life, which robs a person of his discretion, determination, sobriety, tolerance and peace of mind.

Śrila Śrīdhara Svāmī prays,

muñcann aṅga tad aṅga-saṅgam aniśaṁ tvām eva sañcintayan
santaḥ santi yato yato gata-madās tān āśramān āvasan
nityaṁ tan-mukha-paṅkajād vigalita-tvat-puṇya-gāthāmṛta-
srotaḥ-samplava-sampluto nara-hare na syām ahaṁ deha-bhṛt

"My dear Lord, when I will give up all sense gratification and engage incessantly in meditating upon You, and when I will take up residence in the hermitages of saintly devotees free from false pride, then I will become fully immersed in the inundation of nectar pouring from the devotees' lotus mouths as they chant sacred narrations about You. And then, O Lord Narahari, I will never again have to take a material body."

TEXT 36

सत इदमुत्थितं सदिति चेन्ननु तर्कहतं
व्यभिचरति क्व च क्व च मृषा न तथोभययुक् ।
व्यवहृतये विकल्प इषितोऽन्धपरम्परया
भ्रमयति भारती त उरुवृत्तिभिरुक्थजडान् ॥३६॥

sata idam utthitaṁ sad iti cen nanu tarka-hataṁ
vyabhicarati kva ca kva ca mṛṣā na tathobhaya-yuk
vyavahṛtaye vikalpa iṣito 'ndha-paramparayā
bhramayati bhāratī ta uru-vṛttibhir uktha-jaḍān

sataḥ—from that which is permanent; *idam*—this (universe); *utthitam*—arisen; *sat*—permanent; *iti*—thus; *cet*—if (someone proposes); *nanu*—certainly; *tarka*—by logical contradiction; *hatam*—refuted; *vyabhicarati*—it is inconsistent; *kva ca*—in some cases; *kva ca*—in other cases; *mṛṣā*—illusion; *na*—not; *tathā*—so; *ubhaya*—of both (the real and illusion); *yuk*—the conjunction; *vyavahṛtaye*—for the sake of ordinary affairs; *vikalpaḥ*—an imaginary situation; *iṣitaḥ*—desired; *andha*—of blind men; *paramparayā*—by a succession; *bhramayati*—bewilder; *bhāratī*—the words of wisdom; *te*—Your; *uru*—numerous; *vṛttibhiḥ*—with their semantic functions; *uktha*—by ritual utterances; *jaḍān*—dulled.

TRANSLATION

It may be proposed that this world is permanently real because it is generated from the permanent reality, but such an argument is subject to logical refutation. Sometimes, indeed, the apparent nondifference of a cause and its effect fails to prove true, and at other times the product of something real is illusory. Furthermore, this world cannot be permanently real, for it partakes of the natures of not only the absolute reality but also the illusion disguising that reality. Actually, the visible forms of this world are just an imaginary arrangement resorted to by a succession of ignorant persons in order to facilitate their material affairs. With their various meanings and implications, the learned words of Your *Vedas* bewilder all persons whose minds have been dulled by hearing the incantations of sacrificial rituals.

PURPORT

According to Śrīla Viśvanātha Cakravartī Ṭhākura, the *Upaniṣads* teach that this created world is real but temporary. This is the understanding that devotees of Lord Viṣṇu adhere to. But there are also materialistic philosophers, like the proponents of Jaimini Ṛṣi's Karma-mīmāṁsā, who claim that this world is the only reality and exists eternally. For Jaimini, the cycle of karmic action and reaction is perpetual, with no possibility of liberation into a different, transcendental realm. This viewpoint, however, is shown to be fallacious by a careful examination of the Upaniṣadic *mantras,* which contain many descriptions of a higher, spiritual existence. For example, *sad eva saumyedam agra āsīd ekam evādvitīyam:* "My dear boy, the Absolute Truth alone existed prior to this creation, one without a second." (*Chāndogya Up.* 6.2.1) Also, *vijñānam ānandaṁ brahma:* "The supreme reality is divine knowledge and bliss." (*Bṛhad-āraṇyaka Up.* 3.9.34)

In this prayer of the personified *Vedas,* the materialists' argument is summed up in the words *sata idam utthitaṁ sat:* "The visible world is permanently real because it is generated from the permanent reality." In general, this argument goes, that which is produced from a certain thing is composed of that thing. For example, earrings and other ornaments made from gold share gold's substance. Thus, the Mimāṁsā logicians conclude, since the world as we know it is a manifestation of an eternal reality, it is also eternally real. But the Sanskrit ablative expression *sataḥ,* "from the eternal reality," implies a definite separation of cause and effect. Therefore, what is created from *sat,* the permanent reality, must be significantly different from it—in other words, temporary. In this way the argument of the materialists is flawed because it proves just the opposite of what it is intended to prove (*tarka-hatam*), namely that the world as we know it is all that exists, that it is eternal, and that there is no separate, transcendental reality.

In defense, the Mīmāṁsakas may claim that they are not trying to prove nondifference *per se,* but rather trying to disprove the possibility of difference, or in other words, the possibility of any reality separate from the known world. This attempt to support the Mīmāṁsā argument is easily refuted by the phrase *vyabhicarati kva ca:* that is to say, there are counterexamples that deviate from the general rule. Sometimes, indeed, the source is very different from what it produces, as in the case of a man and his young son, or of a hammer and the destruction of a clay pot.

But, the Mīmāṁsakas reply, the creation of the universe is not the same kind of causation as your counterexamples: the father and the hammer are only efficient causes, whereas the *sat* is also this universe's ingredient cause. This reply is anticipated by the words *kva ca mṛṣā* ("and sometimes the effect is illusory"). In the case of the false perception of a snake where there is a rope on the ground, the rope is the snake-illusion's ingredient cause, differing in many respects from the imagined snake, most obviously in its being real.

The Mīmāṁsakas once more rejoin, But the ingredient cause of the illusory snake is not just the rope by itself: it is the rope plus the observer's ignorance (*avidyā*). Since *avidyā* is not a substance, the snake it produces is called an illusion. Yet the same is true, the personified *Vedas* reply, in the case of the universe's creation from *sat* in conjunction with ignorance (*tathobhaya-yuk*); here the unreal element of illusion, Māyā, is the living beings' misconception that their own bodies and other changing material forms are permanent.

But, rejoin the Mīmāṁsakas, our experience of this world is valid because the things we experience are useful for practical activity. If our experience were not valid, we could never be sure that our perceptions corresponded to the facts. We would be like a man who, despite exhaustive examination, would still have to suspect that a rope might be a snake. No, the *śrutis* here answer, the temporary configurations of matter are nonetheless an illusory imitation of the eternal spiritual reality, cleverly concocted to fulfill the conditioned living entities' desire for material activity (*vyavahṛtaye vikalpa iṣitaḥ*). The illusion of this world's permanence is sustained by a succession of blind men who learn the materialistic idea from their predecessors and pass on this illusion to their descendants. Anyone can see that an illusion often continues by the momentum of lingering mental impressions, even when its basis is no longer present. Thus throughout history blind philosophers have misled other blind men by convincing them of the absurd idea that they can reach perfection by engaging in mundane rituals. Foolish people may be willing to exchange counterfeit coins among one another, but a wise man knows that such money is useless for the practical business of buying food, medicine and other necessities. And if given in charity, counterfeit money will earn no pious credit.

But, say the Mīmāṁsakas, how can the sincere performer of Vedic rituals be a deluded fool, since the *Saṁhitās* and *Brāhmaṇas* of the Vedic scriptures establish that the fruits of *karma* are eternal? For example, *akṣayyaṁ ha vai cāturmāsya-yājinaḥ su-kṛtaṁ bhavati:* "For one who observes the Cāturmāsya vows there arises inexhaustible good *karma*," and *apāma somam amṛtā babhūma:* "We have drunk the *soma* and become immortal." (*Ṛg Veda* 8.43.3)

The *śrutis* reply by pointing out that the Personality of Godhead's learned words, comprising the *Vedas,* bewilder those whose weak intelligence has been crushed by the weight of too much faith in *karma.* The specific word used here is *uru-vṛttibhiḥ,* which indicates that the Vedic *mantras,* with their confusing variety of meanings in the semantic modes of *gauṇa, lakṣaṇā* and so on, protect their sublime mysteries from all but those who have faith in Lord Viṣṇu. The *Vedas* do not truly mean to say in their injunctions that the fruits of *karma* are eternal, but only indirectly describe in metaphors the praiseworthiness of regulated sacrifices. The *Chāndogya Upaniṣad* states in no uncertain terms that the results of ritual *karma* are impermanent: *tad yatheha karma-cito lokaḥ kṣīyate evam evāmutra puṇya-cito lokaḥ kṣīyate.* "Just as whatever benefit one works hard to attain in this world is eventually depleted, so whatever life one earns for oneself in the next world by his piety will also eventually end." (*Chāndogya Up.* 8.1.16) According to the testimony of numerous *śruti-mantras,* the entire material universe is but a temporary emanation of the Supreme Truth; the *Muṇḍaka Upaniṣad,* for one, says:

yathorṇa-nābhiḥ sṛjate gṛhṇate ca
yathā pṛthivyām oṣadhayaḥ sambhavanti
yathā sataḥ puruṣāt keśa-lomāni
tathākṣarāt sambhavatīha viśvam

"As a web is expanded and withdrawn by a spider, as plants grow from the earth, and as hair grows from a living person's head and body, so this universe is generated from the inexhaustible Supreme." (*Muṇḍaka Up.* 1.1.7)

Śrīla Śrīdhara Svāmī prays,

udbhūtaṁ bhavataḥ sato 'pi bhuvanaṁ san naiva sarpaḥ srajaḥ
kurvat kāryaṁ apīha kūṭa-kanakaṁ vedo 'pi naivaṁ paraḥ
advaitaṁ tava sat paraṁ tu paramānandaṁ padaṁ tan mudā
vande sundaram indirānuta hare mā muñca mām ānatam

"Although this world has arisen from You, who are the very substance of reality, it is not eternally real. The illusory snake appearing from a rope is not permanent reality, nor are the transformations produced from gold. The *Vedas* never say that they are. The actual, transcendental, nondual reality is Your supremely blissful personal kingdom. To that beautiful abode I offer my obeisances. O Lord Hari, to whom Goddess Indirā always bows down, I also bow to You. Therefore please never release me."

TEXT 37

न यदिदमग्र आस न भविष्यदतो निधनाद्
अनु मितमन्तरा त्वयि विभाति मृषैकरसे ।
अत उपमीयते द्रविणजातिविकल्पपथैर्
वितथमनोविलासमृतमित्यवयन्त्यबुधाः ॥३७॥

na yad idam agra āsa na bhaviṣyad ato nidhanād
anu mitam antarā tvayi vibhāti mṛṣaika-rase
ata upamīyate draviṇa-jāti-vikalpa-pathair
vitatha-mano-vilāsam ṛtam ity avayanty abudhāḥ

na—not; *yat*—because; *idam*—this (universe); *agre*—in the beginning; *āsa*—existed; *na bhaviṣyat*—it will not exist; *ataḥ*—hence; *nidhanāt anu*—after its annihilation; *mitam*—deduced; *antarā*—in the meantime; *tvayi*—within You; *vibhāti*—it appears; *mṛṣā*—false; *eka-rase*—whose experience of spiritual ecstasy is unchanging; *ataḥ*—thus; *upamīyate*—it is understood by comparison; *draviṇa*—of material substance; *jāti*—in the categories; *vikalpa*—of the transformations; *pathaiḥ*—with the varieties; *vitatha*—contrary to fact; *manaḥ*—of the mind; *vilāsam*—fantasy; *ṛtam*—real; *iti*—so; *avayanti*—think; *abudhāḥ*—the unintelligent.

TRANSLATION

Since this universe did not exist prior to its creation and will no longer exist after its annihilation, we conclude that in the interim it is nothing more than a manifestation imagined to be visible within You, whose spiritual enjoyment never changes. We liken this universe to the transformation of various material substances into diverse forms. Certainly those who believe that this figment of the imagination is substantially real are less intelligent.

PURPORT

Having thus defeated all attempts of the ritualists to prove the substantial reality of material creation, the personified *Vedas* now present positive evidence to the contrary—that this world is unreal in that it is temporary. Before the creation of the universe and after its dissolution, only the spiritual reality of the Supreme Lord, along with His abode and entourage, continue to exist. The *śrutis* confirm this: *ātmā vā idam eka evāgra āsīt.* "Prior to the creation of this universe, only the Self existed." (*Aitareya Up.* 1.1) *Nāsad āsīn no sad āsīt tadānīm:* "At that time neither the subtle nor the gross aspects of matter were present." (*Ṛg Veda* 10.129.1)

One can understand the relativity of creation by an analogy. When basic materials like clay and metal are processed and shaped into various products, the created objects exist separately from the clay and metal only in name and form. The basic substance remains unchanged. Similarly, when the energies of the Supreme Lord are transformed into the known things of this world, these things exist separately from Him only in name and form. In the *Chāndogya Upaniṣad* (6.1.4–6), the sage Udālaka explains a similar analogy to his son: *yathā saumyaikena mṛt-piṇḍena sarvaṁ mṛn-mayaṁ vijñātaṁ syād vācārambhaṇaṁ vikāro nāma-dheyaṁ mṛttikety eva satyam.* "For example, my dear boy, by understanding a single lump of clay one can understand everything made from clay. The existence of transformed products is only a creation of language, a matter of assigning designations: the clay alone is real."

In conclusion, there is no convincing evidence that the things of this world are eternal or substantial, while there is overwhelming evidence that they are temporary and conditioned by false designations. Therefore only the ignorant can take the imaginary permutations of matter to be real.

Śrīla Śrīdhara Svāmī prays,

mukuṭa-kuṇḍala-kaṅkaṇa-kiṅkiṇī-
pariṇataṁ kanakaṁ paramārthataḥ
mahad-ahaṅkṛti-kha-pramukhaṁ tathā
nara-harer na paraṁ paramārthataḥ

"Transformations of gold such as crowns, earrings, bangles and ankle bells are not ultimately separate from gold itself. Similarly, the material elements—headed by the *mahat,* false ego and ether—are not ultimately separate from Lord Narahari."

TEXT 38

स यदजया त्वजामनुशयीत गुणांश्च जुषन्
भजति सरूपतां तदनु मृत्युमपेतभगः ।
त्वमुत जहासि तामहिरिव त्वचमात्तभगो
महसि महीयसेऽष्टगुणितेऽपरिमेयभगः ॥३८॥

sa yad ajayā tv ajām anuśayīta guṇāṁś ca juṣan
bhajati sarūpatāṁ tad anu mṛtyum apeta-bhagaḥ
tvam uta jahāsi tām ahir iva tvacam ātta-bhago
mahasi mahīyase 'ṣṭa-guṇite 'parimeya-bhagaḥ

saḥ—he (the individual living entity); *yat*—because; *ajayā*—by the influence of the material energy; *tu*—but; *ajām*—that material energy; *anuśayīta*—lies down next to; *guṇān*—her qualities; *ca*—and; *juṣan*—assuming; *bhajati*—he takes on; *sa-rūpatām*—forms resembling (the qualities of nature); *tat-anu*—following that; *mṛtyum*—death; *apeta*—deprived; *bhagaḥ*—of his assets; *tvam*—You; *uta*—on the other hand; *jahāsi*—leave aside; *tām*—her (the material energy); *ahiḥ*—a snake; *iva*—as if; *tvacam*—its (old, discarded) skin; *ātta-bhagaḥ*—endowed with all assets; *mahasi*—in Your spiritual powers; *mahīyase*—You are glorified; *aṣṭa-guṇite*—eightfold; *aparimeya*—unlimited; *bhagaḥ*—whose greatness.

TRANSLATION

The illusory material nature attracts the minute living entity to embrace her, and as a result he assumes forms composed of her qualities. Subsequently, he loses all his spiritual qualities and must undergo repeated deaths. You, however, avoid the material energy in the same way that a snake abandons its old skin. Glorious in Your possession of eight mystic perfections, You enjoy unlimited opulences.

PURPORT

Although the *jīva* is pure spirit, qualitatively equal with the Supreme Lord, he is prone to being degraded by embracing the ignorance of material illusion. When he becomes entranced by the allurements of Māyā, he accepts bodies and senses that are designed to let him indulge in forgetfulness. Produced from the raw material of Māyā's three modes—goodness, passion and nescience—these bodies envelop the spirit soul in varieties of unhappiness, culminating in death and rebirth.

The Supreme Soul and the individual soul share the same spiritual nature, but the Supreme Soul cannot be entrapped by ignorance like His infinitesimal companion. Smoke may engulf the glow of a small molten sphere of copper, covering its light in darkness, but the vast globe of the sun will never suffer the same kind of eclipse. Māyā, after all, is the Personality of Godhead's faithful maidservant, the outward expansion of His internal, Yogamāyā potency. *Śrī Nārada Pañcarātra* thus states, in a conversation between Śruti and Vidyā,

asyā āvarikā-śaktir
mahā-māyākhileśvarī
yayā mugdhaṁ jagat sarvaṁ
sarve dehābhimāninaḥ

"The covering potency derived from her is Mahā-māyā, the regulator of everything material. The entire universe becomes bewildered by her, and thus every living being falsely identifies with his material body."

Just as a snake casts aside his old skin, knowing that it is not part of his essential identity, so the Supreme Lord always avoids His external, material energy. There is no insufficiency or limit to any of His eightfold mystic opulences, consisting of *aṇimā* (the power to become infinitesimal), *mahimā* (the ability to become infinitely large) and so on. Therefore, the shadow of material darkness has no scope for entering the domain of His unequaled, resplendent glories.

For the sake of those whose realization of spiritual life is only gradually awakening, the *Upaniṣads* sometimes speak in general terms of *ātmā* or Brahman, not openly distinguishing the difference between the superior and inferior souls, the Paramātmā and *jīvātmā*. But often enough they describe this duality in unequivocal terms:

dvā suparṇā sayujā sakhāyā
samānaṁ vṛkṣaṁ pariṣasvajāte
tayor anyaḥ pippalaṁ svādv atty
anaśnann anyo 'bhicākaśīti

"Two companion birds sit together in the shelter of the same *pippala* tree. One of them is relishing the taste of the tree's berries, while the other refrains from eating and instead watches over His friend." (*Śvetāśvatara Up.* 4.6) In this analogy the two birds are the soul and the Supersoul, the tree is the body, and the taste of the berries are the varieties of sense pleasure.

Śrīla Śrīdhara Svāmī prays,

nṛtyantī tava vīkṣaṇāṅgaṇa-gatā kāla-svabhāvādibhir
bhāvān sattva-rajas-tamo-guṇa-mayān unmīlayantī bahūn
mām ākramya padā śirasy ati-bharaṁ sammardayanty āturaṁ
māyā te śaraṇaṁ gato 'smi nṛ-hare tvām eva tāṁ vāraya

"The glance You cast upon Your consort comprises time, the material propensities of the living entities, and so on. This glance dances upon her face, thus awakening the multitude of created entities, who take birth in the modes of goodness, passion and ignorance. O Lord Nṛhari, Your Māyā has put her foot on my head and is pressing down extremely hard, causing me great distress. Now I have come to You for shelter. Please make her desist."

TEXT 39

यदि न समुद्धरन्ति यतयो हृदि कामजटा
दुरधिगमोऽसतां हृदि गतोऽस्मृतकण्ठमणिः ।
असुतृपयोगिनामुभयतोऽप्यसुखं भगवन्न्
अनपगतान्तकादनधिरूढपदाद् भवतः ॥३९॥

yadi na samuddharanti yatayo hṛdi kāma-jaṭā
duradhigamo 'satāṁ hṛdi gato 'smṛta-kaṇṭha-maṇiḥ
asu-tṛpa-yoginām ubhayato 'py asukhaṁ bhagavann
anapagatāntakād anadhirūḍha-padād bhavataḥ

yadi—if; *na samuddharanti*—they do not uproot; *yatayaḥ*—persons in the renounced order of life; *hṛdi*—in their hearts; *kāma*—of material desire; *jaṭāḥ*—the traces; *duradhigamaḥ*—impossible to be realized; *asatām*—for the impure; *hṛdi*—in the heart; *gataḥ*—having entered; *asmṛta*—forgotten; *kaṇṭha*—on one's neck; *maṇiḥ*—a jewel; *asu*—their life airs; *tṛpa*—who gratify; *yoginām*—for practitioners of *yoga;* *ubhayataḥ*—in both (worlds); *api*—even; *asukham*—unhappiness; *bhagavan*—O Personality of Godhead; *anapagata*—not gone away; *antakāt*—from death; *anadhirūḍha*—unobtained; *padāt*—whose kingdom; *bhavataḥ*—from You.

TRANSLATION

Members of the renounced order who fail to uproot the last traces of material desire in their hearts remain impure, and thus You do not allow them to understand You. Although You are present within their hearts, for them You are like a jewel worn around the neck of a man who has totally forgotten it is there. O Lord, those who pratice *yoga* only for sense gratification must suffer punishment both in this life and the next: from death, who will not release them, and from You, whose kingdom they cannot reach.

PURPORT

A mere show of renunciation is not sufficient to gain a person entrance into the kingdom of God. One must undergo a thorough change of heart, symptomized by a complete lack of interest in the self-destructive habits of sense gratification, both gross and subtle. Not only must the true sage refrain from even thinking of illicit sex, meat-eating, intoxication and gambling, but he must also give up his desires for reputation and position. All together these demands add up to a formidable challenge, but the fruits of true renunciation in Kṛṣṇa consciousness are well worth a lifetime of endeavor.

The *Muṇḍaka Upaniṣad* (3.2.2) confirms the statements of this verse: *kāmān yaḥ kāmayate manyamānaḥ sa karmabhir jāyate tatra tatra.* "Even a thoughtful renunciant, if he maintains any worldly desires, will be forced by his karmic reactions to take birth again and again in various circumstances." Philosophers and *yogīs* work hard to become free from birth and death, but because they are unwilling to surrender their proud independence, their meditations are devoid of devotion to the Supreme Lord, and thus they fall short of the perfection of renunciation—pure love of God. This pure love is the only goal of a sincere Vaiṣṇava, and therefore he must vigilantly resist the natural temptations of profit, adoration and distinction, and also the impulse to merge into an all-consuming impersonal oblivion. As Śrīla Rūpa Gosvāmī states in his *Bhakti-rasāmṛta-sindhu* (1.1.11),

anyābhilāṣitā-śūnyaṁ
jñāna-karmādy-anāvṛtam
ānukūlyena kṛṣṇānu-
śīlanaṁ bhaktir uttamā

"When first-class devotional service develops, one must be devoid of all material desires, knowledge obtained by monistic philosophy, and fruitive action. The devotee must constantly serve Kṛṣṇa favorably, as Kṛṣṇa desires."

For those who undergo rigorous *yoga* discipline only to please their senses, prolonged suffering is inevitable. Hunger, disease, the degeneration of old age, injury from accident, violence from others—these are a few of the limitless varieties of suffering one can experience to varying degrees in this world. And ultimately, death awaits, followed by painful punishment for sinful activities. Especially those who have freely indulged in sensual enjoyments at the cost of others' lives can expect punishment so severe it is unimaginable. But the greatest pain of material existence is not misfortune in this life or being sent to hell after death: it is the emptiness of having forgotten one's eternal relationship with the Personality of Godhead.

Śrīla Śrīdhara Svāmī prays,

dambha-nyāsa-miṣeṇa vañcita-janaṁ bhogaika-cintāturaṁ
sammuhyantam ahar-niśaṁ viracitodyoga-klamair ākulam
ājñā-laṅghinam ajñam ajña-janatā-sammānanāsan-madaṁ
dīnānātha dayā-nidhāna paramānanda prabho pāhi mām

"The hypocrite who cheats himself by a pretense of renunciation thinks only of sense enjoyment and thus suffers constantly. Bewildered day and night, he is overwhelmed by the exhausting endeavors he contrives for himself. This fool disobeys Your laws and is corrupted by greed for respect from other fools. O protector of the fallen, O bestower of mercy, O supremely blissful master, please save that person, myself."

TEXT 40

त्वदवगमी न वेत्ति भवदुत्थशुभाशुभयोर्
गुणविगुणान्वयांस्तर्हि देहभृतां च गिरः ।
अनुयुगमन्वहं सगुण गीतपरम्परया
श्रवणभृतो यतस्त्वमपवर्गगतिर्मनुजैः ॥४०॥

tvad-avagamī na vetti bhavad-uttha-śubhāśubhayor
guṇa-viguṇānvayāṁs tarhi deha-bhṛtāṁ ca giraḥ
anu-yugam anv-ahaṁ sa-guṇa gīta-paramparayā
śravaṇa-bhṛto yatas tvam apavarga-gatir manu-jaiḥ

tvat—You; *avagamī*—one who understands; *na vetti*—does not pay regard; *bhavat*—from You; *uttha*—rising; *śubha-aśubhayoḥ*—of the auspiciousness and inauspiciousness; *guṇa-viguṇa*—of good and bad; *anvayān*—to the attributions; *tarhi*—consequently; *deha-bhṛtām*—of embodied living beings; *ca*—also; *giraḥ*—the words; *anu-yugam*—in every age; *anu-aham*—every day; *sa-guṇa*—O You who are endowed with qualities; *gīta*—of recitation; *paramparayā*—by the chain of succession; *śravaṇa*—through hearing; *bhṛtaḥ*—carried; *yataḥ*—because of this; *tvam*—You; *apavarga*—of liberation; *gatiḥ*—the ultimate goal; *manu-jaiḥ*—by human beings, descendants of Manu.

TRANSLATION

When a person realizes You, he no longer cares about his good and bad fortune arising from past pious and sinful acts, since it is You alone who control this good and bad fortune. Such a realized devotee also disregards what ordinary living beings say about him. Every day he fills his ears with Your glories, which are recited in each age by the unbroken succession of Manu's descendants, and thus You become his ultimate salvation.

PURPORT

Text 39 clearly states that impersonalistic renunciants will continue to suffer birth after birth. One may ask if this suffering is justified, since a renunciant's status should exempt him from suffering, whether or not he has a devotional attitude. As the *śruti-mantra* states, *eṣa nityo mahimā brāhmaṇasya na karmaṇā vardhate no kanīyān:* "The perpetual glory of a *brāhmaṇa* is never increased or diminished as a result of any of his activities." (*Bṛhad-āraṇyaka Up.* 4.4.28) To counter the objection thus raised, the personified *Vedas* offer this prayer.

Impersonalistic *jñānīs* and *yogīs* do not qualify for full relief from the reactions of *karma*—a privilege reserved only for those who are *tvad-avagamī*, pure devotees constantly engaged in hearing and chanting topics concerning the Personality of Godhead. The devotees hold firm to the Supreme Lord's lotus feet by their unrelenting Kṛṣṇa consciousness, and so they need not strictly adhere to the ritual commands and prohibitions of the *Vedas*. They can fearlessly ignore the apparent good and bad reactions of the work they do only for the Supreme Lord's pleasure, and they can equally ignore whatever others may say about them, whether praise or condemnation. A humble Vaiṣṇava absorbed in the pleasure of *saṅkīrtana*, glorification of the Lord, pays little heed to praise of himself, which he assumes mistaken, and happily accepts all criticism, which he deems appropriate.

One receives the authorized chanting of the Supreme Lord's glories by faithfully hearing from "the sons of Manu," the disciplic succession of saintly Vaiṣṇavas coming down through the ages. These sages emulate well the example of Svāyambhuva Manu, the forefather of mankind:

ayāta-yāmās tasyāsan
yāmāḥ svāntara-yāpanāḥ
śṛṇvato dhyāyato viṣṇoḥ
kurvato bruvataḥ kathāḥ

"Although Svāyambhuva's life gradually came to an end, his long life, consisting of a *manv-antara* era, was not spent in vain, since he always engaged in hearing, contemplating, writing down and chanting the pastimes of the Lord." (*Bhāg.* 3.22.35)

Even if a neophyte devotee falls from the standards of proper behavior by the force of his past bad habits, the all-merciful Lord will not reject him. As Lord Śrī Kṛṣṇa states,

tair ahaṁ pūjanīyo vai
bhadrakṛṣṇa-nivāsibhiḥ
tad-dharma-gati-hīnā ye
tasyāṁ mayi parāyaṇāḥ

kalinā grasitā ye vai
teṣāṁ tasyām avasthitiḥ
yathā tvaṁ saha putraiś ca
yathā rudro gaṇaiḥ saha
yathā śriyābhiyukto 'haṁ
tathā bhakto mama priyaḥ

"For those who live in Bhadrakṛṣṇa [the district of Mathurā], I am the object of all worship. Even if the residents of that place fail to properly cultivate the religious principles that one should observe in the holy land, they still become devoted to Me just by virtue of living there. Even if Kali [the present age of quarrel] has them in his grip, they still get credit for living in this place. My devotee who lives in Mathurā is just as dear to Me as you [Brahmā] and your sons—Rudra and his followers—and Goddess Śrī and My own self."

Śrīla Śrīdhara Svāmī prays,

avagamaṁ tava me diśa mādhava
sphurati yan na sukhāsukha-saṅgamaḥ
śravaṇa-varṇana-bhāvam athāpi vā
na hi bhavāmi yathā vidhi-kiṅkaraḥ

"O Mādhava, please let Me understand You so that I will no longer experience the entanglement of material pleasure and pain. Or else, just as good, please give me a taste for hearing and chanting about You. In that way I will no longer be a slave to ritual injunctions."

TEXT 41

द्युपतय एव ते न ययुरन्तमनन्ततया
त्वमपि यदन्तराण्डनिचया ननु सावरणाः ।
ख इव रजांसि वान्ति वयसा सह यच्छ्रुतयस्
त्वयि हि फलन्त्यतन्निरसनेन भवन्निधनाः ॥४१॥

dyu-pataya eva te na yayur antam anantatayā
tvam api yad-antarāṇḍa-nicayā nanu sāvaraṇāḥ
kha iva rajāṁsi vānti vayasā saha yac chrutayas
tvayi hi phalanty atan-nirasanena bhavan-nidhanāḥ

dyu—of heaven; *patayaḥ*—the masters; *eva*—even; *te*—Your; *na yayuḥ*—cannot reach; *antam*—the end; *anantatayā*—because of being unlimited; *tvam*—You; *api*—even; *yat*—whom; *antara*—within; *aṇḍa*—of universes; *nicayāḥ*—multitudes; *nanu*—indeed; *sa*—along with; *āvaraṇāḥ*—their outer shells; *khe*—in the sky; *iva*—as; *rajāṁsi*—particles of dust; *vānti*—blow about; *vayasā saha*—with the wheel of time; *yat*—because; *śrutayaḥ*—the *Vedas; tvayi*—in You; *hi*—indeed; *phalanti*—bear fruit; *atat*—of that which is distinct from the Absolute Truth; *nirasanena*—by the elimination; *bhavat*—in You; *nidhanāḥ*—whose ultimate conclusion.

TRANSLATION

Because You are unlimited, neither the lords of heaven nor even You Yourself can ever reach the end of Your glories. The countless universes, each enveloped in its shell, are compelled by the wheel of time to wander within You, like particles of dust blowing about in the sky. The *śrutis*, following their method of eliminating everything separate from the Supreme, become successful by revealing You as their final conclusion.

PURPORT

Now, in their last prayer, the personified *Vedas* draw the conclusion that all *śrutis*, by their various literal and metaphorical references, ultimately describe the Supreme Personality of Godhead's identity, personal qualities and powers. The *Upaniṣads* glorify Him without end: *yad ūrdhvaṁ gārgi divo yad arvāk pṛthivyā yad antarā dyāvā-pṛthivī ime yad bhūtaṁ bhavac ca bhaviṣyac ca.* "My dear daughter of Garga, His greatness encompasses everything above us in heaven, everything below the surface of the earth, everything in between heaven and earth, and everything that has ever existed, exists now or will ever exist." (*Bṛhad-āraṇyaka Up.* 3.8.4)

To illuminate the meaning of this final prayer by the *śrutis*, Śrīla Viśvanātha Cakravartī Ṭhākura presents the following conversation between Lord Nārāyaṇa and the personified *Vedas:* The *Vedas* said, "Lord Brahmā and the other rulers of the heavenly planets have not yet reached the end of Your glories. What can we do, then, since we are insignificant in comparison to these great demigods?"

Lord Nārāyaṇa replied, "No, you *śrutis* are gifted with more sublime vision than the demigods who rule this universe. You will be able to reach the end of My glories if you do not stop now."

"But even You cannot find Your own limit!"

"If that is the case, what do you mean when you call Me omniscient and omnipotent?"

"We conclude that You possess these features from the very fact that You are limitless. Certainly if one is ignorant of something that does not even exist, like a rabbit's horn, that does not detract from his omniscience, and if one fails to find such a nonentity, that does not limit his omnipotence. You are so vast that multitudes of universes float within You. Each of these universes is surrounded by seven shells composed of the material elements, and each of these concentric shells is ten times larger than the one within it. Although we can never fully describe the truth about You, we perfect our existence by declaring that You are the true topic of the *Vedas.*"

"But why do you seem dissatisfied?"

"Because in the *Vedas* Śrīla Vyāsadeva has described the transcendental existence of Brahman, Paramātmā and Bhagavān only briefly. When he saw the need to elaborate on his description of the Supreme, he chose to concentrate on the subject of Brahman, the impersonal aspect of the Supreme known as *tat* ("that"), explaining Brahman by negating whatever is different from it. Just as in a field where a chest of jewels has been accidentally spilled the jewels can be recovered by removing unwanted stones, twigs and refuse, so within the visible realm of Māyā and her creations the Absolute Truth can be found by a process of elimination. Since we *Vedas* cannot possibly enumerate every material category, individual entity, quality and motion in the universe from the beginning to the end of time, and since the truth concerning Brahman, Paramātmā and Bhagavān would still remain untouched even if we described all these things and then discarded them, by this means of investigation we never expect to reach a final definition of You. Only by Your mercy can we make some attempt to approach You, the supremely inaccessible Absolute Truth."

There are many statements of *śruti* that carry on the work of *atan-nirasanam*, the process of distinguishing the Supreme from everything inferior. The *Bṛhad-āraṇyaka Upaniṣad* (3.8.8), for example, states, *asthūlam anaṇu ahrasvam adīrgham alohitam asneham acchāyam atamo 'vāyv anākāśam asaṅgam arasam agandham acakṣuṣkam aśrotram agamano 'tejaskam aprāṇam asukham amātram anantaram abāhyam.* "It is neither big nor small, short nor long, hot nor cool, in shadow nor in darkness. Nor is it the wind or the ether. It is not in contact with anything, and it has no taste, smell, eyes, ears, motion, potency, life air, pleasure, measurement, inside or outside." The *Kena Upaniṣad* (3) declares, *anyad eva tad viditād atho aviditād adhi:* "Brahman is distinct from what is known and also from what is yet to be known." And the *Kaṭha Upaniṣad* (2.14) says, *anyatra dharmād anyatrādharmād anyatrāsmāt kṛtākṛtāt:* "Brahman is outside the scope of religion and irreligion, pious and impious action."

According to the rules of linguistics and logic, a negation cannot be unbounded: there must some positive counterpart of which it is the negation. In the case of the *Vedas'* exhaustive *atan-nirasanam*, their denial that anything material is absolutely real, the counterpart is the Supreme Personality of Godhead, Lord Śrī Kṛṣṇa.

Śrīla Śrīdhara Svāmī prays,

dyu-patayo vidur antam ananta te
na ca bhavān na giraḥ śruti-maulayaḥ
tvayi phalanti yato nama ity ato
jaya jayeti bhaje tava tat-padam

"The gods of heaven do not know Your limit, O endless Lord, and even You do not know it. Because the transcendental words of the topmost *śrutis* become fruitful by revealing You, I offer You my obeisances. Thus I worship You as the Absolute Truth, saying 'All glories to You! All glories to You!'"

TEXT 42

श्रीभगवानुवाच
इत्येतद् ब्रह्मणः पुत्रा आश्रुत्यात्मानुशासनम् ।
सनन्दनमथानर्चुः सिद्धा ज्ञात्वात्मनो गतिम् ॥४२॥

śrī-bhagavān uvāca
ity etad brahmaṇaḥ putrā
āśrutyātmānuśāsanam
sanandanam athānarcuḥ
siddhā jñātvātmano gatim

śrī-bhagavān uvāca—the Supreme Lord (Śrī Nārāyaṇa Ṛṣi) said; *iti*—thus; *etat*—this; *brahmaṇaḥ*—of Brahmā; *putrāḥ*—the sons; *āśrutya*—having heard; *ātma*—about the Self; *anuśāsanam*—instruction; *sanandanam*—the sage Sanandana; *atha*—then; *ānarcuḥ*—they worshiped; *siddhāḥ*—perfectly satisfied; *jñātvā*—understanding; *ātmanaḥ*—their own; *gatim*—ultimate destination.

TRANSLATION

The Supreme Lord, Śrī Nārāyaṇa Ṛṣi, said: Having heard these instructions about the Supreme Self, the Personality of Godhead, the sons of Brahmā now understood their final destination. They felt perfectly satisfied and honored Sanandana with their worship.

PURPORT

Śrīla Jīva Gosvāmī explains that *ātmānuśāsanam* can be understood both as instructions given to benefit the *jīva* souls and as instructions about the living entity's relationship with the foundation of all existence. Similarly, *ātmano gatim* means both the destination of the *jīva* soul and the means of reaching the Supreme Soul. By hearing the twenty-eight prayers of the personified *Vedas*, which comprise the elucidation of the *brahmopaniṣat* spoken at the beginning of this chapter, the sages assembled in Brahmaloka made great progress toward their goal of pure love of God.

TEXT 43

इत्यशेषसमाम्नायपुराणोपनिषद्रसः ।
समुद्धृतः पूर्वजातैर्व्योमयानैर्महात्मभिः ॥४३॥

ity aśeṣa-samāmnāya-
purāṇopaniṣad-rasaḥ

samuddhṛtaḥ pūrva-jātair
vyoma-yānair mahātmabhiḥ

iti—thus; *aśeṣa*—of all; *samāmnāya*—the *Vedas; purāṇa*—and *Purāṇas; upaniṣat*—comprising the confidential mystery; *rasaḥ*—the nectar; *samuddhṛtaḥ*—distilled; *pūrva*—in the distant past; *jātaiḥ*—by those who were born; *vyoma*—in the higher regions of the universe; *yānaiḥ*—who travel; *mahā-ātmabhiḥ*—saintly persons.

TRANSLATION

Thus the ancient saints who travel in the upper heavens distilled this nectarean and confidential essence of all the *Vedas* and *Purāṇas.*

TEXT 44

त्वं चैतद् ब्रह्मदायाद श्रद्धयात्मानुशासनम् ।
धारयंश्चर गां कामं कामानां भर्जनं नृणाम् ॥४४॥

tvaṁ caitad brahma-dāyāda
śraddhayātmānuśāsanam
dhārayaṁś cara gāṁ kāmaṁ
kāmānāṁ bharjanaṁ nṛṇām

tvam—you; *ca*—and; *etat*—this; *brahma*—of Brahmā; *dāyāda*—O heir (Nārada); *śraddhayā*—with faith; *ātma-ānuśāsanam*—instruction in the science of the Self; *dhārayan*—meditating upon; *cara*—wander; *gām*—the earth; *kāmam*—as you wish; *kāmānām*—the material desires; *bharjanam*—which burns up; *nṛṇām*—of men.

TRANSLATION

And as you wander the earth at will, My dear son of Brahmā, you should faithfully meditate on these instructions concerning the science of the Self, which burn up the material desires of all men.

PURPORT

Nārada, the son of Brahmā, heard this account from Śrī Nārāyaṇa Ṛṣi. The epithet *brahma-dāyāda* also means that Nārada attained Brahman effortlessly, just as if it were His inherited birthright.

TEXT 45

श्रीशुक उवाच
एवं स ऋषिणादिष्टं गृहीत्वा श्रद्धयात्मवान् ।
पूर्णः श्रुतधरो राजन्नाह वीरव्रतो मुनिः ॥४५॥

śrī-śuka uvāca
evaṁ sa ṛṣiṇādiṣṭaṁ
gṛhītvā śraddhayātmavān
pūrṇaḥ śruta-dharo rājann
āha vīra-vrato muniḥ

śrī-śukaḥ uvāca—Śukadeva Gosvāmī said; *evam*—in this manner; *saḥ*—he (Nārada); *ṛṣiṇā*—by the sage (Śrī Nārāyaṇa Ṛṣi); *ādiṣṭam*—ordered; *gṛhītvā*—accepting; *śraddhayā*—faithfully; *ātma-vān*—self-possessed; *pūrṇaḥ*—successful in all his purposes; *śruta*—upon what he had heard; *dharaḥ*—meditating; *rājan*—O King (Parīkṣit); *āha*—said; *vīra*—like that of a heroic *kṣatriya; vrataḥ*—whose vow; *muniḥ*—the sage.

TRANSLATION

Śukadeva Gosvāmī said: When Śrī Nārāyaṇa Ṛṣi ordered him in this way, the self-possessed sage Nārada, whose vow is as heroic as a warrior's, accepted the command with firm faith. Now successful in all his purposes, he thought about what he had heard, O King, and replied to the Lord as follows.

TEXT 46

श्रीनारद उवाच
नमस्तस्मै भगवते कृष्णायामलकीर्तये ।
यो धत्ते सर्वभूतानामभवायोशती: कला: ॥४६॥

śrī-nārada uvāca
namas tasmai bhagavate
kṛṣṇāyāmala-kīrtaye
yo dhatte sarva-bhūtānām
abhavāyośatīḥ kalāḥ

śrī-nāradaḥ uvāca—Śrī Nārada said; *namaḥ*—obeisances; *tasmai*—to Him; *bhagavate*—the Supreme Lord; *kṛṣṇāya*—Kṛṣṇa; *amala*—spotless; *kīrtaye*—whose glories; *yaḥ*—who; *dhatte*—manifests; *sarva*—of all; *bhūtānām*—living beings; *abhavāya*—for the liberation; *uśatīḥ*—all-attractive; *kalāḥ*—expansions.

TRANSLATION

Śrī Nārada said: I offer My obeisances to Him of spotless fame, the Supreme Lord Kṛṣṇa, who manifests His all-attractive personal expansions so that all living beings can achieve liberation.

PURPORT

Śrīla Śrīdhara Svāmī remarks that Nārada's addressing Śrī Nārāyaṇa Ṛṣi as an incarnation of Lord Kṛṣṇa is perfectly appropriate, in accordance with the following statement of *Śrīmad-Bhāgavatam* (1.3.28): *ete cāṁśa-kalāḥ puṁsaḥ/ kṛṣṇas tu bhagavān svayam.* "All of the above-mentioned incarnations [including Nārāyaṇa Ṛṣi] are either plenary portions or portions of the plenary portions of the Lord, but Lord Śrī Kṛṣṇa is the original Personality of Godhead."

In his commentary on this verse, Śrīla Viśvanātha Cakravartī has Lord Nārāyaṇa Ṛṣi asking, "Why do you offer obeisances to Kṛṣṇa instead of Me, your *guru,* who am standing here before you?" Nārada explains his action by saying that Lord Kṛṣṇa assumes all-attractive incarnations like Śrī Nārāyaṇa Ṛṣi to end the conditioned souls' material life. By offering obeisances to Lord Kṛṣṇa, therefore, Nārada honors Nārāyaṇa Ṛṣi and all other manifestations of Godhead as well.

This prayer of Nārada's is the essential nectar he has extracted from the personified *Vedas'* prayers, which themselves were churned from the sweet ocean of all secrets of the *Vedas* and *Purāṇas.* As the *Gopāla-tāpanī Upaniṣad* (*Pūrva* 50) recommends, *tasmāt kṛṣṇa eva paro devas taṁ dhyāyet taṁ rasayet taṁ bhajet taṁ yajed iti. oṁ tat sat:* "Therefore Kṛṣṇa is the Supreme Godhead. One should meditate on Him, relish the taste of reciprocating loving exchanges with Him, worship Him and offer sacrifice to Him."

TEXT 47

इत्याद्यमृषिमानम्य तच्छिष्यांश्च महात्मनः ।
ततोऽगादाश्रमं साक्षात्पितुर्द्वैपायनस्य मे ॥४७॥

ity ādyam ṛṣim ānamya
tac-chiṣyāṁś ca mahātmanaḥ
tato 'gād āśramaṁ sākṣāt
pitur dvaipāyanasya me

iti—thus speaking; *ādyam*—foremost; *ṛṣim*—to the sage (Nārāyaṇa Ṛṣi); *ānamya*—bowing down; *tat*—His; *śiṣyān*—to the disciples; *ca*—and; *mahā-ātmanaḥ*—great saints; *tataḥ*—from there (Nārāyaṇāśrama); *agāt*—he went; *āśramam*—to the hermitage; *sākṣāt*—direct; *pituḥ*—of the progenitor; *dvaipāyanasya*—Dvaipāyana Vedavyāsa; *me*—my.

TRANSLATION

[Śukadeva Gosvāmī continued:] After saying this, Nārada bowed down to Śrī Nārāyaṇa Ṛṣi, the foremost of sages, and also to His saintly disciples. He then returned to the hermitage of my father, Dvaipāyana Vyāsa.

TEXT 48

सभाजितो भगवता कृतासनपरिग्रहः ।
तस्मै तद्वर्णयामास नारायणमुखाच्छ्रुतम् ॥४८॥

sabhājito bhagavatā
kṛtāsana-parigrahaḥ
tasmai tad varṇayām āsa
nārāyaṇa-mukhāc chrutam

sabhājitaḥ—honored; *bhagavatā*—by the personal expansion of the Supreme Lord (Vyāsadeva); *kṛta*—having done; *āsana*—of a seat; *parigrahaḥ*—the acceptance; *tasmai*—to him; *tat*—that; *varṇayām āsa*—he described; *nārāyaṇa-mukhāt*—from the mouth of Śrī Nārāyaṇa Ṛṣi; *śrutam*—what he had heard.

TRANSLATION

Vyāsadeva, the incarnation of the Personality of Godhead, respectfully greeted Nārada Muni and offered him a seat, which he accepted. Nārada then described to Vyāsa what he had heard from the mouth of Śrī Nārāyaṇa Ṛṣi.

TEXT 49

इत्येतद्वर्णितं राजन् यन्नः प्रश्नः कृतस्त्वया ।
यथा ब्रह्मण्यनिर्देश्ये निर्गुणेऽपि मनश्चरेत् ॥४९॥

ity etad varṇitaṁ rājan
yan naḥ praśnaḥ kṛtas tvayā
yathā brahmaṇy anirdeśye
nirguṇe 'pi manaś caret

iti—thus; *etat*—this; *varṇitam*—related; *rājan*—O King (Parīkṣit); *yat*—which; *naḥ*—to us; *praśnaḥ*—question; *kṛtaḥ*—made; *tvayā*—by you; *yathā*—how; *brahmaṇi*—in the Absolute Truth; *anirdeśye*—which cannot be described in words; *nirguṇe*—which has no material qualities; *api*—even; *manaḥ*—the mind; *caret*—moves.

TRANSLATION

Thus I have replied to the question You asked me, O King, concerning how the mind can have access to the Absolute Truth, which is indescribable by material words and devoid of material qualities.

TEXT 50

योऽस्योत्प्रेक्षक आदिमध्यनिधने योऽव्यक्तजीवेश्वरो
यः सृष्ट्वेदमनुप्रविश्य ऋषिणा चक्रे पुरः शास्ति ताः ।

यं सम्पद्य जहात्यजामनुशयी सुप्तः कुलायं यथा
तं कैवल्यनिरस्तयोनिमभयं ध्यायेदजस्रं हरिम् ॥५०॥

yo 'syotprekṣaka ādi-madhya-nidhane yo 'vyakta-jīveśvaro
yaḥ sṛṣṭvedam anupraviśya ṛṣiṇā cakre puraḥ śāsti tāḥ
yaṁ sampadya jahāty ajām anuśayī suptaḥ kulāyaṁ yathā
taṁ kaivalya-nirasta-yonim abhayaṁ dhyāyed ajasraṁ harim

yaḥ—who; *asya*—this (universe); *utprekṣakaḥ*—the one who watches over; *ādi*—in its beginning; *madhya*—middle; *nidhane*—and end; *yaḥ*—who; *avyakta*—of the unmanifested (material nature); *jīva*—and of the living entities; *īśvaraḥ*—the Lord; *yaḥ*—who; *sṛṣṭvā*—having sent forth; *idam*—this (universe); *anupraviśya*—entering; *ṛṣiṇā*—along with the *jīva* soul; *cakre*—produced; *puraḥ*—bodies; *śāsti*—regulates; *tāḥ*—them; *yam*—to whom; *sampadya*—by surrendering; *jahāti*—gives up; *ajām*—the unborn (material nature); *anuśayī*—embracing her; *suptaḥ*—a sleeping person; *kulāyam*—his body; *yathā*—as; *tam*—upon Him; *kaivalya*—by His purely spiritual status; *nirasta*—kept away; *yonim*—material birth; *abhayam*—for fearlessness; *dhyāyet*—one should meditate; *ajasram*—incessantly; *harim*—the Supreme Lord Kṛṣṇa.

TRANSLATION

He is the Lord who eternally watches over this universe, who exists before, during and after its manifestation. He is the master of both the unmanifest material energy and the spirit soul. After sending forth the creation He enters within it, accompanying each living entity. There He creates the material bodies and then remains as their regulator. By surrendering to Him one can escape the embrace of illusion, just as a dreaming person forgets his own body. One who wants liberation from fear should constantly meditate upon Him, Lord Hari, who is always on the platform of perfection and thus never subject to material birth.

PURPORT

By glancing upon the dormant universe at the time of sending forth the *jīva* souls into creation, the Supreme Lord provides all their necessities: For those living entities who are fruitive workers, He provides the intelligence and senses needed to achieve success in material work. For those who seek transcendental knowledge, He provides the intelligence by which they can merge into the spiritual effulgence of God, thus attaining liberation. And for the devotees He provides the understanding that leads them to His pure devotional service.

To arrange for these varied facilities, the Lord impels material nature to begin the process of universal evolution. Thus the Lord is the *nimitta-kāraṇam*, or effective cause, of creation. He is also the *upādāna-kāraṇam*, the ingredient cause, inasmuch as everything emanates from Him and He alone is constantly present before, during and after the manifestation of the created cosmos. Lord Nārāyaṇa Himself states this in the *Catuḥ-ślokī Bhāgavatam:*

aham evāsam evāgre
nānyad yat sad-asat-param
paścād ahaṁ yad etac ca
yo 'vaśiṣyate so 'smy aham

"It is I, the Personality of Godhead, who was existing before the creation, when there was nothing but Myself. Nor was there the material nature, the cause of this creation. That which you see now is also I, the Personality of Godhead, and after annihilation what remains will also be I, the Personality of Godhead." (*Bhāg.* 2.9.33) Primeval Māyā and the *jīva* soul may deserve the respective titles of *upādāna* and *nimitta* causes of creation in a relative sense, but the Lord, after all, is the origin of both of them.

Until he chooses to accept the mercy of the Personality of Godhead, the *jīva* soul is *anuśayī,* helplessly bound up in the embrace of illusion. When he turns to the Lord's worship, he becomes *anuśayī* in a different sense: fallen like a rod to pay obeisances at the Lord's feet. By that surrender the soul easily casts illusion aside. Even though the liberated soul may still seem to be living in a material body, the connection he has with it is only an external appearance; he pays no more regard to it than a sleeping man pays to his body while busily engaged far, far away in his dream-world.

One gives up ignorance by abondoning false identification with one's material body. Sometimes one can achieve this state only by a severe effort that takes many lifetimes, but in some cases the Lord may show special consideration for one He favors, regardless of how little credit that soul may have earned by regulated practice. In the words of Śrī Bhīṣmadeva, *yam iha nirīkṣya hatā gatāḥ svarūpam:* "Those who simply saw Kṛṣṇa on the Battlefield of Kurukṣetra attained their original forms after being killed." (*Bhāg.* 1.9.39) That even demons like Agha, Baka and Keśī were liberated by Lord Kṛṣṇa without having performed any spiritual practices is an indication of His unique position as the original Personality of Godhead. Knowing this, we should put aside all fear and doubt and give ourselves fully to the process of devotional service.

As his final words of commentary on this chapter, Śrīla Śrīdhara Svāmī writes,

sarva-śruti-śiro-ratna-
nīrājita-padāmbujam
bhoga-yoga-pradaṁ vande
mādhavaṁ karmi-namrayoḥ

"With their effulgence, the crest jewels among all the *śrutis* offer *ārati* to the lotus feet of Lord Mādhava. I pay homage to Him, who bestows the material enjoyment honored by material workers, and who also grants the divine connection with Him prized by those who bow down to Him with reverence."

Śrīla Viśvanātha Cakravartī Ṭhākura also takes this opportunity to offer this humble prayer:

he bhaktā dvāry ayaṁ cañcad-
vāladhī rauti vo manāk
prasādaṁ labhatāṁ yasmād
viśiṣṭaḥ śveva nāthati

"O devotees, this poor creature is standing at your doorway, waving his tail and barking. Please let him have a little *prasādam* so that he may become exceptional among dogs and get the best of masters as his owner." Here the *ācārya* makes a pun on his own name: *viś*(*iṣṭaḥ*), "exceptional"; *śva*(*iva*), "like a dog"; *nātha*(*ati*), "having a master." Such is the perfection of Vaiṣṇava humility.

Thus end the purports of the humble servants of His Divine Grace A. C. Bhaktivedanta Swami Prabhupāda to the Tenth Canto, Eighty-seventh Chapter, of the Śrīmad-Bhāgavatam, *entitled "The Prayers of the Personified* Vedas."

CHAPTER EIGHTY-EIGHT

Lord Śiva Saved from Vṛkāsura

This chapter describes how it is that the devotees of Viṣṇu obtain liberation, while the devotees of other deities obtain material opulences.

Lord Viṣṇu possesses all opulences, while Lord Śiva lives in poverty. Yet the devotees of Viṣṇu are generally poverty-stricken, while Śiva's attain abundant wealth. When Mahārāja Parīkṣit asked Śukadeva Gosvāmī to explain this puzzling fact, the sage replied as follows: "Lord Śiva manifests as false ego in three varieties, according to the three modes of nature. From this false ego arise the five physical elements and the other transformations of material nature, totaling sixteen. When a devotee of Lord Śiva worships his manifestation in any of these elements, the devotee obtains all sorts of corresponding enjoyable opulences. But because Lord Śrī Hari is transcendental to the modes of material nature, His devotees also become transcendental."

At the end of the performance of his Aśvamedha sacrifices, King Yudhiṣṭhira had asked this same question of Lord Kṛṣṇa, who replied, "When I feel special compassion for someone, I gradually deprive him of his wealth. Then the poverty-stricken man's children, wife and other relations all abandon him. When he again tries to acquire wealth in order to win back his family's favor, I mercifully frustrate him so that he becomes disgusted with fruitive work and befriends My devotees. And at that time I bestow upon him My extraordinary grace; then he can become freed from the bondage of material life and attain to the kingdom of God, Vaikuṇṭha."

Lord Brahmā, Lord Viṣṇu and Lord Śiva can each bestow or withhold favors, but whereas Lord Brahmā and Lord Śiva are satisfied or angered very quickly, Lord Viṣṇu is not. In this regard the Vedic literature relates the following account: Once the demon Vṛka asked Nārada which god was most quickly pleased, and Nārada answered that Lord Śiva was. Thus Vṛkāsura went to the holy place of Kedāranātha and began worshiping Lord Śiva by offering pieces of his own flesh as oblations into the fire. But Śiva did not appear. So Vṛka decided to commit suicide by cutting off his head. Just at the critical moment, Lord Śiva appeared from the sacrificial fire and stopped him, offering the demon whatever boon he chose. Vṛka said, "May death come to whomever I touch upon the head with my hand." Lord Śiva was obliged to fulfill this request, and at once the wicked Vṛka tried to test the benediction by putting his hand on the lord's head. Terrified, Śiva fled for his life, running as far as heaven and the outer limits of the mortal world. Finally the lord reached the planet of Śvetadvīpa, where Lord Viṣṇu resides. Seeing the desperate Śiva from afar, the Lord disguised Himself as a young student and went before Vṛkāsura. In a sweet voice he addressed the demon: "My dear Vṛka, please rest awhile and tell Us what you intend to do." Vṛka was charmed by the Lord's words and revealed everything that had happened. The Lord said, "Ever since Lord Śiva was cursed by Prajāpati Dakṣa, he has become just like a carnivorous hobgoblin. So you shouldn't trust his word. Better to test his benediction by putting your hand on your own head." Bewildered by these words, the foolish demon touched his own head, which immediately shattered and fell to the ground. Cries of "Victory!" "Obeisances!" and "Well done!" were heard from the sky, and the demigods, sages, celestial forefathers and Gandharvas all congratulated the Supreme Lord by raining down flowers upon Him.

TEXT 1

श्रीराजोवाच
देवासुरमनुष्येषु ये भजन्त्यशिवं शिवम् ।
प्रायस्ते धनिनो भोजा न तु लक्ष्म्याः पतिं हरिम् ॥१॥

śrī-rājovāca
devāsura-manuṣyeṣu
ye bhajanty aśivaṁ śivam
prāyas te dhanino bhojā
na tu lakṣmyāḥ patiṁ harim

śrī-rājā uvāca—the King (Parīkṣit) said; *deva*—among demigods; *asura*—demons; *manuṣyeṣu*—and humans; *ye*—who; *bhajanti*—worship; *aśivam*—austere; *śivam*—Lord Śiva; *prāyaḥ*—usually; *te*—they; *dhaninaḥ*—rich; *bhojāḥ*—enjoyers of sense gratification; *na*—not; *tu*—however; *lakṣmyāḥ*—of the goddess of fortune; *patim*—the husband; *harim*—Lord Hari.

TRANSLATION

King Parīkṣit said: Those demigods, demons and humans who worship Lord Śiva, a strict renunciant, usually enjoy wealth and sense gratification, while the worshipers of the Supreme Lord Hari, the husband of the goddess of fortune, do not.

TEXT 2

एतद्वेदितुमिच्छामः सन्देहोऽत्र महान् हि नः ।
विरुद्धशीलयोः प्रभ्वोर्विरुद्धा भजतां गतिः ॥२॥

etad veditum icchāmaḥ
sandeho 'tra mahān hi naḥ
viruddha-śīlayoḥ prabhvor
viruddhā bhajatāṁ gatiḥ

etat—this; *veditum*—to understand; *icchāmaḥ*—we wish; *sandehaḥ*—doubt; *atra*—in this matter; *mahān*—great; *hi*—indeed; *naḥ*—on our part; *viruddha*—opposite; *śīlayoḥ*—whose characters; *prabhvoḥ*—of the two lords; *viruddhā*—opposite; *bhajatām*—of their worshipers; *gatiḥ*—the destinations.

TRANSLATION

We wish to properly understand this matter, which greatly puzzles us. Indeed, the results attained by the worshipers of these two lords of opposite characters are contrary to what one would expect.

PURPORT

The preceding chapter ended with the recommendation that one should always meditate on Lord Hari, the bestower of liberation. In this regard Mahārāja Parīkṣit here expresses a common fear among ordinary people that by becoming a devotee of Lord Viṣṇu one will lose his wealth and social status. For the benefit of such persons of little faith, King Parīkṣit requests Śrīla Śukadeva Gosvāmī to explain an apparent paradox: Lord Śiva, who lives like a beggar, without even a house to call his own, makes his devotees rich and powerful, while Lord Viṣṇu, the omnipotent possessor of all that exists, often reduces His servants to abject poverty. Śukadeva Gosvāmī will respond with reasoned explanations and an ancient account concerning the demon Vṛka.

TEXT 3

श्रीशुक उवाच
शिवः शक्तियुतः शश्वत्त्रिलिंगो गुणसंवृतः ।
वैकारिकस्तैजसश्च तामसश्चेत्यहं त्रिधा ॥३॥

śrī-śuka uvāca
śivaḥ śakti-yutaḥ śaśvat
tri-liṅgo guṇa-saṁvṛtaḥ
vaikārikas taijasaś ca
tāmasaś cety ahaṁ tridhā

śrī-śukaḥ uvāca—Śrī Śuka said; *śivaḥ*—Lord Śiva; *śakti*—with his energy, material nature; *yutaḥ*—united; *śaśvat*—always; *tri*—three; *liṅgaḥ*—whose manifest features; *guṇa*—by the modes; *saṁvṛtaḥ*—prayed to; *vaikārikaḥ*—false ego in the mode of goodness; *taijasaḥ*—false ego in the mode of passion; *ca*—and; *tāmasaḥ*—false ego in mode of ignorance; *ca*—and; *iti*—thus; *aham*—the principle of material ego; *tridhā*—threefold.

TRANSLATION

Śrī Śukadeva said: Lord Śiva is always united with his personal energy, the material nature. Manifesting himself in three features in response to the entreaties of nature's three modes, he thus embodies the threefold principle of material ego in goodness, passion and ignorance.

TEXT 4

ततो विकारा अभवन् षोडशामीषु कञ्चन ।
उपधावन् विभूतीनां सर्वासामश्नुते गतिम् ॥४॥

tato vikārā abhavan
ṣoḍaśāmīṣu kañcana

upadhāvan vibhūtīnāṁ
sarvāsām aśnute gatim

tataḥ—from that (false ego); *vikārāḥ*—transformations; *abhavan*—have manifested; *ṣoḍaśa*—sixteen; *amīṣu*—among these; *kañcana*—any; *upadhāvan*—pursuing; *vibhūtīnām*—of material assets; *sarvāsām*—all; *aśnute*—enjoys; *gatim*—the acquisition.

TRANSLATION

The sixteen elements have evolved as transformations of that false ego. When a devotee of Lord Śiva worships his manifestation in any one of these elements, the devotee obtains all sorts of corresponding enjoyable opulences.

PURPORT

False ego transforms into the mind, ten senses (the eyes, ears, nose, tongue, skin, hands, feet, voice, genitals and anus), and five physical elements (earth, water, fire, air and ether). Lord Śiva appears in a special *liṅga* form in each of these sixteen substances, which are worshiped individually as deities in various sacred locations of the universe. A devotee of Śiva may worship one of his particular *liṅgas* to obtain the mystic opulences pertaining to it. Thus Lord Śiva's *ākāśa-liṅga* bestows the opulences of ether, his *jyotir-liṅga* bestows the opulences of fire, and so on.

TEXT 5

हरिर्हि निर्गुणः साक्षात्पुरुषः प्रकृतेः परः ।
स सर्वदृगुपद्रष्टा तं भजन्निर्गुणो भवेत् ॥५॥

harir hi nirguṇaḥ sākṣāt
puruṣaḥ prakṛteḥ paraḥ
sa sarva-dṛg upadraṣṭā
taṁ bhajan nirguṇo bhavet

hariḥ—the Supreme Lord Hari; *hi*—indeed; *nirguṇaḥ*—untouched by the material modes; *sākṣāt*—absolutely; *puruṣaḥ*—the Personality of

Godhead; *prakṛteḥ*—to material nature; *paraḥ*—transcendental; *saḥ*—He; *sarva*—everything; *dṛk*—seeing; *upadraṣṭā*—the witness; *tam*—Him; *bhajan*—by worshiping; *nirguṇaḥ*—free from the material modes; *bhavet*—one becomes.

TRANSLATION

Lord Hari, however, has no connection with the material modes. He is the Supreme Personality of Godhead, the all-seeing eternal witness, who is transcendental to material nature. One who worships Him becomes similarly free from the material modes.

PURPORT

Lord Viṣṇu is situated in His own transcendental position, beyond the material energy. Why, therefore, should His worship bear the fruit of material opulence? The real fruit of worshiping Lord Viṣṇu is transcendental knowledge. Thus Lord Viṣṇu's worshiper gains the eye of transcendental knowledge instead of being blinded by mundane assets. The Lord being the detached witness of the material creation, His devotee also becomes aloof from the interaction of the Lord's inferior energies.

Śrīla Śrīdhara Svāmī cites the following passage from the Vedic literature:

vastuno guṇa-sambandhe
rūpa-dvayam iheṣyate
tad-dharmāyoga-yogābhyāṁ
bimba-vat pratibimba-vat

"When the absolute reality associates with the modes of nature, He assumes two different kinds of form in this world, according to whether His spiritual qualities are manifest or not. Thus He acts just like a reflection and its further, secondary reflection."

guṇāḥ sattvādayaḥ śānta-
ghora-mūḍhāḥ svabhāvataḥ
viṣṇu-brahma-śivānāṁ ca
guṇa-yantṛ-svarūpiṇām

"The modes of goodness, passion and ignorance, whose individual natures are peaceful, violent and foolish, are personally regulated by Lord Viṣṇu, Lord Brahmā and Lord Śiva, respectively."

nāti-bhedo bhaved bhedo
guṇa-dharmair ihāṁśataḥ
sattvasya śāntyā no jātu
viṣṇor vikṣepa-mūḍhate

"Lord Viṣṇu's peaceful mode of goodness does not differ substantially from His original, spiritual qualities, although it is only a partial manifestation of them within this world. Thus Lord Viṣṇu's mode of goodness is never tainted by agitation [in passion] or delusion [in ignorance]."

rajas-tamo-guṇābhyāṁ tu
bhavetāṁ brahma-rudrayoḥ
guṇopamardato bhūyas
tad-aṁśānāṁ ca bhinnatā

"By the modes of passion and ignorance, on the other hand, the original, spiritual qualities of Lord Brahmā and Lord Rudra are obscured. Thus these spiritual qualities appear only partially, as separated, material qualities."

ataḥ samagra-sattvasya
viṣṇor mokṣa-karī matiḥ
aṁśato bhūti-hetuś ca
tathānanda-mayī svataḥ

"Therefore focusing one's consciousness upon Lord Viṣṇu, the embodiment of all goodness, leads one to liberation. Such God consciousness also generates material success as a by-product, but its proper nature is pure spiritual ecstasy."

aṁśatas tāratamyena
brahma-rudrādi-sevinām
vibhūtayo bhavanty eva
śanair mokṣo 'py anaṁśataḥ

"According to their mode of worship, devotees of Brahmā, Rudra and other demigods obtain the limited success of material opulences. Eventually they may possibly become qualified for full liberation."

This same idea is echoed in the following statement of *Śrīmad-Bhāgavatam* (1.2.23): *śreyāṁsi tatra khalu sattva-tanor nṛṇāṁ syuḥ*. "Of these three [Brahmā, Viṣṇu and Śiva], all human beings can derive ultimate benefit from Viṣṇu, the form of the quality of goodness."

TEXT 6

निवृत्तेष्वश्वमेधेषु राजा युष्मत्पितामहः ।
शृण्वन् भगवतो धर्मानपृच्छदिदमच्युतम् ॥६॥

nivṛtteṣv aśva-medheṣu
rājā yuṣmat-pitāmahaḥ
śṛṇvan bhagavato dharmān
apṛcchad idam acyutam

nivṛtteṣu—when they were completed; *aśva-medheṣu*—his performances of the horse sacrifice; *rājā*—the King (Yudhiṣṭhira); *yuṣmat*—your (Parīkṣit's); *pitāmahaḥ*—grandfather; *śṛṇvan*—while hearing; *bhagavataḥ*—from the Supreme Lord (Kṛṣṇa); *dharmān*—religious principles; *apṛcchat*—he asked; *idam*—this; *acyutam*—of Lord Kṛṣṇa.

TRANSLATION

Your grandfather, King Yudhiṣṭhira, after completing his Aśvamedha sacrifices, asked Lord Acyuta this very same question while hearing the Lord's explanation of religious principles.

TEXT 7

स आह भगवांस्तस्मै प्रीतः शुश्रूषवे प्रभुः ।
नृणां निःश्रेयसार्थाय योऽवतीर्णो यदोः कुले ॥७॥

sa āha bhagavāṁs tasmai
prītaḥ śuśrūṣave prabhuḥ

nṛṇāṁ niḥśreyasārthāya
yo 'vatīrṇo yadoḥ kule

saḥ—He; *āha*—said; *bhagavān*—the Supreme Lord; *tasmai*—to him; *prītaḥ*—pleased; *śuśrūṣave*—who was eager to hear; *prabhuḥ*—his master; *nṛṇām*—of all men; *niḥśreyasa*—of ultimate benefit; *arthāya*—for the sake; *yaḥ*—who; *avatīrṇaḥ*—descended; *yadoḥ*—of King Yadu; *kule*—in the family.

TRANSLATION

This question pleased Śrī Kṛṣṇa, the King's Lord and master, who had descended into the family of Yadu for the purpose of bestowing the highest good on all men: The Lord replied as follows as the King eagerly listened.

TEXT 8

श्रीभगवानुवाच
यस्याहमनुगृह्णामि हरिष्ये तद्धनं शनैः ।
ततोऽधनं त्यजन्त्यस्य स्वजना दुःखदुःखितम् ॥८॥

śrī-bhagavān uvāca
yasyāham anugṛhṇāmi
hariṣye tad-dhanaṁ śanaiḥ
tato 'dhanaṁ tyajanty asya
svajanā duḥkha-duḥkhitam

śrī-bhagavān uvāca—the Personality of Godhead said; *yasya*—whom; *aham*—I; *anugṛhṇāmi*—favor; *hariṣye*—I will take away; *tat*—his; *dhanam*—wealth; *śanaiḥ*—gradually; *tataḥ*—then; *adhanam*—poor; *tyajanti*—abandon; *asya*—his; *sva-janāḥ*—relatives and friends; *duḥkha-duḥkhitam*—who suffers one distress after another.

TRANSLATION

The Personality of Godhead said: If I especially favor someone, I gradually deprive him of his wealth. Then the relatives and friends of such a poverty-stricken man abandon him. In this way he suffers one distress after another.

PURPORT

Devotees of the Supreme Lord experience both happiness and distress—not as consequences of material work but as incidental effects of their loving reciprocation with the Lord. Śrīla Rūpa Gosvāmī, in *Śrī Bhakti-rasāmṛta-sindhu,* his definitive treatise on the process of devotional service, explains how a Vaiṣṇava is relieved of all karmic reactions, including those that have not yet begun to manifest (*aprārabdha*), those that are just about to manifest (*kūṭa*), those that are barely manifesting (*bīja*) and those that have manifested fully (*prārabdha*). As a lotus gradually loses its many petals, so a person who takes shelter of devotional service has all his karmic reactions destroyed.

That devotional service to Lord Kṛṣṇa eradicates all karmic reactions is confirmed in this passage of the *Gopāla-tāpanī śruti* (*Pūrva* 15): *bhaktir asya bhajanaṁ tad ihāmutropādhi-nairāsyenāmuṣmin manaḥ-kalpanam etad eva naiṣkarmyam.* "Devotional service is the process of worshiping the Supreme Lord. It consists of fixing the mind upon Him by becoming disinterested in all material designations, both in this life and the next. It results in the dissolution of all *karma.*" While it is certainly true that those who practice devotional service remain in material bodies and apparently material situations for some time, this is simply an expression of the inconceivable mercy of the Lord, who bestows the fruits of devotion only when it has become pure. In every stage of devotion, however, the Lord watches over His devotee and sees to the gradual elimination of his *karma.* Thus despite the fact that the happiness and distress devotees experience resemble ordinary karmic reactions, they are in fact given by the Lord Himself. As the *Bhāgavatam* (10.87.40) states, *bhavad-uttha-śubhāśubhayoḥ:* A mature devotee recognizes the superficially good and bad conditions he encounters as signs of the direct guidance of his ever well-wishing Lord.

But if the Lord is so compassionate to His devotees, why does He expose them to special suffering? This is answered by an analogy: A very affectionate father takes the responsibility of restricting his children's play and making them go to school. He knows that this is a genuine expression of his love for them, even if the children fail to understand. Similarly, the Supreme Lord Viṣṇu is mercifully strict with all His dependents, not only with immature devotees struggling to become qualified. Even perfect saints like Prahlāda, Dhruva and Yudhiṣṭhira were subjected to great tribulations, all for their glorification. After the

Battle of Kurukṣetra, Śrī Bhīṣmadeva described to King Yudhiṣṭhira his wonder at this:

yatra dharma-suto rājā
gadā-pāṇir vṛkodaraḥ
kṛṣṇo 'strī gāṇḍivaṁ cāpaṁ
suhṛt kṛṣṇas tato vipat

na hy asya karhicid rājan
pumān vetti vidhitsitam
yad-vijijñāsayā yuktā
muhyanti kavayo 'pi hi

"Oh, how wonderful is the influence of inevitable time! It is irreversible—otherwise, how can there be reverses in the presence of King Yudhiṣṭhira, the son of the demigod controlling religion; Bhīma, the great fighter with a club; the great bowman Arjuna with his mighty weapon Gāṇḍiva; and above all, the Lord, the direct well-wisher of the Pāṇḍavas? O King, no one can know the plan of the Lord [Śrī Kṛṣṇa]. Even though great philosophers inquire exhaustively, they are bewildered." (*Bhāg.* 1.9.15-16)

Although a Vaiṣṇava's happiness and distress are felt as pleasure and pain, just like ordinary karmic reactions, they are different in a significant sense. Material happiness and distress, arising from *karma,* leave a subtle residue—the seed of future entanglement. Such enjoyment and suffering tend toward degradation and increase the danger of falling into hellish oblivion. Happiness and distress generated from the Supreme Lord's desires, however, leave no trace after their immediate purpose has been served. Moreover, the Vaiṣṇava who enjoys such reciprocation with the Lord is in no danger of falling down into nescience. As Yamarāja, the lord of death and the judge of all departed souls, declares,

jihvā na vakti bhagavad-guṇa-nāmadheyam
cetaś ca na smarati tac-caraṇāravindam
kṛṣṇāya no namati yac-chira ekadāpi
tān ānayadhvam asato 'kṛta-viṣṇu-kṛtyān

"My dear servants, please bring to me only those sinful persons who do not use their tongues to chant the holy name and qualities of Kṛṣṇa, whose hearts do not remember the lotus feet of Kṛṣṇa even once, and whose heads do not bow down even once before Lord Kṛṣṇa. Send me those who do not perform their duties toward Viṣṇu, which are the only duties in human life. Please bring me all such fools and rascals." (*Bhāg.* 6.3.29)

The beloved devotees of the Lord do not regard as very troublesome the suffering He imposes on them. Indeed, they find that in the end it gives rise to unlimited pleasure, just as a stinging ointment applied by a physician cures his patient's infected eye. In addition, suffering helps protect the confidentiality of devotional service by discouraging intrusions by the faithless, and it also increases the eagerness with which the devotees call upon the Lord to appear. If the devotees of Lord Viṣṇu were complacently happy all the time, He would never have a reason to appear in this world as Kṛṣṇa, Rāmacandra, Nṛsiṁha and so on. As Kṛṣṇa Himself says in *Bhagavad-gītā* (4.8),

paritrāṇāya sādhūnāṁ
vināśāya ca duṣkṛtām
dharma-saṁsthāpanārthāya
sambhavāmi yuge yuge

"To deliver the pious and annihilate the miscreants, as well as to reestablish the principles of religion, I Myself appear, millennium after millennium." And without the Lord's showing Himself on earth in His original form of Kṛṣṇa and in the forms of various incarnations, His faithful servants in this world would have no opportunity to enjoy His *rāsa-līlā* and other pastimes.

Śrīla Viśvanātha Cakravartī here counters a possible objection: "What fault would there be in God's incarnating for some other reason than to deliver saintly persons from suffering?" The learned *ācārya* responds, "Yes, my dear brother, this makes good sense, but you are not expert in understanding spiritual moods. Please listen: It is at night that the sunrise becomes attractive, during the hot summer that cold water gives comfort, and during the cold winter months that warm water is pleasing. Lamplight appears attractive in darkness, not in the glaring light of day, and when one is distressed by hunger, food tastes especially good." In other words, to strengthen his devotees' mood of dependence on Him and longing for Him, the Lord arranges for His devotees to go through some suffering, and when He appears in order to deliver them, their gratitude and transcendental pleasure are boundless.

TEXT 9

स यदा वितथोद्योगो निर्विण्णः स्याद्धनेहया ।
मत्परैः कृतमैत्रस्य करिष्ये मदनुग्रहम् ॥९॥

sa yadā vitathodyogo
nirviṇṇaḥ syād dhanehayā
mat-paraiḥ kṛta-maitrasya
kariṣye mad-anugraham

saḥ—he; *yadā*—when; *vitatha*—useless; *udyogaḥ*—his attempt; *nirviṇṇaḥ*—frustrated; *syāt*—becomes; *dhana*—for money; *īhayā*—with his endeavor; *mat*—to Me; *paraiḥ*—with those who are devoted; *kṛta*—for him who has made; *maitrasya*—friendship; *kariṣye*—I will show; *mat*—My; *anugraham*—mercy.

TRANSLATION

When he becomes frustrated in his attempts to make money and instead befriends My devotees, I bestow My special mercy upon him.

TEXT 10

तद् ब्रह्म परमं सूक्ष्मं चिन्मात्रं सदनन्तकम् ।
विज्ञायात्मतया धीरः संसारात्परिमुच्यते ॥१०॥

tad brahma paramaṁ sūkṣmaṁ
cin-mātraṁ sad anantakam
vijñāyātmatayā dhīraḥ
saṁsārāt parimucyate

tat—that; *brahma*—impersonal Brahman; *paramam*—supreme; *sūkṣmam*—subtle; *cit*—spirit; *mātram*—pure; *sat*—eternal existence;

anantakam—without end; *vijñāya*—understanding with thorough realization; *ātmatayā*—as one's true Self; *dhīraḥ*—sober; *saṁsārāt*—from material life; *parimucyate*—one becomes freed.

TRANSLATION

A person who has thus become sober fully realizes the Absolute as the highest truth, the most subtle and perfect manifestation of spirit, the transcendental existence without end. In this way realizing that the Supreme Truth is the foundation of his own existence, he is freed from the cycle of material life.

TEXT 11

अतो मां सुदुराराध्यं हित्वान्यान् भजते जनः ।
ततस्त आशुतोषेभ्यो लब्धराज्यश्रियोद्धताः ।
मत्ताः प्रमत्ता वरदान् विस्मयन्त्यवजानते ॥११॥

ato māṁ su-durārādhyaṁ
hitvānyān bhajate janaḥ
tatas ta āśu-toṣebhyo
labdha-rājya-śriyoddhatāḥ
mattāḥ pramattā vara-dān
vismayanty avajānate

ataḥ—therefore; *mām*—Me; *su*—very; *durārādhyam*—difficult to worship; *hitvā*—leaving aside; *anyān*—others; *bhajate*—worship; *janaḥ*—the ordinary populace; *tataḥ*—consequently; *te*—they; *āśu*—quickly; *toṣebhyaḥ*—from those who are satisfied; *labdha*—received; *rājya*—royal; *śriyā*—by opulence; *uddhatāḥ*—made arrogant; *mattāḥ*—intoxicated with pride; *pramattāḥ*—negligent; *vara*—of benedictions; *dān*—the givers; *vismayanti*—becoming too bold; *avajānate*—they insult.

TRANSLATION

Because I am difficult to worship, people generally avoid Me and instead worship other deities, who are quickly satisfied. When people receive kingly opulences from these deities, they

become arrogant, intoxicated with pride and neglectful of their duties. They dare to offend even the demigods who have bestowed benedictions upon them.

TEXT 12

श्रीशुक उवाच
शापप्रसादयोरीशा ब्रह्मविष्णुशिवादयः ।
सद्यः शापप्रसादोऽंग शिवो ब्रह्मा न चाच्युतः ॥१२॥

śrī-śuka uvāca
śāpa-prasādayor īśā
brahma-viṣṇu-śivādayaḥ
sadyaḥ śāpa-prasādo 'ṅga
śivo brahmā na cācyutaḥ

śrī-śukaḥ uvāca—Śukadeva Gosvāmī said; *śāpa*—in cursing; *prasādayoḥ*—and showing favor; *īśāḥ*—capable; *brahma-viṣṇu-śiva-ādayaḥ*—Brahmā, Viṣṇu, Śiva and others; *sadyaḥ*—quick; *śāpa-prasādaḥ*—whose curse and benediction; *aṅga*—my dear (King Parīkṣit); *śivaḥ*—Lord Śiva; *brahmā*—Lord Brahmā; *na*—not; *ca*—and; *acyutaḥ*—Lord Viṣṇu.

TRANSLATION

Śukadeva Gosvāmī said: Lord Brahmā, Lord Viṣṇu, Lord Śiva and others are able to curse or bless one. Lord Śiva and Lord Brahmā are very quick to curse or bestow benedictions, my dear King, but the infallible Supreme Lord is not.

TEXT 13

अत्र चोदाहरन्तीममितिहासं पुरातनम् ।
वृकासुराय गिरिशो वरं दत्त्वाप संकटम् ॥१३॥

atra codāharantīmam
itihāsaṁ purātanam
vṛkāsurāya giriśo
varaṁ dattvāpa saṅkaṭam

atra—in this regard; *ca*—and; *udāharanti*—they relate as an example; *imam*—the following; *itihāsam*—historical account; *purātanam*—ancient; *vṛka-asurāya*—to the demon Vṛka; *giri-śaḥ*—Lord Śiva, master of Mount Kailāsa; *varam*—a choice of benedictions; *dattvā*—giving; *āpa*—obtained; *saṅkaṭam*—a dangerous situation.

TRANSLATION

In this connection, an ancient historical account is related concerning how the Lord of Kailāsa Mountain was put into danger by offering a choice of benedictions to the demon Vṛka.

TEXT 14

वृको नामासुरः पुत्रः शकुनेः पथि नारदम् ।
दृष्ट्वाशुतोषं पप्रच्छ देवेषु त्रिषु दुर्मतिः ॥१४॥

vṛko nāmāsuraḥ putraḥ
śakuneḥ pathi nāradam
dṛṣṭvāśu-toṣaṁ papraccha
deveṣu triṣu durmatiḥ

vṛkaḥ—Vṛka; *nāma*—by name; *asuraḥ*—a demon; *putraḥ*—a son; *śakuneḥ*—of Śakuni; *pathi*—on the road; *nāradam*—the sage Nārada; *dṛṣṭvā*—seeing; *āśu*—quickly; *toṣam*—pleased; *papraccha*—he asked about; *deveṣu*—among the lords; *triṣu*—three; *durmatiḥ*—wicked.

TRANSLATION

The demon named Vṛka, a son of Śakuni's, once met Nārada on the road. The wicked fellow asked him which of the three chief gods could be pleased most quickly.

TEXT 15

स आह देवं गिरिशमुपाधावाशु सिद्ध्यसि ।
योऽल्पाभ्यां गुणदोषाभ्यामाशु तुष्यति कुप्यति ॥१५॥

sa āha devaṁ giriśam
upādhāvāśu siddhyasi
yo 'lpābhyāṁ guṇa-doṣābhyām
āśu tuṣyati kupyati

saḥ—he (Nārada); *āha*—said; *devam*—the lord; *giriśam*—Śiva; *upādhāva*—you should worship; *āśu*—quickly; *siddhyasi*—you will become successful; *yaḥ*—who; *alpābhyām*—slight; *guṇa*—by good qualities; *doṣābhyām*—and faults; *āśu*—quickly; *tuṣyati*—is satisfied; *kupyati*—is angered.

TRANSLATION

Nārada told him: Worship Lord Śiva and you will soon achieve success. He quickly becomes pleased by seeing his worshiper's slightest good qualities—and quickly angered by seeing his slightest fault.

TEXT 16

दशास्यबाणयोस्तुष्टः स्तुवतोर्वन्दिनोरिव ।
ऐश्वर्यमतुलं दत्त्वा तत आप सुसंकटम् ॥१६॥

daśāsya-bāṇayos tuṣṭaḥ
stuvator vandinor iva
aiśvaryam atulaṁ dattvā
tata āpa su-saṅkaṭam

daśa-āsya—with ten-headed Rāvaṇa; *bāṇayoḥ*—and with Bāṇa; *tuṣṭaḥ*—satisfied; *stuvatoḥ*—who sang his glories; *vandinoḥ iva*—like minstrels; *aiśvaryam*—power; *atulam*—unequalled; *dattvā*—giving; *tataḥ*—then; *āpa*—he obtained; *su*—great; *saṅkaṭam*—difficulty.

TRANSLATION

He became pleased with ten-headed Rāvaṇa, and also with Bāṇa, when they each chanted his glories, like bards in a royal court. Lord Śiva then bestowed unprecedented power upon each of them, but in both cases he was consequently beset with great difficulty.

PURPORT

Rāvaṇa worshiped Lord Śiva to gain power and then misused that power to uproot the lord's residence, sacred Kailāsa-parvata. On Bāṇāsura's request, Lord Śiva agreed to personally guard Bāṇa's capital, and later he had to fight for Bāṇa against Śrī Kṛṣṇa and His sons.

TEXT 17

इत्यादिष्टस्तमसुर उपाधावत्स्वगात्रतः ।
केदार आत्मक्रव्येण जुह्वानोऽग्निमुखं हरम् ॥१७॥

ity ādiṣṭas tam asura
upādhāvat sva-gātrataḥ
kedāra ātma-kravyeṇa
juhvāno 'gni-mukhaṁ haram

iti—thus; *ādiṣṭaḥ*—instructed; *tam*—him (Lord Śiva); *asuraḥ*—the demon; *upādhāvat*—worshiped; *sva*—his own; *gātrataḥ*—from the bodily limbs; *kedāre*—at the holy place Kedāranātha; *ātma*—his own; *kravyeṇa*—with the flesh; *juhvānaḥ*—offering oblations; *agni*—the fire; *mukham*—whose mouth; *haram*—Lord Śiva.

TRANSLATION

[Śukadeva Gosvāmī continued:] Thus advised, the demon proceeded to worship Lord Śiva at Kedāranātha by taking pieces of flesh from his own body and offering them as oblations into the sacred fire, which is Lord Śiva's mouth.

TEXTS 18–19

देवोपलब्धिमप्राप्य निर्वेदात्सप्तमेऽहनि ।
शिरोऽवृश्चत्सुधितिना तत्तीर्थक्लिन्नमूर्धजम् ॥१८॥
तदा महाकारुणिको स धूर्जटिर्
यथा वयं चाग्निरिवोत्थितोऽनलात् ।
निगृह्य दोर्भ्यां भुजयोर्न्यवारयत्
तत्स्पर्शनाद् भूय उपस्कृताकृतिः ॥१९॥

devopalabdhim aprāpya
nirvedāt saptame 'hani
śiro 'vṛścat sudhitinā
tat-tīrtha-klinna-mūrdhajam

tadā mahā-kāruṇiko sa dhūrjaṭir
yathā vayaṁ cāgnir ivotthito 'nalāt
nigṛhya dorbhyāṁ bhujayor nyavārayat
tat-sparśanād bhūya upaskṛtākṛtiḥ

deva—of the lord; *upalabdhim*—sight; *aprāpya*—not obtaining; *nirvedāt*—out of frustration; *saptame*—on the seventh; *ahani*—day; *śiraḥ*—his head; *avṛścat*—was about to cut off; *sudhitinā*—with a hatchet; *tat*—of that (Kedāranātha); *tīrtha*—in (waters of) the holy place; *klinna*—having wetted; *mūrdha-jam*—the hair of his head; *tadā*—then; *mahā*—supremely; *kāruṇikaḥ*—merciful; *saḥ*—he; *dhūrjaṭiḥ*—Lord Śiva; *yathā*—just as; *vayam*—we; *ca*—also; *agniḥ*—the god of fire; *iva*—appearing like; *utthitaḥ*—risen; *analāt*—from the fire; *nigṛhya*—seizing; *dorbhyām*—with his arms; *bhujayoḥ*—his (Vṛka's) arms; *nyavārayat*—he stopped him; *tat*—his (Lord Śiva's); *sparśanāt*—by the touch; *bhūyaḥ*—again; *upaskṛta*—well formed; *ākṛtiḥ*—his body.

TRANSLATION

Vṛkāsura became frustrated after failing to obtain a vision of the lord. Finally, on the seventh day, after dipping his hair into the holy waters at Kedāranātha and leaving it wet, he took up a hatchet and prepared to cut off his head. But at that very moment the supremely merciful Lord Śiva rose up out of the sacrificial fire, looking like the god of fire himself, and grabbed both arms of the demon to stop him from killing himself, just as we would do. By Lord Śiva's touch, Vṛkāsura once again became whole.

TEXT 20

तमाह चांगालमलं वृणीष्व मे
यथाभिकामं वितरामि ते वरम् ।
प्रीयेय तोयेन नृणां प्रपद्यताम्
अहो त्वयात्मा भृशमर्द्यते वृथा ॥२०॥

tam āha cāṅgālam alaṁ vṛṇīṣva me
yathābhikāmaṁ vitarāmi te varam
prīyeya toyena nṛṇāṁ prapadyatām
aho tvayātmā bhṛśam ardyate vṛthā

tam—to him; *āha*—he (Lord Śiva) said; *ca*—and; *aṅga*—my dear; *alam alam*—enough, enough; *vṛṇīṣva*—please choose a benediction; *me*—from me; *yathā*—howsoever; *abhikāmam*—you desire; *vitarāmi*—I will bestow; *te*—to you; *varam*—your chosen boon; *prīyeya*—I become pleased; *toyena*—with water; *nṛṇām*—from persons; *prapadyatām*—who approach me for shelter; *aho*—ah; *tvayā*—by you; *ātmā*—your body; *bhṛśam*—excessively; *ardyate*—tormented; *vṛthā*—in vain.

TRANSLATION

Lord Śiva said to him: My friend, please stop, stop! Ask from me whatever you want, and I will bestow that boon upon you. Alas, you have subjected your body to great torment for no reason, since I am pleased with a simple offering of water from those who approach me for shelter.

TEXT 21

देवं स वव्रे पापीयान् वरं भूतभयावहम् ।
यस्य यस्य करं शीर्ष्णि धास्ये स म्रियतामिति ॥२१॥

devaṁ sa vavre pāpīyān
varaṁ bhūta-bhayāvaham
yasya yasya karaṁ śīrṣṇi
dhāsye sa mriyatām iti

devam—from the lord; *saḥ*—he; *vavre*—chose; *pāpīyān*—the sinful demon; *varam*—a benediction; *bhūta*—to all living beings; *bhaya*—fear; *āvaham*—bringing; *yasya yasya*—of whomever; *karam*—my hand; *śīrṣṇi*—on the head; *dhāsye*—I place; *saḥ*—he; *mriyatām*—should die; *iti*—thus.

TRANSLATION

[Śukadeva Gosvāmī continued:] The benediction sinful Vṛka chose from the lord would terrify all living beings. Vṛka said, "May death come to whomever I touch upon the head with my hand."

TEXT 22

तच्छ्रुत्वा भगवान् रुद्रो दुर्मना इव भारत ।
ॐ इति प्रहसंस्तस्मै ददेऽहेरमृतं यथा ॥२२॥

tac chrutvā bhagavān rudro
durmanā iva bhārata
om iti prahasaṁs tasmai
dade 'her amṛtaṁ yathā

tat—this; *śrutvā*—hearing; *bhagavān rudraḥ*—Lord Rudra; *durmanāḥ*—displeased; *iva*—as if; *bhārata*—O descendant of Bharata; *om iti*—vibrating the sacred syllable *om* as a sign of assent; *prahasan*—smiling broadly; *tasmai*—to him; *dade*—he gave it; *aheḥ*—to a snake; *amṛtam*—nectar; *yathā*—as.

TRANSLATION

Upon hearing this, Lord Rudra seemed somewhat disturbed. Nonetheless, O descendant of Bharata, he vibrated *om* to signify his assent, granting Vṛka the benediction with an ironic smile, as if giving milk to a poisonous snake.

TEXT 23

स तद्वरपरीक्षार्थं शम्भोर्मूर्ध्नि किलासुरः ।
स्वहस्तं धातुमारेभे सोऽबिभ्यत्स्वकृताच्छिवः ॥२३॥

sa tad-vara-parīkṣārthaṁ
śambhor mūrdhni kilāsuraḥ

sva-hastaṁ dhātum ārebhe
so 'bibhyat sva-kṛtāc chivaḥ

saḥ—he; *tat*—his (Lord Śiva's); *vara*—the benediction; *parīkṣā-artham*—in order to test; *śambhoḥ*—of Lord Śiva; *mūrdhni*—on the head; *kila*—indeed; *asuraḥ*—the demon; *sva*—his own; *hastam*—hand; *dhātum*—to put; *ārebhe*—he tried; *saḥ*—he; *abibhyat*—became afraid; *sva*—by himself; *kṛtāt*—because of what had been done; *śivaḥ*—Lord Śiva.

TRANSLATION

To test Lord Śambhu's benediction, the demon then tried to put his hand on the lord's head. Thus Śiva was frightened because of what he himself had done.

TEXT 24

तेनोपसृष्टः सन्त्रस्तः पराधावन् सवेपथुः ।
यावदन्तं दिवो भूमेः काष्ठानामुदगादुदक् ॥२४॥

tenopasṛṣṭaḥ santrastaḥ
parādhāvan sa-vepathuḥ
yāvad antaṁ divo bhūmeḥ
kāṣṭhānām udagād udak

tena—by him; *upasṛṣṭaḥ*—being pursued; *santrastaḥ*—terrified; *parādhāvan*—fleeing; *sa*—with; *vepathuḥ*—trembling; *yāvat*—as far as; *antam*—the ends; *divaḥ*—of the sky; *bhūmeḥ*—of the earth; *kāṣṭhānām*—and of the directions; *udagāt*—he went swiftly; *udak*—from the north.

TRANSLATION

As the demon pursued him, Lord Śiva fled swiftly from his abode in the north, shaking with terror. He ran as far as the limits of the earth, the sky and the corners of the universe.

TEXTS 25–26

अजानन्तः प्रतिविधिं तूष्णीमासन् सुरेश्वराः ।
ततो वैकुण्ठमगमद् भास्वरं तमसः परम् ॥२५॥

यत्र नारायणः साक्षान् न्यासिनां परमो गतिः ।
शान्तानां न्यस्तदण्डानां यतो नावर्तते गतः ॥२६॥

ajānantaḥ prati-vidhiṁ
tūṣṇīm āsan sureśvarāḥ
tato vaikuṇṭham agamad
bhāsvaraṁ tamasaḥ param

yatra nārāyaṇaḥ sākṣān
nyāsināṁ paramo gatiḥ
śāntānāṁ nyasta-daṇḍānāṁ
yato nāvartate gataḥ

ajānantaḥ—not knowing; *prati-vidhim*—counteraction; *tūṣṇīm*—silent; *āsan*—remained; *sura*—of the demigods; *īśvarāḥ*—the lords; *tataḥ*—then; *vaikuṇṭham*—to Vaikuṇṭha, the kingdom of God; *agamat*—he came; *bhāsvaram*—luminous; *tamasaḥ*—darkness; *param*—beyond; *yatra*—where; *nārāyaṇaḥ*—Nārāyaṇa; *sākṣāt*—directly visible; *nyāsinām*—of *sannyāsīs; paramaḥ*—the Supreme Lord; *gatiḥ*—goal; *śāntānām*—who are peaceful; *nyasta*—who have renounced; *daṇḍānām*—violence; *yataḥ*—from which; *na āvartate*—one does not return; *gataḥ*—having gone.

TRANSLATION

The great demigods could only remain silent, not knowing how to counteract the benediction. Then Lord Śiva reached the luminous realm of Vaikuṇṭha, beyond all darkness, where the Supreme Lord Nārāyaṇa is manifest. That realm is the destination of renunciants who have attained peace and given up all violence against other creatures. Going there, one never returns.

PURPORT

According to Śrīla Śrīdhara Svāmī, Lord Śiva entered the planet of Śvetadvīpa, a special outpost of the spiritual world within the confines of the material universe. There, on a beautiful white island surrounded by the celestial ocean of milk, Lord Viṣṇu rests on the serpent bed of Ananta Śeṣa, making Himself available to the demigods when they need His help.

TEXTS 27–28

तं तथा व्यसनं दृष्ट्वा भगवान् वृजिनार्दनः ।
दूरात्प्रत्युदियाद् भूत्वा बटुको योगमायया ॥२७॥
मेखलाजिनदण्डाक्षैस्तेजसाग्निरिव ज्वलन् ।
अभिवादयामास च तं कुशपाणिर्विनीतवत् ॥२८॥

taṁ tathā vyasanaṁ dṛṣṭvā
bhagavān vṛjinārdanaḥ
dūrāt pratyudiyād bhūtvā
baṭuko yoga-māyayā

mekhalājina-daṇḍākṣais
tejasāgnir iva jvalan
abhivādayām āsa ca taṁ
kuśa-pāṇir vinīta-vat

tam—that; *tathā*—thus; *vyasanam*—danger; *dṛṣṭvā*—seeing; *bhagavān*—the Supreme Lord; *vṛjina*—of distress; *ardanaḥ*—the eradicator; *dūrāt*—from a distance; *pratyudiyāt*—he came before (Vṛkāsura); *bhūtvā*—becoming; *baṭukaḥ*—a young *brāhmaṇa* student; *yoga-māyayā*—by the mystic power of His internal energy; *mekhala*—with a student's belt; *ajina*—deerskin; *daṇḍa*—rod; *akṣaiḥ*—and prayer beads; *tejasā*—by His effulgence; *agniḥ iva*—like fire; *jvalan*—glowing; *abhivādayām āsa*—He respectfully greeted; *ca*—and; *tam*—him; *kuśa-pāṇiḥ*—with *kuśa* grass in His hands; *vinīta-vat*—in a humble manner.

TRANSLATION

The Supreme Lord, who relieves His devotees' distress, had seen from afar that Lord Śiva was in danger. Thus by His mystic Yogamāyā potency He assumed the form of a *brahmacārī* student, with the appropriate belt, deerskin, rod and prayer beads, and came before Vṛkāsura. The Lord's effulgence glowed brilliantly like fire. Holding *kuśa* grass in His hand, He humbly greeted the demon.

PURPORT

Śrīla Viśvanātha Cakravartī quotes the disguised Lord Nārāyaṇa as saying, "For Us seers of the Absolute Truth, all created beings are worthy of respect. And since you are the son of Śakuni, a wise man and performer of great austerities, you certainly deserve the respectful greeting of a young *brahmacārī* like Myself."

TEXT 29

श्रीभगवानुवाच

शाकुनेय भवान् व्यक्तं श्रान्तः किं दूरमागतः ।
क्षणं विश्रम्यतां पुंस आत्मायं सर्वकामधुक् ॥२९॥

śrī-bhagavān uvāca
śākuneya bhavān vyaktaṁ
śrāntaḥ kiṁ dūram āgataḥ
kṣaṇaṁ viśramyatāṁ puṁsa
ātmāyaṁ sarva-kāma-dhuk

śrī-bhagavān uvāca—the Supreme Lord said; *śākuneya*—O son of Śakuni; *bhavān*—you; *vyaktam*—evidently; *śrāntaḥ*—are fatigued; *kim*—for what reason; *dūram*—far; *āgataḥ*—have come; *kṣaṇam*—for a minute; *viśramyatām*—please rest; *puṁsaḥ*—of a person; *ātmā*—body; *ayam*—this; *sarva*—all; *kāma*—desires; *dhuk*—bestowing like a cow's milk.

TRANSLATION

The Supreme Lord said: My dear son of Śakuni, you appear tired. Why have you come such a great distance? Please rest for a minute. After all, it is one's body that fulfills all one's desires.

PURPORT

In *Kṛṣṇa, the Supreme Personality of Godhead,* Śrīla Prabhupāda comments, "Before the demon could argue that he had no time to take rest, the Lord began to inform him about the importance of the body, and the demon was convinced. Any man, especially a demon, takes his body to be very important."

TEXT 30

यदि नः श्रवणायालं युष्मद्व्यवसितं विभो ।
भण्यतां प्रायशः पुम्भिर्धृतैः स्वार्थान् समीहते ॥३०॥

yadi naḥ śravaṇāyālaṁ
yuṣmad-vyavasitaṁ vibho
bhaṇyatāṁ prāyaśaḥ pumbhir
dhṛtaiḥ svārthān samīhate

yadi—if; *naḥ*—Our; *śravaṇāya*—for the hearing; *alam*—suitable; *yuṣmat*—your; *vyavasitam*—intention; *vibho*—O powerful one; *bhaṇyatām*—please tell; *prāyaśaḥ*—usually; *pumbhiḥ*—with persons; *dhṛtaiḥ*—taken help of; *sva*—one's own; *arthān*—purposes; *samīhate*—one accomplishes.

TRANSLATION

O mighty one, please tell Us what you intend to do, if We are qualified to hear it. Usually one accomplishes his purposes by taking help from others.

PURPORT

Even an envious demon will not refuse the help of a *brāhmaṇa's* potency to gain his ends.

TEXT 31

श्रीशुक उवाच
एवं भगवता पृष्टो वचसामृतवर्षिणा ।
गतक्लमोऽब्रवीत्तस्मै यथापूर्वमनुष्ठितम् ॥३१॥

śrī-śuka uvāca
evaṁ bhagavatā pṛṣṭo
vacasāmṛta-varṣiṇā
gata-klamo 'bravīt tasmai
yathā-pūrvam anuṣṭhitam

śrī-śukaḥ uvāca—Śukadeva Gosvāmī said; *evam*—thus; *bhagavatā*—by the Supreme Lord; *pṛṣṭaḥ*—questioned; *vacasā*—with words; *amṛta*—nectar; *varṣiṇā*—which rained; *gata*—gone; *klamaḥ*—his fatigue; *abravīt*—he said; *tasmai*—to Him; *yathā*—as; *pūrvam*—before; *anuṣṭhitam*—executed.

TRANSLATION

Śukadeva Gosvāmī said: Thus questioned by the Personality of Godhead in language that poured down upon him like sweet nectar, Vṛka felt relieved of his fatigue. He described to the Lord everything he had done.

TEXT 32

श्रीभगवानुवाच
एवं चेत्तर्हि तद्वाक्यं न वयं श्रद्दधीमहि ।
यो दक्षशापात्पैशाच्यं प्राप्तः प्रेतपिशाचराट् ॥३२॥

śrī-bhagavān uvāca
evaṁ cet tarhi tad-vākyam
na vayaṁ śraddadhīmahi
yo dakṣa-śāpāt paiśācyaṁ
prāptaḥ preta-piśāca-rāṭ

śrī-bhagavān uvāca—the Supreme Lord said; *evam*—such; *cet*—if; *tarhi*—then; *tat*—his; *vākyam*—in the statements; *na*—not; *vayam*—We; *śraddadhīmahi*—can place faith; *yaḥ*—who; *dakṣa-śāpāt*—by the curse of Dakṣa Prajāpati; *paiśācyam*—the qualities of the Piśācas (a class of carnivorous demons); *prāptah*—obtained; *preta-piśāca*—of the Pretas (ghosts) and Piśācas; *rāṭ*—the king.

TRANSLATION

The Supreme Lord said: If this is the case, We cannot believe what Śiva says. Śiva is the same lord of the Pretas and Piśācas whom Dakṣa cursed to become like a carnivorous hobgoblin.

TEXT 33

यदि वस्तत्र विश्रम्भो दानवेन्द्र जगद्गुरौ ।
तर्ह्यंगाशु स्वशिरसि हस्तं न्यस्य प्रतीयताम् ॥३३॥

yadi vas tatra viśrambho
dānavendra jagad-gurau
tarhy aṅgāśu sva-śirasi
hastaṁ nyasya pratīyatām

yadi—if; *vaḥ*—your; *tatra*—in him; *viśrambhaḥ*—faith; *dānava-indra*—O best of the demons; *jagat*—of the universe; *gurau*—as the spiritual master; *tarhi*—then; *aṅga*—My dear friend; *āśu*—right now; *sva*—your own; *śirasi*—on the head; *hastam*—your hand; *nyasya*—placing; *pratīyatām*—just observe.

TRANSLATION

O best of the demons, if you have any faith in him because he is the spiritual master of the universe, then without delay put your hand on your head and see what happens.

TEXT 34

यद्यसत्यं वचः शम्भोः कथञ्चिद्दानवर्षभ ।
तदैनं जह्यसद्वाचं न यद्वक्तानृतं पुनः ॥३४॥

yady asatyaṁ vacaḥ śambhoḥ
kathañcid dānavarṣabha
tadainaṁ jahy asad-vācaṁ
na yad vaktānṛtaṁ punaḥ

yadi—if; *asatyam*—untrue; *vacaḥ*—the words; *śambhoḥ*—of Lord Śiva; *kathañcit*—in any way; *dānava-ṛṣabha*—O best of the demons; *tadā*—then; *enam*—him; *jahi*—please kill; *asat*—untrue; *vācam*—whose words; *na*—not; *yat*—so that; *vaktā*—he may speak; *anṛtam*—what is false; *punaḥ*—again.

TRANSLATION

If the words of Lord Śambhu prove untrue in any way, O best of the demons, then kill the liar so he may never lie again.

PURPORT

Lord Śiva may have the power to revive himself even after being killed, but at least he will be dissuaded from lying again.

TEXT 35

इत्थं भगवतश्चित्रैर्वचोभिः स सुपेशलैः ।
भिन्नधीर्विस्मृतः शीर्ष्णि स्वहस्तं कुमतिर्न्यधात् ॥३५॥

ittham bhagavataś citrair
vacobhiḥ sa su-peśalaiḥ
bhinna-dhīr vismṛtaḥ śīrṣṇi
sva-hastaṁ kumatir nyadhāt

ittham—in this manner; *bhagavataḥ*—of the Personality of Godhead; *citraiḥ*—wonderful; *vacobhiḥ*—by the words; *saḥ*—he (Vṛka); *su*—very; *peśalaiḥ*—clever; *bhinna*—bewildered; *dhīḥ*—his mind; *vismṛtaḥ*—forgetting; *śīrṣṇi*—on his head; *sva*—his own; *hastam*—hand; *ku-matiḥ*—foolish; *nyadhāt*—placed.

TRANSLATION

[Śukadeva Gosvāmī continued:] Thus bewildered by the Personality of Godhead's enchanting, artful words, foolish Vṛka, without realizing what he was doing, placed his hand on his head.

TEXT 36

अथापतद् भिन्नशिराः व्रजाहत इव क्षणात् ।
जयशब्दो नमःशब्दः साधुशब्दोऽभवद्दिवि ॥३६॥

athāpatad bhinna-śirāḥ
vrajāhata iva kṣaṇāt

jaya-śabdo namaḥ-śabdaḥ
sādhu-śabdo 'bhavad divi

atha—then; *apatat*—he fell down; *bhinna*—shattered; *śirāḥ*—his head; *vraja*—by a lightning bolt; *āhataḥ*—struck; *iva*—as if; *kṣaṇāt*—in a fraction of a second; *jaya*—"victory!"; *śabdaḥ*—the sound; *namaḥ*—"homage!"; *śabdaḥ*—the sound; *sādhu*—"well done!"; *śabdaḥ*—the sound; *abhavat*—happened; *divi*—in the sky.

TRANSLATION

Instantly his head shattered as if struck by a lightning bolt, and the demon fell down dead. From the sky were heard cries of "Victory!" "Obeisances!" and "Well done!"

TEXT 37

मुमुचुः पुष्पवर्षाणि हते पापे वृकासुरे ।
देवर्षिपितृगन्धर्वा मोचितः संकटाच्छिवः ॥३७॥

mumucuḥ puṣpa-varṣāṇi
hate pāpe vṛkāsure
devarṣi-pitṛ-gandharvā
mocitaḥ saṅkaṭāc chivaḥ

mumucuḥ—they released; *puṣpa*—of flowers; *varṣāṇi*—rain; *hate*—having been killed; *pāpe*—the sinful; *vṛka-asure*—demon Vṛka; *deva-ṛṣi*—the celestial sages; *pitṛ*—departed forefathers; *gandharvāḥ*—and singers of heaven; *mocitaḥ*—freed; *saṅkaṭāt*—from danger; *śivaḥ*—Lord Śiva.

TRANSLATION

The celestial sages, Pitās and Gandharvas rained down flowers to celebrate the killing of sinful Vṛkāsura. Now Lord Śiva was out of danger.

TEXTS 38–39

मुक्तं गिरिशमभ्याह भगवान् पुरुषोत्तमः ।
अहो देव महादेव पापोऽयं स्वेन पाप्मना ॥३८॥

हतः को नु महत्स्वीश जन्तुर्वै कृतकिल्बिषः ।
क्षेमी स्यात्किमु विश्वेशे कृतागस्को जगद्गुरौ ॥३९॥

muktaṁ giriśam abhyāha
bhagavān puruṣottamaḥ
aho deva mahā-deva
pāpo 'yaṁ svena pāpmanā

hataḥ ko nu mahatsv īśa
jantur vai kṛta-kilbiṣaḥ
kṣemī syāt kim u viśveśe
kṛtāgasko jagad-gurau

muktam—delivered; *giriśam*—Lord Śiva; *abhyāha*—addressed; *bhagavān puruṣa-uttamaḥ*—the Supreme Personality of Godhead (Nārāyaṇa); *aho*—ah; *deva*—My dear lord; *mahā-deva*—Śiva; *pāpaḥ*—sinful; *ayam*—this person; *svena*—by his own; *pāpmanā*—sins; *hataḥ*—killed; *kaḥ*—what; *nu*—indeed; *mahatsu*—toward elevated saints; *īśa*—O master; *jantuḥ*—living being; *vai*—indeed; *kṛta*—having done; *kilbiṣaḥ*—offense; *kṣemī*—fortunate; *syāt*—can be; *kim u*—what to speak, moreover; *viśva*—of the universe; *īśe*—against the lord (you); *kṛta-āgaskaḥ*—having committed offense; *jagat*—of the universe; *gurau*—the spiritual master.

TRANSLATION

The Supreme Personality of Godhead then addressed Lord Giriśa, who was now out of danger: "Just see, O Mahādeva, My lord, how this wicked man has been killed by his own sinful reactions. Indeed, what living being can hope for good fortune if he offends exalted saints, what to speak of offending the lord and spiritual master of the universe?"

PURPORT

According to Śrīla Viśvanātha Cakravartī, this statement of Lord Viṣṇu's implies a mild scolding: "My dear possessor of unlimited vision, O you of clear intelligence, benedictions should not be given to wicked demons in this way. You could have been killed! But you were only concerned about saving this poor soul, so you disregarded what would happen to you as a result." Thus, Ācārya Viśvanātha Cakravartī points out, Lord Nārāyaṇa's mild rebuke also highlighted Lord Śiva's exceptional compassion.

TEXT 40

य एवमव्याकृतशक्त्युदन्वतः
परस्य साक्षात्परमात्मनो हरेः ।
गिरित्रमोक्षं कथयेच्छृणोति वा
विमुच्यते संसृतिभिस्तथारिभिः ॥४०॥

ya evam avyākṛta-śakty-udanvataḥ
parasya sākṣāt paramātmano hareḥ
giritra-mokṣaṁ kathayec chṛṇoti vā
vimucyate saṁsṛtibhis tathāribhiḥ

yaḥ—whoever; *evam*—thus; *avyākṛta*—inconceivable; *śakti*—of energies; *udanvataḥ*—of the ocean; *parasya*—the Supreme; *sākṣāt*—personally manifest; *parama-ātmanaḥ*—of the Supersoul; *hareḥ*—Lord Hari; *giritra*—of Lord Śiva; *mokṣam*—the saving; *kathayet*—recites; *śṛṇoti*—hears; *vā*—or; *vimucyate*—is freed; *saṁsṛtibhiḥ*—from repeated births and deaths; *tathā*—as well as; *aribhiḥ*—from enemies.

TRANSLATION

Lord Hari is the directly manifest Absolute Truth, the Supreme Soul and unlimited ocean of inconceivable energies. Anyone who recites or hears this pastime of His saving Lord Śiva will be freed from all enemies and the repetition of birth and death.

PURPORT

Śrīla Śrīdhara Svāmī concludes this chapter with the following statement:

bhakta-saṅkaṭam ālokya
kṛpā-pūrṇa-hṛd-ambujaḥ
giritraṁ citra-vākyāt tu
mokṣayām āsa keśavaḥ

"When Lord Keśava saw the danger confronting His devotee, His lotus-like heart became filled with sympathy. Thus He delivered Lord Śiva from the consequences of his own eloquent words."

Thus end the purports of the humble servants of His Divine Grace A. C. Bhaktivedanta Swami Prabhupāda to the Tenth Canto, Eighty-eighth Chapter, of the Śrīmad-Bhagavatam, *entitled "Lord Śiva Saved from Vṛkāsura."*

CHAPTER EIGHTY-NINE

Kṛṣṇa and Arjuna Retrieve a Brāhmaṇa's Sons

This chapter describes how Bhṛgu Muni proved the supremacy of Lord Viṣṇu, and how Lord Kṛṣṇa and Arjuna recovered the dead sons of an aggrieved *brāhmaṇa* in Dvārakā.

Once, long ago, on the shore of the river Sarasvatī, a discussion arose among a group of sages as to which of the three chief lords—Brahmā, Viṣṇu or Śiva—is the greatest. They deputed Bhṛgu Muni to investigate the matter.

Bhṛgu decided to test the lords' tolerance, for that quality is a sure sign of greatness. First he entered the court of Lord Brahmā, his father, without offering him any respect. This enraged Brahmā, who suppressed his anger because Bhṛgu was his son. Next Bhṛgu went to Lord Śiva, his older brother, who rose from his seat to embrace him. But Bhṛgu rejected the embrace, calling Śiva a deviant heretic. Just as Śiva was about to kill Bhṛgu with his trident, Goddess Pārvatī interceded and pacified her husband. Next Bhṛgu went to Vaikuṇṭha to test Lord Nārāyaṇa. Going up to the Lord, who was lying with His head on the lap of the goddess of fortune, Bhṛgu kicked His chest. But instead of becoming angry, both the Lord and His consort stood up and offered Bhṛgu respects. "Welcome," said the Lord. "Please sit down and rest awhile. Kindly forgive us, dear master, for not noticing your arrival." When Bhṛgu went back to the assembly of sages and told them all that had happened, they concluded that Lord Viṣṇu is certainly supreme.

Once in Dvārakā a *brāhmaṇa's* wife gave birth to a son who immediately died. The *brāhmaṇa* took his dead son to the court of King Ugrasena and berated the King: "This duplicitous, greedy enemy of *brāhmaṇas* has caused my son's death by failing to execute his duties properly!" The same misfortune continued to befall the *brāhmaṇa,* and each time he would bring his dead infant's body to the royal court and berate the King. When the ninth son died at birth, Arjuna happened to hear the *brāhmaṇa's* complaint, and he said, "My lord, I will protect your progeny. And if I fail, I will enter fire to atone for my sin."

Some time later, the *brāhmaṇa's* wife was about to give birth for the tenth time. When Arjuna learned of this, he went to the maternity house and enveloped it with a protective cage of arrows. Arjuna's efforts were to no avail, however, for as soon as the child was born and began to cry, it disappeared into the sky. As the *brāhmaṇa* profusely derided Arjuna, the warrior set off for the abode of Yamarāja, the king of death. But Arjuna did not find the *brāhmaṇa's* son there, and even after searching throughout the fourteen worlds he could find no trace of the infant.

Having failed to protect the *brāhmaṇa's* son, Arjuna was now intent on committing suicide by entering the sacred fire. But just as he was about to do so, Lord Kṛṣṇa stopped him and said, "I will show you the *brāhmaṇa's* sons, so please don't despise yourself like this." Lord Kṛṣṇa then took Arjuna onto His transcendental chariot, and the two of them crossed over the seven universal islands with their seven oceans, passed over the Lokāloka mountain range and entered the region of dense darkness. Since the horses could not find their way, Kṛṣṇa sent His blazing Sudarśana disc ahead to pierce the gloom. Gradually they came to the water of the Causal Ocean, within which they found the city of Lord Mahā-Viṣṇu. There they saw the thousand-hooded serpent Ananta, and upon Him lay Mahā-Viṣṇu. The great Lord greeted Śrī Kṛṣṇa and Arjuna, saying "I brought the *brāhmaṇa's* sons here simply because I wanted to see the two of you. Please continue to benefit the people in general by exemplifying religious behavior in your forms of Nara-Nārāyaṇa Ṛṣi."

Lord Kṛṣṇa and Arjuna then took the *brāhmaṇa's* sons, went back to Dvārakā and returned the infants to their father. Having directly experienced the greatness of Śrī Kṛṣṇa, Arjuna was amazed. He concluded that only by the Lord's mercy can a living being exhibit any power or opulence.

TEXT 1

श्रीशुक उवाच

सरस्वत्यास्तटे राजन्नृषयः सत्रमासत ।
वितर्कः समभूत्तेषां त्रिष्वधीशेषु को महान् ॥१॥

śrī-śuka uvāca
sarasvatyās taṭe rājann
ṛṣayaḥ satram āsata
vitarkaḥ samabhūt teṣāṁ
triṣv adhīśeṣu ko mahān

śrī-śukaḥ uvāca—Śukadeva Gosvāmī said; *sarasvatyāḥ*—of the river Sarasvatī; *taṭe*—on the bank; *rājan*—O King (Parīkṣit); *ṛṣayaḥ*—sages; *satram*—a Vedic sacrifice; *āsata*—were performing; *vitarkaḥ*—a disagreement; *samabhūt*—arose; *teṣām*—among them; *triṣu*—among the three; *adhīśeṣu*—chief lords; *kaḥ*—who; *mahān*—the greatest.

TRANSLATION

Śukadeva Gosvāmī said: Once, O King, as a group of sages were performing a Vedic sacrifice on the banks of the Sarasvatī River, a controversy arose among them as to which of the three chief deities is supreme.

PURPORT

The three chief deities mentioned here are Lord Viṣṇu, Lord Brahmā and Lord Śiva.

TEXT 2

तस्य जिज्ञासया ते वै भृगुं ब्रह्मसुतं नृप ।
तज्ज्ञप्त्यै प्रेषयामासुः सोऽभ्यगाद् ब्रह्मणः सभाम् ॥२॥

tasya jijñāsayā te vai
bhṛguṁ brahma-sutaṁ nṛpa
taj-jñaptyai preṣayām āsuḥ
so 'bhyagād brahmaṇaḥ sabhām

tasya—about this; *jijñāsayā*—with the desire of knowing; *te*—they; *vai*—indeed; *bhṛgum*—Bhṛgu Muni; *brahma-sutam*—son of Brahmā; *nṛpa*—O King; *tat*—this; *jñaptyai*—to find out; *preṣayām āsuḥ*—they sent; *saḥ*—he; *abhyagāt*—went; *brahmaṇaḥ*—of Lord Brahmā; *sabhām*—to the court.

TRANSLATION

Eager to resolve this question, O King, the sages sent Lord Brahmā's son Bhṛgu to find the answer. First he went to his father's court.

PURPORT

As Śrīla Prabhupāda explains in *Kṛṣṇa, the Supreme Personality of Godhead,* "The plan decided upon by the sages was for Bhṛgu to test which of the predominating deities possessed the quality of goodness in full." One who is in the mode of goodness possesses such qualities as tolerance and equanimity, whereas those conducted by the modes of passion and ignorance are prone to easily lose their temper.

TEXT 3

न तस्मै प्रह्वणं स्तोत्रं चक्रे सत्त्वपरीक्षया ।
तस्मै चुक्रोध भगवान् प्रज्वलन् स्वेन तेजसा ॥३॥

na tasmai prahvaṇaṁ stotraṁ
cakre sattva-parīkṣayā
tasmai cukrodha bhagavān
prajvalan svena tejasā

na—not; *tasmai*—to him (Brahmā); *prahvaṇam*—bowing down; *stotram*—recitation of prayers; *cakre*—made; *sattva*—his situation in the mode of goodness; *parīkṣayā*—with the aim of testing; *tasmai*—at him; *cukrodha*—became angry; *bhagavān*—the lord; *prajvalan*—becoming inflamed, *svena*—with his own; *tejasā*—passion.

TRANSLATION

To test how well Lord Brahmā was situated in the mode of goodness, Bhṛgu failed to bow down to him or glorify him with prayers. The lord became angry at him, inflamed into fury by his own passion.

TEXT 4

स आत्मन्युत्थितं मन्युमात्मजायात्मना प्रभुः ।
अशीशमद्यथा वह्निं स्वयोन्या वारिणात्मभूः ॥४॥

sa ātmany utthitaṁ manyum
ātmajāyātmanā prabhuḥ
aśīśamad yathā vahniṁ
sva-yonyā vāriṇātma-bhūḥ

saḥ—he; *ātmani*—within himself; *utthitam*—risen; *manyum*—anger; *ātma-jāya*—toward his son; *ātmanā*—by his own intelligence; *prabhuḥ*—the lord; *aśīśamat*—subdued; *yathā*—just as; *vahnim*—fire; *sva*—itself; *yonyā*—whose origin; *vāriṇā*—by water; *ātma-bhūḥ*—self-born Brahmā.

TRANSLATION

Though anger toward his son was now rising within his heart, Lord Brahmā was able to subdue it by applying his intelligence, in the same way that fire is extinguished by its own product, water.

PURPORT

Lord Brahmā is sometimes affected by his contact with the mode of passion. But because he is *ādi-kavi,* the firstborn and foremost learned scholar in the universe, when anger begins to disturb his mind he can control it by means of discriminating self-examination. In this instance he reminded himself that Bhṛgu was his son. Thus in this verse Śukadeva Gosvāmī draws the analogy that Brahmā's own expansion (his son) served to put out his anger just as water, which originally evolved from elemental fire in the primeval creation, puts out a fire.

TEXT 5

ततः कैलासमगमत्स तं देवो महेश्वरः ।
परिरब्धुं समारेभ उत्थाय भ्रातरं मुदा ॥५॥

tataḥ kailāsam agamat
sa taṁ devo maheśvaraḥ
parirabdhuṁ samārebha
utthāya bhrātaraṁ mudā

tataḥ—then; *kailāsam*—to Mount Kailāsa; *agamat*—went; *saḥ*—he (Bhṛgu); *tam*—him; *devaḥ mahā-īśvaraḥ*—Lord Śiva; *parirabdhum*—to embrace; *samārebhe*—attempted; *utthāya*—standing up; *bhrātaram*—his brother; *mudā*—with pleasure.

TRANSLATION

Bhṛgu then went to Mount Kailāsa. There Lord Śiva stood up and happily came forward to embrace his brother.

PURPORT

In the Vedic civilization it is considered very important to properly greet one's family members, especially when one has not seen them for a long time. A worthy son should show respect to his father, a younger brother should honor his older brother, and the older brother should show affection to his younger brother in turn.

TEXTS 6–7

नैच्छत्त्वमस्युत्पथग इति देवश्चुकोप ह ।
शूलमुद्यम्य तं हन्तुमारेभे तिग्मलोचनः ॥६॥
पतित्वा पादयोर्देवी सान्त्वयामास तं गिरा ।
अथो जगाम वैकुण्ठं यत्र देवो जनार्दनः ॥७॥

naicchat tvam asy utpatha-ga
iti devaś cukopa ha
śūlam udyamya taṁ hantum
ārebhe tigma-locanaḥ

patitvā pādayor devī
sāntvayām āsa taṁ girā

atho jagāma vaikuṇṭhaṁ
yatra devo janārdanaḥ

na aicchat—he did not desire this (embrace); *tvam*—you; *asi*—are; *utpatha-gaḥ*—a transgressor of the path (of religion); *iti*—so saying; *devaḥ*—the lord (Śiva); *cukopa ha*—became angry; *śūlam*—his trident; *udyamya*—raising; *tam*—him (Bhṛgu); *hantum*—to kill; *ārebhe*—was about; *tigma*—fierce; *locanaḥ*—whose eyes; *patitvā*—falling; *pādayoḥ*—at (Lord Śiva's) feet; *devī*—Goddess Devī; *sāntvayām āsa*—pacified; *tam*—him; *girā*—with words; *atha u*—then; *jagāma*—(Bhṛgu) went; *vaikuṇṭham*—to the spiritual planet of Vaikuṇṭha; *yatra*—where; *devaḥ janārdanaḥ*—Lord Janārdana (Viṣṇu).

TRANSLATION

But Bhṛgu refused his embrace, telling him, "You are a deviant heretic." At this Lord Śiva became angry, and his eyes burned ferociously. He raised his trident and was about to kill Bhṛgu when Goddess Devī fell at his feet and spoke some words to pacify him. Bhṛgu then left that place and went to Vaikuṇṭha, where Lord Janārdana resides.

PURPORT

In *Kṛṣṇa*, Śrīla Prabhupāda writes, "It is said that an offense can be committed either with the body, with the mind or by speech. Bhṛgu Muni's first offense, committed toward Lord Brahmā, was an offense with the mind. His second offense, committed toward Lord Śiva by insulting him, criticizing him for unclean habits, was an offense by speech. Because the quality of ignorance is prominent in Lord Śiva, when he heard Bhṛgu's insult, his eyes immediately became red with anger. With uncontrollable rage, he took up his trident and prepared to kill Bhṛgu Muni. At that time Lord Śiva's wife, Pārvatī, was present. Her personality is a mixture of the three qualities, and therefore she is called Triguṇa-mayī. In this case, she saved the situation by evoking Lord Śiva's quality of goodness."

Śrīla Jīva Gosvāmī remarks that the Vaikuṇṭha planet referred to here is Śvetadvīpa.

TEXTS 8–9

शयानं श्रिय उत्संगे पदा वक्षस्यताडयत् ।
तत उत्थाय भगवान् सह लक्ष्म्या सतां गतिः ॥८॥
स्वतल्पादवरुह्याथ ननाम शिरसा मुनिम् ।
आह ते स्वागतं ब्रह्मन्निषीदात्रासने क्षणम् ।
अजानतामागतान् वः क्षन्तुमर्हथ नः प्रभो ॥९॥

śayānaṁ śriya utsaṅge
padā vakṣasy atāḍayat
tata utthāya bhagavān
saha lakṣmyā satāṁ gatiḥ

sva-talpād avaruhyātha
nanāma śirasā munim
āha te svāgataṁ brahman
niṣīdātrāsane kṣaṇam
ajānatām āgatān vaḥ
kṣantum arhatha naḥ prabho

śayānam—who was lying down; *śriyaḥ*—of the goddess of fortune; *utsaṅge*—on the lap; *padā*—with his foot; *vakṣasi*—on His chest; *atāḍayat*—he kicked; *tataḥ*—then; *utthāya*—standing up; *bhagavān*—the Personality of Godhead; *saha lakṣmyā*—together with Goddess Lakṣmī; *satām*—of pure devotees; *gatiḥ*—the destination; *sva*—His; *talpāt*—from the bed; *avaruhya*—climbing down; *atha*—then; *nanāma*—He bowed down; *śirasā*—with His head; *munim*—to the sage; *āha*—He said; *te*—to you; *su-āgatam*—welcome; *brahman*—O *brāhmaṇa; niṣīda*—please sit; *atra*—in this; *āsane*—seat; *kṣanam*—for a moment; *ajānatām*—who were unaware; *āgatān*—arrived; *vaḥ*—of you; *ksantum*—forgive: *arhatha*—you should please; *naḥ*—us; *prabho*—O master.

TRANSLATION

There he went up to the Supreme Lord, who was lying with His head on the lap of His consort, Śrī, and kicked Him on the chest. The Lord then rose, along with Goddess Lakṣmī, as a sign of

respect. Coming down from His bedstead, that supreme goal of all pure devotees bowed His head to the floor before the sage and told him, "Welcome, *brāhmaṇa.* Please sit in this chair and rest awhile. Kindly forgive us, dear master, for not noticing your arrival.

PURPORT

According to Śrīla Jīva Gosvāmī, at the time of this pastime Bhṛgu Muni had not yet become a pure Vaiṣṇava; otherwise he would not have acted so rashly toward the Supreme Lord. Not only was Lord Viṣṇu taking rest, but He was lying with His head in His wife's lap. For Bhṛgu to strike Him in this position—and not with his hand but with his foot—was worse than any other offense Bhṛgu could have imagined.

Śrīla Prabhupāda comments, "Of course, Lord Viṣṇu is all-merciful. He did not become angry at the activities of Bhṛgu Muni because Bhṛgu Muni was a great *brāhmaṇa*. A *brāhmaṇa* is to be excused even if he sometimes commits an offense, and Lord Viṣṇu set the example. Yet it is said that from the time of this incident, the goddess of fortune, Lakṣmī, has not been very favorably disposed toward the *brāhmaṇas,* and therefore because the goddess of fortune withholds her benedictions from them, the *brāhmaṇas* are generally very poor."

TEXTS 10–11

पुनीहि सहलोकं मां लोकपालांश्च मद्गतान् ।
पादोदकेन भवतस्तीर्थानां तीर्थकारिणा ॥१०॥
अद्याहं भगवल्ँलक्ष्म्या आसमेकान्तभाजनम् ।
वत्स्यत्युरसि मे भूतिर्भवत्पादहतांहसः ॥११॥

punīhi saha-lokaṁ māṁ
loka-pālāṁś ca mad-gatān
pādodakena bhavatas
tīrthānāṁ tīrtha-kāriṇā

adyāhaṁ bhagaval̐ lakṣmyā
āsam ekānta-bhājanam

vatsyaty urasi me bhūtir
bhavat-pāda-hatāṁhasaḥ

punīhi—please purify; *saha*—along with; *lokam*—My planet; *mām*—Me; *loka*—of various planets; *pālān*—the rulers; *ca*—and; *mat-gatān*—who are devoted to Me; *pāda*—(which has washed) the feet; *udakena*—by the water; *bhavataḥ*—of your good self; *tīrthānām*—of holy places of pilgrimage; *tīrtha*—their sacredness; *kāriṇā*—which creates; *adya*—today; *aham*—I; *bhagavan*—O My lord; *lakṣmyāḥ*—of Lakṣmī; *āsam*—have become; *eka-anta*—exclusive; *bhājanam*—the shelter; *vatsyati*—will reside; *urasi*—on the chest; *me*—My; *bhūtiḥ*—the goddess of fortune; *bhavat*—your; *pāda*—by the foot; *hata*—eradicated; *aṁhasaḥ*—whose sinful reactions.

TRANSLATION

"Please purify Me, My realm and the realms of the universal rulers devoted to Me by giving us the water that has washed your feet. This holy water is indeed what makes all places of pilgrimage sacred. Today, my lord, I have become the exclusive shelter of the goddess of fortune, Lakṣmī; she will consent to reside on My chest because your foot has rid it of sins."

PURPORT

Continuing his comments, Śrīla Prabhupāda says, "The so-called *brāhmaṇas* of the Kali-yuga are sometimes very proud that they can touch the chest of Lord Viṣṇu with their feet. But when Bhṛgu Muni touched the chest of Lord Viṣṇu with his feet, it was different because although it was the greatest offense, Lord Viṣṇu, being greatly magnanimous, did not take it very seriously."

Some editions of *Śrīmad-Bhāgavatam* contain the following verse between Texts 11 and 12, and Śrīla Prabhupāda also includes it in *Kṛṣṇa, the Supreme Personality of Godhead,* his summary study of the Tenth Canto:

atīva-komalau tāta
caraṇau te mahā-mune
ity uktvā vipra-caraṇau
mardayan svena pāṇinā

"[The Lord said to the *brāhmaṇa* Bhṛgu:] 'My dear sir, O great sage, your feet are indeed very tender.' Saying this, Lord Viṣṇu began massaging the *brāhmaṇa's* feet with His own hands."

TEXT 12

श्रीशुक उवाच
एवं ब्रुवाणे वैकुण्ठे भृगुस्तन्मन्द्रया गिरा ।
निर्वृतस्तर्पितस्तूष्णीं भक्त्युत्कण्ठोऽश्रुलोचनः ॥१२॥

śrī-śuka uvāca
evaṁ bruvāṇe vaikuṇṭhe
bhṛgus tan-mandrayā girā
nirvṛtas tarpitas tūṣṇīṁ
bhakty-utkaṇṭho 'śru-locanaḥ

śrī-śukaḥ uvāca—Śukadeva Gosvāmī said; *evam*—in this way; *bruvāṇe*—having spoken; *vaikuṇṭhe*—Lord Viṣṇu; *bhṛguḥ*—Bhṛgu; *tat*—His; *mandrayā*—solemn; *girā*—by the words; *nirvṛtaḥ*—delighted; *tarpitaḥ*—gratified; *tūṣṇīm*—was silent; *bhakti*—with devotion; *ut-kaṇṭhaḥ*—overwhelmed; *aśru*—tears; *locanaḥ*—in whose eyes.

TRANSLATION

Śukadeva Gosvāmī said: Bhṛgu felt satisfied and delighted to hear the solemn words spoken by Lord Vaikuṇṭha. Overwhelmed with devotional ecstasy, he remained silent, his eyes brimming with tears.

PURPORT

Bhṛgu could not offer the Lord any words of praise because his throat was choking with tears of ecstasy. In the opinion of Śrīla Viśvanātha Cakravartī, the sage should not be condemned for his offensive behavior, since his role in this transcendental pastime was arranged by the Personality of Godhead.

TEXT 13

पुनश्च सत्रमाव्रज्य मुनीनां ब्रह्मवादिनाम् ।
स्वानुभूतमशेषेण राजन् भृगुरवर्णयत् ॥१३॥

punaś ca satram āvrajya
munīnāṁ brahma-vādinām
svānubhūtam aśeṣeṇa
rājan bhṛgur avarṇayat

punaḥ—again; *ca*—and; *satram*—to the sacrifice; *āvrajya*—going; *munīnām*—of the sages; *brahma-vādinām*—who were expert in knowledge of the *Vedas; sva*—by himself; *anubhūtam*—experienced; *aśeṣeṇa*—in full; *rājan*—O King (Parīkṣit); *bhṛguḥ*—Bhṛgu; *avarṇayat*—described.

TRANSLATION

O King, Bhṛgu then returned to the sacrificial arena of the wise Vedic authorities and described his entire experience to them.

TEXTS 14–17

तन्निशम्याथ मुनयो विस्मिता मुक्तसंशयाः ।
भूयांसं श्रद्दधुर्विष्णुं यतः शान्तिर्यतोऽभयम् ॥१४॥
धर्मः साक्षाद्यतो ज्ञानं वैराग्यं च तदन्वितम् ।
ऐश्वर्यं चाष्टधा यस्माद्यशश्चात्ममलापहम् ॥१५॥
मुनीनां न्यस्तदण्डानां शान्तानां समचेतसाम् ।
अकिञ्चनानां साधूनां यमाहुः परमां गतिम् ॥१६॥
सत्त्वं यस्य प्रिया मूर्तिर्ब्राह्मणास्त्विष्टदेवताः ।
भजन्त्यनाशिषः शान्ता यं वा निपुणबुद्धयः ॥१७॥

tan niśamyātha munayo
vismitā mukta-saṁśayāḥ
bhūyāṁsaṁ śraddadhur viṣṇuṁ
yataḥ śāntir yato 'bhayam

dharmaḥ sākṣād yato jñānaṁ
vairāgyaṁ ca tad-anvitam
aiśvaryaṁ cāṣṭadhā yasmād
yaśaś cātma-malāpaham

munīnāṁ nyasta-daṇḍānāṁ
śāntānāṁ sama-cetasām
akiñcanānāṁ sādhūnāṁ
yam āhuḥ paramāṁ gatim

sattvaṁ yasya priyā mūrtir
brāhmaṇās tv iṣṭa-devatāḥ
bhajanty anāśiṣaḥ śāntā
yaṁ vā nipuṇa-buddhayaḥ

tat—this; *niśamya*—hearing; *atha*—then; *munayaḥ*—the sages; *vismitāḥ*—amazed; *mukta*—freed; *saṁśayāḥ*—from their doubts; *bhūyāṁsam*—as the greatest; *śraddadhuḥ*—they put their faith; *viṣṇum*—in Lord Viṣṇu; *yataḥ*—from whom; *śāntiḥ*—peace; *yataḥ*—from whom; *abhayam*—fearlessness; *dharmaḥ*—religion; *sākṣāt*—in its direct manifestations; *yataḥ*—from whom; *jñānam*—knowledge; *vairāgyam*—detachment; *ca*—and; *tat*—it (knowledge); *anvitam*—including; *aiśvaryam*—the mystic power (gained by practice of *yoga*); *ca*—and; *aṣṭadhā*—eightfold; *yasmāt*—from whom; *yaśaḥ*—His fame; *ca*—also; *ātma*—of the mind; *mala*—the contamination; *apaham*—which eradicates; *munīnām*—of the sages; *nyasta*—who have given up; *daṇḍānām*—violence; *śāntānām*—peaceful; *sama*—equipoised; *cetasām*—whose minds; *akiñcanānām*—selfless; *sādhūnām*—saintly; *yam*—whom; *āhuḥ*—they call; *paramām*—the supreme; *gatim*—destination; *sattvam*—the mode of goodness; *yasya*—whose; *priyā*—favorite; *mūrtiḥ*—embodiment; *brāhmaṇāḥ*—*brāhmaṇas; tu*—and; *iṣṭa*—worshiped; *devatāḥ*—deities; *bhajanti*—they worship: *anāśiṣaḥ*—without ulterior desires; *śāntāḥ*—those who have attained spiritual peace; *yam*—whom; *vā*—indeed; *nipuṇa*—expert; *buddhayaḥ*—whose faculties of intelligence.

TRANSLATION

Amazed upon hearing Bhṛgu's account, the sages were freed from all doubts and became convinced that Viṣṇu is the greatest Lord. From Him come peace; fearlessness; the essential principles of religion; detachment with knowledge; the eightfold powers of mystic *yoga*; and His glorification, which cleanses the mind of all impurities. He is known as the supreme destination for those

who are peaceful and equipoised—the selfless, wise saints who have given up all violence. His most dear form is that of pure goodness, and the *brāhmaṇas* are His worshipable deities. Persons of keen intellect who have attained spiritual peace worship Him without selfish motives.

PURPORT

By becoming devoted to the Personality of Godhead, one easily attains divine knowledge and detachment from sense gratification, without separate endeavor. As described in the Eleventh Canto of *Śrīmad-Bhāgavatam* (11.2.42),

bhaktiḥ pareśānubhavo viraktir
anyatra caiṣa trika eka-kālaḥ
prapadyamānasya yathāśnataḥ syus
tuṣṭiḥ puṣṭiḥ kṣud-apāyo 'nu-ghāsam

"Devotion, direct experience of the Supreme Lord, and detachment from other things—these three occur simultaneously for one who has taken shelter of the Supreme Personality of Godhead, in the same way that pleasure, nourishment and relief from hunger come simultaneously and increasingly, with each bite, for a person engaged in eating." Similarly, in the First Canto (1.2.7), Śrīla Sūta Gosvāmī states,

vāsudeve bhagavati
bhakti-yogaḥ prayojitaḥ
janayaty āśu vairāgyaṁ
jñānaṁ ca yad ahaitukam

"By rendering devotional service unto the Personality of Godhead, Śrī Kṛṣṇa, one immediately acquires causeless knowledge and detachment from the world."

Lord Śrī Kapila, in His instructions to His mother, Devahūti, proposes that the eightfold powers of *yoga* are also coincidental fruits of devotional service:

atho vibhūtiṁ mama māyāvinas tām
aiśvaryam aṣṭāṅgam anupravṛttam

śriyaṁ bhāgavatīṁ vāspṛhayanti bhadrāṁ
parasya me te 'śnuvate hi loke

"Because he is completely absorbed in thought of Me, My devotee does not desire even the highest benediction obtainable in the upper planetary systems, including Satyaloka. He does not desire the eight material perfections obtained from mystic *yoga*, nor does he desire to be elevated to the kingdom of God. Yet even without desiring them, My devotee enjoys, even in this life, all the offered benedictions." (*Bhāg*. 3.25.37)

Śrīla Viśvanātha Cakravartī points out that in Text 16, three kinds of transcendentalists are named: the *munis*, the *śāntas* and the *sādhus*. These are, in order of increasing importance, persons striving for liberation, those who have attained liberation, and those who are engaged in pure devotional service to Lord Viṣṇu.

TEXT 18

त्रिविधाकृतयस्तस्य राक्षसा असुराः सुराः ।
गुणिन्या मायया सृष्टाः सत्त्वं तत्तीर्थसाधनम् ॥१८॥

tri-vidhākṛtayas tasya
rākṣasā asurāḥ surāḥ
guṇinyā māyayā sṛṣṭāḥ
sattvaṁ tat tīrtha-sādhanam

tri-vidha—of three kinds; *ākṛtayaḥ*—forms; *tasya*—of His; *rākṣasāḥ*—the ignorant spirits; *asurāḥ*—the demons; *surāḥ*—and the demigods; *guṇinyāḥ*—qualified by the material modes; *māyayā*—by His material energy; *sṛṣṭāḥ*—created; *sattvam*—the mode of goodness; *tat*—among them; *tīrtha*—of success in life; *sādhanam*—the means of attainment.

TRANSLATION

The Lord expands into three kinds of manifest beings—the Rākṣasas, the demons and the demigods—all of whom are created by the Lord's material energy and conditioned by her modes. But among these three modes, it is the mode of goodness which is the means of attaining life's final success.

PURPORT

In *Kṛṣṇa* Śrīla Prabhupāda writes, "There are different kinds of people existing in the modes of material nature. Those who are in the mode of ignorance are called *rākṣasas,* those in the mode of passion are called *asuras* [demons], and those in the mode of goodness are called *suras,* or demigods. Under the direction of the Supreme Lord, these three classes of men are created by material nature, but those who are in the mode of goodness have a greater chance to be elevated to the spiritual world, back home, back to Godhead."

TEXT 19

श्रीशुक उवाच
इत्थं सारस्वता विप्रा नृणां संशयनुत्तये ।
पुरुषस्य पदाम्भोजसेवया तद्गतिं गताः ॥१९॥

śrī-śuka uvāca
itthaṁ sārasvatā viprā
nṛṇāṁ saṁśaya-nuttaye
puruṣasya padāmbhoja-
sevayā tad-gatiṁ gatāḥ

śrī-śukaḥ uvāca—Śukadeva Gosvāmī said; *ittham*—in this way; *sārasvatāḥ*—living along the Sarasvatī River; *viprāḥ*—the learned *brāhmaṇas; nṛṇām*—of people in general; *saṁśaya*—the doubts; *nuttaye*—to dispel; *puruṣasya*—of the Supreme Person; *pada-ambhoja*—of the lotus feet; *sevayā*—by service; *tat*—His; *gatim*—destination; *gatāḥ*—attained.

TRANSLATION

Śukadeva Gosvāmī said: The learned *brāhmaṇas* living along the river Sarasvatī came to this conclusion in order to dispel the doubts of all people. Thereafter they rendered devotional service to the Supreme Lord's lotus feet and attained His abode.

TEXT 20

श्रीसूत उवाच
इत्येतन्मुनितनयास्यपद्मगन्ध-
पीयूषं भवभयभित्परस्य पुंसः ।

सुश्लोकं श्रवणपुटैः पिबत्यभीक्ष्णं
पान्थोऽध्वभ्रमणपरिश्रमं जहाति ॥२०॥

śrī-sūta uvāca
ity etan muni-tanayāsya-padma-gandha-
pīyūṣaṁ bhava-bhaya-bhit parasya puṁsaḥ
su-ślokaṁ śravaṇa-puṭaiḥ pibaty abhīkṣṇaṁ
pāntho 'dhva-bhramaṇa-pariśramaṁ jahāti

śrī-sūtaḥ uvāca—Śrī Sūta said; *iti*—thus spoken; *etat*—this; *muni*—of the sage (Vyāsadeva); *tanaya*—of the son (Śukadeva); *āsya*—from the mouth; *padma*—(which is just like) a lotus; *gandha*—with the fragrance; *pīyūṣam*—the nectar; *bhava*—of material life; *bhaya*—fear; *bhit*—which shatters; *parasya*—of the supreme; *puṁsaḥ*—Personality of Godhead; *su-ślokam*—glorious; *śravaṇa*—of the ears; *puṭaiḥ*—through the cavities; *pibati*—drinks; *abhīkṣṇam*—constantly; *pānthaḥ*—a traveler; *adhva*—on the road; *bhramaṇa*—from his wandering; *pariśramam*—the fatigue; *jahāti*—gives up.

TRANSLATION

Śrī Sūta Gosvāmī said: Thus did this fragrant nectar flow from the lotus mouth of Śukadeva Gosvāmī, the son of the sage Vyāsadeva. This wonderful glorification of the Supreme Person destroys all fear of material existence. A traveler who constantly drinks this nectar through his ear-holes will forget the fatigue brought on by wandering along the paths of worldly life.

PURPORT

This narration by Śrīla Śukadeva Gosvāmī is precious in two ways: For those suffering from spiritual infirmity it is an effective tonic to cure the disease of illusion. And for surrendered Vaiṣṇavas it is a delicious and invigorating beverage, fragrant with the aroma of Śrī Śuka's realizations.

TEXT 21

श्रीशुक उवाच
एकदा द्वारवत्यां तु विप्रपत्न्याः कुमारकः ।
जातमात्रो भुवं स्पृष्ट्वा ममार किल भारत ॥२१॥

śrī-śuka uvāca
ekadā dvāravatyāṁ tu
vipra-patnyāḥ kumārakaḥ
jāta-mātro bhuvaṁ spṛṣṭvā
mamāra kila bhārata

śrī-śukaḥ uvāca—Śukadeva Gosvāmī said; *ekadā*—once; *dvāravatyām*—in Dvārakā; *tu*—and; *vipra*—a *brāhmaṇa's;* *patnyāḥ*—of the wife; *kumārakaḥ*—the infant son; *jāta*—born; *mātraḥ*—only; *bhuvam*—the ground; *spṛṣṭvā*—touching; *mamāra*—died; *kila*—indeed; *bhārata*—O descendant of Bharata (Parīkṣit Mahārāja).

TRANSLATION

Śukadeva Gosvāmī said: Once, in Dvārakā, a *brāhmaṇa's* wife gave birth to a son, but the newborn infant died as soon as he touched the ground, O Bhārata.

PURPORT

In this chapter Lord Viṣṇu has been glorified as the Supreme Godhead. Now Śukadeva Gosvāmī is going to identify Lord Kṛṣṇa with that same Personality of Godhead by describing another pastime of His, one which highlighted His unequalled, divine characteristics.

TEXT 22

विप्रो गृहीत्वा मृतकं राजद्वार्युपधाय सः ।
इदं प्रोवाच विलपन्नातुरो दीनमानसः ॥२२॥

vipro gṛhītvā mṛtakaṁ
rāja-dvāry upadhāya saḥ
idaṁ provāca vilapann
āturo dīna-mānasaḥ

vipraḥ—the *brāhmaṇa;* *gṛhītvā*—taking; *mṛtakam*—the corpse; *rāja*—of the King (Ugrasena); *dvāri*—at the door; *upadhāya*—presenting it; *saḥ*—he; *idam*—this; *provāca*—said; *vilapan*—lamenting; *āturaḥ*—agitated; *dīna*—depressed; *mānasaḥ*—whose mind.

TRANSLATION

The *brāhmaṇa* took the corpse and placed it at the door of King Ugrasena's court. Then, agitated and lamenting miserably, he spoke the following.

TEXT 23

ब्रह्मद्विषः शठधियो लुब्धस्य विषयात्मनः ।
क्षत्रबन्धोः कर्मदोषात्पञ्चत्वं मे गतोऽर्भकः ॥२३॥

brahma-dviṣaḥ śaṭha-dhiyo
lubdhasya viṣayātmanaḥ
kṣatra-bandhoḥ karma-doṣāt
pañcatvaṁ me gato 'rbhakaḥ

brahma—against *brāhmaṇas; dviṣaḥ*—hateful; *śaṭha*—duplicitous; *dhiyaḥ*—whose mentality; *lubdhasya*—avaricious; *viṣaya-ātmanaḥ*—addicted to sense gratification; *kṣatra-bandhoḥ*—of an unqualified *kṣatriya; karma*—in the performance of duties; *doṣāt*—because of discrepancies; *pañcatvam*—death; *me*—my; *gataḥ*—met; *arbhakaḥ*—son.

TRANSLATION

[The *brāhmaṇa* said:] This duplicitous, greedy enemy of *brāhmaṇas,* this unqualified ruler addicted to sense pleasure, has caused my son's death by some discrepancies in the execution of his duties.

PURPORT

Presuming that he himself had done nothing to cause his son's death, the *brāhmaṇa* thought it reasonable to blame King Ugrasena. In the Vedic social system, the monarch is considered responsible for everything occurring in his kingdom, good or bad. Even in a democracy, a manager who takes charge of some group or project should accept personal responsibility for any failure rather than, as is so common today, trying to place the blame on his subordinates or superiors.

TEXT 24

हिंसाविहारं नृपतिं दुःशीलमजितेन्द्रियम् ।
प्रजा भजन्त्यः सीदन्ति दरिद्रा नित्यदुःखिताः ॥२४॥

hiṁsā-vihāraṁ nṛpatiṁ
duḥśīlam ajitendriyam
prajā bhajantyaḥ sīdanti
daridrā nitya-duḥkhitāḥ

hiṁsā—violence; *vihāram*—whose sport; *nṛ-patim*—this King; *duḥ-śīlam*—wicked; *ajita*—unconquered; *indriyam*—whose senses; *prajāḥ*—the citizens; *bhajantyaḥ*—serving; *sīdanti*—suffer distress; *daridrāḥ*—poverty-stricken; *nitya*—always; *duḥkhitāḥ*—unhappy.

TRANSLATION

Citizens serving such a wicked king, who takes pleasure in violence and cannot control his senses, are doomed to suffer poverty and constant misery.

TEXT 25

एवं द्वितीयं विप्रर्षिस्तृतीयं त्वेवमेव च ।
विसृज्य स नृपद्वारि तां गाथां समगायत ॥२५॥

evaṁ dvitīyaṁ viprarṣis
tṛtīyaṁ tv evam eva ca
visṛjya sa nṛpa-dvāri
tāṁ gāthāṁ samagāyata

evam—in the same manner; *dvitīyam*—a second time; *vipra-ṛṣiḥ*—the wise *brāhmaṇa; tṛtīyam*—a third time; *tu*—and; *evam eva ca*—just the same way; *visṛjya*—leaving (his dead son); *saḥ*—he; *nṛpa-dvāri*—at the King's door; *tām*—the same; *gāthām*—song; *samagāyata*—he sang.

TRANSLATION

The wise *brāhmaṇa* suffered the same tragedy with his second and third child. Each time, he left the body of his dead son at the King's door and sang the same song of lamentation.

TEXTS 26–27

तामर्जुन उपश्रुत्य कर्हिचित्केशवान्तिके ।
परेते नवमे बाले ब्राह्मणं समभाषत ॥२६॥
किं स्विद् ब्रह्मंस्त्वन्निवासे इह नास्ति धनुर्धरः ।
राजन्यबन्धुरेते वै ब्राह्मणाः सत्रमासते ॥२७॥

tām arjuna upaśrutya
karhicit keśavāntike
parete navame bāle
brāhmaṇaṁ samabhāṣata

kiṁ svid brahmaṁs tvan-nivāse
iha nāsti dhanur-dharaḥ
rājanya-bandhur ete vai
brāhmaṇāḥ satram āsate

tām—that (lamentation); *arjunaḥ*—Arjuna; *upaśrutya*—happening to hear; *karhicit*—once; *keśava*—of Lord Kṛṣṇa; *antike*—in the proximity; *parete*—having died; *navame*—the ninth; *bāle*—child; *brāhmaṇam*—to the *brāhmaṇa; samabhāṣata*—he said; *kim svit*—whether; *brahman*—O *brāhmaṇa; tvat*—your; *nivāse*—at the home; *iha*—here; *na asti*—there is not; *dhanuḥ-dharaḥ*—holding his bow in his hand; *rājanya-bandhuḥ*—a fallen member of the royal order; *ete*—these (*kṣatriyas*); *vaḥ*—indeed; *brāhmaṇāḥ*— (like) *brāhmaṇas; satre*—at a major fire sacrifice; *āsate*—are present.

TRANSLATION

When the ninth child died, Arjuna, who was near Lord Keśava, happened to overhear the *brāhmaṇa* lamenting. Thus Arjuna addressed the *brāhmaṇa:* "What is the matter, my dear *brāhmaṇa*?

Isn't there some lowly member of the royal order here who can at least stand before your house with a bow in his hand? These *kṣatriyas* are behaving as if they were *brāhmaṇas* idly engaged in fire sacrifices.

TEXT 28

धनदारात्मजापृक्ता यत्र शोचन्ति ब्राह्मणाः ।
ते वै राजन्यवेषेण नटा जीवन्त्यसुंभराः ॥२८॥

dhana-dārātmajāpṛktā
yatra śocanti brāhmaṇāḥ
te vai rājanya-veṣeṇa
naṭā jīvanty asum-bharāḥ

dhana—from wealth; *dāra*—wives; *ātmaja*—and children; *apṛktāḥ*—separated; *yatra*—in which (situation); *śocanti*—lament; *brāhmaṇāḥ*—*brāhmaṇas; te*—they; *vai*—indeed; *rājanya-veṣeṇa*—disguised as kings; *naṭāḥ*—actors; *jīvanti*—they live; *asum-bharāḥ*—earning their own livelihood.

TRANSLATION

"The rulers of a kingdom in which *brāhmaṇas* lament over lost wealth, wives and children are merely imposters playing the role of kings just to earn their livelihood.

TEXT 29

अहं प्रजाः वां भगवन् रक्षिष्ये दीनयोरिह ।
अनिस्तीर्णप्रतिज्ञोऽग्निं प्रवेक्ष्ये हतकल्मषः ॥२९॥

ahaṁ prajāḥ vāṁ bhagavan
rakṣiṣye dīnayor iha
anistīrṇa-pratijño 'gniṁ
pravekṣye hata-kalmaṣaḥ

aham—I; *prajāḥ*—the offspring; *vām*—of you two (you and your wife); *bhagavan*—O lord; *rakṣiṣye*—will protect; *dīnayoḥ*—who are wretched; *iha*—in this matter; *anistīrṇa*—failing to fulfill; *pratijñaḥ*—my promise; *agnim*—fire; *pravekṣye*—I will enter; *hata*—destroyed; *kalmaṣaḥ*—whose contamination.

TRANSLATION

"My lord, I will protect the progeny of you and your wife, who are in such distress. And if I fail to keep this promise, I will enter fire to atone for my sin."

PURPORT

Chivalrous Arjuna could not tolerate the shame of being unable to fulfill his promise. As Kṛṣṇa says in *Bhagavad-gītā* (2.34), *sambhāvitasya cākīrtir maraṇād atiricyate:* "For a respected person, dishonor is worse than death."

TEXTS 30–31

श्रीब्राह्मण उवाच
संकर्षणो वासुदेवः प्रद्युम्नो धन्विनां वरः ।
अनिरुद्धोऽप्रतिरथो न त्रातुं शक्नुवन्ति यत् ॥३०॥
तत्कथं नु भवान् कर्म दुष्करं जगदीश्वरैः ।
त्वं चिकीर्षसि बालिश्यात्तन्न श्रद्दध्महे वयम् ॥३१॥

śrī-brāhmaṇa uvāca
saṅkarṣaṇo vāsudevaḥ
pradyumno dhanvināṁ varaḥ
aniruddho 'prati-ratho
na trātuṁ śaknuvanti yat

tat kathaṁ nu bhavān karma
duṣkaraṁ jagad-īśvaraiḥ
tvaṁ cikīrṣasi bāliśyāt
tan na śraddadhmahe vayam

śrī-brāhmaṇaḥ uvāca—the *brāhmaṇa* said; *saṅkarṣaṇaḥ*—Lord Saṅkarṣaṇa (Balarāma); *vāsudevaḥ*—Lord Vāsudeva (Kṛṣṇa); *pradyumnaḥ*—Pradyumna; *dhanvinām*—of bowmen; *varaḥ*—the greatest; *aniruddhaḥ*—Aniruddha; *aprati-rathaḥ*—unrivaled as a chariot fighter; *na*—not;

trātum—to save; *śaknuvanti*—were able; *yat*—inasmuch; *tat*—thus; *katham*—why; *nu*—indeed; *bhavān*—you; *karma*—feat; *duṣkaram*—impossible to be performed; *jagat*—of the universe; *īśvaraiḥ*—by the Lords; *tvam*—you; *cikīrṣasi*—intend to do; *bāliśyāt*—out of naiveté; *tat*—therefore; *na śraddadhmahe*—do not believe; *vayam*—we.

TRANSLATION

The *brāhmaṇa* said: Neither Saṅkarṣaṇa; Vāsudeva; Pradyumna, the best of bowmen; nor the unequalled warrior Aniruddha could save my sons. Then why do you naively attempt a feat that the almighty Lords of the universe could not perform? We cannot take you seriously.

TEXT 32

श्रीअर्जुन उवाच
नाहं संकर्षणो ब्रह्मन्न कृष्णः कार्ष्णिरेव च ।
अहं वा अर्जुनो नाम गाण्डीवं यस्य वै धनुः ॥३२॥

śrī-arjuna uvāca
nāhaṁ saṅkarṣaṇo brahman
na kṛṣṇaḥ kārṣṇir eva ca
ahaṁ vā arjuno nāma
gāṇḍīvaṁ yasya vai dhanuḥ

śrī-arjunaḥ uvāca—Śrī Arjuna said; *na*—not; *aham*—I; *saṅkarṣaṇaḥ*—Lord Balarāma; *brahman*—O *brāhmaṇa; na*—not; *kṛṣṇaḥ*—Lord Kṛṣṇa; *kārṣṇiḥ*—a descendant of Lord Kṛṣṇa; *eva ca*—even; *aham*—I; *vai*—indeed; *arjunaḥ nāma*—the one known as Arjuna; *gāṇḍīvam*—Gāṇḍīva; *yasya*—whose; *vai*—indeed; *dhanuḥ*—bow.

TRANSLATION

Śrī Arjuna said: I am neither Lord Saṅkarṣaṇa, O *brāhmaṇa*, nor Lord Kṛṣṇa, nor even Kṛṣṇa's son. Rather, I am Arjuna, wielder of the Gāṇḍīva bow.

TEXT 33

मावमंस्था मम ब्रह्मन् वीर्यं त्र्यम्बकतोषणम् ।
मृत्युं विजित्य प्रधने आनेष्ये ते प्रजाः प्रभो ॥३३॥

māvamaṁsthā mama brahman
vīryaṁ tryambaka-toṣaṇam
mṛtyuṁ vijitya pradhane
āneṣye te prajāḥ prabho

mā avamaṁsthāḥ—do not belittle; *mama*—my; *brahman*—O *brāhmaṇa; vīryam*—prowess; *tri-ambaka*—Lord Śiva; *toṣaṇam*—which satisfied; *mṛtyum*—death personified; *vijitya*—defeating; *pradhane*—in battle; *āneṣye*—I will bring back; *te*—your; *prajāḥ*—children; *prabho*—O master.

TRANSLATION

Do not minimize my ability, which was good enough to satisfy Lord Śiva, O *brāhmaṇa*. I will bring back your sons, dear master, even if I have to defeat Death himself in battle.

TEXT 34

एवं विश्रम्भितो विप्रः फाल्गुनेन परंतप ।
जगाम स्वगृहं प्रीतः पार्थवीर्यं निशामयन् ॥३४॥

evaṁ viśrambhito vipraḥ
phālgunena parantapa
jagāma sva-gṛhaṁ prītaḥ
pārtha-vīryaṁ niśāmayan

evam—thus; *viśrambhitaḥ*—given faith; *vipraḥ*—the *brāhmaṇa; phālgunena*—by Arjuna; *param*—of enemies; *tapa*—O tormentor (Parīkṣit Mahārāja); *jagāma*—he went; *sva*—to his own; *gṛham*—house; *prītaḥ*—satisfied; *pārtha*—of the son of Pṛthā; *vīryam*—of the prowess; *niśāmayan*—hearing.

TRANSLATION

Thus convinced by Arjuna, O tormentor of enemies, the *brāhmaṇa* went home, satisfied by having heard Arjuna's declaration of his prowess.

TEXT 35

प्रसूतिकाल आसन्ने भार्याया द्विजसत्तमः ।
पाहि पाहि प्रजां मृत्योरित्याहार्जुनमातुरः ॥३५॥

prasūti-kāla āsanne
bhāryāyā dvija-sattamaḥ
pāhi pāhi prajāṁ mṛtyor
ity āhārjunam āturaḥ

prasūti—of giving birth; *kāle*—the time; *āsanne*—being imminent; *bhāryāyāḥ*—of his wife; *dvija*—the *brāhmaṇa; sat-tamaḥ*—most elevated; *pāhi*—please save; *pāhi*—please save; *prajām*—my child; *mṛtyoḥ*—from death; *iti*—thus; *āha*—he said; *arjunam*—to Arjuna; *āturaḥ*—distraught.

TRANSLATION

When the wife of the elevated *brāhmaṇa* was again about to give birth, he went to Arjuna in great anxiety and begged him, "Please, please protect my child from death!"

TEXT 36

स उपस्पृश्य शुच्यम्भो नमस्कृत्य महेश्वरम् ।
दिव्यान्यस्त्राणि संस्मृत्य सज्यं गाण्डीवमाददे ॥३६॥

sa upaspṛśya śucy ambho
namaskṛtya maheśvaram
divyāny astrāṇi saṁsmṛtya
sajyaṁ gāṇḍīvam ādade

saḥ—he (Arjuna); *upaspṛśya*—touching; *śuci*—pure; *ambhaḥ*—water; *namaḥ-kṛtya*—offering obeisances; *mahā-īśvaram*—to Lord Śiva; *divyāni*—celestial; *astrāṇi*—his missile weapons; *saṁsmṛtya*—remembering; *sajyam*—the bowstring; *gāṇḍīvam*—to his bow Gāṇḍīva; *ādade*—he fixed.

TRANSLATION

After touching pure water, offering obeisances to Lord Maheśvara and recollecting the *mantras* for his celestial weapons, Arjuna strung his bow Gāṇḍīva.

PURPORT

The *ācāryas* point out that since the *brāhmaṇa* had disrespected Lord Kṛṣṇa, Arjuna tactfully offered his obeisances instead to Lord Śiva, who had taught Arjuna how to use the *mantras* of the Pāśupāta weapon.

TEXT 37

न्यरुणत्सूतिकागारं शरैर्नानास्त्रयोजितैः ।
तिर्यगूर्ध्वमधः पार्थश्चकार शरपञ्जरम् ॥३७॥

nyaruṇat sūtikāgāraṁ
śarair nānāstra-yojitaiḥ
tiryag ūrdhvam adhaḥ pārthaś
cakāra śara-pañjaram

nyaruṇat—he enveloped; *sūtikā-āgāram*—the house where the birth was taking place; *śaraiḥ*—with arrows; *nānā*—various; *astra*—to missiles; *yojitaiḥ*—attached; *tiryak*—horizontally; *ūrdhvam*—upwards; *adhaḥ*—downwards; *pārthaḥ*—Arjuna; *cakāra*—made; *śara*—of arrows; *pañjaram*—a cage.

TRANSLATION

Arjuna fenced in the house where the birth was taking place by shooting arrows attached to various missiles. Thus the son of Pṛthā constructed a protective cage of arrows, covering the house upwards, downwards and sideways.

TEXT 38

ततः कुमारः सञ्जातो विप्रपत्न्या रुदन्मुहुः ।
सद्योऽदर्शनमापेदे सशरीरो विहायसा ॥३८॥

tataḥ kumāraḥ sañjāto
vipra-patnyā rudan muhuḥ
sadyo 'darśanam āpede
sa-śarīro vihāyasā

tataḥ—then; *kumāraḥ*—the infant; *sañjātaḥ*—born; *vipra*—the *brāhmaṇa's; patnyāḥ*—of the wife; *rudan*—crying; *muhuḥ*—for some time; *sadyaḥ*—suddenly; *adarśanam āpede*—he disappeared; *sa*—along with; *śarīraḥ*—his body; *vihāyasā*—through the sky.

TRANSLATION

The *brāhmaṇa's* wife then gave birth, but after the newborn infant had been crying for a short time, he suddenly vanished into the sky in his selfsame body.

TEXT 39

तदाह विप्रो विजयं विनिन्दन् कृष्णसन्निधौ ।
मौढ्यं पश्यत मे योऽहं श्रद्दधे क्लीबकत्थनम् ॥३९॥

tadāha vipro vijayaṁ
vinindan kṛṣṇa-sannidhau
mauḍhyaṁ paśyata me yo 'haṁ
śraddadhe klība-katthanam

tadā—then; *āha*—said; *vipraḥ*—the *brāhmaṇa; vijayam*—to Arjuna; *vinindan*—criticizing; *kṛṣṇa-sannidhau*—in the presence of Lord Kṛṣṇa; *mauḍhyam*—foolishness; *paśyata*—just see; *me*—my; *yaḥ*—who; *aham*—I; *śraddadhe*—trusted; *klība*—of an impotent eunuch; *katthanam*—the boasting.

TRANSLATION

The *brāhmaṇa* then derided Arjuna in front of Lord Kṛṣṇa: "Just see how foolish I was to put my faith in the bragging of a eunuch!

TEXT 40

न प्रद्युम्नो नानिरुद्धो न रामो न च केशवः ।
यस्य शेकुः परित्रातुं कोऽन्यस्तदवितेश्वरः ॥४०॥

na pradyumno nāniruddho
na rāmo na ca keśavaḥ
yasya śekuḥ paritrātuṁ
ko 'nyas tad-aviteśvaraḥ

na—not; *pradyumnaḥ*—Pradyumna; *na*—not; *aniruddhaḥ*—Aniruddha; *na*—not; *rāmaḥ*—Balarāma; *na*—not; *ca*—also; *keśavaḥ*—Kṛṣṇa; *yasya*—whose (infants); *śekuḥ*—were able; *paritrātum*—to save; *kaḥ*—who; *anyaḥ*—else; *tat*—in this situation; *avitā*—as a protector; *īśvaraḥ*—capable.

TRANSLATION

"When neither Pradyumna, Aniruddha, Rāma nor Keśava can save a person, who else can possibly protect him?

TEXT 41

धिगर्जुनं मृषावादं धिगात्मश्लाघिनो धनुः ।
दैवोपसृष्टं यो मौढ्यादानिनीषति दुर्मतिः ॥४१॥

dhig arjunaṁ mṛṣā-vādaṁ
dhig ātma-ślāghino dhanuḥ
daivopasṛṣṭaṁ yo mauḍhyād
āninīṣati durmatiḥ

dhik—damnation; *arjunam*—on Arjuna; *mṛṣā*—false; *vādam*—whose speech; *dhik*—damnation; *ātma*—of himself; *ślāghinaḥ*—of the glorifier;

dhanuḥ—on the bow; *daiva*—by fate; *upasṛṣṭam*—taken; *yaḥ*—who; *mauḍhyāt*—out of delusion; *āninīṣati*—intends to bring back; *durmatiḥ*—unintelligent.

TRANSLATION

"To hell with that liar Arjuna! To hell with that braggart's bow! He is so foolish that he has deluded himself into thinking he can bring back a person whom destiny has taken away."

TEXT 42

एवं शपति विप्रर्षौ विद्यामास्थाय फाल्गुनः ।
ययौ संयमनीमाशु यत्रास्ते भगवान् यमः ॥४२॥

evaṁ śapati viprarṣau
vidyām āsthāya phālgunaḥ
yayau saṁyamanīm āśu
yatrāste bhagavān yamaḥ

evam—thus; *śapati*—as he cursed him; *vipra-ṛṣau*—the wise *brāhmaṇa; vidyām*—a mystic incantation; *āsthāya*—resorting to; *phālgunaḥ*—Arjuna; *yayau*—went; *saṁyamanīm*—to the heavenly city Saṁyamanī; *āśu*—immediately; *yatra*—where; *āste*—lives; *bhagavān yamaḥ*—Lord Yamarāja.

TRANSLATION

While the wise *brāhmaṇa* continued to heap insults upon him, Arjuna employed a mystic incantation to go at once to Saṁyamanī, the city of heaven where Lord Yamarāja resides.

TEXTS 43–44

विप्रापत्यमचक्षाणस्तत ऐन्द्रीमगात्पुरीम् ।
आग्नेयीं नैरृतीं सौम्यां वायव्यां वारुणीमथ ।
रसातलं नाकपृष्ठं धिष्ण्यान्यन्यान्युदायुधः ॥४३॥

ततोऽलब्धद्विजसुतो ह्यनिस्तीर्णप्रतिश्रुतः ।
अग्निं विविक्षुः कृष्णेन प्रत्युक्तः प्रतिषेधता ॥४४॥

viprāpatyam acakṣāṇas
tata aindrīm agāt purīm
āgneyīṁ nairṛtīṁ saumyāṁ
vāyavyāṁ vāruṇīm atha
rasātalaṁ nāka-pṛṣṭhaṁ
dhiṣṇyāny anyāny udāyudhaḥ

tato 'labdha-dvija-suto
hy anistīrṇa-pratiśrutaḥ
agniṁ vivikṣuḥ kṛṣṇena
pratyuktaḥ pratiṣedhatā

vipra—of the *brāhmaṇa; apatyam*—the child; *acakṣāṇaḥ*—not seeing; *tataḥ*—from there; *aindrīm*—of Lord Indra; *agāt*—he went; *purīm*—to the city; *āgneyīm*—the city of the fire-god; *nairṛtīm*—the city of the subordinate god of death (Nirṛti, who is distinct from Lord Yama); *saumyam*—the city of the moon-god; *vāyavyām*—the city of the wind-god; *vāruṇīm*—the city of the god of the waters; *atha*—then; *rasātalam*—the subterranean region; *nāka-pṛṣṭham*—the roof of heaven; *dhiṣṇyāni*—domains; *anyāni*—others; *udāyudhaḥ*—with weapons held ready; *tataḥ*—from them; *alabdha*—failing to obtain; *dvija*—of the *brāhmaṇa; sutaḥ*—the son; *hi*—indeed; *anistīrṇa*—not having fulfilled; *pratiśrutaḥ*—what he had promised; *agnim*—fire; *vivikṣuḥ*—about to enter; *kṛṣṇena*—by Lord Kṛṣṇa; *pratyuktaḥ*—opposed; *pratiṣedhatā*—who was trying to convince him to desist.

TRANSLATION

Not seeing the *brāhmaṇa's* child there, Arjuna went to the cities of Agni, Nirṛti, Soma, Vāyu and Varuṇa. With weapons at the ready he searched through all the domains of the universe, from the bottom of the subterranean region to the roof of heaven. Finally, not having found the *brāhmaṇa's* son anywhere, Arjuna decided to enter the sacred fire, having failed to keep his promise. But just as he was about to do so, Lord Kṛṣṇa stopped him and spoke the following words.

PURPORT

Śrila Viśvanātha Cakravartī comments that Arjuna trusted Lord Śiva implicitly as his *guru*, and so he did not bother to search out Lord Śiva's celestial abode.

TEXT 45

दर्शये द्विजसूनूंस्ते मावज्ञात्मानमात्मना ।
ये ते नः कीर्तिं विमलां मनुष्याः स्थापयिष्यन्ति ॥४५॥

darśaye dvija-sūnūṁs te
māvajñātmānam ātmanā
ye te naḥ kīrtiṁ vimalāṁ
manuṣyāḥ sthāpayiṣyanti

darśaye—I will show; *dvija*—of the *brāhmaṇa; sūnūn*—the sons; *te*—to you; *mā*—please do not; *avajña*—belittle; *ātmānam*—yourself; *ātmanā*—by your mind; *ye*—who; *te*—these (critics); *naḥ*—of us both; *kīrtim*—the fame; *vimalām*—spotless; *manuṣyāḥ*—men; *sthāpayiṣyanti*—are going to establish.

TRANSLATION

[Lord Kṛṣṇa said:] I will show you the *brāhmaṇa's* sons, so please don't despise yourself like this. These same men who now criticize us will soon establish our spotless fame.

TEXT 46

इति सम्भाष्य भगवानर्जुनेन सहेश्वरः ।
दिव्यं स्वरथमास्थाय प्रतीचीं दिशमाविशत् ॥४६॥

iti sambhāṣya bhagavān
arjunena saheśvaraḥ
divyaṁ sva-ratham āsthāya
pratīcīṁ diśam āviśat

iti—thus; *sambhāṣya*—conferring; *bhagavān*—the Personality of Godhead; *arjunena saha*—with Arjuna; *īśvaraḥ*—the Supreme Lord; *divyam*—divine; *sva*—His; *ratham*—chariot; *āsthāya*—mounting; *pratīcīm*—western; *diśam*—the direction; *āviśat*—He entered.

TRANSLATION

Having thus advised Arjuna, the Supreme Personality of Godhead had Arjuna join Him on His divine chariot, and together they set off toward the west.

TEXT 47

सप्त द्वीपान् ससिन्धूंश्च सप्त सप्त गिरीनथ ।
लोकालोकं तथातीत्य विवेश सुमहत्तमः ॥४७॥

sapta dvīpān sa-sindhūṁś ca
sapta sapta girīn atha
lokālokaṁ tathātītya
viveśa su-mahat tamaḥ

sapta—seven; *dvīpān*—islands; *sa*—with; *sindhūn*—their oceans; *ca*—and; *sapta sapta*—seven each; *girīn*—mountains; *atha*—then; *loka-alokam*—the mountain range separating light from darkness; *tathā*—also; *atītya*—crossing; *viveśa*—He entered; *su-mahat*—vast; *tamaḥ*—darkness.

TRANSLATION

The Lord's chariot passed over the seven islands of the middle universe, each with its ocean and its seven principal mountains. Then it crossed the Lokāloka boundary and entered the vast region of total darkness.

PURPORT

In *Kṛṣṇa, the Supreme Personality of Godhead,* Śrīla Prabhupāda notes, "Kṛṣṇa passed over all these planets and reached the covering of the universe. This covering is described in the *Śrīmad-Bhāgavatam* as great darkness. This material world as a whole is described as dark. In the opening space there is sunlight, and therefore it is illuminated, but in the covering, because of the absence of sunlight, it is naturally dark."

TEXTS 48–49

तत्राश्वाः शैब्यसुग्रीवमेघपुष्पबलाहकाः ।
तमसि भ्रष्टगतयो बभूवुर्भरतर्षभ ॥४८॥
तान् दृष्ट्वा भगवान् कृष्णो महायोगेश्वरेश्वरः ।
सहस्रादित्यसंकाशं स्वचक्रं प्राहिणोत्पुरः ॥४९॥

tatrāśvāḥ śaibya-sugrīva-
meghapuṣpa-balāhakāḥ
tamasi bhraṣṭa-gatayo
babhūvur bharatarṣabha

tān dṛṣṭvā bhagavān kṛṣṇo
mahā-yogeśvareśvaraḥ
sahasrāditya-saṅkāśaṁ
sva-cakraṁ prāhiṇot puraḥ

tatra—at that place; *aśvāḥ*—the horses; *śaibya-sugrīva-meghapuṣpa-balāhakāḥ*—named Śaibya, Sugrīva, Meghapuṣpa and Balāhaka; *tamasi*—in the darkness; *bhraṣṭa*—having lost; *gatayaḥ*—their way; *babhūvuḥ*—became; *bharata-ṛṣabha*—O best of the Bhāratas; *tān*—them; *dṛṣṭvā*—seeing; *bhagavān*—the Personality of Godhead; *kṛṣṇaḥ*—Kṛṣṇa; *mahā*—supreme; *yoga-īśvara*—of masters of *yoga; īśvaraḥ*—the master; *sahasra*—a thousand; *āditya*—suns; *saṅkāśam*—comparable to; *sva*—His personal; *cakram*—disc weapon; *prāhiṇot*—sent; *puraḥ*—in front.

TRANSLATION

In that darkness the chariot's horses—Śaibya, Sugrīva, Meghapuṣpa and Balāhaka—lost their way. Seeing them in this condition, O best of the Bhāratas, Lord Kṛṣṇa, the supreme master of all masters of *yoga*, sent His Sudarśana disc before the chariot. That disc shone like thousands of suns.

PURPORT

Śrīla Viśvanātha Cakravartī gives the following insight into this verse. Lord Kṛṣṇa's horses had descended from Vaikuṇṭha to participate in His earthly pastimes. Since the Lord Himself was pretending to be a finite human being, His steeds now acted confused to enhance the drama of the situation for all who would one day hear this pastime.

TEXT 50

तमः सुघोरं गहनं कृतं महद्
विदारयद् भूरितरेण रोचिषा ।
मनोजवं निर्विविशे सुदर्शनं
गुणच्युतो रामशरो यथा चमूः ॥५०॥

tamaḥ su-ghoraṁ gahanaṁ kṛtaṁ mahad
vidārayad bhūri-tareṇa rociṣā
mano-javaṁ nirviviśe sudarśanaṁ
guṇa-cyuto rāma-śaro yathā camūḥ

tamaḥ—the darkness; *su*—very; *ghoram*—fearsome; *gahanam*—dense; *kṛtam*—a manifestation of the material creation; *mahat*—immense; *vidārayat*—cutting through; *bhūri-tareṇa*—extremely extensive; *rociṣā*—with its effulgence; *manaḥ*—of the mind; *javam*—having the speed; *nirviviśe*—entered; *sudarśanam*—the Sudarśana disc; *guṇa*—from His bowstring; *cyutaḥ*—shot; *rāma*—of Lord Rāmacandra; *śaraḥ*—an arrow; *yathā*—as if; *camūḥ*—at an army.

TRANSLATION

The Lord's Sudarśana disc penetrated the darkness with its blazing effulgence. Racing forward with the speed of the mind, it cut through the fearsome, dense oblivion expanded from primeval matter, as an arrow shot from Lord Rāma's bow cuts through His enemy's army.

TEXT 51

द्वारेण चक्रानुपथेन तत्तमः
परं परं ज्योतिरनन्तपारम् ।
समश्नुवानं प्रसमीक्ष्य फाल्गुनः
प्रताडिताक्षोऽपिदधेऽक्षिणी उभे ॥५१॥

dvāreṇa cakrānupathena tat tamaḥ
paraṁ paraṁ jyotir ananta-pāram
samaśnuvānaṁ prasamīkṣya phālgunaḥ
pratāḍitākṣo 'pidadhe 'kṣiṇī ubhe

dvāreṇa—by the path; *cakra*—the Sudarśana disc; *anupathena*—following; *tat*—that; *tamaḥ*—darkness; *param*—beyond; *param*—transcendental; *jyotiḥ*—light; *ananta*—unlimited; *pāram*—whose expanse; *samaśnuvānam*—all-pervasive; *prasamīkṣya*—beholding; *phālgunaḥ*—Arjuna; *pratāḍita*—pained; *akṣaḥ*—whose eyes; *apidadhe*—he closed; *akṣiṇī*—his eyes; *ubhe*—both.

TRANSLATION

Following the Sudarśana disc, the chariot went beyond the darkness and reached the endless spiritual light of the all-pervasive *brahma-jyoti*. As Arjuna beheld this glaring effulgence, his eyes hurt, and so he shut them.

PURPORT

After breaking through each of the eight concentric shells of the universe, the Sudarśana disc led Lord Kṛṣṇa's chariot into the limitless, self-effulgent atmosphere of the spiritual sky. This journey by Lord Kṛṣṇa and Arjuna to Vaikuṇṭha is also narrated in *Śrī Hari-vaṁśa*, where the Lord is quoted as telling His companion,

brahma-tejo-mayaṁ divyaṁ
mahat yad dṛṣṭavān asi
ahaṁ sa bharata-śreṣṭha
mat-tejas tat sanātanam

"The divine expanse of Brahman effulgence you have seen is none other than Myself, O best of the Bhāratas. It is My own eternal effulgence."

prakṛtiḥ sā mama parā
vyaktāvyaktā sanātanī
tāṁ praviśya bhavantīha
muktā yoga-vid-uttamāḥ

"It comprises My eternal, spiritual energy, both manifest and unmanifest. The foremost *yoga* experts of this world enter within it and become liberated."

sā sāṅkhyānāṁ gatiḥ pārtha
yogināṁ ca tapasvinām
tat paraṁ paramaṁ brahma
sarvaṁ vibhajate jagat
mamaiva tad ghanaṁ tejo
jñātum arhasi bhārata

"It is the supreme goal of the followers of Sāṅkhya, O Pārtha, as well as that of the *yogīs* and ascetics. It is the Supreme Absolute Truth, manifesting the varieties of the entire created cosmos. You should understand this *brahma-jyoti,* O Bhārata, to be My concentrated personal effulgence."

TEXT 52

ततः प्रविष्टः सलिलं नभस्वता
बलीयसैजद्बृहदूर्मिभूषणम् ।
तत्राद्भुतं वै भवनं द्युमत्तमं
भ्राजन्मणिस्तम्भसहस्रशोभितम् ॥५२॥

tataḥ praviṣṭaḥ salilaṁ nabhasvatā
balīyasaijad-bṛhad-ūrmi-bhūṣaṇam
tatrādbhutaṁ vai bhavanaṁ dyumat-tamaṁ
bhrājan-maṇi-stambha-sahasra-śobhitam

tataḥ—from that; *praviṣṭaḥ*—entered; *salilam*—water; *nabhasvatā*—by wind; *balīyasā*—mighty; *ejat*—made to move about; *bṛhat*—huge;

ūrmi—waves; *bhūṣaṇam*—whose ornaments; *tatra*—therein; *adbhutam*—wondrous; *vai*—indeed; *bhavanam*—abode; *dyumat-tamam*—supremely effulgent; *bhrājat*—brilliantly shining; *maṇi*—with gems; *stambha*—of columns; *sahasra*—with thousands; *śobhitam*—made beautiful.

TRANSLATION

From that region they entered a body of water resplendent with huge waves being churned by a mighty wind. Within that ocean Arjuna saw an amazing palace more radiant than anything he had ever seen before. Its beauty was enhanced by thousands of ornamental pillars bedecked with brilliant gems.

TEXT 53

तस्मिन्महाभोगमनन्तमद्भुतं
सहस्रमूर्धन्यफणामणिद्युभिः ।
विभ्राजमानं द्विगुणेक्षणोल्बणं
सिताचलाभं शितिकण्ठजिह्वम् ॥५३॥

tasmin mahā-bhogam anantam adbhutaṁ
sahasra-mūrdhanya-phaṇā-maṇi-dyubhiḥ
vibhrājamānaṁ dvi-guṇekṣaṇolbaṇaṁ
sitācalābhaṁ śiti-kaṇṭha-jihvam

tasmin—there; *mahā*—huge; *bhogam*—a serpent; *anantam*—Lord Ananta; *adbhutam*—amazing; *sahasra*—thousand; *mūrdhanya*—on His heads; *phaṇā*—upon the hoods; *maṇi*—of the gems; *dyubhiḥ*—with the rays of effulgence; *vibhrājamānam*—shining; *dvi*—twice; *guṇa*—as many; *īkṣaṇa*—whose eyes; *ulbaṇam*—frightening; *sita*—white; *acala*—the mountain (namely Kailāsa); *ābham*—whose resemblance; *śiti*—dark blue; *kaṇṭha*—whose necks; *jihvam*—and tongues.

TRANSLATION

In that palace was the huge, awe-inspiring serpent Ananta Śeṣa. He shone brilliantly with the radiance emanating from the gems

on His thousands of hoods and reflecting from twice as many fearsome eyes. He resembled white Mount Kailāsa, and His necks and tongues were dark blue.

TEXTS 54–56

ददर्श तद्भोगसुखासनं विभुं
महानुभावं पुरुषोत्तमोत्तमम् ।
सान्द्राम्बुदाभं सुपिशंगवाससं
प्रसन्नवक्त्रं रुचिरायतेक्षणम् ॥५४॥
महामणिव्रातकिरीटकुण्डल-
प्रभापरिक्षिप्तसहस्रकुन्तलम् ।
प्रलम्बचार्वष्टभुजं सकौस्तुभं
श्रीवत्सलक्ष्मं वनमालयावृतम् ॥५५॥
सुनन्दनन्दप्रमुखैः स्वपार्षदैश्
चक्रादिभिर्मूर्तिधरैर्निजायुधैः ।
पुष्ट्या श्रिया कीर्त्यजयाखिलर्धिभिर्
निषेव्यमानं परमेष्ठिनां पतिम् ॥५६॥

dadarśa tad-bhoga-sukhāsanaṁ vibhuṁ
mahānubhāvaṁ puruṣottamottamam
sāndrāmbudābhaṁ su-piśaṅga-vāsasaṁ
prasanna-vaktraṁ rucirāyatekṣaṇam

mahā-maṇi-vrāta-kirīṭa-kuṇḍala-
prabhā-parikṣipta-sahasra-kuntalam
pralamba-cārv-aṣṭa-bhujaṁ sa-kaustubhaṁ
śrīvatsa-lakṣmaṁ vana-mālayāvṛtam

sunanda-nanda-pramukhaiḥ sva-pārṣadaiś
cakrādibhir mūrti-dharair nijāyudhaiḥ
puṣṭyā śriyā kīrty-ajayākhilardhibhir
niṣevyamānaṁ parameṣṭhināṁ patim

dadarśa—(Arjuna) saw; *tat*—that; *bhoga*—serpent; *sukha*—comfortable; *āsanam*—whose seat; *vibhum*—all-pervasive; *mahā-anubhāvam*—almighty; *puruṣa-uttama*—of Personalities of Godhead; *uttamam*—the supreme; *sāndra*—dense; *ambuda*—a cloud; *ābham*—resembling (with His blue complexion); *su*—beautiful; *piśaṅga*—yellow; *vāsasam*—whose dress; *prasanna*—pleasing; *vaktram*—whose face; *rucira*—attractive; *āyata*—broad; *īkṣaṇam*—whose eyes; *mahā*—great; *maṇi*—of jewels; *vrāta*—with clusters; *kirīṭa*—of His crown; *kuṇḍala*—and earrings; *prabhā*—with the reflected brilliance; *parikṣipta*—scattered about; *sahasra*—thousands; *kuntalam*—whose locks of hair; *pralamba*—long; *cāru*—handsome; *aṣṭa*—eight; *bhujam*—whose arms; *sa*—having; *kaustubham*—the Kaustubha gem; *śrīvatsa-lakṣmam*—and displaying the special mark known as Śrīvatsa; *vana*—of forest flowers; *mālayā*—by a garland; *āvṛtam*—embraced; *sunanda-nanda-pramukhaiḥ*—headed by Sunanda and Nanda; *sva-pārṣadaiḥ*—by His personal associates; *cakra-ādibhiḥ*—the disc and so on; *mūrti*—personal forms; *dharaiḥ*—manifesting; *nija*—His own; *āyudhaiḥ*—by the weapons; *puṣṭyā śriyā kīrti-ajayā*—by His energies Puṣṭi, Śrī, Kīrti and Ajā; *akhila*—all; *ṛdhibhiḥ*—by His mystic powers; *niṣevyamānam*—being served; *parame-sthinām*—of universal rulers; *patim*—the chief.

TRANSLATION

Arjuna then saw the omnipresent and omnipotent Supreme Personality of Godhead, Mahā-Viṣṇu, sitting at ease on the serpent bed. His bluish complexion was the color of a dense raincloud, He wore a beautiful yellow garment, His face looked charming, His broad eyes were most attractive, and He had eight long, handsome arms. His profuse locks of hair were bathed on all sides in the brilliance reflected from the clusters of precious jewels decorating His crown and earrings. He wore the Kaustubha gem, the mark of Śrīvatsa and a garland of forest flowers. Serving that topmost of all Lords were His personal attendants, headed by Sunanda and Nanda; His *cakra* and other weapons in their personified forms; His consort potencies Puṣṭi, Śrī, Kīrti and Ajā; and all His various mystic powers.

PURPORT

Śrīla Prabhupāda mentions that "the Lord has innumerable energies, and they were also standing there personified. The most important among them were as follows: Puṣṭi, the energy for nourishment; Śrī, the energy of beauty; Kīrti, the energy of reputation; and Ajā, the energy of material creation. All these energies are invested in the administrators of the material world, namely Lord Brahmā, Lord Śiva and Lord Viṣṇu, and in the kings of the heavenly planets, Indra, Candra, Varuṇa and the sun-god. In other words, all these demigods, being empowered by the Lord with certain energies, engage in the transcendental loving service of the Supreme Personality of Godhead."

TEXT 57

ववन्द आत्मानमनन्तमच्युतो
जिष्णुश्च तद्दर्शनजातसाध्वसः ।
तावाह भूमा परमेष्ठिनां प्रभुर्
बद्धाञ्जली सस्मितमूर्जया गिरा ॥५७॥

vavanda ātmānam anantam acyuto
jiṣṇuś ca tad-darśana-jāta-sādhvasaḥ
tāv āha bhūmā parameṣṭhināṁ prabhur
baddhāñjalī sa-smitam ūrjayā girā

vavanda—paid homage; *ātmānam*—to Himself; *anantam*—in His boundless form; *acyutaḥ*—infallible Lord Kṛṣṇa; *jiṣṇuḥ*—Arjuna; *ca*—also; *tat*—of Him; *darśana*—by the sight; *jāta*—arising; *sādhvasaḥ*—whose astonishment; *tau*—to the two of them; *āha*—spoke; *bhūmā*—the almighty Lord (Mahā-Viṣṇu); *parame-sthinām*—of the rulers of the universe; *prabhuḥ*—the master; *baddha-añjalī*—who had joined their palms in supplication; *sa*—with; *smitam*—a smile; *ūrjayā*—potent; *girā*—in a voice.

TRANSLATION

Lord Kṛṣṇa offered homage to Himself in this boundless form, and Arjuna, astonished at the sight of Lord Mahā-Viṣṇu, bowed down as well. Then, as the two of them stood before Him with joined palms, the almighty Mahā-Viṣṇu, supreme master of all rulers of the universe, smiled and spoke to them in a voice full of solemn authority.

PURPORT

Śrīla Viśvanātha Cakravartī makes the following observations on this verse: Just as Lord Kṛṣṇa offered obeisances to His own Deity during the worship of Govardhana Hill, so now also He paid homage to His Viṣṇu expansion for the purpose of playing out His pastimes. The Lord is *ananta,* possessed of countless manifestations, and this eight-armed form is among them. He is *acyuta,* "never falling from His position," in the sense that He never stops engaging in His humanlike pastimes as a cowherd boy of Vṛndāvana. Thus to safeguard the special sanctity of His humanlike pastimes as Kṛṣṇa, He offered obeisances to His own plenary expansion.

Lord Mahā-Viṣṇu appeared before Kṛṣṇa and Arjuna as *bhūmā,* the supremely opulent one, and as *parameṣṭhināṁ prabhuḥ,* the Lord of multitudes of Brahmās ruling over millions of universes. With solemn authority He spoke in such a way as to bewilder Arjuna, in obedience to Śrī Kṛṣṇa's intention. His smile hinted at His private thoughts, which Śrīla Viśvanātha Cakravartī has revealed for our benefit: "My dear Kṛṣṇa, by Your desire I will describe My superiority, even though I am Your expansion. At the same time, however, I will subtly imply in My statements the supreme position of Your beauty, character and power and the fact that You are the source from which I emanate. Just see how clever I am—that in front of Arjuna I am confidentially divulging My true identity as nondifferent from You."

TEXT 58

द्विजात्मजा मे युवयोर्दिदृक्षुणा
मयोपनीता भुवि धर्मगुप्तये ।
कलावतीर्णाववनेर्भरासुरान्
हत्वेह भूयस्त्वरयेतमन्ति मे ॥५८॥

dvijātmajā me yuvayor didṛkṣuṇā
mayopanītā bhuvi dharma-guptaye
kalāvatīrṇāv avaner bharāsurān
hatveha bhūyas tvarayetam anti me

dvija—of the *brāhmaṇa; ātma-jāḥ*—the sons; *me*—My; *yuvayoḥ*—you two; *didṛkṣuṇā*—who wanted to see; *mayā*—by Me; *upanītāḥ*—brought; *bhuvi*—on the earth; *dharma*—of the principles of religion; *guptaye*—for the protection; *kalā*—(as My) expansions; *avatīrṇau*—descended; *avaneḥ*—of the earth; *bhara*—who are burdens; *asurān*—the demons; *hatvā*—after killing; *iha*—here; *bhūyaḥ*—again; *tvarayā*—quickly; *itam*—come; *anti*—to the proximity; *me*—My.

TRANSLATION

[Lord Mahā-Viṣṇu said:] I brought the *brāhmaṇa's* sons here because I wanted to see the two of you, My expansions, who have descended to the earth to save the principles of religion. As soon as you finish killing the demons who burden the earth, quickly come back here to Me.

PURPORT

As explained by Śrīla Viśvanātha Cakravartī, the secret import of these words spoken for Arjuna's edification is as follows: "You two, who have descended along with your *kalās,* your personal energies, should kindly return to Me after killing the demons who burden the earth. Please quickly send these demons here to Me for the sake of their liberation." It is stated in *Śrī Hari-vaṁśa* and in the Second Canto of *Śrīmad-Bhāgavatam* that the path of gradual liberation passes through the intermediate station of Lord Mahā-Viṣṇu's abode, outside the eighth shell of the universe.

TEXT 59

पूर्णकामावपि युवां नरनारायणावृषी ।
धर्ममाचरतां स्थित्यै ऋषभौ लोकसंग्रहम् ॥५९॥

pūrṇa-kāmāv api yuvāṁ
nara-nārāyaṇāv ṛṣī
dharmam ācaratāṁ sthityai
ṛṣabhau loka-saṅgraham

pūrṇa—full; *kāmau*—in all desires; *api*—although; *yuvām*—you two; *nara-nārāyaṇau ṛṣī*—as the sages Nara and Nārāyaṇa; *dharmam*—the principles of religion; *ācaratām*—should execute; *sthityai*—for its maintenance; *ṛṣabhau*—the best of all persons; *loka-saṅgraham*—for the benefit of the general populace.

TRANSLATION

Although all your desires are completely fulfilled, O best of exalted personalities, for the benefit of the people in general you should continue to exemplify religious behavior as the sages Nara and Nārāyaṇa.

TEXTS 60–61

इत्यादिष्टौ भगवता तौ कृष्णौ परमेष्ठिना ।
ॐ इत्यानम्य भूमानमादाय द्विजदारकान् ॥६०॥
न्यवर्तेतां स्वकं धाम सम्प्रहृष्टौ यथागतम् ।
विप्राय ददतुः पुत्रान् यथारूपं यथावयः ॥६१॥

ity ādiṣṭau bhagavatā
tau kṛṣṇau parame-ṣṭhinā
oṁ ity ānamya bhūmānam
ādāya dvija-dārakān

nyavartetāṁ svakaṁ dhāma
samprahṛṣṭau yathā-gatam
viprāya dadatuḥ putrān
yathā-rūpaṁ yathā-vayaḥ

iti—with these words; *ādiṣṭau*—instructed; *bhagavatā*—by the Personality of Godhead; *tau*—they; *kṛṣṇau*—the two Kṛṣṇas (Kṛṣṇa and Arjuna); *parame-sthinā*—by the Lord of the supreme kingdom; *om iti*—chanting *om* to signify their agreement; *ānamya*—bowing down; *bhūmānam*—to the almighty Lord; *ādāya*—and taking; *dvija*—of the *brāhmaṇa; dārakān*—the sons; *nyavartetām*—they returned; *svakam*—their own; *dhāma*—to the abode (Dvārakā); *samprahṛṣṭau*—elated; *yathā*—in the same way; *gatam*—as they came; *viprāya*—to the *brāhmaṇa; dadatuḥ*—they gave; *putrān*—his sons; *yathā*—in the same; *rūpam*—forms; *yathā*—with the same; *vayaḥ*—age.

TRANSLATION

Thus instructed by the Supreme Lord of the topmost planet, Kṛṣṇa and Arjuna assented by chanting *om*, and then they bowed down to almighty Lord Mahā-Viṣṇu. Taking the *brāhmaṇa's* sons with them, they returned with great delight to Dvārakā by the same path along which they had come. There they presented the *brāhmaṇa* with his sons, who were in the same infant bodies in which they had been lost.

TEXT 62

निशाम्य वैष्णवं धाम पार्थः परमविस्मितः ।
यत्किञ्चित्पौरुषं पुंसां मेने कृष्णानुकम्पितम् ॥६२॥

niśāmya vaiṣṇavaṁ dhāma
pārthaḥ parama-vismitaḥ
yat kiñcit pauruṣaṁ puṁsāṁ
mene kṛṣṇānukampitam

niśāmya—having seen; *vaiṣṇavam*—of Lord Viṣṇu; *dhāma*—the abode; *pārthaḥ*—Arjuna; *parama*—supremely; *vismitaḥ*—astonished; *yat kiñcit*—whatever; *pauruṣam*—special power; *puṁsām*—belonging to living beings; *mene*—He concluded; *kṛṣṇa*—of Kṛṣṇa; *anukampitam*—the mercy shown.

TRANSLATION

Having seen the domain of Lord Viṣṇu, Arjuna was totally amazed. He concluded that whatever extraordinary power a person exhibits can only be a manifestation of Śrī Kṛṣṇa's mercy.

PURPORT

Śrīla Viśvanātha Cakravartī describes Arjuna's amazement: He thought, "Just see! Even though I am a mere mortal, by Kṛṣṇa's mercy I have seen the Supreme Godhead, the root cause of everything." Then, after a moment, he thought again, "But why did Lord Viṣṇu say that he took away the *brāhmaṇa's* children out of a desire to see Kṛṣṇa? Why would the Supreme Personality of Godhead hanker to see His own expansion? This might be the effect of some peculiar temporary circumstance, but since He said *didṛkṣuṇā* instead of *didṛkṣatā*—where the specific suffix *-ṣuṇā* carries the sense of a permanent characteristic, not a temporary one—it has to be concluded that He has always been wanting to see Kṛṣṇa and myself. Even granted that this is so, why couldn't He simply see Kṛṣṇa at Dvārakā? After all, Lord Mahā-Viṣṇu is the all-pervading creator of the universe, which He holds like an *āmalaka* fruit in His hand. Is it that He could not see Kṛṣṇa in Dvārakā because Kṛṣṇa does not allow anyone to see Him without His special sanction?

"And why, also, would Lord Mahā-Viṣṇu, the compassionate master of all *brāhmaṇas,* have repeatedly tormented an elevated *brāhmaṇa,* year after year? He must have acted in this unusual way only because He could not give up His extreme eagerness to see Kṛṣṇa. All right, He may have acted improperly for that reason, but why couldn't He have sent a servant to kidnap the *brāhmaṇa's* sons? Why did He Himself have to come to Dvārakā? Was stealing them out of Lord Kṛṣṇa's capital so difficult that no one but Viṣṇu Himself could hope to accomplish it? I can understand that He intended to cause so much distress to a *brāhmaṇa* of Lord Kṛṣṇa's city that Kṛṣṇa would be unable to tolerate it; then He would grant Lord Viṣṇu His audience. Lord Viṣṇu inspired the distressed *brāhmaṇa* to pour out his complaints to Kṛṣṇa in person. Thus it is clear that Śrī Kṛṣṇa's status of Godhood is superior to Lord Mahā-Viṣṇu's."

Having thought in this way, Arjuna was totally amazed. He asked Lord Kṛṣṇa whether these were actually the facts of the matter, and the Lord replied, as related in the *Hari-vaṁśa,*

mad-darśanārthaṁ te bālā
hṛtās tena mahātmanā
viprārtham eṣyate kṛṣṇo
mat-samīpaṁ na cānyathā

"It was to see Me that He, the Supreme Soul, stole the children. He believed, 'Only on a *brāhmaṇa's* behalf will Kṛṣṇa come to see Me, not otherwise.' "

Śrīla Viśvanātha Cakravartī states that Lord Kṛṣṇa further told

Arjuna, "I did not go there, however, for the *brāhmaṇa's* sake; I went there, My friend, just to save your life. If it had been for the *brāhmaṇa's* sake that I traveled to Vaikuṇṭha, I would have done so after his first child was abducted."

According to Śrīla Śrīdhara Svāmī, although this pastime occurred before the Battle of Kurukṣetra, it is recounted here at the end of the Tenth Canto under the general heading of the supremacy of Lord Kṛṣṇa's glories.

TEXT 63

इतीदृशान्यनेकानि वीर्याणीह प्रदर्शयन् ।
बुभुजे विषयान् ग्राम्यानीजे चात्युर्जितैर्मखैः ॥६३॥

itīdṛśāny anekāni
vīryāṇīha pradarśayan
bubhuje viṣayān grāmyān
īje cāty-urjitair makhaiḥ

iti—thus; *īdṛśāni*—like this; *anekāni*—many; *vīryāṇi*—feats of valor; *iha*—in this world; *pradarśayan*—exhibiting; *bubhuje*—(Lord Kṛṣṇa) enjoyed; *viṣayān*—objects of sense pleasure; *grāmyān*—ordinary; *īje*—He performed worship; *ca*—and; *ati*—extremely; *urjitaiḥ*—potent; *makhaiḥ*—with Vedic fire sacrifices.

TRANSLATION

Lord Kṛṣṇa exhibited many other, similar heroic pastimes in this world. He apparently enjoyed the pleasures of ordinary human life, and He performed greatly potent fire sacrifices.

TEXT 64

प्रववर्षाखिलान् कामान् प्रजासु ब्राह्मणादिषु ।
यथाकालं यथैवेन्द्रो भगवान् श्रैष्ठ्यमास्थितः ॥६४॥

pravavarṣākhilān kāmān
prajāsu brāhmaṇādiṣu

yathā-kālaṁ yathaivendro
bhagavān śraiṣṭhyam āsthitaḥ

pravavarṣa—He rained down; *akhilān*—all; *kāmān*—desired things; *prajāsu*—upon His subjects; *brāhmaṇa-ādiṣu*—beginning with the *brāhmaṇas; yathā-kālam*—at the suitable times; *yathā eva*—in the same way; *indraḥ*—(as) Indra; *bhagavān*—the Personality of Godhead; *śraiṣṭhyam*—in His supremacy; *āsthitaḥ*—situated.

TRANSLATION

The Lord having demonstrated His supremacy, at suitable times He showered down all desirable things upon the *brāhmaṇas* and His other subjects, just as Indra pours down his rain.

TEXT 65

हत्वा नृपानधर्मिष्ठान् घातयित्वार्जुनादिभिः ।
अञ्जसा वर्तयामास धर्मं धर्मसुतादिभिः ॥६५॥

hatvā nṛpān adharmiṣṭhān
ghātayitvārjunādibhiḥ
añjasā vartayām āsa
dharmaṁ dharma-sutādibhiḥ

hatvā—having killed; *nṛpān*—kings; *adharmiṣṭhān*—most irreligious; *ghātayitvā*—having them killed; *arjuna-ādibhiḥ*—by Arjuna and others; *añjasā*—easily; *vartayām āsa*—He caused to be carried out; *dharmam*—the principles of religion; *dharma-suta-ādibhiḥ*—by Yudhiṣṭhira (the son of Dharma) and others.

TRANSLATION

Now that He had killed many wicked kings and engaged devotees such as Arjuna in killing others, the Lord could easily assure

the execution of religious principles through the agency of such pious rulers as Yudhiṣṭhira.

Thus end the purports of the humble servants of His Divine Grace A. C. Bhaktivedanta Swami Prabhupāda to the Tenth Canto, Eighty-ninth Chapter, of the Śrīmad-Bhāgavatam, *entitled "Kṛṣṇa and Arjuna Retrieve a* Brāhmaṇa's *Sons."*

CHAPTER NINETY

Summary of Lord Kṛṣṇa's Glories

This chapter describes how Lord Kṛṣṇa enjoyed with His queens in the lakes of Dvārakā. It also relates the queens' ecstatic prayers in the mood of intense separation from Him, and summarizes the Lord's pastimes.

Lord Śrī Kṛṣṇa continued to reside in His opulent capital of Dvārakā, together with the Yadus and His queens. He would enjoy sporting with His wives in the ponds on the palace grounds, squirting water on them with a syringe and being squirted in turn. With His graceful gestures, loving words and sidelong glances, He would enchant their hearts. In this way the queens would become totally absorbed in thoughts of Him. Sometimes, after playing with the Lord in the water, they would address various creatures—*kurarī* and *cakravāka* birds, the ocean, the moon, a cloud, a cuckoo, a mountain, a river and so on—declaring their great attachment to Śrī Kṛṣṇa on the pretext of commiserating with these creatures.

Lord Kṛṣṇa begot ten sons in the womb of each of His queens. Among these sons, Pradyumna was foremost, being equal to His father in all transcendental qualities. Pradyumna married Rukmī's daughter, and from her womb Aniruddha was born. Aniruddha then married Rukmī's granddaughter and begot Vajra, who was the only Yadu prince to survive the battle of iron clubs at Prabhāsa. From Vajra descended the remainder of the Yadu dynasty, beginning with Pratibāhu. The members of the Yadu dynasty are virtually innumerable; indeed, just to educate their children the Yadus employed 38,800,000 teachers.

Before Lord Kṛṣṇa appeared, many demons took birth in human families to harass the people of the world and destroy brahminical culture. To subdue them, the Lord ordered the demigods to descend into the Yadu dynasty, which then expanded into 101 clans. All of the Yadus recognized Śrī Kṛṣṇa as the Supreme Personality of Godhead and had unflinching faith in Him. While resting, eating, walking and so on, which they often did in His company, they would forget their own bodies in their transcendental happiness.

The Tenth Canto concludes with this promise of success for the sincere hearer: "By regularly hearing, chanting and meditating on the beautiful topics of Lord Mukunda with ever-increasing sincerity, a mortal being will attain the divine kingdom of the Lord, where the inviolable power of death holds no sway."

TEXTS 1–7

श्रीशुक उवाच

सुखं स्वपुर्यां निवसन् द्वारकायां श्रियः पतिः ।
सर्वसम्पत्समृद्धायां जुष्टायां वृष्णिपुंगवैः ॥१॥
स्त्रीभिश्चोत्तमवेषाभिर्नवयौवनकान्तिभिः ।
कन्दुकादिभिर्हर्म्येषु क्रीडन्तीभिस्तडिद्द्युभिः ॥२॥
नित्यं संकुलमार्गायां मदच्युद्भिर्मतङ्गजैः ।
स्वलंकृतैर्भटैरश्वै रथैश्च कनकोज्ज्वलैः ॥३॥
उद्यानोपवनाढ्यायां पुष्पितद्रुमराजिषु ।
निर्विशद्भृंगविहगैर्नादितायां समन्ततः ॥४॥
रेमे षोडशसाहस्रपत्नीनामेकवल्लभः ।
तावद्विचित्ररूपोऽसौ तद्गेहेषु महर्द्धिषु ॥५॥
प्रोत्फुल्लोत्पलकह्लारकुमुदाम्भोजरेणुभिः ।
वासितामलतोयेषु कूजद्द्विजकुलेषु च ॥६॥
विजहार विगाह्याम्भो ह्रदिनीषु महोदयः ।
कुचकुंकुमलिप्तांगः परिरब्धश्च योषिताम् ॥७॥

śrī-śuka uvāca
sukhaṁ sva-puryāṁ nivasan
dvārakāyāṁ śriyaḥ patiḥ
sarva-sampat-samṛddhāyāṁ
juṣṭāyāṁ vṛṣṇi-puṅgavaiḥ

strībhiś cottama-veṣābhir
nava-yauvana-kāntibhiḥ
kandukādibhir harmyeṣu
krīḍantībhis taḍid-dyubhiḥ

nityaṁ saṅkula-mārgāyāṁ
mada-cyudbhir mataṅ-gajaiḥ
sv-alaṅkṛtair bhaṭair aśvai
rathaiś ca kanakojjvalaiḥ

udyānopavanāḍhyāyāṁ
puṣpita-druma-rājiṣu
nirviśad-bhṛṅga-vihagair
nāditāyāṁ samantataḥ

reme ṣoḍaśa-sāhasra-
patnīnām eka-vallabhaḥ
tāvad vicitra-rūpo 'sau
tad-geheṣu maharddhiṣu

protphullotpala-kahlāra-
kumudāmbhoja-reṇubhiḥ
vāsitāmala-toyeṣu
kūjad-dvija-kuleṣu ca

vijahāra vigāhyāmbho
hradinīṣu mahodayah
kuca-kuṅkuma-liptāṅgaḥ
parirabdhaś ca yoṣitām

śrī-śukaḥ uvāca—Śukadeva Gosvāmī said; *sukham*—happily; *sva*—in His own; *puryām*—city; *nivasan*—residing; *dvārakāyām*—in Dvārakā; *śriyaḥ*—of the goddess of fortune; *patiḥ*—the master; *sarva*—all; *sampat*—in opulent features; *samṛddhāyām*—which was rich; *juṣṭā-yām*—populated; *vṛṣṇi-puṅgavaiḥ*—by the most prominent of the Vṛṣṇis; *strībhiḥ*—by women; *ca*—and; *uttama*—excellent; *veṣābhiḥ*—whose dress; *nava*—new; *yauvana*—of youth; *kāntibhiḥ*—whose beauty; *kanduka-ādibhiḥ*—with balls and other toys; *harmyeṣu*—on the rooftops; *krīḍantībhiḥ*—playing; *taḍit*—of lightning; *dyubhiḥ*—whose effulgence; *nityam*—always; *saṅkula*—crowded; *mārgāyām*—whose roads; *mada-cyudbhiḥ*—exuding *mada; matam*—intoxicated; *gajaiḥ*—with elephants; *su*—well; *alaṅkṛtaiḥ*—ornamented; *bhaṭaiḥ*—with foot-soldiers; *aśvaiḥ*—horses; *rathaiḥ*—chariots; *ca*—and; *kanaka*—with gold; *ujjvalaiḥ*—

brilliant; *udyāna*—with gardens; *upavana*—and parks; *āḍhyāyām*—endowed; *puṣpita*—flowering; *druma*—of trees; *rājiṣu*—which had rows; *nirviśat*—entering (therein); *bhṛṅga*—by bees; *vihagaiḥ*—and birds; *nāditāyām*—filled with sound; *samantataḥ*—on all sides; *reme*—He enjoyed; *ṣoḍaśa*—sixteen; *sāhasra*—thousand; *patnīnām*—of wives; *eka*—the only; *vallabhaḥ*—beloved; *tāvat*—that many; *vicitra*—variegated; *rūpaḥ*—having personal forms; *asau*—He; *tat*—their; *geheṣu*—in the residences; *mahā-ṛddhiṣu*—richly furnished; *protphulla*—blooming; *utpala*—of water lilies; *kahlāra*—white lotuses; *kumuda*—night-blooming lotuses; *ambhoja*—and day-blooming lotuses; *reṇubhiḥ*—by the pollen; *vāsita*—made aromatic; *amala*—pure; *toyeṣu*—in bodies of water; *kūjat*—cooing; *dvija*—of birds; *kuleṣu*—where there were flocks; *ca*—and; *vijahāra*—He sported; *vigāhya*—diving; *ambhaḥ*—into the water; *hradinīṣu*—in rivers; *mahā-udayaḥ*—the all-powerful Lord; *kuca*—from their breasts; *kuṅkuma*—by the red cosmetic powder; *lipta*—smeared; *aṅgaḥ*—His body; *parirabdhaḥ*—embraced; *ca*—and; *yoṣitām*—by the women.

TRANSLATION

Śukadeva Gosvāmī said: The master of the goddess of fortune resided happily in His capital city, Dvārakā, which was endowed with all opulences and populated by the most eminent Vṛṣṇis and their gorgeously dressed wives. When these beautiful women in the bloom of youth would play on the city's rooftops with balls and other toys, they shone like flashing lightning. The main streets of the city were always crowded with intoxicated elephants exuding *mada*, and also with cavalry, richly adorned infantrymen, and soldiers riding chariots brilliantly decorated with gold. Gracing the city were many gardens and parks with rows of flowering trees, where bees and birds would gather, filling all directions with their songs.

Lord Kṛṣṇa was the sole beloved of His sixteen thousand wives. Expanding Himself into that many forms, He enjoyed with each of His queens in her own richly furnished residence. On the grounds of these palaces were clear ponds fragrant with the pollen of blooming *utpala*, *kahlāra*, *kumuda* and *ambhoja* lotuses and filled with flocks of cooing birds. The almighty Lord

would enter those ponds, and also various rivers, and enjoy sporting in the water while His wives embraced Him, leaving the red *kuṅkuma* from their breasts smeared on His body.

PURPORT

One rule of poetic composition practiced by Vaiṣṇava authors is *madhureṇa samāpayet:* "A literary work should conclude in a mood of special sweetness." Śrīla Śukadeva Gosvāmī, the most tasteful narrator of transcendental topics, has accordingly included in this last chapter of the Tenth Canto of *Śrīmad-Bhāgavatam* a description of Lord Kṛṣṇa's water sports in the attractive setting of Dvārakā, followed by the rapturous prayers of the Lord's queens.

TEXTS 8–9

उपगीयमानो गन्धर्वैर्मृदंगपणवानकान् ।
वादयद्भिर्मुदा वीणां सूतमागधवन्दिभिः ॥८॥
सिच्यमानोऽच्युतस्ताभिर्हसन्तीभिः स्म रेचकैः ।
प्रतिषिञ्चन् विचिक्रीडे यक्षीभिर्यक्षराडिव ॥९॥

upagīyamāno gandharvair
mṛdaṅga-paṇavānakān
vādayadbhir mudā vīṇāṁ
sūta-māgadha-vandibhiḥ

sicyamāno 'cyutas tābhir
hasantībhiḥ sma recakaiḥ
pratiṣiñcan vicikrīḍe
yakṣībhir yakṣa-rāḍ iva

upagīyamānaḥ—being glorified by song; *gandharvaiḥ*—by Gandharvas; *mṛdaṅga-paṇava-ānakān*—*mṛdaṅga*, *paṇava* and *ānaka* drums; *vādayadbhiḥ*—who were playing; *mudā*—joyfully; *vīṇām*—*vīṇas; sūta-māgadha-vandibhiḥ*—by Sūta, Māgadha and Vandi reciters; *sicyamānaḥ*—being squirted with water; *acyutaḥ*—Lord Kṛṣṇa; *tābhiḥ*—by them (His wives); *hasantībhiḥ*—who were laughing; *sma*—indeed; *recakaiḥ*—with syringes; *pratiṣiñcan*—squirting back at them; *vicikrīḍe*—He sported; *yakṣībhih*—with Yakṣī nymphs; *yakṣa-rāṭ*—the lord of the Yakṣas (Kuvera); *iva*—like.

TRANSLATION

As Gandharvas joyfully sang His praises to the accompaniment of *mṛdaṅga, paṇava* and *ānaka* drums, and as professional reciters known as Sūtas, Māgadhas and Vandīs played *vīṇās* and recited poems praising Him, Lord Kṛṣṇa would play with His wives in the water. Laughing, the queens would squirt water on Him with syringes, and He would squirt them back. Thus Kṛṣṇa would sport with His queens in the same way that the lord of the Yakṣas sports with the Yakṣī nymphs.

TEXT 10

ताः क्लिन्नवस्त्रविवृतोरुकुचप्रदेशाः
सिञ्चन्त्य उद्धृतबृहत्कवरप्रसूनाः ।
कान्तं स्म रेचकजिहीर्षययोपगुह्य
जातस्मरोत्स्मयलसद्वदना विरेजुः ॥१०॥

tāḥ klinna-vastra-vivṛtoru-kuca-pradeśāḥ
siñcantya uddhṛta-bṛhat-kavara-prasūnāḥ
kāntaṁ sma recaka-jihīrṣayayopaguhya
jāta-smarotsmaya-lasad-vadanā virejuḥ

tāḥ—they (Lord Kṛṣṇa's queens); *klinna*—wet; *vastra*—whose clothes; *vivṛta*—revealed; *ūru*—thighs; *kuca*—of their breasts; *pradeśāḥ*—the area; *siñcantyaḥ*—sprinkling; *uddhṛta*—scattered; *bṛhat*—large; *kavara*—from the braids of their hair; *prasūnāḥ*—whose flowers; *kāntam*—their consort; *sma*—indeed; *recaka*—His syringe; *jihīrṣayayā*—with the desire of taking away; *upaguhya*—embracing; *jāta*—arisen; *smara*—of feelings of lust; *utsmaya*—with wide smiles; *lasad*—glowing; *vadanāḥ*—whose faces; *virejuḥ*—they appeared resplendent.

TRANSLATION

Under the drenched clothing of the queens, their thighs and breasts would become visible. The flowers tied in their large braids would scatter as they sprayed water on their consort, and on the plea of trying to take away His syringe, they would embrace Him. By His touch their lusty feelings would increase, causing their faces to beam with smiles. Thus Lord Kṛṣṇa's queens shone with resplendent beauty.

TEXT 11

कृष्णस्तु तत्स्तनविषज्जितकुंकुमस्रक्-
क्रीडाभिषंगधुतकुन्तलवृन्दबन्धः ।
सिञ्चन्मुहुर्युवतिभिः प्रतिषिच्यमानो
रेमे करेणुभिरिवेभपतिः परीतः ॥११॥

kṛṣṇas tu tat-stana-viṣajjita-kuṅkuma-srak
krīḍābhiṣaṅga-dhuta-kuntala-vṛnda-bandhaḥ
siñcan muhur yuvatibhiḥ pratiṣicyamāno
reme kareṇubhir ivebha-patiḥ parītaḥ

kṛṣṇaḥ—Lord Kṛṣṇa; *tu*—and; *tat*—their; *stana*—from the breasts; *viṣajjita*—becoming attached; *kuṅkuma*—the *kuṅkuma* powder; *srak*—on whose flower garland; *krīḍā*—in the sport; *abhiṣaṅga*—due to His absorption; *dhuta*—shaken; *kuntala*—of the locks of hair; *vṛnda*—of the mass; *bandhaḥ*—the arrangement; *siñcan*—sprinkling; *muhuḥ*—repeatedly; *yuvatibhiḥ*—by the young women; *pratiṣicyamānaḥ*—being sprinkled in return; *reme*—He enjoyed; *kareṇubhiḥ*—by she-elephants; *iva*—as; *ibha-patiḥ*—the king of elephants; *parītaḥ*—surrounded.

TRANSLATION

Lord Kṛṣṇa's flower garland would become smeared with *kuṅkuma* from their breasts, and His abundant locks of hair would become disheveled as a result of His absorption in the game. As the Lord repeatedly sprayed His young consorts and

they sprayed Him in turn, He enjoyed Himself like the king of elephants enjoying in the company of his bevy of she-elephants.

TEXT 12

नटानां नर्तकीनां च गीतवाद्योपजीविनाम् ।
क्रीडालंकारवासांसि कृष्णोऽदात्तस्य च स्त्रियः ॥१२॥

naṭānāṁ nartakīnāṁ ca
gīta-vādyopajīvinām
krīḍālaṅkāra-vāsāṁsi
kṛṣṇo 'dāt tasya ca striyaḥ

naṭānām—to the male performers; *nartakīnām*—the female performers; *ca*—and; *gīta*—by singing; *vādya*—and playing musical instruments; *upajīvinām*—who earned their livelihoods; *krīḍā*—from His sports; *alaṅkāra*—the ornaments; *vāsāṁsi*—and garments; *kṛṣṇaḥ*—Lord Kṛṣṇa; *adāt*—gave; *tasya*—His; *ca*—and; *striyaḥ*—wives.

TRANSLATION

Afterward, Lord Kṛṣṇa and His wives would give the ornaments and clothing they had worn during their water sports to the male and female performers, who earned their livelihoood from singing and from playing instrumental music.

TEXT 13

कृष्णस्यैवं विहरतो गत्यालापेक्षितस्मितैः ।
नर्मक्ष्वेलिपरिष्वंगैः स्त्रीणां किल हृता धियः ॥१३॥

kṛṣṇasyaivaṁ viharato
gaty-ālāpekṣita-smitaiḥ
narma-kṣveli-pariṣvaṅgaiḥ
strīṇāṁ kila hṛtā dhiyaḥ

kṛṣṇasya—of Lord Kṛṣṇa; *evam*—thus; *viharataḥ*—who was sporting; *gati*—by the movements; *ālāpa*—conversing; *īkṣita*—glancing; *smitaiḥ*—

and smiling; *narma*—by the jokes; *kṣveli*—playful exchanges; *pari-ṣvaṅgaiḥ*—and embraces; *strīṇām*—of the wives; *kila*—indeed; *hṛtāḥ*—stolen; *dhiyaḥ*—the hearts.

TRANSLATION

In this way Lord Kṛṣṇa would sport with His queens, totally captivating their hearts with His gestures, talks, glances and smiles, and also with His jokes, playful exchanges and embraces.

TEXT 14

ऊचुर्मुकुन्दैकधियो गिर उन्मत्तवज्जडम् ।
चिन्तयन्त्योऽरविन्दाक्षं तानि मे गदतः शृणु ॥१४॥

ūcur mukundaika-dhiyo
gira unmatta-vaj jaḍam
cintayantyo 'ravindākṣaṁ
tāni me gadataḥ śṛṇu

ūcuḥ—they spoke; *mukunda*—upon Lord Kṛṣṇa; *eka*—exclusively; *dhiyaḥ*—whose minds; *giraḥ*—words; *unmatta*—crazed persons; *vat*—as; *jaḍam*—stunned; *cintayantyaḥ*—thinking; *aravinda-akṣam*—about the lotus-eyed Lord; *tāni*—these (words); *me*—from me; *gadataḥ*—who am telling; *śṛṇu*—please hear.

TRANSLATION

The queens would become stunned in ecstatic trance, their minds absorbed in Kṛṣṇa alone. Then, thinking of their lotus-eyed Lord, they would speak as if insane. Please hear these words from me as I relate them.

PURPORT

Śrīla Viśvanātha Cakravartī Ṭhākura explains that this superficial appearance of insanity in Lord Kṛṣṇa's queens, as if they had become intoxicated by *dhattūra* or some other hallucinogenic drug, was in fact the manifestation of the sixth progressive stage of pure love of Godhead, technically known as *prema-vaicitrya.* Śrīla Rūpa Gosvāmī refers to this variety of *anurāga* in his *Ujjvala-nīlamaṇi* (15.134):

priyasya sannikarṣe 'pi
premotkarṣa-svabhāvataḥ
yā viśleṣa-dhiyārtis tat
prema-vaicitryam ucyate

"When, as a natural by-product of one's extreme love, one feels the distress of separation even in the direct presence of the beloved, this state is called *prema-vaicitrya.*"

TEXT 15

महिष्य ऊचु:
कुररि विलपसि त्वं वीतनिद्रा न शेषे
स्वपिति जगति रात्र्यामीश्वरो गुप्तबोधः ।
वयमिव सखि कच्चिद् गाढनिर्विद्धचेता
नलिननयनहासोदारलीलेक्षितेन ॥१५॥

mahiṣya ūcuḥ
kurari vilapasi tvaṁ vīta-nidrā na śeṣe
svapiti jagati rātryām īśvaro gupta-bodhaḥ
vayam iva sakhi kaccid gāḍha-nirviddha-cetā
nalina-nayana-hāsodāra-līlekṣitena

mahiṣyaḥ ūcuḥ—the queens said; *kurari*—O *kurarī* bird (female osprey); *vilapasi*—are lamenting; *tvam*—you; *vīta*—deprived; *nidrā*—of sleep; *na śeṣe*—you cannot rest; *svapiti*—is sleeping; *jagati*—(somewhere) in the world; *rātryām*—during the night; *īśvaraḥ*—the Supreme Lord; *gupta*—hidden; *bodhaḥ*—whose whereabouts; *vayam*—we; *iva*—just as; *sakhi*—O friend; *kaccit*—whether; *gāḍha*—deeply; *nirviddha*—pierced; *cetāḥ*—whose heart; *nalina*—(like) a lotus; *nayana*—whose eyes; *hāsa*—smiling; *udāra*—liberal; *līlā*—playful; *īkṣitena*—by the glance.

TRANSLATION

The queens said: O *kurarī* bird, you are lamenting. Now it is night, and somewhere in this world the Supreme Lord is asleep in a hidden place. But you are wide awake, O friend, unable to fall asleep. Is it that, like us, you have had your heart pierced to the core by the lotus-eyed Lord's munificent, playful smiling glances?

PURPORT

Śrīla Viśvanātha Cakravartī explains that the transcendental madness (*unmāda*) of the queens filled them with such ecstasy that they saw their own mood reflected in everyone and everything else. Here they point out to the *kurarī* bird, whom they take to be sorrowing over separation from Lord Kṛṣṇa, that if the Lord actually had any concern for her or themselves, He would not be sleeping comfortably at that moment. They warn the *kurarī* not to expect Kṛṣṇa to hear her lamentation and show some mercy. In case the *kurarī* might think that Kṛṣṇa is sleeping with His queens, they deny this by saying that He is *gupta-bodha:* His whereabouts are unknown to them. He is out in the world somewhere this night, but they have no idea where to go looking for Him. "Ah, dear bird," they cry, "even though you are a simple creature, your heart has been deeply pierced, just like ours. You must have had some contact, then, with our Kṛṣṇa. What keeps you from giving up your hopeless attachment to Him?"

TEXT 16

नेत्रे निमीलयसि नक्तमदृष्टबन्धुस्
त्वं रोरवीषि करुणं बत चक्रवाकि ।
दास्यं गता वयमिवाच्युतपादजुष्टां
किं वा स्रजं स्पृहयसे कवरेण वोढुम् ॥१६॥

netre nimīlayasi naktam adṛṣṭa-bandhus
tvaṁ roravīṣi karuṇaṁ bata cakravāki
dāsyaṁ gatā vayam ivācyuta-pāda-juṣṭāṁ
kiṁ vā srajaṁ spṛhayase kavareṇa voḍhum

netre—your eyes; *nimīlayasi*—you keep closed; *naktam*—during the night; *adṛṣṭa*—not seen; *bandhuḥ*—whose beloved; *tvam*—you; *roravīṣi*—are crying; *karuṇam*—pitifully; *bata*—alas; *cakravāki*—O *cakravākī* (female crane); *dāsyam*—servitude; *gatā*—attained; *vayam iva*—like us; *acyuta*—of Kṛṣṇa; *pāda*—by the feet; *juṣṭām*—honored; *kim*—perhaps; *vā*—or; *srajam*—the flower garland; *spṛhayase*—you desire; *kavareṇa*—in the braid of your hair; *voḍhum*—to carry.

TRANSLATION

Poor *cakravākī*, even after closing your eyes, you continue to cry pitifully through the night for your unseen mate. Or is it that, like us, you have become the servant of Acyuta and hanker to wear in your braided hair the garland He has blessed with the touch of His feet?

TEXT 17

भो भोः सदा निष्टनसे उदन्वन्न्
अलब्धनिद्रोऽधिगतजागरः ।
किं वा मुकुन्दापहृतात्मलाञ्छनः
प्राप्तां दशां त्वं च गतो दुरत्ययाम् ॥१७॥

bho bhoḥ sadā niṣṭanase udanvann
alabdha-nidro 'dhigata-prajāgaraḥ
kiṁ vā mukundāpahṛtātma-lāñchanaḥ
prāptāṁ daśāṁ tvaṁ ca gato duratyayām

bhoḥ—dear; *bhoḥ*—dear; *sadā*—always; *niṣṭanase*—you are making a loud sound; *udanvan*—O ocean; *alabdha*—not obtaining; *nidraḥ*—sleep; *adhigata*—experiencing; *prajāgaraḥ*—insomnia; *kim vā*—or else, perhaps; *mukunda*—by Kṛṣṇa; *apahṛta*—taken away; *ātma*—personal; *lāñchanaḥ*—marks; *prāptām*—obtained (by us); *daśām*—the condition; *tvam*—you; *ca*—also; *gataḥ*—have reached; *duratyayām*—impossible to become freed from.

TRANSLATION

Dear ocean, you are always roaring, not sleeping at night. Are you suffering insomnia? Or is it that, as with us, Mukunda has taken your insignias and you are hopeless of retrieving them?

PURPORT

Śrīla Śrīdhara Svāmī states that Lord Kṛṣṇa's queens here confuse the sea surrounding Dvārakā with the celestial Ocean of Milk, from which Lakṣmī and the Kaustubha gem arose long ago. These were taken (*apahṛta*) by Lord Viṣṇu, and they now reside on His chest. The queens presume that the ocean is anxious to see once again the mark of Lakṣmī's residence and the Kaustubha jewel on the Lord's chest, and they express their sympathy by saying that they also want to see these marks. But the queens desire even more to see the *kuṅkuma* marks on the Lord's chest, which He "took" from their breasts when they last embraced Him.

TEXT 18

त्वं यक्ष्मणा बलवतासि गृहीत इन्दो
क्षीणस्तमो न निजदीधितिभिः क्षिणोषि ।
कच्चिन्मुकुन्दगदितानि यथा वयं त्वं
विस्मृत्य भोः स्थगितगीरुपलक्ष्यसे नः ॥१८॥

tvaṁ yakṣmaṇā balavatāsi gṛhīta indo
kṣīṇas tamo na nija-dīdhitibhiḥ kṣiṇoṣi
kaccin mukunda-gaditāni yathā vayaṁ tvaṁ
vismṛtya bhoḥ sthagita-gīr upalakṣyase naḥ

tvam—you; *yakṣmaṇā*—by consumption; *bala-vatā*—powerful; *asi*—are; *gṛhītaḥ*—seized; *indo*—O moon; *kṣīṇaḥ*—emaciated; *tamaḥ*—darkness; *na*—not; *nija*—your; *dīdhitibhiḥ*—with the rays; *kṣiṇoṣi*—you destroy; *kaccit*—whether; *mukunda-gaditāni*—the statements made by Mukunda; *yathā*—like; *vayam*—us; *tvam*—you; *vismṛtya*—forgetting; *bhoḥ*—dear one; *sthagita*—stunned; *gīḥ*—whose speech; *upalakṣyase*—you appear; *naḥ*—to us.

TRANSLATION

My dear moon, having contracted a severe case of tuberculosis, you have become so emaciated that you fail to dispel the darkness with your rays. Or is it that you appear dumbstruck because, like us, you cannot remember the encouraging promises Mukunda once made to you?

TEXT 19

किं न्वाचरितमस्माभिर्मलयानिल तेऽप्रियम् ।
गोविन्दापांगनिर्भिन्ने हृदीरयसि नः स्मरम् ॥१९॥

kiṁ nv ācaritam asmābhir
malayānila te 'priyam
govindāpāṅga-nirbhinne
hṛdīrayasi naḥ smaram

kim—what; *nu*—indeed; *ācaritam*—action done; *asmābhiḥ*—by us; *malaya*—of the Malaya mountain range; *anila*—O wind; *te*—to you; *apriyam*—displeasing; *govinda*—of Kṛṣṇa; *apāṅga*—by the sidelong glances; *nirbhinne*—which has been shattered; *hṛdi*—in the hearts; *īrayasi*—you are inspiring; *naḥ*—our; *smaram*—lust.

TRANSLATION

O Malayan breeze, what have we done to displease you, so that you stir up lust in our hearts, which have already been shattered by Govinda's sidelong glances?

TEXT 20

मेघ श्रीमंस्त्वमसि दयितो यादवेन्द्रस्य नूनं
श्रीवत्सांकं वयमिव भवान् ध्यायति प्रेमबद्धः ।
अत्युत्कण्ठः शवलहृदयोऽस्मद्विधो बाष्पधाराः
स्मृत्वा स्मृत्वा विसृजसि मुहुर्दुःखदस्तत्प्रसंगः ॥२०॥

megha śrīmaṁs tvam asi dayito yādavendrasya nūnaṁ
śrīvatsāṅkaṁ vayam iva bhavān dhyāyati prema-baddhaḥ

aty-utkaṇṭhaḥ śavala-hṛdayo 'smad-vidho bāṣpa-dhārāḥ
smṛtvā smṛtvā visṛjasi muhur duḥkha-das tat-prasaṅgaḥ

megha—O cloud; *śrī-man*—O honored one; *tvam*—you; *asi*—are; *dayitaḥ*—dear friend; *yādava-indrasya*—of the chief of the Yādavas; *nūnam*—certainly; *śrīvatsa-aṅkam*—upon the one who bears (on His chest) the special mark known as Śrīvatsa; *vayam*—we; *iva*—just as; *bhavān*—your good self; *dhyāyati*—meditate; *prema*—by pure love; *baddhaḥ*—bound; *ati*—extremely; *utkaṇṭhaḥ*—eager; *śavala*—distraught; *hṛdayaḥ*—whose heart; *asmat*—as our (hearts); *vidhaḥ*—in the same manner; *bāṣpa*—of tears; *dhārāḥ*—torrents; *smṛtvā smṛtvā*—repeatedly remembering; *visṛjasi*—you release; *muhuḥ*—again and again; *duḥkha*—misery; *daḥ*—giving; *tat*—with Him; *prasaṅgaḥ*—association.

TRANSLATION

O revered cloud, you are indeed very dear to the chief of the Yādavas, who bears the mark of Śrīvatsa. Like us, you are bound to Him by love and are meditating upon Him. Your heart is distraught with great eagerness, as our hearts are, and as you remember Him again and again you shed a torrent of tears. Association with Kṛṣṇa brings such misery!

PURPORT

The *ācāryas* explain this verse as follows: The cloud acts as the friend of Lord Kṛṣṇa by shielding Him from the scorching rays of the sun, and certainly such an earnest well-wisher of the Lord must constantly meditate on Him with concern for His welfare. Although the cloud shares the Lord's blue complexion, it is Lord Kṛṣṇa's distinctive features, such as His Śrīvatsa mark, that especially attract him to this meditation. But what is the result? Simply unhappiness: the cloud is depressed and thus constantly sheds tears on the pretext of raining. "So," the queens advise him, "it would be better for you not to take much interest in Kṛṣṇa."

TEXT 21

प्रियरावपदानि भाषसे मृतसञ्जीविकयानया गिरा ।
करवाणि किमद्य ते प्रियं वद मे वल्गितकण्ठ कोकिल ॥२१॥

priya-rāva-padāni bhāṣase
mṛta-sañjīvikayānayā girā
karavāṇi kim adya te priyaṁ
vada me valgita-kaṇṭha kokila

priya—dear; *rāva*—of him whose sounds; *padāni*—the vibrations; *bhāṣase*—you are uttering; *mṛta*—the dead; *sañjīvikayā*—which brings back to life; *anayā*—in this; *girā*—voice; *karavāṇi*—I should do; *kim*—what; *adya*—today; *te*—for you; *priyam*—pleasing; *vada*—please tell; *me*—me; *valgita*—sweetened (by these sounds); *kaṇṭha*—O you whose throat; *kokila*—O cuckoo.

TRANSLATION

O sweet-throated cuckoo, in a voice that could revive the dead you are vibrating the same sounds we once heard from our beloved, the most pleasing of speakers. Please tell me what I can do today to please you.

PURPORT

As Śrīla Viśvanātha Cakravartī explains, though the song of a cuckoo is very pleasant, Lord Kṛṣṇa's wives perceive it as painful because it reminds them of their beloved Kṛṣṇa and exacerbates their pain of separation.

TEXT 22

न चलसि न वदस्युदारबुद्धे
क्षितिधर चिन्तयसे महान्तमर्थम् ।
अपि बत वसुदेवनन्दनाङ्घ्रिं
वयमिव कामयसे स्तनैर्विधर्तुम् ॥२२॥

na calasi na vadasy udāra-buddhe
kṣiti-dhara cintayase mahāntam artham
api bata vasudeva-nandanāṅghriṁ
vayam iva kāmayase stanair vidhartum

na calasi—you do not move; *na vadasi*—you do not speak; *udāra*—magnanimous; *buddhe*—whose intelligence; *kṣiti-dhara*—O mountain;

cintayase—you are thinking; *mahāntam*—great; *artham*—about a matter; *api bata*—perhaps; *vasudeva-nandana*—of the darling son of Vasudeva; *aṅghrim*—the feet; *vayam*—we; *iva*—just as; *kāmayase*—you desire; *stanaiḥ*—on your breasts (peaks); *vidhartum*—to hold.

TRANSLATION

O magnanimous mountain, you neither move nor speak. You must be pondering some matter of great importance. Or do you, like us, desire to hold on your breasts the feet of Vasudeva's darling son?

PURPORT

Here the word *stanaiḥ*, "on your breasts," refers to the mountain's peaks.

TEXT 23

शुष्यद्ध्रदाः करशिता बत सिन्धुपत्न्यः
सम्प्रत्यपास्तकमलश्रिय इष्टभर्तुः ।
यद्वद्वयं मधुपतेः प्रणयावलोकम्
अप्राप्य मुष्टहृदयाः पुरुकर्शिताः स्म ॥२३॥

śuṣyad-dhradāḥ karaśitā bata sindhu-patnyaḥ
sampraty apāsta-kamala-śriya iṣṭa-bhartuḥ
yadvad vayaṁ madhu-pateḥ praṇayāvalokam
aprāpya muṣṭa-hṛdayāḥ puru-karśitāḥ sma

śuṣyat—drying up; *hradāḥ*—whose lakes; *karaśitāḥ*—shriveled up; *bata*—alas; *sindhu*—of the ocean; *patnyaḥ*—O wives; *samprati*—now; *apāsta*—lost; *kamala*—of lotuses; *śriyaḥ*—whose opulence; *iṣṭa*—beloved; *bhartuḥ*—of the husband; *yadvat*—just as; *vayam*—we; *madhu-pateḥ*—of Kṛṣṇa, the Lord of Madhu; *praṇaya*—loving; *avalokam*—the glance; *aprāpya*—not obtaining; *muṣṭa*—cheated; *hṛdayāḥ*—whose hearts; *puru*—thoroughly; *karśitāḥ*—emaciated; *sma*—we have become.

TRANSLATION

O rivers, wives of the ocean, your pools have now dried up. Alas, you have shriveled to nothing, and your wealth of lotuses has vanished. Are you, then, like us, who are withering away because of not receiving the affectionate glance of our dear husband, the Lord of Madhu, who has cheated our hearts?

PURPORT

During the summer the rivers do not receive downpours of water provided by their husband, the ocean, via the clouds. But the real reason for the rivers' emaciation, as the queens see it, is that they have failed to obtain the loving glance of Lord Kṛṣṇa, the reservoir of all happiness.

TEXT 24

हंस स्वागतमास्यतां पिब पयो ब्रूह्यंग शौरेः कथां
दूतं त्वां नु विदाम कच्चिदजितः स्वस्त्यास्त उक्तं पुरा ।
किं वा नश्चलसौहृदः स्मरति तं कस्माद् भजामो वयं
क्षौद्रालापय कामदं श्रियमृते सैवैकनिष्ठा स्त्रियाम् ॥२४॥

haṁsa svāgatam āsyatāṁ piba payo brūhy aṅga śaureḥ kathāṁ
dūtaṁ tvāṁ nu vidāma kaccid ajitaḥ svasty āsta uktaṁ purā
kiṁ vā naś cala-sauhṛdaḥ smarati taṁ kasmād bhajāmo vayaṁ
kṣaudrālāpaya kāma-daṁ śriyam ṛte saivaika-niṣṭhā striyām

haṁsa—O swan; *su-āgatam*—welcome; *āsyatām*—please come and sit down; *piba*—please drink; *payaḥ*—milk; *brūhi*—tell us; *aṅga*—dear one; *śaureḥ*—of Śauri; *kathām*—news; *dūtam*—messenger; *tvām*—you; *nu*—indeed; *vidāma*—we recognize; *kaccit*—whether; *ajitaḥ*—the unconquerable one; *svasti*—well; *āste*—is; *uktam*—spoken; *purā*—long ago; *kim*—whether; *vā*—or; *naḥ*—to us; *cala*—fickle; *sauhṛdaḥ*—whose friendship; *smarati*—He remembers; *tam*—Him; *kasmāt*—for what reason; *bhajāmaḥ*—should worship; *vayam*—we; *kṣaudra*—O servant of Him who is petty; *ālāpaya*—tell Him to come; *kāma*—desire; *dam*—who bestows; *śriyam*—the goddess of fortune; *ṛte*—without; *sā*—she; *eva*—alone; *eka-niṣṭhā*—exclusively devoted; *striyām*—among women.

TRANSLATION

Welcome, swan. Please sit here and drink some milk. Give us some news of the descendant of Śūra, dear one. We know you are His messenger. Is that invincible Lord doing well, and does that unreliable friend of ours still remember the words He spoke to us long ago? Why should we go and worship Him? O servant of a petty master, go tell Him who fulfills our desires to come here without the goddess of fortune. Is she the only woman exclusively devoted to Him?

PURPORT

Śrīla Viśvanātha Cakravartī relates the following conversation between the queens and the swan:

The queens ask, "Is the unconquerable Lord doing well?"

The swan replies, "How can Lord Kṛṣṇa be doing well without you, His beloved consorts?"

"But does He even remember what He once told one of us, Śrīmatī Rukmiṇī? Does He recall that He said, 'In all My palaces I see no other wife as dear as you'?" [*Bhāg*. 10.60.55: *na tvādṛśīṁ praṇayiṇīṁ gṛhiṇīṁ gṛheṣu paśyāmi*]

"He does indeed remember this, and that is just why He sent me here. You should all go to Him and engage in His devotional service."

"Why should we go worship Him if He refuses to come here to be with us?"

"But my dear oceans of compassion, He is suffering so much from your absence! How can He be saved from this distress?"

"Just listen, O servant of a petty master: tell Him to come here, as He should. If He is suffering from lusty desires, He has only Himself to blame, since He Himself is the creator of Cupid's power. We self-respecting ladies are not going to yield to His demand that we go seek Him out."

"So be it; then I will take my leave."

"No, one minute, dear swan. Ask Him to come to us here, but without the goddess of fortune, who always cheats us by keeping Him all to herself."

"Don't you know that Goddess Lakṣmī is devoted exclusively to the Lord? How could He give her up like that?"

"And is she the only woman in the world who is completely sold out to Him? What about us?"

TEXT 25

श्रीशुक उवाच
इतीदृशेन भावेन कृष्णे योगेश्वरेश्वरे ।
क्रियमाणेन माधव्यो लेभिरे परमां गतिम् ॥२५॥

śrī-śuka uvāca
itīdṛśena bhāvena
kṛṣṇe yogeśvareśvare
kriyamāṇena mādhavyo
lebhire paramāṁ gatim

śrī-śukaḥ uvāca—Śukadeva Gosvāmī said; *iti*—speaking thus; *īdṛśena*—with such; *bhāvena*—ecstatic love; *kṛṣṇe*—for Kṛṣṇa; *yoga-īśvara*—of masters of *yoga; īśvare*—the master; *kriyamāṇena*—behaving; *mādhavyaḥ*—the wives of Lord Mādhava; *lebhire*—they attained; *paramām*—ultimate; *gatim*—the goal.

TRANSLATION

Śukadeva Gosvāmī said: By thus speaking and acting with such ecstatic love for Lord Kṛṣṇa, the master of all masters of mystic *yoga*, His loving wives attained the ultimate goal of life.

PURPORT

According to Ācārya Śrī Jīva Gosvāmī, here Śukadeva Gosvāmī uses the present tense of the word *kriyamāṇena* to indicate that the Lord's queens attained His eternal abode immediately, without delay. By this insight the *ācārya* helps refute the false notion that after Lord Kṛṣṇa's departure from this world, some primitive cowherds kidnapped His queens while they were under the protection of Arjuna. In fact, as the self-realized Vaiṣṇava commentators elsewhere explain, Lord Kṛṣṇa Himself appeared in the guise of the thieves who abducted the queens. For further information on this subject, see Śrīla Prabhupāda's purport to *Śrīmad-Bhāgavatam* 1.15.20.

Śrīla Viśvanātha Cakravartī remarks that the supreme goal attained by these exalted women was not the liberation of the impersonal *yogīs* but the perfect state of *prema-bhakti,* pure loving devotion. Indeed, since they were already imbued with divine love of God from the very beginning, they possessed transcendental bodies of eternity, knowledge and bliss, in which they were fully able to relish the pleasure of reciprocating with the Supreme Lord in his most intimate, sweet pastimes. Specifically, in the opinion of Śrīla Viśvanātha Cakravartī, their love of God matured into the ecstasy of madness in pure love (*bhāvonmāda*), just as the *gopīs'* love did when Kṛṣṇa disappeared from their midst during the *rāsa* dance. At that time the *gopīs* experienced the full development of ecstatic madness, which they expressed in their inquiries from the various creatures of the forest and in such words as *kṛṣṇo 'haṁ paśyata gatim:* "I am Kṛṣṇa! Just see how gracefully I move!" (*Bhāg.* 10.30.19) Similarly, the *vilāsa,* or flourishing transformation, of the ecstatic love of Lord Dvārakādhīśa's principal queens has produced the *prema-vaicitrya* symptoms they have exhibited here.

TEXT 26

श्रुतमात्रोऽपि यः स्त्रीणां प्रसह्याकर्षते मनः ।
उरुगायोरुगीतो वा पश्यन्तीनां च किं पुनः ॥२६॥

śruta-mātro 'pi yaḥ strīṇāṁ
prasahyākarṣate manaḥ
uru-gāyoru-gīto vā
paśyantīnāṁ ca kiṁ punaḥ

śruta—heard about; *mātraḥ*—merely; *api*—even; *yaḥ*—who (Lord Kṛṣṇa); *strīṇām*—of women; *prasahya*—by force; *ākarṣate*—attracts; *manaḥ*—the minds; *uru*—numerous; *gāya*—by songs; *uru*—in numerous ways; *gītaḥ*—sung about; *vā*—on the other hand; *paśyantīnām*—of those women who see him; *ca*—and; *kim*—what; *punaḥ*—more.

TRANSLATION

The Lord, whom countless songs glorify in countless ways, forcibly attracts the minds of all women who simply hear about Him. What to speak, then, of those women who see Him directly?

TEXT 27

याः सम्पर्यचरन् प्रेम्णा पादसंवाहनादिभिः ।
जगद्गुरुं भर्तृबुद्ध्या तासां किं वर्ण्यते तपः ॥२७॥

yāḥ samparyacaran premṇā
pāda-saṁvāhanādibhiḥ
jagad-guruṁ bhartṛ-buddhyā
tāsāṁ kiṁ varṇyate tapaḥ

yāḥ—who; *samparyacaran*—perfectly served; *premṇā*—with pure love; *pāda*—His feet; *saṁvāhana*—by massaging; *ādibhiḥ*—and so forth; *jagat*—of the universe; *gurum*—the spiritual master; *bhartṛ*—as their husband; *buddhyā*—with the attitude; *tāsām*—of them; *kim*—how; *varṇyate*—can be described; *tapaḥ*—the austere penances.

TRANSLATION

And how could one possibly describe the great austerities that had been performed by the women who perfectly served Him, the spiritual master of the universe, in pure ecstatic love? Thinking of Him as their husband, they rendered such intimate services as massaging His feet.

TEXT 28

एवं वेदोदितं धर्ममनुतिष्ठन् सतां गतिः ।
गृहं धर्मार्थकामानां मुहुश्चादर्शयत्पदम् ॥२८॥

evaṁ veditaṁ dharmam
anutiṣṭhan satāṁ gatiḥ
gṛhaṁ dharmārtha-kāmānāṁ
muhuś cādarśayat padam

evam—in this manner; *veda*—by the *Vedas; uditam*—spoken; *dharmam*—the principles of religion; *anutiṣṭhan*—executing; *satām*—of saintly devotees; *gatiḥ*—the goal; *gṛham*—one's home; *dharma*—of religiosity; *artha*—economic development; *kāmānām*—and sense gratification; *muhuḥ*—repeatedly; *ca*—and; *ādarśayat*—He demonstrated; *padam*—as the place.

TRANSLATION

Thus observing the principles of duty enunciated in the *Vedas*, Lord Kṛṣṇa, the goal of the saintly devotees, repeatedly demonstrated how one can achieve at home the objectives of religiosity, economic development and regulated sense gratification.

TEXT 29

आस्थितस्य परं धर्मं कृष्णस्य गृहमेधिनाम् ।
आसन् षोडशसाहस्रं महिष्यश्च शताधिकम् ॥२९॥

āsthitasya paraṁ dharmaṁ
kṛṣṇasya gṛha-medhinām
āsan ṣoḍaśa-sāhasraṁ
mahiṣyaś ca śatādhikam

āsthitasya—who was situated in; *param*—the highest; *dharmam*—religious principles; *kṛṣṇasya*—of Lord Kṛṣṇa; *gṛha-medhinām*—of those in the household order of life; *āsan*—there were; *ṣoḍaśa*—sixteen; *sāhasram*—thousand; *mahiṣyaḥ*—queens; *ca*—and; *śata*—one hundred; *adhikam*—plus.

TRANSLATION

While fulfilling the highest standards of religious householder life, Lord Kṛṣṇa maintained more than 16,100 wives.

TEXT 30

तासां स्त्रीरत्नभूतानामष्टौ याः प्रागुदाहृताः ।
रुक्मिणीप्रमुखा राजंस्तत्पुत्राश्चानुपूर्वशः ॥३०॥

tāsāṁ strī-ratna-bhūtānām
aṣṭau yāḥ prāg udāhṛtāḥ
rukmiṇī-pramukhā rājaṁs
tat-putrāś cānupūrvaśaḥ

tāsām—among them; *strī*—of women; *ratna*—gems; *bhūtānām*—who were; *aṣṭau*—eight; *yāḥ*—who; *prāk*—previously; *udāhṛtāḥ*—described; *rukmiṇī-pramukhāḥ*—headed by Rukmiṇī; *rājan*—O King (Parīkṣit); *tat*—their; *putrāḥ*—sons; *ca*—also; *anupūrvaśaḥ*—in consecutive order.

TRANSLATION

Among these jewellike women were eight principal queens, headed by Rukmiṇī. I have already described them one after another, O King, along with their sons.

TEXT 31

एकैकस्यां दश दश कृष्णोऽजीजनदात्मजान् ।
यावत्य आत्मनो भार्या अमोघगतिरीश्वरः ॥३१॥

ekaikasyāṁ daśa daśa
kṛṣṇo 'jījanad ātmajān
yāvatya ātmano bhāryā
amogha-gatir īśvaraḥ

eka-ekasyām—in each one of them; *daśa daśa*—ten each; *kṛṣṇaḥ*—Kṛṣṇa; *ajījanat*—begot; *ātma-jān*—sons; *yāvatyaḥ*—as many as; *ātmanaḥ*—His; *bhāryāḥ*—wives; *amogha*—never frustrated; *gatiḥ*—whose effort; *īśvaraḥ*—the Supreme Lord.

TRANSLATION

The Supreme Lord Kṛṣṇa, whose endeavor never fails, begot ten sons in each of His many wives.

PURPORT

The total number of Lord Kṛṣṇa's sons was thus 161,080, and He also had a daughter by each wife.

TEXT 32

तेषामुद्दामवीर्याणामष्टादश महारथाः ।
आसन्नुदारयशसस्तेषां नामानि मे शृणु ॥३२॥

teṣām uddāma-vīryāṇām
aṣṭā-daśa mahā-rathāḥ
āsann udāra-yaśasas
teṣāṁ nāmāni me śṛṇu

teṣām—of these (sons); *uddāma*—unlimited; *vīryāṇām*—whose prowess; *aṣṭā-daśa*—eighteen; *mahā-rathāḥ*—*mahā-rathas,* the highest class of chariot warriors; *āsan*—were; *udāra*—widespread; *yaśasah*—whose fame; *teṣām*—their; *nāmāni*—names; *me*—from me; *śṛṇu*—hear.

TRANSLATION

Among these sons, all possessing unlimited valor, eighteen were *mahā-rathas* of great renown. Now hear their names from me.

TEXTS 33–34

प्रद्युम्नश्चानिरुद्धश्च दीप्तिमान् भानुरेव च ।
साम्बो मधुर्बृहद्भानुश्चित्रभानुर्वृकोऽरुणः ॥३३॥
पुष्करो वेदबाहुश्च श्रुतदेवः सुनन्दनः ।
चित्रबाहुर्विरूपश्च कविर्न्यग्रोध एव च ॥३४॥

pradyumnaś cāniruddhaś ca
dīptimān bhānur eva ca
sāmbo madhur bṛhadbhānuś
citrabhānur vṛko 'ruṇaḥ

puṣkaro vedabāhuś ca
śrutadevaḥ sunandanaḥ
citrabāhur virūpaś ca
kavir nyagrodha eva ca

pradyumnaḥ—Pradyumna; *ca*—and; *aniruddhaḥ*—Aniruddha; *ca*—and; *dīptimān bhānuḥ*—Dīptimān and Bhānu; *eva ca*—also; *sāmbaḥ madhuḥ bṛhat-bhānuḥ*—Sāmba, Madhu and Bṛhadbhānu; *citra-bhānuḥ vṛkaḥ aruṇaḥ*—Citrabhānu, Vṛka and Aruṇa; *puṣkaraḥ veda-bāhuḥ ca*—Puṣkara and Vedabāhu; *śrutadevaḥ sunandanaḥ*—Śrutadeva and Sunandana; *citra-bāhuḥ virūpaḥ ca*—Citrabāhu and Virūpa; *kaviḥ nyagrodhaḥ*—Kavi and Nyagrodha; *eva ca*—also.

TRANSLATION

They were Pradyumna, Aniruddha, Dīptimān, Bhānu, Sāmba, Madhu, Bṛhadbhānu, Citrabhānu, Vṛka, Aruṇa, Puṣkara, Vedabāhu, Śrutadeva, Sunandana, Citrabāhu, Virūpa, Kavi and Nyagrodha.

PURPORT

In the opinion of Śrīla Viśvanātha Cakravartī, the Aniruddha mentioned here is Lord Kṛṣṇa's son, not His well-known grandson through Pradyumna.

TEXT 35

एतेषामपि राजेन्द्र तनुजानां मधुद्विषः ।
प्रद्युम्न आसीत्प्रथमः पितृवद् रुक्मिणीसुतः ॥३५॥

eteṣām api rājendra
tanu-jānāṁ madhu-dviṣaḥ
pradyumna āsīt prathamaḥ
pitṛ-vad rukmiṇī-sutaḥ

eteṣām—of these; *api*—and; *rāja-indra*—O most eminent of kings; *tanu-jānām*—sons; *madhu-dviṣaḥ*—of Kṛṣṇa, enemy of the demon Madhu; *pradyumnaḥ*—Pradyumna; *āsīt*—was; *prathamaḥ*—first; *pitṛ-vat*—just like His father; *rukmiṇī-sutaḥ*—son of Rukmiṇī.

TRANSLATION

O best of kings, of these sons begotten by Lord Kṛṣṇa, the enemy of Madhu, the most prominent was Rukmiṇī's son Pradyumna. He was just like His father.

TEXT 36

स रुक्मिणो दुहितरमुपयेमे महारथः ।
तस्यां ततोऽनिरुद्धोऽभून्नागायुतबलान्वितः ॥३६॥

sa rukmiṇo duhitaram
upayeme mahā-rathaḥ
tasyāṁ tato 'niruddho 'bhūt
nāgāyuta-balānvitaḥ

saḥ—He (Pradyumna); *rukmiṇaḥ*—of Rukmī (the oldest brother of Rukmiṇī); *duhitaram*—the daughter, Rukmavatī; *upayeme*—married; *mahā-rathaḥ*—the great chariot warrior; *tasyām*—in her; *tataḥ*—then; *aniruddhaḥ*—Aniruddha; *abhūt*—was born; *nāga*—of elephants; *ayuta*—ten thousand; *bala*—with the strength; *anvitaḥ*—endowed.

TRANSLATION

The great warrior Pradyumna married Rukmī's daughter [Rukmavatī], who gave birth to Aniruddha. He was as strong as ten thousand elephants.

TEXT 37

स चापि रुक्मिणः पौत्रीं दौहित्रो जगृहे ततः ।
वज्रस्तस्याभवद्यस्तु मौषलादवशेषितः ॥३७॥

sa cāpi rukmiṇaḥ pautrīṁ
dauhitro jagṛhe tataḥ
vajras tasyābhavad yas tu
mauṣalād avaśeṣitaḥ

saḥ—he (Aniruddha); *ca*—and; *api*—furthermore; *rukmiṇaḥ*—of Rukmī; *pautrīm*—the granddaughter, Rocanā; *dauhitraḥ*—(Rukmī's) daughter's son; *jagṛhe*—took; *tataḥ*—then; *vajraḥ*—Vajra; *tasya*—as his son; *abhavat*—took birth; *yaḥ*—who; *tu*—but; *mauṣalāt*—after the pastime in which the Yadus slaughtered each other with iron clubs; *avaśeṣitaḥ*—remained.

TRANSLATION

Rukmī's daughter's son [Aniruddha] married Rukmī's son's daughter [Rocanā]. From her was born Vajra, who would remain among the few survivors of the Yadus' battle with clubs.

TEXT 38

प्रतिबाहुरभूत्तस्मात्सुबाहुस्तस्य चात्मजः ।
सुबाहोः शान्तसेनोऽभूच्छतसेनस्तु तत्सुतः ॥३८॥

pratibāhur abhūt tasmāt
subāhus tasya cātmajaḥ
subāhoḥ śāntaseno 'bhūc
chatasenas tu tat-sutaḥ

prati-bāhuḥ—Pratibāhu; *abhūt*—came; *tasmāt*—from him (Vajra); *su-bāhuḥ*—Subāhu; *tasya*—his; *ca*—and; *ātma-jaḥ*—son; *su-bāhoḥ*—from Subāhu; *śānta-senaḥ*—Śāntasena; *abhūt*—came; *śata-senaḥ*—Śatasena; *tu*—and; *tat*—his (Śāntasena's); *sutaḥ*—son.

TRANSLATION

From Vajra came Pratibāhu, whose son was Subāhu. Subāhu's son was Śāntasena, from whom Śatasena was born.

TEXT 39

न ह्येतस्मिन् कुले जाता अधना अबहुप्रजाः ।
अल्पायुषोऽल्पवीर्याश्च अब्रह्मण्याश्च जज्ञिरे ॥३९॥

na hy etasmin kule jātā
adhanā abahu-prajāḥ
alpāyuṣo 'lpa-vīryāś ca
abrahmaṇyāś ca jajñire

na—not; *hi*—indeed; *etasmin*—in this; *kule*—family; *jātāḥ*—appearing; *adhanāḥ*—poor; *a-bahu*—not having many; *prajāḥ*—children; *alpa-*

āyuṣaḥ—short-lived; *alpa*—small; *vīryāḥ*—whose prowess; *ca*—and; *abrahmaṇyāḥ*—not devoted to the brahmincal class; *ca*—and; *jajñire*—were born.

TRANSLATION

No one born in this family was poor in wealth or progeny, short-lived, weak or neglectful of brahminical culture.

TEXT 40

यदुवंशप्रसूतानां पुंसां विख्यातकर्मणाम् ।
संख्या न शक्यते कर्तुमपि वर्षायुतैर्नृप ॥४०॥

yadu-vaṁśa-prasūtānām
puṁsām vikhyāta-karmaṇām
saṅkhyā na śakyate kartum
api varṣāyutair nṛpa

yadu-vaṁśa—in the Yadu dynasty; *prasūtānām*—of those who were born; *puṁsām*—men; *vikhyāta*—famous; *karmaṇām*—whose deeds; *saṅkhyā*—the counting; *na śakyate*—cannot; *kartum*—be done; *api*—even; *varṣa*—in years; *ayutaiḥ*—tens of thousands; *nṛpa*—O King (Parīkṣit).

TRANSLATION

The Yadu dynasty produced innumerable great men of famous deeds. Even in tens of thousands of years, O King, one could never count them all.

TEXT 41

तिस्रः कोटच: सहस्राणामष्टाशीतिशतानि च ।
आसन् यदुकुलाचार्याः कुमाराणामिति श्रुतम् ॥४१॥

tisraḥ koṭyaḥ sahasrāṇām
aṣṭāśīti-śatāni ca

āsan yadu-kulācāryāḥ
kumārāṇām iti śrutam

tisraḥ—three; *koṭyaḥ*—(times) ten million; *sahasrāṇām*—thousand; *aṣṭā-aśīti*—eighty-eight; *śatāni*—hundreds; *ca*—and; *āsan*—were; *yadu-kula*—of the Yadu family; *ācāryāḥ*—teachers; *kumārāṇām*—for the children; *iti*—thus; *śrutam*—has been heard.

TRANSLATION

I have heard from authoritative sources that the Yadu family employed 38,800,000 teachers just to educate their children.

TEXT 42

संख्यानं यादवानां कः करिष्यति महात्मनाम् ।
यत्रायुतानामयुतलक्षेणास्ते स आहुकः ॥४२॥

saṅkhyānaṁ yādavānāṁ kaḥ
kariṣyati mahātmanām
yatrāyutānām ayuta-
lakṣeṇāste sa āhukaḥ

saṅkhyānam—the counting; *yādavānām*—of the Yādavas; *kaḥ*—who; *kariṣyati*—can do; *mahā-ātmanām*—of the great personalities; *yatra*—among whom; *ayutānām*—of tens of thousands; *ayuta*—(times) ten thousand; *lakṣeṇa*—with (three) hundred thousand (persons); *āste*—was present; *saḥ*—he; *āhukaḥ*—Ugrasena.

TRANSLATION

Who can count all the great Yādavas, when among them King Ugrasena alone was accompanied by an entourage of thirty trillion attendants?

PURPORT

Śrīla Viśvanātha Cakravartī explains why specifically thirty trillion, rather than an indefinite number of tens of trillions, is stated here to be the number of King Ugrasena's attendants. He does so by citing the interpretational rule of *kapiñjalādhikaraṇa,* the logic of "referring to pigeons": Somewhere in the *Vedas* is found the injunction that "one should sacrifice some pigeons." This plural number should be taken to mean not an indiscriminate number of pigeons, but precisely three of them, since the *Vedas* never leave any matter vague. The rules of Mimāṁsā interpretation take three as the default number when no specific number is given.

TEXT 43

देवासुराहवहता दैतेया ये सुदारुणाः ।
ते चोत्पन्ना मनुष्येषु प्रजा दृप्ता बबाधिरे ॥४३॥

devāsurāhava-hatā
daiteyā ye su-dāruṇāḥ
te cotpannā manuṣyeṣu
prajā dṛptā babādhire

deva-asura—among the demigods and demons; *āhava*—in wars; *hatāḥ*—killed; *daiteyāḥ*—demons; *ye*—who; *su*—very; *dāruṇāḥ*—ferocious; *te*—they; *ca*—and; *utpannāḥ*—arose; *manuṣyeṣu*—among human beings; *prajāḥ*—the populace; *dṛptāḥ*—arrogant; *babādhire*—they troubled.

TRANSLATION

The savage descendants of Diti who had been killed in past ages in battles between the demigods and demons took birth among human beings and arrogantly harassed the general populace.

TEXT 44

तन्निग्रहाय हरिणा प्रोक्ता देवा यदोः कुले ।
अवतीर्णाः कुलशतं तेषामेकाधिकं नृप ॥४४॥

tan-nigrahāya hariṇā
proktā devā yadoḥ kule

avatīrṇāḥ kula-śataṁ
teṣām ekādhikaṁ nṛpa

tat—of them; *nigrahāya*—for the subduing; *hariṇā*—by Lord Kṛṣṇa; *proktāḥ*—told; *devāḥ*—the demigods; *yadoḥ*—of Yadu; *kule*—in the family; *avatīrṇāḥ*—descended; *kula*—of clans; *śatam*—one hundred; *teṣām*—their; *eka-adhikam*—plus one; *nṛpa*—O King (Parīkṣit).

TRANSLATION

To subdue these demons, Lord Hari told the demigods to descend into the dynasty of Yadu. They comprised 101 clans, O King.

TEXT 45

तेषां प्रमाणं भगवान् प्रभुत्वेनाभवद्धरिः ।
ये चानुवर्तिनस्तस्य ववृधुः सर्वयादवाः ॥४५॥

teṣāṁ pramāṇaṁ bhagavān
prabhutvenābhavad dhariḥ
ye cānuvartinas tasya
vavṛdhuḥ sarva-yādavāḥ

teṣām—for them; *pramāṇam*—authority; *bhagavān*—Lord Kṛṣṇa; *prabhutvena*—on account of His being the Supreme Personality of Godhead; *abhavat*—was; *hariḥ*—Lord Hari; *ye*—they who; *ca*—and; *anuvartinaḥ*—personal associates; *tasya*—His; *vavṛdhuḥ*—prospered; *sarva*—all; *yādavāḥ*—the Yādavas.

TRANSLATION

Because Lord Kṛṣṇa is the Supreme Personality of Godhead, the Yādavas accepted Him as their ultimate authority. And among them, all those who were His intimate associates especially flourished.

TEXT 46

शय्यासनाटनालापक्रीडास्नानादिकर्मसु ।
न विदुः सन्तमात्मानं वृष्णयः कृष्णचेतसः ॥४६॥

śayyāsanāṭanālāpa-
krīḍā-snānādi-karmasu
na viduḥ santam ātmānaṁ
vṛṣṇayaḥ kṛṣṇa-cetasaḥ

śayyā—of sleeping; *āsana*—sitting; *aṭana*—walking; *ālāpa*—conversing; *krīḍā*—playing; *snāna*—bathing; *ādi*—and so on; *karmasu*—in the activities; *na viduḥ*—they were not aware of; *santam*—present; *ātmānam*—their own selves; *vṛṣṇayaḥ*—the Vṛṣṇis; *kṛṣṇa*—(absorbed) in Kṛṣṇa; *cetasaḥ*—whose minds.

TRANSLATION

The Vṛṣṇis were so absorbed in Kṛṣṇa consciousness that they forgot their own bodies while sleeping, sitting, walking, conversing, playing, bathing and so on.

TEXT 47

तीर्थं चक्रे नृपोनं यदजनि यदुषु स्वःसरित्पादशौचं
विद्विट्स्निग्धाः स्वरूपं ययुरजितपरा श्रीर्यदर्थेऽन्ययत्नः ।
यन्नामामंगलघ्नं श्रुतमथ गदितं यत्कृतो गोत्रधर्मः
कृष्णस्यैतन्न चित्रं क्षितिभरहरणं कालचक्रायुधस्य ॥४७॥

tīrthaṁ cakre nṛponaṁ yad ajani yaduṣu svaḥ-sarit pāda-śaucaṁ
vidviṭ-snigdhāḥ svarūpaṁ yayur ajita-parā śrīr yad-arthe 'nya-yatnaḥ
yan-nāmāmaṅgala-ghnaṁ śrutam atha gaditaṁ yat-kṛto gotra-dharmaḥ
kṛṣṇasyaitan na citraṁ kṣiti-bhara-haraṇaṁ kāla-cakrāyudhasya

tīrtham—sacred place of pilgrimage; *cakre*—made; *nṛpa*—O King (Parīkṣit); *ūnam*—lesser; *yat*—which (glories of Lord Kṛṣṇa); *ajani*—He took birth; *yaduṣu*—among the Yadus; *svaḥ*—of heaven; *sarit*—the river;

pāda—whose feet; *śaucam*—(the water) which washes; *vidviṭ*—enemies; *snigdhāḥ*—and loved ones; *svarūpam*—whose personal form; *yayuḥ*—attained; *ajita*—who is undefeated; *parā*—and supremely perfect; *śrīḥ*—the goddess of fortune; *yat*—whose; *arthe*—for the sake; *anya*—of others; *yatnaḥ*—endeavor; *yat*—whose; *nāma*—name; *amaṅgala*—inauspiciousness; *ghnam*—which destroys; *śrutam*—heard; *atha*—or else; *gaditam*—chanted; *yat*—by whom; *kṛtaḥ*—created; *gotra*—among the lines of descent (of various sages); *dharmaḥ*—the religious principles; *kṛṣṇasya*—for Lord Kṛṣṇa; *etat*—this; *na*—not; *citram*—wonderful; *kṣiti*—the earth's; *bhara*—of the burden; *haraṇam*—the removal; *kāla*—of time; *cakra*—the wheel; *āyudhasya*—whose weapon.

TRANSLATION

The heavenly Ganges is a holy place of pilgrimage because her waters wash Lord Kṛṣṇa's feet. But when the Lord descended among the Yadus, His glories eclipsed the Ganges as a holy place. Both those who hated Kṛṣṇa and those who loved Him attained eternal forms like His in the spiritual world. The unattainable and supremely self-satisfied goddess of fortune, for the sake of whose favor everyone else struggles, belongs to Him alone. His name destroys all inauspiciousness when heard or chanted. He alone has set forth the principles of the various disciplic successions of sages. What wonder is it that He, whose personal weapon is the wheel of time, relieved the burden of the earth?

PURPORT

From beginning to end, the Tenth Canto of *Śrīmad-Bhāgavatam* has been exclusively dedicated to reciting the pastimes of Lord Kṛṣṇa in Vṛndāvana, Mathurā and Dvārakā. As Śrīla Viśvanātha Cakravartī points out, this verse sums up the Tenth Canto by mentioning five special glories of Śrī Kṛṣṇa that even His expansions, plenary portions and incarnations do not display.

First, Lord Kṛṣṇa's reputation eclipsed that of the holy Ganges when He descended into the Yadu dynasty. Previous to this, mother Ganges was the most sacred of all *tīrthas,* being the water that had bathed Lord Vāmanadeva's lotus feet. Another river, the Yamunā, became even greater than the Ganges by contacting the dust from Śrī Kṛṣṇa's feet in the districts of Vraja and Mathurā:

gaṅgā-śata-guṇā prāyo
māthure mama maṇḍale
yamunā viśrutā devi
nātra kāryā vicāraṇā

"The renowned Yamunā in My domain of Mathurā is hundreds of times greater than the Ganges. About this there can be no dispute, O goddess." (*Varāha Purāṇa*)

Second, Lord Kṛṣṇa gave liberation not only to His surrendered devotees but also to those who considered themselves His enemies. Devotees like the cowherd girls of Vraja and others attained His personal association by entering into His eternal pleasure pastimes in the spiritual world, while inimical demons killed by Him attained the *sāyujya-mukti* of merging into His divine form. When He was present on this earth, Lord Kṛṣṇa's compassion extended to His family, friends and servants, and also to His enemies and their families, friends and servants. Great authorities like Lord Brahmā have mentioned this fact: *sad-veṣād iva pūtanāpi sa-kulā tvām eva devāpitā.* "My Lord, You have already given Yourself to Pūtanā and her family members simply because she dressed herself as a devotee." (*Bhāg.* 10.14.35)

Third, Goddess Lakṣmī, Lord Nārāyaṇa's constant companion, whom great demigods serve menially to win her slight favor, was unable to win the privilege of joining the intimate company of Lord Kṛṣṇa's devotees in Vraja. Despite her eagerness to participate in the *rāsa* dance and other pastimes enacted by Śrī Kṛṣṇa, and despite the severe austerities she underwent to achieve that end, she could not transcend her natural mood of reverence. The sweetness and intimacy Lord Kṛṣṇa manifested in Vṛndāvana constitute a unique kind of opulence found nowhere else, even in Vaikuṇṭha. As Śrī Uddhava says,

yan martya-līlaupayikaṁ sva-yoga-
māyā-balaṁ darśayatā gṛhītam
vismāpanaṁ svasya ca saubhagarddheḥ
paraṁ padaṁ bhūṣaṇa-bhūṣaṇāṅgam

"To exhibit the strength of His spiritual potency, Lord Kṛṣṇa manifested a form just suitable for His humanlike pastimes in the material world. This form was wonderful even for Him and was the supreme abode of the wealth of good fortune. Its limbs were so beautiful that they increased the beauty of the ornaments worn on different parts of His body." (*Bhāg.* 3.2.12)

Fourth, the name *Kṛṣṇa* is superior to the name *Nārāyaṇa* and to those of all of Lord Kṛṣṇa's other expansions. These two syllables—*kṛṣ* and *ṇa*—combine together to destroy all inauspiciousness and illusion. When recited, the name *Kṛṣṇa* becomes *śruta-matha*; that is to say, the recitation of Kṛṣṇa's name totally crushes (*mathnāti*) the excellence of all other spiritual practices described in the revealed scriptures (*śruta*). In the words of the *Brahmāṇḍa Purāṇa,*

sahasra-nāmnāṁ puṇyānāṁ
trir āvṛttyā tu yat phalam
ekāvṛttyā tu kṛṣṇasya
nāmaikaṁ tat prayacchati

"By uttering the single name of Kṛṣṇa just once, one attains the same benefit as that gained by reciting Lord Viṣṇu's thousand names three times."

Fifth, Lord Kṛṣṇa solidly reinstated *dharma*, the bull of religion, on his four legs of compassion, austerity, cleanliness and truth. Thus *dharma* could once again become *go-tra*, the protector of the earth. Śrī Kṛṣṇa also established the religious function of Govardhana-pūjā to honor His favorite hill, the cows and the *brāhmaṇas*. He also became the hill (*gotra*) Himself, assuming its form to accept the cowherds' offerings. Moreover, He cultivated the *dharma*, or loving nature, of Vraja's divine cowherds (*gotras*), whose love for Him has never been equaled.

These are just a few of the wonderful features of Lord Kṛṣṇa's unique personality.

TEXT 48

जयति जननिवासो देवकीजन्मवादो
यदुवरपरिषत्स्वैर्दोर्भिरस्यन्नधर्मम् ।
स्थिरचरवृजिनघ्नः सुस्मितश्रीमुखेन
व्रजपुरवनितानां वर्धयन् कामदेवम् ॥४८॥

jayati jana-nivāso devakī-janma-vādo
yadu-vara-pariṣat svair dorbhir asyann adharmam
sthira-cara-vṛjina-ghnaḥ su-smita-śrī-mukhena
vraja-pura-vanitānāṁ vardhayan kāma-devam

jayati—eternally lives gloriously; *jana-nivāsaḥ*—He who lives among human beings like the members of the Yadu dynasty and is the ultimate resort of all living entities; *devakī-janma-vādaḥ*—known as the son of Devakī (No one can actually become the father or mother of the Supreme Personality of Godhead. Therefore *devakī-janma-vāda* means that He is *known* as the son of Devakī. Similarly, He is also known as the son of mother Yaśodā, Vasudeva and Nanda Mahārāja.); *yadu-vara-pariṣat*—served by the members of the Yadu dynasty or the cowherd men of Vṛndāvana (all of whom are constant associates of the Supreme Lord and are the Lord's eternal servants); *svaiḥ dorbhiḥ*—by His own arms, or by His devotees like Arjuna who are just like His own arms; *asyan*—killing; *adharmam*—demons or the impious; *sthira-cara-vṛjina-ghnaḥ*—the destroyer of all the ill fortune of all living entities, moving and not moving; *su-smita*—always smiling; *śrī-mukhena*—by His beautiful face; *vraja-pura-vanitānām*—of the damsels of Vṛndāvana; *vardhayan*—increasing; *kāma-devam*—the lusty desires.

TRANSLATION

Lord Śrī Kṛṣṇa is He who is known as *jana-nivāsa*, the ultimate resort of all living entities, and who is also known as Devakī-nandana or Yaśodā-nandana, the son of Devakī and Yaśodā. He is the guide of the Yadu dynasty, and with His mighty arms He kills everything inauspicious, as well as every man who is impious. By His presence He destroys all things inauspicious for all living entities, moving and inert. His blissful smiling face always increases the lusty desires of the *gopīs* of Vṛndāvana. May He be all glorious and happy!

PURPORT

The translation and word meanings for this verse are taken from Śrīla Prabhupāda's English rendering of *Śrī Caitanya-caritāmṛta* (*Madhya* 13.79).

According to Śrīla Viśvanātha Cakravartī, Śrīla Śukadeva Gosvāmī has composed this beautiful verse to console those who lament the fact that Lord Kṛṣṇa did not continue to manifest His intimate pastimes down to the present time. Here Śrī Śukadeva reminds his listeners that the Lord is eternally present in this world—in His holy abode, His name and the recitation of His glories. This idea is expressed by the word *jayati* ("He is victorious"), which is in the present tense rather than the past.

Śrīla Prabhupāda explains this verse as follows in *Kṛṣṇa:* "Śrīla Śukadeva Gosvāmī thus concludes his description of the superexalted position of Lord Kṛṣṇa by glorifying Him in the following way: 'O Lord Kṛṣṇa, all glories unto You. You are present in everyone's heart as Paramātmā. Therefore You are known as Jananivāsa, one who lives in everyone's heart.' As confirmed in the *Bhagavad-gītā, īśvaraḥ sarva-bhūtānāṁ hṛd-deśe 'rjuna tiṣṭhati:* The Supreme Lord in His Paramātmā feature lives in everyone's heart. This does not mean, however, that Kṛṣṇa has no separate existence as the Supreme Personality of Godhead. The Māyāvādī philosophers accept the all-pervading feature of Parabrahman, but when Parabrahman, or the Supreme Lord, appears, they think that He appears under the control of material nature. Because Lord Kṛṣṇa appeared as the son of Devakī, the Māyāvādī philosophers accept Kṛṣṇa to be an ordinary living entity who takes birth within this material world. Therefore Śukadeva Gosvāmī warns them: *devakī-janma-vādaḥ,* which means that although Kṛṣṇa is famous as the son of Devakī, actually He is the Supersoul, or the all-pervading Supreme Personality of Godhead.

"The devotees, however, take this word *devakī-janma-vādaḥ* in a different way. The devotees understand that actually Kṛṣṇa was the son of mother Yaśodā. Although Kṛṣṇa first of all appeared as the son of Devakī, He immediately transferred Himself to the lap of mother Yaśodā, and His childhood pastimes were blissfully enjoyed by mother Yaśodā and Nanda Mahārāja. This fact was also admitted by Vasudeva himself when he met Nanda Mahārāja and Yaśodā at Kurukṣetra. He admitted that Kṛṣṇa and Balarāma were actually the sons of mother Yaśodā and Nanda Mahārāja. Vasudeva and Devakī were only Their official father and mother....

"Śukadeva Gosvāmī then glorifies the Lord as one who is honored by the *yadu-vara-pariṣat,* the assembly house of the Yadu dynasty, and as the killer of different kinds of demons. Kṛṣṇa, the Supreme Personality of Godhead, could have killed all the demons by employing His different material energies, but He wanted to kill them personally in order to give them salvation. There was no need of Kṛṣṇa's coming to this material world to kill the demons. Simply by His willing, many hundreds and thousands of demons could have been killed without His personal endeavor. But actually He descended for His pure devotees, to play as a child with mother Yaśodā and Nanda Mahārāja and to give pleasure to the inhabitants of Dvārakā. By killing the demons and by giving protection to the devotees, Lord Kṛṣṇa established the real religious principle, which is simply love of God. By following the factual religious principles of love of God, even the living entities known as *sthira-cara* were also delivered from all material contamination and were transferred to the spiritual kingdom. *Sthira* means the trees and plants, which cannot move, and *cara* means the moving animals, specifically the cows. When Kṛṣṇa was present, He delivered all the trees, monkeys and other plants and animals who happened to see Him and serve Him both in Vṛndāvana and Dvārakā.

"Lord Kṛṣṇa is especially glorified for His giving pleasure to the *gopīs* and the queens of Dvārakā. Śukadeva Gosvāmī glorifies Lord Kṛṣṇa for His enchanting smile, by which He enchanted not only the *gopīs* of Vṛndāvana but also the queens at Dvārakā. The exact words used in this connection are *vardhayan kāmadevam*. In Vṛndāvana as the boyfriend of many *gopīs* and in Dvārakā as the husband of many queens, Kṛṣṇa increased their lusty desires to enjoy with Him. For God realization or self-realization, one generally has to undergo severe austerities and penances for many, many thousands of years, and then it may be possible to realize God. But the *gopīs* and the queens of Dvārakā, simply by enhancing their lusty desires to enjoy Kṛṣṇa as their boyfriend or husband, received the highest type of salvation."

In this way Śrīla Prabhupāda wonderfully illuminates the meaning of this verse by Śukadeva Gosvāmī, which summarizes Lord Kṛṣṇa's pastimes.

TEXT 49

इत्थं परस्य निजवर्त्मरिरक्षयात्त-
लीलातनोस्तदनुरूपविडम्बनानि ।
कर्माणि कर्मकषणानि यदूत्तमस्य
श्रूयादमुष्य पदयोरनुवृत्तिमिच्छन् ॥४९॥

itthaṁ parasya nija-vartma-rirakṣayātta-
līlā-tanos tad-anurūpa-viḍambanāni
karmāṇi karma-kaṣaṇāni yadūttamasya
śrūyād amuṣya padayor anuvṛttim icchan

ittham—(described) in this manner; *parasya*—of the Supreme; *nija*—His own; *vartma*—path (of devotional service); *rirakṣayā*—with the desire of protecting; *ātta*—who has assumed; *līlā*—for pastimes; *tanoḥ*—various personal forms; *tat*—to each of these; *anurūpa*—suitable; *viḍambanāni*—imitating; *karmāṇi*—activities; *karma*—the reactions of material work; *kaṣaṇāni*—which destroy; *yadu-uttamasya*—of the best of the Yadus; *śrūyāt*—one should hear; *amuṣya*—His; *padayoḥ*—of the feet; *anuvṛttim*—the privilege of following; *icchan*—desiring.

TRANSLATION

To protect the principles of devotional service to Himself, Lord Kṛṣṇa, the best of the Yadus, accepts the pastime forms that have been glorified here in the *Śrīmad-Bhāgavatam*. One who desires to faithfully serve His lotus feet should hear of the activities He performs in each of these incarnations—activities that suitably imitate those of the forms He assumes. Hearing narrations of these pastimes destroys the reactions to fruitive work.

TEXT 50

मर्त्यस्तयानुसवमेधितया मुकुन्द-
श्रीमत्कथाश्रवणकीर्तनचिन्तयैति ।
तद्धाम दुस्तरकृतान्तजवापवर्गं
ग्रामाद्वनं क्षितिभुजोऽपि ययुर्यदर्थाः ॥५०॥

martyas tayānusavam edhitayā mukunda-
śrīmat-kathā-śravaṇa-kīrtana-cintayaiti
tad-dhāma dustara-kṛtānta-javāpavargaṁ
grāmād vanaṁ kṣiti-bhujo 'pi yayur yad-arthāḥ

martyaḥ—a mortal; *tayā*—by such; *anusavam*—constantly; *edhita-yā*—increasing; *mukunda*—about Lord Kṛṣṇa; *śrīmat*—beautiful; *kathā*—of the topics; *śravaṇa*—by hearing; *kīrtana*—chanting; *cintayā*—and meditating; *eti*—goes; *tat*—His; *dhāma*—to the abode; *dustara*—unavoidable; *kṛta-anta*—of death; *java*—of the force; *apavargam*—the place of cessation; *grāmāt*—from one's mundane home; *vanam*—to the forest; *kṣiti-bhujaḥ*—kings (like Priyavrata); *api*—even; *yayuḥ*—went; *yat*—whom; *arthāḥ*—for the sake of obtaining.

TRANSLATION

By regularly hearing, chanting and meditating on the beautiful topics of Lord Mukunda with ever-increasing sincerity, a mortal being will attain the divine kingdom of the Lord, where the inviolable power of death holds no sway. For this purpose, many persons, including great kings, abandoned their mundane homes and took to the forest.

PURPORT

For the *Śrīmad-Bhāgavatam's* Tenth Canto, this verse is the *phala-śruti,* the promise of success given to one who hears it. The process of devotional service begins with hearing topics about the Supreme Lord. When one has heard these topics properly, he can then proceed to chant them for others' benefit and reflect on their significance. This leads to faithful adherence to the principles of devotional service, which culminates in absolute faith in Lord Kṛṣṇa. Such perfect faith gives one the right to enter the Lord's intimate service and, in due course of time, return to one's eternal, spiritual life in one of the Lord's personal domains.

Humbly offering his comments on the Tenth Canto at the lotus feet of his worshipable Lord, Śrīla Viśvanātha Cakravartī prays,

mad-gavīr api gopālaḥ
svī-kuryāt kṛpayā yadi
tadaivāsāṁ payaḥ pītvā
hṛṣyeyus tat-priyā janāḥ

"If Lord Gopāla mercifully accepts the cows of my words, then His dear devotees may enjoy the pleasure of drinking their milk—the nectar produced by hearing them."

Thus end the purports of the humble servants of His Divine Grace A. C. Bhaktivedanta Swami Prabhupāda to the Tenth Canto, Ninetieth Chapter, of the Śrīmad-Bhāgavatam, *entitled "Summary of Lord Kṛṣṇa's Glories."*

The Tenth Canto of *Śrīmad-Bhāgavatam* was completed on December 27, 1988, the anniversary of Śrīla Bhaktisiddhānta Sarasvatī Ṭhākura's disappearance.

Appendixes

His Divine Grace
A. C. Bhaktivedanta Swami Prabhupāda

His Divine Grace A. C. Bhaktivedanta Swami Prabhupāda appeared in this world in 1896 in Calcutta, India. He first met his spiritual master, Śrīla Bhaktisiddhānta Sarasvatī Gosvāmī, in Calcutta in 1922. Bhaktisiddhānta Sarasvatī, a prominent religious scholar and the founder of sixty-four Gauḍīya Maṭhas (Vedic institutes), liked this educated young man and convinced him to dedicate his life to teaching Vedic knowledge. Śrīla Prabhupāda became his student, and eleven years later (1933) at Allahabad he became his formally initiated disciple.

At their first meeting, in 1922, Śrīla Bhaktisiddhānta Sarasvatī Ṭhākura requested Śrīla Prabhupāda to broadcast Vedic knowledge through the English language. In the years that followed, Śrīla Prabhupāda wrote a commentary on the *Bhagavad-gītā*, assisted the Gauḍīya Maṭha in its work and, in 1944, started *Back to Godhead*, an English fortnightly magazine. Maintaining the publication was a struggle. Single-handedly, Śrīla Prabhupāda edited it, typed the manuscripts, checked the galley proofs and even distributed the individual copies. Once begun, the magazine never stopped; it is now being continued by his disciples in the West and is published in over thirty languages.

Recognizing Śrīla Prabhupāda's philosophical learning and devotion, the Gauḍīya Vaiṣṇava Society honored him in 1947 with the title "Bhaktivedanta." In 1950, at the age of fifty-four, Śrīla Prabhupāda retired from married life, adopting the *vānaprastha* (retired) order to devote more time to his studies and writing. Śrīla Prabhupāda traveled to the holy city of Vṛndāvana, where he lived in very humble circumstances in the historic medieval temple of Rādhā-Dāmodara. There he engaged for several years in deep study and writing. He accepted the renounced order of life (*sannyāsa*) in 1959. At Rādhā-Dāmodara, Śrīla Prabhupāda began work on his life's masterpiece: a multivolume commentated translation of the eighteen-thousand-verse *Śrīmad-Bhāgavatam* (*Bhāgavata Purāṇa*). He also wrote *Easy Journey to Other Planets*.

After publishing three volumes of the *Bhāgavatam*, Śrīla Prabhupāda came to the United States, in September 1965, to fulfill the mission of his spiritual master. Subsequently, His Divine Grace wrote more than sixty volumes of authoritative commentated translations and summary studies of the philosophical and religious classics of India.

When he first arrived by freighter in New York City, Śrīla Prabhupāda was practically penniless. Only after almost a year of great difficulty did he establish the International Society for Krishna Consciousness, in July of 1966. Before his passing away on November 14, 1977, he guided the Society and saw it grow to a worldwide confederation of more than one hundred *āśramas*, schools, temples, institutes and farm communities.

In 1968 Śrīla Prabhupāda created New Vrindaban, an experimental Vedic community in the hills of West Virginia. Inspired by the success of New Vrindaban, now a thriving farm community of more than two thousand acres, his students have since founded several similar communities in the United States and abroad.

In 1972 His Divine Grace introduced the Vedic system of primary and secondary education in the West by founding the Gurukula school in Dallas, Texas. Since then, under his supervision, his disciples have established children's schools throughout the United States and the rest of the world, with the principal educational center now located in Vṛndāvana, India.

Śrīla Prabhupāda also inspired the construction of several large international cultural centers in India. The center at Śrīdhāma Māyāpur in West Bengal is the site for a planned spiritual city, an ambitious project for which construction will extend over many years to come. In Vṛndāvana, India, are the magnificent Kṛṣṇa-Balarāma Temple and International Guesthouse and the Śrīla Prabhupāda Memorial and Museum. There is also a major cultural and educational center in Bombay. Other centers are planned in a dozen important locations on the Indian subcontinent.

Śrīla Prabhupāda's most significant contribution, however, is his books. Highly respected by the academic community for their authority, depth and clarity, they are used as standard textbooks in numerous college courses. His writings have been translated into over fifty languages. The Bhaktivedanta Book Trust, established in 1972 to publish the works of His Divine Grace, has thus become the world's largest publisher of books in the field of Indian religion and philosophy.

In just twelve years, in spite of his advanced age, Śrīla Prabhupāda circled the globe fourteen times on lecture tours that took him to six continents. In spite of such a vigorous schedule, Śrīla Prabhupāda continued to write prolifically. His writings constitute a veritable library of Vedic philosophy, religion, literature and culture.

References

The purports of *Śrīmad-Bhāgavatam* are all confirmed by standard Vedic authorities. The following authentic scriptures are cited in this volume. For specific page references, consult the general index.

Agni Purāṇa
Aitareya Upaniṣad
Bahv-ṛca Brāhmaṇa
Baudhāyana-dharma-śāstra
Bhagavad-gītā
Bhakti-rasāmṛta-sindhu
Brahma Upaniṣad
Brahmāṇḍa Purāṇa
Brahma-saṁhitā
Bṛhad-āraṇyaka Upaniṣad
Brhad-gautamīya-tantra
Bṛhaspati-saṁhitā
Caitanya-caritāmṛta
Chāndogya Upaniṣad
Gopāla-tāpanī Upaniṣad
Govinda-bhāṣya
Hari-vaṁśa
Īśopaniṣad
Jyotī-rāga
Kaṭha Upaniṣad
Kena Upaniṣad
Kṛṣṇa, the Supreme Personality of Godhead
Laghu-bhāgavatāmṛta
Mahābhārata
Mahā-nārāyaṇa Upaniṣad
Mahā-vāmana Purāṇa
Mahā-varāha Purāṇa
Muṇḍaka Upaniṣad
Nārada Pañcarātra
Nyāya-sūtra
Padma Purāṇa
Pūrva-mīmāṁsā-sūtra
Rāmāyaṇa
Ṛg Veda
Ṛg-veda-bhāṣya
Sāṅkhya-kārikā
Śaṭapatha Brāhmaṇa
Śrīmad-Bhāgavatam
Śvetāśvatara Upaniṣad
Taittirīya Brāhmaṇa

Taittirīya Upaniṣad

Ujjvala-nīlamaṇi

Vaiśeṣika-sūtra

Vaiṣṇava-toṣaṇī

Vājasaneyī Saṁhitā

Vedānta-sūtra

Vedārtha-saṅgraha

Viṣṇu Purāṇa

Yoga-sūtra

Glossary

A

Ācārya—an ideal teacher, who teaches by his personal example; a spiritual master.

Akṣauhiṇī—a military division consisting of 21,870 chariots, 21,870 elephants, 109,350 infantrymen and 65,610 horses.

Āśrama—one of the four spiritual orders according to the Vedic social system: *brahmacarya* (student life), *gṛhastha* (householder life), *vānaprastha* (retirement) and *sannyāsa* (renunciation); also, a place where spiritual practices are executed.

B

Brahmacārī—one in the first order of spiritual life; a celibate student of a spiritual master.

Brāhma-muhūrta—the period of the day just before dawn. It is especially favorable for spiritual practices.

Brāhmaṇa—a person wise in Vedic knowledge, fixed in goodness and knowledgeable of Brahman, the Absolute Truth; a member of the first Vedic social order.

C

Cakra—one of six centers of vital energy located in the body.

Cāmara—a yak-tail fan used in Deity worship.

Caṇḍāla—an outcaste or untouchable; a dog-eater.

Catuḥ-ślokī Bhāgavatam—the four verses of *Śrīmad-Bhāgavatam* (2.9.33-36) spoken by Lord Kṛṣṇa to Brahmā, which summarize that scripture's entire philosophy.

D

Dhotī—a simple garment worn by men in Vedic culture.

Durgā—the personified material energy and the wife of Lord Śiva.

Dvāpara-yuga—the third in the cycle of four ages. It lasts 864,000 years.

E

Ekādaśī—a special day for increased remembrance of Kṛṣṇa that comes on the eleventh day after both the full and new moon. Abstinence from grains and beans is prescribed.

G

Gandharvas—demigod singers and musicians.
Gāyatrī mantra—the Vedic prayer chanted silently by *brāhmaṇas* at sunrise, noon and sunset.
Gopīs—Kṛṣṇa's cowherd girlfriends, who are His most surrendered and confidential devotees.

J

Jīva (jīvātmā)—the living entity, who is an eternal individual soul, part and parcel of the Supreme Lord.
Jñāna—transcendental knowledge.

K

Karma—material, fruitive activity and its reactions; also, fruitive actions performed in accordance with Vedic injunctions.
Karma-yoga—the path of God realization through dedicating the fruits of one's work to God.
Kṣatriya—a warrior or administrator; the second Vedic social order.

M

Mahābhārata—Vyāsadeva's epic history of greater India, which includes the events of the Kurukṣetra war and the narration of *Bhagavad-gītā*.
Mantra—a transcendental sound or Vedic hymn that can deliver the mind from illusion.

P

Purāṇas—eighteen literary supplements to the *Vedas*, discussing such topics as the creation of the universe, incarnations of the Supreme Lord and demigods, and the history of dynasties of saintly kings.

R

Rākṣasas—man-eating demons.
Ṛṣi—a sage.

S

Sac-cid-ānanda—eternal, blissful and full of knowledge.
Sādhu—a saintly person.
Sāṅkhya—analytical discrimination between spirit and matter.
Smṛti—revealed scriptures supplementary to the *śruti*, or original Vedic scriptures, which are the *Vedas* and *Upaniṣads*.
Śruti—knowledge via hearing; also, the original Vedic scriptures (the *Vedas* and *Upaniṣads*), given directly by the Supreme Lord.
Sudarśana cakra—the disc weapon of the Supreme Lord.
Śūdra—a laborer, the fourth Vedic social order.
Svayaṁ-vara—the ceremony in which a princess is allowed to choose her husband.
Śvetadvīpa—the spiritual planet where Lord Viṣṇu resides within the material universe.

T

Timiṅgila—a huge aquatic monster that can swallow whales.
Tīrtha—a holy place of pilgrimage.
Tulasī—a sacred plant dear to Lord Kṛṣṇa and worshiped by His devotees.

U

Uttamaḥśloka—the Supreme Lord, Kṛṣṇa, who is worshiped by select poetry.

V

Vaijayantī—a garland containing flowers of five colors and reaching down to the knees. It is worn by Lord Kṛṣṇa.
Vaikuṇṭha—the spiritual world, where there is no anxiety.
Vaiṣṇava—a devotee of Lord Viṣṇu, or Kṛṣṇa.
Vaiśya—a farmer or merchant; the third Vedic social order.

Varṇas—the four Vedic social-occupational divisions of society, distinguished by quality of work and situation in the modes of nature (*guṇas*). *See also: Brāhmaṇa; Kṣatriya; Vaiśya; Śūdra*

Varṇāśrama-dharma—the Vedic social system of four social and four spiritual orders. *See also: Varṇas; Āśrama*

Vedas—the four original revealed scriptures (*Ṛg, Sāma, Atharva* and *Yajur*).

Viṣṇu-tattva—the status or category of Godhead; primary expansions of the Supreme Lord.

Y

Yoga—spiritual discipline undergone to link oneself with the Supreme.

Yogī—a transcendentalist striving for union with the Supreme.

Sanskrit Pronunciation Guide

Throughout the centuries, the Sanskṛit language has been written in a variety of alphabets. The mode of writing most widely used throughout India, however, is called *devanāgarī*, which means, literally, the writing used in "the cities of the demigods." The *devanāgarī* alphabet consists of forty-eight characters: thirteen vowels and thirty-five consonants. Ancient Sanskrit grammarians arranged this alphabet according to practical linguistic principles, and this order has been accepted by all Western scholars. The system of transliteration used in this book conforms to a system that scholars in the last fifty years have accepted to indicate the pronunciation of each Sanskrit sound.

Vowels

अ a आ ā इ i ई ī उ u ऊ ū ऋ ṛ

ॠ ṝ ऌ ḷ ए e ऐ ai ओ o औ au

Consonants

Gutturals:	क ka	ख kha	ग ga	घ gha	ङ ṅa
Palatals:	च ca	छ cha	ज ja	झ jha	ञ ña
Cerebrals:	ट ṭa	ठ ṭha	ड ḍa	ढ ḍha	ण ṇa
Dentals:	त ta	थ tha	द da	ध dha	न na
Labials:	प pa	फ pha	ब ba	भ bha	म ma
Semivowels:	य ya	र ra	ल la	व va	
Sibilants:	श śa	ष ṣa	स sa		
Aspirate:	ह ha	Anusvāra: ं ṁ	Visarga: ः ḥ		

Numerals

० -0 १-1 २-2 ३-3 ४-4 ५-5 ६-6 ७-7 ८-8 ९-9

The vowels are written as follows after a consonant:

ा ā ि i ी ī ु u ू ū ृ ṛ ॄ ṝ े e ै ai ो o ौ au

For example: क ka का kā कि ki की kī कु ku कू kū
कृ kṛ कॄ kṝ के ke कै kai को ko कौ kau

Generally two or more consonants in conjunction are written together in a special form, as for example: क्ष kṣa त्र tra

The vowel "a" is implied after a consonant with no vowel symbol.

The symbol virāma (्) indicates that there is no final vowel: क्

The vowels are pronounced as follows:

a — as in but
ā — as in far but held twice as long as a
ai — as in aisle
au — as in how
e — as in they
i — as in pin
ī — as in pique but held twice as long as i
ḷ — as in lree
o — as in go
ṛ — as in rim
ṝ — as in reed but held twice as long as ṛ
u — as in push
ū — as in rule but held twice as long as u

The consonants are pronounced as follows:

Gutturals
(pronounced from the throat)
k — as in kite
kh — as in Eckhart
g — as in give
gh — as in dig-hard
ṅ — as in sing

Labials
(pronounced with the lips)
p — as in pine
ph — as in up-hill (not f)
b — as in bird
bh — as in rub-hard
m — as in mother

Cerebrals
(pronounced with tip of tongue against roof of mouth)

ṭ — as in **t**ub
ṭh — as in ligh**t-h**eart
ḍ — as in **d**ove
ḍh — as in re**d-h**ot
ṇ — as in si**ng**

Dentals
(pronounced as cerebrals but with tongue against teeth)

t — as in **t**ub
th — as in ligh**t-h**eart
d — as in **d**ove
dh — as in re**d-h**ot
n — as in **n**ut

Aspirate

h — as in **h**ome

Anusvāra

ṁ — a resonant nasal sound like in the French word *bon*

Palatals
(pronounced with middle of tongue against palate)

c — as in **ch**air
ch — as in staun**ch-h**eart
j — as in **j**oy
jh — as in he**dgeh**og
ñ — as in ca**ny**on

Semivowels

y — as in **y**es
r — as in **r**un
l — as in **l**ight
v — as in **v**ine, except when preceded in the same syllable by a consonant, then like in s**w**an

Sibilants

ś — as in the German word *sprechen*
ṣ — as in **sh**ine
s — as in **s**un

Visarga

ḥ — a final **h**-sound: **aḥ** is pronounced like **aha**; **iḥ** like **ihi**

There is no strong accentuation of syllables in Sanskrit, or pausing between words in a line, only a flowing of short and long (twice as long as the short) syllables. A long syllable is one whose vowel is long (**ā, ai, au, e, ī, o, ṝ, ū**) or whose short vowel is followed by more than one consonant (including **ḥ** and **ṁ**). Aspirated consonants (consonants followed by an **h**) count as single consonants.

Index of Sanskrit Verses

This index constitutes a complete listing of the first and third lines of each of the Sanskrit poetry verses of this volume of *Śrīmad-Bhāgavatam*, arranged in English alphabetical order. The first column gives the Sanskrit transliteration; the second, the chapter-verse reference. Apostrophes are alphabetized as *a*'s.

B

C

L

M

O

P

Index of Verses Quoted

This index lists the verses quoted in the purports and footnotes of this volume of *Śrīmad-Bhāgavatam*. Numerals in boldface type refer to the first or third lines of verses quoted in full; numerals in roman type refer to partially quoted verses.

General Index

Numerals in boldface type indicate references to translations of the verses of *Śrīmad-Bhāgavatam.*

B

E

F

H

I

J

K

M

N

O

S

T

W

Y